W9-CRE-174

THE WAY
THINGS
WORK

An Illustrated Encyclopedia

of Technology

SIMON AND SCHUSTER · NEW YORK

All rights reserved including the right of reproduction in whole or in part in any form. Original German language edition entitled *Wie funktioniert das?* Copyright © Bibliographisches Institut AG, Mannheim, 1963. This translation and adaptation from the revised edition by C. van Amerongen, M.Sc., A.M.I.C.E., Copyright © 1967 George Allen & Unwin Ltd. Published in Great Britain as *The Universal Encyclopedia of Machines or how things work*.

Published by Simon and Schuster
Rockefeller Center, 630 Fifth Avenue
New York, New York 10020

SIXTH PRINTING

Library of Congress Catalog Card Number: 67-27972
Manufactured in the United States of America
Printed by The Murray Printing Company, Forge Village, Mass.
Bound by H. Wolff, New York

FOREWORD

THIS VOLUME is not a reference book in the ordinary sense. It has been designed, instead, to give the layman an understanding of *how things work*, from the simplest mechanical functions of modern life to the most basic scientific principles and complex industrial processes that affect our well-being. The result is, we believe, a unique book—a graphic and original introduction to the modern world of technology.

When it was originally published, in Germany, this book was called *Wie funktioniert das? (How Does It Work?)*. That question remains the key to the purpose and layout of the book. Here you will find the answer to the question posed by the inquisitive child who wants to know how a vacuum cleaner or a refrigerator works, or by you yourself, puzzled by the complexities of lasers or the secrets of Polaroid color photography. A page of descriptive text faces the coloured drawing to which it refers. Certain common principles have prompted the grouping on successive pages of related machines in which these principles are applied. Thus, for example, an entry on Light introduces a group of entries running in sequence from lenses and telescopes to cameras and colour television, etc. The various subjects are shown in the list of contents, overleaf, and may prove useful for cross-reference purposes. In addition, there is a full index at the end of the book, in which both machines and topics are listed alphabetically.

The translation and adaptation of this book from the original German into English was conceived and carried out as a joint Anglo-American project, every effort being made to make the book useful to both American and British readers. In certain places, British terminology has been used which may be unfamiliar to the American reader. Wherever possible, such places have been footnoted to give the American equivalent, so that the information contained in THE WAY THINGS WORK is accessible to readers on both sides of the Atlantic.

THE PUBLISHERS

CONTENTS

8

DISTILLATION

When a liquid is heated, the molecules of the liquid begin to perform increasingly violent movements. They collide with other molecules which are not yet in violent motion, and in the end some of the molecules attain such high velocities that they burst through the surface film of the liquid (Fig. 1). They thus escape from the liquid as a gas. When they encounter the molecules of a colder medium, these escaped molecules part with some of their kinetic energy, coalesce, and finally form water droplets. This process can be observed when water is boiled in a kettle: the water vapour, or steam, which emerges from the kettle condenses against the kitchen windows. Similarly, water which is evaporated by the sun's heat will, on cooling when it rises to great altitudes, similarly condense into tiny droplets (clouds) which may eventually coalesce into larger drops that fall as rain. In chemical technology this process is performed in a distilling apparatus (Fig. 2) which, if it is of large size, is known as a distilling column (Fig. 3). In this way distillation is used for separating evaporable substances from non-evaporable ones, or separating substances which evaporate easily from others which evaporate less easily. Distillation is therefore a process for the separation of substances according to their volatility. The portion which evaporates when heat is applied and which is subsequently condensed by cooling it in coolers is called the distillate; the portion which does not evaporate is called the distillation residue. Distillation is one of the most important methods of purifying volatile substances and has been practised for thousands of years. High-efficiency distillation columns used in the chemical industry may be over 300 ft. high and as much as 16 ft. thick. They are employed more particularly in the petroleum industry for the production of power gases, fuels, lubricating oils, etc., but distillation is, for example, also an essential process in the manufacture of alcohol.

However, distillation can be used only for the separation of substances whose respective boiling points differ at least $0 \cdot 5 - 1^\circ$ C, unless additives can be used to facilitate the process in special cases (extractive distillation). According to Raoult's Law, a proportion of the substance with the higher boiling point will—depending on its quantity and vapour pressure—be intermingled with the vapour of the substance with the lower boiling point, so that the latter substance will always to a greater or less extent be contaminated by the higher-boiling substance. By returning a portion of the distillate of the lower-boiling substance to the head of the column, however, the separation efficiency can be improved, as for example in rectifying installations (Fig. 3).

Every distilling plant comprises a source of heat and an evaporator (continuous-flow heater, still, distilling flask, retort). For the separation of more volatile mixtures a fractionating unit is attached to the evaporator, so that a distillation equilibrium is established depending upon the qualitative and quantitative composition of the mixture and the effect upon the temperature and pressure. Finally, the distillate is passed to a cooler, where it is cooled, and is then wholly or partially removed. In difficult separation processes a proportion of the distillate (depending upon the nature of the problem and the separation efficiency of the column) is returned to the column. Various forms of distillation are distinguished: one-way, vacuum, molecular, pressure and dry distillation. In the last-mentioned process a non-volatile substance, such as wood, is split up into distillable components by the application of heat.

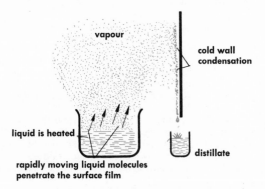

Fig. 1   PROCESSES OCCURRING IN DISTILLATION

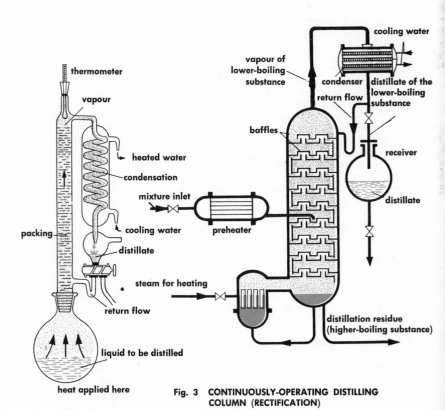

thermometer

vapour

heated water

condensation

mixture inlet

cooling water

packing

distillate

steam for heating

return flow

liquid to be distilled

heat applied here

preheater

Fig. 2   MODERN DISTILLING APPARATUS

cooling water

vapour of
lower-boiling
substance

condenser

return flow

baffles

distillate of the
lower-boiling
substance

receiver

distillate

distillation residue
(higher-boiling substance)

Fig. 3   CONTINUOUSLY-OPERATING DISTILLING
COLUMN (RECTIFICATION)

11

CENTRIFUGE

A centrifuge is an apparatus intended mainly for the separation of heterogeneous mixtures (liquid-solid, e.g., sugar crystals in molasses) and liquid mixtures (e.g., liquids of different specific gravity which are not soluble in one another, such as fat in milk).

The physical principle on which the functioning of the centrifuge is based can be explained by first considering what happens when grains of sand suspended in water settle to the bottom. When sand is stirred up in a jar containing water, the force of gravity will exercise a more powerful attraction on each individual sand grain than on the water particles because a grain of sand has a greater mass than the surrounding water particles. The sand grains are therefore pulled down to the bottom of the jar. This is called sedimentation. After a time the system comes to rest; we then see that two layers have formed in the jar: on the bottom is the settled sand, and over this is the water. A similar separation can also be produced in a centrifuge. Indeed, it can be speeded up by subjecting the grains of sand (or other particles of matter suspended in the liquid) to a centrifugal force instead of gravitational force. Centrifugal forces come into play when a drum containing the mixture to be separated is rotated at high speed about its longitudinal axis. The magnitude of the centrifugal force, which is directed outward from the centre of rotation, is determined mainly by the speed of rotation of the drum—for the same reason that the iron ball which is being swung round and round (Fig. 2) will (for a given angle of elevation) fly farther, when it is released, in proportion as the athlete spins round faster.

If the rotating drum is unperforated, the components of the mixture to be separated will, under the action of the centrifugal force, be deposited layerwise—according to the size of the particles and their specific gravity—against the wall of the drum. The materials with the highest specific gravity or whose particles have the greatest mass will, generally speaking, be sedimented closest to the wall of the rotating drum (Fig. 3). The separated layers can be removed from the latter through stationary tubes provided for the purpose.

Another type of centrifuge (intended more particularly for the continuous separation of the components of a liquid emulsion) is shown in Fig. 4a. The mixture is fed continuously through a spout into the rotating drum, which is equipped internally with conical plates arranged one above the other. The lighter liquid flows upwards along the backs of the plates and emerges from the centrifuge. The heavier liquid is flung to the periphery of the centrifuging drum, and the conically shaped casing of the drum deflects it upwards, where it emerges through another outlet (Fig. 4b).

In centrifuges operating on the filter principle the drum is perforated and may be covered with filter cloth. When the drum rotates, the solid particles are retained at the inner wall of the drum, whereas the liquid goes through the perforations and is thus hurled out of the drum and removed from the casing of the centrifuge (the well-known domestic spin dryer operates in this way). Fig. 5 shows an industrial centrifuge of this kind. Such a machine is usually run intermittently, i.e., it is filled with the mixture to be centrifuged; on completion of the treatment, the drum is stopped and the sedimented material is removed from the wall. In the continuous-action centrifuge for the separation of a solid from a liquid, the drum is provided internally with stationary scrapers which continuously remove the solid material.

As a rule, the drum is driven by an electric motor through a gear unit (worm gear, bevel gear) or belt which rotates the shaft on which the drum is mounted. At the point where this shaft enters the fixed casing of the machine a stuffing box (which forms a seal) must be provided.

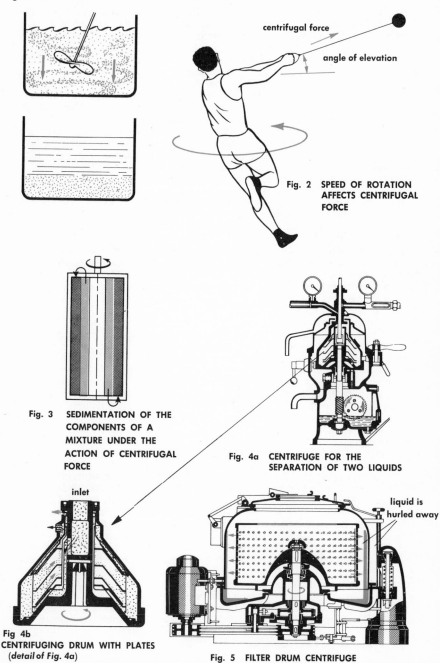

Fig. 1   SEDIMENTATION OF A HEAVY SOLID IN A LIQUID

centrifugal force

angle of elevation

Fig. 2   SPEED OF ROTATION
AFFECTS CENTRIFUGAL
FORCE

Fig. 3   SEDIMENTATION OF THE
COMPONENTS OF A
MIXTURE UNDER THE
ACTION OF CENTRIFUGAL
FORCE

Fig. 4a   CENTRIFUGE FOR THE
SEPARATION OF TWO LIQUIDS

inlet

liquid is
hurled away

Fig 4b
CENTRIFUGING DRUM WITH PLATES
(detail of Fig. 4a)

Fig. 5   FILTER DRUM CENTRIFUGE

FIRE EXTINGUISHERS

Any ordinary combustion process is usually initiated by decomposition of the combustible material as a result of heating, which is usually confined to a small local area and which may be due to friction, irradiation, chemical oxidation, action of sparks or flames. This decomposition produces combustible gases which ignite because they react violently with the oxygen of the air. The reaction produces heat which causes further decomposition of the material and thus produces more gas. Eventually the temperature rises so high that the residue from the initial decomposition due to heat (namely, the carbon, which at first remains unaffected by the heat) also begins to burn, producing a large amount of heat in the process. This continuously liberated heat keeps the combustion process going until the combustible material, or the oxygen needed to sustain the process, has been consumed. Fire extinguishing agents must therefore either cool the combustible material, or they must cover this material with a firmly adhering non-inflammable coating, or they must rarify or displace the oxygen from the focus of the outbreak. As there are, for example, combustible substances which themselves contain the oxygen necessary to sustain combustion, and as it is of considerable importance—from the point of view of fire-fighting—whether the burning substance is liquid or solid, whether it is miscible with water, or whether it is lighter or heavier than the fire extinguishing agent, there must obviously be different kinds of extinguishing agents and different fire-fighting methods.

The carbon tetrachloride extinguisher (Fig. 1) contains anything from 0.5 to 6 litres[1] of this chemical (with certain additives), which is forced out of the extinguisher by the gas pressure from a cylinder of liquefied carbon dioxide. Carbon tetrachloride vaporises completely at 76.5° C, producing a heavy incombustible vapour. This kind of extinguisher is more particularly suitable for putting out fires in machinery and electrical installations. The carbon dioxide extinguisher (Fig. 2) contains 5 to 6 litres of carbon dioxide under high pressure. It is expanded to atmospheric pressure in the "snow tube", where the greater part rapidly vaporises and, in doing so, extracts so much heat from the surroundings that the rest of the carbon dioxide (about 30 %) is cooled to solid carbon dioxide snow (−79° C). This "snow" is sprayed on to the fire by the carbon dioxide gas and causes a lowering of the temperature to below the ignition point; it also displaces oxygen. This is an all-purpose extinguisher.

The water type fire extinguisher (Fig. 3) contains 6 to 12 litres of water containing dissolved sodium bicarbonate. When the pin is struck, it shatters a flask of concentrated sulphuric acid inside the extinguisher. The acid reacts with the sodium bicarbonate, whereby a large quantity of carbon dioxide is evolved which forces the water at high pressure out of the discharge pipe. Because of its high heat of evaporation, water exerts a powerful cooling action; besides, the water vapour displaces oxygen. Water is useless and, indeed, dangerous as an extinguishing agent for fighting a fire in electrical installations or when inflammable solvents catch fire.

The dry chemical extinguisher (Fig. 4) contains 4 to 12 kg of sodium bicarbonate which is hurled into the blaze by the gas pressure developed by liquefied carbon dioxide or nitrogen. In the fire the sodium bicarbonate is decomposed into soda (which covers the combustible material with an air-excluding crust) and into water vapour and carbon dioxide (which displaces the oxygen and therefore smothers the fire). The application of this type of extinguisher will depend upon the nature and place of the fire (secondary damage). In the larger foam type fire extinguishers (Fig. 5) an air- or nitrogen-filled foam is produced. The foaming agent may, for example, consist of a decomposed protein substance (such as horn waste). The foam is stabilised by the admixture of urea, plastics, etc. It exercises a smothering and cooling action on the fire. Foam extinguishers can be used for any fire-fighting purpose, other than for putting out fires in machinery and electrical equipment.

---

1. One litre equivalent to 1.0567 liquid quarts.

Fig. 1   CARBON TETRACHLORIDE EXTINGUISHER   Fig. 2   CARBON DIOXIDE EXTINGUISHER

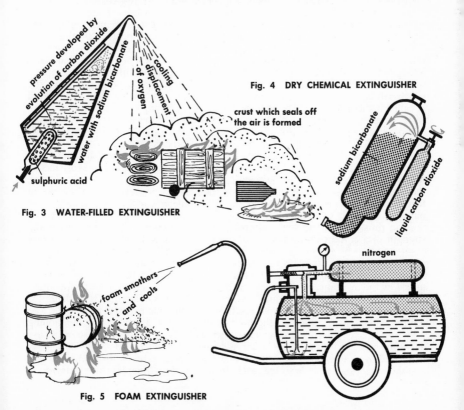

Fig. 4   DRY CHEMICAL EXTINGUISHER

Fig. 3   WATER-FILLED EXTINGUISHER

Fig. 5   FOAM EXTINGUISHER

TEMPERATURE MEASURING INSTRUMENTS

The functioning principle of an ordinary *thermometer* is based on the property of thermal expansion possessed by most substances, i.e., they expand when heated and contract on cooling.

The commonest type of thermometer is the mercury thermometer. It consists of a capillary tube (a tube with a very small bore) which is sealed at its upper end and is enlarged into a spherical or cylindrical bulb at its lower end. This bulb is filled with mercury. When this is heated, it expands and rises in the tube. Because of the very small bore of the latter, even a small increase in the volume of the mercury will cause it to rise quite appreciably. The thermometer is calibrated between two fixed reference points: the freezing point and the boiling point of water at normal atmospheric pressure (760 mm mercury; see page 220). The difference in level in the mercury column between these two points is divided into 100 equal parts, each division being one degree on the centigrade scale (1° C). On the Fahrenheit scale the difference between the two fixed reference points is divided into 180 parts, each division being one degree Fahrenheit (1° F), the freezing point and boiling point of water on this scale being 32° F and 212° F respectively. On the Réamur scale the corresponding temperatures are 0° R and 80° C, i.e., this scale is divided into 80 degrees between freezing and boiling. Mercury is not suitable for thermometers used for measuring very low temperatures, as mercury itself solidifies at −39° C. Such thermometers are filled with coloured alcohol, which has a substantially lower freezing point. The lowest conceivable temperature is the absolute zero, corresponding to −273.16° C. Absolute temperature is measured with respect to the absolute zero in degrees Kelvin, i.e., −273.16° = 0° K.

Thermocouple: If the ends of two wires of dissimilar metals or metal alloys (e.g., copper and constantan or copper and iron) are soldered together (Fig. 2a) and if one soldered junction is kept at a constant temperature, while the other junction is heated, a thermo-electric potential difference develops between the two junctions. This potential difference (voltage) is greater according as the difference in temperature between the junctions is greater and can be read on a voltmeter (Fig. 2b), which can be calibrated to give temperature readings. An arrangement of this kind is called a thermocouple. The voltage produced by a single thermocouple is very small (a few millivolts). To obtain a higher voltage, a number of thermocouples can be arranged in series (Fig. 3), with alternate hot and cold junctions. In this way a so-called thermopile, or thermo-electric battery, is obtained.

The *resistance thermometer* (Fig. 5) is a device whose operation depends upon the variation of the electrical resistance of a wire with temperature. Most metals become more resistant to the passage of an electric current as they become hotter, the increase in resistance being (within certain limits) proportional to the rise in temperature. The resistance used in the thermometer consists of a platinum or nickel wire and is so designed that its resistance at 0° C is 100 ohms. The variations in resistance due to temperature changes are measured as variations in the strength of a current by means of, for example, a crossed-coil instrument, whose pointer deflects by an amount governed by the ratio of the currents flowing through the two coils. The current in one of the coils is kept constant by means of a resistance which is unaffected by temperature; the current in the other coil is determined by the resistance of the thermometer wire which varies with the temperature.

A *bimetallic thermometer* comprises two strips of dissimilar metals soldered together. These metals have different coefficients of thermal expansion and therefore undergo different increases in length on heating. Fig. 4 illustrates the functioning principle of a temperature measuring device embodying a bimetallic spiral whose curvature varies with the temperature and causes a pointer to deflect. The scale is calibrated by establishing the positions of the pointer at certain known temperatures and then marking the scale so that each division corresponds, say, to one degree.

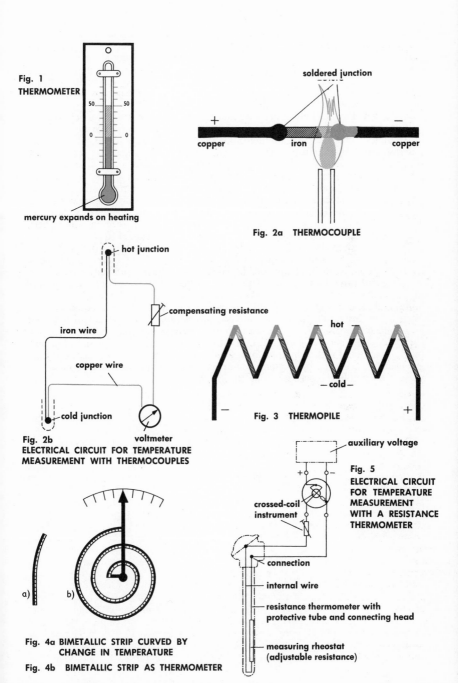

Fig. 1
THERMOMETER

mercury expands on heating

soldered junction

+ copper   iron   copper −

Fig. 2a   THERMOCOUPLE

hot junction

compensating resistance

iron wire

copper wire

cold junction

voltmeter

Fig. 2b
ELECTRICAL CIRCUIT FOR TEMPERATURE
MEASUREMENT WITH THERMOCOUPLES

hot

—cold—

Fig. 3   THERMOPILE

−   +

auxiliary voltage

Fig. 5
ELECTRICAL CIRCUIT
FOR TEMPERATURE
MEASUREMENT
WITH A RESISTANCE
THERMOMETER

+   −

crossed-coil
instrument

connection

internal wire

resistance thermometer with
protective tube and connecting head

measuring rheostat
(adjustable resistance)

a)   b)

Fig. 4a BIMETALLIC STRIP CURVED BY
CHANGE IN TEMPERATURE

Fig. 4b   BIMETALLIC STRIP AS THERMOMETER

17

DRY ICE

"Dry ice" is a name sometimes applied to compressed carbon dioxide "snow", i.e., solid carbon dioxide with a temperature of $-79°$ C. Under normal conditions carbon dioxide is a colourless and odourless gas with a density about $1\frac{1}{2}$ times as high as that of air. Like water (and indeed all other substances), it can occur in the gaseous, liquid or solid state, depending on the physical conditions. In addition, carbon dioxide possesses the property of sublimation, i.e., it can pass directly from the solid to the gaseous state without becoming liquid.

Under which conditions of pressure and temperature a particular state occurs is indicated by the vapour pressure curve (Figs. 1 and 2). In accordance with the lines in the vapour pressure diagram, the transition from one state to the other, in conjunction with absorption or release of heat. Of particular interest is the so-called triple point, where all the three states—gaseous, liquid, solid—can co-exist simultaneously. For example, the triple point for water is located at a pressure of 4.6 mm mercury column (approx. 6/1000 atm.; Fig. 1) and 0.01° C. On the other hand, for CO_2 this point is located at 5.1 atm. and $-56.2°$ C. The vapour pressure curve indicates the relationship between the boiling point of a substance and the pressure. Thus, water (Fig. 1) boils at 100° C at a pressure of 1 atm. (=normal atmospheric pressure); carbon dioxide (Fig. 2) "boils" at 0° C at a pressure of 60 atm.

To make carbon dioxide snow, carbon dioxide is cooled at high pressure (up to 70 atm.) and liquefies in consequence. Further cooling takes the carbon dioxide to the triple point. Now the compressed liquid carbon dioxide is suddenly expanded by spraying and turns into "snow". This happens because the evaporation of part of the liquid causes intensive cooling of the rest (see page 36). The dividing line between liquid and solid in Fig. 2 is crossed: the carbon dioxide turns from liquid to solid. To achieve this result, the carbon dioxide gas is liquefied by means of three- or four-stage compressors (see page 46) with intermediate and final cooling, the liquid carbon dioxide then being expanded in a tower (on the right in Fig. 3). About one-third of the liquid is thereby transformed into snow; the other two-thirds turn into gas, which is removed by suction, recompressed, and returned to the process. The snow is pressed into blocks weighing 50–250 lb.

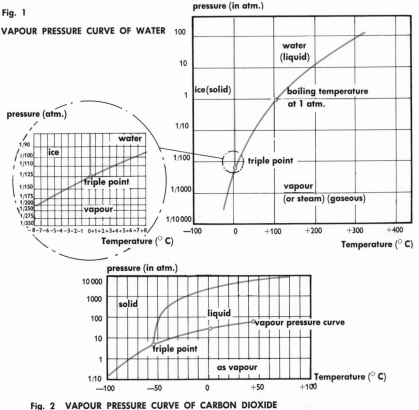

Fig. 1

VAPOUR PRESSURE CURVE OF WATER

pressure (in atm.)

100

10

1

1/10

1/100

1/1000

1/10000

water
(liquid)

ice(solid)

boiling temperature
at 1 atm.

triple point

vapour
(or steam) (gaseous)

-100   0   +100   +200   +300   +400

Temperature ($^\circ$ C)

pressure (atm.)

1/90
1/100
1/110
1/125
1/150
1/175
1/200
1/250
1/275
1/350

ice   water

triple point

vapour

-8 -7 -6 -5 -4 -3 -2 -1 0 +1 +2 +3 +4 +5 +6 +7 +8

Temperature ($^\circ$ C)

pressure (in atm.)

10 000

1000

100

10

1

1/10

solid

liquid

vapour pressure curve

triple point

as vapour

-100   -50   0   +50   +100

Temperature ($^\circ$ C)

Fig. 2   VAPOUR PRESSURE CURVE OF CARBON DIOXIDE
(CO_2)

gasometer

cooling

compressor

carbon dioxide
(gaseous)

carbon dioxide
(gaseous)

1st stage   2nd stage   3rd stage

liquid
carbon
dioxide

nozzle

carbon
dioxide
snow

recompression

ice press

block of dry ice

Fig. 3   MANUFACTURE OF DRY ICE
(*schematic*)

19

THERMOSTAT

A thermostat is a device for maintaining a temperature constant at a desired value. For this purpose it is equipped with a temperature sensing unit which detects any deviation of the actual temperature from the desired value and transmits information on this to a device which cancels the deviation. The sensing unit may be a tube filled with a liquid, a bimetallic strip or a spring bellows. The simplest device of this kind is the *direct*-acting thermostat. It makes use of the fact that nearly all liquids expand on heating (Fig. 1). The thermostat itself consists of a tube filled with a liquid which expands very considerably when it is heated (Fig. 2). The connection to the control device which actuates the valve in the hot-water supply pipe (for example) is established by a capillary tube which is also filled with liquid. If the air temperature in the room under thermostatic control rises above the desired level, the liquid in the sensing unit expands, overcomes the restraining force of a spring on the valve, and throttles or closes the latter. As a result of this, the flow of hot water (or other heating medium) is reduced, and less heat is supplied to the room. Because of this the temperature in the room will go down after a time, so that the liquid cools and contracts. The spring load on the valve once again exceeds the pressure exerted by the liquid and opens the valve. In this way the temperature in the room is kept constant within fairly narrow limits. The desired value of the temperature is set on a graduated scale which has been calibrated by the makers. By rotation of the screw on the control device the valve spring is compressed to a greater or less extent by the liquid, so that the valve correspondingly opens more or less. The flow rate of the hot water thus increases or decreases, causing the temperature level in the room to rise or to fall (Fig. 2). A different type of device is the *indirect*-acting thermostat, which uses an auxiliary source of power (e.g., electricity or compressed air) for transmitting the impulses for effecting the change in temperature. In a device of this kind the sensing unit actuates a contact, i.e., an electrical contact is closed (Fig. 3), so that, for example, an electromagnetically controlled valve of the heating system is opened or closed. For instance, if the above mentioned liquid-filled sensing unit is employed, the expansion of the liquid due to a rise in temperature closes the contact. The electric current which then energises the electromagnetic valve will close the latter. When the temperature falls, the reverse process takes place. When the pre-set minimum temperature is reached, and the liquid in the sensing unit has contracted a certain amount, the circuit is broken, so that the electromagnet now ceases to keep the valve closed. Consequently the hot water flows through the system once again.

Another type of sensing unit is the so-called bimetallic strip (Fig. 4b). This consists of two thin strips of different metals bonded one against the other to form a composite strip. These metals undergo different amounts of thermal expansion. One end of the bimetallic strip is fixed. When the temperature rises, one metal expands more than the other, causing the strip to curve, so that its free end actuates a contact (Fig. 4a).

A third type of sensing unit consists of a resilient bellows filled with a volatile liquid or a gas (Fig. 4c). When the temperature rises, the increase in volume of the vapour or gas in the bellows causes the latter to expand and actuate a contact. A fall in temperature has the opposite effect, i.e., the bellows contracts and may (as in the example illustrated) actuate another contact.

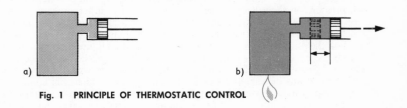

a)   b)

Fig. 1   PRINCIPLE OF THERMOSTATIC CONTROL

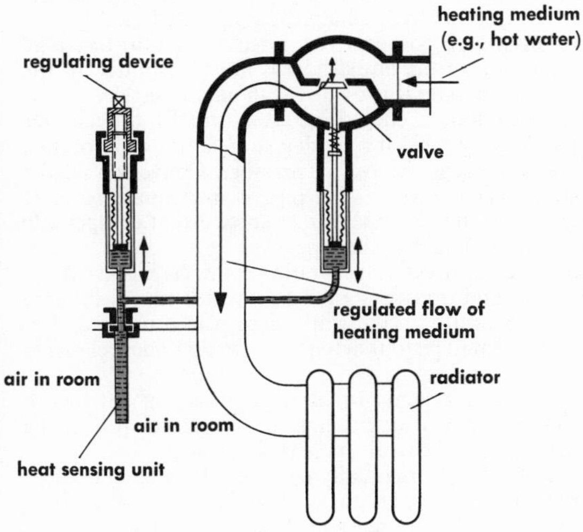

regulating device

heating medium
(e.g., hot water)

valve

regulated flow of
heating medium

air in room

air in room

radiator

heat sensing unit

Fig. 2   THERMOSTAT FOR SPACE HEATING CONTROL
(*direct action*)

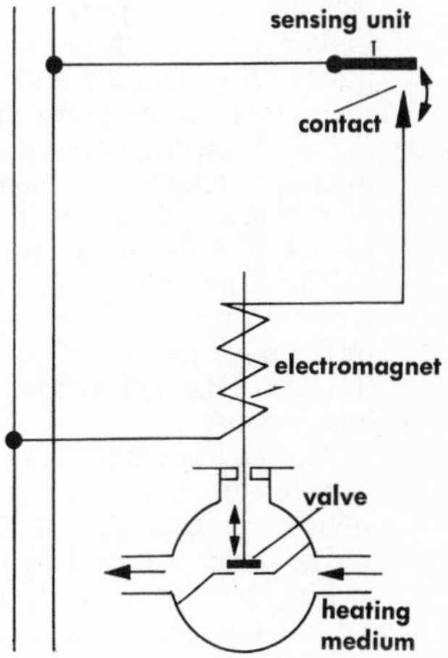

sensing unit

contact

electromagnet

valve

heating
medium

Fig. 3   DIAGRAM OF A
DIRECT-ACTING THERMOSTAT

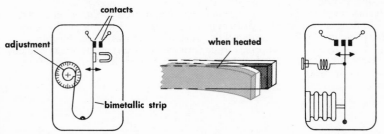

contacts

adjustment

bimetallic strip

when heated

Fig. 4a   BIMETALLIC SENSING UNIT

Fig. 4b   PRINCIPLE OF THE
BIMETALLIC STRIP

Fig. 4c   BELLOWS-TYPE
SENSING UNIT

21

PRESSES

Presses provide a means of compressing and shaping components by exerting a high pressure on them. Depending on their method of functioning, a distinction is to be made between hydraulic and mechanical presses. *Hydraulic presses* use a gas or a liquid (usually water) as the power-transmitting medium. Their operation is based on the phenomenon that the pressure exerted on a liquid or gaseous medium which is compressed in a cylinder is of the same magnitude at all points of the cylinder. "Pressure" is defined as force acting per unit of area. If the liquid is compressed by means of a small piston in a small cylinder which is in communication with a large cylinder closed by a large piston (as in Fig. 1), then the situation will be as follows: on one side a small force acts upon a small area (i.e., the small piston) and produces a certain pressure. On the other side this pressure acts upon a large area (i.e., the large piston). A large force can therefore be developed by the large piston (since pressure is force per unit of area, then force must be pressure times area). The volume that is displaced by these two piston movements is, however, the same in both cylinders, i.e., the small piston has to travel a great distance to make the large piston move only a short distance. A hydraulic press is operated, not by one, but usually by three small pistons which consecutively force water into the large cylinder. To ensure that the pulsation of the liquid flow is not transmitted to the main cylinder of the press, the delivery pipe is provided with an air vessel which is partly filled with air and has a cushioning effect (Fig. 2). Normally this air has the same pressure as that in the delivery pipe. If a sudden surge of pressure occurs, the air is further compressed and absorbs the rise in pressure. Conversely, if the quantity of hydraulic medium delivered through the pipe is inadequate to meet brief high demands, the air pressure in the air vessel can to some extent compensate for this by boosting the pressure of the liquid in the pipe.

When the water pump (i.e., the small pressure generating cylinder) is started up, it fills the main cylinder with water and produces a pressure which causes the ram of the press to descend and exert pressure on the work-piece placed under it. Retraction of the ram is effected by two small pistons actuated by water under relatively low pressure.

Mechanical presses have various drive systems. In the screw press (Fig. 3a) a screw spindle is rotated in a fixed nut, whereby a longitudinal force is developed in the spindle, one end of which thrusts against the work-piece laid under it.

The upper end of the spindle of a simple manually-operated press as illustrated in Fig. 3b (known as a "fly press") is provided with a cross-piece for rotating it.

On the larger presses the upper end of the screw spindle is provided with a large flywheel which, when it is rotating, contains a large reserve of stored-up energy. This energy is transmitted through the spindle to the work-piece. The flywheel is driven by a friction wheel. Retraction is effected by another friction wheel, which drives the flywheel in the opposite direction (Fig. 3a).

A further modification of the mechanically driven press is the eccentric press (Fig. 4) and the crank press (Fig. 5). In both cases a large flywheel is driven by a motor or other prime mover. When the ram of the press strikes the work-piece, the rotational energy of the flywheel produces a torque (twisting moment) in the shaft, whereby a relatively large force is developed at the eccentric or at the crank. This force is imparted to the work-piece.

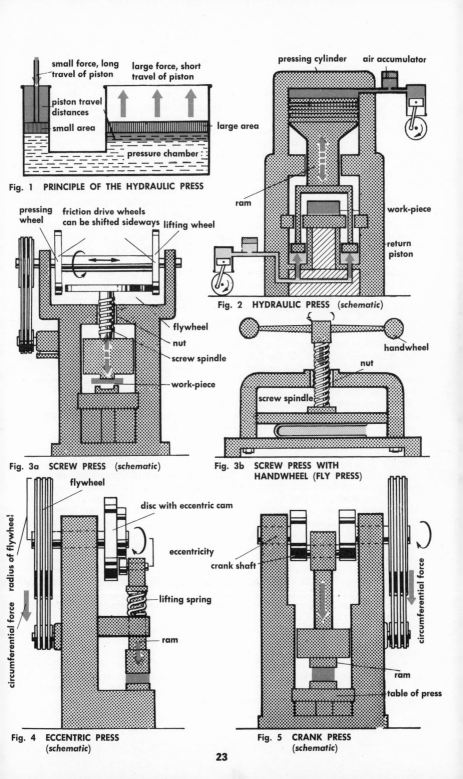

small force, long travel of piston

large force, short travel of piston

piston travel distances

small area

large area

pressure chamber

Fig. 1 PRINCIPLE OF THE HYDRAULIC PRESS

pressing cylinder

air accumulator

ram

work-piece

return piston

Fig. 2 HYDRAULIC PRESS (*schematic*)

pressing wheel

friction drive wheels can be shifted sideways

lifting wheel

flywheel

nut

screw spindle

work-piece

Fig. 3a SCREW PRESS (*schematic*)

handwheel

nut

screw spindle

Fig. 3b SCREW PRESS WITH HANDWHEEL (FLY PRESS)

flywheel

disc with eccentric cam

eccentricity

crank shaft

lifting spring

ram

circumferential force

radius of flywheel!

circumferential force

ram

table of press

Fig. 4 ECCENTRIC PRESS (*schematic*)

Fig. 5 CRANK PRESS (*schematic*)

23

PUMPS

Pumps are used for the transport of liquids or gases through pipes. The general principle is as follows: on one hand, a suction is produced, whereby the liquid is drawn in; on the other hand, an excess pressure to overcome the counter pressure is developed, causing the fluid (liquid or gas) to be forced away. According to the various operating principles, several types of pump are to be distinguished: 1. Piston pumps, which operate with reciprocating (up-and-down or to-and-fro) or rotating pistons. 2. Centrifugal pumps, which operate with rotating blades. 3. Jet pumps, which utilise the energy of flowing fluids.

1. *Piston pumps*: Consider a piston in a cylinder, as in Fig. 1. When the piston moves to the right from its extreme left initial position, water flows into the vacant space that is formed in the cylinder. This happens because the atmospheric pressure acting upon the surface of the water outside the pump forces water up the pipe into the cylinder, in which the outward stroke of the piston has produced a vacuum (or, at any rate, a lowering of pressure). Theoretically the atmospheric pressure can sustain a column of water 33 ft. in height. A pump would thus have a "suction head" of 33 ft., i.e., it would be able to draw water up to a height of 33 ft. into the cylinder. However, the fact that water has a certain vapour pressure and encounters resistance in the suction pipe, reduces the actual suction head to usually somewhere around 23 ft. (Fig. 2). When the piston has travelled to its farthest position, it changes its direction and starts to move back to the left. This produces a higher pressure in the cylinder and causes the inlet valve to close and the delivery valve to open. The latter valve remains closed during the suction stroke of the piston, as the pressure in the delivery pipe is higher than in the cylinder. The piston now pushes the liquid out of the cylinder, against the pressure in the delivery pipe. Special forms of the piston pump are the lifting pump, which discharges the liquid when the piston rises (Fig. 3); the diaphragm pump, in which a flexible diaphragm takes the place of the piston, this diaphragm being moved to and fro by an actuating rod (Fig. 4); and the vane pump, in which instead of a piston there is a vane which is swung to and fro in a circular casing (Fig. 5); the inlet valves are installed in a fixed partition of the casing, while the delivery valves are in the vane.

2. *Centrifugal pumps*: A centrifugal pump is very similar to a Francis turbine (see page 50) operating "in reverse". In a turbine the water drives a runner wheel[1], whereas in a pump a similar wheel fitted with vanes and known as an impeller imparts motion to the water (or other fluid). A piston pump delivers the water in a pulsating stream, but a centrifugal pump gives a steady flow. The pressure for achieving the required "delivery head" is produced by centrifugal acceleration of the fluid in the rotating impeller. The fluid flows axially towards the impeller, is deflected by it, and flows out through the aperatures between the vanes. Thus the fluid undergoes a change in direction and is accelerated. This produces an increase in pressure at the pump outlet. On leaving the impeller, the fluid may first pass through a ring of fixed vanes which surrounds the impeller and is known as a diffuser. In this device with its gradually widening passages the velocity of the liquid is reduced, its kinetic energy being converted into pressure energy. This conversion is completed in the volute of the pump, i.e., the gradually widening spiral casing (Fig. 6). It should be noted that in some pumps there is no diffuser, the fluid passing directly from the impeller to the volute. Pumps of the kind described here cannot, however, produce high delivery heads. A higher delivery head can be obtained by means of a multistage centrifugal pump in which two or more impellers are mounted one behind the other (compare Fig. 8 with Fig. 7).

As a rule, centrifugal pumps are not self-priming, i.e., they are unable to draw in the fluid on first being started up, because when the impeller is revolving in air in the "empty" casing, it cannot develop sufficient suction. These pumps therefore have to be primed (filled with water) for starting.

1. Rotor in U.S.A.

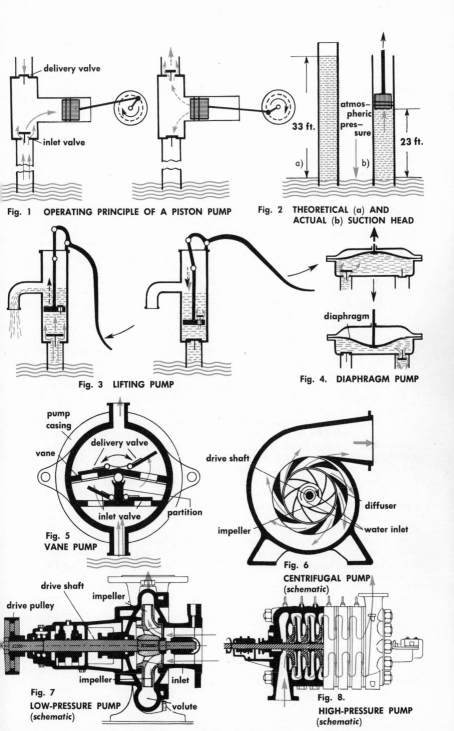

Fig. 1   OPERATING PRINCIPLE OF A PISTON PUMP

delivery valve

inlet valve

Fig. 2   THEORETICAL (a) AND ACTUAL (b) SUCTION HEAD

atmospheric pressure

33 ft.

23 ft.

a)   b)

Fig. 3   LIFTING PUMP

diaphragm

Fig. 4.   DIAPHRAGM PUMP

pump casing

vane

delivery valve

inlet valve

partition

Fig. 5 VANE PUMP

drive shaft

diffuser

impeller

water inlet

Fig. 6 CENTRIFUGAL PUMP (*schematic*)

drive shaft

impeller

drive pulley

impeller

inlet

volute

Fig. 7 LOW-PRESSURE PUMP (*schematic*)

Fig. 8. HIGH-PRESSURE PUMP (*schematic*)

COMPRESSORS (PISTON COMPRESSORS)

Compressors are machines for the compression of gases and vapours (to pressures of 2000 atm. and higher). Piston compressors are used for producing the highest pressures, whereas centrifugal compressors (see page 264) are used for low to medium pressures.

Fig. 1 shows a piston compressor. The crankshaft is driven by a suitable prime mover (electric motor, steam engine, internal combustion engine, etc.). A connecting rod between the crankshaft and the piston transforms the rotary motion of the former into a to-and-fro motion of the piston in the cylinder. The valves are spring-loaded and react to variations in pressure produced by the piston movement. In performing the suction stroke the piston causes a lowering of pressure in the cylinder, so that the inlet valve (Fig. 2) opens against the restraining pressure of its spring and allows the gas to flow into the cylinder. Then, when the piston begins to form its return stroke (compression stroke), the inlet closes because of the increase in pressure within the cylinder. When the piston has completed this stroke, i.e., has arrived at "top dead centre", the pressure of the gas compressed in the cylinder is so high that the delivery valve opens against the restraining pressure of its spring, allow the gas to flow into the delivery pipe. The spring of the delivery valve need not be as powerful as might at first be supposed. Actually there is also a pressure acting in the delivery pipe, at the rear of the valve, and this pressure is only a little below that which is produced by the compression stroke of the piston. Also, it is this pressure in the delivery pipe that keeps the delivery valve closed during the suction stroke. Usually, the compressor feeds the compressed gas into an intermediate vessel—called a receiver in the case of an air compressor—from which it is supplied to consumer equipment.

The operating cycle of a compressor is characterised by the so-called indicator diagram (Fig. 3). It shows the relation between pressure and volume during one revolution of the crankshaft, i.e., during one to-and-fro movement of the piston. Line 1 represents the suction stroke: the gas volume in the cylinder increases while the (low) pressure remains constant. Line 2 represents the compression: the pressure rises while the volume decreases. Then comes the discharge of the compressed gas, represented by line 3: the volume of the cylinder decreases at constant (high) pressure. Line 4 shows that when the piston performs the suction stroke (i.e., travels to the right), the inlet valve cannot immediately open, as the residual gas in the cylinder at the end of the compression stroke must expand until the pressure in the cylinder has fallen below the pressure in the inlet pipe. Not till then does the inlet valve open. Since the piston must not actually strike the end of the cylinder, there is always some dead space and therefore an undesirable gas residue, so that only a portion of the suction stroke is really utilised for drawing gas into the cylinder. If high pressures are required, compression will have to be achieved in several stages, i.e., the gas is passed from one cylinder to the next (Fig. 4). As gases become heated when they are compressed, it is necessary to provide cooling between the successive stages (Fig. 4a). These multi-stage compressors are usually of the double-acting type, i.e., when the piston travels in one direction, the gas is compressed on one side and suction is produced on the other side of the piston: the opposite occurs during the return stroke.

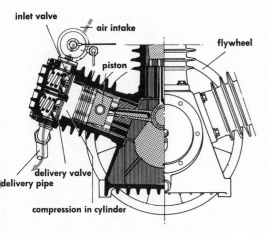

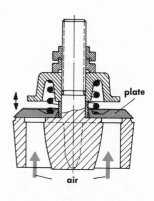

Fig. 1 SECTION THROUGH A COMPRESSOR

Fig. 2 VALVE

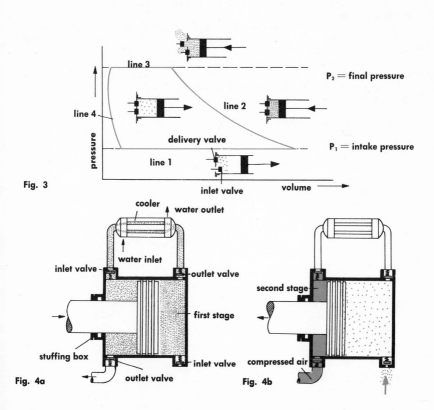

Fig. 3

Fig. 4a

Fig. 4b

27

PETROLEUM

About 300 million years ago the conditions for the subsequent formation of petroleum (mineral oil) were established in shallow coastal waters by the teeming tiny creatures and plants that lived and died in vast numbers. The ooze formed on the bottom by the remains of these organisms was unable to decompose because of lack of oxygen. As a result of climatic changes, these coastal areas became buried under layers of earth, and the organic remains were subjected to high pressures and temperatures over periods of millions of years. The fats, carbohydrates and proteins were thereby subjected to conditions in which they were decomposed and underwent extensive chemical changes. As a result of these changes, a large number of compounds were formed which all enter into the composition of petroleum (alkanes, aromatic compounds, sulphur compounds, etc.). As the conditions of decomposition varied from one region to another, petroleum found in different parts of the world tends to vary considerably in composition. In some places the decomposition was a very intensive process, with the result that natural gas and petroleum particularly rich in aromatic compounds (benzene derivatives) were formed. In addition to pressure and heat, it is certain that catalysts, ferments and especially bacteria have affected the chemical composition of petroleum crude oils.

The world's petroleum reserves are estimates at upward of 40 milliard[1] tons, and production is running at well over 1 milliard tons per year. Unless extensive new deposits are found (under the seas, in desert regions), it seems likely that the world's recoverable reserves of petroleum will be exhausted in something like half a century from now.

A vast variety of products is obtained from petroleum: petrol (gasoline) for aircraft and vehicles, fuel oil for heating and steam-raising, diesel oil, etc. Also, numerous organic chemicals are manufactured from petroleum and are processed into a wide range of products: synthetic rubber, pesticides, synthetic fibres, solvents, drugs, etc. Large-scale exploitation of the world's petroleum reserves started about a hundred years ago and is now a major factor in the power resources available to modern man.

1. A milliard is equivalent to one billion in U.S.A.

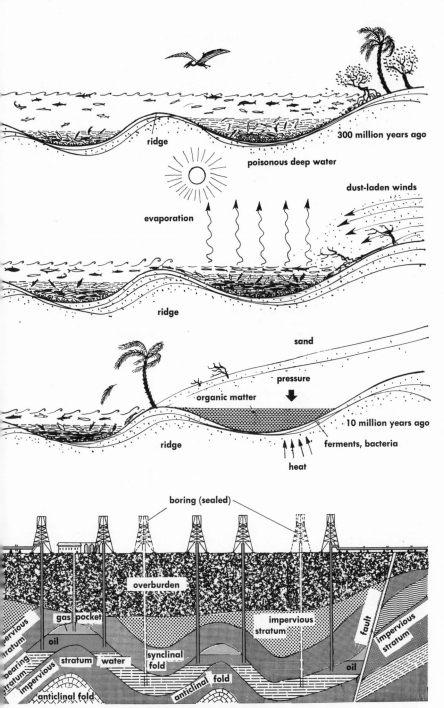

ridge

300 million years ago

poisonous deep water

evaporation

dust-laden winds

ridge

sand

pressure

organic matter

10 million years ago

ferments, bacteria

heat

ridge

boring (sealed)

overburden

impervious stratum

gas pocket

oil

impervious stratum

fault

impervious stratum

oil-bearing stratum

stratum water

synclinal fold

oil

impervious stratum

anticlinal fold

anticlinal fold

petroleum deposits (schematic)

29

PETROLEUM DISTILLATION

Petroleum is a complex mixture of hydrocarbons of varying volatility, together with small quantities of substances which contain oxygen, nitrogen, sulphur and ash derived from the vegetable and animal organisms from which the petroleum was formed (see page 28). The crude oil, which is conveyed to the refinery by pipeline, oil tanker or tank wagon, first has water and solid contaminants removed from it by sedimentation and is then split up by fractional distillation (see page 10). The crude oil is pumped through tube stills in which it is heated to 280°–300° C. It is then admitted to a large fractionating column in which the gases, the readily volatile petrol constituents, and the kerosene (paraffin oil) are distilled off. The remaining distillation residue, which is already of a viscous consistency, is pumped through a second tube still, in which it is reheated, and is then passed to a second fractionating column. In this column, which operates under vacuum, various grades of oil are distilled off (gas oil, diesel oil, cylinder oil, machine oil, etc.), while asphalt, mineral pitch, coke-like residues and inorganic matter remain behind. Except for the gas, nearly all the petroleum fractions require further processing whereby their content of deleterious impurities (ash, sulphur and nitrogen compounds, "gumming" and polymerising substances) is reduced or these impurities are removed altogether, either by chemical conversion (treatment with appropriate chemicals) or by physical adsorption with such substances as active charcoal, silica gel, kieselguhr (diatomaceous earth), fuller's earth, etc. Many petroleum fractions have to be treated with additives in order to acquire the desired properties. For example, petrol (gasoline) must undergo further chemical processing to give it good anti-knock and ignition properties, reduce its odour, and make it resistant to ageing. Similarly, machine oils have to be non-resinous, pale-coloured, odourless and oxidation-resistant; additives which further improve the properties of the oil are also employed.

Despite the separation of the multiple mixture of which petroleum consists into a number of fractions, each of which contains fewer constituents than the initial crude petroleum, each fraction still comprises many different constituents (for example, petrol contains upwards of a hundred). The correct fractionation of petroleum is therefore a difficult art which, in addition to the necessary knowledge, involves the use of much complex measuring equipment and costly apparatus. For instance, petroleum contains corrosive substances. Because of this the giant modern petroleum fractionating columns are made of special high-grade steel. Their operation is well-nigh fully automatic.

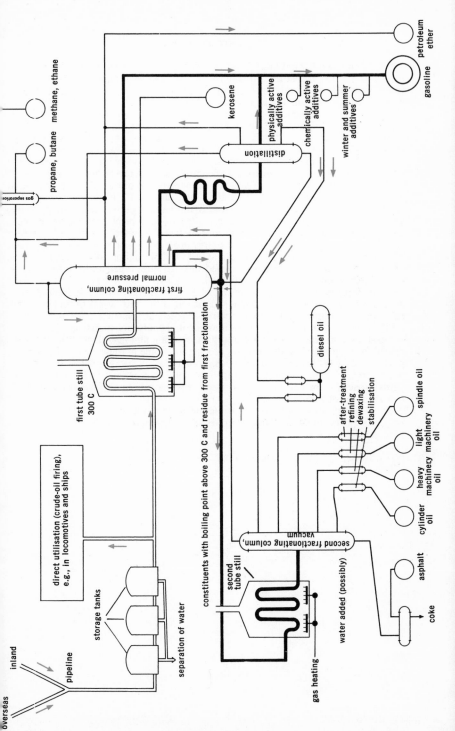

overseas

inland

pipeline

storage tanks

separation of water

direct utilisation (crude-oil firing), e.g., in locomotives and ships

first tube still 300 C

first fractionating column, normal pressure

gas separator

propane, butane   methane, ethane

kerosene

distillation

physically active additives

chemically active additives

winter and summer additives

gasoline

petroleum ether

constituents with boiling point above 300 C and residue from first fractionation

diesel oil

second fractionating column, vacuum

second tube still

gas heating

water added (possibly)

after-treatment
refining
dewaxing
stabilisation

spindle oil

light machinery oil

heavy machinery oil

cylinder oil

asphalt

coke

NATURAL GAS

Something like 700 milliard[1] cubic yards of gas a year are produced by gas wells in various parts of the world. Most of this is combustible gas now generally referred to as "natural gas" ("marsh gas" is an older name for very much the same thing); it consists of 80–95% methane, a hydrocarbon.

Some natural gas wells also produce incombustible or highly toxic gases such as carbon dioxide, sulphur dioxide, hydrogen sulphide and others, in rare cases also inert gases (noble gases) such as helium, neon and argon. The sulphurous gases for the most part are of volcanic origin and are formed deep down in the earth's crust. Natural gas in the more specific sense of a combustible hydrogen (largely methane) is usually found in regions where petroleum is also likely to occur. Many gas wells produce so-called "wet" natural gas containing petrol vapour which can be separated and utilised. For example, in the United States, up to 10% of the country's petrol consumption is supplied from this source. In dry natural gas, in addition to methane, small quantities of the following gases are often found to be present: carbon monoxide, hydrogen, helium, neon, argon, and nitrogen. Natural gas provides a very significant part of the raw material for energy production: in terms of energy content, the annual output of natural gas corresponds to 350 million tons of coal. A large proportion of the natural gas is conveyed through huge pipelines from the wells to the industrial centres and major cities, where it is used for industrial and domestic heating. A proportion is also used as fuel for gas engines which drive electricity-generating plant. Also, an increasing proportion of the natural gas output is chemically processed into motor fuels (petrol, diesel oil), plastics, man-made fibres, synthetic rubber, anti-freeze preparations, alcohols, solvents, insecticides, etc.

Besides the naturally existing gas wells, increasing numbers of artificial wells are drilled for tapping the underground gas supplies. Some of these wells deliver gas at pressures of 2000 lb./in^2. and upwards. Sometimes former gas-fields (worked out wells) are used as underground storage reservoirs—sometimes of $1\frac{1}{2}$ milliard cubic yards capacity—for natural gas which may first have been chemically cleaned and had their petrol content removed.

Large quantities of natural gas are found at the foot of the Western Pyrenees. In recent years, too, very large supplies of natural gas have been discovered in Holland.

1. A milliard is equivalent to one billion in U.S.A.

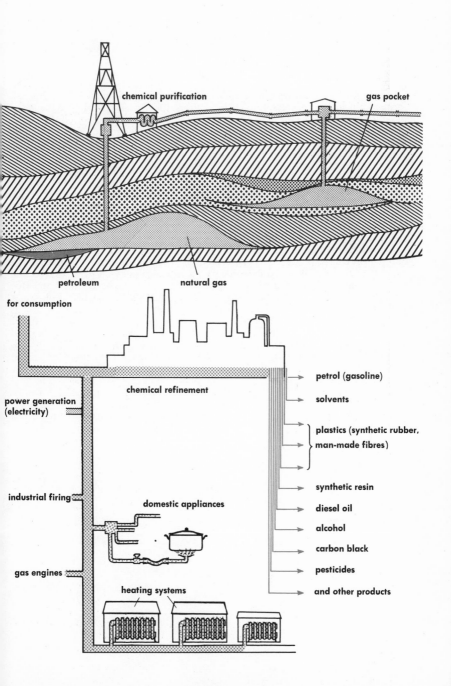

chemical purification

gas pocket

petroleum

natural gas

for consumption

chemical refinement

petrol (gasoline)

solvents

plastics (synthetic rubber, man-made fibres)

power generation (electricity)

synthetic resin

diesel oil

industrial firing

domestic appliances

alcohol

carbon black

pesticides

gas engines

heating systems

and other products

TOWN GAS[1]

Town gas is a combustible and toxic mixture comprising 50% hydrogen, 20–30% methane, 7–17% carbon monoxide, 3% carbon dioxide, 8% nitrogen and 2% hydrocarbons. Furthermore, town gas contains ammonia, sulphur, hydrocyanic acid, benzene and other substances. Sulphur (in the form of strong-smelling chemical compounds) produces the characteristic "gas smell"; indeed, sometimes the smell is deliberately added to provide a warning in the event of the escape of gas. Detoxicated gas contains little or no carbon monoxide. It is distributed to the consumers through pipelines at a pressure of at least about 1 lb./in². The quality of the gas is rated in terms of its calorific value, i.e., the amount of heat that is produced when one cubic foot of gas is burned with air. The calorific value ranges from 450 to 500 B.T.U. per cubic foot.

Because of its carbon monoxide content, town gas is highly poisonous, and because of its content of combustible gases it is highly explosive when mixed with air. If several cubic yards of gas are allowed to escape into a room, an explosive mixture will be formed, which can be ignited even by a tiny electric spark, such as may, for instance, be caused by a door bell or a telephone ringing.

Town gas is a fuel gas. The term "coal gas" is sometimes applied to it, denoting that it is produced mostly from coal. One way to produce this gas is to heat rough coal to a temperature of 1000°–1200° C, out of contact of air, in a chamber called a retort, which may be of the inclined type. In this process, up to about 500 cu. ft. of town gas can be produced from 100 lb. of dry coal with a low ash content. What remains of the coal after extraction of the gas is called coke. In other gas-making processes the coal is not heated by the external application of heat, but is converted into gas by partial combustion with oxygen and chemical reaction with water vapour. The crude gas produced must be carefully purified: in particular, it is necessary to remove volatile sulphur and nitrogen compounds. In many cases the "water gas" or "producer gas" obtained in this way is used as an admixture to coal gas (up to 40% being added). Fuel gases from oil refineries (which gases are produced by gasification of petroleum) or natural gas are playing an increasingly important part in town gas supply. Despite its dangerous character, town gas is unlikely to be entirely superseded by electricity in the foreseeable future. Gas will be able to hold its own because of its relatively low cost and the convenience with which it can be distributed through pipes. At the same time, the large quantities of carbon dioxide and the by no means inconsiderable quantities of sulphur dioxide, which are formed in the combustion of gas, add to the pollution of the atmosphere of our towns.

1. Coal gas in U.S.A.

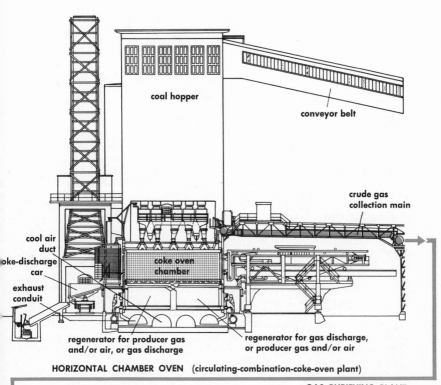

coal hopper

conveyor belt

crude gas
collection main

cool air
duct

coke-discharge
car

exhaust
conduit

coke oven
chamber

regenerator for producer gas
and/or air, or gas discharge

regenerator for gas discharge,
or producer gas and/or air

HORIZONTAL CHAMBER OVEN (circulating-combination-coke-oven plant)

GAS PURIFYING PLANT

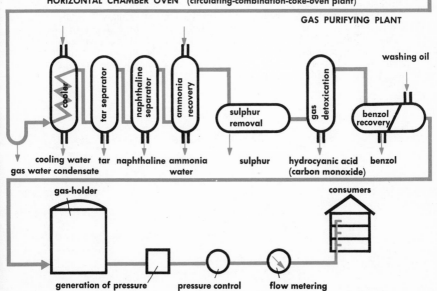

washing oil

cooler

tar separator

naphthaline separator

ammonia recovery

sulphur removal

gas detoxication

benzol recovery

cooling water tar naphthaline ammonia
gas water condensate
water

sulphur

hydrocyanic acid
(carbon monoxide)

benzol

gas-holder

consumers

generation of pressure

pressure control

flow metering

35

NATURAL PETROL (GASOLINE)

A distinction is made between synthetic petrol, which is produced from coal and other raw materials by chemical processes, and natural petrol, most of which is obtained as a substance already present in petroleum (mineral oil). The name "petrol" (or "gasoline") denotes a mixture of liquid, volatile hydrocarbons or, to be more precise, a mixture of alkanes, naphthenes and aromatic compounds with boiling points between 40° and 180° C. "Hydrocarbons" is a general designation for chemical compounds which consist solely of the elements hydrogen and carbon and which readily burn to produce carbon dioxide and water if they are mixed with a sufficient quantity of air and then ignited. Petrol for use as a fuel for internal combustion engines is produced by the following process:

The petroleum is pumped from the well through pipelines to storage tanks at the port of shipment, where the crude oil undergoes a preliminary purification treatment. Tankers convey the crude oil to other ports, where it is discharged into storage tanks. From here it is distributed to the refineries, e.g., through pipelines. At the refinery the petroleum is preheated in heat exchangers, then passed to tube stills, where it is heated to a high temperature in special steel tubes. These stills are fired with oil which is likewise obtained from the crude oil. The crude oil, heated to a temperature of several hundred degrees, expands in the distilling column, where it is separated into the fractions: power gas (1% of the total quantity), light petrol (5%) and petrol (10%). The remaining 82% of the original quantity is again passed through the tube still, is reheated to a high temperature, and is passed to a distilling column in which a vacuum is applied, because the distillation temperature can be kept considerably lower when the vacuum is employed. In this second column 20% of the original quantity of crude oil is split up into petrol, 15% into fuel oils and 20% into lubricating oil. The residue, about 27%, provides tar, pitch and coke or undergoes further processing whereby, in some cases, more petrol is produced. However, such petrol is more properly to be regarded as synthetic petrol. The various petrol fractions are mixed and refined; the composition of the mixture depends on the time of year (in the winter the proportion of light petrol in the mixture is higher than in the summer). "Refinement" involves various processing treatments whereby the quality of the petrol as a motor fuel is improved, e.g., it comprises the admixture of aromatic compounds, anti-knock agents, anti-oxidants (ageing inhibitors), etc. The final result must be a volatile fuel which must, among other properties, have a minimum octane number of 80 to 90, ignites easily, does not gasify at room temperature, does not develop "gumming", does not smell objectionably, and burns without residue. Such a mixture of substances is of extremely complex composition, comprising over two hundred individual constituents.

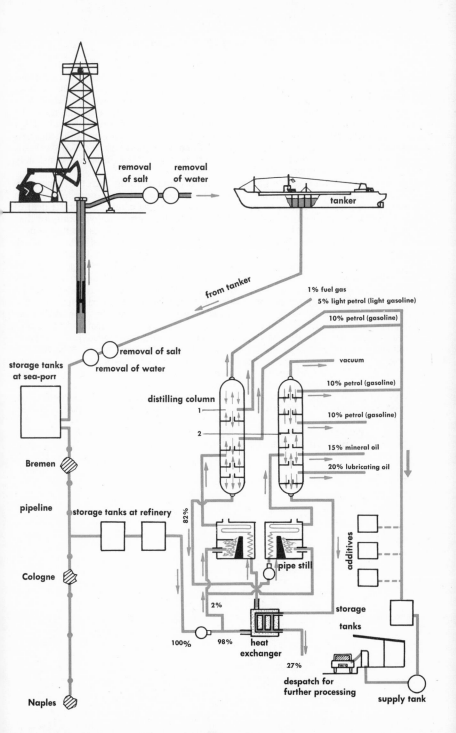

removal of salt   removal of water

tanker

from tanker

1% fuel gas
5% light petrol (light gasoline)
10% petrol (gasoline)

removal of salt
removal of water

storage tanks at sea-port

distilling column
1
2

vacuum
10% petrol (gasoline)
10% petrol (gasoline)
15% mineral oil
20% lubricating oil

Bremen

pipeline   storage tanks at refinery

82%

additives

Cologne

pipe still

2%

storage tanks

100%   98%   heat exchanger

27%

despatch for further processing

supply tank

Naples

37

SYNTHETIC PETROL (GASOLINE)

In some countries without petroleum resources of their own the production of "synthetic" petrol from coal or from gases containing carbon is of considerable importance. But even in countries which are well supplied with petroleum, a certain amount of synthetic petrol is usually added to the natural product. Synthetic petrol is manufactured either from coal or from natural gas or from petroleum fractions. In the last-mentioned case the designation "synthetic" is appropriate only if the initial substance is gaseous or of low volatility. Crude oil residues and other residues rich in carbon can be converted into petrol. Such petrol, too, can be called synthetic.

Petrol is a high-energy mixture of hydrocarbons consisting of molecules containing 5 to 12 carbon atoms and 12 to 26 hydrogen atoms.

Coal contains only very little hydrogen. To convert it into petrol it is therefore necessary to introduce hydrogen into the compounds. This is done under high pressure and temperature and in the presence of active catalysts. A great deal of petrol used to be produced by so-called catalytic high pressure hydration. In that process it took 4 tons of coal to produce 1 ton of petrol, pressures up to 700 atm. and temperatures of 410°–460° C being employed. The coal was dried, pulverised, and mixed with heavy oil to form a thick slurry. Catalysts were added, and about 70,000 cu. ft. of hydrogen gas per ton of coal was forced in. The hydrogen was produced from coal and water, the carbon monoxide formed in this process being utilised as fuel gas or converted. Synthetic petrol is also manufactured from water and coal by a process in which carbon monoxide and hydrogen are produced from coke, raw brown coal or brown coal briquettes and, after careful cleaning, are passed over catalysts at low pressure. Solid hydrocarbons, in addition to petrol and other products, are formed in this process. In a more recently developed process, gases containing carbon monoxide are conducted, together with water, over suitable catalysts. The resulting reactions produce petrol, as well as acids, alcohols and other substances. Also, petrol is produced from unsaturated hydrocarbon gases with the aid of catalysts. However, since such synthetic petrols are more expensive to produce than petrols from petroleum, in Western Europe synthetic petrol is nowadays of importance only as an additive for natural petrols so as to adjust their properties to meet the exacting requirements of modern internal combustion engines. For this purpose, synthetic petrols having a high octane number (a criterion for the anti-knock properties) are particularly valuable.

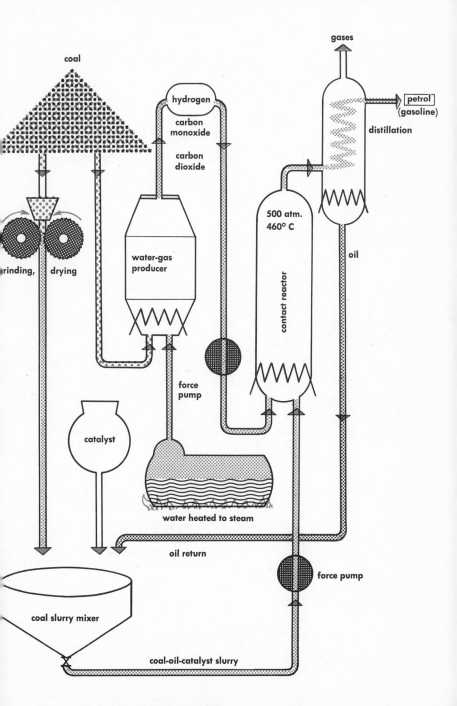

coal

hydrogen

carbon monoxide

carbon dioxide

grinding, drying

water-gas producer

force pump

catalyst

water heated to steam

oil return

coal slurry mixer

coal-oil-catalyst slurry

gases

petrol (gasoline)

distillation

500 atm. 460° C

contact reactor

oil

force pump

STEAM BOILERS

In industrial plants where large quantities of high-pressure steam are required for a wide variety of purposes the steam is generated in boilers at pressures of about 175–600 lb./in^2. (in power stations: up to about 2400 lb./in^2.).

The various types of boiler differ fundamentally in the method whereby the heat of the furnace and flue gases causes the water to boil. In the elementary form of "boiler", the domestic kettle (Fig. 1), the heat of the flames is applied to the bottom of the receptacle containing the water. In a simple steam-generating boiler this same principle is applied, and in so-called fire tube boilers the hot furnace gases pass through tubes in the water space (fire tubes). The advantage of this type of boiler is its simple operation. On the other hand, their steam-generating efficiency is relatively low because of the limited grate area and the slow water circulation. Also, it has the disadvantages of having a low operating pressure and taking up much space. For these reasons such boilers are nowadays used only in locomotives or in installations which require fairly small quantities of steam.

Modern high-efficiency boilers, capable of very quickly coping with high peak loads, are of the water-tube type. In such boilers the water is evaporated in tubes which are arranged inside a heated chamber in which they are exposed to the radiant heat of the flames and the hot flue gases. They are constructed as boilers with steeply inclined water tubes (e.g., Stirling boiler, Fig. 2) or with tubes set at a relatively low inclination (e.g., Babcock and Wilcox boiler, Fig. 3). The tubes are interconnected at their ends by so-called headers, which are usually set at right angles to the tubes. The boiler feed-water, preheated by the flue gases, enters the upper steam drum from where it flows through unheated or only slightly heated tubes to the lower headers or drums. From here it ascends into the water tubes, in which it is evaporated and is returned in the form of a water-and-steam mixture to the upper drum. In the latter the steam is separated from the entrained water and flows through the superheater tubes, which are heated by flue gases of sufficiently high temperature. The steam then flows to the consumer equipment. The separated water, together with additional water, flows back to the lower headers or drums, and the cycle is repeated.

The boilers referred to here are heated with coal or oil. A coal-fired boiler is usually provided with a so-called mechanical stoker, a frequently employed form of which is the chain grate (Fig. 4). This device consists of a slowly moving endless chain of grate bars. The coal fed on to one end of the grate is burned in the furnace. The residual matter, slag and ash fall off the other end of the chain into the ashpit. To control the combustion process, air is blown from below through the grate. In other types of firing system pulverised coal, together with air, is blown into the combustion chamber of the furnace, where it burns at temperatures of about 1800° C. Again, in other systems finely divided ("atomised") fuel oil is sprayed through nozzles into the combustion chamber. The latter is lined with refractory material (fireclay brick), in which water pipes are embedded. These absorb the radiant heat, protect the lining and, in addition, produce steam.

Special boilers can generate high-pressure steam (150–350 lb./in^2.). In such boilers the water is circulated by pumping (forced-circulation boilers, Fig. 5), whereby the quantity of water circulated is six or seven times as large as that corresponding to the evaporative capacity. Alternatively, the water is pumped straight through the boiler tubes ("once-through" or flash boiler, Fig. 6).

Fig. 1   KETTLE

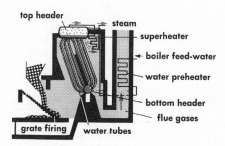

Fig. 2   STIRLING BOILER

top header
steam
superheater
boiler feed-water
water preheater
bottom header
flue gases
grate firing   water tubes

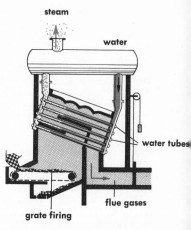

Fig. 3   BABCOCK & WILCOX BOILER

steam
water
water tubes
flue gases
grate firing

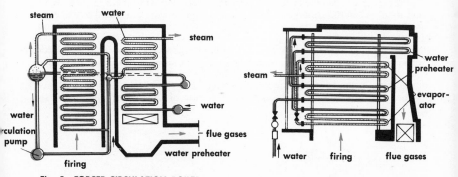

Fig. 4   CHAIN GRATE FIRING SYSTEM

coal feed
ash removal
air   grate movement

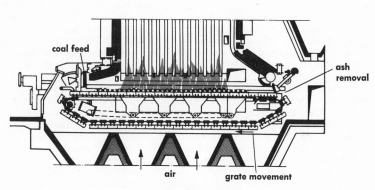

Fig. 5   FORCED-CIRCULATION BOILER

steam
water
steam
water
circulation pump
water preheater
flue gases
firing

Fig. 6   ONCE-THROUGH BOILER

steam
water preheater
evaporator
water   firing   flue gases

41

STEAM ENGINE

A steam engine utilises the energy contained in steam under high pressure. The energy that is released when steam expands is made to produce rotary motion which can be used for the driving of machinery. The steam from the boiler is admitted into the cylinder in which there is a piston and in which the steam expands, causing the piston to move (Fig. 1a). When the piston has travelled to the end of the cylinder and thus completed its stroke (Fig. 1b), the now expanded steam is allowed to escape from the cylinder. At the same time the steam is changed over, live steam under pressure being admitted to the other side of the piston, causing the latter to travel back, past its starting point (Fig. 1c), until it has reached the other end of its stroke (Fig. 1d). A steam engine of this kind is called "double-acting" because the force of the steam is applied alternately on two sides of the piston. While the piston is being forced in one direction by the expanding steam, the spent steam is pushed out of the cylinder on the other side of the piston. Reversing, i.e., the change-over of the steam supply so as to ensure the admission of live steam to the appropriate side of the piston and the discharge of the spent steam on the other side, is effected automatically by a control device called a slide valve. On some steam engines, valves are similar in principle to those used in internal combustion engines. The commonest type is the flat slide valve (often called a "D-slide valve") (Fig. 2). It alternately covers the steam inlet port and the exhaust port. During the piston movement the slide valve opens the exhaust port for the escape of the spent steam behind the piston (Figs. 2a and 2b). The slide valve must therefore always be in such a position that it connects the working side of the piston to the live steam supply, and opens the exhaust port on the other side to enable the steam to escape into the exhaust channel. The valve does this by moving to-and-fro at the same rate as the piston. It is controlled through a linkage system from the crankshaft in such a manner that the valve moves in the opposite direction to the piston (Fig. 3). The spent steam that emerges from the cylinder is passed to a condenser where it is cooled and thereby precipitated as water. In some cases (e.g., steam locomotives) it is, instead, discharged direct into the atmosphere.

The term "compound steam engine" refers to an engine in which the steam is expanded in several cylinders (usually three), in successive stages. As a rule, all three pistons have the same length of stroke, since they drive the same crankshaft. However, as the volume of the steam increases as the result of expansion, i.e., when its pressure is reduced, the second (or medium-pressure) stage has a larger piston diameter than the first stage (the high-pressure stage). The third (or low-pressure) stage has a piston of still larger diameter than the second stage. The transmission of power and motion from the piston to the crankshaft is effected through a crosshead (a reciprocating block sliding between guides) which forms the junction piece between the piston-rod and the connecting-rod. One end of the latter is pivotably connected to the crosshead and the other end is connected to the circumference of a wheel or to a crank of the crankshaft. When the piston and, with it, the piston rod and crosshead move to-and fro, the crosshead transmits this movement to the crankshaft or wheel and thus produces rotation. One end of the crankshaft is provided with a flywheel to ensure smooth running, free from jerkiness due to the reciprocating motion of the piston. Nowadays steam engines are used only in cases where slow-running machinery with varying power requirements has to be driven, e.g., for winding gear in coal mines, ships' propulsion machinery, rollers, etc. Even the best steam engines have an efficiency of only 15–18% in terms of utilisation of the energy contained in the coal.

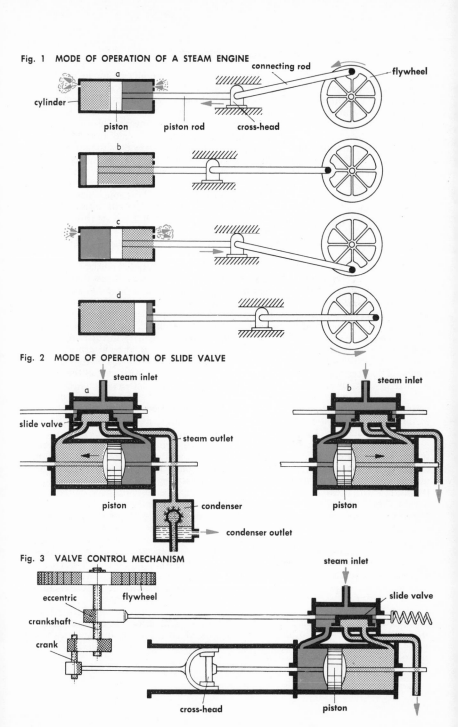

Fig. 1 MODE OF OPERATION OF A STEAM ENGINE

connecting rod
flywheel
cylinder
a
piston
piston rod
cross-head

b

c

d

Fig. 2 MODE OF OPERATION OF SLIDE VALVE

steam inlet
a
slide valve
steam outlet
piston
condenser
condenser outlet

steam inlet
b
piston

Fig. 3 VALVE CONTROL MECHANISM

steam inlet
eccentric
flywheel
slide valve
crankshaft
crank
cross-head
piston

43

STEAM TURBINES

In a steam turbine the energy in steam under pressure is used for producing a mechanical rotary motion which is usually employed for electric power generation. The steam is discharged in the form of a high-velocity jet from a nozzle and impinges upon blades mounted on a wheel, whereby the latter is caused to rotate. In order to convert the pressure energy of the steam as efficiently as possible into kinetic energy, so-called Laval nozzles are employed comprising an inlet portion, a constricted throat and a gradually widening outlet (Fig. 1). As a result of the constriction of the passage followed by the widened outlet portion (diffuser), the pressure of the steam flowing through this nozzle is converted into velocity. The higher the velocity of the steam is, the larger is the force that the jet of steam is able to exert upon any obstacle it encounters. Also, it very much depends upon how much the steam is thereby deflected from its original path. If a wheel is provided with a set of blades which deflect the steam into very nearly the circumferential direction (Fig. 2), then the steam will exert upon the wheel a force in the circumferential direction, causing it to rotate (Fig. 3). In order to achieve the fullest possible utilisation of the energy contained in the steam, a number of successive stages are usually arranged one behind the other. The wheels provided with blading are mounted on the same shaft and therefore all revolve at the same speed. The rotating assembly as a whole is called the rotor. The decrease in pressure and the increase in diameter of the successive blade wheels is effected in definite and carefully calculated stages. Theoretically the entire pressure of the steam (e.g., 1500 lb./in.^{2}) can be expanded to atmospheric pressure in a single nozzle and be converted into velocity. In that case the blade wheel would have to revolve at a very high circumferential velocity in order to attain reasonable efficiency. Such a high velocity would, however, present a number of technical difficulties and involve the risk of destruction of the machine by the large centrifugal forces that would arise. Turbines embodying the utilisation of the energy in successive stages are designed according to various alternative principles:

1. Velocity staging: In this arrangement the entire steam pressure is, indeed, converted into velocity in one nozzle, but this velocity is utilised in stages in a number of blade rings (rows of moving blades mounted on the same shaft (Curtis turbine, Fig. 4).

2. Pressure staging: The steam is expanded in a nozzle, and the resulting velocity is used up in driving a blade ring mounted behind the nozzle. The steam then passes through guide blading which functions as a nozzle and in which the steam is again expanded a little and the velocity used for driving another blade ring (Fig. 2). This alternating sequence of stationary nozzles and rotating blades is continued until the entire steam pressure has been used up. The same quantity of steam (in terms of weight) flows successively through all the blade rings that make up the turbine rotor. However, the stage-by-stage reduction of the high initial pressure of the steam is associated with a progressive increase in volume, and for this reason the flow sections between the blades of the successive rows of blading must become correspondingly larger. For this reason the blade rings at the end of the turbine are of larger outside diameter than those at the beginning (impulse turbines).

3. Reaction staging: In this system the pressure is converted into velocity not only in nozzles or guide blades, but also in the blade rings of the rotor (reaction turbines).

Steam turbines can also be classified according to the utilisation of the steam pressure drop. For instance, a condensing turbine (Fig. 5) utilises the entire available drop from high pressure to the vacuum in the condenser; a back-pressure turbine utilises only the top part, whereas an exhaust-steam turbine utilises only the bottom part of the pressure drop.

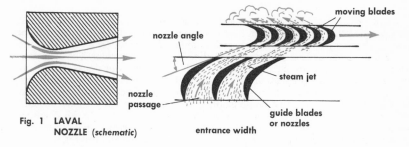

Fig. 1 **LAVAL NOZZLE** (*schematic*)

nozzle angle

nozzle passage

entrance width

moving blades

steam jet

guide blades or nozzles

Fig. 2 **DEFLECTION OF THE STEAM JET**
(*pressure staging*)

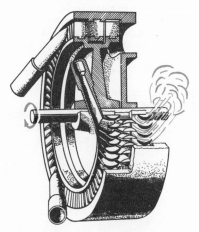

Fig. 3 **DRIVE OF A WHEEL WITH ROTOR BLADES** (*schematic*)

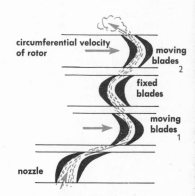

circumferential velocity of rotor

moving blades 2

fixed blades

moving blades 1

nozzle

Fig. 4 **DOUBLE-ROW CURTIS TURBINE**
(*velocity staging*)

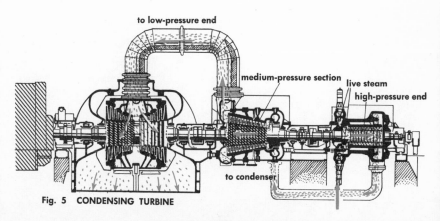

to low-pressure end

medium-pressure section

live steam
high-pressure end

to condenser

Fig. 5 **CONDENSING TURBINE**

45

GAS TURBINES

Gas turbines are driven by the combustion gases from liquid fuels. In construction and operation they resemble steam turbines (see page 44) in that a flowing medium with a high energy content—i.e., the combustion gases—produces a rotary motion as a result of being deflected by rings of blading mounted on a rotor. The operation of a gas turbine is shown schematically in Fig. 1: the compressor draws in fresh air and compresses it to a pressure of 50–75 lb./in.^{2}; the air is forced by the compressor through a heat exchanger (the regenerator) where it is preheated by the heat that is still present in the exhaust combustion gases emerging from the turbine; and finally the preheated air is admitted into the combustion chamber. In this chamber liquid fuel is burned, thereby producing gases with a temperature of about 650° C. These combustion gases flow at high velocity into the turbine and drive it.

The turbine itself, the compressor, and the electric generator are all mounted on one shaft. The turbine cannot transmit its entire power output to the generator, for a substantial proportion is needed for driving the compressor. The turbine is started with the aid of an electric motor which first has to set the compressor in motion, in order to produce compressed air and supply it to the combustion chamber so as to enable the combustion gases to be formed. Only then can the turbine start running. Fig. 2 shows the main features of a gas turbine. The most familiar form of gas turbine is the jet propulsion engine for aircraft (see page 562). This is a particular specialised form of turbine, however. Ordinary gas turbines are used only in cases where the liquid fuels they use are cheaper than coal.

Another type of gas turbine is the hot-air turbine (Fig. 3). Here the rotary is produced, not by combustion gases, but by air which is heated in a heat exchanger by the hot combustion gases. This hot air recirculates continuously, i.e., it is drawn into the compressor again after leaving the turbine. However, the air must be cooled before entering the compressor, otherwise the blading of the latter would soon be destroyed as a result of operating at excessively high temperatures.

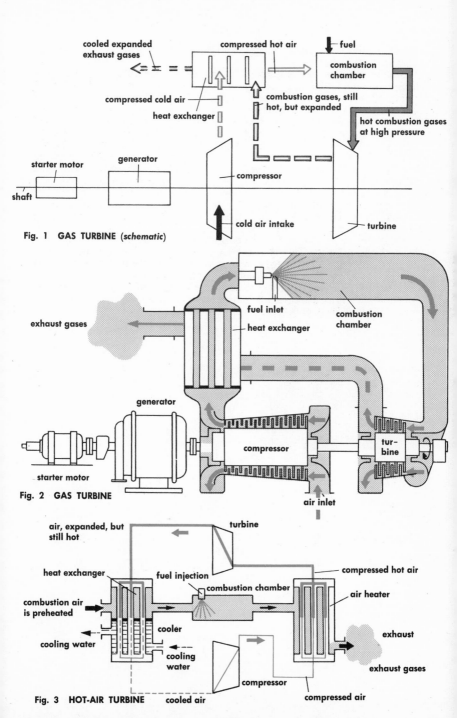

Fig. 1 GAS TURBINE (*schematic*)

cooled expanded exhaust gases
compressed hot air
fuel
combustion chamber
compressed cold air
heat exchanger
combustion gases, still hot, but expanded
hot combustion gases at high pressure
starter motor
generator
compressor
shaft
cold air intake
turbine

Fig. 2 GAS TURBINE

fuel inlet
combustion chamber
exhaust gases
heat exchanger
generator
compressor
tur-bine
starter motor
air inlet

Fig. 3 HOT-AIR TURBINE

air, expanded, but still hot
turbine
heat exchanger
fuel injection
combustion chamber
compressed hot air
air heater
combustion air is preheated
cooler
cooling water
exhaust
cooling water
exhaust gases
cooled air
compressor
compressed air

47

WATER TURBINES (PELTON)

In water turbines the kinetic energy of flowing or falling water is converted into mechanical rotary motion.

The oldest form of "water turbine" is the water wheel. The natural head— difference in water level—of a stream is utilised to drive it. In its conventional form the water wheel is made of wood and is provided with buckets or vanes round the periphery. The water thrusts against these, causing the wheel to rotate. The latter drives the millstones (or sometimes other machinery). In the case of an "overshot wheel" the water pours on to the buckets from above. If the water thrusts against the vanes on the underside of the water wheel, as in Fig. 1, it is called an "undershot wheel". The principle of the old water wheel is embodied in the modern Pelton wheel (Fig. 2), which consists of a wheel provided with spoon-shaped buckets round the periphery (Fig. 3). A high-velocity jet of water emerging from a nozzle impinges on the buckets and sets the wheel in motion. The speed of rotation is determined by the flow rate and the velocity of the water; it is controlled by means of a needle in the nozzle (the turbine operates most efficiently when the wheel rotates at half the velocity of the jet). If the load on the wheel suddenly decreases, the jet deflectors partially divert the jet issuing from the nozzle until the jet needle has appropriately reduced the flow (Fig. 4). This arrangement is necessary because if, in the event of sudden load decrease, the jet needle were suddenly closed, the flow of water would be reduced too abruptly, causing harmful "water hammer" phenomena in the water system. In most cases the control of the deflector is linked to an electric generator.

A Pelton wheel is used in cases where large heads of water are available. The water is discharged from the high-level reservoir through pipes to the turbine.

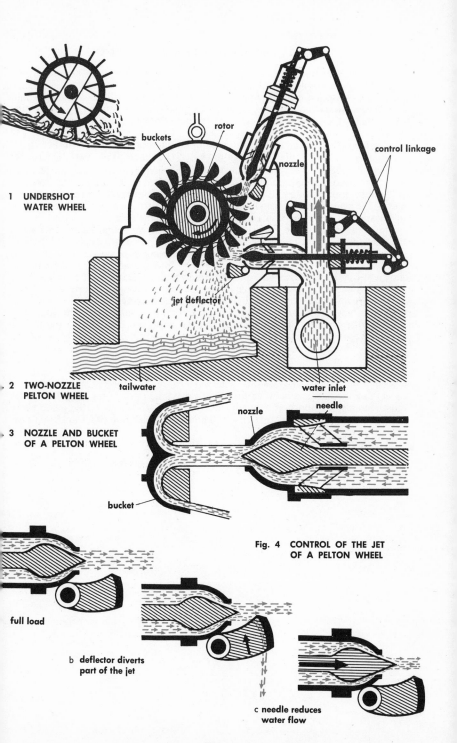

1 UNDERSHOT WATER WHEEL

buckets

rotor

nozzle

control linkage

jet deflector

2 TWO-NOZZLE PELTON WHEEL

tailwater

water inlet

3 NOZZLE AND BUCKET OF A PELTON WHEEL

nozzle

needle

bucket

Fig. 4 CONTROL OF THE JET OF A PELTON WHEEL

full load

b deflector diverts part of the jet

c needle reduces water flow

49

WATER TURBINES (FRANCIS, KAPLAN)

In the great majority of cases (large and small water flow rates and heads) the type of turbine employed is the *Francis* or *radial-flow turbine*. The significant difference in relation to the Pelton wheel is the water is diverted inside the turbine. This diversion takes place at right angles to the direction of entry (Fig. 1), causing the runner—the turbine rotor—to spin round. The water first enters the volute, which is an annular channel surrounding the runner, and then flows between the fixed guide vanes, which give the water the optimum direction of flow. It then enters the runner and flows radially through the latter, i.e., towards the centre. The runner is provided with curved vanes upon which the water impinges. The guide vanes are so arranged that the energy of the water is largely converted into rotary motion and is not consumed by eddies and other undesirable flow phenomena causing energy losses. The guide vanes are usually adjustable so as to provide a degree of adaptability to variations in the water flow rate and in the load of the turbine.

The guide vanes in the Francis turbine are the elements that direct the flow of the water, just as the nozzle of the Pelton wheel does. The water is discharged through an outlet from the centre of the turbine. The main features of a water turbine of this type are illustrated schematically in Fig. 1. The volute, guide vanes and runner are shown in Fig. 1a. The diversion of the water at right angles to its direction of entry is clearly indicated in Fig. 1b, which is a cross-section through the turbine.

For very low heads and high flow rates—e.g., at barrages[1] in rivers—a different type of turbine, the *Kaplan* or *propeller turbine* is usually employed. It is rather like the propeller of a ship operating in reverse: the ship's propeller rotates and thrusts the water away behind it, thus causing the ship to move forward (see page 546), in the Kaplan turbine the water flows through the propeller and sets the latter in rotation. The water enters the turbine laterally (Fig. 2), is deflected by the guide vanes, and flows axially through the propeller. For this reason, these machines are referred to as axial-flow turbines. The flow rate of the water through the turbine can be controlled by varying the distance between the guide vanes; the pitch of the propeller blades must then also be appropriately adjusted (Fig. 3). Each setting of the guide vanes corresponds to one particular setting of the propeller blades in order to obtain high efficiency.

The runner of a water turbine drives a shaft which is coupled, directly or through gearing, to an electric generator (see page 64).

1. Dams in U.S.A.

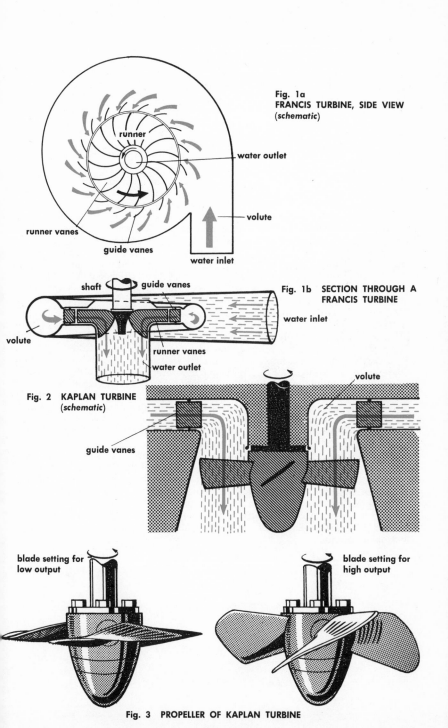

Fig. 1a
FRANCIS TURBINE, SIDE VIEW
(*schematic*)

runner

water outlet

volute

runner vanes

guide vanes

water inlet

shaft   guide vanes

Fig. 1b   SECTION THROUGH A
FRANCIS TURBINE

water inlet

volute

runner vanes

water outlet

Fig. 2   KAPLAN TURBINE
(*schematic*)

guide vanes

volute

blade setting for
low output

blade setting for
high output

Fig. 3   PROPELLER OF KAPLAN TURBINE

51

FUEL CELL

A fuel cell is a device in which the energy released in the oxidation of a conventional fuel is made directly available in the form of an electric current. It thus avoids the wasteful detour of the conventional thermal power stations, i.e., the generation of electricity via the "inferior" thermal energy. Although the principle of the fuel cell was formulated by W. Ostwald as long ago as 1894, it is only in recent years that some success has been achieved in the construction of efficient cells of this kind. In the fuel cell constructed by Baur and Ehrenberg in 1911 (Fig. 1) a carbon rod serves as the fuel. It functions as the anode, introducing C^{++++} ions into the solution. This necessitates an operating temperature of $1000°$–$1100°$ C. The electrolyte is molten soda. The cathode, consisting of molten silver, forms O^{--} ions from the oxygen that is continuously injected. According to the equation $C^{++++} + 2O^{--} = CO_2$, the reaction product obtained is carbon dioxide, just as in ordinary combustion. For every carbon atom that is converted, four electrons are given off to the carbon rod and four electrons are withdrawn from the oxygen electrode. These electrons can produce a current in an external circuit. According to this conception, a coal-burning stove is an internally short-circuited fuel cell. The major disadvantage of the fuel cell described above is the high temperature and, consequently, the very short service life of the materials employed. Less severe conditions can be achieved by using gases (hydrogen, in particular) as the fuel. Thus, the Bacon fuel cell (H_2O_2 cell) (Fig. 2) produces current densities of up to about $6\frac{1}{2}$ amp./in.^{2} at a temperature of $240°$ C. The pressure of the aqueous electrolytes does, however, rise to 1000 lb./in.^{2} and upwards. The ionisation of the gas fed to the cell is effected at diffusion electrodes of nickel. These are porous sintered components which on one side are connected to the gas supply and on the other side are in contact with the electrolyte. The active region is at the boundary of the three phases gas/electrode/electrolyte. To make this boundary as long as possible, all the pores must have the same optimum diameter, as is clarified by Fig. 3 (principle of homoporosity). In order completely to obviate the passage of unutilised gas through the pores, each electrode is provided with a fine-pored cover layer (double-layer electrode). As a result of the high catalytic activity of the electrodes employed, the cell can operate already at room temperature. The H_2O_2 cell designed by Justi and Winsel (Fig. 4), which is known as the dissolved fuel cell, also operates at ordinary temperatures. In this cell the oxygen electrodes contain Raney silver and the hydrogen electrodes contain Raney nickel as the catalyst. Already at temperatures below $100°$ C (and at atmospheric pressure, too!) this cell attains current density values almost as high as those of the Bacon cell. The fundamental voltage is over 90% of the theoretically attainable voltage of 1.23 volt. The electrodes employed are described as "double-skeleton catalyst electrodes". Because of their great catalytic activity, they are able to dehydrate liquid organic fuels (e.g., methanol). This results in the relatively simple constructional features of the dissolved fuel cell (Fig. 5). The alcohol serving as fuel is mixed with the electrolyte (potassium hydroxide solution).

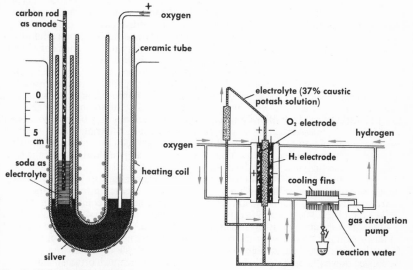

Fig. 1 HIGH-TEMPERATURE CELL ACCORDING
TO BAUR AND EHRENBERG

carbon rod
as anode
oxygen
ceramic tube
0
5
cm
soda as
electrolyte
heating coil
silver

Fig. 2 HIGH-PRESSURE CELL WITH
POROUS NICKEL ELECTRODES
ACCORDING TO F. T. BACON

electrolyte (37% caustic
potash solution)
O₂ electrode
hydrogen
oxygen
H₂ electrode
cooling fins
gas circulation
pump
reaction water

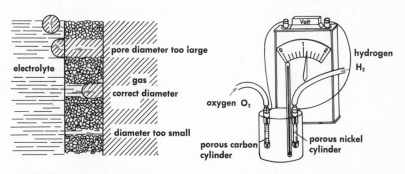

Fig. 3 GAS DIFFUSION ELECTRODE WITH
PORES OF DIFFERENT WIDTHS

electrolyte
pore diameter too large
gas
correct diameter
diameter too small

Fig. 4 H₂O₂ CELL ACCORDING TO
JUSTI AND WINSEL

Volt
hydrogen
H₂
oxygen O₂
porous carbon
cylinder
porous nickel
cylinder

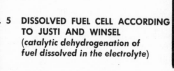

Fig. 5 DISSOLVED FUEL CELL ACCORDING
TO JUSTI AND WINSEL
(catalytic dehydrogenation of
fuel dissolved in the electrolyte)

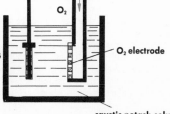

O₂
O₂ electrode
caustic potash solution
and alcohol

NUCLEAR REACTOR

The nuclear reactor serves to convert nuclear energy (atomic energy) into thermal energy. The nuclei of atoms consist, broadly speaking, of the elementary particles named protons and neutrons. The protons have a positive electric charge, whereas the neutrons have no charge, i.e., they are electrically neutral. Very powerful forces of attraction act between these particles (collectively referred to as "nucleons") and hold them together in the nucleus. Heavy atomic nuclei are, however, not so stable as light ones, because in the former the repulsive forces exerted by the protons loosen the structure of the nucleus. For this reason it is possible to cause fission of heavy nuclei—such as those of uranium 235—by bombarding them with free neutrons. In Fig. 1 a neutron is shown hitting a nucleus of uranium 235. The latter is set vibrating as a result of this impact, and these vibrations may become so violent that the nucleus is split up into several parts, e.g., into a barium and a krypton nucleus. The "fission products" travel at considerable velocity, collide with matter somewhere in the reactor, and give off their kinetic energy as heat. This is the conversion of nuclear energy into heat. In addition to the fission products and heat formed in the fission of uranium, however, two fresh neutrons are also formed, which in turn can cause the fission of more uranium atoms. In this way the *chain reaction* is initiated; this is illustrated in Fig. 2: the neutron coming from the left strikes the U 235 nucleus and briefly forms the intermediate product U 236, which disintegrates spontaneously into strontium and xenon. Three neutrons are released in this fission process. In order to be able to utilise these neutrons, which are emitted from the parent nucleus at high velocity, for further fissile processes, they have to be slowed down ("moderated"). Low-velocity neutrons are much better suited to split atoms than high-velocity neutrons are. The slower neutrons can interact with the uranium nucleus for a greater length of time, whereas faster neutrons are in the vicinity of the nucleus for too short a time to initiate the fission process. The velocity of the neutrons is moderated by causing them to collide with light atoms, large numbers of which must be incorporated in the reactor for this purpose. Materials consisting of such light atoms are, for example, graphite and water. The neutrons which have been slowed down in this way will then cause fission of further U 235 nuclei. Each fission process gives birth to fresh electrons, so that the chain reaction is self-sustaining and the reactor is consequently kept in operation.

Fig. 3 is a schematic illustration of a nuclear reactor—in this case a water-moderated reactor. The actual reactor core is shown on the left. The uranium is installed in the form of metallic rods in a vessel filled with water. The fission takes place within the uranium. The neutrons which are released in the process are diffused through the uranium and into the surrounding water, where they collide with the light hydrogen and oxygen atoms and are moderated, i.e., they lose velocity.

These slowed-down neutrons re-enter the uranium rods with a certain probability and they there cause fresh fission reactions to take place. The fission products formed as a result of these give off their energy to the uranium, which in turn transmits it to the water. The latter is circulated by a pump through a heat exchanger, in which it transfers the heat to a secondary thermal circuit. To ensure that the reactor will not stop functioning nor become excessively overheated, the rate of neutron formation inside it has to be controlled with considerable accuracy. This is done by means of the control rods, which consist of a neutron-absorbing material and which are inserted into the reactor core to an accurately variable depth. This depth of penetration must be just enough to ensure that, on an average, per fission only one neutron remains available to produce another fission reaction. Since the fission products are highly radioactive, the reactor must be enclosed in a thick casing of concrete called the "shield". In the so-called boiling water reactor (Fig. 4) the water is allowed to evaporate inside the reactor itself, the steam being utilised in the primary circuit; in principle, no heat exchanger is needed.

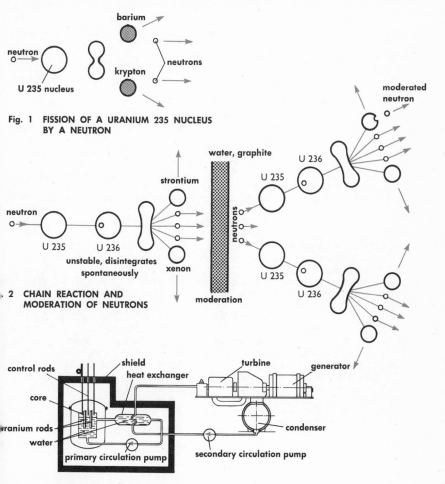

Fig. 1 FISSION OF A URANIUM 235 NUCLEUS
BY A NEUTRON

2 CHAIN REACTION AND
MODERATION OF NEUTRONS

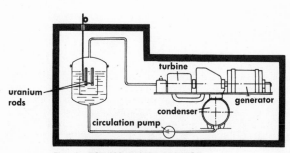

Fig. 3 WATER-MODERATED REACTOR
(*schematic*)

Fig. 4 BOILING WATER REACTOR
(*schematic*)

ELECTROSTATICS I

Matter is composed of neutral atoms. The electrical neutrality of the atoms is due to the fact that the positive charge of the nucleus of the atom is compensated by the negative charge of the electrons that surround it. The outermost electron may either be only loosely connected to the rest of the atom (Fig. 1a) or be more firmly embedded in it (Fig. 1b). Atoms of the first type tend to part with electrons to adjacent atoms, while those of the second type tend to tear electrons away from adjacent atoms. It is because of this phenomenon that, for example, glass becomes positively charged when it is rubbed with a silk cloth (Fig. 2a), whereas ebonite acquires a negative charge on being rubbed with a woollen cloth (Fig. 2b). If two small balls, suspended pendulum wise, are given electric charges of the same sign (e.g., by touching each ball with a glass or ebonite rod charged by friction in the manner described), they will be pushed some distance apart by the mutually repellent force exerted by the two similarly charged balls, as in Figs. 3a and 3b. On the other hand two oppositely charged balls will attract each other, as in Fig. 3c, and when they come into contact, their charges will neutralise each other. A positive charge means that there is a deficiency of electrons; a negative charge means that there is a surplus of electrons in relation to the neutral condition of the atoms. Electrons are the elementary particles of electricity. Each electron has a charge $e = 1.602 \times 10^{-19}$ Coulomb, a rest mass $m_0 = 0.9108 \times 10^{-27}$ grammes, and a radius of 2.82×10^{-13} cm.

Since similar charges repel each other, the electrons so arrange themselves at the surface of an electrical conductor (e.g., a metal ball) that the space inside it contains no charge and is thus entirely free from electrical forces (Figs. 4a and 4b). When a charged conductor is brought near an uncharged (neutral) one, a separation of charges is induced on the latter (Fig. 5a). If the first conductor has a positive charge, then the initially neutral conductor will become negatively charged on the side facing the positive conductor, while the other side will acquire a positive charge of the same magnitude. This positive charge can be discharged to the earth (Fig. 5b), and the second, initially neutral conductor will then remain negatively charged (Fig. 5c). This method of charging is known as electrostatic induction. The repulsion of similar charges may produce repellent forces of considerable magnitude at pointed extremities, where the electrons become concentrated and are actually discharged from the conductor (Fig. 6), so that they can, as it were, be sprayed on to a neutral conductor, which in turn will acquire a charge of the same sign (in this case negative) as that of the first conductor.

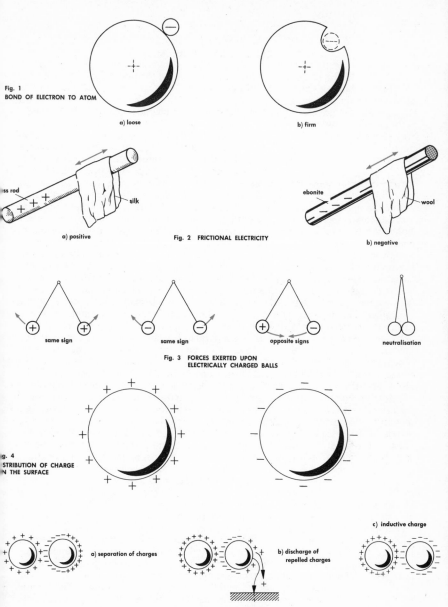

Fig. 1
BOND OF ELECTRON TO ATOM

a) loose

b) firm

glass rod

silk

a) positive

Fig. 2   FRICTIONAL ELECTRICITY

ebonite

wool

b) negative

same sign

same sign

opposite signs

neutralisation

Fig. 3   FORCES EXERTED UPON
ELECTRICALLY CHARGED BALLS

Fig. 4
DISTRIBUTION OF CHARGE
ON THE SURFACE

a) separation of charges

b) discharge of
repelled charges

c) inductive charge

Fig. 5   ELECTROSTATIC INDUCTION

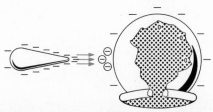

Fig. 6   POINT EFFECT

ELECTROSTATICS II

The Van de Graaff generator (Fig. 1) makes use of the possibility of spraying an electric charge from sharp points of a conductor. The charge is thus applied to a belt conveyor made of an insulating material, which conveys the charge into the interior of a spherical conductor of large radius, where the charge is collected by a "comb" of pointed electrodes. More and more electricity is collected in this way from the travelling belt and is accumulated at the surface of the large sphere, which thus acquires a very high charge. The power output from this electrostatic generator is not very large, for the charge accumulated by this method cannot sustain a current of any significant magnitude. On the other hand, very high voltages can be obtained (of the order of some millions of volts). The voltage can be further increased by installing the generator in an enclosed space in which the air pressure is increased above the normal atmospheric pressure, so that the spark-over voltage to earthed components is increased. The amount of electric charge that can be stored up in a body is called the *capacity* of that body. A *condenser* (or capacitor) is a device specifically intended to store up an electrical charge. Its capacity is determined mainly by the action of electrostatic induction. It consists essentially of two conducting surfaces (plates) which are insulated from each other (Fig. 2a). In the case of a variable condenser the area (F) of these surfaces and/or their distance apart (d_1, d_2) can be varied. Obviously, the quantity of electricity that can be stored up by induction will be greater according as F is larger and the gap d between the condenser plates is smaller. The capacity of a plate condenser is therefore proportional to F and inversely proportional to d. High-capacity condensers are composed of "plates" consisting of rolled-up thin metal foils separated by sheets of paper as the insulating medium. The capacity of a condenser may be compared with the cubic capacity of a tank, which depends on the area of the bottom and on the height (Fig. 2b). If a small ball pendulum is attached to a conductor and the latter is charged with electricity, the pendulum will acquire a deflection (due to electrical repulsion) which is proportional to the magnitude of the charge (Fig. 3a). There is an analogy with the pressure of water in a tank, which pressure can be measured by means of a mercury manometer (or pressure gauge) (Fig. 3b). The pressure of the water corresponds to the electric potential or voltage (the unit of measurement being the volt). The voltage (U) is associated with the electric charge Q (measured in coulombs) and the capacity C of a conductor (measured in farads) by the following relation: $U = Q/C$. In the space which surrounds an electrically charged body an electric potential occurs which is proportional to the charge Q and inversely proportional to the distance r from the centre of the body ($U \approx Q/r$). The electrical condition produced in a space by the presence of electrically charged bodies is called an *electric field* (Fig. 4). Points which all have the same potential (voltage) are located on equipotential surfaces. Forces always act in the direction of the potential gradient. The electric force which is exerted upon a charge of unit magnitude in an electric field is called the field strength (or field intensity). It is always directed perpendicularly to the equipotential surfaces. The lines of force in an electric field represent the direction of the force at any point on their length. The properties of an electric field can be described in terms of the equipotential surfaces and lines of force. The lines of force are conceived as emerging from positive charges and disappearing into negative charges.

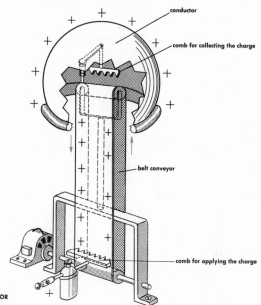

conductor

comb for collecting the charge

belt conveyor

comb for applying the charge

Fig. 1   VAN DE GRAAFF GENERATOR

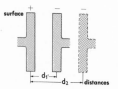

surface

d_1 — d_2 — distances

Fig. 2a   ELECTRIC CAPACITY

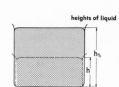

heights of liquid

h_1

h

Fig. 2b   HYDRAULIC CAPACITY

comparison between electrostatic and hydrostatic phenomena

U

Fig. 3a   ELECTRIC VOLTAGE U

Fig. 3b   HYDROSTATIC PRESSURE

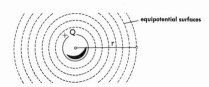

equipotential surfaces

Q

r

Fig. 4   ELECTRIC FIELD

ELECTRODYNAMICS

If two electrostatically charged conductors differing in potential ($U_1 > U_2$) are interconnected by means of a metal wire, charge equalisation in the form of an electric current will occur until the two conductors have acquired the same potential (Fig. 1a). This process is comparable to the flow which occurs when a tank containing a liquid is connected by means of a pipe to another tank, situated at lower level, so that there is what is known as a pressure gradient between the two tanks (Fig. 1b). To obtain a sustained flow of electricity – i.e., an electric current – it is necessary to maintain the potential difference between the two conductors. In the case of the Van de Graaff generator (see page 58) this is achieved by the continuous input of electric charge by the belt conveyor (Fig. 2a). In the hydraulic analogy of the two tanks the same effect would be produced by a pump (or, to make the analogy even closer, by a bucket elevator which raises the liquid from the lower level to the higher level) (Fig. 2b). However, the flow or electricity differs from the flow of a liquid in that it produces a magnetic field around it. The relation between the direction of current and the polarity of the magnetic field is conveniently expressed by the "corkscrew rule": A current following the direction of twist of a corkscrew (clockwise direction) produces magnetic lines of force in the direction of its thrust, i.e., the south pole faces the observer. Conversely, if a current flows through a conductor in the direction of thrust of the corkscrew, the direction of rotation ("screwing-in" direction) corresponds to the direction of the magnetic lines of force surrounding that conductor. The presence of this magnetic field can be demonstrated, for example, by the deflection of a compass needle (Fig. 3a). The effect of an electric current flowing through a coil of wire is to produce a magnetic field similar to that of a bar magnet (Fig. 3b). The magnetic effect of a coil can be intensified by causing the magnetic flux (i.e., the lines of force conceived as a "flow" from one pole of the magnetic to the other) to pass through a core consisting of a material whose magnetic resistance is lower than that of air. The most suitable substance for the purpose is iron. A coil provided with an iron core is called an electromagnet (Fig. 4a). Frequently two electromagnets are joined together by a yoke, i.e., an iron bar forming a magnetic path (Fig. 4b). In an arrangement of this kind the two coils are wound in opposite directions so that they have a free north pole and a free south pole respectively. The magnetic lines of force are conceived as flowing from the north pole to the south pole. Magnetism is always associated with dipoles, i.e., there are always two poles; there are no free positive and negative magnetic charges similar to electrostatic charges.

(Continued)

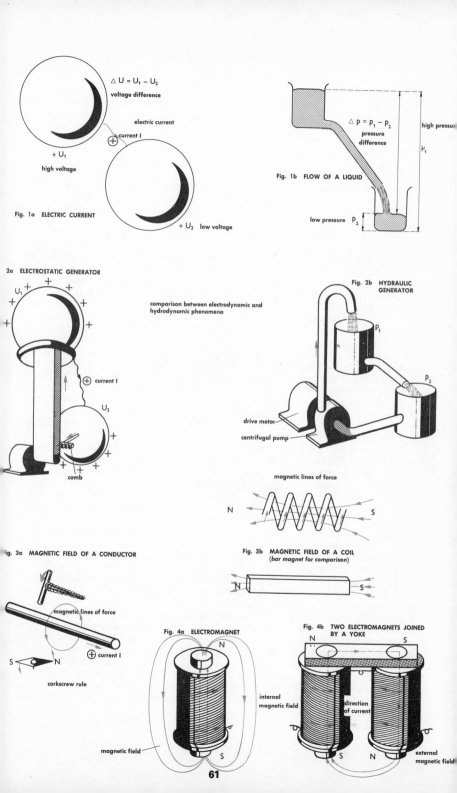

$\triangle U = U_1 - U_2$
voltage difference

electric current

⊕ current I

+ U_1

high voltage

Fig. 1a ELECTRIC CURRENT

+ U_2 low voltage

$\triangle P = P_1 - P_2$
pressure difference

high pressu

P_1

Fig. 1b FLOW OF A LIQUID

low pressure P_2

2a ELECTROSTATIC GENERATOR

U_1

comparison between electrodynamic and hydrodynamic phenomena

⊕ current I

U_2

comb

Fig. 2b HYDRAULIC GENERATOR

P_1

P_2

drive motor

centrifugal pump

magnetic lines of force

N   S

Fig. 3a MAGNETIC FIELD OF A CONDUCTOR

Fig. 3b MAGNETIC FIELD OF A COIL
(bar magnet for comparison)

N   S

magnetic lines of force

⊕ current I

S   N

corkscrew rule

Fig. 4a ELECTROMAGNET

N

internal magnetic field

magnetic field

S

Fig. 4b TWO ELECTROMAGNETS JOINED BY A YOKE

N   S

direction of current

S   N

external magnetic field

The phenomena associated with the flow of electricity in metallic conductors can be explained with the aid of the interaction of the elementary electric charge of the electron with the atoms of the metals. For convenience, the electrons are assumed to have a spherical shape. A metal very widely employed for the conduction of electricity is copper. It has a crystalline structure (Fig. 1). The nucleus of the copper atom contains 29 positive elementary charges, which are neutralised by 29 negatively charged electrons. The 29th (outermost) electron is only very loosely connected to the atomic nucleus. Even at room temperature the thermal energy is great enough to enable the copper atoms to perform vibrations about their position of rest in the crystal lattice. As a result, these loosely connected electrons are, as it were, shaken off and thus become available as free carriers of negative electric charge for the conduction of electricity. These electrons are "quasi-free", i.e., they are repeatedly captured and released again. In the crystal lattice they behave rather like a gas in a container; for this reason the term "electron gas" is sometimes employed (Fig. 2). When a potential difference is applied between the ends of a conductor, electrons go from the negative to the positive pole (Fig. 3). The flow of electrons thus moves in the direction opposite to that of the current as conventionally defined. The behaviour of an electron stream in a magnetic field is shown in Fig. 4, where a single individual electron (e.g., emitted by an incandescent wire in a vacuum) traverses a constant magnetic field. The electron itself is surrounded by its own magnetic field, which is superimposed upon the main field. Under the conditions considered, the magnetic field strength above the electron path is thereby intensified, and the field strength below it is reduced. The resulting field strength gradient causes the electron to move in a curved path. In the interior of a metal conductor this gives rise to a difference in potential, or voltage, between the upper and the lower face of the conductor (Fig. 5). This phenomenon is called the Hall effect, after its discoverer.

The electron theory of metallic conductivity also enables *induction* to be explained in terms that can be visualised. By induction is understood the occurrence of electric potential differences and currents as a result of mechanical movements of conductors in a magnetic field.

As shown in Fig. 6, a piece of metal can be conceived as a kind of container which is filled with "electron gas" and which, for the purpose of the present explanation, is assumed to be moving in a constant magnetic field. As a result of this motion the electrons in the metal will tend to follow downward-curving paths and thus concentrate at the lower end, so that this end will acquire a negative potential in relation to the upper end of the piece of metal. If the two ends are interconnected by a wire which extends far outside the magnetic field, an induction current will flow through this wire so long as the piece of metal continues to move through the magnetic field. In general, the current will flow so long as the amount of magnetic flux intersecting the plane of a circuit (which in its simplest form is merely a loop of wire) varies. The variation of the flux can be obtained either by varying the area enclosed within the circuit (this is the principle applied in the electric generator) or by varying the magnetic field strength and thus causing changes in the density of the flux (as in the transformer: see page 92). The operating principle of the *generator* is illustrated in Fig. 7a: The amount of magnetic flux passing through the plane of the rotating loop of wires varies periodically from zero to its maximum value, according as the plane of the loop is parallel or perpendicular to the magnetic lines of force. An electric current which varies periodically in direction (*alternating current*) is thereby induced in the loop. This current is collected by means of contact rings (known as slip-rings) and flows through the external circuit (Fig. 7b). The collector may also be in the form of a so-called commutator consisting of a number of separate segments (Fig. 7c, showing only two segments), whereby a (pulsating) *direct current* is obtained. See also pages 64 and 68.

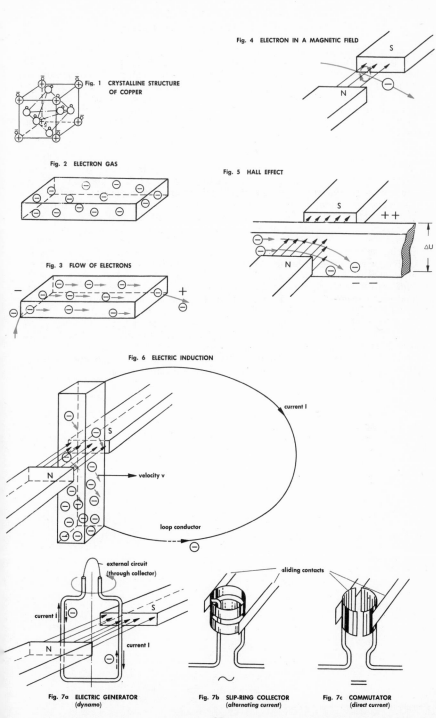

Fig. 1 CRYSTALLINE STRUCTURE OF COPPER

Fig. 2 ELECTRON GAS

Fig. 3 FLOW OF ELECTRONS

Fig. 4 ELECTRON IN A MAGNETIC FIELD

Fig. 5 HALL EFFECT

Fig. 6 ELECTRIC INDUCTION

current I

velocity v

loop conductor

external circuit (through collector)

sliding contacts

current I

current i

current I

Fig. 7a ELECTRIC GENERATOR (dynamo)

Fig. 7b SLIP-RING COLLECTOR (alternating current)

Fig. 7c COMMUTATOR (direct current)

ELECTRIC GENERATOR (DYNAMO)

Generators are machines used for the large-scale production of electrical energy. Their operation is based on the principle of electrical induction (see also page 62), whereby a periodic flow of electricity is produced in a loop-type conductor as a result of the periodic variation of the flux of the magnetic lines of force passing through this loop. To do this, we can either cause the loop to rotate in a constant magnetic field or, alternatively, the loop can be kept stationary and the magnetic field rotated. In the former arrangement the "loop" is formed by the armature windings on the rotor which revolves between the fixed magnetic poles of the stator. In the latter arrangement the armature is stationary, and the magnetic poles (on a so-called "magnet wheel") revolve instead; the stator consists of an iron ring with induction coils mounted on the inside; the magnetic poles on the rotor move past the ends of these coils at a very short distance from them (Figs. 1 and 3). In this case the current produced by the generator is taken direct from the stator, without the aid of special current collectors (brushes). For this reason this form of construction is particularly suitable for the generation of high-voltage alternating current. The sparking that occurs at high voltages (around 20,000 volts) in large generators would destroy the brushes. The relatively low output of direct current needed for producing the rotating magnetic field is fed to the rotor by means of slip-rings and carbon or copper-mesh brushes (Fig. 3). The successive coils in Fig. 1 are wound in alternate directions, which ensures that the generated current always flows in the same direction. High-duty generators are usually coupled directly—on the same shaft—to steam or water turbines. Usually, a small direct-current dynamo for producing the magnetic field is also mounted on the driving shaft (Fig. 2). In the older type of power station with reciprocating steam engines, the rotor of the generator is generally constructed as a flywheel with the magnetic pole windings round its rim. Fig. 3 shows a smaller generator which likewise operates on the principle described above (rotating magnetic field, stationary armature winding). In this case the magnet wheel is in the form of a two-part T-rotor.

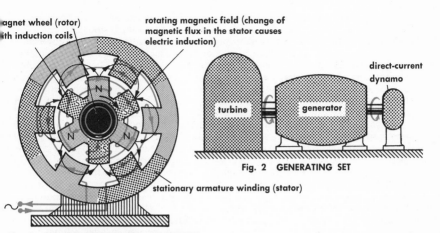

magnet wheel (rotor) with induction coils

rotating magnetic field (change of magnetic flux in the stator causes electric induction)

direct-current dynamo

turbine   generator

Fig. 2   GENERATING SET

stationary armature winding (stator)

Fig. 1   ALTERNATING-CURRENT GENERATOR
(*internal pole machine, schematic*)

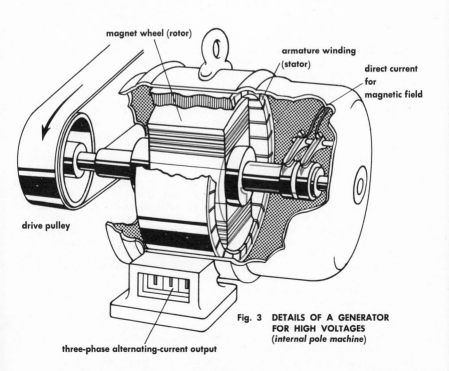

magnet wheel (rotor)

armature winding (stator)

direct current for magnetic field

drive pulley

three-phase alternating-current output

Fig. 3   DETAILS OF A GENERATOR FOR HIGH VOLTAGES
(*internal pole machine*)

65

BATTERY, ACCUMULATOR (DIRECT CURRENT)

If two different metals are immersed in an aqueous solution—i.e., a solution of a substance in water—which can conduct electricity (e.g., dilute sulphuric acid), they will have a different tendency to dissolve in the liquid. The two metals thereby acquire electric charges of different sign. As a result of this chemical process, a difference in voltage occurs because one of the metals appears positive or negative in relation to the other. In this respect the various metals or other conductors can be arranged in a so-called electrochemical or electromotive series in which each metal has a higher potential—i.e., appears electrically positive—in relation to the next metal: carbon, gold, silver, copper, tin, lead, iron, zinc.

A combination of two metals (the electrodes) in an aqueous solution for producing electrical energy from chemical energy is sometimes called a galvanic cell. One such cell is the voltaic cell (Fig. 1) in which the two metals are copper $(+)$ and zinc $(-)$ and the solution in which they are immersed is dilute sulphuric acid. If an incandescent lamp (for example) is connected to the two poles of the cell, an electric current will flow. The lamp and connecting wires form the external part of the electric circuit, which is completed in the interior of the cell by the conducting liquid (which is called the electrolyte). The flow of current inside the cell causes polarisation, i.e., bubbles of gas are deposited on the electrodes, with the result that the internal resistance is increased and the flow of current is, after a time, greatly reduced. In particular, the hydrogen gas that is evolved at the anode (the positive pole) must be removed if the cell is to go on functioning properly. In the Leclanché cell (Fig. 2), the undesirable polarisation is prevented by a mixture of manganese dioxide and graphite as depolarisers which, in a simple form of this cell, are contained in a linen bag which encloses the carbon anode. Cells of this kind are nowadays sometimes used for supplying the current to work an electric bell. It consists of a carbon anode with the depolariser, a zinc cathode (negative pole), and an ammonium chloride solution as the electrolyte. The potential difference between the poles of the Leclanché cell is 1.3 volts. The size of the cell does not affect this voltage, but it does determine the intensity of the current (amperage) it can give. The chemical energy that is converted into electrical energy when the cell is in operation is obtained from the zinc electrode, which dissolves and is thus consumed. This process is irreversible, and the zinc must therefore be renewed from time to time. The depolariser is also consumed and requires occasional renewal. Cells in which the electrodes are consumed are called primary cells. On the other hand, a secondary cell can be restored to its original state by charging, i.e., passing an electric current through it, so that the electrodes are regenerated. Cells of this latter type, usually grouped in batteries of two or more, are called accumulators (storage batteries). A commonly used type of accumulator has electrodes consisting of lead plates; the electrolyte is dilute sulphuric acid (Figs. 3 and 4). A layer of lead sulphate is formed on these plates. When the accumulator is charged, the layer on the anode plate is transformed into brown lead dioxide, while the cathode is reduced to grey lead. Electrical energy (the charging current) is converted into chemical energy. In the charged accumulator, one electrode thus consists of lead and the other of lead dioxide; these electrodes, together with the electrolyte, then function as a voltaic cell. The stored (accumulated) chemical energy is converted back into electrical energy (discharging). The accumulator is widely used for technical purposes. Besides the familiar lead accumulator there are several other kinds, including the nickel–iron (Ni–Fe) accumulator, which has potassium hydroxide as electrolyte. The lead accumulator produces a potential difference of about 2 volts; for the nickel–iron accumulator it is 1.36 volts. Secondary as well as primary cells are also manufactured as so-called "dry" cells, in which the electrolyte is in the form of a paste instead of a liquid. Higher voltages are obtained by connecting two or more cells in series (Fig. 5), higher current intensities by connecting them in parallel (Fig. 6). All cells produce direct current, i.e., an electric current which flows constantly in one direction (as opposed to alternating current: see page 62). The term "battery" denotes a group of two or more primary or secondary cells, connected in series or in parallel.

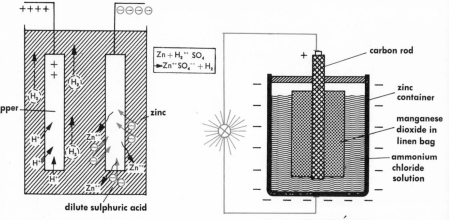

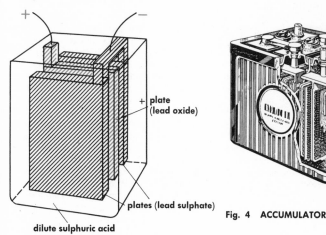

$$Zn + H_2^{++} SO_4 \\ \rightarrow Zn^{++} SO_4^{--} + H_2$$

pper — zinc — H[2]

H⁺ — Zn⁺⁺

H⁺ — Zn⁺⁺

H⁺ — Zn⁺⁺

dilute sulphuric acid

Fig. 1 VOLTAIC CELL

carbon rod

zinc container

manganese dioxide in linen bag

ammonium chloride solution

Fig. 2 LECLANCHÉ CELL

+ plate (lead oxide)

plates (lead sulphate)

dilute sulphuric acid

Fig. 3 ACCUMULATOR (*principle*)

Fig. 4 ACCUMULATOR (*automobile battery*)

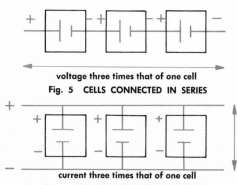

voltage three times that of one cell

Fig. 5 CELLS CONNECTED IN SERIES

current three times that of one cell

Fig. 6 CELLS CONNECTED IN PARALLEL

ALTERNATING CURRENT, THREE-PHASE CURRENT, ELECTROMAGNETIC WAVES

When electrical energy is produced by induction in a generator, a primary alternating voltage is produced which causes an alternating current to flow in an external circuit (Fig. 1a; see page 64). The presence of capacity and self-induction in the circuit may cause phase displacements between the voltage and the current (Fig. 1b). The product of voltage and current is the power. In a case where the voltage and the current have the same algebraic sign, the power is positive (Fig. 1a). If a phase displacement between current and voltage occurs, they are liable to be of different sign, in which case the power becomes negative. Because of these negative values, the active power (true power) of alternating current which is not in phase (Fig. 1b) is smaller than that of current which is in phase (Fig. 1a). If the current is displaced a quarter period in relation to the voltage, then there will be no active power at all; in that case only the so-called idle current (wattless current) flows through the circuit. The reduction in power that occurs as a result of phase displacement is expressed by the power factor cos ϕ (electric power N = U. I. cos ϕ).

If three alternating currents have phase displacements of 120° in relation to one another, then at any particular instant the sum of their currents or of their voltages will be zero (Fig. 2a). Instead of six, only three conductors are required for the transmission of these three currents if either "star" connection (Fig. 2b) or "delta" connection (Fig. 2c) is employed for the conductors.

If three electromagnets arranged as shown in Fig. 2d are energised by three such alternating currents (which together are referred to as "three-phase alternating current"), the maximum values of the current in the three electromagnet coils will occur successively, with a phase displacement of 120° in relation to one another. This has the effect of producing a rotating magnetic field. A so-called "squirrel-cage" rotor, for instance, can be made to rotate in such a magnetic field, so that this principle can very suitably be applied to the construction of three-phase electric motors.

Alternating currents are characterised by their frequency, i.e., the number of cycles (or double waves) per second. The term "period" signifies the time occupied by one complete cycle. The unit of frequency is the hertz, which is equal to one cycle per second. Low-frequency alternating current is a term applicable to frequencies up to 20,000 hertz.[1]) Ordinary alternating current from the mains has a frequency of 50[2] hertz. The electric railways in certain countries operate at a frequency of 16⅔ hertz. High-frequency alternating currents up to several gigahertz (1 gigahertz = 1 milliard[3] hertz)—are used in communication engineering and more particularly in radio communication. This is because an alternating current produces an electromagnetic field which varies with the frequency of the current and which is propagated through space with the velocity of light, i.e., 180,000 miles per second. With low-frequency alternating current the energy that is transmitted into space has sufficient time to return to the electrical conductor each time the alternating current changes its direction of flow. With very high frequencies, on the other hand, the change of direction takes place before the whole of the energy has had time to return. A proportion of the energy is therefore, as it were, cut off and is transmitted into space as *electromagnetic radiation*. Because of the periodic character of this radiation, it is referred to as an "electromagnetic vibration", and because of its similarity with the propagation of a wave in water, it is also called an "electromagnetic wave".

(Continued)

---

1. The usual subdivision of frequency ranges is: low frequency up to 20,000 hertz; medium frequency from 20,000 to 30,000 hertz; high frequency from 30,000 to 3000 megahertz (=3000 million hertz); beyond this is the range known as hyperfrequency.
2. 60 in U.S.A.
3. One billion in U.S.A.

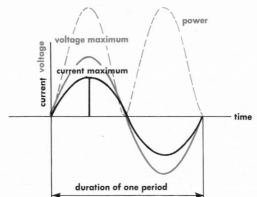

Fig. 1a TIME GRAPH OF AN ALTERNATING CURRENT

power

voltage maximum

current maximum

current voltage

time

duration of one period

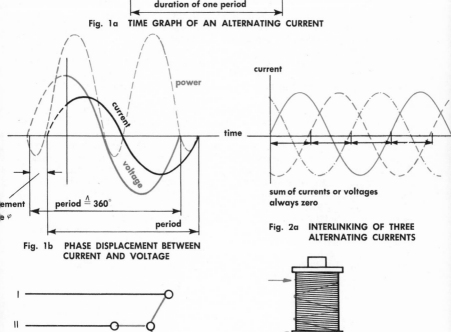

power

current

voltage

ement
e φ

period ≙ 360°

period

Fig. 1b PHASE DISPLACEMENT BETWEEN
CURRENT AND VOLTAGE

current

time

sum of currents or voltages
always zero

Fig. 2a INTERLINKING OF THREE
ALTERNATING CURRENTS

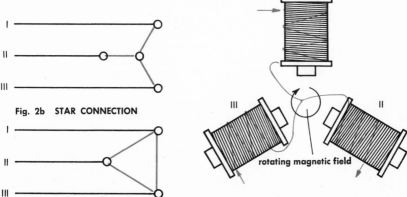

I

II

III

Fig. 2b STAR CONNECTION

I

II

III

Fig. 2c DELTA CONNECTION

III

II

rotating magnetic field

The generation of electromagnetic waves is therefore always associated with the existence of a high-frequency alternating current whose energy is radiated into space. This radiation process, which depends on the frequency of the alternating current that produces it, can best be demonstrated with reference to the so-called Hertz dipole (Fig. 3a). This device consists of a conductor whose length is related to the length of the period—more commonly known as the *wavelength*—of the electromagnetic wave produced. The wavelength is found as the velocity of propagation (= distance travelled per second) divided by the frequency (= number of periods or cycles per second). If a high-frequency alternating current is passed through this conductor (or is produced in the latter by induction), a high-frequency alternating electromagnetic field will be formed around it, as shown in Fig. 3a. The emission of electromagnetic waves at the critical distance r_k is illustrated in Fig. 3b. If one end of a dipole is earthed, we have the simplest form of an *aerial* (antenna). A circuit whose electrical and magnetic properties (capacity and self-induction respectively) are tuned to the frequency of the alternating current—i.e., is in resonance with it— is called an *oscillating circuit*. The latter comprises a condenser and a self-induction coil. Once it is charged, the condenser discharges itself through the coil, so that electrical energy that was stored up in the condenser is converted into magnetic energy. After the discharge of the condenser has taken place, the magnetic field breaks down and induces a current in the coil. This current gives the condenser a charge of opposite sign to its original charge. If no losses occurred, the charge would go on oscillating—changing its sign—indefinitely. The frequency of this oscillation, and therefore the frequency of the alternating current that is produced, is higher in proportion as the capacity C and the self-induction L are lower (Fig. 4a). The oscillation period T is given by the formula $T = 2\pi\sqrt{LC}$.

If the plates of the condenser are separated, as in Fig. 4b, they can be conceived as the "aerial" and "earth" respectively. This principle of the aerial (antenna) is further illustrated in Figs. 4c and 4d. In these cases the electric field of the condenser is utilised for the transmission and reception of the electromagnetic energy in the form of waves. A coil wound round an open frame (directive aerial) (Fig. 4e) can be used for receiving the magnetic portion of the field. The frame is rotated to the position where maximum variation of the magnetic flux is obtained.

An important piece of equipment for producing hyper-frequency oscillations (see page 76 *et seq.*) is the cavity resonator. Fig. 4f shows how such a resonator can be conceived as being evolved from an oscillating circuit of minimum capacity and self-induction. The lateral wall of the "box" corresponds to the self-induction and the end surfaces correspond to the capacity.

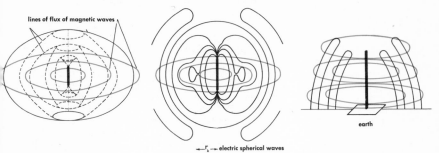

lines of flux of magnetic waves

Fig. 3a SPHERICAL WAVE SYSTEM
AROUND A HERTZ DIPOLE

Fig. 3b EMISSION OF WAVES

←—r_k—→ electric spherical waves

Fig. 3c DIPOLE EARTHED ON ONE SIDE
(antenna)

earth

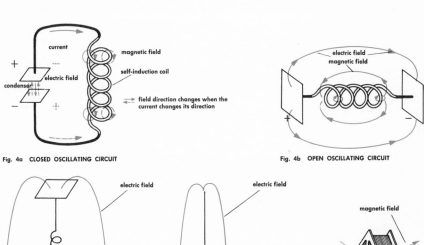

current

magnetic field

self-induction coil

electric field

condenser

+

−

→ field direction changes when the
current changes its direction

Fig. 4a CLOSED OSCILLATING CIRCUIT

electric field
magnetic field

+

−

Fig. 4b OPEN OSCILLATING CIRCUIT

electric field

earth

Fig. 4c ANTENNA

electric field

earth

Fig. 4d ANTENNA

magnetic field

induced current

Fig. 4e DIRECTIVE ANTENNA

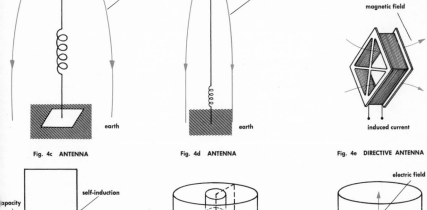

capacity

self-induction

rotation produces cavity with
"pegs" (determining the capacity)

When the "pegs"
disappear
(reduction of the capacity)
a pure cavity resonator
is obtained

electric field

magnetic field

Fig. 4f CAVITY RESONATOR

71

ALTERNATING CURRENT, THREE-PHASE CURRENT,
ELECTROMAGNETIC WAVES: TRANSMITTERS, RECEIVERS

Oscillating circuits are used, in the form of aerials, as transmitting and receiving devices for electromagnetic energy in radio transmitters and receivers. As the emission of electromagnetic waves constantly withdraws energy from the oscillating circuit of the transmitter and therefore damps it, it is necessary constantly to supply fresh energy to it. This is done by means of a triode or a transistor in a feedback circuit (Figs. 1, 2 and 6). As a result of induction, a grid voltage is produced which supplies a correctly synchronised high-frequency alternating current to the oscillating circuit in the anode circuit or collector circuit. By means of a suitably connected microphone the transmitted wave is amplitude-modulated or frequency-modulated. In radio engineering "modulation" means that the pattern of the current variations or impulses are superimposed upon the carrier wave. With amplitude modulation it is the amplitude of the high-frequency carrier wave that is modified; on the other hand, with frequency modulation, the frequency of the carrier wave is varied in accordance with the frequency pattern of the sound waves (speech or music) to be transmitted. In the receiver the oscillating circuit is tuned to the frequency of the incoming wave, whose energy produces a synchronous high-frequency alternating current in the oscillating circuit. The alternating voltage associated with this current is used to control the anode current or collector current through the agency of the grid (Figs. 3 and 4) or the emitter (Fig. 5). The high-frequency alternating current component that is superimposed on the anode direct current is fed to a loudspeaker through a resistance or a transformer (Figs. 3, 4 and 5). The cases considered here relate to high-frequency amplification. If rectification is applied before amplification, the process is called low-frequency amplification. Cf. radio receiver (page 84), thermionic tube (page 74), and semiconductors (page 82).

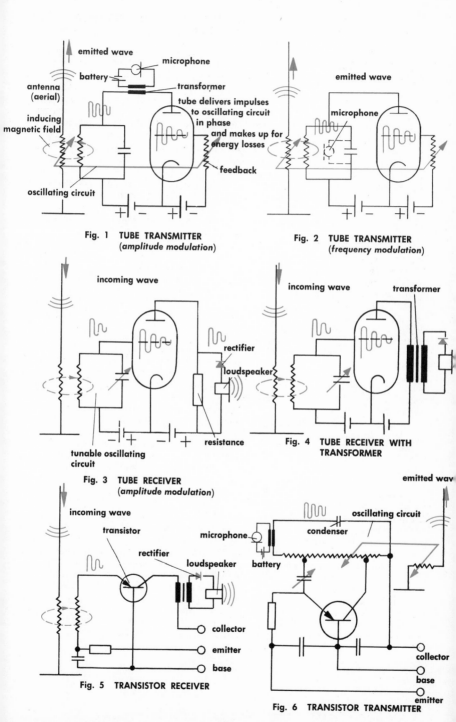

Fig. 1 TUBE TRANSMITTER
(*amplitude modulation*)

emitted wave
microphone
battery
transformer
tube delivers impulses
to oscillating circuit
in phase
and makes up for
energy losses
feedback
antenna
(aerial)
inducing
magnetic field
oscillating circuit

Fig. 2 TUBE TRANSMITTER
(*frequency modulation*)

emitted wave
microphone

Fig. 3 TUBE RECEIVER
(*amplitude modulation*)

incoming wave
rectifier
loudspeaker
tunable oscillating
circuit
resistance

Fig. 4 TUBE RECEIVER WITH
TRANSFORMER

incoming wave
transformer

Fig. 5 TRANSISTOR RECEIVER

incoming wave
transistor
rectifier
loudspeaker
collector
emitter
base

Fig. 6 TRANSISTOR TRANSMITTER

emitted wave
oscillating circuit
microphone
condenser
battery
collector
base
emitter

73

THERMIONIC (VACUUM) TUBE

The "free" electrons which are present in the crystal lattice of a metal can be liberated by the addition of energy. The simplest way to do this is by heating the metal to incandescence. The emission of the electrons can in that case suitably be conceived as a kind of evaporation process (Fig. 1). As a result of collisions between the atoms of the metal—which are in a state of increased thermal agitation (heat motion) because of the heat applied—high-energy electrons are released, which can break out from the surface of the metal and escape despite the restraining effect of the attractive force exerted by the positive ions remaining behind in the metal. This emission of electrons from an incandescent metal (usually an electrically-heated filament) can most suitably be made to take place in a vacuum. This prevents oxidation of the very hot surface of the metal and allows the electrons to emerge unobstructed, i.e., without colliding with, or being neutralised by, gas molecules and ions of the air. A device which fulfils this requirement is the thermionic tube (or thermionic valve). It must contain at least two electrodes; also, it may have one or more additional electrodes for controlling the stream of free electrons flowing inside it. The simplest form, with only two electrodes, is the diode valve (or merely "diode") (Fig. 2). The hot cathode, connected to the negative pole of a battery, faces the anode (positive electrode) which draws electrons towards it from the cathode. On their way from the cathode to the anode the electrons form a negative space charge, which can be influenced by the electric fields of other electrodes (and also by magnetic fields; cf. magnetron, page 76). The simplest thermionic tube of this kind is the triode, which has a third electrode, the control grid. The latter allows the electrons to pass through it and controls them by appropriately modifying the space charge. The circuit connections for a triode of this kind are shown in Fig. 3. The effect of the grid upon the space charge is clarified in Fig. 4. Variations in the grid voltage strengthen or weaken the space charge and thus vary the density of the stream of electrons flowing to the anode. The cathode of the triode in Fig. 4 shows a particular feature in that the electrons are not emitted by the hot glowing filament itself, but by a coating of barium oxide which is (indirectly) heated by the filament. The oxide cathode offers two advantages: for one thing, it emits electrons already at a relatively low temperature (feeble red heat), so that the heat losses are lower; secondly, it forms an equipotential surface, so that the conditions of emission are the same for all the electrons. This latter condition is not satisfied if the electrons are emitted by the filament itself because a voltage drop occurs between its ends. The control performance of a triode can be judged from so-called characteristic curves. Each of these curves is obtained by measuring the current I_a flowing from the anode and also measuring the grid voltage U_g (this is the voltage which is applied to the grid at $\pm$ in Fig. 3) while the anode voltage U_a is kept constant at one particular value. One such curve can be plotted for each of a number of values of the anode voltage (U_{a1}, U_{a2}, U_{a3}). From the characteristic curves thus obtained (Fig. 5) it is possible to deduce certain characteristic quantities (e.g., the slope S) which can be used for describing the behaviour of the thermionic tube. By applying negative grid voltages, the flow of electrons can be completely inhibited; on the other hand, for high positive values of the grid voltage the electron flow must attain a maximum (saturation) value when the space charge has become exhausted and all the electrons emitted by the cathode reach the anode. The increase in the anode current from zero up to its saturation value is approximately linear.

The thermionic tube has the property of unipolar conductivity, i.e., the electrons can flow in one direction only, namely, from the (hot) cathode to the (cold) anode. For this reason, thermionic tubes can also serve as rectifiers (see page 80).

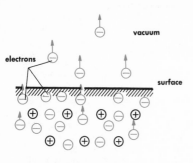

Fig. 1 EMISSION OF ELECTRONS FROM
A HOT METAL

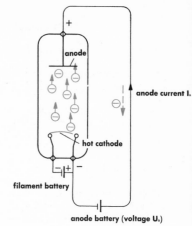

Fig. 2 DIODE

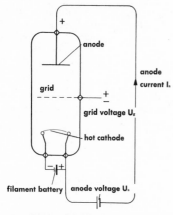

Fig. 3 TRIODE

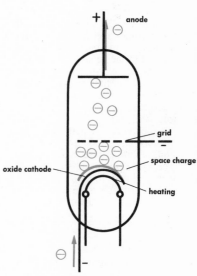

Fig. 4 EFFECT OF THE GRID ON THE
SPACE CHARGE

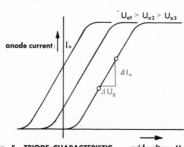

Fig. 5 TRIODE CHARACTERISTIC   grid voltage U_g
STEEPNESS S = $\triangle I_a / \triangle U_g$

75

ULTRA-HIGH FREQUENCY VIBRATIONS

If variations occur in the electron density or the electron velocity of a stream of electrons, portions of the electromagnetic field which always surrounds the electron stream will become detached at the same rhythm, or frequency, as the variations and will—more particularly if the variations occur periodically—cause emission of electromagnetic vibrations. Such vibrations are thus invariably associated with the existence of a high-frequency alternating current. Conditions for the detachment of the electromagnetic field are more favourable according as the frequency is higher, because the individual phases will, on reversal, encounter an already changed situation (cf. page 68). The frequency of the alternating current which supplies the energy will depend on the inductance and capacitance (or capacity) of the circuit which generates and gives forth the electromagnetic energy. High frequencies, i.e., short wavelengths, will therefore be obtained more particularly by reducing the self-inductance and capacitance of the oscillating circuit and by using a set of apparatus that produces periodic variations of electron density and electron velocity (Figs. 1 and 2). Fig. 2 shows the so-called three-point circuit (1-2-3), in which the inductance of the terminal wires (L_A and L_G) provides the self-inductance and a very small condenser (C) merely serves to separate the anode and cathode. The self-inductances of the tubes serve as the capacitances of the oscillating circuits. If the inductance and capacitance are still further reduced (shorter terminal wires, smaller condenser), the finite transit time of the electrons will disturb the onset of the vibrations. If the transit time exceeds the oscillation period (which is the reciprocal value of the frequency) of the oscillating circuit, phase displacements will occur which may be likened to the behaviour of a swing which is being pushed at intervals of time which are shorter than its swinging period. To make a virtue of necessity, investigators either chose the transit time itself as the oscillation period (Barkhausen–Kurz oscillations; Fig. 3) or shortened the distances between the grid and the cathode, the electrodes being constructed as discs for the sake of better mechanical stability (disc-seal triodes; Fig. 4). In the first-mentioned case the grid must have a positive, but the anode a negative voltage, in order to make the electrons oscillate to and fro between the anode and cathode (and pass through the grid while doing so). The highest frequencies attainable with a triode are in the region of about 10^4 megahertz. The grid-to-cathode spacing of 15 microns (0.015 mm = 0.0006 inch) presents a technical limit to a further increase in frequency.

The next step in the process of development was to produce the periodic vibrations of the electron stream without the help of a material grid. A stream of electrons can be forced to perform a periodic motion other than oscillation, namely, movement along a circular or spiral path. This led to the construction of the *magnetron*. The permanent magnetic field with constant field strength functions as a virtual grid. The rotational frequency of the electrons on circular paths between anode and cathode determines the frequency of the electromagnetic vibrations (Figs. 5a–5c).

(Continued)

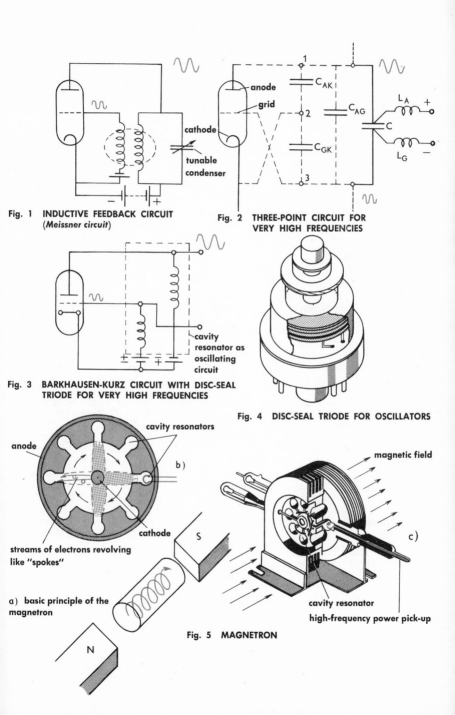

Fig. 1 INDUCTIVE FEEDBACK CIRCUIT (*Meissner circuit*)

cathode

tunable condenser

Fig. 2 THREE-POINT CIRCUIT FOR VERY HIGH FREQUENCIES

anode

grid

C_{AK}

C_{AG}

C_{GK}

L_A

L_G

C

+

−

cavity resonator as oscillating circuit

Fig. 3 BARKHAUSEN-KURZ CIRCUIT WITH DISC-SEAL TRIODE FOR VERY HIGH FREQUENCIES

Fig. 4 DISC-SEAL TRIODE FOR OSCILLATORS

cavity resonators

anode

b)

cathode

streams of electrons revolving like "spokes"

a) basic principle of the magnetron

S

N

magnetic field

c)

cavity resonator

high-frequency power pick-up

Fig. 5 MAGNETRON

Further increases in the frequencies attainable with the magnetron (see page 76) can be achieved by reducing the size of the operative components. There is obviously a technical limit to what can be done in this direction. In the arrangement shown in Fig. 1 an electron beam of constant velocity is directed into a cavity resonator (cf. page 70) which modulates the velocity of the electrons in the rhythm of the voltage impressed upon it. On the way from the cathode to the anode variations of density occur on account of the different electron transit times as a result of their different velocities, the electrons are periodically compressed to "electron packets". The intensified alternating current energy is abstracted from the beam in a second cavity resonator and fed to an aerial (antenna). Control is effected by feedback by means of a hollow waveguide to the input cavity resonator. A velocity-modulated tube of this kind is called a *klystron*. The *travelling-wave tube* (Fig. 2) utilises the fact that an electric field prefers a metallic path to a vacuum. If the metallic spiral which guides the field has a pitch of $\frac{1}{13}$, the field will have a velocity component whose magnitude in the flow direction of the electrons is equal to $\frac{1}{13}$ of the velocity of light and thus has about the same value as the electrons accelerated by about 1500 volts, which interact with the field. With electron tubes of this kind it is possible to attain ultra-high frequencies corresponding to wavelengths in the millimetre range. This already brings us into the range of long-wave heat radiation, i.e., the range of atomic phenomena. The next step, therefore, was to enable atomic electromagnetic radiation to be controlled at will. This can be achieved by means of the molecular oscillators (known as *masers* and *lasers* respectively.*) Masers differ from lasers in the wavelength range of the radiation emitted: it consists of microwaves in the case of the maser, and of light waves in the case of the laser. The principle is indicated in the atomic diagram in Fig. 3. Three possible different energy states I, II, III (stable electron orbits) occur around a positive atomic nucleus. The pump radiation (I) raises electrons from state I to state III, with the result that more electrons than the number corresponding to temperature equilibrium will be in state III. There they form a supply of electrons in readiness to move into state II, from where the electrons—under the action of an excitation radiation (2)—pass back to state I, this being accompanied by the emission of radiation (3).

The entire process (pumping, excitation, emission) takes place so rapidly that the equalisation due to thermal energy has not yet been accomplished. For this reason amplifiers and transmitters which operate on the maser or laser principle are practically noiseless, i.e., they do not exhibit the disturbances caused by the thermal oscillatory motion of the electrons (thermal noise; cf. page 118), which can otherwise be eliminated only by cooling to a temperature close to absolute zero ($-273°$ C). With these devices it is possible to detect power outputs of as low as 10^{-28} Watts. Because of its atomic character, the maser or laser radiation has an extremely constant frequency and sharp concentration of the radiation into a beam. Fig. 4 shows the technical form of construction of a ruby maser.

---

* These names are abbreviations of "microwave amplification by stimulated emission of radiation" and "light amplification by stimulated emission of radiation".

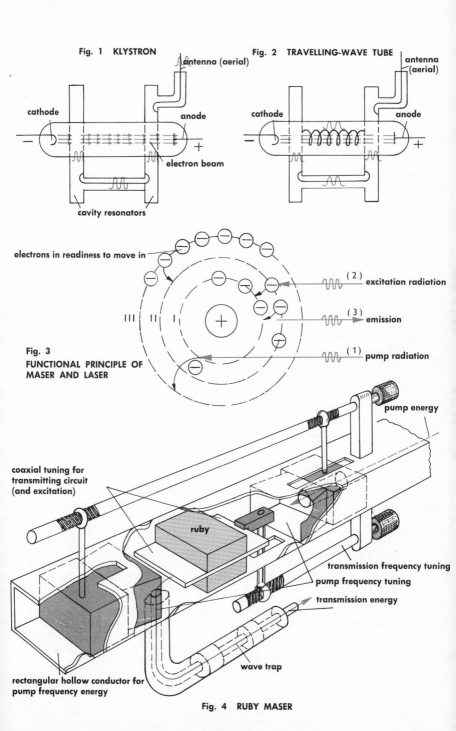

Fig. 1 KLYSTRON

antenna (aerial)

cathode

anode

electron beam

cavity resonators

Fig. 2 TRAVELLING-WAVE TUBE

antenna (aerial)

cathode

anode

electrons in readiness to move in

(2) excitation radiation

(3) emission

Fig. 3
FUNCTIONAL PRINCIPLE OF
MASER AND LASER

(1) pump radiation

III II I

pump energy

coaxial tuning for
transmitting circuit
(and excitation)

ruby

transmission frequency tuning

pump frequency tuning

transmission energy

rectangular hollow conductor for
pump frequency energy

wave trap

Fig. 4 RUBY MASER

79

RECTIFIER

A rectifier is a device which allows an electric current to pass in one direction but not in the opposite direction. A mechanical analogy is, for example, a venetian blind (Fig. 1).

A vacuum tube rectifier always has a cathode (K), which is almost invariably a filament heated by current, and an anode (A). The cathode emits electrons which either rush at high velocity straight to the anode and thus establish the conductive connection directly to the anode (in the case of high-vacuum tubes), or, alternatively, ionise the gas that is present in the tube (in gas-filled tubes). High-vacuum rectifier tubes can be used only for relatively small currents. Fig. 2 shows the principle of a rectifier in its simplest form (one-way rectifier): as the rectifier tube allows current to pass in one direction only (Fig. 3), a pulsating direct current is produced in the circuit; this current is "smoothed" by the condenser.

Gas-filled rectifier tubes (the gas filling usually consists of mercury vapour or an inert gas, e.g., argon or helium) differ in their functional behaviour from high-vacuum tubes. When a low anode voltage is applied, at first only a weak current will flow, as the gas retards rather than assists the movements of the emitted electrons. On increasing the voltage, however, so high a velocity is imparted to the electrons that they ionise the gas atoms as a result of colliding with them: a powerful current suddenly flows: the tube "ignites". The internal resistance of a conductive path through an ionised gas is substantially lower than that of an electron stream, and the power output is therefore higher. Fig. 4 shows the technical form of construction of a large rectifier. It is intended more particularly for three-phase alternating current and is accordingly provided with three anodes.

Besides the thermionic rectifiers described above, semiconductors (see page 82) are also used as rectifier elements.

A characteristic feature of semiconductors is that their low electric conductivity can be substantially modified by the addition of minute quantities of impurities. If the crystals are contaminated by the intentional addition of impurities, the conductivity is very greatly increased. For instance, one part in ten thousand of boron can increase the conductivity of silicon one million times. Depending on the kind of impurity, a positively conducting (P-type) or a negatively conducting (N-type) semiconductor can be obtained. The direction of flow of the electrons can be controlled in this way. If a P-type and an N-type semiconductor layer are in contact with each other in, for example, a germanium crystal, then such a crystal will have rectifying properties (Fig. 6; semiconductor diode).

If an external voltage is so applied to a semiconductor diode that the negative pole is in contact with the N-type layer and the positive pole is in contact with the P-type layer (Fig. 6a), then the negative charge carriers of the N-type layer and the positive charge carriers of the P-type layer are forced to the middle of the crystal— where the P–N boundary is located—because charges of similar sign repel each other. At the boundary an intensive interchange of electrons and "holes" (equivalent to positive electronic charges) occurs, so that a strong current flows. If the polarity of the externally applied voltage is reversed (Fig. 6b), the negative and positive charge carriers are drawn away from the boundary zone because charges of dissimilar sign attract each other. At the boundary—the so-called blocking layer—there are now no charge carriers available, and no current can flow.

Fig. 5 shows the characteristic of a semiconductor diode. The voltage and the current have been plotted in a co-ordinate system. It appears that the current increases when the voltage is raised towards positive values, but that the current remains zero when negative voltages are applied (though some current may flow when the negative voltage is further increased to a high value).

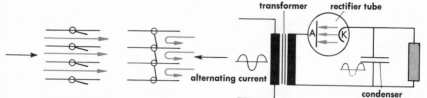

Fig. 1 VENETIAN BLIND AS "RECTIFIER"

transformer   rectifier tube

alternating current

condenser

Fig. 2 SIMPLE ONE-WAY RECTIFIER TUBE

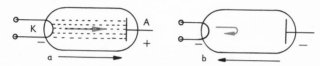

Fig. 3 DIAGRAM OF RECTIFIER TUBE: *current*
can flow in direction (a) but not in direction (b)

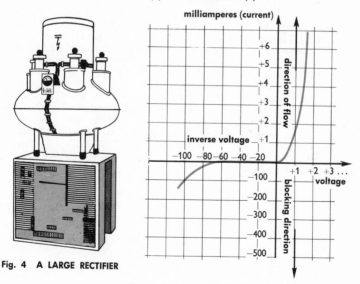

milliamperes (current)

+6
+5
+4
+3
+2
+1

direction of flow

inverse voltage

−100 −80 −60 −40 −20

+1 +2 +3 ...
voltage

−100
−200
−300
−400
−500

blocking direction

Fig. 4 A LARGE RECTIFIER

Fig. 5 CHARACTERISTIC OF A SEMI-CONDUCTOR DIODE

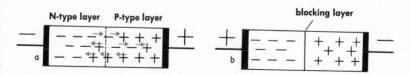

N-type layer   P-type layer

blocking layer

Fig. 6 RECTIFYING ACTION OF A SEMI-CONDUCTOR

SEMICONDUCTORS

In contrast with metals, semiconductors contain only a relatively small number of quasi-free electrons (see page 62) at room temperature. The conductivity of semiconductors is therefore of the order of 10^{-5} times as low as that of metals. It can be increased by breaking up the electronic double bonds which normally exist between the tetravelent atoms of semiconductors, as represented in the crystal lattice diagrams (Figs. 1 and 2). Commonly used semiconductors are germanium (Ge), silicon (Si) and various others. By the incorporation of impurities, i.e., foreign atoms of higher or lower valence, which function as points of disturbance in the crystal lattice (Fig. 4), the conductivity properties of semiconductors can be varied within very wide limits. A donor impurity makes electronic conduction possible by providing free electrons; an acceptor impurity captures electrons. Positive conduction occurs as the result of a deficiency of electrons: there is a flow of positive charges ("holes"); negative conduction occurs as the result of a surplus of electrons. Where positively and negatively conducting zones meet each other, the transition region constitutes a layer of high electric resistance (blocking layer) (Fig. 6). When a voltage is applied, the concentration of positive and negative charges in the transition region can be increased (flow direction of current) or decreased (blocking direction). Figs. 3 and 5 show the conditions within the so-called energy level diagram. The range ΔE is known as the "forbidden band". The ordinate is the electron energy E, the abscissa represents the longitudinal extension x. Semiconductor elements comprising a transition from positive to negative conduction are called *semiconductor diodes*, while those which comprise two such transitions are called *transistors*. The transistor (Fig. 7) is a semiconductor triode. Its three electrodes are respectively called the emitter, the base and the collector. The significant feature is that the base should be narrow (50 microns) so as to enable the charge carriers from the emitter to pass through the boundary layer 1 and traverse the base, so that they can thus affect the processes taking place at the boundary layer 2. Control of the passage of current between base and collector is thereby achieved. This enables the transistor to be employed for purposes of amplification and the generation of oscillations. It is progressively superseding the thermionic valves or tubes (see page 74). Besides taking up far less space, transistorised systems have the advantage of dispensing with the filament current. Cf. rectifiers, page 80.

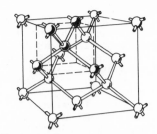

Fig. 1   CRYSTAL STRUCTURE OF A SEMI-CONDUCTOR

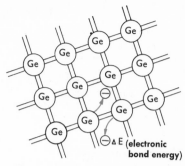

Fig. 2   CRYSTAL LATTICE DIAGRAM

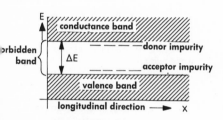

Fig. 3   ELECTRON BAND MODEL OF A SEMI-CONDUCTOR

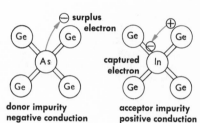

donor impurity
negative conduction

acceptor impurity
positive conduction

Fig. 4   DONOR AND ACCEPTOR IMPURITIES

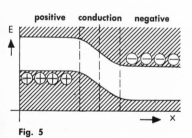

Fig. 5

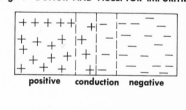

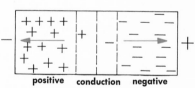

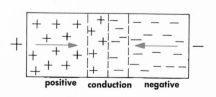

Fig. 6   FORMATION AND VARIATION OF TRANSITION REGION

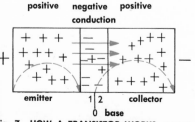

Fig. 7   HOW A TRANSISTOR WORKS: *current in collector circuit controlled by conduction in emitter circuit*

RADIO RECEIVER

The radio receiver in its simplest form comprises an input circuit for tuning in to the frequencies of the various transmitters to be received, the demodulation circuit for separating the audio-frequency vibrations from the high-frequency carrier, a low-frequency amplifier stage, and the loudspeaker. The amplifier elements (high-vacuum tubes or transistors) are supplied with the necessary operating voltages by a suitable device. Corresponding to the frequency bands on which the various transmitters operate, receivers are equipped to receive long waves (150–285 kilohertz), medium waves (up to 1605 kilohertz), short waves (6 to 21.4 megahertz), and ultra-short waves (up to 100 megahertz). Long, medium and short wave reception function with a channel spacing of 9 kilohertz and with amplitude modulation (see page 72). The channel spacing in the ultra-short wave range is 300 kilohertz, and in this range frequency modulation is employed (see page 72). Reception here is usually better than in the other ranges, because high audio frequencies, which considerably affect the sound pattern, can also be transmitted. Besides, atmospheric disturbances, which have an amplitude-modulating effect, are of hardly any significance to this kind of reception.

The propagation conditions of the four radio waves ranges determine their possibilities of application and the purposes for which they are used. Long and medium wave transmitters send out a direct wave, which travels along the earth's surface, and an indirect wave. In general, only the direct wave is received (which has a range of up to some hundreds of miles); the indirect wave, which is reflected back from the Heaviside layer (an electrically conducting layer about 55 to 85 miles above the earth's surface), makes much larger ranges possible. In the short wave range, only indirect waves are used. Ultra-short waves are propagated in a quasi-optical manner (the waves travel in straight paths), so that they cannot travel beyond the optical horizon. To extend the range as much as possible, the transmitting antenna is installed at the top of a high mast or building.

The more tuning circuits that there are arranged in series in the radio receiver, the greater is the selectivity. In order to obviate manual tuning of the many circuits required, the superheterodyne receiver was developed (Fig. 1). A receiver of this kind comprises an oscillator which generates its own high-frequency oscillation, which is mixed with the oscillation received from the transmitter. The two circuits are so tuned by means of (rotary) variable condensers mounted on the same spindle[1] that the difference of the two frequencies is always the same. All the following circuits (intermediate frequency filters) have been pre-adjusted to this frequency difference by the manufacturer. In this way a high selectivity is obtained and yet only two circuits have to be tuned. Because of the considerably higher carrier frequency in the ultra-short wave range, receivers for this range require small tuning circuits which are usually installed as complete assemblies. In general, however, the variable condensers are mounted on the same spindle, like those used in medium wave receivers (cf. Fig. 2).

The low-frequency or audio-frequency part of the receiver is generally separated into a number of channels for high-pitched and low-pitched tones. Also, separate speakers for high and low notes are employed. In addition to the equipment described here, there is of course a wide range of special receiving equipment designed for the particular purpose for which it is intended. Cf. Alternating current, three-phase current. electromagnetic waves, page 68 *et seq.*

---

1. Shaft in U.S.A.

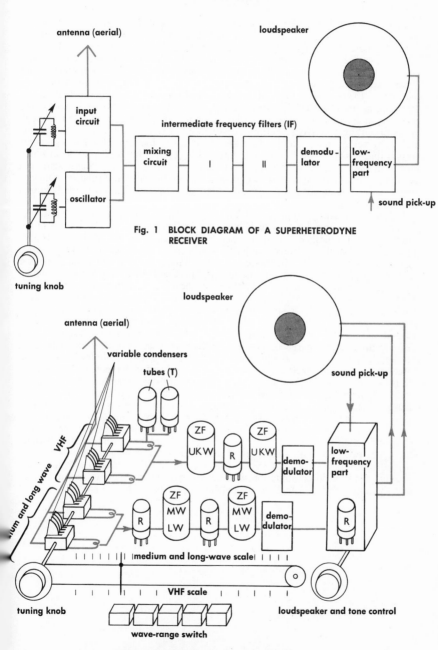

antenna (aerial)

loudspeaker

input circuit

intermediate frequency filters (IF)

mixing circuit

I

II

demodu-lator

low-frequency part

oscillator

sound pick-up

tuning knob

Fig. 1 BLOCK DIAGRAM OF A SUPERHETERODYNE RECEIVER

loudspeaker

antenna (aerial)

variable condensers

tubes (T)

sound pick-up

VHF

ZF UKW

R

ZF UKW

demo-dulator

low-frequency part

medium and long wave

ZF MW LW

R

ZF MW LW

demo-dulator

R

R

medium and long-wave scale

VHF scale

tuning knob

loudspeaker and tone control

wave-range switch

Fig. 2 DIAGRAM SHOWING MAIN COMPONENTS OF A RADIO RECEIVER

85

LOUDSPEAKER

A loudspeaker is a device for converting variations of electric energy into corresponding variations of acoustic energy, i.e., sound. Its task is therefore similar to that of a telephone receiver (cf. page 112), except that the sound produced is much louder. In fact, the early loudspeakers were designed like large telephone receivers (Fig. 1): mounted in front of the poles of a permanent magnet whose field is strengthened and weakened by the speaker current passing through coils is a metal diaphragm which vibrates to the rhythm of the field strength variations and transmits these vibrations to the air as sound waves. To improve the effect, a conical horn is fitted in front of the diaphragm. Because of the restraint of the diaphragm at its edges, where it is gripped in its mounting, the fidelity of the reproduction is adversely affected, however. The further development of the loudspeaker therefore had to aim at achieving, as far as possible, unrestrained vibration of the diaphragm. The first loudspeakers in which this principle was applied were constructed as shown in Fig. 2: the "diaphragm" is a resiliently mounted paper cone which is set in motion by the armature which is energised by the speaker current which here, too, can vibrate freely in the field of a permanent magnet.

A further advance is represented by the dynamic loudspeakers (also known as moving-coil loudspeakers). In such speakers the "armature" which vibrates in the magnetic field consists of a coil attached to the conical diaphragm. In the electro-dynamic speaker (Fig. 3) the moving coil oscillates inside an electromagnet which is energised with direct current, while in the permanent-magnet moving-coil speaker (Fig. 4) the coil oscillates in an annular cavity of a specially-shaped permanent magnet.

All the loudspeakers described above use the electrodynamic principle for the conversion of electrical oscillations into mechanical vibrations which in turn produce sound waves in the air. Crystal loudspeakers (Fig. 5) and electrostatic loudspeakers (Fig. 6) are based on different principles. The crystal loudspeaker utilises the piezo-electric effect, i.e., the phenomenon that certain crystals (quartz, Seignette salt) develop an electric charge or potential difference when subjected to mechanical pressure and conversely undergo changes in thickness (and thus produce mechanical forces) when they are electrically charged by the application of a potential difference. Thus, when an alternating voltage is applied, the crystal undergoes periodic variations in thickness, i.e., thickness oscillations, which are transmitted to the loudspeaker diaphragm (Fig. 5). The electrostatic loudspeaker makes use of the electrostatic attractive and repulsive forces to which a diaphragm is subjected in the electric field of a condenser when the voltage applied to the latter is made to vary. The condenser plates are perforated, so that the sound waves can emerge through them. The two last-mentioned types of loudspeaker are more particularly suitable for the reproduction of high frequencies. In high-fidelity ("hi-fi") systems these speakers are used in combination with electrodynamic speakers to obtain sound-reproduction with a very high degree of accuracy (cf. page 314 *et seq.*).

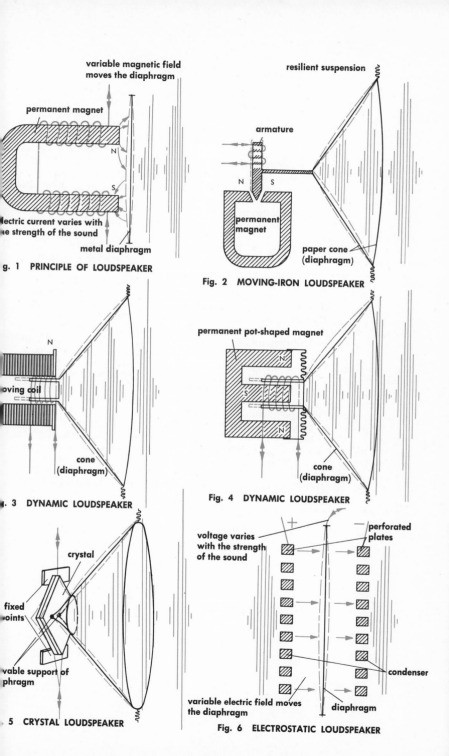

variable magnetic field
moves the diaphragm

permanent magnet

N

S

electric current varies with
the strength of the sound

metal diaphragm

Fig. 1 PRINCIPLE OF LOUDSPEAKER

resilient suspension

armature

N   S

permanent
magnet

paper cone
(diaphragm)

Fig. 2 MOVING-IRON LOUDSPEAKER

N

moving coil

cone
(diaphragm)

Fig. 3 DYNAMIC LOUDSPEAKER

permanent pot-shaped magnet

N

S

N

cone
(diaphragm)

Fig. 4 DYNAMIC LOUDSPEAKER

crystal

fixed
points

movable support of
diaphragm

Fig. 5 CRYSTAL LOUDSPEAKER

voltage varies
with the strength
of the sound

+   −   perforated
plates

condenser

variable electric field moves
the diaphragm

diaphragm

Fig. 6 ELECTROSTATIC LOUDSPEAKER

OVERHEAD TRANSMISSION LINES

The electric power from the generating stations, which are situated in regions where coal or water power is readily available, is distributed by long-distance transmission lines. These are usually of the overhead type consisting of conductors ("wires") suspended from lattice steel towers. According to Ohm's law ($U = R.I$, where U is the voltage, R is the resistance, and I is the current strength) the voltage drop is greater in proportion as the resistance (i.e., the length) of the line is greater and the current strength (amperage) is higher. For this reason it is endeavoured to keep these two electrical quantities as small as possible. With regard to reducing the resistance, one is soon up against a limit, because for reasons of economy and weight it is of course not possible to increase the thickness of the conductors indefinitely. As for the current, however, this can be considerably reduced by using alternating current in conjunction with transformation (see page 92). The voltage drop along the transmission line is thereby also reduced.

A simple example is illustrated in Fig. 1: a 220 kilowatt generator supplies a current of 1000 A at 220 V to the primary circuit of a high-tension transformer which increases the voltage a thousandfold and whose 220 kilowatt output is transmitted through a long-distance power line as a current of 1 A at 220,000 V. Before the electric power is supplied to the consumer, its voltage is transformed down in the ratio of 1000 to 1, so that a current of 1000 A at 220 V is again obtained. In actual practice the high tension of 220,000 V is usually first transformed down to 20,000 or 6000 V as an intermediate stage, which is used for local distribution lines, the final "step-down" of the voltage to 220 V[1] being performed in a second transformation stage at or near the consumer's premises. Since the resistance of a power line to alternating current is higher than its resistance to direct current, the use of alternating current involves additional losses. Such losses could be avoided by using high-tension direct current, but this calls for dependable high-duty rectifier equipment (see page 80). Long-distance power transmission with direct current is in fact being tried out experimentally in various countries.

The high-tension power transmission lines of the various generating stations are interconnected in a network known as the "grid". A system of this kind, of course, requires elaborate switchgear. High-tension switchgear and transformer equipment is very often installed (suitably sealed against moisture, etc.) in the open air.

Fig. 3 schematically illustrates the distribution of electricity by means of transmission lines and transformers from the power station to the individual consumers.

1. Consumer transmission lines carry 120 volts in U.S.A.

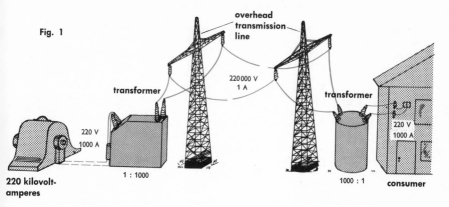

Fig. 1

overhead transmission line

transformer

220 000 V
1 A

transformer

220 V
1000 A

220 V
1000 A

220 kilovolt-amperes

1 : 1000

1000 : 1

consumer

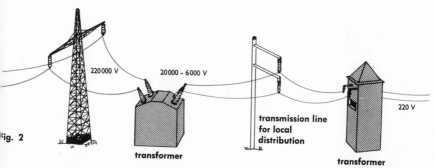

220 000 V

20 000 - 6 000 V

transmission line for local distribution

220 V

Fig. 2

transformer

transformer

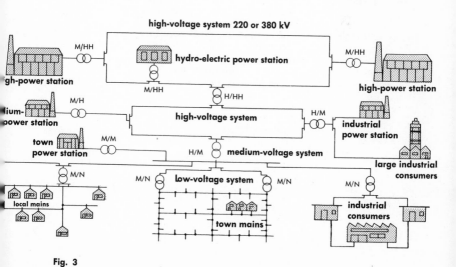

high-voltage system 220 or 380 kV

M/HH

hydro-electric power station

M/HH

gh-power station

M/HH

high-power station

M/H

H/HH

high-voltage system

H/M

ium-power station

industrial power station

town power station

M/M

H/M

medium-voltage system

large industrial consumers

M/N

M/N

low-voltage system

M/N

M/N

local mains

town mains

industrial consumers

Fig. 3

HH = very high voltage   H = high voltage   M = medium voltage   N = low voltage

/ = is transformed to   ⊖ = transformation

89

EARTHING (GROUNDING)

The substances of which the earth's crust consists mostly have a moderate degree of electric conductivity. Besides, the water which is often abundantly present in the soil contains salts in solution and thus forms an electrolyte which conducts electricity fairly well. This means that electric currents can pass through the soil if differences in potential (voltage) occur at various points of the earth's surface. Conversely, any potential difference will be immediately equalised, so that this surface in effect constitutes an equipotential surface (i.e., with a potential which is the same at all points). Since measurements of potential are merely relative, the earth's potential is adopted as a reference value and is, for the sake of convenience, taken as zero. Electrical equipment or conductors which are connected to the earth are said to be "earthed" or "grounded" (Figs. 1 and 2), which means that no difference of potential in relation to the earth can occur in them. Earthing thus provides a safeguard against electric shocks to anyone who happens to touch the metal parts concerned. A person who touches a "live" metal part which is not earthed is liable to receive a shock (possibly a fatal one).

Earthing can also be utilised for obtaining a "field-free" or "zero field" space, i.e., a space in which there is no electric field that might, for example, disturb delicate electrical measurements. For this purpose the walls of the laboratory are lined with wire netting or metal plates (and the doors and windows are also covered in this way) which are electrically interconnected and earthed. The room is then enclosed in equipotential surfaces which have the same potential as the earth, i.e., zero potential, so that no potential gradient (differences in potential from one point to another) and therefore no electric field can develop inside it. Faraday was the first to apply this principle, and for this reason a space screened against external fields is called a Faraday cage (in particular, this term is applied to an earthed wire cage surrounding apparatus to be protected from outside influence) (Fig. 3). The "pollution" of the atmosphere with electromagnetic fields from a multitude of radio and television transmitters has made Faraday's discovery a particularly important one for various present-day scientific and technical purposes. The all-metal body of a modern motor car also forms a kind of Faraday cage and provides excellent protection for the occupants against external electrostatic influences (lightning, in particular); besides, present-day motor tyres contain carbon black which makes the rubber conductive to electricity and thus ensures adequate earthing. The prerequisite for effective earthing is that the contact resistance between the earth wire and the soil should be very low, i.e., very good contact should be provided. Various methods of establishing a good earth connection are illustrated in Figs. 4a–4c: wide metal strips (4a) or metal rods (4c) well spread out and buried deep in the ground; connection to an underground metallic pipe system (e.g., water supply pipes) (4b).

Fig. 1 ELECTRIC APPLIANCE EARTHED BY MEANS OF A PROTECTIVE PLUG

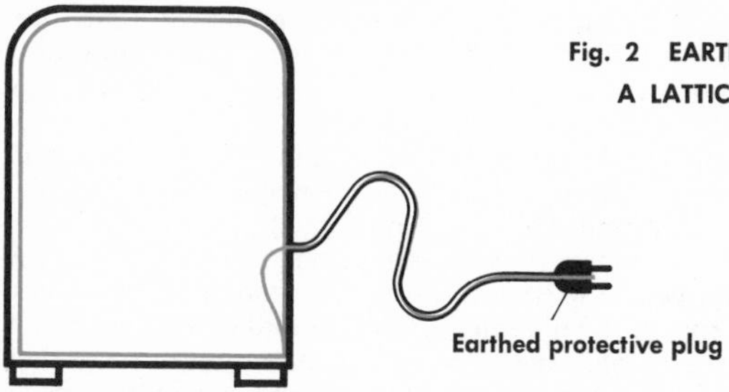

Earthed protective plug

Fig. 2 EARTHING OF A LATTICE PYLON

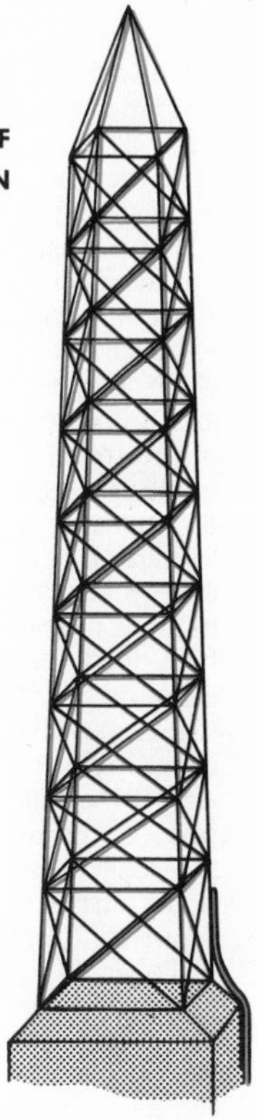

Fig. 3 FARADAY CAGE
(*field-free space inside it*)

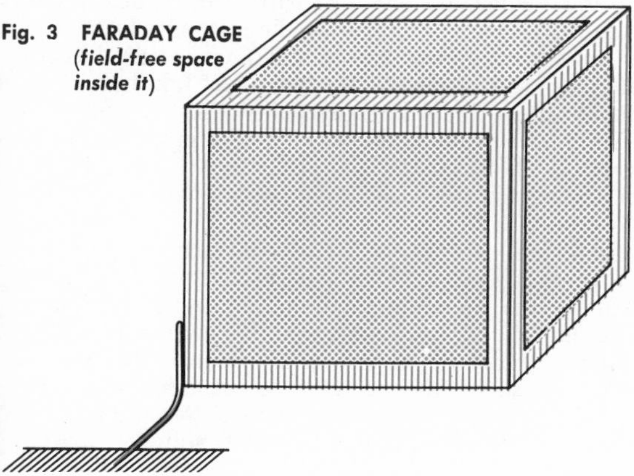

Fig. 4 EARTH CONNECTION

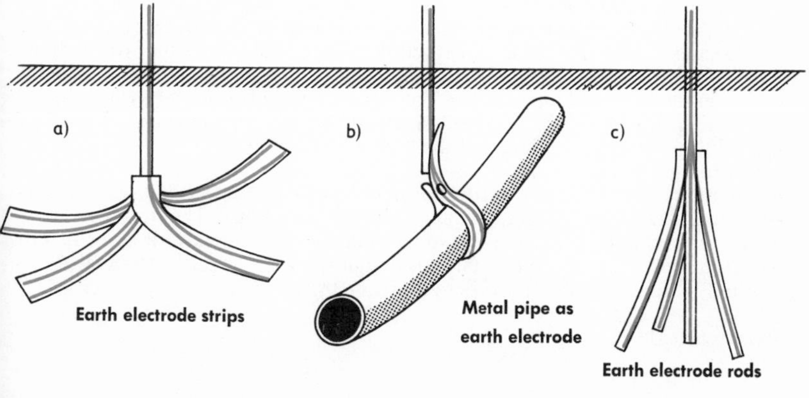

a)

Earth electrode strips

b)

Metal pipe as earth electrode

c)

Earth electrode rods

TRANSFORMER

Transformers are used for "stepping up" alternating current (and three-phase current) to high voltages for long-distance power transmission—in order to minimise the relative voltage losses—and also for "stepping down" the voltage at the point of consumption (see page 88).

The principle underlying the operation of a transformer is closely associated with Faraday's law of induction, which states that when the magnetic flux enclosed within a circuit varies, an electric current which is proportional to the rate of variation is induced in the circuit. If the magnetic flux variation is produced by means of an electromagnet coil energised by alternating (primary winding of the transformer), an induced electric current can be obtained from a second coil (secondary winding of the transformer) through which the varying magnetic flux from the first coil is made to pass. The two coils, i.e., the primary and the secondary winding, are mounted on the same iron core, so as to obtain maximum concentration of the flux. Transformation is characterised by its very high efficiency (98–99%), practically the only energy losses associated with low-frequency alternating current being heat losses, namely, heat developed in the resistance of the copper windings (copper losses) and heat due to eddy currents set up in the iron core (iron losses). To minimise the eddy currents, the core is laminated, i.e., it is made up of a number of thin iron plates which are insulated from one another. The iron losses additionally comprise so-called hysteresis losses. Ideally: $U_1.I_1 = U_2.I_2$ (input voltage × input current = output voltage × output current). The ratio $U_1:U_2$ is determined solely by the ratio of the number of turns of the primary and secondary winding respectively; it is called the transformation ratio. Thus, if the secondary winding has twice as many turns as the primary winding, the output voltage will be twice as high as the input voltage, but the output current will be only half the input current (see Fig. 1).

To step up (increase) the voltage, the secondary winding of the transformer has a larger number of turns of wire than the primary winding. To step down (decrease) the voltage before the current is supplied to the consumer, a transformer is used whose primary winding contains a larger number of turns than the secondary winding. For local distribution in a town the high voltage of the power grid is transformed down to, say, 6000 volts and this in turn is reduced to 220[1] volts for distribution to individual consumers within the limited area served by the final step-down transformer. A low-voltage device such as an electric bell (see page 256) often obtains its electricity from the mains through a small transformer of its own (called a bell transformer) which gives current at 4–8 volts. Such a transformer is often of the kind known as an auto-transformer, which has only one winding, part of which forms the secondary, while the whole forms the primary, or vice versa. Its principle is illustrated in Figs. 3a and 3b. It is cheaper in construction than a transformer with two windings, and the copper losses are lower. The ignition coil of an internal combustion engine operates on the same principle, except that it is a step-up transformer which has to deliver a high voltage for the sparking plugs. In this case the low (primary) voltage is applied to part of the winding and the high (secondary) voltage is taken from the whole winding (see page 482).

A commonly employed type of transformer is shown in Fig. 2. It is wound in concentric form, the primary winding being within the secondary. The iron core forms a double closed magnetic circuit (and is laminated, as already described). For practical purposes this is a more efficient design than the so-called toroidal transformer in Fig. 1, which merely serves to illustrate the principle.

1. 110/120 volts in U.S.A.

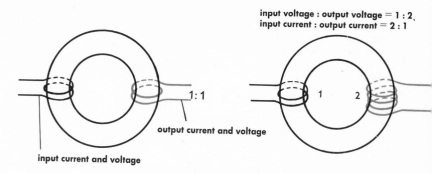

input voltage : output voltage $= 1 : 2$
input current : output current $= 2 : 1$

1 : 1

output current and voltage

input current and voltage

Fig. 1   TOROIDAL TRANSFORMER

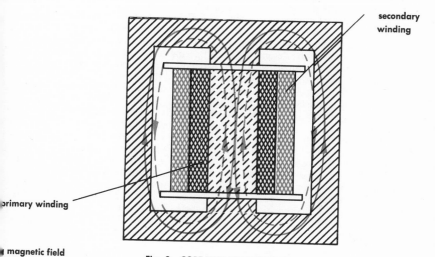

secondary
winding

primary winding

magnetic field
ns largely within the
nd causes electric
ion in the secondary winding

Fig. 2   CORE-TYPE TRANSFORMER

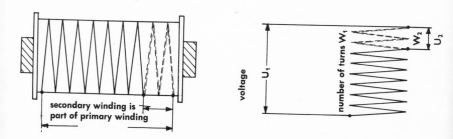

secondary winding is
part of primary winding

Fig. 3a   AUTO-TRANSFORMER

Fig. 3b   DIAGRAM SHOWING PRINCIPLE OF
AUTO-TRANSFORMER

RELAY

A relay is an electric switching device comprising one or more contacts which open or close circuits. The switching device is mostly actuated by an electromagnet which closes or opens the contacts by means of a movable armature which it attracts or releases. However, there are also relays which are operated by other than electromagnetic forces, e.g., electrical attraction forces or mechanical forces such as the flexural force of a bimetallic strip in a thermo-relay (cf. thermostat, page 20).

In this article only the electromagnetic relay will be described. In a variety of forms it plays a very important part in many branches of electrical engineering (telecommunication, automatic control, computers, etc.).

Three electromagnetic relays differing in the design of the armature are illustrated in Figs. 1–3. Each relay has a coil of wire with an iron core and an iron yoke which carries the movable armature (or may be an integral feature of the latter). The yoke, which serves as an easy path for the magnetic flux, imparts the polarity of the rear end of the core to the armature, which is thus powerfully attracted by the opposite polarity of the front end of the core. To prevent the armature from remaining sticking to the core by the action of remanent magnetism (the residual magnetism which remains in the core even when no current is flowing in the coil), a small separator stud made of a non-magnetic material (brass) maintains an air gap between the armature and the electromagnet core. The current for energising the coil is supplied through the connections designated as "soldering lugs". In the relay in Fig. 1 the contacts are normally open: when the relay coil is energised, the core attracts the armature, which presses the bottom contact up and thus closes the contacts, so that current then flows through the working circuit by way of the connections 1 and 2. Several sets of contacts can be installed in a relay, as in Figs. 2 and 3; these are simultaneously actuated when the relay is energised. These include normally closed contacts, which open only when the relay is energised and then break the working circuit in which they are installed (connections 2 and 3). A type of relay which is used particularly in telegraphy is the polarised relay (Fig. 4). The armature, which carries the contacts at its front end, is suspended from a torsion wire and receives the polarity of a magnetic north pole from the suitably mounted permanent magnet. The rear end of the armature extends into a gap in an iron yoke with magnetic south polarity. Mounted on this yoke is the relay coil which produces the controlling magnetic flux. The superposition of the magnetic fluxes, and therefore of the forces exerted, is shown in Fig. 4. A relay of this kind responds differently to energising currents flowing in different directions.

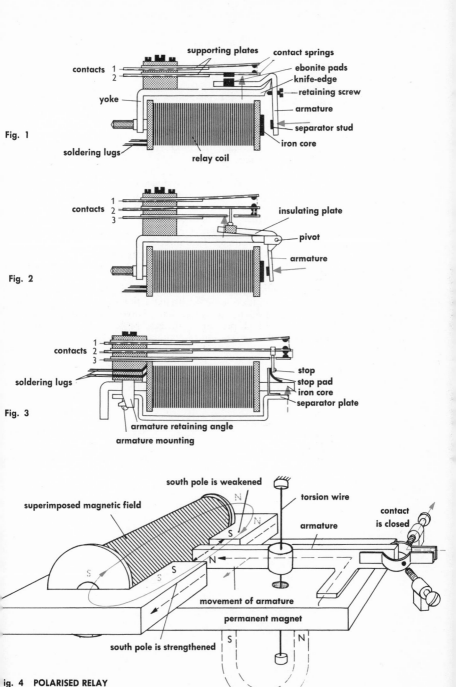

Fig. 1

contacts 1
2

supporting plates
contact springs
ebonite pads
knife-edge
retaining screw
armature
separator stud
iron core

yoke

soldering lugs
relay coil

Fig. 2

contacts 1
2
3

insulating plate
pivot
armature

Fig. 3

contacts 1
2
3

soldering lugs

stop
stop pad
iron core
separator plate

armature retaining angle
armature mounting

Fig. 4   POLARISED RELAY

south pole is weakened
superimposed magnetic field
torsion wire
contact is closed
armature
movement of armature
permanent magnet
south pole is strengthened

95

SWITCH

A switch is a general name for a device used for effecting the completion and interruption of an electric circuit. Fig. 1 shows a very simple switch for low voltage current. This type is extensively used in telecommunication engineering and for many other purposes, e.g., in bell circuits. The switch lever is conductively connected to the contact K and can be connected to either of two alternative circuits by setting it in the position I or II. A switch of this kind is unsuitable for heavy currents because considerable sparking would occur, more particularly on interruption of the current, and this could give rise to dangerous arc formation. To prevent this, the interruption of the current must be accomplished as speedily as possible. For this reason knife switches are used. One such switch is shown in Fig. 2. The switch blade is connected to the lever by a spring. When the operating lever is pulled out, the spring is tensioned and then quickly pulls the blade out of the contact: the brief interruption spark then cannot develop into an arc. Another way to prevent arcing at the contacts is embodied in the mercury switch, which is filled with a protective gas (inert gas, nitrogen) (Fig. 3). The switches used for domestic lighting purposes are turn switches, tumbler switches or push-button switches (Figs. 4–6). In all three types the interruption of the current is effected suddenly, by a kind of spring operated trigger action which ensures rapid separation of the contacts, so that no harmful arcing occurs. Switches for very strong currents are usually of the electromagnetically operated type (Fig. 7). High tension switchgear is often of the oil break type, i.e., the contacts are separated under oil for the quick and effective extinction of the arc; the oil also serves as insulation (Fig. 8). Switches for very high voltages are often of the gas-blast type, in which a blast of high pressure hydrogen, air or other gas is directed on to the arc at the moment of separation of contacts to accelerate its extinction (Fig. 9).

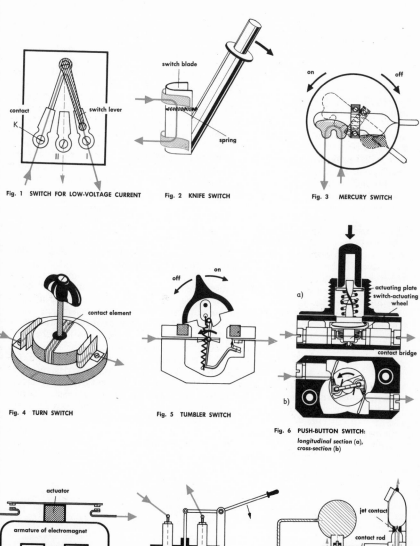

Fig. 1   SWITCH FOR LOW-VOLTAGE CURRENT

contact

switch lever

K

II   I

Fig. 2   KNIFE SWITCH

switch blade

spring

Fig. 3   MERCURY SWITCH

on

off

Fig. 4   TURN SWITCH

contact element

Fig. 5   TUMBLER SWITCH

off   on

Fig. 6   PUSH-BUTTON SWITCH:
longitudinal section (a),
cross-section (b)

a)

actuating plate
switch-actuating
wheel

contact bridge

b)

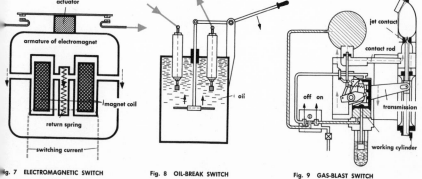

Fig. 7   ELECTROMAGNETIC SWITCH

actuator

armature of electromagnet

magnet coil

return spring

switching current

Fig. 8   OIL-BREAK SWITCH

oil

Fig. 9   GAS-BLAST SWITCH

jet contact

contact rod

off   on

transmission

working cylinder

SHORT-CIRCUIT (FUSE)

If the poles of an electric current source are interconnected by a short thick metal bar providing an easy path for the current (Fig. 1a), a very strong current will flow and the conductors (wires or cables) will become very hot, with an attendant fire hazard. According to Ohm's Law, the relationship between the voltage (U), the amperage or current strength (I) and the resistance (R) is as follows; $U = I.R$ or $I = U/R$. From this it appears that if the resistance in an electric circuit becomes abnormally low in consequence of some accidental cause, the current strength will increase considerably. This phenomenon is called *short circuit*. It is liable to occur more particularly in faulty leads or in electrical appliances such as a standard lamp whose flexible supply cord ("flex") is subjected to frequent bending, as a result of which the insulation between the two wires becomes damaged and allows them to touch each other, so that short circuit occurs. Damage due to short circuit is prevented by the inclusion of fuses in electric circuits. The simplest kind of fuse is merely a length of thin wire which, in the event of a short circuit, is heated rapidly by the ensuing high current and melts away, thus interrupting the circuit (Fig. 1b). Fig. 2 shows a more sophisticated fuse embodying this principle. The essential component is the fuse cartridge containing the fuse element (fusible wire or strip) embedded in sand. The rating of the fuse element, i.e., the current strength at which it will melt, will depend on the operating conditions and the degree of safeguard to be provided. A "blown" fuse is recognisable by the fact that a small coloured distinctive disc on the front of the fuse has dropped off. The disc serves as a colour code for the fuse rating, e.g., a green disc for a 6-amp. fuse, a red disc for a 10-amp. fuse, etc. When a fuse has blown, the fuse cartridge must be removed and a new cartridge inserted (of course, after the fault which caused the short circuit has been traced and remedied). The need for fitting a new cartridge is obviated in the automatic cut-out (or automatic circuit breaker) (Figs. 3a and 3b). In a device of this kind a switch is held in the "on" position by means of a catch. The catch can be withdrawn either by the action of an electromagnet or a bimetallic strip. When this happens, the switch is released and springs open, thereby interrupting the circuit. The electromagnet is so designed that it is actuated by the current in the circuit as soon as this current exceeds a certain predetermined value. In the other type, the heat produced by the excessive current in the event of short circuit causes the bimetallic strip to bend and thus interrupt the flow of current. When the cause of the short circuit has been eliminated, the automatic cut-out can be re-set in its operating position by actuation of a push-button. A second push button may be provided, to enable the cut-out to be "tripped" manually, so as to break the circuit at will.

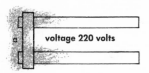
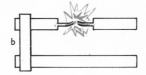

voltage 220 volts

Fig. 1   PRINCIPLE OF A FUSE

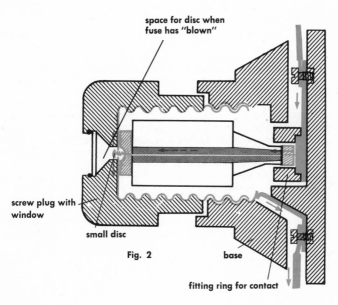

space for disc when
fuse has "blown"

screw plug with
window

small disc

Fig. 2

base

fitting ring for contact

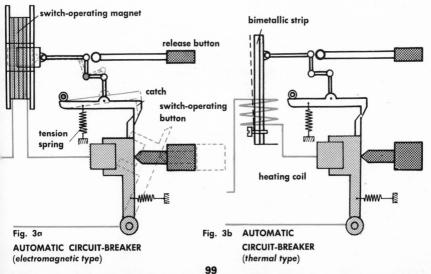

switch-operating magnet

release button

catch

switch-operating
button

tension
spring

Fig. 3a
AUTOMATIC CIRCUIT-BREAKER
(electromagnetic type)

bimetallic strip

heating coil

Fig. 3b AUTOMATIC
CIRCUIT-BREAKER
(thermal type)

ELECTRIC ARC, ARC LAMP

The electric discharge in the form of an arc is allied to the gas discharge which takes place when electricity is passed through rarefied gases and which is the underlying principle of fluorescent lamps (see page 104). The arc discharge occurs when two carbon electrodes are brought into contact with each other and are then moved apart a distance of about one eighth of an inch (the voltage should be at least 55 volts). Just before the carbon rods separate and direct material contact between them is broken, such a high electric resistance is developed at their boundary that the tips of the carbons begin to glow. This is associated with the emission of electrons (see page 74), which, because of the high emission temperatures (up to 4000° C), produces a high degree of ionisation of the air. (With direct current the electrons are emitted from the cathode, i.e., the negative electrode; with alternating current the emission occurs at both electrodes alternately). As a result of this ionisation, the air in the immediate vicinity of the carbon tips becomes conductive to electricity, so that the current will continue to flow when the electrodes are no longer actually touching each other. The bombardment of electrons to which it is exposed causes the positive electrode (anode), in particular, to become white hot, and a "crater" forms at its tip. In the actual arc itself, which merely gives off yellowish violet light, the gas molecules of the air dissociate. They lose some of their enveloping electrons and form a mixture of positive ions (electrically charged atoms) and electrons (negatively charged), which is externally neutral and which, on account of its particular properties, is called *thermal plasma* (Fig. 1). The temperature of this gaseous state can be determined by spectroscopic investigations of its dissociated condition. It is found to be between 20,000° and 50,000° C in the arc. In the arc lamp the arc serves as a source of light, but most of the light comes from the incandescent tips of the carbons (Fig. 2) and especially from the positive crater if the arc lamp is fed with direct current (Fig. 3). As the carbons burn away, they have to be fed forward so as to keep the gap between them fairly constant. If this gap becomes too large, the arc will be extinguished. In modern arc lamps the electrode feed is performed automatically (Fig. 4). The springs F_1 and F_2 keep the carbons in contact with each other when the lamp is not functioning. When the current is switched on, the electromagnets E_1 and E_2 draw the carbons apart and thereby strike the arc. If the rate of burning away is too low, the resistance of the arc will increase. As a result, the current will become weaker, the pull exerted by the electromagnets will diminish, and the springs will draw the carbons closer together. This kind of control mechanism is still sometimes used in arc lamps of cinema projectors, but high-pressure gas discharge lamps are now superseding the arc lamp for this purpose.

In electric furnaces the intense heat developed by the arc discharge is utilised for the melting of metals such as steel. If the material to be melted is a poor conductor of electricity, the heat radiated by the arc formed between two carbon electrodes is used to melt it (Fig. 5). On the other hand, if the material does conduct electricity, then the arc discharge may either be passed direct from the electrodes to the material (Fig. 6) or the electrodes may be actually buried in the material (Fig. 7). In both cases the considerable heat developed in the electrodes helps the current to generate heat in the material and thus attain the melting temperature.

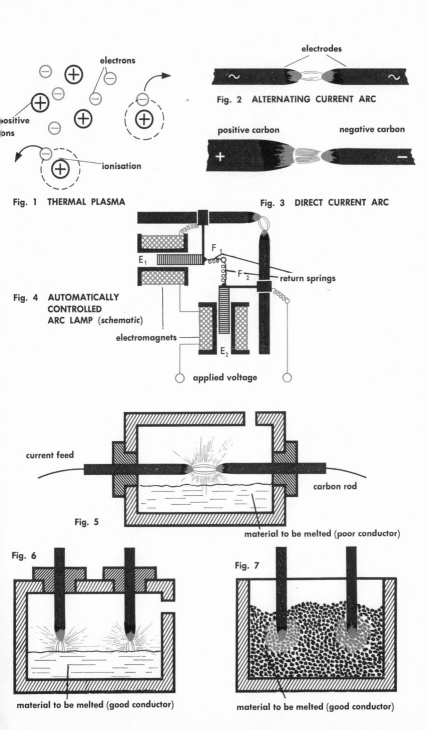

electrons

positive ions

ionisation

Fig. 1 THERMAL PLASMA

electrodes

Fig. 2 ALTERNATING CURRENT ARC

positive carbon

negative carbon

Fig. 3 DIRECT CURRENT ARC

Fig. 4 AUTOMATICALLY
CONTROLLED
ARC LAMP (*schematic*)

E_1

F_1

F_2 — return springs

electromagnets

E_2

applied voltage

current feed

carbon rod

Fig. 5

material to be melted (poor conductor)

Fig. 6

material to be melted (good conductor)

Fig. 7

material to be melted (good conductor)

PHOTO-ELECTRIC CELLS

The functioning of a photo-electric cell (or photocell) which is, for example, an important component of an exposure meter (see page 180), is based on photo-electric effects.

The electrons in a metal can have energy supplied to them by radiation, e.g., light rays. This is known as photo-electric effect. The energy of a light quantum (photon) is imparted to the most loosely bound electron of an atom (Fig. 1a). This energy may be sufficient to liberate the electron but not enough to eject it entirely from the metal (Fig. 1b) (photo conductive effect); alternatively, it may be sufficient not only to liberate the electron but also to cause it to be ejected into the vacuum (Fig. 1c) (normal photo-electric effect). The energy balance of the elementary process involved is given by Einstein's equation:

$$hv = A + \tfrac{1}{2} m_e v^2$$

where hv denotes the energy of the photon, in which v is the frequency of the light radiation and h is Planck's constant ($h = 6.625 \times 10^{-27}$ erg-seconds), A denotes the photo-electric work function (i.e., the energy required by a photon to eject an electron from a metal), m_e denotes the mass of the electron, and v its velocity in vacuum. The normal photo-electric effect is applied in the *photo-electric cell* (Fig. 2a). The light-sensitive photo-cathode, which is usually installed in an evacuated glass tube, may consist of a very thin film of cesium deposited by vaporisation on to an oxidised silver base. For greater sensitivity the glass tube may be filled with an inert gas at low pressure. A battery in the external circuit serves to amplify the current by ionisation of the gas filling.

The photo-conductive effect is utilised in the *photo-conductive cell* (Fig. 2b). The sensitive material usually employed in this case is cadmium sulphide or cadmium selenide. These substances undergo changes in resistance in the ratio of $10^9 : 1$ between the extremes of darkness and maximum exposure to light.

When the photo-conductive effect occurs at the P-N boundary of semiconductors (see page 82) or at the boundary between a semiconductor and a metal (e.g., cuprous oxide and copper), a potential difference will develop: this is known as the photo voltaic effect, and a cell of this kind is called a photo-voltaic cell (Fig. 2c). The cells represented in Figs. 2a and 2c generate an electromotive force on their own account, causing a current to flow in the circuit even if no battery is included in the circuit, whereas the photo-conductive cell (Fig. 2b) requires an auxiliary voltage provided by a battery. Photo-electric cells are used for a wide variety of purposes in control engineering, for precision measuring devices, in exposure meters used in photography, etc. They are also used in "solar batteries" as sources of electric power for rockets and satellites used in space research. For this purpose silicon photo-electric cells are used; about 10% of the radiation energy which they absorb is converted into electric energy.

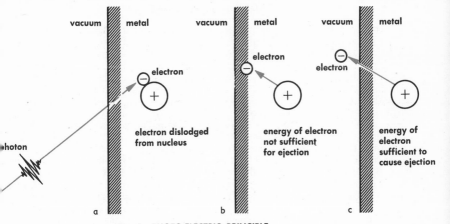

vacuum | metal

electron

electron dislodged
from nucleus

vacuum | metal

electron

energy of electron
not sufficient
for ejection

vacuum | metal

electron

energy of
electron
sufficient to
cause ejection

photon

a

b

c

Fig. 1   PHOTO-ELECTRIC PRINCIPLE

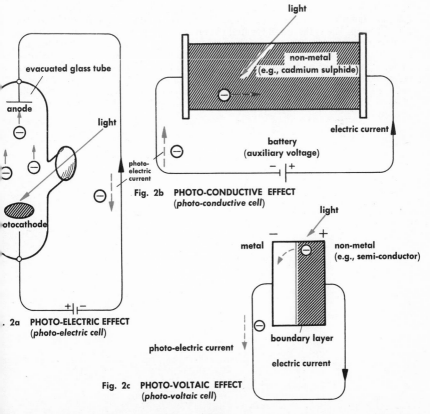

evacuated glass tube

anode

light

photocathode

photo-
electric
current

Fig. 2a   PHOTO-ELECTRIC EFFECT
(*photo-electric cell*)

light

non-metal
(e.g., cadmium sulphide)

electric current

battery
(auxiliary voltage)

Fig. 2b   PHOTO-CONDUCTIVE EFFECT
(*photo-conductive cell*)

light

metal

non-metal
(e.g., semi-conductor)

boundary layer

electric current

photo-electric current

Fig. 2c   PHOTO-VOLTAIC EFFECT
(*photo-voltaic cell*)

103

FLUORESCENT LAMP

The fluorescent lamp is a gas discharge tube whose output of light is so increased by special means that it can be used for lighting purposes. The inner surface of the wall of the tube is coated with a light-emitting substance—usually fluorescent or phosphorescent metallic salts (calcium tungstate, zinc sulphide, zinc silicate). The tube is filled with mercury vapour at extremely low pressure. The electrons ejected from the incandescent electrodes (see page 74) collide with the mercury atoms and cause these to emit radiation which consists for the most part of ultraviolet rays, which are invisible. The visible portion of the mercury vapour rays is situated in the green and blue range of the spectrum (see page 134) and gives a pale light. The ultra-violet light strikes the fluorescent substance with which the wall of the tube is coated and causes this substance to emit radiation with a longer wavelength in the visible range of the spectrum—i.e., the coating transforms the invisible rays into visible light. By suitable choice of the fluorescent substance, this light can be given any desired colour. The lamp has to be operated with a choke,[1] which prevents a harmful rise in voltage and serves to ignite the lamp. For this purpose a small auxiliary glow lamp provided with a thermal contact is connected in parallel with the main lamp. When the current is switched on, the glow lamp first lights up (the bimetallic thermal contact is then open). This causes the bimetallic strip to warm up and close the contact, with the result that the glow lamp is short-circuited and the cathodes of the main lamp receive the full current that makes them incandescent. The bimetallic strip cools and breaks the contact. Through the agency of the choke this interruption of the circuit produces a voltage surge which is high enough to initiate the discharge in the fluorescent lamp itself. Because it is bypassed by the main lamp, the small auxiliary lamp then ceases to function. The bimetallic strip (cf. page 20) keeps the contact open. The cathodes of the main lamp are kept glowing at white heat by the impingement of positive mercury ions, and the lamp thus continues to function and emit light in the manner described. The light of a fluorescent lamp is not produced by an incandescent body (such as the filament of an ordinary electric lamp), but is emitted as a result of the excitation of atoms (namely, those of the mercury vapour and the fluorescent coating) and is extremely economical. Because of the large light-emitting area, a fluorescent lamp gives a pleasant light which produces only soft shadows.

1. Starter in U.S.A.

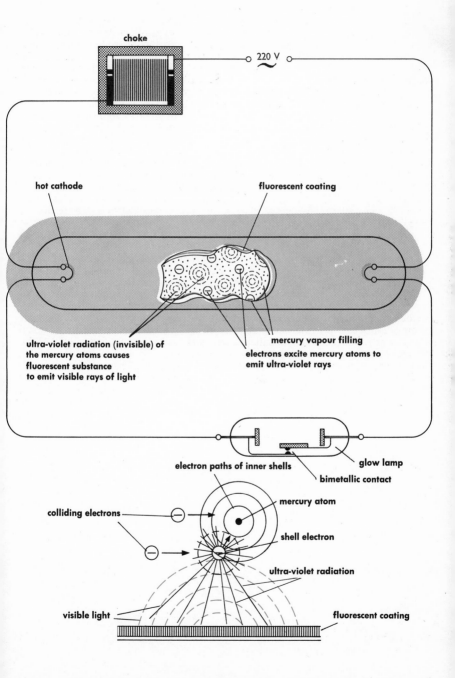

choke

220 V

hot cathode

fluorescent coating

ultra-violet radiation (invisible) of
the mercury atoms causes
fluorescent substance
to emit visible rays of light

mercury vapour filling

electrons excite mercury atoms to
emit ultra-violet rays

glow lamp

bimetallic contact

electron paths of inner shells

colliding electrons

mercury atom

shell electron

ultra-violet radiation

visible light

fluorescent coating

X-RAYS

When a stream of very fast high-energy electrons strikes a metallic electrode (anode), the electrons are slowed down, and some of them penetrate into the metal (Fig. 1). The sudden "braking" of the electrons produces an electromagnetic radiation of very short wavelength: X-rays or Röentgen rays. This radiation is generated by electrons penetrating into the metal and interacting with the metal atoms. It shows well-defined wavelengths which are characteristic of the structure of the metal forming the anode: a high-energy electron which penetrates into the metal atom may dislodge one of the inner electrons of that atom; the vacant place is taken by one of the outer electrons which thus leaps from an outer to an inner "shell" and, in doing so, emits energy in the form of radiation, i.e., X-rays.

These rays were discovered by W. Röntgen, a German physicist, in 1895. Their nature was unknown to him, and he accordingly referred to them as "X-rays", a name which has persisted more particularly in the English-speaking countries. Technical forms of construction of X-ray tubes are illustrated in Figs. 3 and 4. As a rule, the stream of electrons (such electrons issuing from a cathode are called "cathode rays") is not directed against the actual anode, but against the anticathode, which forms a target for bombardment. The impingement of the electrons against the anticathode causes the latter to become very hot, and it may be necessary to cool it or to design it as a rotating anode, so that the cathode rays are always beamed on a fresh area of the anode surface (cf. page 438).

Because of their short wavelength (10^{-8} to 10^{-12} cm) X-rays can pass through objects which are opaque to ordinary light, and shadow images of such objects can be made visible on a fluorescent screen coated with barium platinocyanide. When X-rays pass through crystalline substances, diffraction phenomena occur which reveal the wave character of this radiation. An interference pattern (cf. page 134) composed of a regular arrangement of dots can be formed on a photographic plate, and these provide information as to the crystal structure of the material concerned. Such diffraction patterns were first studied scientifically by M. von Laue, and they are known as Laue X-ray patterns (Fig. 5).

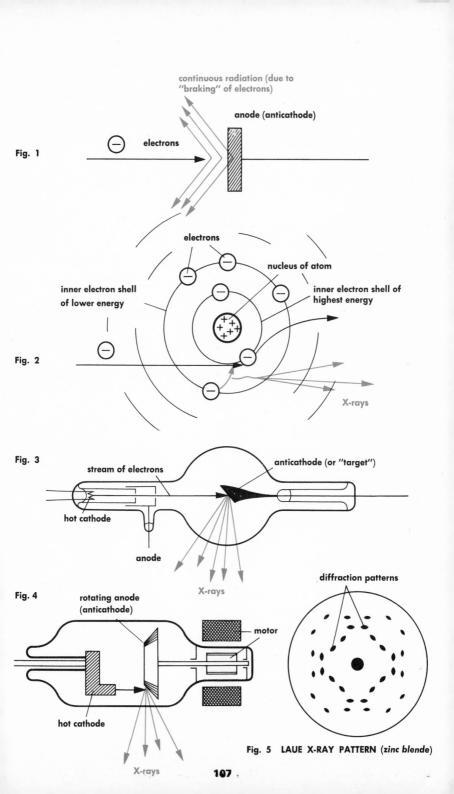

continuous radiation (due to "braking" of electrons)

anode (anticathode)

electrons

Fig. 1

electrons

nucleus of atom

inner electron shell of lower energy

inner electron shell of highest energy

Fig. 2

X-rays

Fig. 3

stream of electrons

anticathode (or "target")

hot cathode

anode

X-rays

Fig. 4

rotating anode (anticathode)

motor

hot cathode

X-rays

diffraction patterns

Fig. 5 LAUE X-RAY PATTERN (zinc blende)

107

CYCLOTRONS AND SIMILAR DEVICES

Scientists engaged in research into the structure of the atom use high-energy "projectiles" for bombarding the atom. Elementary particles (e.g., electrons) make very suitable projectiles because they mostly have an electric charge, so that they can be accelerated by electromagnetic fields. The acceleration is usually produced by causing the particles to travel in circular paths, and for this reason the various machines used for the purpose are known collectively as "circular accelerators".

The *betatron* (Fig. 1) resembles a transformer (see page 92) in its general construction: an iron core is provided with an exciting winding (corresponding to the primary winding of a transformer) through which an alternating current flows. Instead of a secondary winding, however, the betatron has an evacuated annular tube into which electrons are shot. In consequence of magnetic induction (see page 62), an annular alternating electric field (rotational field) is produced in the tube. This field, whose direction is perpendicular to that of the magnetic field, can have a retarding as well as an accelerating effect on the electrons. Since acceleration is required, an intermittent mode of operation is applied. The electrons are shot into the annular tube at the instant when the alternating electric field attains its maximum strength. During the next quarter period of the alternating field strength the electrons are accelerated by the field, while the field strength continuously decreases. The electrons must be removed from the annular tube not later than the end of this quarter period, for otherwise they would be decelerated in the following half period.

According to the conventional theory of electrodynamics the rotational frequency of an electrically charged particle travelling in a circular orbit in a magnetic field is independent of the radius of its orbit. The energy of the particle increases with its velocity. The operation of the *cyclotron* is based on these principles. The evacuated acceleration chamber is mounted in a homogeneous magnetic field between the poles of a powerful electromagnet, as shown in Fig. 2a. The actual vacuum chamber is shown (in plan) in Fig. 2b. Ions (electrically charged atoms) are produced by a source at the centre of the chamber and are forced to travel along circular orbits by the magnetic field. As their circular frequency is constant, the ions can be accelerated by means of a high-frequency alternating electric field of the same frequency. This is done with the aid of two hollow semicircular electrodes (called "dees") to which a high-frequency oscillating voltage is applied. Each time an ion passes from one dee into the other, it is accelerated by the electric field that exists in the gap between the two dees. This does not cause any change in the rotational frequency, but it does increase the velocity of the ion, with the result that the radius of its orbit increases. The ion thus progressively acquires more and more energy and moves into orbits of increasingly large radius, i.e., it moves in a spiral path, until it is finally deflected (by means of a deflecting condenser) out of the vacuum chamber at the periphery.

Whereas the cyclotron is used for the acceleration of particles in the low velocity range, the *synchrotron* (Fig. 3) is an accelerator for particles with velocities approaching the velocity of light. The operating principle of the two machines is very similar, however. As distinct from what happens in the cyclotron, in the synchrotron both the orbit radius of the particle and the rotational frequency remain constant, whereas the magnetic field increases (just as in the betatron). The fact that the energy of the particles increases despite the fact that their velocity remains nearly constant is something that can be explained only with the aid of the relativity theory: when the particle velocity becomes almost equal to the velocity of light, even a small increase in velocity will result in a considerable increase in the mass (and therefore the energy) of the particle. The gain in energy achieved in the synchrotron is therefore due, not to a velocity increase, but to an increase in mass.

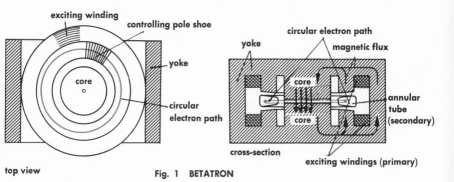

Fig. 1   BETATRON

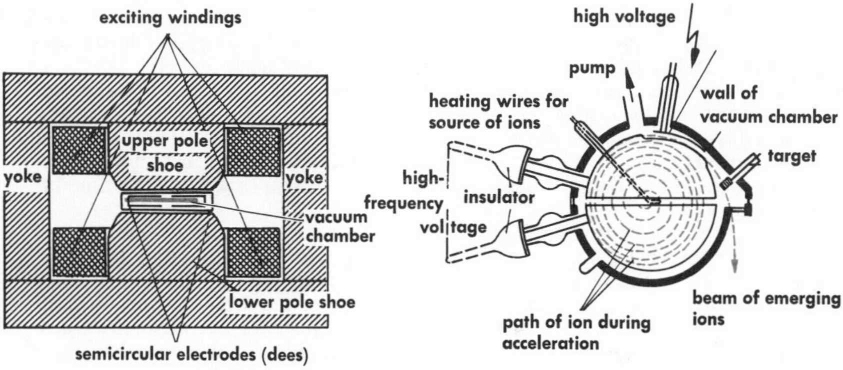

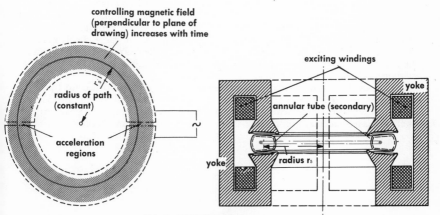

Fig. 2   CYCLOTRON

Fig. 3   SYNCHROTRON

TELECOMMUNICATION

Telecommunication, in its widest sense, is as old as mankind's need for ways and means of exchanging information over long distances. In ancient times and during the middle ages, visual signals were usually employed for the purpose, in the form of beacon fires lit on top of towers or on hills and visible a long way off. Of course, only a limited number of prearranged messages could be communicated by such means. A later and more sophisticated method of visual signalling was the semaphore, a device provided with movable arms which could be set in various positions to spell out letters and words. Signalling by means of flags or lamps, and the hoisting and lowering of signal balls, as are still commonly employed in navigation, also belong to the general category of communication by visual signals. Telecommunication in the modern sense developed only after the discovery of the magnetic effect of electric current. The first telegraph consisted of a compass needle which was deflected by the magnetic field produced by electric currents which flowed through the circuit whenever the transmitting key was depressed and contact established (Fig. 1). A further advance in electrical telecommunication was the invention of the Morse telegraph: an electromagnetically actuated stylus records long and short dashes—forming a code named Morse code after its inventor—on a moving strip of paper (cf. page 114). In the latter half of the last century a further advance was made by the invention of the telephone (and microphone) so that it then became possible to transmit speech-modulated current fluctuations over long distances (Fig. 3).

The current fluctuations are transmitted either through overhead wires, through cables, or through the medium of radio communication (Fig. 4). The electric current or the radio waves can be modulated in various ways to carry the message: amplitude modulation (Fig. 5), i.e., variations in current strength, or frequency modulation, i.e., variations in the timing of the zero values of the current (Fig. 6), or pulse modulation (Fig. 7).

As the transmission of messages over long distances, whether by cable or by radio, is very expensive, the problem of simultaneous multiple utilisation had to be tackled. It was solved by means of carrier wave communication: a high-frequency current is modulated in various frequency ranges. For telephony a band width of 3600 cycles/sec. is adopted for each range and is adequate for the intelligible transmission of speech. Each range of this kind is comparable to a wire or cable and is called a channel. The frequency band of a telephony channel can, for example, be subdivided into 24 telegraphy channels. In this way it is possible to cater for the needs of subscribers to the teleprinter (telex) system. Filtering out the individual channels is done by means of electric filter systems. For the transmission of the high-frequency carrier oscillations the cables are of the so-called coaxial type (Fig. 8): a flexible metal sheath contains a coaxial conductor which is held in position by highly insulating material. As a rule, the cable also contains various subsidiary wires for low-frequency, i.e., direct, transmission purposes. In a coaxial cable of this kind up to 2880 telephony channels can be accommodated in the coaxial conductor and in the subsidiary wires. The coaxial core (tube) is additionally suitable for the transmission of a television channel.

Fresh possibilities in electric telecommunication have been opened up by pulse techniques and other modern developments which form the basis of data processing (see page 298). Also, practical applications of masers and lasers (see page 78) are likely to leave their mark on present-day telecommunication methods.

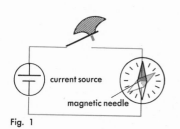

current source

magnetic needle

Fig. 1

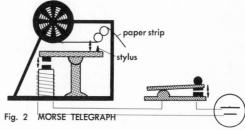

paper strip

stylus

Fig. 2 MORSE TELEGRAPH

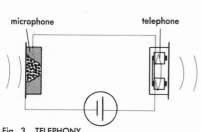

microphone

telephone

Fig. 3 TELEPHONY

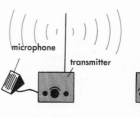

microphone

transmitter

receiver

loudspeaker

Fig. 4 RADIO COMMUNICATION

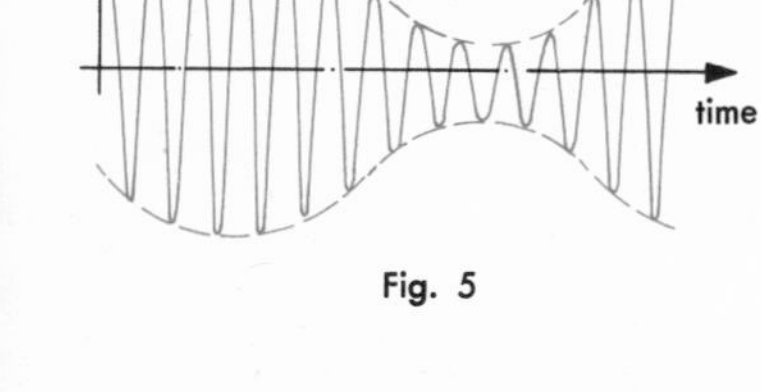

current strength

low-frequency vibration (message)

high-frequency carrier wave

time

Fig. 5

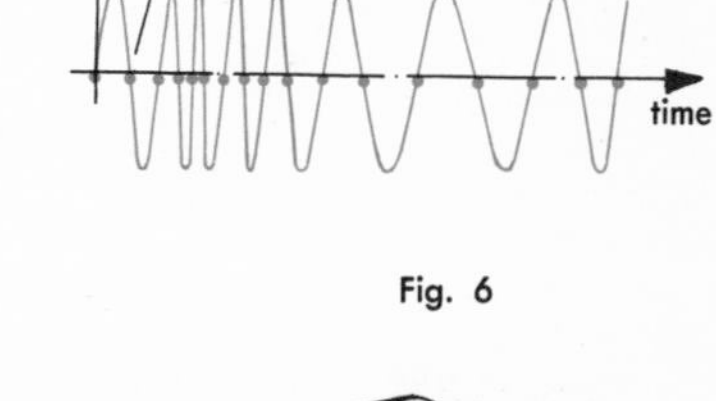

current strength

low-frequency vibration (message)

high-frequency carrier wave

passage through zero

time

Fig. 6

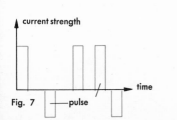

current strength

time

Fig. 7   pulse

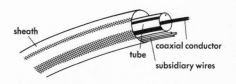

sheath

coaxial conductor

tube

subsidiary wires

Fig. 8 COAXIAL CABLE

TELEPHONES AND TELEPHONE EXCHANGES

The basic problem in telephony consists in converting acoustic into electric energy and vice versa. The first part of the problem is solved by means of the carbon microphone in which carbon granules are compressed to a greater or less degree by a diaphragm, so that their resistance varies with the acoustic pressure. This in turn produces corresponding fluctuations in the current, which are transmitted—through a transformer called a repeating coil—to the telephone receiver. The latter comprises a U-shaped permanent magnet whose legs are provided with coils which are energised by the telephone current. The fluctuations in the strength of the magnetic field, and these correspondingly move the steel diaphragm, which in turn transmits its vibrations to the air in the form of audible sound waves (Fig. 1). As an alternative to the carbon microphone the condenser microphone may be employed (Fig. 2). This is a more sensitive instrument. Its diaphragm, in conjunction with a fixed counter electrode, forms a condenser whose capacity varies with the vibrations of the diaphragm. The direct voltage applied in the circuit thereby has an alternating voltage superimposed upon it.

The interconnection of two subscribers in the central battery system is indicated diagrammatically in Fig. 3. With manual switching (Fig. 4) the connection with the desired subscriber is effected through various exchanges (local exchange, trunk exchange, zone centre, trunk exchange, local exchange). The connections are routed through subscriber's lines (AL), interoffice trunks (VL), and trunk lines (FL). In the automatic long distance service the connections are nowadays still usually established by means of mechanical selector units (two-motion selectors). When the subscriber dials the desired number, electrical impulses, corresponding to the respective numbers, are transmitted along the telephone line and actuate a selector at the telephone exchange (Figs. 5 and 6).

A selector is an automatically actuated multiple contact switch or other device which makes contact with any desired circuit. In the two-motion type the wiper can move vertically step by step from one tier of contacts to another, and at each tier it can swing horizontally to any particular contact. These movements are controlled by the current impulses transmitted by dialling. For each figure dialled, a corresponding number of impulses of current reaches the selector, causing the wiper to move automatically to the correct tier and to the correct individual contact corresponding to the figure dialled.

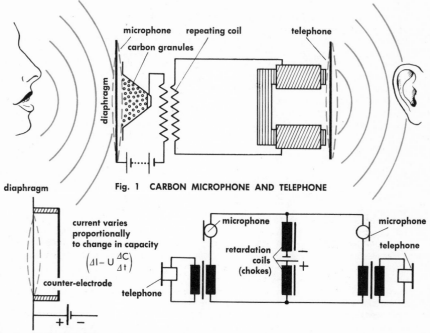

Fig. 1 CARBON MICROPHONE AND TELEPHONE

current varies
proportionally
to change in capacity

$$\left(\Delta I = U\,\frac{\Delta C}{\Delta t}\right)$$

Fig. 2 CONDENSER MICROPHONE

Fig. 3 CENTRAL BATTERY SYSTEM

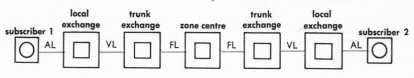

Fig. 4 MANUAL SWITCHING

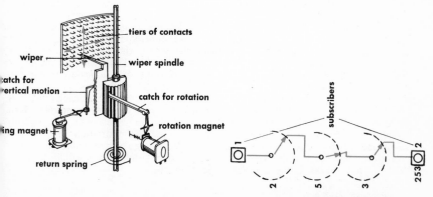

Fig. 5 TWO-MOTION SELECTOR

Fig. 6 SELECTOR UNIT FOR THREE-STAGE CONNECTION

113

TELEGRAPHY, TELETYPEWRITER

After the discovery of electromagnetism in the first part of the nineteenth century, inventors strove to utilise it for the transmission of messages by electricity. After the promising tests carried out by Gauss and Weber at the University of Göttingen, Germany, in 1833, Morse developed a reliably functioning telegraph apparatus and a workable code (Morse alphabet). In its present form the Morse apparatus has a strip of paper which is unwound from a supply reel and slides past an inked printing wheel. When at rest, this wheel does not touch the paper strip, but when a message is being received, the wheel is pressed against the moving strip for shorter or longer periods of time by means of an electromagnet, so that a series of "dots" and "dashes" are produced (Fig. 1). The International Morse code is as follows:

Alphabet   *Numerals*

a	· –	h	· · · ·	q	– – · –	1	· – – – –
ä	· – · –	i	· ·	r	· – ·	2	· · – – –
å	· – – · –	j	· – – –	s	· · ·	3	· · · – –
b	– · · ·	k	– · –	t	–	4	· · · · –
c	– · – ·	l	· – · ·	u	· · –	5	· · · · ·
ch	– – – –	m	– –	ü	· · – –	6	– · · · ·
d	– · ·	n	– ·	v	· · · –	7	– – · · ·
e	·	ñ	– – · – –	w	· – –	8	– – – · ·
é	· · – · ·	o	– – –	x	– · · –	9	– – – – ·
f	· · – ·	ö	– – – ·	y	– · – –	0	– – – – –
g	– – ·	p	· – – ·	z	– – · ·		

Punctuation marks

apostrophe	· – – – – ·	hyphen	– · · · · –	question mark	· · – – · ·
colon	– – – · · ·	parenthesis	– · – – · –	quotation mark	· – · · – ·
comma	– – · · – –	period	· – · – · –	*Distress signal (SOS)*	· · · – – – · · ·

Subsequent inventors aimed at achieving direct transmission of characters, i.e., letters of the alphabet, instead of having to use a code. The latest stages in this process of development are the Hell printing telegraph (Fig. 2) and the teletypewriter (or teleprinter) (Fig. 3). Both these devices make use of an alphabet produced by current impulses on the step-by-step principle. This alphabet operates with a five-unit code comprising seven current steps and five separating steps. The trains of impulses are timed by means of synchronised camshafts rotating in the transmitting and in the receiving instrument respectively (7 r.p.m.). The various code signals (characters) correspond to different notches in the permutation bars in the transmitter. When the keys are depressed, these bars shift to different positions and thereby control the current impulses sent (Fig. 3a). In the receiver, slotted combination bars are similarly so displaced in relation to one another that only that type bar which corresponds to the transmitted code signal engages with the slots in the bars and thus prints a particular character on a sheet or strip of paper (Fig. 3b). These bar movements are produced by an electromagnet. The teletypewriter looks like a large desk typewriter. One and the same apparatus can be used for transmitting and receiving.

Another branch of telegraphy is picture telegraphy (or phototelegraphy[1]): a photograph attached to a revolving drum is scanned point by point in a spiral pattern by a beam of light. The reflected light causes photo-electric cells (see page 102) to produce currents of varying strength which correspond to the variations in brightness of the individual points of the photograph (Fig. 4a). At the receiving end, a glow lamp transforms the current variations into variations of brightness of a light spot (P) which is focused on to photographic paper (Fig. 4b).

1. Wire-photo in U.S.A.

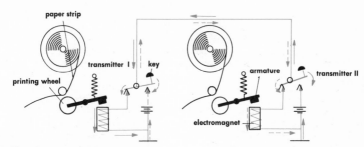

1 MORSE TELEGRAPHY WITH OPEN-CIRCUIT WORKING

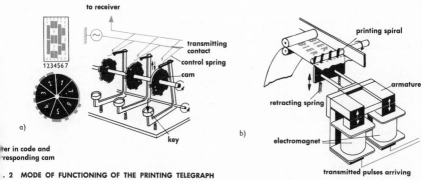

ter in code and
rresponding cam

2 MODE OF FUNCTIONING OF THE PRINTING TELEGRAPH

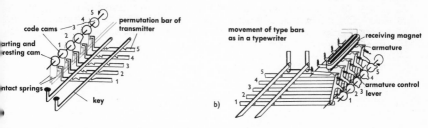

3 MODE OF FUNCTIONING OF THE TELETYPEWRITER

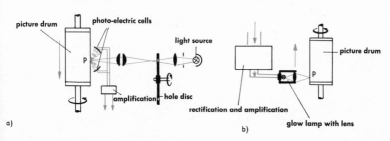

4 MODE OF FUNCTIONING OF THE PHOTOTELEGRAPH

RADAR

The name "radar" has been derived from the initial letters of the phrase "radio detecting and ranging'. It denotes a method of scanning the surrounding space by means of high-frequency radio waves which are sent out from a powerful transmitter and are reflected by any objects which they encounter. The reflected beam is picked up by a receiver; its strength and direction gives information on the size, distance, altitude, etc. of the object.

If, for example, an observer in an aircraft wishes to survey by radar the terrain over which he is flying (Fig. 1), a rotating radar beam is directed downward from the aircraft. The beam scans a circular area in the form of a sector which sweeps round and round. Depending on the nature of the reflecting objects (in this case these are located on the surface of the earth), the intensity of the reflected beam will vary (Fig. 2). The transmission and reception of the high-frequency waves are effected in the radar apparatus (Fig. 3). The radar waves are generated in the transmitter, which is equipped with radio tubes of special design (klystron, magnetron: see page 76 *et seq*). The transmitting antenna usually also functions as the receiving antenna (periodic change-over). The reflected beam is picked up by the receiver and the corresponding electric currents are used to deflect an electron beam in a cathode-ray tube (see page 126). The beam is so deflected that it scans the luminescent screen from the centre to the edge while it rotates at the same speed as the antenna. An echo picked up by the receiver strengthens the flow of electrons in the tube, causing a point of light to appear on the screen and to remain visible by phosphorescent afterglow until fresh echoes are picked up on the next revolution of the scanning antenna. In this way the points of light build up a picture of the area (or space) scanned by the radar beam. The brightness of the display of the signal (the radar echo) on the luminescent screen of the cathode ray tube depends on the reflecting power of the object with regard to the high-frequency radio waves sent out by the radar transmitter. For this reason a radar image generally looks quite different from an optical image, though as a rule they will have the same outlines (Fig. 4).

Most radar sets employ pulse radar. This is so called because the transmitter sends out short intense bursts or pulses of energy with a relatively long interval between pulses. The receiver is active during this interval. When sufficient time has elapsed to permit the reception of echoes from the most distant objects of interest, the transmitter sends another short pulse, and the cycle repeats.

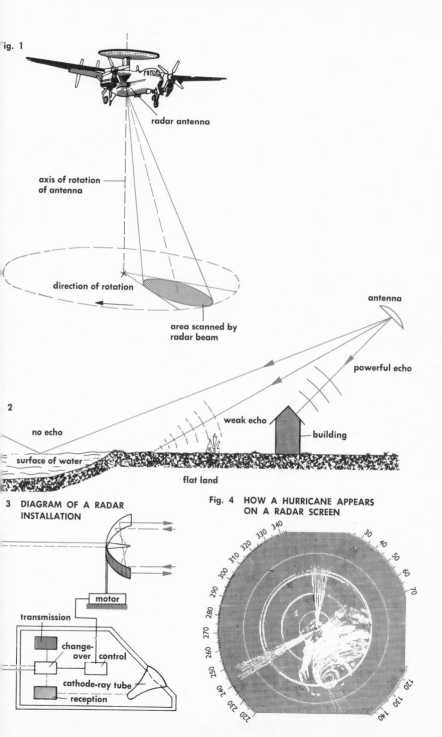

Fig. 1

radar antenna

axis of rotation
of antenna

direction of rotation

area scanned by
radar beam

antenna

powerful echo

2

weak echo

no echo

building

surface of water

flat land

3 DIAGRAM OF A RADAR
   INSTALLATION

Fig. 4 HOW A HURRICANE APPEARS
        ON A RADAR SCREEN

motor

transmission

change-
over

control

cathode-ray tube

reception

117

PHOTOMULTIPLIER

An electron multiplier is a device which employs secondary emission (the ejection of electrons as a result of the impact of charged particles) from solids to produce current amplification. A photomultiplier is an electron multiplier tube in which the bombarding electrons initiating the cascade are due to photo-emission, i.e., the emission of electrons from a substance by subjecting it to electro-magnetic radiation such as light, X-rays, etc. Magnesium oxide and caesium oxide layers exhibit a particularly strong secondary emission of electrons. The number of secondary electrons released depends upon the kinetic energy of the primary electrons (the bombarding electrons) and therefore upon the voltage whereby the primary electrons are accelerated. At low voltages, on an average, less than one secondary electron is released per incident primary electron. Only when the secondary emission factor is larger than unity, i.e., when the number of secondary electrons is greater than the number of primary electrons, can one speak of "multiplication". This usually occurs at acceleration voltages above 100 volts (for the primary electrons). For magnesium and caesium oxide layers the secondary emission factor has values above 10, i.e., a more than tenfold multiplication is obtained. The multiplication can be further increased by connecting a number of secondary emission electrodes in series.

If the beam of photo-electrically liberated primary electrons is allowed to impinge upon a row of electrodes provided with a secondary emission coating, amplification values up to 10^9 times the primary radiation can be obtained. The irregularity of the electron flow which is affected by thermal phenomena (thermal noise) sets a limit to further multiplication. The electrodes can be formed as wire gauze electrodes (Fig. 1) or as hollow electrodes (Fig. 2). If need be magnetic deflection can be employed (Fig. 3). In nuclear physics the photo-multiplier plays an important part in the recording of scintillations which are produced by high-energy particles. It is also used as a highly sensitive photometer. In television engineering the photo-multiplier is used in connection with the transmission of cine films and as an important component of camera tubes based on the orthicon principle (see page 124).

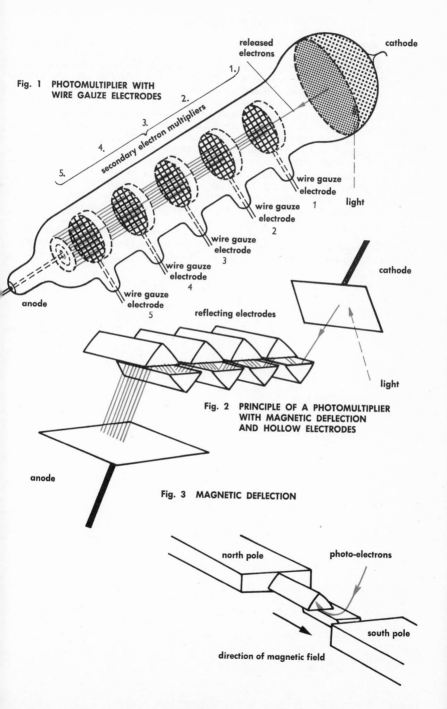

Fig. 1 PHOTOMULTIPLIER WITH WIRE GAUZE ELECTRODES

released electrons

cathode

1.
2.
3.
4.
5.

secondary electron multipliers

wire gauze electrode 1

wire gauze electrode 2

wire gauze electrode 3

wire gauze electrode 4

wire gauze electrode 5

light

anode

reflecting electrodes

cathode

light

Fig. 2 PRINCIPLE OF A PHOTOMULTIPLIER WITH MAGNETIC DEFLECTION AND HOLLOW ELECTRODES

anode

Fig. 3 MAGNETIC DEFLECTION

north pole

photo-electrons

south pole

direction of magnetic field

119

MAGIC EYE

The name "magic eye" is popularly applied to the electron-ray tube, a device which gives a visual indication of correct tuning in radio receivers and correct adjustment of the microphone output to obtain a good recording in tape recorders. The electron-ray tube consists of a triode (an electron tube with cathode, control grid and anode: see page 74) and a cathode ray tube (see page 126). The latter comprises a fluorescent screen which is bombarded by electrons emitted by an incandescent cathode; they are accelerated by an anode and are controlled by another electrode (indicator grid). The two parts, i.e., the triode and the cathode ray tube, have separate grids, but share a common, indirectly-heated cathode and have a common anode voltage. The anode of the electron-ray tube comprises two control fins which are conductively connected to the anode of the triode. The fluorescent screen symmetrically surrounds the dark red glowing indirectly-heated cathode, whose light is screened by a cap. The image on the screen in the zero position is shown in Fig. 1b: wide dark sectors are separated by narrow luminous ones. When the receiver is correctly tuned, the luminous sectors open to maximum width.

A further development of this device is the dual electron-ray tube, which allows of coarse and fine adjustment (for powerful and medium-power transmitters). It contains two triode systems and two pairs of anode fins. The fluorescent pattern for various conditions is illustrated in Figs. 2a, 2b and 2c.

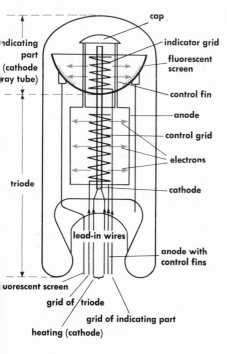

cap

indicating part (cathode ray tube)

indicator grid

fluorescent screen

control fin

anode

control grid

electrons

cathode

triode

lead-in wires

anode with control fins

fluorescent screen

grid of triode

grid of indicating part

heating (cathode)

Fig. 1a   MAGIC EYE (*schematic*)

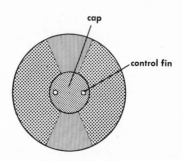

cap

control fin

Fig. 1b   ZERO POSITION

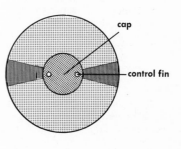

cap

control fin

Fig. 1c   CORRECTLY TUNED

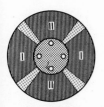

a) zero position

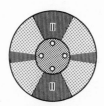

b) range I adjustment (medium-power transmitter)

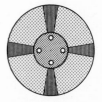

c) range II adjustment (powerful transmitter)

Fig. 2   IMAGES FORMED BY DUAL ELECTRON-RAY TUBE

BLACK-AND-WHITE TELEVISION

Television utilises the cinematographic projection principle in that it, too, operates at a picture rate of at least 25 per second and thus produces the visual impression of continuous motion. Just as in the half-tone screens used in photo-engraving (see page 416), in which the different light and shade values of a photograph are reproduced by a pattern of dots, in television the image is likewise analysed into a large number of "picture elements", the principle of which is illustrated in Fig. 1. This means that the picture must be divided into a number of lines (e.g., 625), and each line must contain several hundred individually identifiable half-tone light values. This is known as "scanning". To obtain a reasonably good picture, the image must be thus analysed into at least 100,000 (and preferably 200,000) picture elements. In the television camera (iconoscope, Fig. 2; for further details see page 124) the image is focused on to a plate called the signal plate whose surface is covered with a mosaic of photosensitive points. Each of these points, corresponding to one picture element, acquires a positive electric charge whose magnitude depends on the strength of the illumination falling on it (Fig. 3). An electron beam, forming a scanning spot on the signal plate, zig-zags its way, line by line, across the plate every 1/25 second[1] and thus discharges each photosensitive point 25 times per second. Each point thus gives an electric impulse whose strength corresponds to the strength of illumination at that point at that particular instant. These impulses (forming the picture signal) are amplified and transmitted. In the television receiver the incoming impulses, after amplification, are fed to the control electrode of the picture tube (cathode ray tube; see page 126) (Fig. 4) in which an electron beam is zig-zagged across a fluorescent screen synchronously with the beam in camera tube and with an intensity varying with the strength of the electric impulses. In this way a pattern of luminous points of varying brightness, and formed in rapid succession, is produced on the screen, thus making the picture that the viewer sees.

The picture signal (Fig. 5) can be conveyed to the receiver by cable (coaxial cables are employed), but they are usually transmitted by means of waves similar to those used in ordinary radio broadcasting, but of shorter wavelength. These high-frequency short waves are only able to travel in straight paths from the transmitter, so that, because of the earth's curvature, the range is, broadly speaking, limited to the visual horizon. It is for this reason that television transmitters are installed on tall masts or towers, which have to be spaced about fifty miles apart in order to provide good television coverage throughout a region (Fig. 6).

1. 1/30 second in U.S.A.

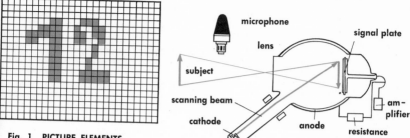

Fig. 1   PICTURE ELEMENTS

Fig. 2   TELEVISION CAMERA (iconoscope)
AND MICROPHONE

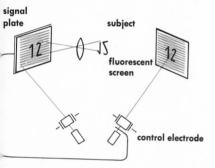

Fig. 3   ICONOSCOPE (transmission) AND
CATHODE RAY TUBE (reception)

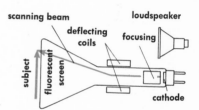

Fig. 4   SOUND AND PICTURE REPRO-
DUCTION AT RECEIVER (loudspeaker and cathode ray tube)

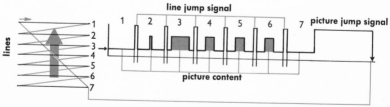

Fig. 5   SCANNING OF AN IMAGE AND CORRESPONDING
ELECTRIC SIGNALS

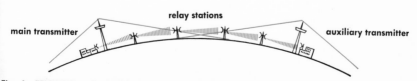

Fig. 6   TELEVISION TRANSMISSION WAVES TRAVEL IN STRAIGHT PATHS; RELAY STATIONS
AND AUXILIARY TRANSMITTERS ARE THEREFORE REQUIRED

TELEVISION CAMERA TUBES

The *iconoscope*, invented some forty years ago and now obsolescent, is the oldest electronic analysing device for converting the optical image in the television camera into a sequence of electric signals. It proved to be much more efficient than the older mechanical scanning devices, which it entirely superseded in the nineteen-thirties. The essential component of the iconoscope is the signal plate, whose front face is covered with a mosaic consisting of hundreds of thousands of tiny globules of silver, which are so treated during manufacture that each globule has a surface of the oxides of silver and cesium. A lens focuses an optical image on the mosaic, the whole surface of which acquires a positive photo-electric charge whose distribution matches the distribution of light in the image (Fig. 1). The mosaic is scanned line by line by a narrow beam of electrons which is moved across the image. When this beam hits a globule, the latter is discharged. The individual silver oxide coatings act as one electrode of a condenser, the other electrode of which is the metallic signal plate (separated from the globules by a sheet of mica) (Fig. 2). Each time a globule is discharged, it gives an electrical impulse (Fig. 3). The translation of the televised scene into its electrical counterpart thus results in a sequence of electrical impulses known as the television picture signal.

The line-by-line, left-to-right, top-to-bottom dissection and reconstitution of television images is known as scanning. The agent which disassembles and reassembles the light values along each line is called the scanning spot (produced by a beam of electrons), and the path it follows is the scanning pattern. The spot is moved from left to right and then returned rapidly, while extinguished and inactive, from right to left. At the same time, the spot is moved comparatively slowly from top to bottom.

The first successor to the iconoscope was the *orthicon*, in which the mosaic is similar to that of the iconoscope, but is composed of squares of photosensitive material. The signal plate is formed by a transparent metal coating on the reverse side. A further development is embodied in the *image orthicon*, which is notable for its very high sensitivity to light. It is similar to the orthicon, but includes an additional electrical-imaging process and comprises an amplifier based on the phenomenon of electron multiplication. The electron multiplier increases the strength of the picture signal by several thousand times, whereby the very high sensitivity is obtained.

Another television camera tube is the *vidicon*, whose function is based on the phenomenon of photoconductivity. In its early forms its action was rather slow, and it was limited to industrial applications, traffic supervision, etc. Later developments overcame this drawback. The signal plate in the vidicon is a transparent metallic coating on which is a layer of photoconductive material (a complex compound of selenium) whose electrical resistance is high in the dark but diminishes as the light increases. The optical image induces a pattern of varying conductivity which corresponds to the distribution of brightness in the image. The conduction paths through the photoconductive layer allow positive charge from the signal plate to pass through the layer. An electron beam neutralises the positive charge on each point of the electrical image, and the resulting change in potential is transferred by "condenser" action to the signal plate (on the same principle as in the iconoscope). An advantage of the vidicon is that it can be constructed to a very small size, so that small and relatively inexpensive lenses can be used.

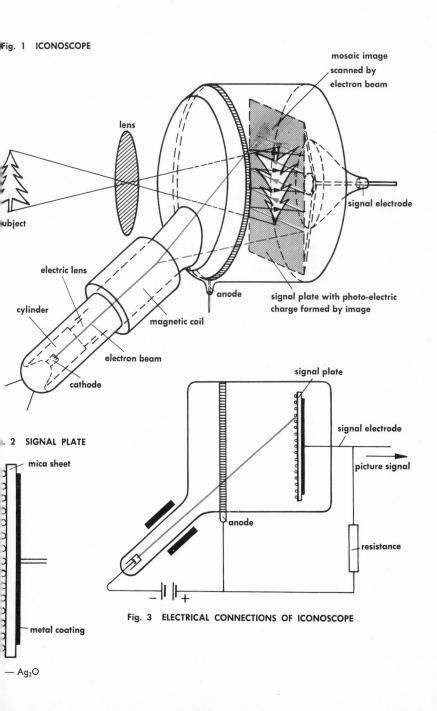

Fig. 1   ICONOSCOPE

mosaic image
scanned by
electron beam

lens

object

signal electrode

electric lens

cylinder

cathode

electron beam

magnetic coil

anode

signal plate with photo-electric
charge formed by image

2   SIGNAL PLATE

mica sheet

metal coating

— Ag₂O

signal plate

signal electrode

picture signal

anode

resistance

— || ||+

Fig. 3   ELECTRICAL CONNECTIONS OF ICONOSCOPE

125

TELEVISION PICTURE TUBE

The television picture tube (cathode-ray tube) is equipped with an electron gun, comprising a hot cathode which emits electrons. These are concentrated into a beam which is moved to and fro by a deflecting system and appears as a spot of light on a fluorescent screen. Concentration of the emitted electrons into a beam is done by electrodes which function as an electric lens, or by a concentrating coil functioning as a magnetic lens (Fig. 2). Electrostatic deflection of the beam in two directions for scanning is obtained by means of two mutually perpendicular pairs of plates (electrodes) (Fig. 1) or by means of a magnetic deflecting coil (Fig. 2). The advantage of magnetic over electrostatic deflection is that larger deflection angles can be achieved at low voltages. This in turn enables the tube to be made shorter, so that the television set can be of "flatter" construction. The scanning spot of the electron beam moves to and fro across the screen, line by line, in synchronisation with the scanning spot in the television camera. The fluorescent screen, which is inside the tube, consists of a coating of chemicals (of which, for example, zinc sulphide may be a major constituent) which glow under the impact of high-speed electrons. The colour of the fluorescence can be modified by certain admixtures to the coating. The concentration of the electron beam in the "electric lens" is achieved by means of the electric field which is formed between the earthed cylinder (zero potential) and the anode plate (positive potential). The lines of force pass through the hole at the centre of the anode, and the equipotential surfaces are curved rather in the manner of an optical lens (cf. page 128 and page 144). With magnetic concentration the electrons travel along spiral paths (cf. page 76). Scanning by electrostatic deflection of the electrons in the field of the two pairs of deflecting plates is comparable to the fall of a body in a gravitational field. Each individual electron describes a parabolic path. In the case of magnetic deflection a similar effect is achieved by causing the electrons to travel along a spiral path for some distance. Magnetic scanning is accomplished by two sets of electromagnet coils wound on a core of magnetic material. Deflection of the beam occurs by virtue of the fact that an electron in motion through a magnetic field experiences a force at right angles both to its direction of motion and to the direction of the magnetic lines of force.

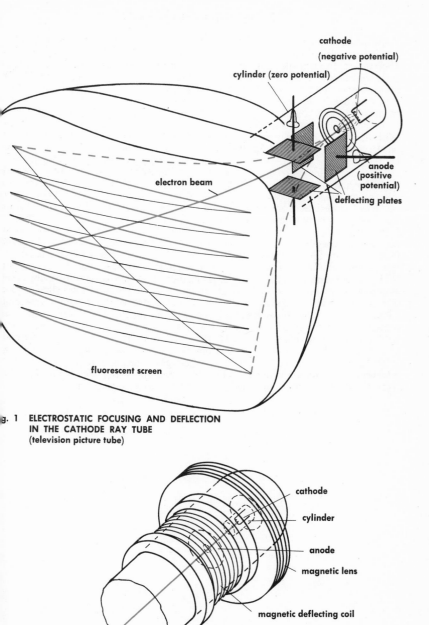

cathode
(negative potential)

cylinder (zero potential)

electron beam

anode
(positive
potential)

deflecting plates

fluorescent screen

**g. 1 ELECTROSTATIC FOCUSING AND DEFLECTION
IN THE CATHODE RAY TUBE**
(television picture tube)

cathode

cylinder

anode

magnetic lens

magnetic deflecting coil

g. 2 MAGNETIC FOCUSING AND DEFLECTION DEVICES

127

IMAGE CONVERTER TUBE

An image converter tube is an apparatus which converts images of an optically non-observable kind of radiation into images which come within the range of optical observation. In principle (Fig. 1) it consists of a thin photocathode which reacts to invisible radiation. The electron image which is formed is projected on to the fluorescent screen by means of magnetic or electric focusing lenses (Figs. 2 and 3) and thus produces an optically visible image. For the conversion of X-rays a converter tube is used which contains a thin aluminium foil (Fig. 4) one side of which is provided with the fluorescent screen, while the other side constitutes the photocathode. With the aid of the X-ray image converter tube the original silhouette images can be electronically intensified. In this way, for instance, a sufficiently bright image can be obtained even with a low radiation dose which is quite harmless to the patient.

The mode of functioning of the image converter tube is based on the properties of electric and magnetic lenses (cf. page 144) whereby electron beams emitted from an (electronic) image point can be gathered and focused at another point. The concept of "lens" is derived from conventional optics and refers to devices whose only features in common with optical lenses are that they are able to focus rays, though in this case these are electron rays, not light rays. With the electric lens the focusing action is obtained by means of an electrical field (e.g., between two coaxial cylindrical electrodes, one of which has a higher potential than the other) which has curved equipotential surfaces (surfaces of constant potential or voltage) that are comparable to the curved surfaces of a lens (Fig. 2). Each individual electron performs vibrations of diminishing amplitude as it travels along in the direction of the cylinder axes. The electron beam, consisting of vast numbers of electrodes, thus assumes a tapering tubular shape, i.e., it converges and is focused. The functioning of a magnetic lens is even less like that of an ordinary optical lens (Fig. 3). In the longitudinal magnetic field, which is approximately parallel to their direction of flight, the electrons describe spiral paths. All electrons which start from one and the same point may travel along different spiral paths, but will eventually converge at one point. In this sense there is a focusing—i.e., image-forming—effect. Magnetic lenses are preferable to electrical ones because they can be operated at lower and therefore less dangerous voltages

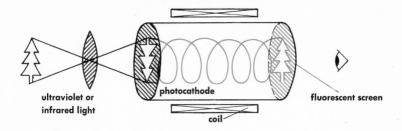

Fig. 1   PRINCIPLE OF IMAGE CONVERTER TUBE

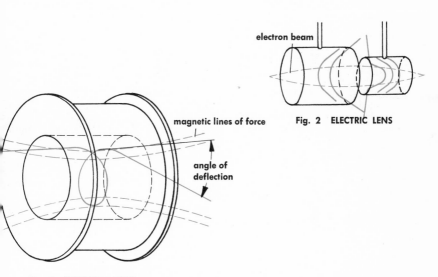

Fig. 2   ELECTRIC LENS

Fig. 3   MAGNETIC LENS

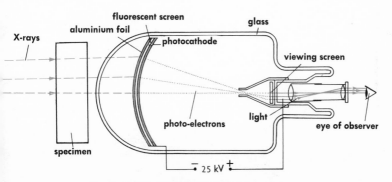

Fig. 4   X-RAY CONVERTER TUBE (schematic)

EIDOPHOR SYSTEM

The eidophor system is a projection television system, i.e., it enables enlarged television pictures to be projected on to a screen. An ordinary television picture (see page 122) derives its brightness from the fluorescence of a screen bombarded by electrons; with the eidophor system, on the other hand, a very powerful source of light is controlled by the television signal picked up by the receiver. The light emitted by an arc lamp (which in the case of colour television is passed through a colour filter disc) is directed on to the screen by means of two grating screens (Fig. 1)—or, alternatively, a grating mirror silvered on the back (Fig. 2)—through an oil film and a projection lens. The oil film is given an electric charge of varying intensity, depending on the brightness value of the incoming signal, by an electron beam which is controlled by this signal. As a result of the electrostatic repulsion forces, the oil film thereby acquires varying degrees of curvature. The curved surface produces a change in the optical image formed by the light which passes through or is reflected by it. The light reflected by the bars of the grating mirror will, on its return path after being reflected by the oil film, pass with varying intensity through the gaps in the mirror, so that the stream of light is controlled by the television signal. In consequence of the scanning by means of the electron beam an electrical charge pattern is formed which corresponds to the brightness values of the image. This varying pattern of electrical charge in turn controls the light emitted by the light source which projects the greatly enlarged image on to the screen. The light rays which are unaffected by the charge pattern are retained by the grating screen (Fig. 1) or by the grating mirror (Fig. 2).

The apparatus represented diagrammatically in Fig. 2 must, of course, be accommodated in a high-vacuum enclosure to enable electronic control to be effected. The electrical charge of the oil film dies away gradually; for this reason the film is made to rotate slowly away from under the controlling electron beam, and a smoothing blade ensures that the film is given a fresh, electrically discharged surface before it is again exposed to the electron beam.

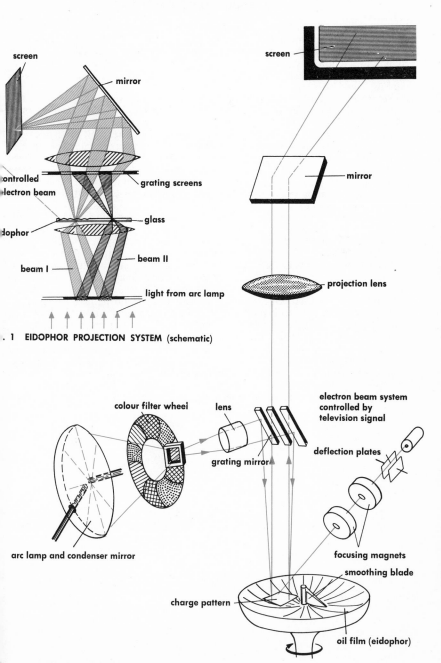

screen

mirror

controlled
electron beam

grating screens

glass

eidophor

beam II

beam I

light from arc lamp

Fig. 1 EIDOPHOR PROJECTION SYSTEM (schematic)

screen

mirror

projection lens

electron beam system
controlled by
television signal

deflection plates

colour filter wheel

lens

grating mirror

focusing magnets

smoothing blade

arc lamp and condenser mirror

charge pattern

oil film (eidophor)

Fig. 2 EIDOPHOR EQUIPMENT

STROBOSCOPIC EFFECTS

Stroboscopic effects have a physiological basis. The human sense of vision is so slow to react to light stimuli that it is unable to separate two different light impulses reaching the eye within a very short period of time (less than $\frac{1}{10}$ second). A succession of impulses following one another at such brief intervals are observed by the eye as a continuous unbroken sequence (principle of cinematography and television; cf. Figs. 2 and 3).

Stroboscopic phenomena in a more restricted sense occur in cases where two periodic motions which differ slightly in their timing, or which are performed synchronously, are superimposed one upon the other. An example is provided by the glow lamp in Fig. 1, which is fed with alternating current (50 cycles/sec.) and emits 100 light impulses (brief flashes) every second. This intermittent light is beamed on to a revolving disc provided with two dark-coloured sectors. If the disc is rotated exactly 180° (half a revolution) during the interval of darkness (Fig. 1b) between light maxima (Figs. 1a and 1c), the observer will see a stationary two-pointed star. The speed of rotation of the disc is then 50 revolutions per second. If the speed is a little below this value the double sector will appear to be rotating in a direction opposite to the direction of the rotation of the disc; if the speed of the disc is a little above 50 revolutions per second, the double sector will appear to be rotating in the direction of rotation of the disc. In the former case the disc has not quite rotated through 180° when the next light maximum occurs; in the latter case the disc has rotated a little more than 180°. Such stroboscopic effects are sometimes seen in the cinema when the frequency with which the successive images are projected on to the screen is superimposed on the speed of rotation of, for example, the spokes of a wheel. When that happens, the wheel appears to be revolving backwards.

Examples of stroboscopic phenomena in the more general sense are afforded by the toy called a stroboscope (Fig. 2) or the little books with pictures which appear to move when the pages are flicked (Fig. 3). In the stroboscopic toy a succession of pictures, each corresponding to a stage of movement, is viewed through rotating slots, with the result that an impression of continuous motion is obtained. In engineering, stroboscopes are used for measuring and checking the speeds of rotation of shafts and other parts of machinery; they are also used for apparently slowing down periodically repetitive motions and thus enable them to be observed more conveniently.

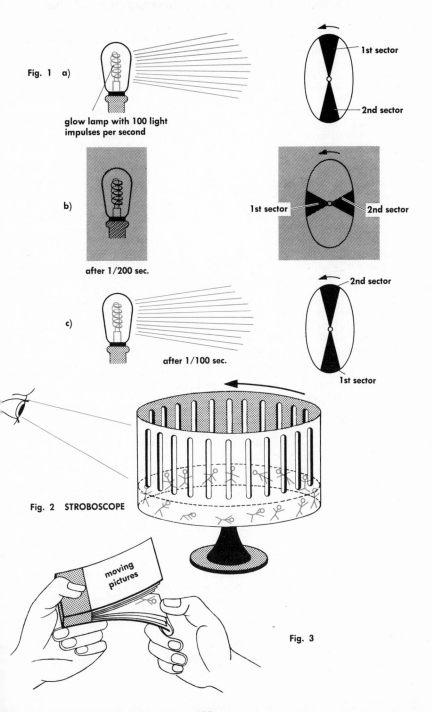

Fig. 1 a)

glow lamp with 100 light impulses per second

1st sector

2nd sector

b)

after 1/200 sec.

1st sector   2nd sector

c)

after 1/100 sec.

2nd sector

1st sector

Fig. 2   STROBOSCOPE

moving pictures

Fig. 3

133

REFLECTION, REFRACTION AND DIFFRACTION OF LIGHT

When a ray of light strikes the boundary surface of two different transparent media, e.g., on passing from air into a block of glass, a proportion of the light is reflected back into the first medium. The rest penetrates into the second medium, but it undergoes a change of direction in doing so: it is refracted. These two phenomena of reflection and refraction are indicated in Fig. 1. The ray r is so reflected that the angle α which it forms with the perpendicular of incidence l (i.e., a line perpendicular to the boundary surface) is equal to the angle α formed by the incident ray e (angle of incidence = angle of reflection). The incident ray e, the perpendicular of incidence l, the reflected ray r, and the refracted ray g are all situated in the same plane. The mathematical relation that exists between the angle of incidence α and the refraction angle β is known as the law of refraction: $\sin\alpha/\sin\beta = n$. This ratio n is called the index of refraction.

On undergoing refraction, white light is broken up into a number of different colours, the spectral colours (Fig. 2): a spectrum is formed (Fig. 3). Red light undergoes the least, violet light undergoes the greatest amount of diffraction (dispersion). If the light rays corresponding to the various spectral colours are combined by means of a lens, white light is obtained again. The same result can even be obtained with only two spectral colours (in a certain intensity ratio) if these are complementary to each other (complementary colours). Each spectral colour corresponds to a particular wavelength of light. The spectrum of an incandescent solid or liquid substance or a very highly compressed gas is continuous: it contains all wavelengths (comprising "all the colours of the rainbow" from red to violet). The fact that particular wavelengths are nevertheless absent from the solar spectrum (there are individual dark lines, known as Fraunhofer lines) is due to absorption of these wavelengths in the outer, gaseous part of the sun. Under normal conditions, incandescent gases emit light of particular, definite wavelengths; the spectrum takes the form of a line spectrum, consisting of individual spectral lines (in the case of atoms), or a band spectrum (in the case of molecules) which comprises a large number of spectral lines spaced close together. These wavelengths can similarly be absorbed by the gas. Every chemical element, when it is in the gaseous state, produces a characteristic spectrum whereby it can be detected (spectrum analysis; Kirchhoff and Bunsen, 1859). A spectroscope is used for the purpose (Fig. 4).

If an object of sufficiently small dimensions is placed in the path of light rays, it does not cast a sharply outlined geometrical shadow (as would correspond to rectilinear propogation of light). Instead, we observe a certain arrangement of light and dark areas (e.g., stripes). Such deviation from the rectilinear path is called diffraction. This phenomenon can be explained only in terms of the wave theory of light: superposition of individual light waves (interference). An arrangement of very narrow, closely spaced gaps or slits forms a so-called diffraction grating (Fig. 5). If white light is directed on to a diffraction grating, it will likewise produce a spectrum, because the directions in which the bright areas occur are dependent on the wavelength. However, in contrast with what happens in refraction, in diffraction the red light undergoes a greater deflection from its original direction than does the violet light with its shorter wavelength.

The small annular haloes, or coronas, which sometimes appear round the sun and moon are diffraction phenomena caused by tiny water droplets in the upper atmosphere. For this reason the outer edge of such a halo displays a (faint) red colour. On the other hand, large haloes are phenomena due to refraction and reflection of light by ice crystals (usually in the form of cirro-stratus clouds). The colour sequence in such haloes, if it is perceptible at all, is the reverse of that in small haloes, i.e., red is on the inside and violet on the outside of the ring. A rainbow is the result of a combination of refraction, reflection and diffraction phenomena. The blue colour of the sky is due to scattering of sunlight on its way through the atmosphere, in which process the shorter wavelengths (blue light) are more strongly scattered than the longer wavelengths (red light).

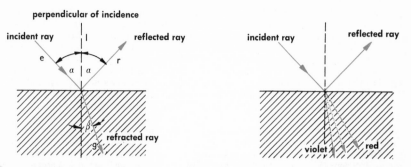

perpendicular of incidence

incident ray | | reflected ray

e | | r

α | α

β

g refracted ray

Fig. 1 REFLECTION AND REFRACTION

incident ray | reflected ray

violet | red

Fig. 2 BREAKING-UP OF LIGHT ON REFRACTION

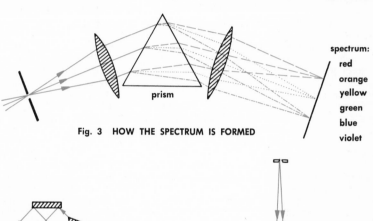

prism

spectrum:
red
orange
yellow
green
blue
violet

Fig. 3 HOW THE SPECTRUM IS FORMED

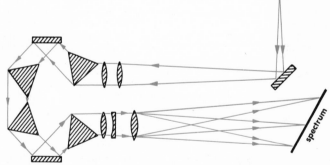

spectrum

Fig. 4 PRINCIPLE OF A SPECTROSCOPE

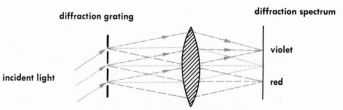

diffraction grating

diffraction spectrum

incident light

violet

red

Fig. 5 HOW A DIFFRACTION SPECTRUM IS FORMED

LENSES

When rays of light pass through a prism, they undergo a change of direction: they are always deflected away from the refractive edge (see page 134). It is possible to conceive an assembly of prisms, arranged as shown in Fig. 1a, whose respective refractive surfaces progressively become more nearly parallel to each other towards the middle: light rays passing through the outer prisms will undergo the greatest amount of refraction, with consequent deflection of their path towards the centre, whereas the middle prism with its two parallel surfaces causes no deflection at all. When a beam of parallel rays passes through these prisms, the rays are all deflected towards the axis and converge at one point (F'). Rays emerging from a point P are also so deflected by the prisms that they converge at a point P'. A lens can be conceived as consisting of a large number of such prisms placed close up against one another, so that their surfaces merge into a continuous spherical surface. A lens of this kind, which collects the rays and concentrates them at one point, is called a convergent lens. Since it is thicker in the middle than at the edge, it is known as a *convex lens*.

In the case of a *concave lens*, which is thinner in the middle than at the edge, similar considerations show that all rays diverge from the centre (Fig. 1b). Hence such a lens is called a divergent lens. After undergoing refraction, parallel rays appear to come from one point (F), while rays emerging from a point will, after passing through the lens, appear to emerge from another point (see Fig. 3b). Fig. 2 shows the various shapes of convex and concave lenses. The last lens in each group has surfaces curved in the same direction but having different radii of curvature; these are known as meniscus lenses and are used more particularly in spectacles (see page 140).

The properties of lenses are determined by the law of refraction: Rays parallel to the axis of a convex lens are refracted by the lens so as to converge at a point F, called the focus or focal point. Conversely, rays which pass through (or emerge from) become parallel after being refracted by the lens. Rays which pass through the centre of the lens continue with their direction unchanged. In the case of a concave lens, rays parallel to the axis are refracted in such a manner that they appear to emerge from a single point, which here again is called the focus. With the aid of these optical properties of lenses it is possible to construct the path of the rays and determine the position of the image that the lens will form of any particular point of an object (Figs. 3a and 3b). A convex lens generally produces a *real image* which is formed at the point of convergence of the rays and can be made visible by projecting it on to a screen. On the other hand, a concave lens produces a *virtual image*, from which the light rays appear to diverge. Such an image cannot be formed on a screen.

The positions of the image and the object in the case of a thin lens are determined by the following simple formula:

$$\frac{1}{g} + \frac{1}{b} = \frac{1}{f} = D$$

(g = object distance; b = image distance; f = focal distance or focal length). Instead of the focal length, its (refractive) power is expressed in dioptres. The shorter the focal length of a lens is, the greater is its power. A convergent lens of 1 metre focal length is said to have a power of $+1$ dioptre. The power of a convergent lens of 0.2 m focal length is $+5$ dioptres. The power of a divergent lens is expressed as a negative quantity; the focal distance of such a lens is likewise negative, which means that b must also have a negative value, as the virtual image is located on the same side of the lens as the object is.

Single lenses are affected by errors due to physical causes which prevent truly accurate convergence of the light rays. The sharpness of the image can be improved by using a combination of two or more lenses whose errors compensate one another (see page 152).

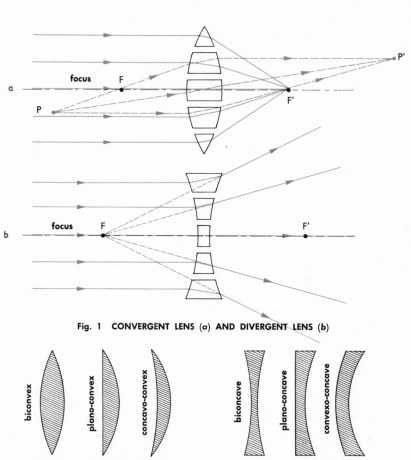

Fig. 1 CONVERGENT LENS (a) AND DIVERGENT LENS (b)

biconvex   plano-convex   concavo-convex

Fig. 2a CONVERGENT LENSES

biconcave   plano-concave   convexo-concave

Fig. 2b DIVERGENT LENSES

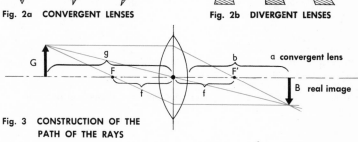

Fig. 3 CONSTRUCTION OF THE PATH OF THE RAYS

a convergent lens

B real image

b divergent lens

virtual image

137

MIRRORS

Reflection occurs at smooth surfaces. The law of reflection states: the incident ray, the perpendicular to the reflecting surface, and the reflected ray are situated in one plane. The angle of reflection is equal to the angle of incidence (Fig. 1).

Plane mirror

Rays emerge from the object in all directions. If a beam of rays from the object is reflected by a plane mirror, the rays will change their direction but will, after doing so, continue on their divergent paths. They do not converge and therefore cannot produce a real image. They all appear to come from a point located behind the mirror, i.e., from the virtual image of the object. The virtual image is at the same distance behind the reflecting surface as the object is in front of it.

Curved mirror

If a spherical reflecting surface is conceived as being composed of a vast number of tiny plane surfaces, of which each is perpendicular to a radius of the sphere, then the law of reflection can be applied to such a mirror. Obviously, a ray of light directed through the centre of curvature M will be reflected back in its own direction. At each point the reflected ray forms the same angle with the radius as does the incident ray, so that rays parallel to the principal axis will converge at one point located midway between the mirror and its centre of curvature. This point of convergence is the focus or focal point (F) of the concave mirror. The focal length of such a mirror is equal to half the radius of curvature. Conversely, all rays passing through, or emerging from, the focus will be reflected in a direction parallel to the principal axis. Fig. 2 shows the construction of the ray paths associated with a convergent (concave) mirror. The formula linking the positions of the object and image is similar to that already given for lenses:

$$\frac{1}{g} + \frac{1}{b} = \frac{1}{f} = \frac{2}{r}$$

(g = object distance; b = image distance; f = focal distance or focal length = $\frac{1}{2}r$; and r = radius of curvature). In the case of a divergent (convex) mirror a virtual image is formed behind the mirror; the focal length and image distance then both occur as negative quantities in the above equation.

Driving mirrors in motor cars are sometimes of the convex type (example 1), forming a virtual image of reduced size but covering a wide field of vision behind the vehicle. A shaving mirror (example 2) is a concave mirror. The user comes within its focal distance, with the result that he sees the upright and enlarged virtual image of his face in the mirror.

The constructions for determining the position of the image carried out in the accompanying drawings are in each case based on the choice of two particularly convenient rays, namely, the ray parallel to the principal axis and the ray passing through the focal point of the mirror.

The use of mirrors in the reflecting telescope is explained on page 146.

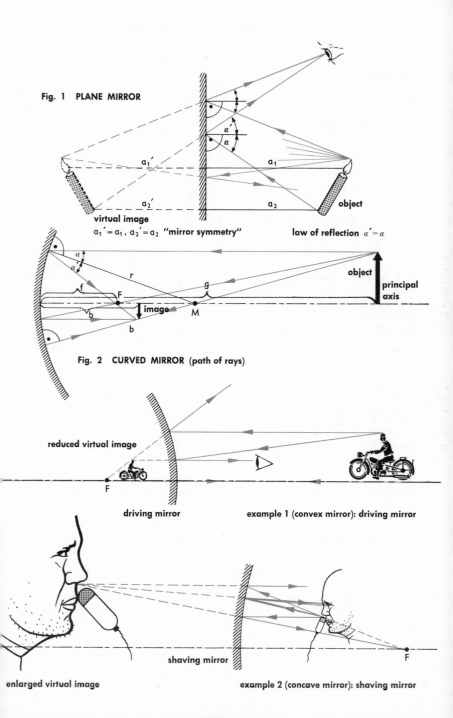

Fig. 1   PLANE MIRROR

virtual image
$a_1' = a_1$, $a_2' = a_2$ "mirror symmetry"

object

law of reflection $\alpha' = \alpha$

Fig. 2   CURVED MIRROR (path of rays)

object

principal axis

image

reduced virtual image

driving mirror

example 1 (convex mirror): driving mirror

enlarged virtual image

shaving mirror

example 2 (concave mirror): shaving mirror

139

SPECTACLES (EYEGLASSES)

When a person has normal eyesight, the image of a distant object (theoretically at infinity) is formed accurately on the retina of the eye, i.e., the focus (see page 136) is located on the retina (Fig. 1). Since the image distance—the distance from lens to retina—is predetermined by the size of the eyeball, the image of an object nearer the eye can be sharply focussed on the retina only by reduction of the focal length of the lens, by increasing its refractive power (see page 136). This is achieved by the action of a muscle, which increases the curvature of the lens. When a distant object is observed, the radius of curvature of the front surface of the lens is about 10 mm (0.4 in.). To adjust the focus to an object only 4 inches away, this radius of curvature must be reduced to about half this amount. This adjustment of the eye to varying distances is called "accommodation" (Fig. 2).

However, not all human eyes are "normal" in that they behave as represented in Figs. 1 and 2. If the distance between the lens and the retina is too large, the image of a distant object will be formed not on, but in front of, the retina (Fig. 3). To form a sharply focused image, the object must be at a shorter distance from the lens, i.e., the eye is only able to form a clear image of objects within this latter distance. Such a person is said to be *short-sighted*. This defect can be corrected by spectacles (Fig. 3). Light rays coming from infinity are made slightly divergent by the lens, so that it is as if they come from an object situated closer to the eye. By thus interposing a lens with negative refractive power between the eye and the object, the combined system of glass lens and eye lens has its focus located on the retina.

If the eyeball is too short for the focal length of the lens, the person is said to be *far-sighted* (Fig. 4); his eyes must accommodate to get even a distant object properly in focus (whereas a normal eye lens is "at rest", i.e., does not have to accommodate, when viewing objects at infinity), while near-by objects cannot be seen sharply at all. This condition is corrected by means of spectacles fitted with convergent lenses. The combined system of glass lens and eye lens is again so contrived that the focus is on the retina, so that distant objects can be viewed without the strain of constant accommodation.

The amplitude of accommodation of the human eye, i.e., the limits of distance within which an object must lie in order to enable a sharp image to be formed on the retina, diminishes with age. This is because the lens grows less flexible, so that its curvature becomes more difficult to vary. A person with normal eyesight may, at the age of 55, be unable to bring objects less than about 3 ft. away sharply into focus, and he will require reading-glasses (compare Fig. 5 with Fig. 2).

Loss of power of accommodation can to some extent be compensated by spectacles fitted with bifocal lenses. These act as weak lenses when the gaze is directed straight ahead and as strong ones when the gaze is directed downward for reading or working. Trifocals are also sometimes used. The accommodation amplitude of the eye and the refractive power of spectacle lenses is measured in dioptres (see page 136).

In the defect known as astigmatism the refracting surfaces of the eye have unequal curvature, which prevents the focusing of light rays to a common point on the retina. Correction is achieved by means of spectacles whose lenses embody a combination of spherical and cylindrical curvature, so contrived that the combined system comprising glass lens and eye lens has the correct spherical curvature.

Contact lenses, as an alternative to conventional spectacles, are lenses worn on the eyeball. All visual conditions correctible by spectacles can also be corrected by contact lenses. These were first introduced towards the end of the previous century and were made of glass. Today they are made of plastics.

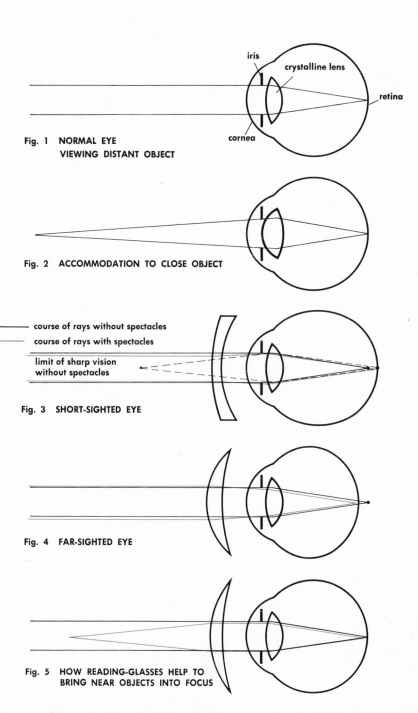

Fig. 1 NORMAL EYE
VIEWING DISTANT OBJECT

iris

crystalline lens

retina

cornea

Fig. 2 ACCOMMODATION TO CLOSE OBJECT

——— course of rays without spectacles
——— course of rays with spectacles

limit of sharp vision
without spectacles

Fig. 3 SHORT-SIGHTED EYE

Fig. 4 FAR-SIGHTED EYE

Fig. 5 HOW READING-GLASSES HELP TO
BRING NEAR OBJECTS INTO FOCUS

MAGNIFYING GLASS AND MICROSCOPE

How clearly the human eye can distinguish details on any particular object depends on the visual angle under which they are observed. Distant objects appear small, and to see them better we use a telescope, which increases the visual angle (see page 146). In the case of very small objects the visual angle remains too small even when they are viewed from the shortest possible distance at which they can be brought into sharp focus by the unaided eye (approx. 6–15 in.). If an object is brought still closer to the eye, the visual angle does indeed increase, but the eye is then no longer able to see it distinctly. With the aid of a magnifying glass or a microscope, however, it is possible to bring the object very close to the eye and yet view it as though it were comfortably within the eye's range of accommodation (i.e., the range of distance within which it can produce a sharply focused image on the retina). The "magnifying power" of a microscope or magnifying glass is the ratio of the apparent size of the image of an object formed by the instrument to that of the object seen by the naked eye. For the purpose of this definition it is assumed that the object would be examined by the naked eye at the least distance of distinct vision, conventionally assumed to be 25 cm (about 10 in.). Thus, for instance, a microscope with a magnifying power of 300 will show an object 300 times as large as it would appear to the naked eye from a distance of 25 cm.

The *magnifying glass* (Fig. 1) consists of a convergent lens (or a convergent system of lenses) of short focal length. The object to be examined is placed within the focal distance, so that a magnified upright virtual image is formed approximately at a distance at which the eye can see it most distinctly. A magnifying glass is similar to reading glasses (see page 140) in that it enables the eye to take a close look at objects while remaining accommodated to a greater distance.

In a *microscope* (Fig. 2) magnification takes place in two stages. In the case of a telescope the object is a long distance away; the real image formed by the object lens (which has a long focal length) is formed approximately at the rear focal point. On the other hand, in the case of a microscope the objective (object glass) has a very short focal length (ranging approximately from $1\frac{3}{4}$ in. to 0.06 in.); the object is placed so close to the front focal point of this lens that the image distance is much greater than the focal length. As a rule, the latter is predetermined by the length of the microscope tube, which is usually about $6\frac{1}{2}$ in. Hence the real intermediate image (for the above-mentioned focal lengths) is about $2\frac{1}{2}$ to 100 times as large as the object viewed. In the plane of the intermediate image are the field of vision diaphragm and, in some microscopes for special purposes, measuring scales, measuring grids, or similar optical aids. The intermediate image is examined through a magnifying glass, the ocular (eyepiece), which is mounted at the top of the tube and which further magnifies the image. For example, the objective of a microscope has a magnifying power of 40 × and the ocular has a magnifying power of 10 ×; in that case the overall magnification will be 400 ×. With an objective and ocular of 100 × and 25 × magnifying respectively, a magnification of 2500 × would be obtained. However, an ordinary optical microscope of such power is of little practical value. Because of the wave character of light, it is possible only to distinguish details of a size down to approximately the wavelength of light $(0.0004 - 0.0007\,\text{mm} = 0.000016 - 0.000028\,\text{in.})$. For practical purposes this limits the maximum useful magnification to about 2000 ×. Much higher magnifications are attainable with the electron microscope, which uses electron rays of much shorter wavelength than visible light rays (see page 144). An important part in connection with the satisfactory functioning of the microscope is played by the condenser, i.e., the lens or lenses which serves to direct the light on to the object and to illuminate it intensively and uniformly in such a manner that nearly all of this light is transmitted into the object glass of the microscope.

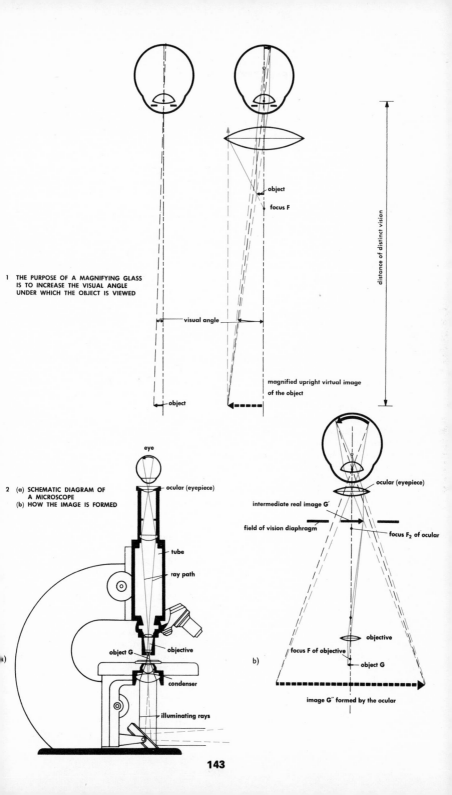

1 THE PURPOSE OF A MAGNIFYING GLASS
IS TO INCREASE THE VISUAL ANGLE
UNDER WHICH THE OBJECT IS VIEWED

object

focus F

distance of distinct vision

visual angle

magnified upright virtual image
of the object

object

eye

2 (a) SCHEMATIC DIAGRAM OF
A MICROSCOPE
(b) HOW THE IMAGE IS FORMED

ocular (eyepiece)

tube

ray path

object G

objective

condenser

illuminating rays

ocular (eyepiece)

intermediate real image G'

field of vision diaphragm

focus F₂ of ocular

objective

focus F of objective

object G

b)

image G'' formed by the ocular

143

ELECTRON MICROSCOPE

As the resolving power of the light microscope is limited by the wavelength of light (see page 142), efforts were made to utilise rays of shorter wavelength which can also be deflected and be used to form images. This possibility is presented by electron beams, i.e., free electrons which are accelerated to high velocities on traversing an electric field. Depending on the velocity of the electrons, such beams can be considered to have a certain wavelength; under particular conditions they behave as though they were of an undulatory character, i.e., composed of waves. As an electron has a negative electric charge, it undergoes acceleration on passing through an electric field (Fig. 1)—for example, it is attracted towards the positive plate of a condenser or, in general, it is accelerated in the direction of higher voltage (higher potential); when travelling in the opposite direction, it will be retarded. In an electric field all points having the same voltage are conceived as being connected by so-called equipotential lines. If an electron passes obliquely through an electric field (e.g., between two electrically charged wire grids, Fig. 2), it will undergo an additional acceleration towards the lines of higher potential: it changes its direction of motion, i.e., it is "refracted". On the basis of this principle, electrostatic "lenses" for electrons were constructed—in analogy with glass lenses for light—from spherically curved grids of wire netting (Fig. 3). However, electronic lenses of this kind have disadvantages, and for this reason the lenses now employed are based on tubes (Fig. 4) or diaphragms with apertures (Fig. 5). The fact that, although the equipotential lines present a symmetrical pattern, the concentrating and the dispersing action do not cancel each other out is because the electrons traverse the dispersing region at higher velocity, so that they undergo less deflection. Besides electrostatic lenses, there are also magnetic lenses. The function of a magnetic lens is based on the following principle: A moving electron is the most elementary form of an electric current; it is therefore surrounded by a magnetic field. When the magnetic field associated with an electric current interacts with another magnetic field, forces are exerted on the conductor through which the current flows. This is the basic principle of all electric motors and generators. For the same reason an electron travelling in a magnetic field undergoes a change of direction. To obtain high field strengths, magnetic lenses are made of iron-encased coils provided with a narrow gap (Fig. 6).

In principle the construction of an electron microscope—with electrostatic or with magnetic lenses—is very similar to that of a light microscope for photographic recordings (Figs. 7a, 7b, 7c): The electrons are emitted by the incandescent cathode, accelerated, and concentrated by the condenser on to the object to be examined. The object—a bacterium, a virus or a so-called replica—is supported on an extremely thin collodion film. (A replica is an envelope of carbon or some other suitable substance formed on the surface of a metal or mineral and then removed for observation under the electron microscope). Depending on the thickness and composition of the object, the electron rays undergo varying degrees of attenuation. The objective lens forms them into the enlarged intermediate image. This in turn is used to form a further enlarged image by the projector lens system. This image may be projected on to a fluorescent screen (for visual observation) or on to a photographic plate sensitive to electron rays.

Green light has a wavelength of around 1/2000 millimetre. Electrons accelerated with 50,000 volts have a 100,000 times smaller wavelength. Because of this extremely short wavelength, the resolving power of an electron microscope is very much greater than that of a light microscope. In combination with further enlargement of the photographic image, magnifications ranging from 100,000x to 500,000x can be obtained.

Fig. 1 ELECTRON IN AN ELECTRIC FIELD

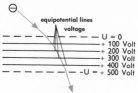

equipotential lines
voltage

U = 0
+ 100 Volt
+ 200 Volt
+ 300 Volt
+ 400 Volt
−U = + 500 Volt

Fig. 2 "REFRACTION" OF THE ELECTRON BEAM

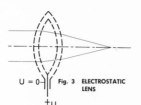

U = 0

+U

Fig. 3 ELECTROSTATIC LENS

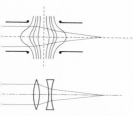

4 TUBULAR ELECTRONIC LENS COMPARED WITH A CORRESPONDING SYSTEM OF OPTICAL LENSES

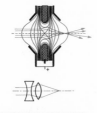

Fig. 5 DIAPHRAGM TYPE ELECTRONIC LENS COMPARED WITH A CORRESPONDING SYSTEM OF OPTICAL LENSES

Fig. 6 IRON-ENCASED COIL AS A MAGNETIC LENS

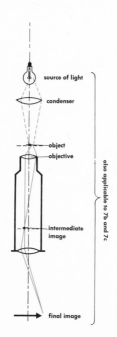

source of light

condenser

object
objective

also applicable to 7b and 7c

intermediate image

final image

Fig. 7a OPTICAL MICROSCOPE

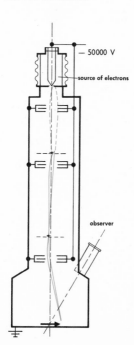

− 50000 V

source of electrons

observer

Fig. 7b ELECTROSTATIC ELECTRON MICROSCOPE (diaphragm type lens)

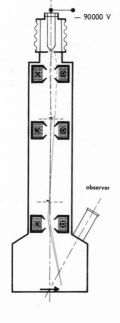

− 90000 V

observer

Fig. 7c MAGNETIC ELECTRON MICROSCOPE (coil type lens)

TELESCOPES

Telescopes are often said to "enlarge things" or "bring distant objects nearer". Actually they increase the visual angle. We are accustomed to judging the size or distance of objects by the angle under which we see them (Fig. 1).

In principle, all refracting telescopes (as distinct from reflecting telescopes) comprise an *objective* (object glass), which is directed towards the object to be observed, and an *ocular* (eyepiece), to which the observer applies his eye. The rays coming from the distant object are almost parallel; they converge to form an image at the focus of the objective (cf. lenses, page 136). This point also coincides with the focus of the ocular, so that the rays emerging from the latter are again parallel. The observer thus sees the object as though it were at infinity, but under a larger angle than without the aid of the telescope. The magnification is defined as the ratio of the focal length of the objective (f_1) to that of the ocular (f_2), i.e., the ratio f_1/f_2.

In the so-called Galilean telescope (named after Galileo, the great Italian scientist and astronomer) (Fig. 2) the ocular is a divergent lens. This system produces an upright image. This arrangement is nowadays used more particularly in opera-glasses, which are low-powered binoculars (usually with a magnification of $2\frac{1}{2}$ ×).

The so-called *Keplerian telescope* (named after the German astronomer Kepler) (Fig. 3) has a convergent lens for its ocular. The fact that the intermediate image in this type of instrument is a real image is a great advantage: everything located in the plane of this image appears sharp and as though it were at infinity. For this reason a diaphragm is installed in this plane, so as to form a sharp boundary to the field of vision. Also, crosswires or a glass measuring scale or some other device—depending on the purpose for which the telescope is used—may be installed here. The inverted position of the image is no objection when the telescope is used for astronomical observations. For terrestrial use, however, it is necessary to introduce an extra lens to produce a second intermediate image, this time in the upright position. For this purpose the "terrestrial telescope" is provided with an additional convergent lens between the objective and the ocular (Fig. 4). This intermediate lens does not enlarge the image formed by the objective, but merely "brings it the right way up". The drawback of this type of telescope is that, because of the intermediate inversion of the image, the instrument has a rather large overall length. For this reason the tube is often of collapsible construction, consisting of segments which can be slid into one another ("telescoped"). The old portable telescope constructed on this principle has now largely been superseded by prismatic binoculars (page 148).

It is impracticable to make lenses of more than about 40 in. diameter. For this reason, in very large astronomical telescopes a concave mirror instead of a lens is used as the objective (the big mirror of the world's largest telescope, at Mount Palomar in the U.S.A., has a diameter of 200 in.) Fig. 5 shows the principle of the reflecting telescope, and Fig. 6 gives an example of a combination of a concave main mirror and a convex collecting mirror; the overall length of the instrument is quite small.

In astronomical telescopes used for photographic purposes the photographic plate is placed direct in the image plane of the objective.

The principle of the reflecting telescope with its conveniently short construction length has also been introduced into ordinary photography. Fig. 7 shows the optical arrangement of a miniature camera comprising a mirror objective with a focal length of 20 in. and an aperture of $f/4.5$. It consists of two glass mirrors and four low-powered correcting lenses.

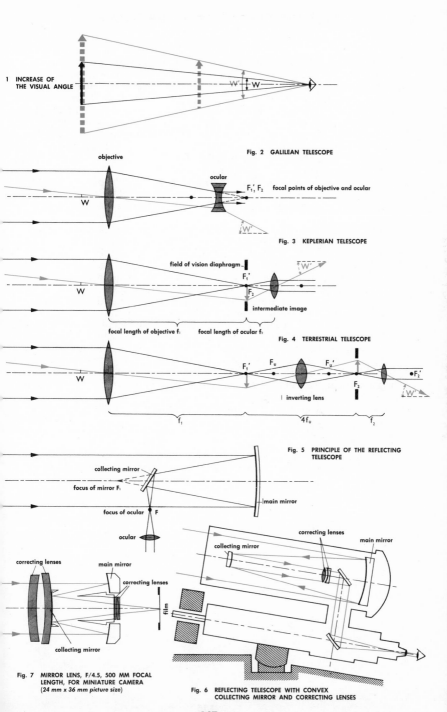

1 INCREASE OF THE VISUAL ANGLE

Fig. 2 GALILEAN TELESCOPE

objective

ocular

F_1', F_2 focal points of objective and ocular

Fig. 3 KEPLERIAN TELESCOPE

field of vision diaphragm

F_1'

F_2

intermediate image

focal length of objective f_1 focal length of ocular f_2 Fig. 4 TERRESTRIAL TELESCOPE

F_1' F_u F_u' F_2 F_2'

inverting lens

f_1 $4f_u$ f_2

Fig. 5 PRINCIPLE OF THE REFLECTING TELESCOPE

collecting mirror

focus of mirror F_1

focus of ocular   F

ocular

main mirror

correcting lenses

collecting mirror

correcting lenses

main mirror

correcting lenses

main mirror

correcting lenses

film

collecting mirror

Fig. 7 MIRROR LENS, F/4.5, 500 MM FOCAL LENGTH, FOR MINIATURE CAMERA (24 mm x 36 mm picture size)

Fig. 6 REFLECTING TELESCOPE WITH CONVEX COLLECTING MIRROR AND CORRECTING LENSES

TELESCOPES: PRISMATIC BINOCULARS

Prismatic binoculars (or, in its single form, the prismatic telescope) comprises an objective and an ocular, like the astronomical telescope (see page 146). The latter, however, produces an inverted image. In the prismatic telescope the image is brought into the upright position by means of prisms. Fig. 1. shows how a beam of light is twice deflected at right angles in a prism (by total reflection at the boundary surfaces), with the result that "top" and "bottom" are interchanged. However, in order to rectify the inverted image formed by the objective, it is necessary also to interchange "left" and "right". For this reason the light is passed through a second reversing prism (Fig. 2). In comparison with the terrestrial telescope (page 146) there is a very substantial saving in the overall length of the instrument. Besides, the two object lenses are spaced farther apart than the eyepieces; this makes for better stereoscopic seeing. Fig. 4 shows the course of rays in prismatic binoculars. The point of convergence of the rays in front of the ocular marks the position of the intermediate image. Here, too, is located the diaphragm forming the boundary of the field vision.

The magnification of a telescope is usually indicated in combination with the diameter of the objective. For instance, 8×30 means the magnification is $8 \times$ (eight times) and that the objective has a diameter of 30 mm. The ratio of objective diameter to magnification—i.e., in this case $30/8 = 3.75$—is an important criterion. It means that the beam of rays emerging from the so-called exit pupil of the instrument has a diameter of 3.75 mm. The exit pupil is the image of the eight times larger entrance pupil. These two pupils can be seen on looking into the ocular or the objective from a distance of about 12 inches. The amount of light entering the human eye, too, is controlled by the pupil; in feeble light its diameter may be as much as 8 mm, but in bright sun it diminishes to 1.5 mm. The light-gathering power of a telescope or field-glass is therefore best utilised when the beam of rays emerging from the ocular has the same diameter of the pupil of the observer's eye. So-called "night-glasses" are characterised, for example, by the data 7×50, i.e., the magnification is $7 \times$ and the objective diameter ($=$ entrance pupil) is 50 mm. In moonlight the entire emergent beam enters the observer's eye (Fig. 3a). On the other hand, if the instrument is used in bright sunlight, the pupil of the eye is, say, 2 mm in diameter (Fig. 3b), so that then only $\frac{1}{13}$ of the instrument's light-gathering power is utilised. As the amount of light passing through the aperture is proportional to the area thereof, the light-gathering power of a telescope is designated by the square of the diameter of the exit pupil, e.g., $7.14 \times 7.14 = 51.5$.

In twilight, objects are distinguished better according as they appear larger and brighter. It is known that the perceptibility increases approximately in proportion to the square root of the product of objective diameter and magnification, e.g.,

$$\sqrt{30} \times 8 = 15.5; \qquad \sqrt{50} \times 7 = 18.7.$$

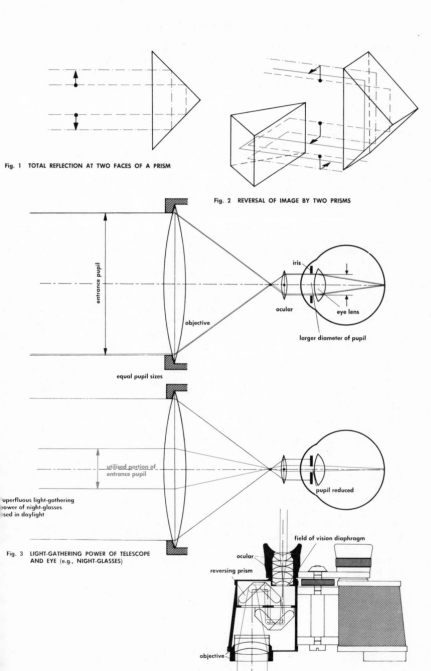

Fig. 1   TOTAL REFLECTION AT TWO FACES OF A PRISM

Fig. 2   REVERSAL OF IMAGE BY TWO PRISMS

entrance pupil

objective

iris

ocular

eye lens

larger diameter of pupil

equal pupil sizes

utilised portion of
entrance pupil

pupil reduced

superfluous light-gathering
power of night-glasses
used in daylight

Fig. 3   LIGHT-GATHERING POWER OF TELESCOPE
AND EYE (e.g., NIGHT-GLASSES)

field of vision diaphragm

ocular

reversing prism

objective

Fig. 4   PRISMATIC BINOCULARS

149

CAMERAS: GENERAL INTRODUCTION

A camera is a device consisting essentially of a light-tight box which has an opening covered by a lens in one wall; this lens forms a real image of the object upon a plate or film of light-sensitive material disposed inside the box. A modern camera consists of a body, or housing, with the film holder and the film feed mechanism, the lens, the shutter, the distance setting (possibly also a rangefinder), and the viewfinder for composing the picture. A small portion of the light from the object is momentarily allowed to form a real image on the photographic plate or film. The simplest method of forming an image of this kind is by means of a "pinhole" diaphragm, containing a hole of 0.016 in. diameter, on the front of the light-tight box. On this principle it is possible to construct a so-called pinhole camera (Fig. 1). From each point of the object a ray of light passes through the hole and strikes the photographic plate, where it makes an image of that point. Each point of the object is, admittedly, projected on to the plate as a small elliptical spot of light, and the adjacent ellipses merge together, so that a blurred image is formed. Besides, a pinhole camera has a low light intensity, i.e., it has a very low-speed "lens" (the pinhole), which means that long exposure times are necessary for obtaining adequate blackening of the plate. Sharper images are obtained by using an objective consisting of a lens or, preferably, a set of lenses (elements) mounted one behind the other. In that case the light coming from each point of the object to be photographed is focused by the lens and concentrated as a corresponding point on the photographic plate. In a box camera (Fig. 2) the aperture and therefore the light-transmitting power of the lens are fixed. This type of camera usually has a single or a two-element lens. In more advanced cameras both the aperture and the exposure time can be varied to suit the lighting conditions and/or the movement (if any) of the object (moving objects must be photographed with short exposures in order to obtain sharp images on the plate or film). The lenses in these more elaborate cameras usually consist of three or more elements. Cameras using the larger sizes of film are usually constructed as bellows-type folding cameras (Fig. 3). Smaller cameras are often of the tube type (Fig. 4). This latter form of construction, as applied to so-called miniature cameras, has important optical advantages (short focal length, larger angular field and the resultant advantages. High-class models are equipped with coupled rangefinders, interchangeable lenses, and shutters with speeds up to $\frac{1}{1250}$ second. The twin-lens reflex camera (Fig. 5) comprises a camera part and a viewfinder part. The distance setting for the two parts is coupled, so that the sharply focused image which is formed on the ground-glass screen of the viewfinder is also formed on the film plane. The lenses of the two parts have exactly the same focal length. As a rule, the viewfinder lens has greater light-transmitting power than the camera lens, as this makes for quicker and sharper focusing. All twin-lens reflex cameras take $2\frac{1}{4}$ in. $\times$ $2\frac{1}{4}$ in. photographs. The single-lens reflex camera (Fig. 6) has only one lens. This lens first serves for focusing the image on a ground-glass screen (or in a prism viewfinder); then, when the image has been focused, the deviating mirror (set at 45°) is swung upwards, enabling the image to be formed on the film plane. The stop value (aperture) is set before the exposure is made. When the shutter is released, the deviating mirror is automatically swung out of the way, and the shutter, which in such cameras is usually of the focal plane type, i.e., mounted directly in front of the film (see page 160), momentarily exposes the film. Then, when the film is wound on for the following shot and the shutter is thereby automatically cocked, the mirror is lowered again for focusing the next picture.

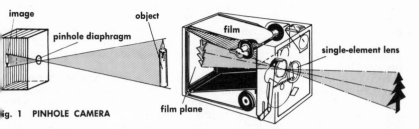

Fig. 1 PINHOLE CAMERA

image — pinhole diaphragm — object

Fig. 2 BOX CAMERA

film — single-element lens — film plane

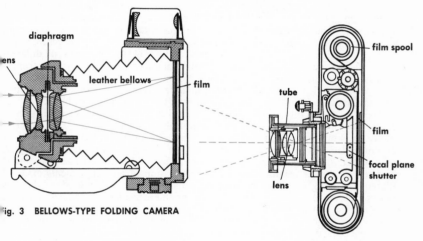

diaphragm — lens — leather bellows — film

Fig. 3 BELLOWS-TYPE FOLDING CAMERA

film spool — tube — film — focal plane shutter — lens

Fig. 5 TWIN-LENS REFLEX CAMERA

Fig. 4 TUBE-TYPE CAMERA

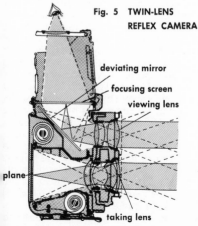

deviating mirror — focusing screen — viewing lens — plane — taking lens

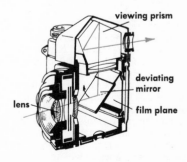

viewing prism — deviating mirror — lens — film plane

Fig. 6 SINGLE-LENS REFLEX CAMERA

PHOTOGRAPHIC LENSES

The most important component of a camera is the objective or, as it is more familiarly called, the lens. The lens should form a sharp, even, undistorted and bright image over the entire picture size.

The simplest conceivable "lens" is merely a small hole—a "pinhole"—which forms an image on the back wall of the camera (where the photographic plate or film is mounted) because light travels in a straight path (Fig. 1). However, a photograph taken with a pinhole camera is not very sharp, as a point is reproduced in the image as a spot of light which can never be smaller than the pinhole itself. Also, because of the very small size of the hole, its light-transmitting power is extremely low (see page 162).

Because of its ability to concentrate the rays in a beam of light at one point, a lens is the obviously suitable device for forming a suitably sharp and bright image in a camera. Fig. 2. shows diagrammatically how the image is formed by the lens (see page 136). However, rays entering the lens at wide angles in relation to the optical axis are not ideally concentrated at one point: the deviations from the ideal image are called lens errors (or lens aberrations). The principal errors are: spherical aberration (Fig. 3; the marginal rays are focused at a point closer to the lens), astigmatism and curvature of the image field (Fig. 4; two mutually perpendicular rays passing obliquely through a lens are concentrated on two curved surfaces of different curvature), coma (comet-like elongation of points outside the centre of the image), distortion (Fig. 5), chromatic aberration (Fig. 6; light rays of different colours are not focused at the same point: light of longer wavelength is less strongly refracted than shorter-wave light; see page 134).

If a convergent lens is combined with a suitable divergent lens, which is so shaped as to have half the (negative) refractive power of the convergent lens but is made of glass with twice the colour dispersion, the refractive power of the lens combination is halved, but the chromatic aberration is entirely eliminated (Fig. 7). A lens (or, strictly speaking, an objective comprising two elements) of this kind is called an achromatic lens. Its two component elements are usually cemented together (Fig. 8), and it is used for box cameras with apertures up to $f/9$. The other lens errors can be corrected by similar means, i.e., by the combination of several elements made of different kinds of glass possessing different optical properties. Hundreds of varieties of glass differing in refractive index and dispersion are available to the lens designer. By varying the number of lenses ("elements"), the type of glass, the radii of curvature, the lens thicknesses, and the air gaps (if any) between the elements, it is possible to reduce the optical errors to acceptable values.

Besides the other errors, anastigmatism is a defect which is particularly necessary to eliminate in the case of a "fast" lens, i.e., a lens with a high light-transmitting power. A lens corrected in this way is called an anastigmatic lens (or "anastigmat"). Some fundamental forms of lens in this category have proved satisfactory. Thus, the so-called "triplet" (Fig. 9) is fitted as the standard lens in nearly all cameras in the medium price range, with apertures of $f/3.5$ or $f/2.8$ (see page 162) and focal lengths of 45 to 50 mm. These lenses are known by various proprietary names (e.g., Agnar, Apotar, Cassar, Lanthar, Novar, Pantar, Radionar, Reomar, Triotar). An important form of camera lens is the cemented four-element triplet (Fig. 10), which usually has an aperture $f/2.8$ and a focal length of 50 mm; for larger sizes of camera these lenses have an aperture of $f/3.5$ for a focal length of 75 mm or $f/4.5$ for a focal length in 105–300 mm range (e.g., Elmar, Skopar, Solinar, Tessar, Xenar, Ysarex). Also, there are five-element variants (e.g., Apo-Lanthar, Elmarit, Heliar), and four- to seven-element variants of the Sonnar lens, which can hardly be classed as triplets at all. For large angular fields, symmetrical arrangements of the lens elements facilitate the correction of the image defects. Most of the fast lenses used in miniature cameras, with apertures of about $f/2$, are of the *Gauss double anastigmat* type (Fig. 11) (e.g., Biotar, Heligon, Pancolar, some Planar lenses, Auto-Quinon, Solagon, Ultron, Xenon). In some lenses a seventh or indeed an eighth element is added in order to obtain good correction even at the highest light-transmitting power ($f/2$ to $f/1.4$) (Nokton, some Planar lenses, Septon, Summicron, Summilux). For further combinations see the article on interchangeable lenses (page 156).

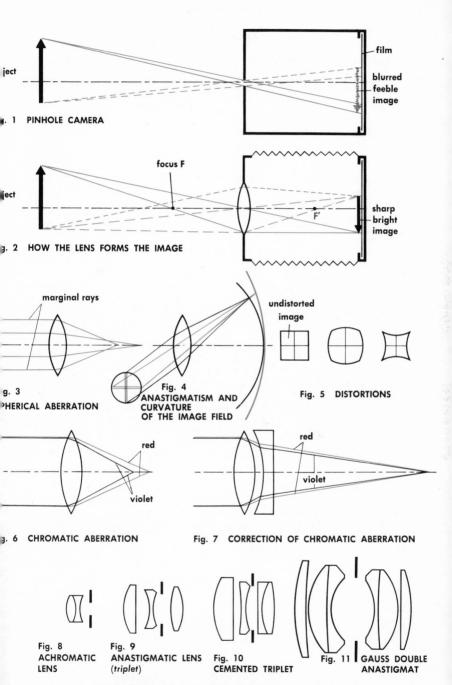

Fig. 1 PINHOLE CAMERA

object — film / blurred feeble image

Fig. 2 HOW THE LENS FORMS THE IMAGE

object — focus F / F' / sharp bright image

Fig. 3 SPHERICAL ABERRATION

marginal rays

Fig. 4 ANASTIGMATISM AND CURVATURE OF THE IMAGE FIELD

Fig. 5 DISTORTIONS

undistorted image

Fig. 6 CHROMATIC ABERRATION

red / violet

Fig. 7 CORRECTION OF CHROMATIC ABERRATION

red / violet

Fig. 8 ACHROMATIC LENS

Fig. 9 ANASTIGMATIC LENS (*triplet*)

Fig. 10 CEMENTED TRIPLET

Fig. 11 GAUSS DOUBLE ANASTIGMAT

basic forms of photographic lenses (in each case the object to be photographed is assumed to be situated to the left of the lens)

FOCAL DISTANCE AND SIZE OF IMAGE

The size of the image in a camera is determined by the distance between the lens and the film plane.

Fig. 1a shows the conditions in a camera provided with a "standard lens", while Fig. 1b is a diagram of a camera with a "wide-angle lens". The latter has a wider angular field, but the actual image size is the same (for the same film size). From Fig. 1c we see: the image size B bears the same ratio to the subject size G as does the image distance b to the subject distance g:

$$\frac{B}{G} = \frac{b}{g} \quad \text{or alternatively:} \quad \frac{B}{b} = \frac{G}{g}$$

For large "taking distances" (distance from camera to subject) the image distance b is approximately equal to the focal length f (cf. the article on lenses, page 136); hence the image size is, generally speaking, proportional to the focal length: a short focal length produces a small image of the subject; if the focal length is, say, three times as large, the image will also be three times as large (Figs. 3a and 3b; principle of wide-angle and telephoto photographs).

The image size must now be considered in relation to the picture size. The focal length of a "standard lens" is about equal to the diagonal of the picture size, i.e., a miniature camera or a plate camera with standard lenses both form an image of a section of space whose diagonal is therefore approximately equal to the distance from the camera. This corresponds to an angular field of 53° over the diagonal. The usual standard lenses have an angular field in the range of 45° to 60°, corresponding to focal lengths of 45–50 mm for miniature cameras with picture size 24 mm × 36 mm (diagonal 43 mm), 75–85 mm for picture size 6 cm × 6 cm (diagonal 85 mm), and 135–150 mm for picture size g × 12 cm (diagonal 150 mm).

The question as to the angular field for which a lens system is corrected is of significance only with regard to cameras having extension bellows, because in such cameras a lens of the same focal length is used as a telephoto lens for a roll film size, as a standard lens with reserve scope for adjustment, or as a wide-angle lens for a larger plate size, provided that the camera is suitably designed for such a large angular field (Fig. 2). In a miniature camera the lens is normally mounted in a tube of appropriate length and is corrected exactly for the angle of the particular picture size employed (see the article on interchangeable lenses (page 156).

If different focal lengths are used at one and the same view point, the image size will be altered, but not the perspective effect: in that case a photograph taken with a telephoto lens will be no different from a wide-angle photograph which is subsequently enlarged (Figs. 3a and 3b). A much more favourable method is to use different focal lengths to alter the perspective by changing the distance. Figs. 3b and 3c show how the size ratio between foreground and background is reversed: the distance to the foreground subject V is adapted to the focal length so that the image V^1 retains its size; the distance between the foreground and the background does not change, however, so that here the change affects the scale of the image.

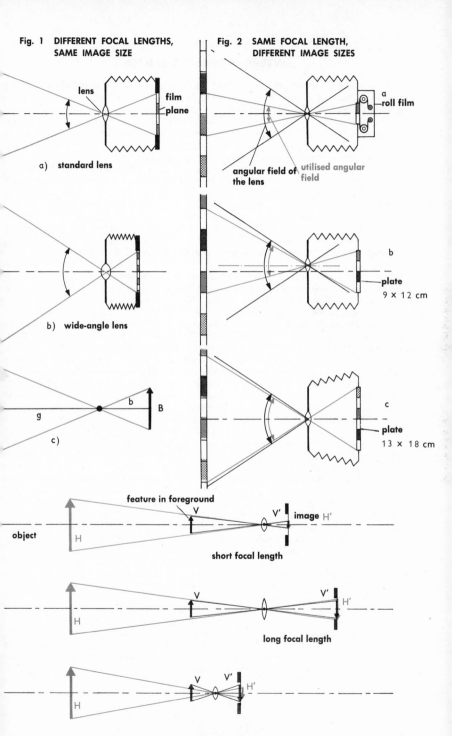

Fig. 1 DIFFERENT FOCAL LENGTHS, SAME IMAGE SIZE

lens
film
plane

a) standard lens

b) wide-angle lens

g   b   B

c)

Fig. 2 SAME FOCAL LENGTH, DIFFERENT IMAGE SIZES

a
roll film

angular field of the lens   utilised angular field

b
plate
9 × 12 cm

c
plate
13 × 18 cm

feature in foreground
object
H   V   V'   image H'

short focal length

H   V   V'   H'

long focal length

H   V V'   H'

Fig. 3 FOCAL LENGTH AND PERSPECTIVE

155

INTERCHANGEABLE LENSES

Some cameras are so constructed that the focal length can be changed, in order to enable the scale of the picture (or image) to be suited to the size of the subject and to modify the perspective (cf. page 154).

The systems for changing the focal length and the construction of these interchangeable lenses will here be explained with reference to the three focal lengths most commonly employed for miniature cameras (wide angle lens approx. 35 mm, standard lens approx. 50 mm, portrait lens approx. 85 mm).

Unlimited possibility of changing the lenses is afforded by the focal plane shutter (cf. page 160, Fig. 1). In this example the standard lens (1b) is a triplet with a cemented rear element. Because of its shorter focal length, the wide angle lens (Fig. 1a) is mounted closer to the film plane, whereas the telephoto lens (1c), with its greater focal length, has a correspondingly longer tube. For cameras fitted with focal plane shutters there are lenses with focal lengths ranging from 21 mm to 600 mm. Indeed, there are special lenses with focal lengths of as little as 8 mm or as much as 2000 mm, corresponding to a scale ranging from 0.16 to 40 times in relation to the standard lens.

Single-lens reflex cameras require a certain amount of space for the collapsible mirror behind the lens, and this "width of cut" represents a minimum distance between the back of the lens and the image. Similar limitations occur in the case of a camera with a diaphragm shutter (cf. page 158) if it is designed for interchangeable lenses: instead of being mounted between the lenses, the shutter must then be installed directly behind the interchangeable lens, so as to ensure that even with very short exposures there is not too much lack of sharpness at the corners of the picture. If this requirement is fulfilled for the standard lens (2b), then the width of cut, i.e., the distance between the back of the lens and the image, will be predetermined, just as in the mirror reflex camera. However at some additional cost it is nevertheless possible to make a wide angle lens whose focal length is shorter than the width of cut (Fig. 2a). Greatly simplified, this lens could be described as a standard lens in which the path of the rays is modified by the divergent element. The arrangement illustrated in (2c) is a "true telephoto lens" in that it comprises a "positive" (convergent) and a "negative" (divergent) set of lenses; together these form a system having a large focal length, in the manner of a Galilean telescope (see page 146). This form of construction has the advantage of requiring only a relatively short construction length (cf. Figs 2c and 1c).

A third possibility is the so-called convertible lens. The lens with shutter and diaphragm is permanently connected to the body of the camera (just as in a camera without interchangeable lenses), only the front element of the lens being interchanged. The combinations illustrated in Figs. 3a and 3c correspond approximately to the wide angle lens and the telephoto lens of Figs. 2a and 2c respectively. It is on this principle, too, that the functioning of the so-called "zoom lens", which allows of "infinitely variable" control of focal length, is based. Fig. 4 shows a lens of this kind in the "telephoto" setting. The front set of lenses as a whole is positive, whereas the rear set is negative. By and large, the lens resembles a telephoto lens as shown in Fig. 2c. Now if the two movable sets of lenses are slid backwards (towards the camera) a continuous transition is effected until an arrangement rather like that in Fig. 2a is reached, i.e., the lens now functions as a wide angle lens.

Zoom lenses with large focal length ranges—e.g., 8 to 48 mm for 8 mm cine film—are now extensively used on television cameras and narrow-gauge cine cameras. For the latter class of cameras the cost of such lenses is not prohibitively high (because of the small picture size), and attractive or interesting effects in motion pictures can be obtained by means of zoomed shots.

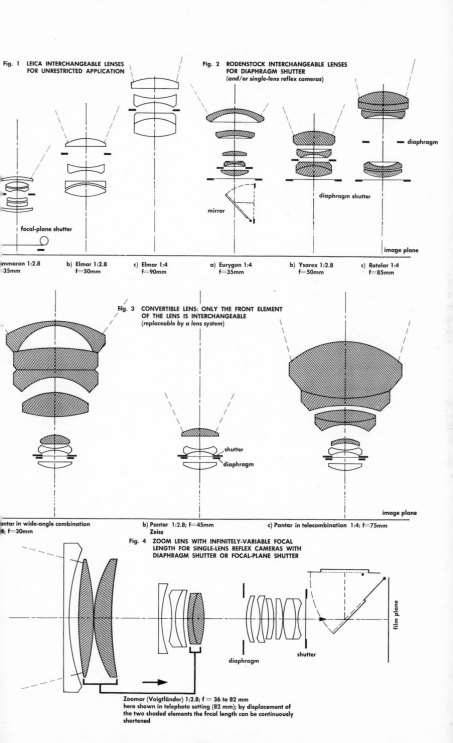

Fig. 1 LEICA INTERCHANGEABLE LENSES FOR UNRESTRICTED APPLICATION

Fig. 2 RODENSTOCK INTERCHANGEABLE LENSES FOR DIAPHRAGM SHUTTER
(and/or single-lens reflex cameras)

— diaphragm

diaphragm shutter

mirror

focal-plane shutter

image plane

mmaron 1:2.8   b) Elmar 1:2.8   c) Elmar 1:4   a) Eurygon 1:4   b) Ysarex 1:2.8   c) Rotelar 1:4
35mm   f=50mm   f=90mm   f=35mm   f=50mm   f=85mm

Fig. 3 CONVERTIBLE LENS: ONLY THE FRONT ELEMENT OF THE LENS IS INTERCHANGEABLE
(replaceable by a lens system)

shutter

diaphragm

image plane

antar in wide-angle combination   b) Pantar 1:2.8; f=45mm   c) Pantar in telecombination 1:4; f=75mm
; f=30mm   Zeiss

Fig. 4 ZOOM LENS WITH INFINITELY-VARIABLE FOCAL LENGTH FOR SINGLE-LENS REFLEX CAMERAS WITH DIAPHRAGM SHUTTER OR FOCAL-PLANE SHUTTER

film plane

diaphragm

shutter

Zoomar (Voigtländer) 1:2.8; f = 36 to 82 mm
here shown in telephoto setting (82 mm); by displacement of
the two shaded elements the focal length can be continuously
shortened

157

DIAPHRAGM SHUTTERS

The function of a camera shutter is to admit the light rays to the film for a controlled—and usually very brief—length of time. Diaphragm shutters are usually in the form of a "between-the-lens" shutter, i.e., the shutter is mounted in the diaphragm plane between the individual elements which the compound lens of the camera is composed. In particular cases, however, the shutter may be located directly behind the lens.

This type of shutter comprises a number of thin steel plates (usually five), known as shutter leaves or shutter blades, which rotate about pivots in such a way that they open out in a direction away from the optical axis, i.e., from the centre of the lens outwards, and then, on completion of the exposure, close the lens by moving back towards the centre. Before the exposure is made, the shutter has to be cocked by tensioning a spring ("pre-set shutter"). This cocking operation is often coupled with the film advance motion. Simple "everset" shutters (with speeds of approx. $\frac{1}{30}$ to $\frac{1}{125}$ sec.) are cocked only when the releaser is depressed. The functioning of the shutter is shown simplified, with reference only to one shutter leaf instead of the actual five leaves, in Figs. 1a to 1d. In Fig. 1a the shutter is still closed. Now the drive element rotates in the arrowed direction (Fig. 1b) and thrusts against the shutter-opening pin of the actuating ring, causing the latter to rotate anti-clockwise. Other pins mounted on this ring engage with slots in the shutter leaves and cause these to swing about their respective pivots. In Fig. 1c the shutter is fully opened. Further rotation of the drive element is now prevented by an escapement mechanism, which is really a kind of clockwork in which an oscillating anchor controls the movements of the cog-wheels. When the exposure period (up to 1 sec.) has ended and the escapement has run down, the drive element continues its rotation in the same direction as before. A projection on the drive element now thrusts against the shutter-closing pin on the actuating ring and causes this ring to rotate in the reverse direction, so that the shutter leaves close again.

The actual opening and closing movements are accomplished in about 2 milliseconds ($=\frac{2}{1000}$ sec., see Fig. 2a). The "shutter open" time regulated by the escapement is therefore about 2 milliseconds shorter than the nominal exposure time to which the shutter mechanism has been set. For very short exposures ($\frac{1}{50}$ sec. and less; Fig. 2b) the escapement is disconnected and an auxiliary spring speeds up the shutter movements still more.

Some cameras are equipped with a self-timer (automatic release). When this device is used, actuation of the releaser first sets a delayed-action mechanism in motion which initiates the movement of the shutter leaves after an interval of 5 to 10 seconds.

For flashlight photography the actual flash must be synchronised with the opening of the shutter. Most shutters are provided with a so-called X contact which establishes electrical contact at the instant when the shutter is fully opened (electronic flash). "Fully synchronised" shutters are additionally equipped with an M contact, which ignites the flash about 16 milliseconds earlier, so as to give the somewhat slower flash produced by a flashbulb sufficient time to attain its maximum intensity (cf. page 182).

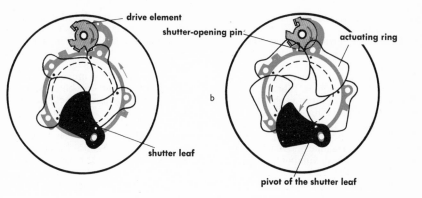

b

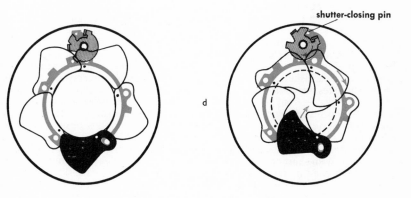

d

Fig. 1   SEQUENCE OF MOVEMENTS OF A SHUTTER LEAF

Fig. 2   LIGHT FLUX / TIME DIAGRAM OF A DIAPHRAGM
SHUTTER

159

FOCAL PLANE SHUTTERS

If the camera is fitted with interchangeable lenses for long and short focal lengths respectively, or if the camera is to be used with close-up adapter rings and bellows attachment, or mounted on a microscope, then it must be equipped with a shutter which moves in a plane just in front of the film. A shutter of this kind is known as a focal plane shutter.

A focal plane shutter comprises two opaque roller blinds which move in the same guide tracks (Fig. 1). When the shutter release is actuated, the first blind is drawn aside and rolled on to a spool by means of a spring. After a certain pre-set interval of time the second blind unrolls at the same speed and covers the film again. The two blinds thus form a slit which travels across the film gate. If the shutter has been set to a long exposure (Fig. 2), the second roller blind will wait a relatively long time before following the first blind; in that case the slit is very wide. With a short exposure the second blind will quickly follow the first, so that only a very narrow moving slit is formed (Fig. 3).

The roller blinds may be designed to move either longitudinally across the picture area, i.e., a distance of 36 mm (as in Fig. 1), or transversely, i.e., a distance of 24 mm (as in Fig. 4). Most focal plane shutters of the roller blind type are designed to operate at speeds down to $\frac{1}{1000}$ sec. Such short exposures are obtained by narrowing down the slit, as already explained, while the speed of travel of the blinds remain the same. The entire duration of the exposure procedure is therefore substantially longer than $\frac{1}{1000}$ sec. If the subject of the photograph is moving rapidly past the camera, the image it forms on the film will be travelling either "along with" or "against" the direction of movement of the slit. This could cause a certain distortion (elongation or shortening) of the image, as was indeed found to occur in the older large cameras equipped with such shutters. However, in modern miniature cameras using 35 mm film the slit takes less than $\frac{1}{50}$ sec. to travel across the picture area. The image of a fast-moving object in front of the camera, such as a racing car, which takes, say, $\frac{1}{5}$ sec. to traverse the picture area would therefore undergo a distortion of 10%. The vehicle would have to be travelling very fast indeed for this effect to be objectionably noticeable.

The operating time of the shutter is, however, a very significant factor in flashlight photography. With short exposure times the brightness of the flashbulb must remain approximately constant for at least the length of time required for the slit to traverse the image. With an electronic flash or flashbulb with a very short flash period this condition would not be fulfilled, and in that case only a narrow strip of the film (corresponding to the width of the shutter slit at the actual time of the flash) would be exposed. To synchronise the camera to flashlight equipment of this kind it is therefore necessary so to adjust the exposure time that the slit width exceeds the width of the film gate at the instant of flash. In modern cameras this exposure time is about $\frac{1}{50}$ sec.

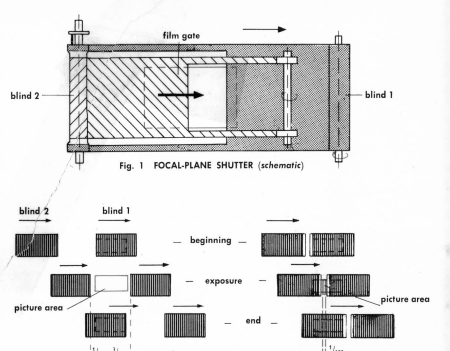

Fig. 1 FOCAL-PLANE SHUTTER (*schematic*)

blind 2

film gate

blind 1

blind 2   blind 1

— beginning —

picture area   — exposure —   picture area

— end —

$^1/_{100}$ $^3/_{100}$

0 $^2/_{100}$ $^4/_{100}$

$^1/_{100}$

0 $^2/_{100}$

Fig. 2 MOTION OF THE BLINDS FOR
LONG EXPOSURE (1/25 sec.)

Fig. 3 MOTION OF THE BLINDS FOR
SHORT EXPOSURE (1/200 sec.)

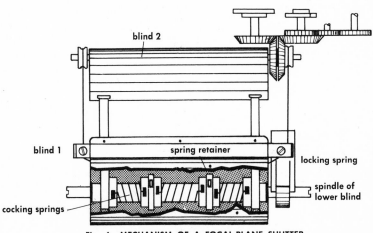

blind 2

blind 1   spring retainer

locking spring

spindle of
lower blind

cocking springs

Fig. 4 MECHANISM OF A FOCAL-PLANE SHUTTER

SPEED OF A CAMERA LENS

The "speed" or light-transmitting power of a lens can be visualised by conceiving the camera as a closed chamber with an opening (a window) at one end (Fig. 1). The wall opposite the window will receive more light in proportion as the window is larger and the distance from the wall to the window is less. All the light rays entering the eye of an observer standing at the rear wall of the chamber will form a cone whose base is bounded by the edges of the window. The larger the window is, the wider will be the cone and the greater will be the amount of light entering the observer's eye. The ratio of the diameter of window opening (assuming it to be circular) to the length of the chamber is therefore a criterion of the "width" of the cone of light rays.

In a camera the rear wall is formed by the film, each point of which receives a quantity of light corresponding to the width (or diameter) of the aperture. Normally the distance between the lens and the film is approximately equal to the focal length of the lens. The larger the lens is, the more light it can transmit into the camera. For this reason the transmitting power of a lens is characterised by the ratio of the diameter of the effective aperture to the focal length. This is called the lens aperture ratio or relative aperture of the lens (Fig. 2). For example, if a camera lens has an aperture of 25 mm diameter and a focal length of 50 mm, its aperture ratio is $25:50 = 1:2$, where the figure 2 is the so called "f-number" (often designated as $f/2$). If the aperture is reduced to 12.5 mm, by appropriately altering the aperture setting (i.e., by closing the stop or diaphragm), then the ratio will become $12.5:50 = 1:4$, i.e., $f/4$. The aperture with half the diameter has only a quarter of the area of the initial aperture and therefore admits only a quarter of the initial amount of light into the camera (Fig. 2b). The f-numbers (aperture settings) of a camera lens are usually so arranged that each next higher f-number corresponds to a reduction of about one-half in the light-transmitting power of the lens, e.g.:

aperture (f-number)	1.4	2	2.8	4	5.6	8	11	16
relative brightness	1	$\frac{1}{2}$	$\frac{1}{4}$	$\frac{1}{8}$	$\frac{1}{16}$	$\frac{1}{32}$	$\frac{1}{64}$	$\frac{1}{128}$

Hence a lens with $f/2.8$ is sixteen times "faster" than one with $f/11$. If, for instance, an exposure time of $\frac{1}{500}$ sec. is sufficient at $f/2.8$, it will be necessary to give sixteen times as long an exposure at $f/11$, i.e., about $\frac{1}{30}$ sec. For a telephoto lens with a focal length of, say, 100 mm to have the same speed as the above-mentioned normal lens of 50 mm focal length, it will have to have twice the diameter of lens (Fig. 3). This larger lens will transmit four times as much light, but as the image formed on the film is twice as large linearly, i.e., has four times the area of the image formed by the normal lens, the brightness remains the same. With close-up photography (Fig. 4) the distance between the lens and the film will become larger than the focal length of the lens, so that the cone of illumination becomes narrower and the actual light-transmitting effect of the lens diminishes even though the aperture is not altered. If supplementary lenses are used for close-up work, however, the focal length of the lens system as a whole is thereby reduced, but not the distance from lens to film; the actual light-transmitting effect is therefore not reduced. In the case of a compound lens it is not possible to determine the effective aperture merely from the diameters of the component elements and the diameter of the diaphragm. The effective aperture is called the "entrance pupil"; it depends on the diaphragm and forms the boundary of the beam of rays which is concentrated on the film.

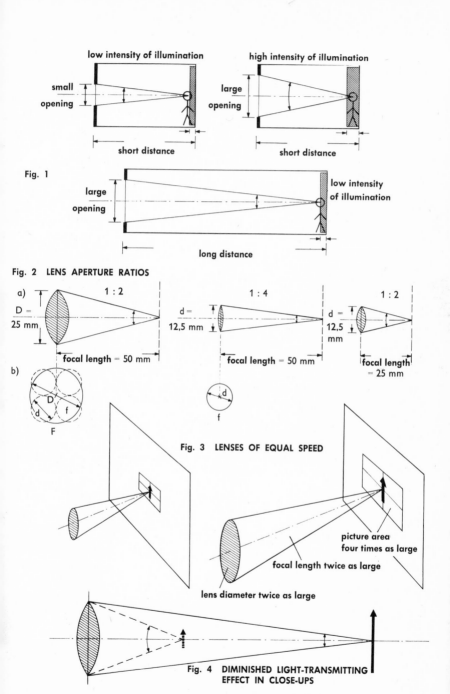

low intensity of illumination

high intensity of illumination

small opening

large opening

short distance

short distance

Fig. 1

large opening

low intensity of illumination

long distance

Fig. 2 LENS APERTURE RATIOS

a)

1 : 2

D = 25 mm

focal length = 50 mm

1 : 4

d = 12,5 mm

focal length = 50 mm

1 : 2

d = 12,5 mm

focal length = 25 mm

b)

D

d

f

F

d

f

Fig. 3 LENSES OF EQUAL SPEED

picture area four times as large

focal length twice as large

lens diameter twice as large

Fig. 4 DIMINISHED LIGHT-TRANSMITTING EFFECT IN CLOSE-UPS

163

COLOUR PRINTING

Colour printing in the present context refers to the production of photo-engraved colour plates by means of the three- and four-colour processes.

If an area is covered with a mosaic-like pattern of dots in the three primary colours (yellow, red, blue) (Fig. 1c) and is viewed from a sufficiently long distance (so that the individual points cannot be separately distinguished), it appears grey. If numerous dots in two primary colours are placed side by side (Fig. 1c, lower squares) they will, when viewed from a distance, appear as a mixed (or compound) colour. This apparent merging of colours to give the appearance of another colour is one of the fundamental principles of colour printing. The first step in preparing four-colour printing plates from the original painting or photographic transparency is to make colour-separation negatives by means of colour filters on the camera. A different filter is used for each colour negative. Each filter allows only its complementary colour to pass. To make a negative for the blue printing plate, a red filter is used; for the yellow printing plate, a blue-violet filter; for the red printing plate, a green filter. A pale yellow filter is used for obtaining the black values. These various colour negatives are shown in Figs. 1b, 2b and 3b; the colours of the corresponding filters are shown in Figs. 1a, 2a and 3a. The purpose of the black plate (Fig. 4) is to cover certain white areas of the base (i.e., the paper on which the picture is printed) and to give depth and detail to the picture.

The negatives are developed, printed on metal, and etched in much the same way as when making a monochrome halftone plate. The plates are inked and printed in the sequence shown (Fig. 1–Fig. 4), each being superimposed exactly upon the other. The picture is successively thus built up step by step, as shown in Figs. 2c, 3c and 5. The surface of each printing plate is composed of a large number of dots, these being formed by a special process. When the four colours from the plates are superimposed, the resulting print contains not only the four colours, but also the compound colours formed by the blending of these. Fig. 6 is an enlarged detail of Fig. 5 and shows how this effect is obtained.

To achieve good results, it is of course essential to make the successive coloured impressions register exactly one upon the other. The coloured inks must be clear and clean, and variations in the shade and intensity of the colours must be avoided. In some cases, to obtain very high quality, it may be necessary to employ auxiliary colours. Sometimes, too, the colour negatives may have to be retouched by hand.

1 a

1 b

1 c

2 a

2 b

2 c

3 a

3 b

3 c

4

5

6

COLOUR TELEVISION

A certain type of colour television camera contains three image orthicon tubes (see page 124). By means of a system of mirrors and colour filters the first tube forms a red image (R), the second forms a green image (G), and the third forms a blue image (B). The three camera tubes have essentially identical scanning patterns, so that the picture signals developed by the respective tubes represent images which are identical except that they differ in colour. (See Fig. 1).

By means of an electric transmission system the primary colour signals E_R, E_G and E_B are simultaneously fed to three colour picture tubes and converted back into three separate colour images (red, green and blue). By means of a system of colour-selective (dichroic) mirrors the viewer sees the three pictures as one superimposed picture in which the three colours are blended to give additively mixed colours, just as in colour printing (see page 165).

In the system developed by the National Television System Committee (NTSC system) in the United States, the E_R, E_G, E_B signals (primary colour signals) are converted by a device called a colour coder into a luminance (i.e., brightness or "brilliance") signal, E_Y and a chrominance signal. Chrominance comprises two independent characteristic quantities: "hue" and "saturation". The luminance signal can be received by an ordinary (monochrome) television receiver and produces a black-and-white picture. This technique comprising a luminance and a chrominance transmission is known as compatible colour television. The luminance signal is subtracted from the primary colour signals, and the colour-difference signals thus obtained are then further combined to produce two signals E_I and E_Q, which are then mixed with the chrominance subcarrier signal. This signal is amplitude-modulated in accordance with the saturation values and phase-modulated in accordance with the hues. The luminance and chrominance components are combined to form the overall colour picture signal, which is then transmitted. The picture signal wave is a composite wave in which the chrominance wave is superimposed upon part of the luminance wave.

(Continued)

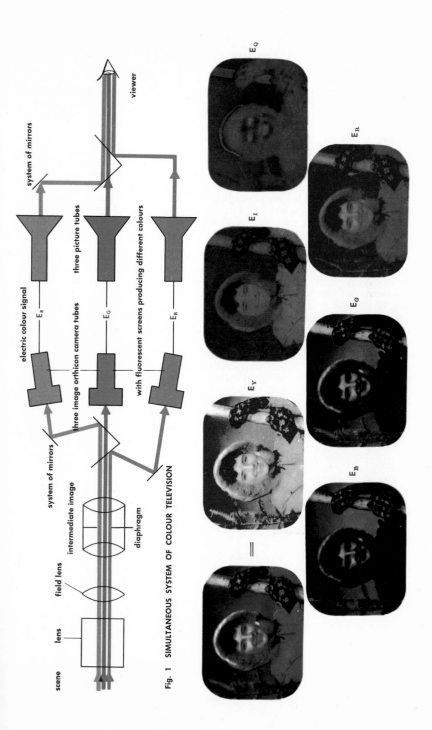

Fig. 1 SIMULTANEOUS SYSTEM OF COLOUR TELEVISION

scene

lens

field lens

intermediate image

diaphragm

system of mirrors

three image orthicon camera tubes

electric colour signal

E_R

E_G

E_B

three picture tubes

with fluorescent screens producing different colours

system of mirrors

viewer

E_Y =

E_I

E_Q

E_R

E_G

E_B

167

COLOUR TELEVISION
(continued)

The primary colour signals, which have been recast into luminance and chrominance components at the transmitter have to be reconverted into primary colour signals at the receiver before they can be applied to the colour picture tube. Instead of using three picture tubes as in the system outlined above, the NTSC system uses only one picture tube, known as a shadow-mask tube, which contains three electron guns which produce three separate electron beams, which move simultaneously in the scanning pattern over the viewing screen and which respectively produce a red, a green and a blue image. The screen is composed of three separate sets of uniformly distributed phosphor dots. The dots of each set glow in a different colour. Electrons discharged by the gun controlled by the red primary colour signal impinge only on the red-glowing phosphor dots and are prevented from impinging on the green- and blue-glowing dots by a mask which contains about 200,000 tiny holes, each of which is accurately aligned with the different coloured phosphor dots on the screen. Similarly, the electrons from the two other guns fall only on the green and the blue dots respectively. In this way three separate primary colour images are formed simultaneously. The dots producing the three different colours are so small and so close together that the eye does not see them as separate points of light.

In the colour television receiver the luminance component is applied simultaneously to all three electron guns of the picture tube. The receiver contains circuits which perform the inverse operations of the addition and subtraction circuits at the transmitter. In this way three colour-difference signals are obtained (the difference between the luminance signal and the primary colour signals). The three colour-difference signals are applied to the respective electron guns in addition to the luminance signal. The net control signal applied to each gun corresponds to the primary colour signal coming from the respective camera tube.

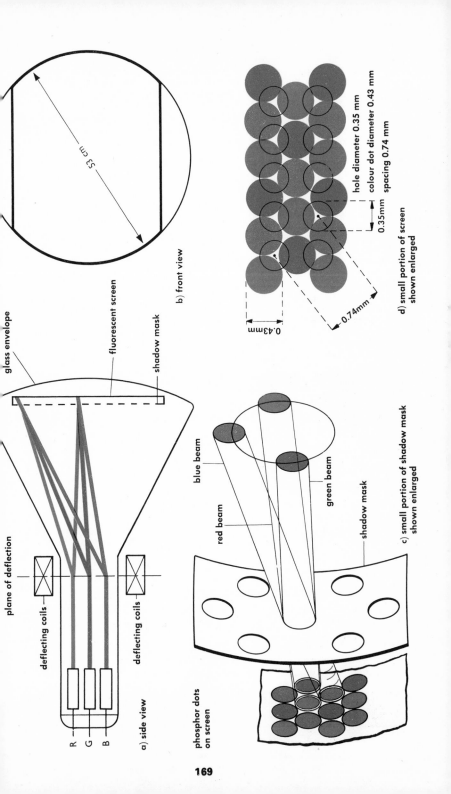

glass envelope

plane of deflection

fluorescent screen

shadow mask

b) front view

53 cm

deflecting coils

deflecting coils

R
G
B

a) side view

blue beam

red beam

green beam

shadow mask

c) small portion of shadow mask
shown enlarged

phosphor dots
on screen

hole diameter 0.35 mm
colour dot diameter 0.43 mm
spacing 0.74 mm

0.35mm

0.43mm

0.74mm

d) small portion of screen
shown enlarged

COLOUR PHOTOGRAPHY

There are many different processes of colour photography, which differ in detail but they can be divided into two main groups: additive processes (for transparencies only) and subtractive processes (for transparencies and also for paper prints). In all cases the fundamental principle is the same: images in three primary colours must be obtained which, in combination with one another, produce the desired colour picture. The individual processes differ in that, for example, the subject may be photographed three times in succession in three different colours (e.g., yellow, green, red) or that, alternatively, the three films are exposed simultaneously in a special camera fitted with a system of lenses and mirrors for achieving this result, or again that only one film is used, which is provided with three superimposed layers of emulsion, each sensitive to a different colour. The principles whereby the three single-colour images are combined to produce the final result also varies from one process to another. The reversal process and the negative-positive process described here belong to the group of subtractive processes, which are now used almost exclusively for colour prints on paper and transparencies for still and motion-picture projection.

The emulsion layers incorporate chemicals which, on exposure to light, form dyes to a degree corresponding to the amount of light. Most modern colour photographic processes embody this principle of dye formation, which is based on the fact that when a developer reacts with silver bromide to reduce it to silver, the resulting oxidised developer can react with certain dye-forming chemicals (called couplers) to form dyes. The developers used are diamines.

In a well-known type of colour film the film is coated with three emulsion layers which respond respectively to blue, green and red light. A yellow filter layer is inter-

a) Colours in the subject to be photographed

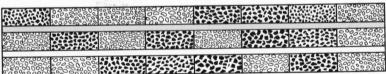

b) Layers in the film after the first (black and white) development: black grains represent developed silver, light grains represent residual silver bromide, yellow filter layer still present

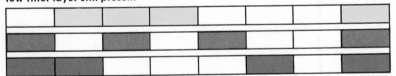

c) The same film after processing: colour developed at the residual silver bromide, silver and yellow filter layer dissolved out

d) Colours in the finished film

posed between the blue-sensitive top layer and the two other layers in order to prevent blue light from reaching these. Positive pictures are obtained directly by reversal. First, the film is developed to give a negative in all three layers, followed by exposure to red light through the base, and again developing; then exposure to blue light through the front, again followed by developing. The silver in all three layers is bleached out, leaving the dyes to form the colour picture (see illustration below).

In another process, called the negative-positive process, the film is coated with red-, green- and blue-sensitive layers. After exposure, the film is processed with a developer which produces silver plus dye images in each layer. The silver is removed, and a colour negative is obtained. The dyes formed in each layer have the colour complementary to the colour of the light that caused it to be formed. Thus, blue light produces a yellow dye, green light a purple dye, and red light a blue-green dye. Thus all the colours in the negative are complementary to those in the subject photographed. The negative is printed on to paper coated with a similar set of emulsion layers, so that prints are obtained in which the original colours of the subject are reproduced (see illustration). In a refinement of this process the film has an extra layer in which a black-and-white negative can be developed. This acts as a mask and improves the colour quality of the print.

The coloured diagrams show how the final colour reproduction is obtained. If small blue and yellow dots are situated close beside one another, the overall visual impression is of a green colour. This is the principle of additive colour blending. However, the final transparencies or prints obtained in colour photography comprise superimposed single-colour layers which are partly transparent. The layers act as filters, so that only those rays of light which are not absorbed by these layers reach the eye. This is the principle of subtractive colour blending.

a) Colours in the subject to be photographed

b) Layers in the finished negative

c) Finished negative: colours are complementary to those in the subject

d) Layers in the finished positive

e) Colours in the finished positive

POLAROID-LAND COLORFILM

The processing of ordinary colour films to produce the final result—the colour positive—is a fairly laborious procedure, involving a number of operations performed under carefully controlled chemical and temperature conditions and with meticulous timing.

On the other hand, the colour photography process developed by Dr. Land produces a colour positive in only one minute. The film is coated with three colour-sensitive layers containing silver halide crystals, three layers containing dyes and developers, and two intermediate layers. Blue light acts upon the blue-sensitive layer I; green light passes unhindered to the green-sensitive layer IV; red light passes through both these layers to the red-sensitive layer VII. Now a strip is pulled out of the camera, causing a viscous developer-activating paste to be squeezed out of a capsule, while steel rollers press the negative layer (with the squeezed-on paste) firmly on to the so-called positive layer. The latter comprises the colour reception layer, an intermediate layer, and an acid layer for neutralising and stabilising the colour image. The activating paste diffuses quickly into the negative layer and first enters the blue sensitive layer I, where it develops the silver halide crystals; then it liberates a yellow dye in layer II, passes through the intermediate layer III, develops the silver halide crystals in the green-sensitive layer IV, liberates a purple dye in layer V, passes through the intermediate layer VI, develops the silver halide crystals in the red-sensitive layer VII, and finally reaches the layer VIII, where a blue-green dye is liberated. All the dye molecules liberated by the paste from the compounds in which they were previously held in a latent form are now free to diffuse in all directions. Where they encounter a grain of silver (into which a silver halide particle which was exposed to light has been converted by the developing action) they are retained and held by it. Those dye molecules which encounter no silver grains continue their migration until they reach the positive layer, where they, too, are held.

(Continued)

Fig. 1 EXPOSURE OF EIGHT-LAYER FILM

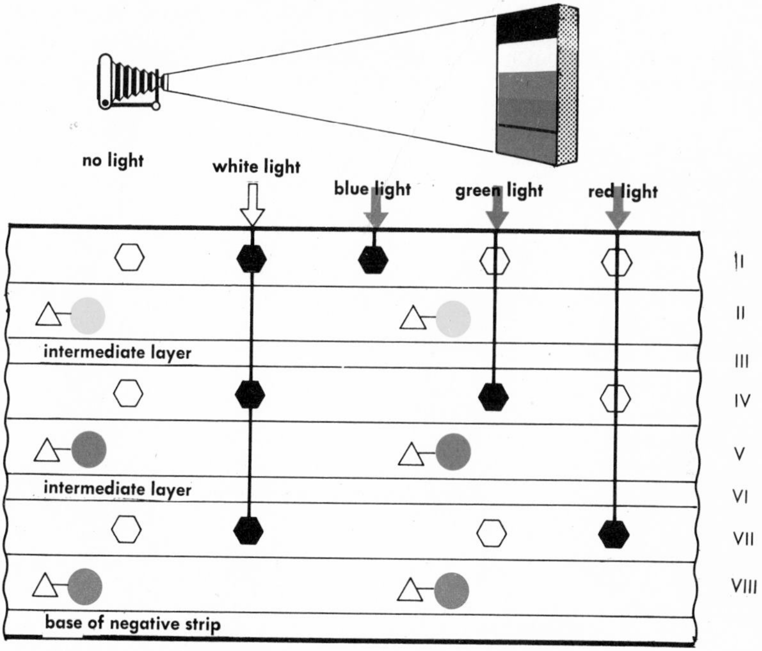

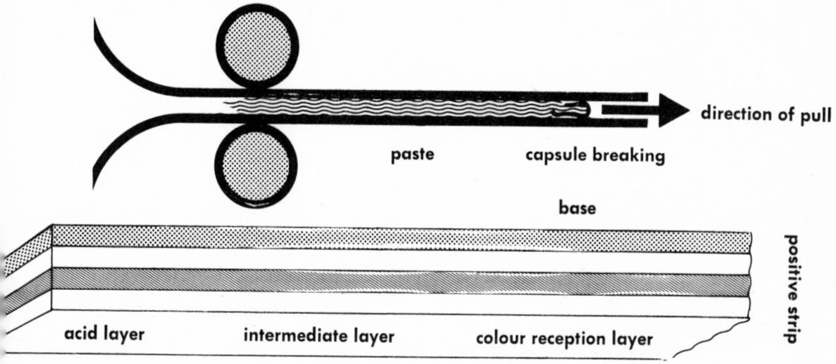

no light   white light   blue light   green light   red light

I
II
intermediate layer   III
IV
V
intermediate layer   VI
VII
VIII
base of negative strip

direction of pull

paste   capsule breaking

base

positive strip

acid layer   intermediate layer   colour reception layer

Fig. 2 THREE-LAYER POSITIVE STRIP IS PRESSED AGAINST
NEGATIVE STRIP; DEVELOPER-ACTIVATING PASTE
SERVES AS "GLUE"

173

POLAROID-LAND COLORFILM
(continued)

How is the colour image produced? Where red light has fallen on the film, the blue-green dye from layer VIII is held by the silver grains in layer VII. Since the red light had no effect on the layers IV and I (these being sensitive to green and blue respectively) the purple and the yellow dye respectively liberated in the layers V and II can pass freely to the colour-holding positive layer. Yellow and purple mixed produce the red colour in the positive layer. Blue light affects only the blue-sensitive layer I, and the yellow dye formed in the adjacent layer is retained and held by the grains of silver in layer I. But now the purple dye from layer V and the blue-green dye from layer VIII can pass unhindered to the positive layer, where the two dyes are held: purple and blue-green mixed produce blue. Similarly, green light affects on the green-sensitive layer IV; the silver grains in that layer retain and hold only the purple dye, whereas the blue-green and the yellow dye travel unhindered to the positive layer, where their mixture produces green. In the case of white light all the dyes are retained, because this light affects all three colour-sensitive layers. In the shadows ("black"), no dye is retained, and all three dyes reach the positive layer: their mixture produces black. Finally, water is formed in an alkali-neutralising process and serves to wash the positive. The process is illustrated schematically in the accompanying diagrams.

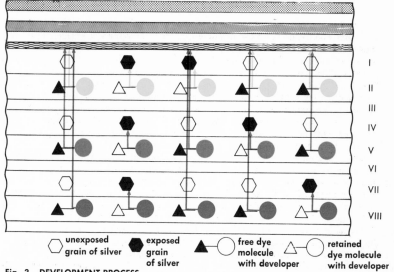

I	
II	
III	
IV	
V	
VI	
VII	
VIII	

⬡ unexposed grain of silver   ⬢ exposed grain of silver   ▲─◯ free dye molecule with developer   △─◯ retained dye molecule with developer

Fig. 3   DEVELOPMENT PROCESS

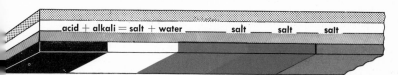

acid + alkali = salt + water _____ salt ____ salt ____ salt

Fig. 4   FINALLY DEVELOPED POSITIVE

175

AUTOMATIC EXPOSURE CONTROL

The object of automatic exposure control is to make things easier for the amateur photographer who has no relish for, or interest in, the technicalities of working a camera. He is thus spared the trouble of determining the correct exposure and of selecting and setting the aperture (f-number) and shutter speed.

The various systems are all derived from one simple principle: the basis is a built-in exposure meter which detects the brightness of the subject to be photographed. In many 8 mm cine cameras the light received by the meter is transformed into a force which is directly applied to the adjustment of the lightly constructed moving diaphragm. However, in larger standard-size cameras an auxiliary force is needed for adjusting the iris diaphragm and shutter speed. This force is provided either by the user of the camera when he presses the release button, or it is stored up in a spring which is wound beforehand.

When the camera is pointed at the subject, the needle of the measuring device of the exposure meter inside the camera will be deflected a greater or less amount, depending on the brightness. When the release button is actuated, the needle is first arrested by a stirrup bar which presses against it and thereby holds it immovable. This position of the needle determines the exposure value. Then a scanner arm is moved until it touches the arrested needle. At the other end of the scanner are the devices which set the exposure time and the aperture.

The three most frequently encountered methods of automatic exposure control will now be further explained with reference to the somewhat simplified accompanying diagrams:

1. Diaphragm control: To adapt the lens to the brightness conditions, only the aperture is varied. Before the exposure, the lens is set to its maximum aperture. On release, the diaphragm ring is rotated until the toothed stop ratchet engages with a pawl mounted on the scanner. This will occur at an earlier or later instant, depending on the position of the exposure meter needle detected by the scanner arm, and the size of the aperture will accordingly be larger or smaller (alternatively, the scanner may directly control the diaphragm).

The exposure time is always the same. When the user loads his camera with a certain type of film and sets the camera to the film speed (sensitivity of the film), he really selects the shutter speed appropriate to that film. For example, a film of 18 DIN will require an exposure time of $\frac{1}{125}$ sec., while a 15 DIN film, which is only about half as sensitive, will require $\frac{1}{60}$ sec. The exposure time is accordingly adjusted automatically over the aperture range from, say, $f/2.8$ to $f/22$. If a more sensitive film is used, it does not enable photographs to be taken under poorer lighting conditions, but it does enable the exposure time to be reduced (e.g., to $\frac{1}{500}$ sec. for a 24 DIN film), which is essential for photographing fast-moving objects, as in the case of sports events.

2. Programme control of diaphragm and shutter speed: The exposure meter measures the brightness and its needle position is scanned as already described. In this system, however, a so-called programme ring is rotated, which effects continuous adjustment of the shutter speed and the aperture through the agency of control cams and rods; for example:

$$2.8 \quad 2.8 \to 4 \quad 5.6 \quad 5.6 \to 8 \quad 8 \to 11 \quad 11 \to 16 \to 22$$
$$\frac{1}{30} \to \frac{1}{60} \quad \frac{1}{60} \quad \frac{1}{60} \to \frac{1}{125} \quad \frac{1}{125} \to \frac{1}{250} \quad \frac{1}{250} \to \frac{1}{500} \quad \frac{1}{500} \quad \frac{1}{500}$$

This range of values shows that first the shutter speed is increased (i.e., the exposure time is shortened) as a precaution against blurring of the picture as a result of shaking the camera. Then, when the lens has been stopped down to give better depth of field (see page 178)—at about $f/8$, say—the exposure times are further shortened for photographing fast-moving objects. The film speed has already been taken into account in scanning the exposure meter needle, the meter having first (at the time of loading the camera with that particular film) been appropriately pre-set to that film speed.

3. Exposure time pre-selection and diaphragm control: With this system the user of the camera can choose the exposure time and the aperture for himself. The exposure time ring is coupled to the DIN (or ASA film speed) ring, so that any alteration to the shutter adjustment will automatically also adjust the exposure meter mechanism. The exposure meter needle gives readings on a scale of aperture settings (f-numbers) seen in the viewfinder. By altering the exposure time, it is also possible to pre-select the aperture, which constantly adjusts itself to the light conditions.

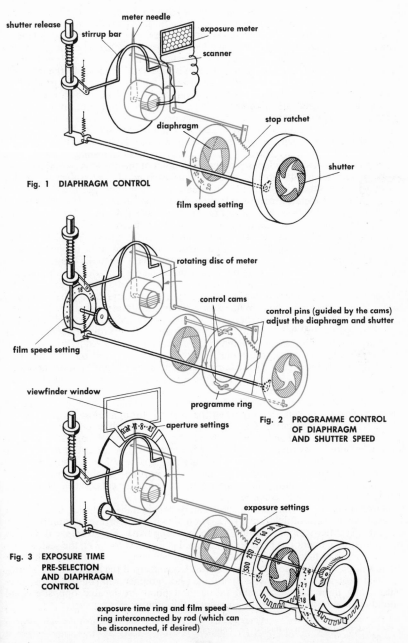

shutter release

stirrup bar

meter needle

exposure meter

scanner

stop ratchet

diaphragm

shutter

Fig. 1 DIAPHRAGM CONTROL

film speed setting

rotating disc of meter

control cams

control pins (guided by the cams)
adjust the diaphragm and shutter

film speed setting

viewfinder window

aperture settings

programme ring

**Fig. 2 PROGRAMME CONTROL
OF DIAPHRAGM
AND SHUTTER SPEED**

exposure settings

**Fig. 3 EXPOSURE TIME
PRE-SELECTION
AND DIAPHRAGM
CONTROL**

exposure time ring and film speed
ring interconnected by rod (which can
be disconnected, if desired)

177

DEPTH OF FIELD (DEPTH OF FOCUS)

By depth of field (or depth of focus) in photography is understood the range of distances within which the subject must be located in relation to the camera in order to produce a reasonably sharply focused image.

According to the well-known formula for lenses $\dfrac{1}{g} + \dfrac{1}{b} = \dfrac{1}{f}$

(see page 136), only one object plane (G_e) is sharply focused in the image plane (B_e) (Fig. 1). Objects which are farther away from the lens than the distance G_e have a larger image distance so that the image-forming rays of light converge at a plane B_n behind the image plane B_e to which the lens has been focussed. The image actually formed on B_e (i.e., on the film) will therefore not be in focus but will, instead, be somewhat blurred. Similarly, the image of an object which is closer to the lens than the distance G_e will have a shorter image distance and at a plane B_w in front of the plane B_e. The image actually formed on B_e will therefore likewise be blurred.

In reality, however, there is some latitude. The sharpness of vision of the human eye has its limitations, and some lack of sharpness in the image can be tolerated without being objectionably noticeable as blurring of the picture. Just how much lack of sharpness is acceptable will depend on how much the picture is to be enlarged and on how much importance the observer attaches to distinguishing minute details in the picture. In a sharply focused image each point of the object is reproduced as a point in the image. If the image is out of focus, each point is reproduced as a tiny circle of finite diameter in the image. For amateur photographic purposes a diameter of $\frac{1}{20}$ mm is considered a permissible limit for this so-called "circle of confusion" for 6 cm × 6 cm (pictures and $\frac{1}{30}$ mm for miniature size (24 mm × 36 mm).

The size of the circle of confusion depends on three factors:

1. The distance: The farther a point is located away from the object plane (G_e) on which the camera has been focused, the farther will its image be outside the corresponding image plane (B_e) (Fig. 2). The closer the object* is to the lens, the greater will its image distance vary. For this reason the available depth of field beyond the focused distance is always greater than that in front of the focused distance; for example, when the camera is focused on an object 20 m away, the depth of field may range from 10 m to infinity. With close-ups the depth of field diminishes considerably and may be no more than a few centimetres or indeed a few millimetres.

2. The aperture: When the camera is stopped down (i.e., the diaphragm is closed), the cone of light rays is narrowed and the circle of confusion is reduced in diameter. In Fig. 2 the reproduction of the points III and IV was too blurred, but after the aperture has been reduced (Fig. 3), the corresponding circles of confusion are no larger than those of I' and II' previously. (The circles of confusion associated with I' and II' have similarly been reduced).

3. The focal length (Figs. 4a and 4b; cf. page 136): As already stated, the image distance varies very considerably when the object is brought close to the lens. An object which is at a distance of, say, 5 m from the camera will be practically located at infinity for a wide-angle lens with a focal length of 35 mm (cf. page 154), whereas for a telephoto lens with a focal length of 500 mm it will be almost in the close-up range. Hence wide-angle lenses and lenses of short focal length have a greater depth of field. Of course, this advantage is cancelled if, in order to obtain the same size of image, the picture subsequently has to be considerably enlarged or the camera has to be brought closer to the subject.

Depth-of-field tables for camera lenses can be based on these considerations. Most lenses have a depth-of-field scale (Fig. 5) on which the apertures (f-numbers) are indicated symmetrically in relation to the focussing mark. For example, if the lens of a miniature camera has been set to $f/11$ and is focussed to 3.3 m, the scale shows that the depth of field extends from 2.2 to 6.8 m, meaning that anything within this range will be within reasonably sharp focus. Conversely, if the subject to be photographed is of some considerable depth, the photographer will rotate the distance-setting ring until the nearest and the farthest point are located opposite equal f-numbers, and he will then set the aperture to this number.

* The term "object" is used in optics generally; more particularly in photography the term "subject" is used to denote the person or thing to be photographed.

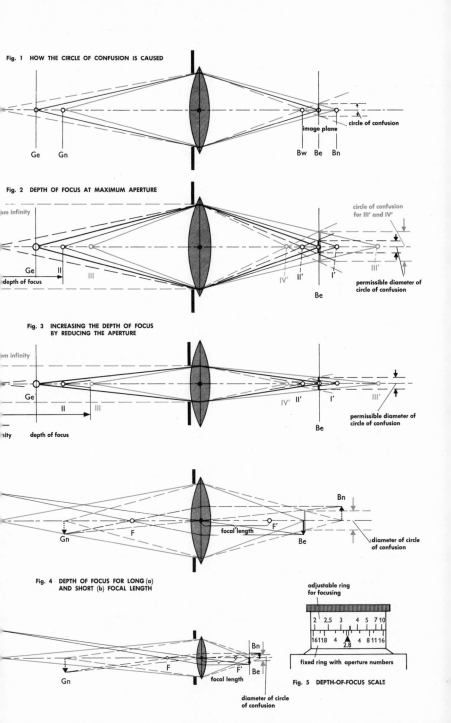

Fig. 1 HOW THE CIRCLE OF CONFUSION IS CAUSED

circle of confusion

image plane

Ge   Gn

Bw Be Bn

Fig. 2 DEPTH OF FOCUS AT MAXIMUM APERTURE

from infinity

circle of confusion
for III' and IV'

Ge   II

III

IV' II' I'

III'

depth of focus

permissible diameter of
circle of confusion

Be

Fig. 3 INCREASING THE DEPTH OF FOCUS
BY REDUCING THE APERTURE

from infinity

Ge

II   III

IV' II' I'

III'

permissible diameter of
circle of confusion

infinity   depth of focus

Be

Bn

Gn   F   focal length   F'

Be

diameter of circle
of confusion

Fig. 4 DEPTH OF FOCUS FOR LONG (a)
AND SHORT (b) FOCAL LENGTH

adjustable ring
for focusing

Bn

Gn   F   focal length   F' Be

2 2,5 3   4 5 7 10
16 11 8   4   ▲   8 11 16
              2,8

fixed ring with aperture numbers

diameter of circle
of confusion

Fig. 5 DEPTH-OF-FOCUS SCALE

179

EXPOSURE METER

In photography, exposure meters are used for determining the correct exposure time for a pre-selected aperture (f-number) and a given film speed. Besides optical exposure meters, electric exposure meters are now predominantly used. The light reflected from the subject into the meter is converted into a feeble electric current by means of a photo-electric cell (cf. page 102). This current is measured by the deflection of a needle or pointer, the deflection being larger or smaller according to the brightness of the subject. The precise exposure time (for the given film speed and aperture setting) is indicated on an appropriate scale.

The two principal parts of an electric exposure meter are the photo-electric cell and the measuring device. A device for admitting the light and a contrivance for obtaining the required readings are additional features. The light which enters through a honeycomb lens and a cellular grid strikes the photo-electric cell (the object of the lens and grid is to confine the angle of entry of the light approximately to the angular field of a normal camera lens). The photo-electric cell consists of an iron plate provided with a thin coating of selenium, which in turn is covered with a coating of platinum of such extreme thinness (about $\frac{1}{100000}$ mm) as to be transparent to light. When light strikes the selenium, electrons are released in the latter. These enter the platinum coating and, as a result, an electric current—a very feeble one, it is true—will flow in a circuit connecting the platinum and the iron plate. The light striking the selenium thus produces an electric current; this current is stronger in proportion as the light intensity (i.e., the brightness of the subject) is greater, and vice versa. If a small current measuring instrument is included in the circuit, the pointer of this instrument will provide an indication of the strength of the current. The appropriate exposure times for various aperture settings can then be read from a special scale which is adjustable to the deflection of the pointer. Pre-adjustment to the appropriate film speed (sensitivity of the film) is provided.

Fig. 2 shows the internal parts of a well known type of exposure meter. The adjusting knob is turned until the curved line marked on the roller rotated by this knob coincides with the intersection of the pointer with the reference line. At the same time, bevel gears connected to the adjusting knob cause a flexible band, on which the exposure times and exposure values are marked, to move in relation to the fixed scale of f-numbers. The roller with the curve is adjustable to suit the particular speed (sensitivity) of the film used.

In other exposure meters the arrangement of the scales of exposure times and f-numbers may be rather different, though the general principle is the same as that described.

Instead of selenium photo-electric cells, so-called photo-resistances are nowadays used in some exposure meters (Fig. 4). A photo-resistance does not convert light into electrical energy but undergoes a change in electrical resistance when light strikes it. The resistance to the passage of current diminishes with increasing light intensity, so that the current—which has to be provided by an auxiliary source such as a small battery—becomes stronger. Meters of this type can be made sufficiently sensitive to respond to very weak light (e.g., moonlight).

The exposure meter is mostly used by pointing it at the subject to be photographed (reflected light measurement). Alternatively, the light that actually illuminates the subject may be measured. This includes the light reflected from adjacent objects. For this reason a so-called incident light attachment or a light diffuser is used, enabling light to be directed into the meter over a much wider angle of entry (Fig. 4).

With regard to built-in exposure meters for automatic exposure control, see page 176.

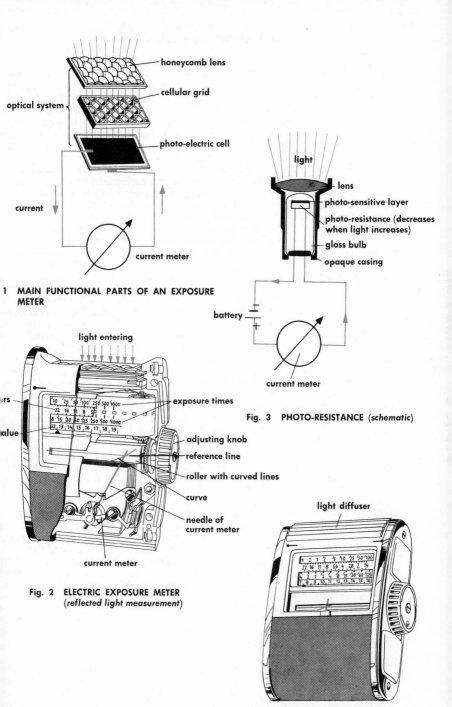

honeycomb lens

cellular grid

optical system

photo-electric cell

current

current meter

1 MAIN FUNCTIONAL PARTS OF AN EXPOSURE METER

light

lens

photo-sensitive layer

photo-resistance (decreases when light increases)

glass bulb

opaque casing

battery

current meter

Fig. 3 PHOTO-RESISTANCE (*schematic*)

light entering

rs

exposure times

alue

adjusting knob

reference line

roller with curved lines

curve

needle of current meter

current meter

Fig. 2 ELECTRIC EXPOSURE METER
(*reflected light measurement*)

light diffuser

Fig. 4 ELECTRIC EXPOSURE METER
(*incident light measurement*)

181

FLASH BULBS AND FLASH GUNS

Flash bulbs are required to produce the greatest possible light flux (measured in lumens) in the fraction of a second during which the shutter of the camera is open. The total quantity of light emitted by a bulb during this period is measured in lumen-seconds. The light is produced by the combustion of a coil of aluminium-magnesium wire or zirconium wire with oxygen. An electric current impulse from the flash contact in the camera causes a tungsten filament to glow and ignite small pellets of a substance similar in composition to the head of a match, which in turn ignite the metal wire coil. The oxygen filling in the bulb has a pressure of less than 1 atm., which ensures that the glass bulb will not shatter as a result of the increase in pressure due to the explosion-like combustion process. As a further precaution the bulb is coated internally and externally with a transparent lacquer which prevents glass splinters from flying about. For colour photography there are flashbulbs with a blue-tinted lacquer which ensures that the light emitted has a spectrum composition more or less similar to that of daylight. Inside the bulb is an indicator bead of a blue cobalt salt which turns pink as the result of penetration of atmospheric moisture into the bulb if the latter should become defective by developing a leak either during manufacture or during subsequent handling.

The light-time curves (Fig. 2) give information on the light efficiency and the application purpose of flashbulbs. Of especial importance to synchronisation with the camera shutter is the peak value., i.e., the length of time between the closing of the contact and the maximum light intensity. For ordinary type M flashbulbs it is 18 milliseconds. Most diaphragm shutters have "X synchronisation": contact is made as soon as the shutter is fully open (Fig. 3a). In order that the entire "firing" process of the flashbulb is completed while the camera lens is open, the shutter speed must be at least 30 milliseconds (about $\frac{1}{30}$ sec.). For use with faster shutter speeds many cameras are additionally equipped with a so-called "M" contact, which comes into operation 16 milliseconds before the lens is fully open, so that the shutter opens only a short time before the peak value is reached and only that part of the firing process which corresponds to maximum flash intensity is utilised (Fig. 3b). For comparison, the light-time curve for an electronic flash (see page 184) is also shown in the two diagrams: with "X" synchronisation it is possible to use diaphragm shutters up to $\frac{1}{500}$ sec.; in that case, if the contact is inadvertently set to "M", no light from the flashbulb will reach the film.

With focal-plane shutters the shutter action takes about $\frac{1}{20}$ to $\frac{1}{60}$ sec. to accomplish and shorter exposures can be obtained only by narrowing the slit (see page 160). For this reason the flashbulb employed should have a wider firing curve, so as to ensure that the light intensity on the film at the moving slit is constant over the entire width of the picture.

If the exposure time is longer than the firing time of the flashbulb, the exposure will depend solely on the aperture setting. The aperture (f-number) is calculated from the "guide number" for the type of film used, the formula being: f-number = guide number divided by distance (in metres). To understand the significance of the guide number it must be borne in mind that the intensity of illumination decreases in proportion to the square of the distance from the light source and that the speed (transmitting power) of a lens likewise decreases with the square of the f-number. The two quantities are linked by the guide number whose square is proportional to the quantity of light. For instance, the intensity of illumination at a distance of 5 m is only a quarter of that at 2.5 m. The transmitting power of the lens at $f/4$ is four times as high as that at $f/8$. This means that $f/4$ at 5 m gives the same exposure as $f/8$ at 2.5 m. Both settings can be used with a flash having a guide number of 20. Other possible settings in this case are $f/2.8$ at 7 m or $f/5.6$ at 3.5 m.

Ignition used to be effected by directly short-circuiting the battery through the flashbulb (Fig. 4a). Nowadays small dry batteries, usually of 22.5 volts, are used which charge a condenser when the flashbulb is inserted (Fig. 4b); because of the high resistance in the charging circuit, this current remains so feeble that it does not ignite the bulb. When the shutter is released, the contact in the camera connects the condenser directly to the bulb, and the sudden discharge causes ignition of the latter.

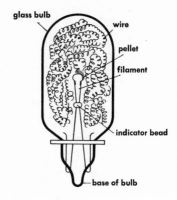

glass bulb
wire
pellet
filament
indicator bead
base of bulb

Fig. 1 FLASHBULB

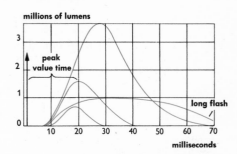

millions of lumens

peak
value time

long flash

milliseconds

Fig. 2 LIGHT-TIME CURVES OF FLASHBULBS

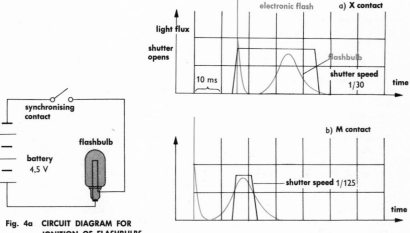

electronic flash
a) X contact

light flux

shutter
opens

flashbulb

10 ms

shutter speed
1/30

time

b) M contact

shutter speed 1/125

time

Fig. 3 FLASH SYNCRONISATION WITH
DIAPHRAGM SHUTTER

synchronising
contact

flashbulb

battery
4,5 V

Fig. 4a CIRCUIT DIAGRAM FOR
IGNITION OF FLASHBULBS
DIRECT FROM THE BATTERY

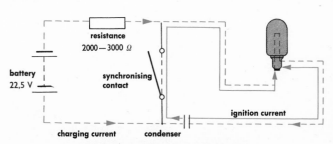

resistance
2000 — 3000 Ω

battery
22,5 V

synchronising
contact

ignition current

charging current   condenser

Fig. 4b CIRCUIT DIAGRAM FOR IGNITION OF
FLASHBULBS THROUGH A CONDENSER

ELECTRONIC FLASH

The "electronic flash" used in modern flashlight photography produces a high-intensity source of light of very short duration which has much in common with a flash of lighting. In a thunderstorm, lightning is caused when a cloud becomes electrically charged, for example, in relation to the earth; the cloud and the earth can be conceived as the plates of a giant condenser. If the voltage becomes too high, a flash-over occurs: the gas of the atmosphere becomes temporarily conductive to electricity, and a tremendous surge of current occurs which lasts a very short time. In the electronic flash this effect is simulated by discharging a condenser through a gaseous atmosphere. The apparatus must therefore generate the requisite high voltage and enable the flash to be produced at the desired instant (Fig. 1). Older types of apparatus operated at some thousands of volts, but the more recent ones usually operate at 500 volts. Portable sources of electric current (dry batteries or accumulators), however, supply direct current at very low voltages. Only an alternating current can be stepped up to a higher voltage by means of a transformer. The direct must therefore first be converted into an alternating current. This is done either by means of a so-called "chopper" which changes the polarity (i.e., the direction of flow) of the current about 200 times per second by mechanical action or by means of a transistor circuit which achieves a similar effect (in modern equipment the latter method is almost exclusively employed). The alternating current thus obtained is raised to the required high voltage by means of a transformer (see page 92). A rectifier then converts it back into direct current.

This high-voltage direct current charges a condenser whose two poles are connected to the electrodes of the flash tube. The flash tube and ignition device are in the flash holder. Also, there are modern very small electronic flash sets in which the generator equipment and the reflector are combined into a single unit. The flash tube is filled with an inert gas, usually xenon, which does not conduct electricity. The final voltage at the condenser, and therefore at the electrodes, is attained after a charging time of about 3 to 15 sec. This voltage is not so high, however, that it can by itself initiate a discharge through the flash tube. When the camera shutter is released, the synchronising contact of the shutter causes a small ignition condenser to discharge through one winding of the ignition coil. As a result of this, a high voltage (about 10,000 volts) is induced at that instant in the other winding. This high voltage impulse, which is applied between the ignition electrode and the negative electrode of the flash tube, ionises the inert gas and makes it conductive to electricity, so that the condenser can discharge itself through the tube. During a period of about $\frac{1}{1000}$ sec. the stored-up electrical energy flows through the flash tube as a high-intensity current (of about 100 amps and more), during which time it causes the gas to glow brightly.

The light emitted by the electronic flash has approximately the same spectrum composition as daylight. For colour photography the usual daylight colour film should accordingly be used.

For synchronisation with the shutter of the camera and for calculating the aperture setting from the "guide number", see page 182.

Fig. 1 ELECTRONIC FLASH (*schematic*)

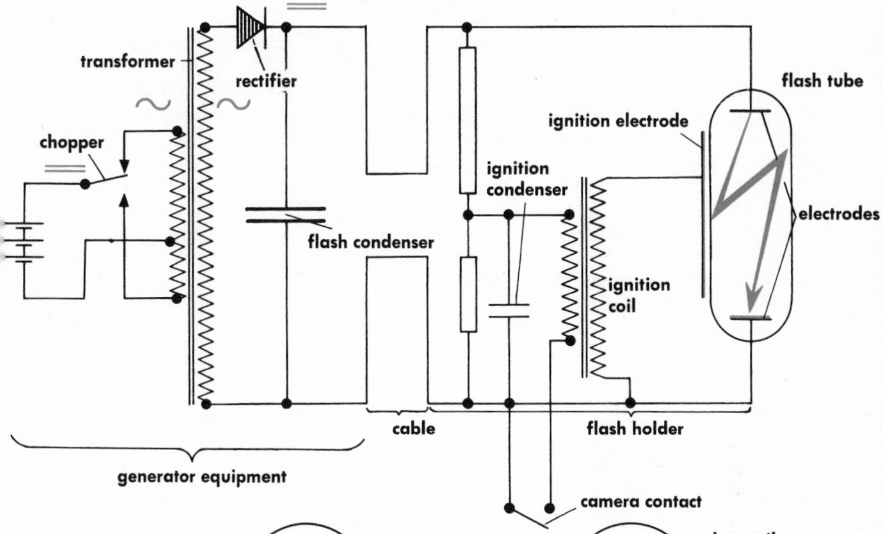

transformer
rectifier
flash tube
ignition electrode
chopper
ignition condenser
electrodes
flash condenser
ignition coil
cable
flash holder
generator equipment
camera contact

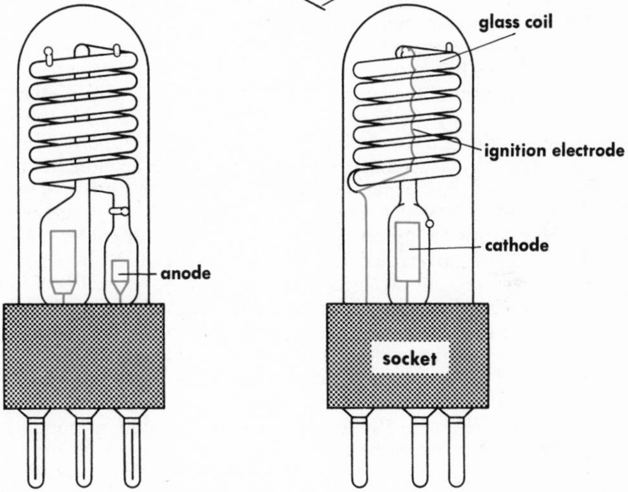

glass coil
ignition electrode
cathode
anode
2 HIGH-VOLTAGE FLASH TUBE
socket

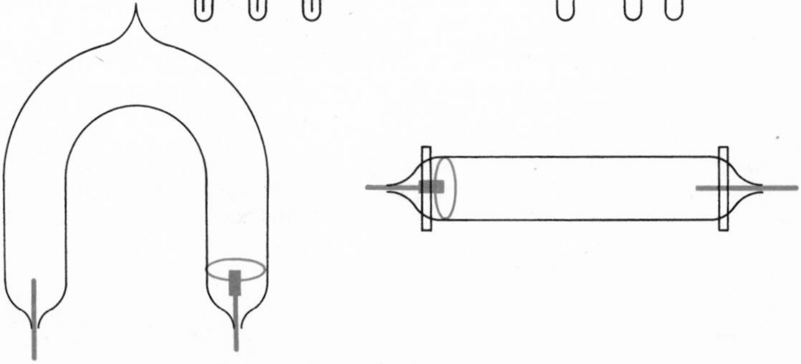

Fig. 3 FLASH TUBES USED IN MODERN AMATEUR EQUIPMENT
(*drawn to a much larger scale than Fig. 2*)

185

RANGEFINDER

When subjects close to the camera are photographed with large apertures (low f-numbers), the depth of field (see page 178) is very small. A mere rough estimate of the distance is generally too inaccurate, and for this reason high-class cameras are equipped with built-in rangefinders. The principle of the rangefinder is rather like that of binocular vision: when an observer looks at a very distant object, his two eyes look in parallel directions; if the object comes nearer, the eyes turn inwards, and they do this more and more in proportion as the distance to the object decreases. The angle between the lines of sight is therefore a measure for the distance (Fig. 1).

Similarly, the rangefinder has two "eyes" or sight openings: one of these is the normal viewfinder, whose optical axis is accurately parallel to that of the camera lens; the other is located at the other end of the "base" and produces a second image (the rangefinder image). The rays of light which form the rangefinder image are reflected by a mirror to the viewfinder, where it is superimposed upon the viewfinder image by means of a semi-transparent mirror (Fig. 2a). In the eyepiece of the viewfinder the photographer thus sees two images, one over the other. This is known as coincident image (Fig. 2b). If the two rays entering the viewfinder and the second "eye" of the rangefinder are parallel (i.e., if they both come from a very distant object), the two superimposed images will accurately coincide and thus appear as one image. An object close to the camera will, however, produce two images which are displaced in relation to each other. To bring them into exact coincidence, the second ray will have to be deflected through a certain angle until it, too, passes through the object. The magnitude of this angle is a measure of the distance to the object in question. The angular rotation of the component which produces this deflection can therefore be coupled to a distance scale (in metres or feet) or directly to the focusing mechanism of the lens. The deflection may be produced by means of a swivelling mirror (Fig. 2a). Greater precision is attainable with the swivelling wedge type rangefinder (Fig. 3) because here the deflecting component has to be rotated through a substantially larger angle to produce a given deflection. In this device two cylindrical lenses, one of which rotates within the other, form a prism of variable refractive power. In Fig. 3 the base with the two fixed mirrors consists of a glass rod for greater strength. In other forms of construction the pair of cylindrical lenses (or sometimes only one swivelling cylindrical lens) is mounted between the mirrors. In the rotating wedge rangefinder (Fig. 4) two circular wedges can be rotated 180° in relation to each other in both directions. In one extreme position they together form a double wedge; in the intermediate position they form a plano parallel plate; and in the other extreme position they form a double wedge which deflects light in the opposite direction. Because of its complicated mechanism, this type has now largely been superseded by the simpler lever-action rangefinders. For the same reason the so-called split-image rangefinder (Fig. 5a) has now largely disappeared, although it is a very convenient one to use because of the clear image it produces in the rangefinder. In this type the image is split into a top and bottom half which are displaced in relation to each other and which have to be brought into coincidence with each other (Fig. 5b).

Nearly all mirror-reflex cameras are now equipped with a focusing aid which, because of its similar action, is often referred to as a "split-image rangefinder". This device comprises two clear glass wedges which are so cemented in position that their point of intersection is accurately located in the plane of the focusing screen. If the image has been sharply focused on the screen, the wedges have practically no effect; the farther the image is away from this plane, the more the two parts of the image are displaced in relation to each other as a result of the deflecting action of the wedges.

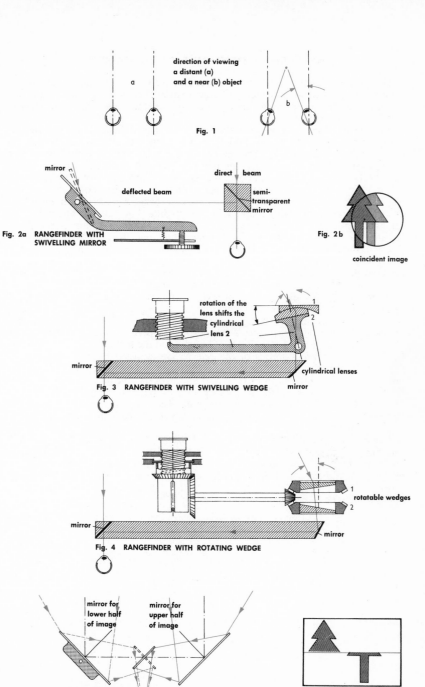

direction of viewing
a distant (a)
and a near (b) object

a

b

Fig. 1

mirror

deflected beam

direct beam

semi-transparent mirror

Fig. 2a RANGEFINDER WITH SWIVELLING MIRROR

Fig. 2b

coincident image

rotation of the lens shifts the cylindrical lens 2

mirror

cylindrical lenses

mirror

Fig. 3 RANGEFINDER WITH SWIVELLING WEDGE

rotatable wedges

mirror

mirror

Fig. 4 RANGEFINDER WITH ROTATING WEDGE

mirror for lower half of image

mirror for upper half of image

Fig. 5a SPLIT-IMAGE RANGEFINDER

Fig. 5b

split image

187

CINE CAMERA (MOTION PICTURE CAMERA)

There is no difference in principle between an ordinary "still" camera and a cine camera, except that the latter takes a large number of pictures in rapid succession, so that when these are appropriately projected on the screen, an impression of continuous motion is produced.

Fig. 1 shows how the film is run through the camera. The feed spool carries the unexposed film, which is unwound from this spool by the sprocket wheel and moved along to the film gate. The sprocket is driven by a small electric motor or a spring motor. Guide plates keep the film engaged with the sprocket. A pressure plate keeps the film perfectly flat as it moves past the film gate. After exposure, the film is advanced a distance corresponding to one image by the feeding claw. As this movement occurs intermittently, whereas the sprocket rotates continuously, the film must comprise relieving loops. While the feeding claw pulls the film along, the rotary disc shutter covers the film gate and then exposes it for a certain length of time (about $\frac{1}{32}$ to $\frac{1}{50}$ sec.). The feeding claw and the shutter must therefore be interadjusted.

The feeding claw is secured at its pivot; its lever is movable (Fig. 2). The hook engages with the perforation of the film and moves the latter forward a certain distance, as the other end of the claw performs an eccentric motion. In narrow-gauge cine cameras the film is held stationary for as long a time as is necessary for the exposure. The rotary disc shutter therefore performs the function of covering the film—i.e., preventing light entering the camera—during the film advance movement. It consists of a circular disc (Fig. 3) with cut-out sectors. With 16 exposures per second a sector of 180° corresponds to an exposure speed of $\frac{1}{32}$ sec. Fig. 4 shows the interrelated operations of covering the film gate and the film advance movement.

The various running speeds of the camera are adjusted by means of a small governor (Fig. 5). Small centrifugal weights attached to a plate are slidably mounted on a shaft. In the neutral position (Fig. 5a) a spring pushes the plate to the right. Now if the shaft rotates (Fig. 5b) the weights are flung outwards by centrifugal action and pull the plate to the left until it strikes a stop. The position of this stop therefore determines the speed of rotation of the shaft, which will be higher according as the stop is farther to the left.

Slow-motion and time-lapse effects are determined by the ratio of the speed of shooting the film to the speed of projecting it. If the film is run through the camera at a lower speed (i.e., a lower footage per second) than through the projector, the movements of the subject which has been filmed will be seen speeded up. Conversely, slow-motion is obtained by running the film through the camera at a higher speed than through the projector.

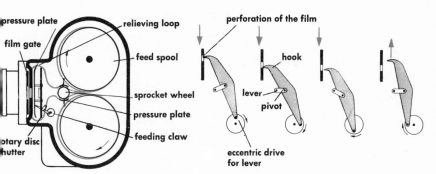

Fig. 1   SCHEMATIC DIAGRAM OF A CINE CAMERA

pressure plate
film gate
relieving loop
feed spool
sprocket wheel
pressure plate
feeding claw
rotary disc shutter

Fig. 2   HOW THE FEEDING CLAW WORKS

perforation of the film
hook
lever
pivot
eccentric drive for lever

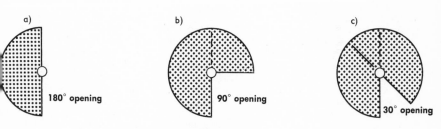

a) 180° opening

b) 90° opening

c) 30° opening

Fig. 3   ROTARY DISC SHUTTER

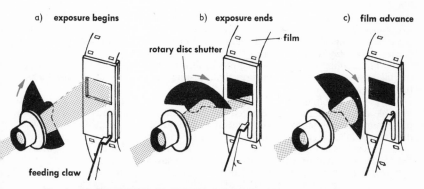

a)   exposure begins

b)   exposure ends

film

rotary disc shutter

c)   film advance

feeding claw

Fig. 4   CO-ORDINATION OF SHUTTER OPERATION AND FILM ADVANCE

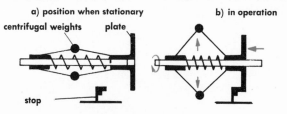

a) position when stationary

centrifugal weights   plate

b) in operation

stop

Fig. 5   SPEED GOVERNOR

CINE PROJECTOR

The cine projector (movie projector) operates on the same principle as the cine camera (see page 188). But whereas in the camera the light rays from the subject are concentrated on the film by the lens, in the projector the rays from a source of light pass through the film image and are projected by the lens on to a screen.

The construction of a cine projector is shown schematically in Fig. 1. Each image on the film is projected on to the screen for a short time, and the film then moves on so as to bring the next image into position for projection. During this movement the film gate of the projector is obscured. To ensure that there is always sufficient slack in the film—because the feed sprocket rotates at a constant rate, whereas the feeding mechanism operates intermittently—a loop of film must be formed between the sprocket and the film gate.

The feeding mechanism which moves the film along may be in the form of a claw (Fig. 2). The lower end of the claw is eccentrically mounted on a disc which rotates at a uniform speed. In addition, the claw is pivoted at the centre. As a result, the head performs the motion indicated in Fig. 2: the points of the claw engage with the perforations in the film and, with each movement, pull it down a distance corresponding exactly to one image. During the time when the image is being projected, the film is stationary and the head of the feeding claw returns to its initial position. A different type of feeding mechanism embodies a so-called maltese cross (Fig. 3). This device is mounted just above the lower film loop and is driven by a constantly rotating disc provided with an eccentric pin. The maltese cross in turn drives a sprocket whose teeth engage with the perforations of the film. Fig. 3a shows the cross in the stationary position. The eccentric pin then engages with the slot in the cross and rotates it with a jerking movement which is imparted to the sprocket (Fig. 3b).

During the time when the film is being moved along, the film gate must be obscured. This is done by the rotary disc shutter, whose mode of functioning is illustrated in Fig. 4. As a result of the intermittent covering and uncovering of the film by this revolving shutter, a flicker effect is produced on the screen. This effect is more pronounced according as the projector light beam is obscured less frequently. To reduce flicker, the image which is being projected is also obscured for part of the time that it is in position at the film gate. For this purpose a three-blade shutter is used, especially with the smaller film sizes.

The film coming from the feeding mechanism forms a loop and then passes over the take-up sprocket, which ensures that, despite the pull exerted by the take-up reel, the lower film loop always remains the same size.

The path of the light rays in the projector is shown in Figs. 1 and 5. The largest possible amount of the light emitted by the projector lamp must be utilised for projection. The condenser lens concentrates the light which is emitted in the forward direction, while the collecting mirror behind the lamp reflects the rearward emitted light. This concave mirror is so mounted that the filament of the lamp is located at the centre of curvature of the mirror. By this means uniform illumination of the film image is obtained. Projector lenses are usually of fairly simple construction (large focal length, small angular field). Projectors are driven by electric motors. A fan or blower for cooling the lamp and film guide equipment is usually mounted on the drive shaft of the motor.

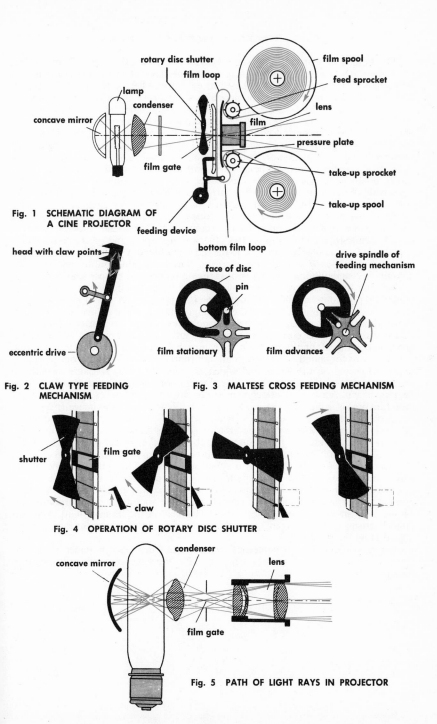

rotary disc shutter
film loop
lamp
condenser
concave mirror
film spool
feed sprocket
lens
film
pressure plate
film gate
take-up sprocket
take-up spool

Fig. 1 SCHEMATIC DIAGRAM OF A CINE PROJECTOR

feeding device
bottom film loop

head with claw points
face of disc
pin
drive spindle of feeding mechanism
eccentric drive
film stationary
film advances

Fig. 2 CLAW TYPE FEEDING MECHANISM

Fig. 3 MALTESE CROSS FEEDING MECHANISM

shutter
film gate
claw

Fig. 4 OPERATION OF ROTARY DISC SHUTTER

concave mirror
condenser
lens
film gate

Fig. 5 PATH OF LIGHT RAYS IN PROJECTOR

191

The filming and projection system described in this article arose from the fact that the "aspect ratio" (width-to-height ratio of the picture) of the conventional cinema does not correspond at all well to the normal field of vision of the human eye. In addition, it was felt to be necessary to improve the quality of the sound, especially with regard to its directional effect (stereophonic sound).

CinemaScope is the proprietary name of a filming and projection system which, by means of special optical equipment, enables cinematographic pictures of great width to be reproduced on a wide screen. The system operates with single-track optical sound reproduction or, better, with multi-channel magnetic sound reproduction in which the source of the sound (loudspeakers installed behind the screen) corresponds to the visual image. CinemaScope film and standard film are both 35 mm wide. When sound film was first introduced in cinematography the frame lines (the strips between the successive frames or pictures on the film) had been substantially widened in order to retain the same aspect ratio of the picture, which had had to be made narrower in order to accommodate the sound track on the film. The CinemaScope picture utilises this otherwise lost space and reverts to the image height that was formerly employed in the old silent film days. The four sound tracks of the CinemaScope system with magnetic sound reproduction are necessary for obtaining "stereophonic" sound with lifelike qualities and proper spatial relationships. The sound is recorded on magnetic tape by three microphones installed in different positions, so that the sounds picked up by each microphone differ in intensity and timing (because of the varying distance to the source of the sound) from those picked up by the other microphones. When the film is subsequently shown, the sound is correspondingly reproduced by three sets of loudspeakers installed on the left and right and at the centre, behind the screen. The fourth sound track is used for sound effects which are not represented as coming from the actual scene projected on the screen and which are reproduced by speakers installed in various parts of the auditorium. The camera for taking CinemaScope films is equipped with an optical attachment called an anamorphotic system, which has the function of squeezing the image together sideways, i.e., the image is distorted by reducing the horizontal scale in relation to the vertical scale. When the film is projected, the process is reversed: the projector is fitted with an anamorphotic system which "stretches" the picture so as to obtain the correct proportions on the screen. Anamorphotic systems may be composed of lenses (Fig. 2), mirrors (Fig. 3) or prisms (Fig. 4). In Fig. 2 the two cylindrical lenses of the anamorphotic system are mounted in front of the projection lens and produce their optical effect by expanding the picture in the horizontal direction (expansion factor 2). An anamorphotic mirror system functions in much the same way as an anamorphotic lens system, but involves a certain vertical displacement of the beam of light. Anamorphotic prisms have the advantage that the magnification of the system can be varied by rotating the prisms.

For physiological and geometrical reasons the CinemaScope screen should be curved. This curvature is particularly essential if the screen is of the reflecting type (cf. page 194).

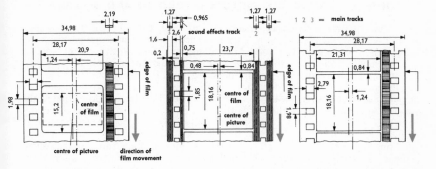

Fig. 1a DIMENSIONS OF STANDARD FILM (in mm)

Fig. 1b DIMENSIONS OF CINEMASCOPE FILM WITH FOUR MAGNETIC SOUND TRACKS

Fig. 1c DIMENSIONS OF CINEMASCOPE FILM WITH OPTICAL SOUND TRACK

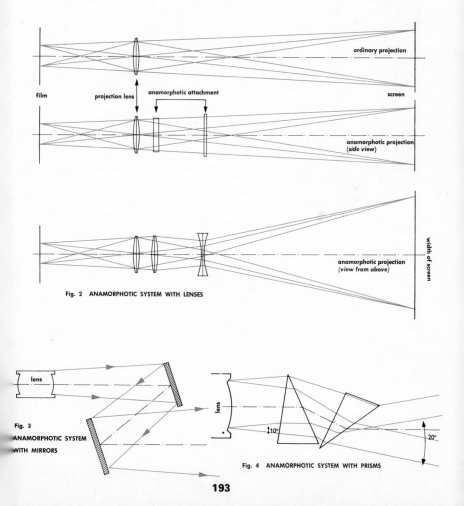

Fig. 2 ANAMORPHOTIC SYSTEM WITH LENSES

Fig. 3 ANAMORPHOTIC SYSTEM WITH MIRRORS

Fig. 4 ANAMORPHOTIC SYSTEM WITH PRISMS

WIDE SCREEN MOTION PICTURES: TODD-AO AND CINERAMA

Another modern wide-screen system is Todd-AO. Like the Cinerama system described below, the object is to give the audience a sense of personal participation in the action of the film. The Todd-AO system uses a film which is about twice as wide as standard film, i.e., about 70 mm (Figs. 1a and 1b). Because of the larger picture area, only a moderate amount of enlargement in projection is possible, and this makes for better picture definition on the screen. The sound is recorded on six magnetic sound tracks by means of six microphones. Five tracks correspond to the various directions of the scene, while the sixth track is used for sound effects (cf. page 192). The camera used for filming in Todd-AO is of special design, because of the wide film used and the effect to be achieved: wide-angle lenses are employed (shooting angles of up to 128°; cf. page 154). The most striking feature of the system is the greatly curved wide screen. The audience's sense of direct participation in the scenes shown is very largely attributable to this curvature of the screen. This is bound up with the physiological and psychological processes of visual perception.

Objects projected near, say, the extreme left-hand edge of a flat wide screen will appear considerably compressed in the lateral direction to an observer seated on the extreme right in the front part of the auditorium (Fig. 2a). This distortion is partly corrected by the considerable curvature of the screen. The same is true of the distortions due to the projection itself. The curvature of the screen also avoids or reduces the amount of accommodation to varying distances that the observer's eye has to perform when viewing the picture as a whole. If the screen were made of a white, diffusely reflecting material, the various parts of a curved screen would reflect light towards one another, resulting in a considerable loss of picture definition (Fig. 2b). This disadvantage can most be overcome by using a screen whose surface is provided with a large number of vertical ridges (formed of white plastic), as shown in cross-section in Fig. 2c: the light which strikes any particular point on such a screen is almost entirely reflected towards the audience.

As distinct from the Todd-AO system, which uses only a single camera and a single projector, the Cinerama system makes use of three cameras and three projectors for 35 mm film. The lenses of the triple camera cover a field of 146°, which corresponds approximately to the field of vision of the human eye. In the cinema the three separate but synchronised films are projected simultaneously on to a semicircular panoramic screen (Fig. 3). The sound system of Cinerama is similar to that of Todd-AO, i.e., six magnetic sound tracks comprising five main tracks and one effects track, except that the sound is reproduced by running a separate "blind" film, with sound recording only, through a special fourth projector.

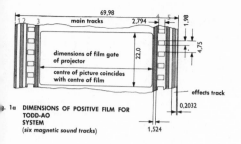

Fig. 1a DIMENSIONS OF POSITIVE FILM FOR TODD-AO SYSTEM
(six magnetic sound tracks)

main tracks

69,98

2,794

1,98

4,75

22,0

dimensions of film gate of projector

centre of picture coincides with centre of film

effects track

0,2032

1,524

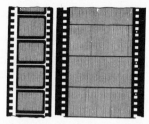

Fig. 1b STANDARD FILM COMPARED WITH TODD-AO COPY

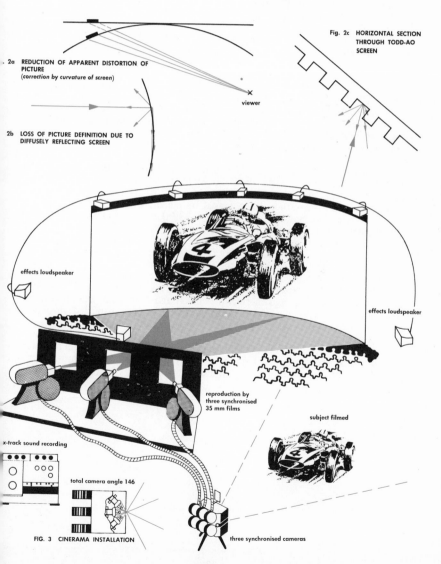

Fig. 2c HORIZONTAL SECTION THROUGH TODD-AO SCREEN

2a REDUCTION OF APPARENT DISTORTION OF PICTURE
(correction by curvature of screen)

2b LOSS OF PICTURE DEFINITION DUE TO DIFFUSELY REFLECTING SCREEN

viewer

effects loudspeaker

effects loudspeaker

reproduction by three synchronised 35 mm films

subject filmed

x-track sound recording

total camera angle 146

FIG. 3 CINERAMA INSTALLATION

three synchronised cameras

PROJECTORS: EPISCOPE AND DIASCOPE

The *episcope* is a projector for opaque flat pictures (paper prints, pages of books, etc.). Its mode of operation is shown schematically in Fig. 1. The efficiency (light yield) of the episcope, i.e., the ratio of the brightness of the image on the screen to the power output of the projection lamp, is relatively poor. This is due to the multiple reflections that some of the light has to undergo inside the apparatus. The filament of the lamp sends rays out in all directions. Only a small proportion of these rays directly impinges upon the picture to be projected. The larger proportion is directed on to the picture by reflectors. From each individual point of the picture rays are sent out in all directions, and only a fraction of these rays passes through the lens and is projected on to the screen via the reversing mirror. A large proportion of the rays is thrown back on to the picture by the reflectors. The light efficiency can be improved by skilful arrangement of the reflectors and by the use of wide-angle lenses of high light-transmitting power. The instrument illustrated in Fig. 2 is known as an "epidiascope"; it can alternatively be used for the projection of transparent slides.

The *diascope*, or slide projector, is intended for the projection of transparencies (diapositives, negatives). Its principal parts the light source with a concave collecting mirror (Fig. 3), the condenser and the projection lens. The source of light (usually an incandescent lamp with a coiled filament) emits light in all directions. The light which strikes the concave mirror is reflected and focused in the plane of the filament. The light emitted in the forward direction encounters the condenser, which in the larger projectors comprises two plano-convex lenses (double condenser). It collects the rays over a large angle and forms the image of the filament at a point located within the projection lens system. The condenser ensures uniformly bright illumination of the entire area of the slide. The light efficiency of a projector is higher according as the angle of the beam of light admitted by the condenser is larger. This angle can, for instance, be increased by placing the condenser closer to the lamp. The refractive power of the condenser will then have to be greater, since the distance from the lamp to the projection lens must remain the same. This requirement can be fulfilled by means of a meniscus lens which is interposed between the double condenser and the lamp (Fig. 5). The efficiency is thereby increased; the image of the lamp filament within the projection lens system is larger. However, because of the shorter distance between lamp and condenser, the amount of heat from the lamp that is absorbed by the condenser becomes greater. The condenser lenses consequently undergo thermal expansion and must be so mounted that this expansion can freely take place. Some of the heat is transmitted through the condenser lenses, however. To protect the slide, a plate of special heat-absorbing glass is installed inside the condenser. This plate itself becomes very hot, and for this reason it is often composed of a number of strips in order to prevent the internal thermal stresses becoming too high and fracturing the glass. Fig. 4 shows a section through the epidiascope functioning as a diascope.

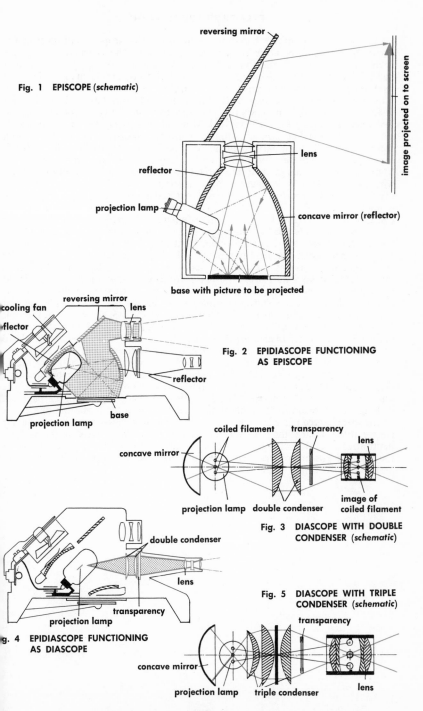

Fig. 1 EPISCOPE (*schematic*)

reversing mirror

lens

reflector

projection lamp

concave mirror (reflector)

image projected on to screen

base with picture to be projected

cooling fan

reversing mirror

lens

reflector

projection lamp

base

reflector

Fig. 2 EPIDIASCOPE FUNCTIONING AS EPISCOPE

coiled filament

transparency

lens

concave mirror

projection lamp   double condenser

image of coiled filament

Fig. 3 DIASCOPE WITH DOUBLE CONDENSER (*schematic*)

double condenser

lens

transparency

projection lamp

Fig. 4 EPIDIASCOPE FUNCTIONING AS DIASCOPE

Fig. 5 DIASCOPE WITH TRIPLE CONDENSER (*schematic*)

transparency

concave mirror

projection lamp   triple condenser

lens

197

ELECTROPHOTOGRAPHY

Ordinary photography is based on the light-sensitive properties of silver halides and more particularly silver bromide (see page 200). The image is developed b chemical processes performed in the liquid phase. Electrophotography, on the othe hand, is based on photo-electric and electrostatic effects, and the image is develope by a dry process. The light-sensitive layer in this case is formed by the surface of photo-semiconductor (cf. page 102). Such semiconductors have a very high dark resistance (up to 10^{14} ohm), whereas exposure to light greatly lowers the resistanc (by a factor ranging from 10^5 to 10^7). Materials possessing this property are, fo example, selenium (Se), cadmium sulphide (CdS), and zinc oxide (ZnO). Thin seleniun coatings applied to an earthed metal base have proved particularly suitable fo electrophotography. Sensitisation is achieved by spraying positively charged ion from a corona discharge on to the surface. To this end, a network of thin paralle wires is suspended a short distance from the surface. The wires are given a potentia of about + 8000 volts (Fig. 1a). As a result of this, the surface of the coating is charge to about + 600 volts in relation to its back, where a corresponding negative inductiv charge is produced (Fig. 1b). On exposure to light, a discharge occurs in those part of the coating where the light impinges and thus lowers the resistance, so that a equalisation of electric charge between front and back of the coating occurs. I Fig. 2a it is assumed that light impinges on the left-hand and right-hand side of th semiconductor, but that the centre remains unexposed to light. The "image" formed latently as a pattern of electric charges of varying magnitude. It is "developed by means of a very fine-grained electrically charged powder (e.g., coloured plastic which is called the toner. The movement of these powder particles (approx. $\frac{1}{1000}$ mr diameter) is represented in Fig. 2a. Depending on the electric charge of the tone particles, it is possible to bring out and make visible a positive or a negative portio of the invisible pattern of charges. By electrical means this pattern can be transferre to insulating surfaces (e.g., paper) as often as may be desired and can be develope there. Fixation is effected by heating, whereby the particles of plastic are melte so that they no longer need the electrostatic forces in order to remain adhering t the surface of the paper. The electrical conductivity is produced by means of photo ionisation due to a photo-electric effect (Fig. 2b): a light quantum (cf. page 102 dislodges an electron from an atom and thereby causes the formation of a pair c electrically charged particles. The negative electron neutralises a positive elementar charge at the surface; the positively charged atomic nucleus travels to the back an neutralises a negative charge there. The formation of a visible image respectively i the negative-positive process and in the positive-positive process is illustrated dia grammatically in Fig. 3a and Fig. 3b.

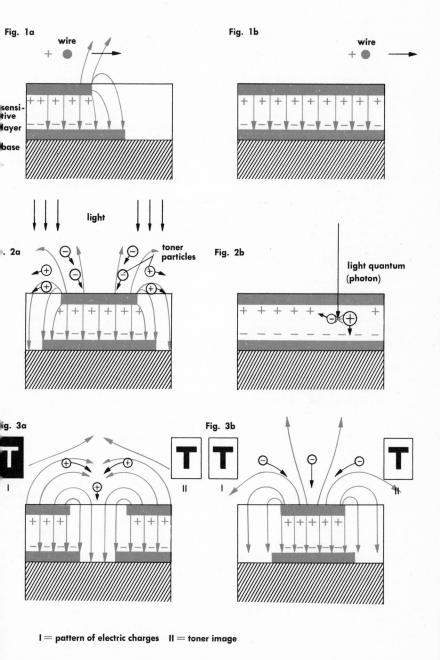

Fig. 1a

wire

+ ●

sensi-
tive
layer

base

+ + + +

− − − −

Fig. 1b

wire

+ ●

+ + + + + + + +

− − − − − − − −

light

Fig. 2a

toner
particles

⊖   ⊖   ⊖   ⊕
  ⊕   ⊖   ⊕
⊕   ⊕

+ + + + + +

− − − − − −

Fig. 2b

light quantum
(photon)

+ + + +   ⊖⊕   +

− − −   ↓   − −

Fig. 3a

T

⊕   ⊕
    ⊕

+ + +   + + +

− − −   − − −

I

Fig. 3b

T | T

⊖   ⊖   ⊖

+ + + + +

− − − − −

T

I   II

I = pattern of electric charges   II = toner image

199

BLACK-AND-WHITE FILM

Black-and-white film is a highly light-sensitive photographic material which is sold commercially in the form of roll films, plates or photographic papers. It is used for black-and-white photography.

The film usually consists of a very thin base made of cellulose acetate, nitrocellulose (cellulose nitrate) or metal. The light-sensitive emulsion is applied to a thin dark-coloured intermediate layer (anti-halo layer). The emulsion is in the form of a very thin coating consisting of 40% silver bromide crystals, 50% gelatine (as a binder) and 10% water. In complete darkness the silver bromide is emulsified in gelatine solution and, together with further additives, is applied by machine to the film or plate. The size of the tiny silver bromide crystals determines the light-sensitivity ("speed") and the resolving power of the emulsion coating. A coarse particle is highly light-sensitive; on the other hand, its optical resolving power is low. Pictures taken with coarse-grained film cannot be greatly enlarged, as the enlargement obtained would be too "grainy". The silver bromide emulsion is not equally sensitive to all colours of light. Yellow-green, yellow, orange and red colour shades could not be photographed on such film. For this reason the coating is chemically sensitised by the addition of minute quantities of gold, mercury and other heavy metal ions to the silver bromide and by feeble reaction with sulphide ions. Also, the coating is physically sensitised by the addition of pigmental sensitisers and thus made sensitive to a wider range of hues. Orthochromatic film is sensitive to the blue-green-yellow range of light, orthopanchromatic film is sensitive to these colours and additionally extends the range to orange, while panchromatic film is sensitive to the whole range of visible light including red. There are, furthermore, special kinds of photographic film with widely varying sensitivity properties for scientific research purposes.

The photographic image is formed by the light rays which come from the subject (i.e., the object being photographed) and are focused on the light-sensitive coating of the film by the lens system of the camera. Each ray of light that strikes the film encounters silver bromide crystals, which are thereby activated. The exposed film is then developed in a development bath, which is a solution of a chemical reducing agent (developer). The latter reduces the activated silver bromide particles to black metallic silver. Silver bromide which has not been activated by exposure to light is not reduced by the developer and can be dissolved out of the emulsion coating by immersion of the developed film in a fixing bath, which contains a solvent (usually solium hyposulphite or "hypo") that dissolves unexposed silver bromide.

After the developer and fixing solutions have been washed out of the film and the latter has dried, the result obtained is the negative. (What has been described here is the simplest procedure; for special purposes the negative can be subjected to various intermediate chemical and heat treatments, etc.) On a negative the shadows appear as "white" (transparent) areas, while the highlights appear black. If the negative is placed in contact with photographic paper (positive paper) and exposed to light, then the areas of this paper under the (dark) highlights in the negative will receive little light, while the areas under the (white) shadows in the negative will be strongly exposed. On developing this photographic paper, a "print" is obtained in which the exposed areas come out dark, while the unexposed areas remain white, and of course those areas which are somewhere between deep shadow and bright highlight come out in various intermediate shades of grey. The dark and light areas of the negative are thus reversed in the printing process.

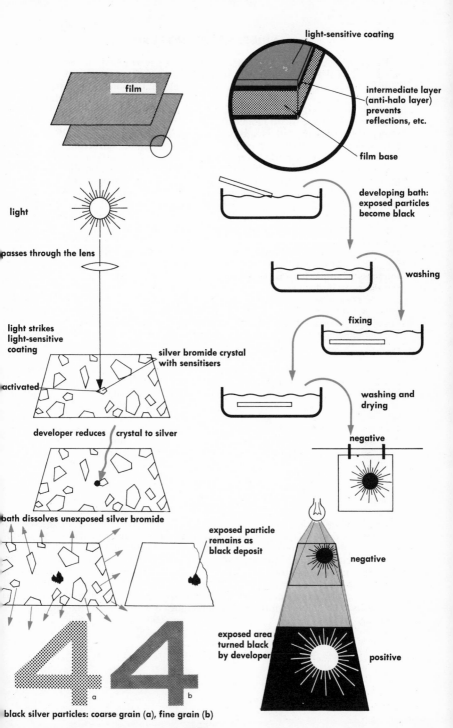

film

light-sensitive coating

intermediate layer (anti-halo layer) prevents reflections, etc.

film base

developing bath: exposed particles become black

washing

fixing

washing and drying

negative

light

passes through the lens

light strikes light-sensitive coating

activated

silver bromide crystal with sensitisers

developer reduces crystal to silver

bath dissolves unexposed silver bromide

exposed particle remains as black deposit

negative

exposed area turned black by developer

positive

black silver particles: coarse grain (a), fine grain (b)

201

NOISE, SOUND INTENSITY

By noise is understood sound consisting of a mixture of airborne vibrations which is completely irregular with regard to sound intensity, frequency and phase. Noise is usually regarded as a nuisance and may, if the sound intensities involved are very high, cause damage to the organs of hearing. Such objectionable noise is, for example, caused when a piece of sheet metal is struck with a hammer (Fig. 1a). When the sound intensity is plotted as a function of time, the curve obtained presents a very irregular shape with jagged peaks and valleys (Fig. 1b). To provide protection against noise is an important function of modern structural engineering. For example, in offices in which the rattle of typewriters would produce unbearable conditions if it were reflected back from the walls, the ceilings and, if need be, the walls can be lined with sound-absorbing panels (Fig. 2). The actual sound-absorbing material, e.g., glass wool or rock wool, is interposed between the ceiling (or wall) itself and an inner skin formed of perforated plates secured at a certain distance from the wall face. The sound waves which pass through the perforations are absorbed by the glass wool or similar absorbing material. The result is a remarkable reduction of noise. According to the Weber-Fechner law of hearing, the apparent loudness of a sound— i.e., the intensity of the acoustic perception—is approximately proportional to the logarithm of the intensity of the stimulus (sound intensity). The unit of objective loudness or sound level is the phon. The loudness, in phons, of a sound is equal to the intensity in decibels of a sound of frequency 1000 cycles/sec. which seems as loud to the ear as the given sound. Two sound intensities, P_1 and P_2, are said to differ by n decibels when $n = 10 \log_{10} P_2/P_1$, where P_2 is the intensity of the sound under consideration and P_1 is the intensity of the reference sound level.

The following table gives typical loudness values, in phons, for a number of sound sources:

air raid siren	135 phons
aircraft at take-off	130 phons
pneumatic hammer	120 phons
hooter	110 phons
engineering shop	100 phons
underground railway train	95 phons
heavy lorry (truck)	90 phons
motor cycle	85 phons
moped (motor bike)	80 phons
office	75 phons
road traffic	70 phons
transformer	60 phons
rustling leaves	30 phons
soundproofed room	10 phons

Loudness values in excess of 130 phons produce a sensation of acute discomfort. Continuous noise in excess of 100 phons may cause hearing damage. The sound-level scale from 1 to 140 phons comprises the intensity ratio of $1:10^{14}$. Objective measurement of sound intensity can be carried out by means of a Rayleigh disc (Fig. 4). This is a small thin disc which is suspended from a fine thread of glass or quartz and is placed at an angle of 45° to the direction of propagation of the sound waves. The disc experiences a torque and strives to place itself at right angles to the waves. The amount of rotation it undergoes is a measure of the intensity. See also page 518.

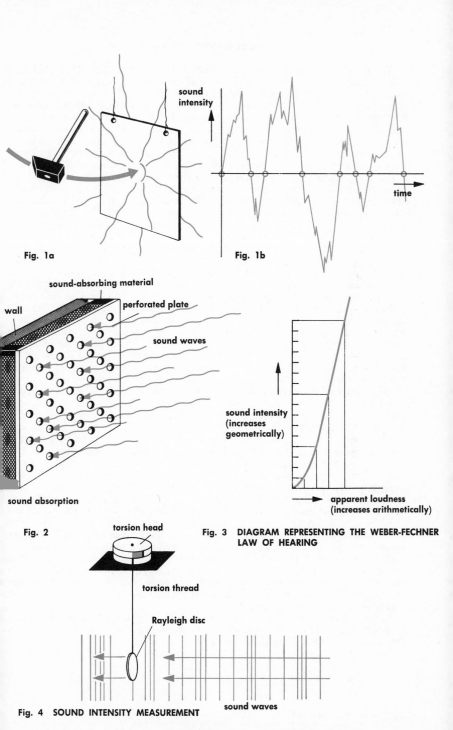

Fig. 1a

Fig. 1b

sound-absorbing material

wall

perforated plate

sound waves

sound absorption

Fig. 2

torsion head

Fig. 3 DIAGRAM REPRESENTING THE WEBER-FECHNER LAW OF HEARING

sound intensity (increases geometrically)

apparent loudness (increases arithmetically)

torsion thread

Rayleigh disc

sound waves

Fig. 4 SOUND INTENSITY MEASUREMENT

RESONANCE, ECHO

By resonance is understood the phenomenon that structures capable of oscillation will oscillate in sympathy with relatively feeble external forces which act periodically and whose oscillation period coincides with that of the resonating structure. While it is resonating, the structure stores up energy. Under certain circumstances the amount of energy stored up in this way may become so great that it brings about the destruction or collapse of the structure. A simple example of a resonating structure is a child's swing (Fig. 1a). It is a pendulum which is given a push or a thrust in the swinging direction each time it reaches its maximum deflection. Its energy build-up, i.e., its resonance, is directly evident from the increasing amplitude of the deflection of the swing. Another example is a liquid in a U-shaped tube (Fig. 1b). The liquid can be set in motion by blowing into one end of the tube, and by blowing it periodically at the appropriate instant, the amplitude of its oscillations is progressively increased. The oscillations do not, however, go on increasing indefinitely, but are limited by energy losses—in this case more particularly by losses due to friction of the liquid on the wall of the tube. Resonance of a magnetically polarised steel spring can be induced by the fluctuating magnetic field of an electromagnet energised by an alternating current (Fig. 2a). This resonance effect is, for example, utilised in frequency meters. The conception of resonance had its origin in the science of acoustics. Fig. 2b illustrates an acoustic resonator, a device known as Kundt's tube, which is used for measuring the wavelength of sound waves. Projecting into the glass tube is one end of a metal rod which is held gripped in the middle. Longitudinal vibrations are set up in this rod by rubbing it with a cloth sprinkled with powdered rosin. The end of the rod in the tube is provided with a disc which in turn transmits the vibrations to the air in the tube. The effective length of the tube can be varied by means of an adjustable disc at the other end. The vibrations (sound waves) are reflected by this disc, and on suitably adjusting its position, a stationary wave will be produced in the tube, and resonance occurs. This happens when the distance between the two discs is equal to an odd multiple of one-quarter of the wavelength of the sound waves set up in the tube (see also page 210), and vibration nodes and antinodes are formed. These can be indicated by introducing a small quantity of some suitably light powder (e.g., lycopodium powder) into the tube. The powder congregates in a heap at each node. The nodes are thus made "visible", and the distance between them can be measured. The distance between two successive nodes is equal to half the wavelength of the sound waves set up in the tube. Resonance effects are also observed in connection with electromagnetic phenomena. The most well known and important example is the excitation of an electromagnetic oscillatory circuit, comprising a self-inductance L and capacity C, by an alternating voltage (Fig. 3). In the circuit the energy oscillates between its electrical state in the condenser (Fig. 3a) and its magnetic state in the magnetic field of self-induction (Fig. 3b). If the natural period of vibration (and therefore the frequency) of the oscillatory circuit corresponds to that of the alternating voltage, resonance will occur. The circuit will in that case absorb the maximum amount of energy from the source of energy that produces the excitation. Radio transmitters and receivers are tuned with the aid of this resonance effect (cf. page 70 and page 532). To prevent the energy attaining disastrously high values, resistances are included in the circuit; these cause energy losses in the form of heat.

Another phenomenon that acoustic and electric vibrations have in common is echo, i.e., the reflection of sound waves or electromagnetic waves from obstacles they encounter (Fig. 4). See also page 116.

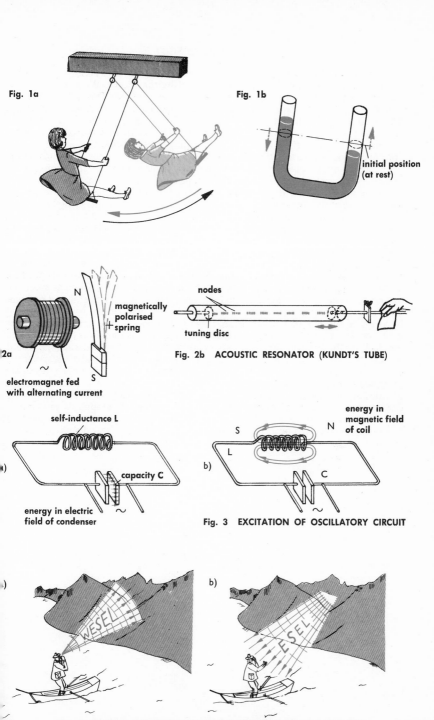

Fig. 1a

Fig. 1b

initial position
(at rest)

N

magnetically
polarised
spring

nodes

tuning disc

2a

electromagnet fed
with alternating current

S

Fig. 2b   ACOUSTIC RESONATOR (KUNDT'S TUBE)

self-inductance L

capacity C

energy in electric
field of condenser

energy in
magnetic field
of coil

S   N

L

C

b)

Fig. 3   EXCITATION OF OSCILLATORY CIRCUIT

a)   b)

WESEL   ESEL

Fig. 4   ECHO IS REFLECTION OF SOUND WAVES FROM AN OBSTACLE

205

DOPPLER EFFECT

When a vibrating source of waves is approaching an observer, the frequency observed is higher than the frequency emitted by the source. When the source is receding, the observed frequency is lower than that emitted. This is known as the Doppler effect, or Doppler's principle, and is named after an Austrian physicist who lived in the first half of the 19th century. Figs. 1 and 2 will help to explain this phenomenon. When a whistling locomotive (or any other sound source) approaches a stationary observer (Fig. 1), more density concentrations reach his ear than when both the sound source and the observer are stationary. As the pitch depends on the frequency (number of vibrations per second), the sound from the approaching locomotive's whistle has a higher pitch than the sound coming from the same whistle when the locomotive is stationary in relation to the observer. Similarly, when the locomotive is receding, its whistle sounds with a lower note. At the instant when the locomotive passes the observer, the note of the whistle is heard to change to a lower pitch. The same effect is observed when we are passed by a fast-moving hooting car in the street, or when the observer is moving fast in relation to a stationary sound source (e.g., a motor cyclist approaching a siren, as in Fig. 2).

The Doppler effect is widely used in astronomy for measuring the velocity at which distant stars or nebulae are approaching or receding. These motions produce a shift in the position of lines in their spectra (see page 134). A particular spectrum line corresponds to a certain definite light wavelength. If the star emitting the light is moving away from us, its light rays have a longer wavelength (lower frequency) by virtue of the Doppler principle, and this is manifested in a general shift of the spectrum lines towards the red end of the spectrum. This is known as the "red shift". Similarly, in the spectrum of a star moving towards us, the characteristic lines would show a "blue shift", i.e., they would be displaced towards the blue end of the spectrum, corresponding to shorter wavelengths and higher frequencies. These phenomena are indicated in Fig. 3. A remarkable thing about the spectra of the spiral nebulae (the galaxies of stars far out in space beyond our own Milky Way system) is that they all display the red shift and must therefore—on the basis of Doppler's principle—all be moving away from us. The theory of the "expanding universe" is based on this phenomenon. However, this interpretation of the red shift is disputed by some authorities.

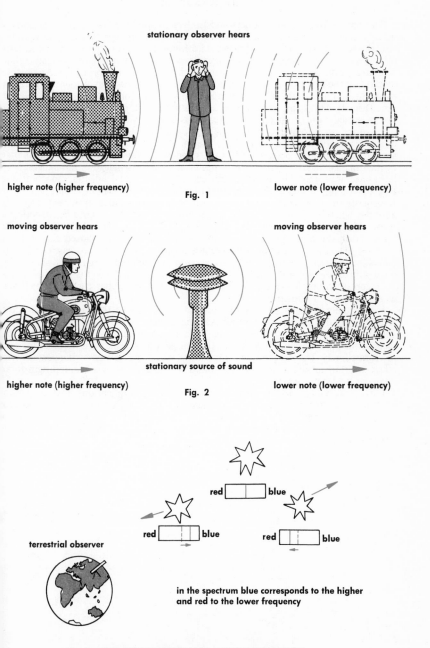

stationary observer hears

higher note (higher frequency)

Fig. 1

lower note (lower frequency)

moving observer hears

moving observer hears

stationary source of sound

higher note (higher frequency)

Fig. 2

lower note (lower frequency)

terrestrial observer

red | blue

red | blue

red | blue

in the spectrum blue corresponds to the higher and red to the lower frequency

Fig. 3   RED SHIFT INTERPRETED AS DOPPLER EFFECT

ULTRASONICS

The term ultrasonics (or supersonics) refers to sound vibrations—variations o density in elastic media (e.g., air)—whose frequencies are beyond the auditory limit i.e., above approx. 20,000 cycles/sec. The highest ultrasonic frequencies hithert attained are of the order of 10 million cycles/sec. Such high-frequency elastic vibra tions are produced in various ways, based on different physical principles. An obviou method, in the first place, is to extend the old acoustic principle of sound generation by means of pipes to the ultrasonic range. This can be done by means of the Galto pipe (Fig. 1). This is a pipe (cf. page 210) in which the position of the gap and li can be varied by micrometer adjustment. It is blown by compressed air and enable ultra-sound with frequencies up to 30,000 cycles/sec. to be produced. Higher fre quencies can be attained by making use of other phenomena, namely, magneto striction and the piezoelectric effect (cf. page 86). Magnetostriction is the chang in the dimensions of a ferromagnetic material when it is placed in a magnetic field If the latter is produced by an alternating current, the material will undergo vibrations Fig. 2 is a diagrammatic representation of a magnetostriction ultrasonic generator It consists of 0.1–0.3 mm (0.004–0.012 in.) thick nickel plates, insulated from on another, whereby the eddy current losses are reduced. The general construction i rather like that of a transformer (page 92). The arrangement of the windings, a indicated in the diagram, causes the magnetic field to form a closed circuit in th stack of plates. Utilising this principle, ultrasonic waves with frequencies of up t 200,000 cycles/sec. can be produced. The sound is radiated—e.g., in air or water— in two directions (upward and downward in Fig. 2). If radiation is required in on direction only, one face must be provided with a foam rubber cushion, which act as a screen impervious to sound.

Even higher frequencies can be attained by means of the piezoelectric effect A circular quartz plate—cut from a hexagonal quartz crystal in the manner shown i Fig. 3—is so gripped at its edge (Fig. 4) that thin metal foils on the two circula faces of the plate impart a high-frequency charge to it and that it is nevertheless abl to vibrate freely. The high-frequency thickness vibrations caused by the piezoelectri effect are transmitted to the air in a sound box and thence via a diaphragm to a adjacent medium (e.g., water).

Ultrasonic vibrations are used in many technical applications, including non destructive testing of materials, degasification of liquids, echo-sounding, and als in therapeutic medicine. Certain nocturnal animals, such as bats, make use o ultrasonic vibrations to guide their movements in the dark on the radar principl (cf. page 116).

Fig. 1 GALTON PIPE

Fig. 2 MAGNETOSTRICTION ULTRASONIC
GENERATOR (schematic)

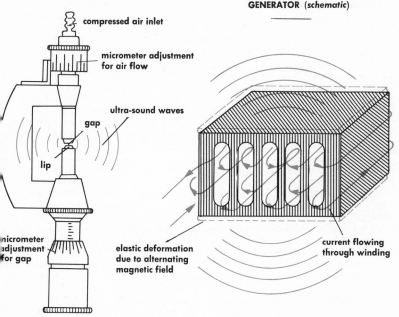

compressed air inlet

micrometer adjustment
for air flow

ultra-sound waves

gap

lip

micrometer
adjustment
for gap

elastic deformation
due to alternating
magnetic field

current flowing
through winding

Fig. 3 PLATE CUT FROM
QUARTZ CRYSTAL

Fig. 4 PIEZOELECTRIC SOUND TRANSMITTER

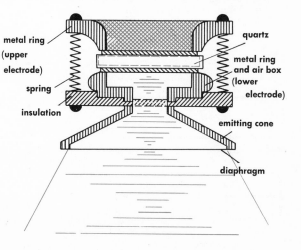

metal ring
(upper
electrode)

spring

insulation

quartz

metal ring
and air box
(lower
electrode)

emitting cone

diaphragm

ORGAN PIPES

If a vibrating tuning fork is held over a glass cylinder, the column of air in the cylinder will, if it is of appropriate length, resonate with the fork. The length (l) of the air column can be adjusted by pouring water into the cylinder so as to make it an odd multiple (n) of one-quarter of the wavelength (λ) of the note produced by the tuning fork, i.e., $l = n\,\lambda/4$, where n denotes an odd integer; in that case resonance will occur (see page 204). This means that the column of air vibrates "in tune" with the tuning fork, so that the sound emitted by the fork is strengthened. The air in the glass cylinder forms what are known as stationary waves, with nodes and antinodes. At the nodes the air in the cylinder is at rest, whereas it moves to and fro, i.e., it is in a state of vibration, at the antinodes. Fig. 1 shows the arrangement of the nodes and antinodes associated with the second harmonic vibration (the second overtone). The fundamental vibration and the first harmonic vibration in an open-ended pipe or cylinder are indicated in the diagram at the foot of this page. At the antinodes the air periodically increases and decreases in density, in time with the frequency of the vibration.

The operation of all wind instruments for producing sounds is based on resonance vibrations. These vibrations can be generated by two different methods: a stream of air issuing from a gap flows past a sharp-edged lip and produces a vortex motion of the air (labial organ pipe, Fig. 2a; flute, Fig. 3); alternatively, a stream of air is periodically interrupted by means of a vibrating tongue of wood or metal, known as a reed (reed pipe, Fig. 2b). In the organ pipe the air first enters a chamber in which the air is stored up; it then flows through a gap and impinges on a lip which causes vortexes to form. These generate resonance vibrations in the air column in the pipe, whose length (l) is a multiple of half the wavelength, i.e., $l = n\,\lambda/2$, where n is an integer. In Fig. 2 the conditions corresponding to the second harmonic, or overtone, are represented. The flute (Fig. 3) functions on the same principle as the organ pipe. When all the holes are closed, the flute gives its fundamental note, i.e., the note with the lowest frequency and associated with the greatest length of the vibrating column of air. When one of the holes is opened, a higher note is heard according as the vibrating air column is shorter. In the reed pipe (Fig. 2b) the air causes a resilient tongue, called a reed, to close an opening and thus cut off the air flow. As soon as this happens, the reed springs back, and the action is thus repeated periodically, whereby vibrations are set up in the funnel-shaped pipe above the reed. The reed pipe principle is employed in various musical instruments, such as clarinet, oboe, harmonium and mouth-organ.

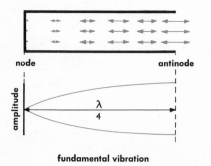

node   antinode

$$\frac{\lambda}{4}$$

fundamental vibration

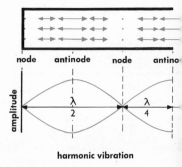

node   antinode   node   antino

$$\frac{\lambda}{2} \qquad \frac{\lambda}{4}$$

harmonic vibration

of a column of air open at one end

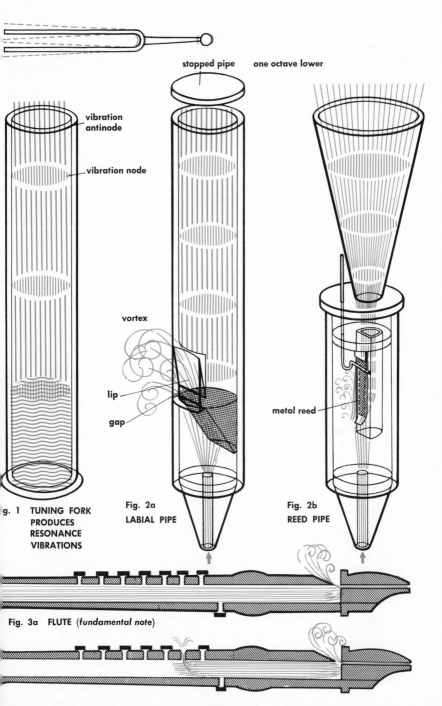

stopped pipe   one octave lower

vibration
antinode

vibration node

vortex

lip

gap

metal reed

Fig. 1   TUNING FORK
PRODUCES
RESONANCE
VIBRATIONS

Fig. 2a
LABIAL PIPE

Fig. 2b
REED PIPE

Fig. 3a   FLUTE (*fundamental note*)

Fig. 3b   FLUTE (*note one octave higher than in* Fig. 3a)

SCALES AND WEIGHING MACHINES

The force with which the earth attracts an object, i.e., the gravitational force exerted upon it, is called weight. This force is proportional to the mass (the amount of matter) in the object and to the gravitational acceleration. However, the acceleration of gravity is not exactly the same in all parts of the world: its value is a little higher at the poles than at the equator; in other words, the same object at the poles of the earth has a somewhat greater weight than it has at the equator.

The simplest form of weighing device is the equal-armed beam scale (or balance) (Fig. 1). It consists of a beam pivotably mounted on a knife-edge fulcrum at the centre. Attached to the centre of the beam is a pointer which points vertically downwards when the scale is in equilibrium (Fig. 1a). For proper functioning of the scale it is essential that the centre of gravity of the beam is located lower than the pivot (fulcrum). For this reason the pointer is provided with a vertically slidable weight. The beam is in equilibrium when the clockwise rotating moment (load on right-arm × length of right arm) is equal to the anti-clockwise rotating moment (load on left arm × length of left arm); since the two arms of the beam are equal, the scale will be in equilibrium when the weight of the object to be weighed is equal to that of the weights placed in the other pan. The sensitivity of the beam scale is lower according as the centre of gravity of the beam is located lower down. From Fig. 1b it is apparent that, when the weight on the pointer is lowered, the lever arm of this weight in relation to the pivot will, for the same angle of tilt of the beam, be increased from a to b. The beam will in fact rotate about the pivot until b becomes equal to a, so that the deflection of the pointer decreases, although the loads on the two pans of the scale are the same as before.

The equal-armed scale requires a set of weights at least as heavy as the heaviest load to be weighed. For the weighing of heavier objects, scales having arms of unequal length are therefore used. The weights are suspended from the longer arm, and the object is suspended from the shorter arm. For equilibrium, the forces (loads) acting upon the two arms have to be inversely proportional to the lengths of the arms. Thus, in the weighbridge illustrated in Fig. 2, the weight needed to balance the load is only one-tenth of the latter if the machine is so designed that $l = 10 \times a$ and $a:b = c:d$. The platform weighing machine illustrated in Fig. 3 is of the pendulum type, i.e., it is equipped with a counterbalancing pendulum instead of a pan for weights. The deflection of the pendulum (and therefore of the lever attached to it) provides an indication of the magnitude of the load placed on the weighing platform. To alter the range of the machine, a sliding weight can be moved along a lever.

In the case of the letter balance (Fig. 4) the rods interconnecting the various pivots form a parallelogram in all positions. When a load is placed on the platform, the lever arm of the counterbalancing weight in relation to the pivot increases, so that the deflection provides a measure of the magnitude (i.e., the weight) of the load.

Another type of scale is the spring balance (Fig. 5). In this device the extension of the spring is proportional to the magnitude of the load suspended from it. The scale can be directly graduated in weight units. The familiar "bathroom scales" are also based on the spring balance principle. Here, too, the extension or deflection of a spring is transmitted to a scale whose markings give a direct reading of the weight (Fig. 6).

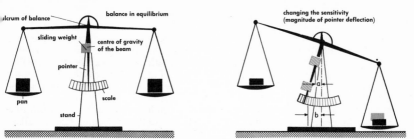

Fig. 1 EQUAL-ARMED BEAM SCALE

fulcrum of balance
balance in equilibrium
sliding weight
centre of gravity of the beam
pointer
scale
pan
stand

changing the sensitivity
(magnitude of pointer deflection)
a
b

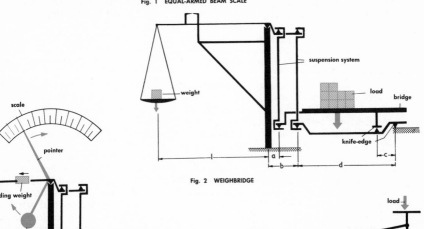

suspension system
weight
load
bridge
knife-edge
l
a
b
d
c

Fig. 2 WEIGHBRIDGE

scale
pointer
sliding weight
pendulum

Fig. 3 PENDULUM TYPE WEIGHING MACHINE

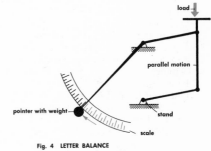

load
parallel motion
pointer with weight
stand
scale

Fig. 4 LETTER BALANCE

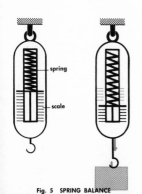

spring
scale

Fig. 5 SPRING BALANCE

100
90
80
70
60
50
40
30
20
10
spring
pinion
toothed rack
pointer
pull-rod

Fig. 6 SPRING BALANCE WITH CIRCULAR SCALE

CLOCKS AND WATCHES

Any periodically repeated phenomenon can be utilised for time measurement, so long as the duration of the period remains accurately constant. In early timepieces the periodic movement was performed by a pendulum (Fig. 1). The weight which drives the watch is applied to the circumference of the spindle, causing it to rotate. This rotation is, however, arrested by the anchor, which is linked to the pendulum and which periodically engages with, and releases, a toothed wheel called the escape wheel (the combination of escape wheel and anchor is called the escapement). Each time the pendulum reaches its maximum amplitude, one of the projections (called pallets) of the anchor releases a tooth of the escape wheel, allowing this wheel to rotate a corresponding amount. Its rotation is therefore performed in a series of jerks, controlled by the anchor and pendulum, and this rotation is transmitted to the hands of the clock through a train of gear wheels. Friction would soon cause the pendulum to stop swinging if it were not given an impulse at regular intervals to keep it in motion, just as a child's swing has to be pushed each time it reaches it's full amplitude (Fig. 2). In the pendulum clock an impulse is imparted to the pendulum by the escape wheel (which is driven by the weight) through the pallets. The frequency (number of swings per second) of the pendulum can be varied by sliding the bob of the pendulum up or down on its rod. Lowering the bob makes the pendulum swing more slowly, and vice versa. In this way the period (time of oscillation) of the pendulum can be adjusted and, the clock itself thus be regulated. In watches the controlling action of the pendulum is performed by a device called the balance (Fig. 3). Attached to the spindle of the balance is a spiral spring, named the balance spring or hairspring, which controls the oscillations of the balance. Attached to the balance is a pin which engages with the lever. With each oscillation of the lever the pallets release the escape wheel, allowing it to rotate a distance corresponding to one tooth. At the same time an impulse from the escape wheel (which is driven by the mainspring) is transmitted to the balance through the lever and pin and thereby keeps the balance in motion. The function of the latter is thus entirely analogous to that of the pendulum in a pendulum clock. The type of escapement illustrated in Fig. 3 is the so-called lever escapement; it was invented about two hundred years ago, and is now widely employed; there are several other types of escapement for watches. The balance performs five to-and-fro movements per second, i.e., the second hand moves in five tiny jerks each second. The escape wheel drives the minute hand and hour hand through a train of gear wheels.

The transmission of the movement of the minute wheel and hour wheel to the hands of the watch is shown in Fig. 4. The minute wheel performs one complete revolution per hour, and so does the minute hand, which is mounted on the same spindle. During the same length of time the hour wheel and hour hand perform only one-twelfth of a revolution.

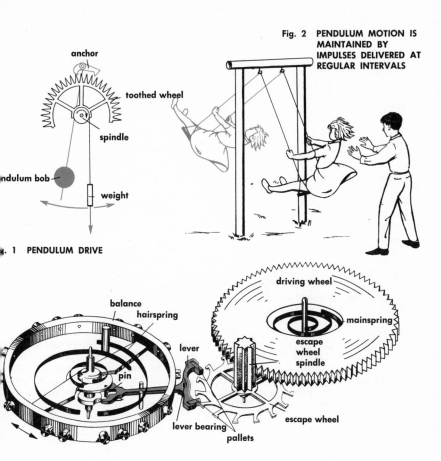

anchor

toothed wheel

spindle

pendulum bob

weight

Fig. 1 PENDULUM DRIVE

Fig. 2 PENDULUM MOTION IS MAINTAINED BY IMPULSES DELIVERED AT REGULAR INTERVALS

balance
hairspring

lever

pin

lever bearing

pallets

driving wheel

mainspring

escape wheel spindle

escape wheel

Fig. 3 DRIVE MECHANISM OF A WATCH

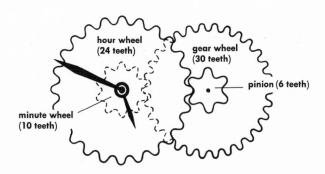

hour wheel (24 teeth)

gear wheel (30 teeth)

pinion (6 teeth)

minute wheel (10 teeth)

Fig. 4 TRANSMISSION OF MOTION FROM THE MINUTE AND HOUR WHEELS TO THE HANDS

QUARTZ CLOCK

In every method of measuring time a periodically recurring process is used as the basis of the measurement. In clocks and watches the periodic recurrence is provided by the swinging pendulum or the oscillating balance (see page 215).

Essentially, any periodic process can be used for controlling a timepiece. In the device called the "quartz clock" these consist of the "thickness vibrations" that quartz (and certain other crystals) perform under particular conditions. The principle of such vibrations can best be illustrated by a very simple example: when a jelly pudding is struck with a spoon (Fig. 1), it begins to wobble. These movements are a kind of thickness vibrations. If the jelly is struck at regular intervals corresponding to its vibration frequency, the amplitude of the vibrations will increase to such an extent that the pudding may actually break up. A quartz crystal cut in a certain way exhibits a similar effect. In this case, however, the excitation of the crystal is not done by mechanical impulses but by periodic electric charging (Fig. 2). For this purpose a phenomenon known as the *piezoelectric* effect is utilised: when the crystal is subjected to alternate compressive and tensile strains, opposite electric charges are produced on different faces; conversely, when electric charges are applied to these faces of the crystal, the latter undergoes expansion and contraction. By this means the crystal can be set vibrating. The frequency of these thickness vibrations depends solely on the dimensions of the crystal and can be given any desired value by appropriately choosing these dimensions. For a given set of conditions the frequency is extremely constant. A quartz crystal can thus be used as a highly accurate regulator for an electric oscillatory circuit (Fig. 3).

The quartz clock comprises a tube (or valve) transmitter (Fig. 4), or a transistorised transmitter (cf. page 72), whose oscillatory circuit is controlled by a quartz crystal. At the output end (A) an alternating voltage with a frequency possessing a high degree of constancy is obtained. This output can be fed through frequency reducing circuits, or be supplied to a high-frequency motor, and thus be used to drive a normal clock. The time-keeping accuracy is very high (to within one ten-thousandth of a second over a period of months). Quartz clocks have acquired importance as master clocks for public timekeeping purposes and for keeping the frequencies of radio transmitters constant.

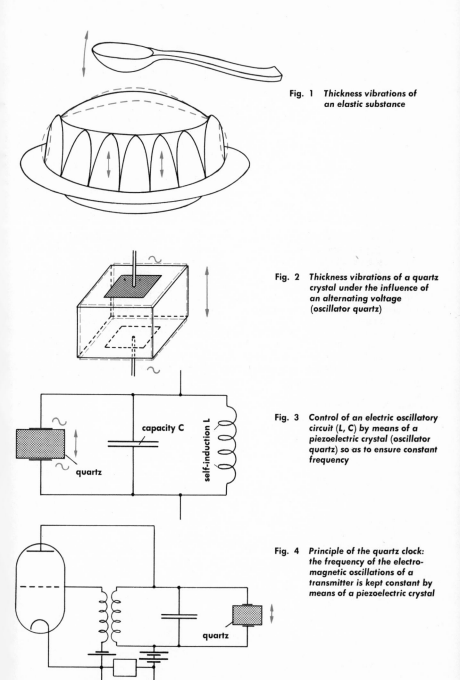

Fig. 1 *Thickness vibrations of an elastic substance*

Fig. 2 *Thickness vibrations of a quartz crystal under the influence of an alternating voltage (oscillator quartz)*

capacity C

self-induction L

~

quartz

Fig. 3 *Control of an electric oscillatory circuit (L, C) by means of a piezoelectric crystal (oscillator quartz) so as to ensure constant frequency*

Fig. 4 *Principle of the quartz clock: the frequency of the electromagnetic oscillations of a transmitter is kept constant by means of a piezoelectric crystal*

quartz

output   A

ATOMIC CLOCK

The atomic clock is the most accurate time measuring device at present known. Whereas the accuracy attainable with high-precision pendulum clocks is about 10^{-7} (i.e., an error of 3 seconds per year), the accuracy of the quartz clock (see page 216) is 100–1000 times greater. However, quartz clocks have the great disadvantage that their vibration frequency changes in course of time. Hence the frequency has to be checked from time to time and readjusted. This is done with the aid of an atomic clock, in which the frequency is determined by molecular vibrations and remains constant. The accuracy of the atomic clock is about ten times as great as that of the quartz clock.

The operating principle of an ammonia atomic clock is as follows:

Gaseous ammonia (NH_3) is introduced through the nozzle on the left in Fig. 1. The nozzle consists of a number of very fine parallel passages, and the molecules travelling to the right enter the focusing device, which consists of a number of metal cylinders (usually four) charged to a high voltage. Among the NH_3 molecules are some with a higher and some with a lower energy content. Both kinds of molecule have a dipole moment, i.e., they align themselves in an electric field in such a manner that the high-energy molecules dispose themselves against the direction of the field, whereas the low-energy molecules dispose themselves in that direction. Because of these properties of the NH_3 molecule, it is possible, with the aid of the very inhomogeneous field in the focusing device, to separate the high-energy molecules from the low-energy ones, so that the former are thrust towards the central area by the electric field, while the latter are thrust outwards (Fig. 2). The high-energy molecules are collected by the focusing device and directed into a cavity resonator (see page 70). The resonator is a metal box in which a stationary high-frequency wave can be formed with the aid of a feedback system. Activated by this wave, the high-energy NH_3 molecules acquire vibrations of about 24 milliard[1] cycles/sec. and give off their energy to the wave, which is thereby amplified. This high-frequency energy has a frequency which remains very accurately constant, thus providing the basis for the time measurement.

1. A milliard is equivalent to one billion in U.S.A.

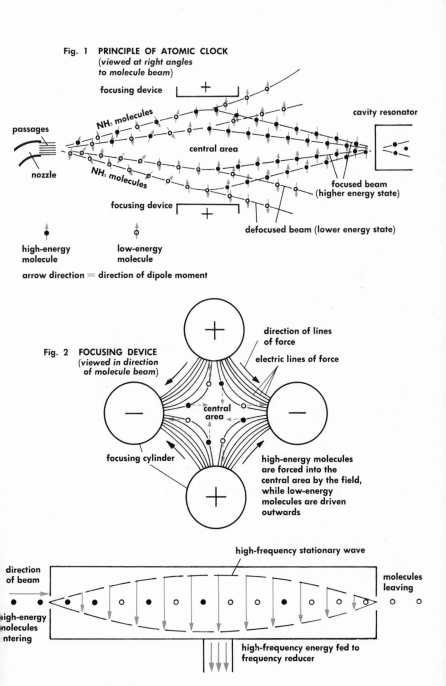

Fig. 1 PRINCIPLE OF ATOMIC CLOCK
(*viewed at right angles to molecule beam*)

focusing device

NH_3 molecules

central area

cavity resonator

passages

nozzle

NH_3 molecules

focused beam (higher energy state)

focusing device

defocused beam (lower energy state)

high-energy molecule

low-energy molecule

arrow direction = direction of dipole moment

Fig. 2 FOCUSING DEVICE
(*viewed in direction of molecule beam*)

direction of lines of force

electric lines of force

central area

focusing cylinder

high-energy molecules are forced into the central area by the field, while low-energy molecules are driven outwards

high-frequency stationary wave

direction of beam

molecules leaving

high-energy molecules entering

high-frequency energy fed to frequency reducer

Fig. 3 CAVITY RESONATOR

219

BAROMETER

A barometer is a device for measuring atmospheric pressure. The average atmospheric pressure at sea level is 1 atmosphere, which is the pressure that will support a column of mercury 760 mm (29.92 inches) high, i.e., about 1 kg/cm^2 (14.7 lb./in.^{2}). This would correspond to the pressure exerted by a column of air about 5 miles (8 km) high if its density were constant and equal to that at sea level. (Actually the depth of the atmosphere is substantially greater, as the density diminishes with increasing altitude). This explains why the atmospheric pressure on the top of a mountain is lower. If the mountain is, say, 10,000 ft. (3000 m) high, the column of air pressing down at the top is only about 3 miles (assuming constant density) (Fig. 1). Actually the atmospheric pressure at any particular altitude is never constant, but varies by relatively small amounts about the average. These variations provide data for weather forecasts.

When a rubber suction pad is pressed against a smooth wall (Fig. 2), it will remain adhering to the wall. By pressing the pad down flat against the wall surface the air is expelled from the cavity under the pad and a vacuum is formed there. The air pressure which originally acted in that cavity now no longer thrusts against the inside of the pad. When the latter is released, it will remain in the compressed position because the air pressure acts on the outside only and thus presses the edge of the pad down so firmly that no air will penetrate into the cavity, which therefore remains void of air. The external air pressure thus keeps the suction pad firmly pressed against the wall.

Difference of air pressure is also utilised when we drink a liquid through a straw. Air is sucked out of the straw, and the atmospheric air pressure, which acts upon the surface of the liquid in the glass, will force the liquid up through the straw (Fig. 3). If a long glass tube, which is sealed at one end and open at the other, is filled with mercury and is then stood upright, with the open end downwards, in a dish containing mercury, then so much mercury will flow out of the tube until a column of mercury not more than 760 mm in height above the mercury surface in the dish remains (Fig. 4). The air pressure which acts upon the surface of the mercury in the dish is therefore able to hold up a 760 mm high mercury column. If the same experiment were carried out with water instead of mercury, the tube would have to be at least 33.9 ft. (10.33 m) high; and a column of air would have to be 5 miles high to exert a pressure of the same magnitude (Fig. 5). A mercury-filled tube over 760 mm in length as described above, represents the simplest form of the mercury barometer. The tube contains no air; the space above the mercury column is a vacuum.

Modern barometers are mostly of the aneroid type. An aneroid barometer (Fig. 6) consists of a hermetically sealed metal box, exhausted of air. The top and bottom of this box are thin corrugated plates. In the interior of the box is a spring which strives to force the top and bottom plates apart, against the external air pressure. If this air pressure decreases, the springs can expand; if it increases, the spring is compressed. The movement of the top plate is transmitted through a train of levers to a pointer which indicates the atmospheric pressure on an appropriately graduated scale.

The unit of atmospheric pressure usually employed in meteorology is the millibar. It is approximately equal to $\frac{1}{32}$ inch of mercury (actually a mercury column of 750 mm corresponds to 1000 millibars).

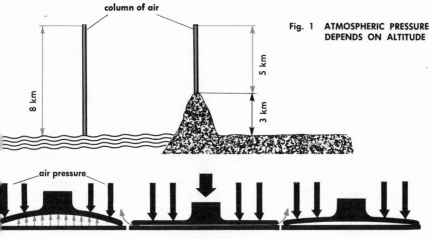

column of air

Fig. 1 ATMOSPHERIC PRESSURE
DEPENDS ON ALTITUDE

8 km

5 km

3 km

air pressure

Fig. 2 RUBBER SUCTION PAD

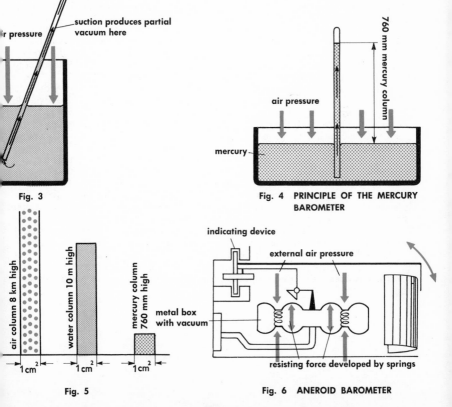

air pressure

suction produces partial
vacuum here

Fig. 3

760 mm mercury column

air pressure

mercury

Fig. 4 PRINCIPLE OF THE MERCURY
BAROMETER

air column 8 km high

water column 10 m high

mercury column
760 mm high

1cm   2

1cm   2

1cm   2

Fig. 5

indicating device

external air pressure

metal box
with vacuum

resisting force developed by springs

Fig. 6 ANEROID BAROMETER

221

ELECTRICITY METERS (ENERGY METERS)

Electricity meters are used for measuring the "quantity" of electricity consumed in houses and factories. What the meter actually measures is the electric energy that passes through the circuit. For direct current the energy is $A = V.I.t$, and for single-phase alternating current it is $A = V.I.t \cos \phi$ (cf. page 68), where V is the voltage, I is the current strength, t is the time, and $\cos \phi$ is the power factor. In the case of direct current the energy can be metered by determining the value of $I.t$ by means of an ampere-hour meter, so long as the voltage V in the mains is kept constant. In alternating-current supply systems, however, only watt-hour meters are used.

Fig. 1 illustrates the principle of the electrolytic meter, which can be used only for alternating current. It is now obsolete, but its mode of functioning is of some interest. A closed glass vessel contains an electrolyte consisting of a solution of a mercury salt. Part of the consumer current flows through this electrolyte; at the cathode a quantity of mercury proportional to the value of $I.t$ is deposited. The mercury collects in the bottom part of the vessel. The scale is graduated in kWh. The mercury can subsequently be retrieved and returned to the top compartment.

Fig. 2a shows a motor-type ampere-hour meter. It is in effect a small direct-current motor. The armature, or rotor, is an aluminium disc mounted in the field of a permanent magnet. The disc contains three coils which are supplied with current from a commutator consisting of three sectors. The current to the rotor coils is proportional to the total current passing through the consumer installation, from which it is branched off (Fig. 2b). Since the field strength of the permanent magnet is constant, the speed of rotation of the rotor is proportional to the current strength. The counting mechanism connected to the rotor shaft counts the revolutions, which correspond to the product $I.t$. If, instead of the permanent magnet, an electromagnet is used to produce the magnetic field, and if the consumer voltage V is applied to this coil, then the speed of rotation of the rotor is proportional both to V and to I, and therefore to the product $V.I$. In that case the counting mechanism directly records the energy $V.I.t$. The ampere-hour meter has thus become a true watt-hour meter.

The kind of meter nowadays generally used for alternating current is the induction meter (Fig. 3). It has no commutator. There are two electromagnets. The coil of one of these is energised by the consumer current; the other magnet coil is connected to the consumer voltage. If the current and the voltage in the consumer circuit are in phase with each other (see page 68), then the current in the voltage coil, and therefore the magnetic field of this coil, will have a lag of one-quarter period (90°) in relation to that of the current coil. The interaction of the two coils produces a moving magnetic field which induces eddy currents in the light aluminium rotor disc. These currents cause the disc to rotate in the direction of motion of the moving field. The speed of rotation of the disc is proportional to the strengths of the two magnetic fields, but it is also dependent upon the phase displacement of these fields (and therefore upon the power factor $\cos \phi$). This will readily be understood when one considers the case where the consumer installation has a 90° phase displacement between V and I (i.e., $\cos \phi = 0$); when this happens the two magnetic fields in the meter will be in phase, so that the rotor will then cease to rotate. The braking magnet (on the right in Fig. 3) constantly produces eddy currents in the rotor; these damp the rotation and thereby ensure that the rotor stops instantly when the consumer current ceases to flow.

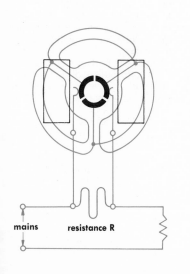

separator

electrolyte

mercury

electrolyte

anode (+)

cathode (−)

scale

Fig. 1   ELECTROLYTIC METER

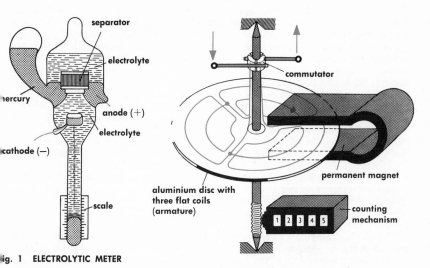

commutator

permanent magnet

aluminium disc with
three flat coils
(armature)

counting
mechanism

Fig. 2a   MOTOR-TYPE METER (*schematic*)

mains

resistance R

Fig. 2b   WIRING DIAGRAM OF A
MOTOR-TYPE METER

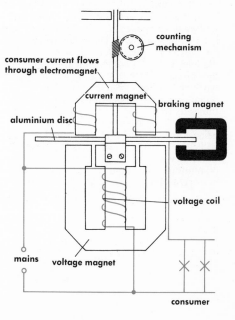

counting
mechanism

consumer current flows
through electromagnet

current magnet

braking magnet

aluminium disc

voltage coil

mains   voltage magnet

consumer

Fig. 3   INDUCTION METER

GAS METERS

Gas meters are either of the "dry" or the "wet" type. The *"dry" gas meter* comprises two chambers of known volume, which are separated from each other by a leather diaphragm. Both chambers have inlet and outlet valves. The pressure of the gas causes the chambers to be alternately filled and emptied, whereby the diaphragm is alternately stretched and relaxed. These movements of the diaphragm are transmitted to a lever system which controls the valves of the chambers. The filled chamber controls the mechanism of the other chamber, which is about to be filled.

In order to keep the flow of gas through the meter as continuous as possible, two two-chamber systems are combined into a unit. Figs. 1a–c illustrate some stages in the alternate filling and emptying operations of the system. In Fig. 1a, measuring chamber Ia is full of gas. Just previously to this the control mechanism of chamber I effected the change-over of the valve so as to let gas flow into chamber IIb. When this chamber has filled up, the valve *a* opens chamber Ib further. It closes the latter again as soon as chamber IIa begins to fill up (Fig. 1b). Fig. 1c shows chamber Ib completely closed by the valve, while chamber IIa is in the final stage of filling. In this stage chamber Ib begins to empty its contents; at the same time, the diaphragm, acting through the crank mechanism, has set the valve *a* so as to let gas into chamber Ia. As chamber Ia fills up, the diaphragm *a* so actuated the valve *b* that chamber IIa is emptied and chamber IIb fills up.

The rate of emptying and filling of the chambers corresponds to the rate of rise and fall of the diaphragms; this rate, which is therefore a measure of the volume of gas consumed, is transmitted to a counting mechanism. This type of meter is able to measure even very small rates of gas flow with considerable accuracy, but at high rates of flow the accuracy diminishes because the valves can then no longer be changed over quickly enough. The meter is very reliable and unlikely to develop disorders, and for this reason it is widely used for metering domestic supplies.

The *"wet" gas meter* operates on the same principle as the drum type rotary meter for liquids (see page 226). The Crossley meter is an extensively used type. Its principle is illustrated in Fig. 2. The drum, which contains four compartments with inlet and outlet slots or holes, rotates half immersed in water, which acts as a seal. As soon as the inlet hole of a compartment emerges from the water, gas flows into it and fills the compartment as the water level in it goes down. When the outlet hole of the compartment emerges from the water, the gas flows out through this hole. Residual gas remaining in the compartment is forced out by the inflowing water as the drum continues its rotation.

In Fig. 2, compartment I of the meter is completely filled with water. The gas is being forced out of compartment II by the water. Compartment III is full of gas, and compartment IV, whose inlet hole has just emerged from the water, is beginning to fill up with gas. The gas pressure causes the rotation of the drum. The number of revolutions is recorded by a counting mechanism whose readings show the amount of gas consumed.

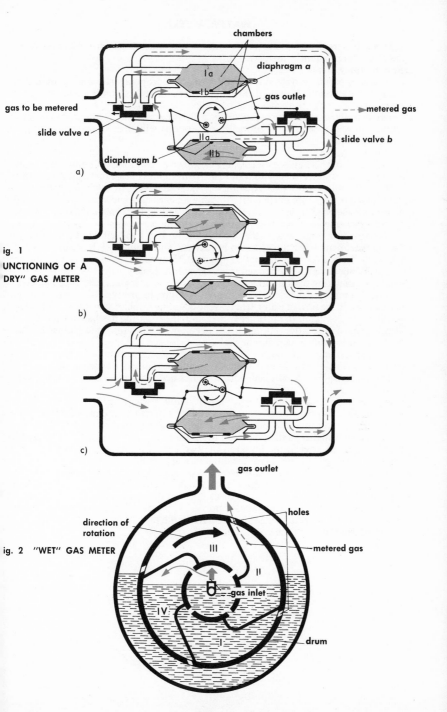

chambers

diaphragm a

gas outlet

gas to be metered

metered gas

slide valve a

slide valve b

diaphragm b

a)

fig. 1
FUNCTIONING OF A
"DRY" GAS METER

b)

c)

gas outlet

direction of
rotation

holes

fig. 2   "WET" GAS METER

metered gas

III

II

gas inlet

IV

I

drum

225

WATER METERS

Water meters used for measuring water consumption may function according to either of two different principles:

Rate-of-flow meters:

In devices of this kind the flowing water rotates a propeller whose speed of rotation (r.p.m.) is measured. A certain flow rate (cubic feet per second) corresponds to a certain speed of the propeller. The propeller speed indicator can therefore be calibrated directly in cubic feet per second (or gallons per second). A counting mechanism which totals the number of propeller revolutions will thus show the quantity of water consumed.

Volumetric meters:

In devices of this category a rotating chamber or container of known volumetric capacity is constantly filled with water and then empties itself. Here again the number of rotations is a measure of the quantity of water that flows through the meter. Volumetric meters are more particularly suitable for measuring low rates of flow. In the drum type meter (Fig. 1) the water enters the drum at the central inlet and fills one of the measuring compartments. The compartment is so designed that, as it fills up, the weight of the water makes the drum rotate (in Fig. 1 the left-hand deeper part of the compartment, when full of water, is heavier). The rotation of the drum causes the the water to flow out of the outlet opening. Meanwhile the next compartment is already being filled with water entering at the central inlet.

For the metering of domestic water supplies the rotating impeller type of meter is frequently employed. These devices are of two types. In one type (Fig. 2) the impeller is immersed in the flow of water, whereas the counting mechanism and dial are housed in a dry compartment. In the other type (Fig. 3) the counting mechanism and dial are also immersed. The latter type has better accuracy, but has the disadvantage that dirt in the water is liable to clog up the dial.

Woltmann meters are used for the metering of larger quantities of water, especially in industry (Fig. 4). This kind of meter consists essentially of a straight length of pipe in which a propeller is installed, which rotates and transmits its motion through a worm gear.

A different type of metering device is the Venturi meter (Fig. 5). It is based on the principle that different flow velocities produce different amounts of suction. The Venturi meter comprises a pipe formed with a constriction or "waist". The flow velocity at B is higher than at either of the sections A, and the suction (measured by the difference in level in the liquid in the two legs of the U-tube manometer) at B is correspondingly greater. Since the difference in pressure between B and A depends on the flow velocity, it must also depend on the quantity of water passing through the pipe per unit of time (flow rate in cu. ft./sec. = cross-sectional area of pipe in ft.^{2} × flow velocity in ft./sec.). Hence this pressure difference provides a measure for the flow rate. In the gradually tapered portion of the pipe downstream of B the velocity of the water is reduced and the pressure in the pipe restored to the value it had before passing through the constriction.

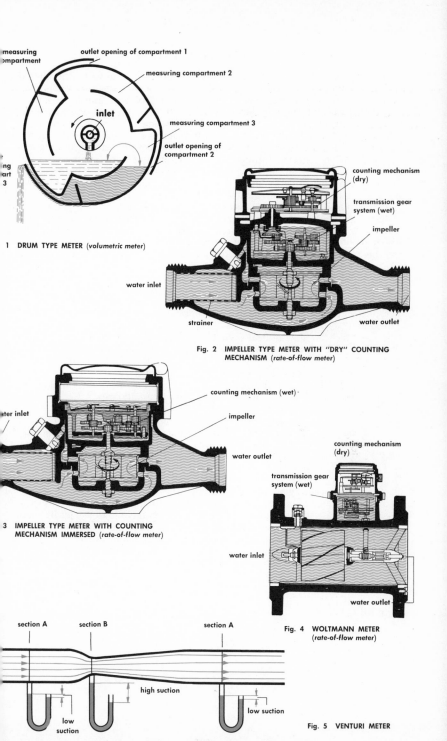

measuring compartment

outlet opening of compartment 1

measuring compartment 2

inlet

measuring compartment 3

outlet opening of compartment 2

measuring compartment 3

1 DRUM TYPE METER (*volumetric meter*)

counting mechanism (dry)

transmission gear system (wet)

impeller

water inlet

strainer

water outlet

Fig. 2 IMPELLER TYPE METER WITH "DRY" COUNTING MECHANISM (*rate-of-flow meter*)

counting mechanism (wet)

impeller

water inlet

water outlet

3 IMPELLER TYPE METER WITH COUNTING MECHANISM IMMERSED (*rate-of-flow meter*)

counting mechanism (dry)

transmission gear system (wet)

water inlet

water outlet

Fig. 4 WOLTMANN METER (*rate-of-flow meter*)

section A

section B

section A

high suction

low suction

low suction

Fig. 5 VENTURI METER

227

THERMAL INSULATION

If two bodies with different temperatures can exchange heat with each other, they will finally both acquire the same temperature at some intermediate value between their original temperatures. There are three kinds of heat transfer: convection, radiation, and conduction. In the case of convection (Fig. 1), heat transfer is effected by the flow of a gas or a liquid caused by local heating and the effect of gravity (e.g., when a room is heated by warm air rising from a stove or a radiator, water heating; cf. page 240 *et seq.*). Thermal radiation is independent of heat-transmitting matter and can also be effected through vacuum. Every hot body emits rays (electromagnetic waves) (Fig. 2) which are located in the infra-red portion of the spectrum, i.e., they have wavelengths longer than those of visible light rays. Bodies which absorb a large amount of radiation (e.g., soot) also re-emit a large amount of radiation. On the other hand, a suitably transparent body will, in general, allow radiant heat to pass and will undergo only a slight rise in temperature in consequence.

Transfer of heat by conduction occurs in the interior of solid bodies (Fig. 3) and also in liquids and gases. The rate of transfer will depend on the thermal conductivity, the thermal capacity of the materials, and the temperature difference. In building construction the thermal conductivity is a criterion for the heat insulating capacity of a material, which is important with regard to the loss of heat through the walls of a building. In metric units, thermal conductivity is expressed as the amount of heat (kcal)[1] which flows through 1 m^3 cube of a material in a time of 1 hour when the temperature difference between the two opposite faces of the cube is constantly maintained at 1° C. The "cube" must be conceived as a 1 m^2 area of a 1 m thick wall through which the flow of heat occurs. Steel has a thermal conductivity of about 50 kcal/m^3h °C; the corresponding figure for natural stone is about 2.5, for concrete about 1.5, for brickwork about 0.75, for glass about 0.70, for wood about 0.15, and for cork panels about 0.035. In British units the conductivity is usually expressed as the heat (in B.T.U.[2]) that is transmitted through 1 sq.ft. of a 1 ft. thick wall in 1 hour for a temperature difference of 1° F between the two wall faces.

The heat capacity (kcal per °C) of a body is the amount of heat that must be added to it, or abstracted from it, so as to produce a change of 1° C in its temperature. The thermal resistivity is the reciprocal of the thermal conductivity and provides a direct indication of the heat-insulating power of a material: the thicker the layer of material and the lower its thermal conductivity, the higher will be its resistivity (Fig. 4).

The best heat insulator is a vacuum (in combination with efficient protection against heat transfer by radiation). An important application is, for example, the vacuum flask, a double-walled glass vessel, the cavity between the two walls being exhausted of air (and silvered to minimise losses of heat due to radiation), so that this vacuum serves to insulate the contents of the flask and keep them hot or cold. In building construction, heat insulation is obtained by using materials which are poor conductors of heat, especially materials containing a large number of air-filled voids or pores. Since air itself is a poor conductor of heat, such materials are good insulators. Air as a heat-insulating substance is also utilised in cavity walls, i.e., brick walls consisting of an outer and an inner "leaf" separated by an air gap.

1. Kilo calories.
2. 1 B.T.U. = 0.252 kcal.

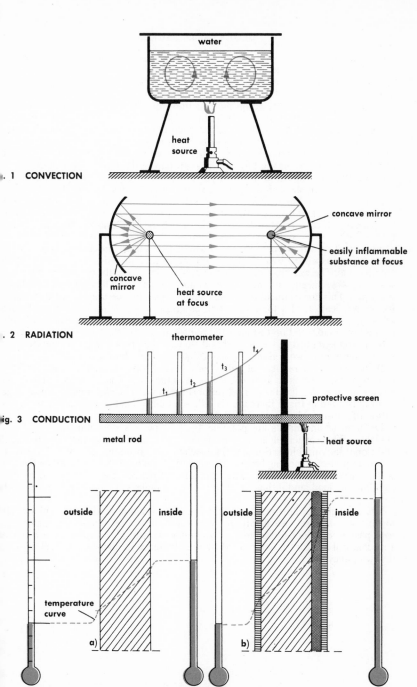

water

heat source

Fig. 1 CONVECTION

concave mirror

easily inflammable substance at focus

concave mirror

heat source at focus

Fig. 2 RADIATION

thermometer

t_1 t_2 t_3 t_4

protective screen

Fig. 3 CONDUCTION

metal rod

heat source

outside inside outside inside

temperature curve

a) b)

Fig. 4 EXAMPLES OF TEMPERATURE GRADIENTS IN A WALL:
(a) without insulation; (b) with insulating backing and facing

229

BLOCK AND TACKLE

A block and tackle arrangement is an extensively applied mechanical device which is used for lifting loads and hauling. It comprises two or more pulley blocks and a length of rope that passes round the pulleys. With its aid it is possible to lift heavy loads by the application of only a relatively small force. The mechanical principle of equilibrium based on the equation: force × arm of the force = load × arm of the load is illustrated in Figs. 1a and 1b. In Fig. 1a there is obviously no equilibrium, but in Fig. 1b the equilibrium equation is satisfied, i.e., one boy at a distance from the pivot of the see-saw (the fulcrum of the pivot) will counterbalance two boys (of the same weight as the other) at a distance $\frac{1}{2} l$ from the pivot. It will also be apparent that if the boy on the right-hand side descends a distance s, the boys on the left will rise a distance $\frac{1}{2} s$. The product of the force (i.e., the weight moved) times the distance is therefore the same on both sides. This product—force × distance—is called "work". A similar situation presents itself when a rope carrying a weight at each end is passed round pulleys. In Fig. 2 there is no equilibrium, since the left-hand load is twice as large as the right-hand load and the lever arm (equal to the radius of the pulley) is the same for both loads (just as in Fig. 1a). In the arrangement shown in Fig. 3 there is a top "fixed" pulley and a moving pulley, the latter being suspended by two "falls" of rope, in each of which acts a pull equal to half the load. The sole function of the top pulley is to change the direction of the rope so that the force needed on the right to balance the left-hand load can act as a downward pull. This arrangement therefore enables a load of a certain weight to be raised by the application of a force only half as great as that load. Thus a mechanical advantage is gained, but there is no saving in the amount of work, because in order to raise the load a certain distance, the right-hand end of the rope (where the lifting force is applied) must move twice that distance. The product of force and distance, i.e., the amount of work done, is therefore the same in both cases.

By increasing the number of pulleys and falls of rope, the mechanical advantage is increased according to $W = nP$, where W is the load, P is the force applied, and n is the number of falls of rope that support the moving block. Thus, in the arrangement illustrated in Fig. 6 there are six falls, enabling a load to be lifted by the application of a force only one-sixth as large.

Different arrangements are possible. In the type of system illustrated in Fig. 4 (which can be conceived as derived from Fig. 3 as the fundamental case) each additional moving block doubles the mechanical advantage, i.e., $W = 2^m P$, where m is the number of moving blocks. Thus, in Fig. 4 we have $W = 2^2 P = 4P$ or $P = \frac{1}{4} W$. If there were a third moving pulley similarly suspended, the force would be one eighth of the load, and if there were four moving pulleys, it would be one-sixteenth etc.

The arrangement illustrated in Fig. 5 is known as a differential pulley block. The top block comprises two firmly interconnected pulleys of different diameter. The rope passes continuously round the two pulleys shown. This arrangement provides a mechanical advantage determined by the difference in diameter $(R - r)$ between the two pulleys.

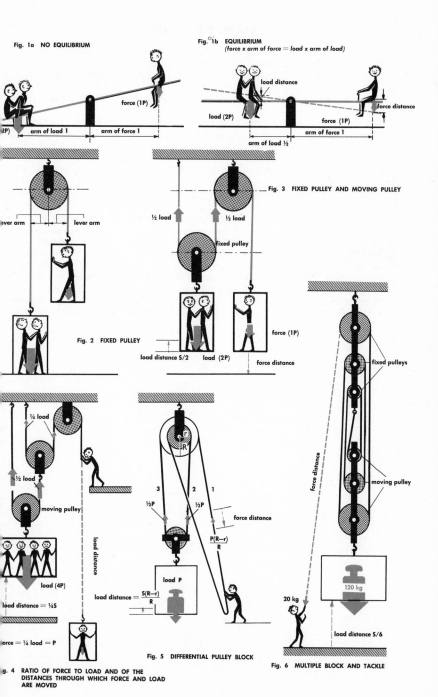

Fig. 1a NO EQUILIBRIUM

force (1P)

2P) arm of load 1 arm of force 1

Fig. 1b EQUILIBRIUM
(force x arm of force = load x arm of load)

load distance

force distance

load (2P) force (1P)

arm of load ½ arm of force 1

lever arm lever arm

Fig. 2 FIXED PULLEY

½ load ½ load

fixed pulley

force (1P)

load distance S/2 load (2P) force distance

Fig. 3 FIXED PULLEY AND MOVING PULLEY

¼ load

½ load

moving pulley

load (4P)

load distance

load distance = ¼S

orce = ¼ load = P

3 2 1

½P ½P force distance

$\frac{P(R-r)}{R}$

load P

load distance = $\frac{S(R-r)}{R}$

Fig. 5 DIFFERENTIAL PULLEY BLOCK

fixed pulleys

force distance

moving pulley

120 kg

20 kg

load distance S/6

Fig. 6 MULTIPLE BLOCK AND TACKLE

g. 4 RATIO OF FORCE TO LOAD AND OF THE
DISTANCES THROUGH WHICH FORCE AND LOAD
ARE MOVED

PNEUMATIC HAMMER

A pneumatic hammer delivers a large number of blows in rapid succession. These blows are delivered by a piston which moves to and fro in a cylinder and is worked by compressed air. The piston strikes the upper end of a tool inserted in the front of the appliance. Various kinds of tool can be fitted, so that the appliance can be used not merely as a hammer, but as a pick, a concrete breaker, a digging tool, etc.

The compressed air is supplied through a hose from a compressor (see page 26). When the inlet valve is opened by means of the lever mounted within the handle (Fig. 2), the air flows through the diaphragm valve into the outer air compartment. The diaphragm valve is convex, so that it can rock to and fro. In Fig. 2 this valve is in the position where it opens the inlet passage to the outer compartment. From here the air flows into the inner compartment from below and forces the piston upwards. The air above in the space above the piston undergoes compression, so that it forms an air cushion which somewhat softens the impact of the return movement of the piston. At the same time, this air acts against the underside of the diaphragm valve and tilts it the other way, with the result that the inlet passage to the outer compartment is closed and the inlet passage to the inner compartment is opened (Fig. 3). The compressed air is thereby admitted to the top of the piston and forces it downwards, so that it strikes the upper end of the tool. Both during the downward and during the upward stroke of the piston the expanded exhaust air is discharged into the exhaust air compartment and thence into the open air.

All pneumatic tools of the hammer or drill type function on the principle described here, though there are differences of detail in the design of the valves.

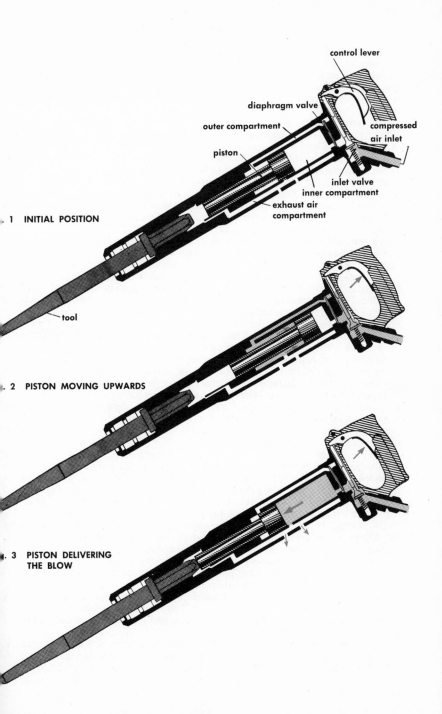

control lever

diaphragm valve

outer compartment

piston

compressed
air inlet

inlet valve

inner compartment

exhaust air
compartment

1 INITIAL POSITION

tool

2 PISTON MOVING UPWARDS

3 PISTON DELIVERING
THE BLOW

233

CRANES

Cranes are of many different kinds, depending on the purpose for which they are intended and on the magnitude of the loads to be handled. They may be mobile or stationary. The load is picked up by means of such attachments as hooks or tongs (for individual loads) or by means of buckets, skips or grabs (for bulk materials). A special lifting attachment, used mainly for the handling of scrap iron, is the lifting magnet. These attachments are usually suspended from wire ropes which pass round various pulley systems and are wound on hoist drums which are driven by electric motors. The principles of the pulley block (see page 230) are often embodied in the lifting tackle of cranes.

A major distinction can be made between bridge cranes and jib cranes. A crane of the bridge type has a trolley, or crab, which travels along a track and carries the winch that lifts the load. The commonest form of bridge crane is the overhead travelling crane used in factories, workshops, etc. Such a crane usually consists of a "bridge", comprising two girders, each end of which is mounted on a truck which travels on an overhead track extending the length of the building. The crab can travel to and fro on a transverse track installed on these girders. The combined movements of the crab and of the crane as a whole enable the lifting hook to be brought into position at any desired point in the building.

A jib crane has an arm—called the jib (or boom)—which can usually perform a "slewing" motion, i.e., rotate horizontally about a vertical pivot (the "king pin") mounted in the substructure of the crane. In addition, the jib is often able to perform a "luffing" (or "derricking") motion, i.e., it can be raised or lowered by varying its angle of inclination. The combination of these two motions enables the hook to be brought into position at any desired point within a certain radius. A type of jib crane used on construction sites for tall buildings is the tower crane (Fig. 1). Another type of jib crane is the so-called level-luffing crane, which is so designed that, by means of some form of compensating mechanism, the load moves in a horizontal path when the jib is luffed (raised or lowered); this arrangement has certain technical and operational advantages, especially in quay cranes used for loading and unloading ships at ports. Fig. 2 shows a particular form of level-luffing crane which has what is known as a double-lever jib. In this crane the compensating action is obtained by the movements of the jib lever. An advantage of this crane is that its projecting jib lever provides a greater amount of lateral clearance than an ordinary straight jib, so that there is ample space for handling bulky loads.

Every crane has a certain lifting capacity, ranging from a few tons to many hundreds of tons, depending on the type of crane and the purpose for which it is intended. In jib cranes the capacity usually varies with the radius, which depends on the slope of the jib. When the latter is raised to a steep slope, the radius—the distance from the load to the centre of the king pin—is small, and the crane can then carry a heavier load than when the jib is lowered to its farthest extent and the radius is large. This difference in lifting capacity at different radii is determined by the stability of the crane, i.e., its safety against overturning. The weight of the load (suspended from the jib) multiplied by the radius constitutes the overturning moment. The latter is counterbalanced by a heavy counterweight which is located a certain distance rearward from the king pin and develops a counterbalancing moment. This counterweight may be mounted on the substructure or on a special secondary jib projecting to the rear and is sometimes movable, so that the counterbalancing moment can be varied within certain limits. The overturning moment must always be smaller than the counterbalancing moment, and for this reason only a certain maximum load is permissible at a certain radius.

Besides hooks, a variety of lifting and handling devices can be attached to cranes. An important device for picking up bulk materials such as coal, ore, etc. is the grab (Fig. 3). It consists of two shells which can open and close to pick up the load and subsequently discharge it. These movements are produced by the actuation of the holding rope and the closing rope.

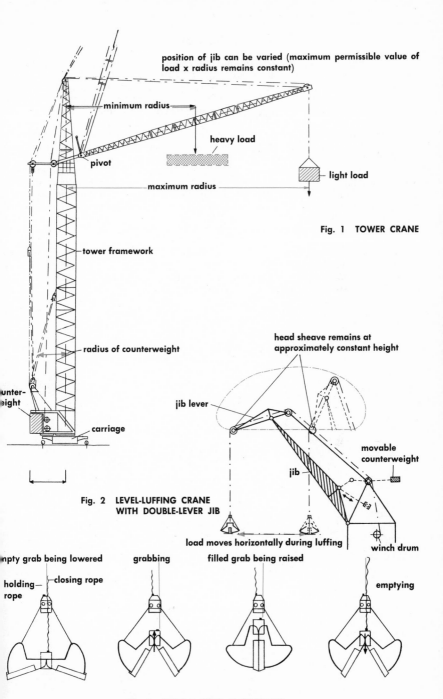

position of jib can be varied (maximum permissible value of load x radius remains constant)

minimum radius

heavy load

pivot

light load

maximum radius

Fig. 1   TOWER CRANE

tower framework

radius of counterweight

head sheave remains at approximately constant height

counter-weight

jib lever

carriage

movable counterweight

jib

Fig. 2   LEVEL-LUFFING CRANE WITH DOUBLE-LEVER JIB

load moves horizontally during luffing

winch drum

empty grab being lowered

grabbing

filled grab being raised

holding-rope

closing rope

emptying

Fig. 3   HOW A GRAB IS OPERATED

235

LIGHTNING CONDUCTOR

A lightning conductor, or lightning rod, comprises a system of metal conductors whose purpose is to provide an easy path to earth for a lightning discharge striking the highest points of a building. In this way the discharge takes place through the conductor instead of through the building, so that the latter is safeguarded from damage. To perform this function, the lightning conductor must, of course, be properly earthed (grounded) (Fig. 1). The principle of the lightning conductor was discovered by Benjamin Franklin in the 18th century. The system consists of pointed air terminals (rods) mounted on the ridges of roofs, on chimneys, etc. Lightning conductors do not prevent lightning strokes, but exert a local influence to direct strokes to the air terminals and thence safely to earth. To help them perform this function the air terminals are provided with sharp points. At these points the lines of force of the electric field are closely concentrated (Fig. 2), so that ionisation of the air around the points takes place, i.e., electrons (negatively charged particles) become dislodged from atoms, with the result that the latter are left with a positive charge, thereby making the air conductive to electricity and providing an easier path for the lightning discharge (Fig. 3).

Steel-framed buildings generally need no special lightning protection, as the frame itself provides a suitable path for the lightning discharge to earth. Isolated buildings, such as farm buildings, run a greater risk of being struck by lightning than buildings of similar size and height in built-up areas.

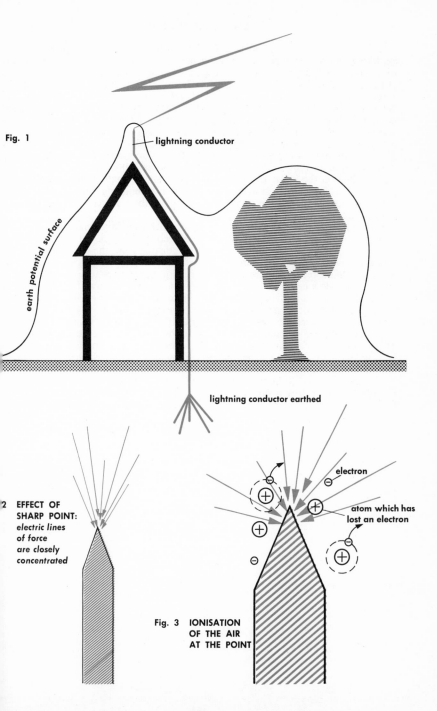

Fig. 1

lightning conductor

earth potential surface

lightning conductor earthed

2 EFFECT OF
SHARP POINT:
electric lines
of force
are closely
concentrated

electron

atom which has
lost an electron

Fig. 3   IONISATION
OF THE AIR
AT THE POINT

237

LIFT (ELEVATOR)

A lift (or elevator, as it is called in the United States) is a power-operated device for lifting and lowering passengers from one level to another; it comprises a car which runs between guide rails and is suspended from steel hoisting ropes. The weight of the car and its load is approximately counterbalanced by a counterweight. The weight to be hoisted by the drive motor is therefore never the total weight of car and passengers but only the relatively small difference between the counterweight and the weight of the loaded car (this latter weight will, of course, vary to some extent according to the number of passengers carried at any given time). The car is braked by means of electromagnets acting upon the drive shaft of the hoist pulley. The creep motion of the car before stopping at a floor is obtained by changing over to a lower speed of the motor. The switches which automatically effect this speed change are installed on the inside of the lift shaft. Similar automatic switches unlock the door or gate of the lift when it stops at a floor of the building. When the lift passes a floor without stopping, the device which actuates these switches is rendered temporarily inoperative.

Some lifts are equipped with a safety rope which runs in an endless loop round pulleys at the top and bottom of the shaft respectively (Fig. 2). This rope is secured to the lift car. In the event of fracture of the hoisting rope, the car will drop. This causes the pulleys of the safety rope to rotate more rapidly. A centrifugal governor (see page 188) connected to the top safety rope pulley then actuates a switch which sets the car safety device in operation. This causes powerful jaws to grip the guide rails and thus arrest the descent of the car. Various other safety devices are provided on modern lifts, including limit switches to prevent over-travel of the car, door interlocks to prevent the car from starting until the doors are securely closed, etc.

A type of lift still sometimes employed is the so-called paternoster lift (Fig. 3). This is a continuous elevating device for passengers, which consists essentially of two endless chains between which the cars are suspended and which are so arranged that the cars go up on one side and down on the other side. The two chains are driven by a motor installed at the top of the building. The cars travel continuously, but at a low speed, so that there is sufficient time to step in and out of them at the successive floors. In modern buildings such devices have largely been superseded by escalators (see page 540).

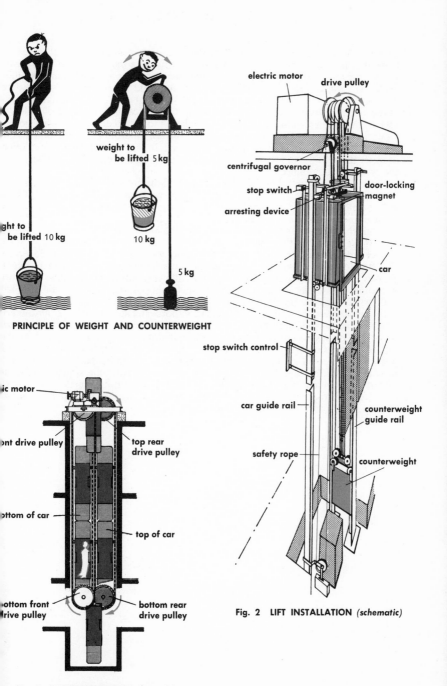

electric motor

drive pulley

centrifugal governor

stop switch

door-locking magnet

arresting device

car

PRINCIPLE OF WEIGHT AND COUNTERWEIGHT

weight to be lifted 5 kg

weight to be lifted 10 kg

10 kg

5 kg

stop switch control

car guide rail

counterweight guide rail

safety rope

counterweight

ic motor

ont drive pulley

top rear drive pulley

bottom of car

top of car

bottom front drive pulley

bottom rear drive pulley

Fig. 2   LIFT INSTALLATION (schematic)

Fig. 3   PATERNOSTER LIFT (schematic)

239

HOT-WATER HEATING (GRAVITY SYSTEMS)

In a heating system operated with hot water the water serves as the medium for carrying the heat to all parts of the building. Heating causes nearly all substances to expand. This is also true of water. A result of this phenomenon is that the specific gravity, or the weight per unit volume, of water decreases when its temperature is raised, i.e., warm water is specifically lighter than cold water. Fig. 1 illustrates the principle of hot-water heating. When the tank shown at the bottom left-hand corner of the system is heated, the hot water rises in the vertical pipe (because of its lower specific gravity, which makes it "float" in relation to the colder water), while cooler ("heavier") water descends in the right-hand vertical pipe and enters the tank where it is in turn heated and rises in the pipe on the left. In this way a constant circulation of water through the pipes and through the radiator in the top right-hand corner of the system is maintained.

In the domestic central heating system in Fig. 2 the hot water from the boiler rises through the flow pipe and circulates through the radiators. In these it gives off heat and therefore cools. It thus becomes specifically heavier and descends by gravity through the return pipes to the boiler, where it is heated and resumes its circulation through the system. For efficient circulation the boiler must obviously be located at the lowest point of the system.

In gravity systems the water is heated to about 90° C when it rises in the flow pipe. The radiators are so designed that the temperature of the water going down the return pipes is about 70° C. Venting the system, i.e., allowing entrapped air in the radiators to escape, is essential to ensure efficient functioning. A vent pipe may be installed at the top of the system; the radiators may be provided with individual venting cocks.

In the simplest form of gravity-circulation hot-water heating (Fig. 2) all the hot water ascends to roof level through the flow pipe and then flows down through return pipes and passes successively through the radiators on the various floors of the building. The disadvantage is that the radiators on the lower floors receive colder water than those on the upper floors and therefore have to be made larger in order to compensate for this. For this reason the so-called two-pipe system (Fig. 3) is preferred, in which each radiator has its own individual hot-water feed instead of (in the case of the radiators on the lower floor in Fig. 2) receiving water which has already passed through another radiator.

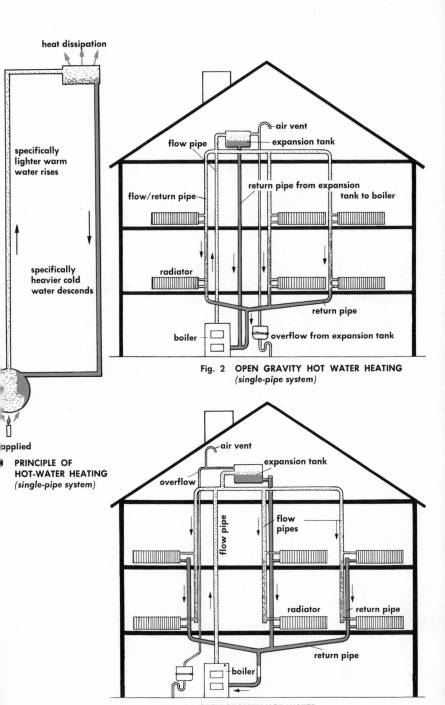

heat dissipation

specifically
lighter warm
water rises

specifically
heavier cold
water descends

applied

PRINCIPLE OF
HOT-WATER HEATING
(single-pipe system)

air vent

expansion tank

flow pipe

return pipe from expansion
tank to boiler

flow/return pipe

radiator

return pipe

boiler

overflow from expansion tank

Fig. 2 OPEN GRAVITY HOT WATER HEATING
(single-pipe system)

air vent

expansion tank

overflow

flow pipe

flow
pipes

radiator

return pipe

return pipe

boiler

Fig. 3 OPEN GRAVITY HOT-WATER
HEATING (two-pipe system)

HOT-WATER HEATING (PUMPED CIRCULATION SYSTEMS)

Gravity systems rely entirely on the difference in specific gravity between hotter and colder water to produce the desired circulation and are especially suitable for small buildings and also for large buildings which are concentrated on plan. For large, sprawling complexes of buildings more efficient circulation can be achieved by means of an electrically driven centrifugal pump (cf. page 24). Pipes of smaller diameter than in gravity-circulation systems can be employed.

The pump may be installed either in the flow pipe (i.e., in the pipe extending from the boiler to the radiators) or in the return pipe. In the former arrangement the pump sucks hot water from the boiler and forces it through the pipes into the radiators, whence it returns to the boiler. When the pump is in the return pipe, it sucks the cooled water from the radiators and forces it into the boiler. In the simplest arrangement for a pumped-circulation hot-water heating system the radiators on successive floors are connected in series (single-pipe system, Fig. 1).

The two-pipe system with pumped circulation is similar in principle to the gravity system (see page 240). In addition, the pump may be installed in the flow pipe or in the return pipe (Fig. 3 and Fig. 2), as already stated. In the two-pipe system the hot water that flows into the radiators and the cooled water that flows out of them are conveyed through two different pipelines. The installations described here are known as low-pressure systems, i.e., they are in open communication with the external air through a vent pipe from the expansion tank.

Hot-water heating systems can be automatically controlled, i.e., the room temperature can be kept constant at any desired value by means of thermostats (see page 20). These devices are pre-set to the desired temperature, and when the actual temperature rises above, or falls below, this value, the thermostats transmit impulses which control the valves which in turn control the flow of hot water to the radiators or control the firing of the boiler itself by appropriately varying the fuel supply rate or (in the case of coal-fired systems) the combustion air rate. In the case of pumped circulation it is, alternatively, possible to control the hot-water flow by varying the speed of the pump.

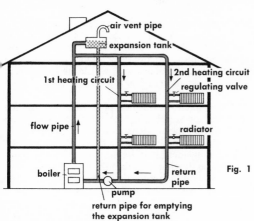

Fig. 1 **SINGLE-PIPE PUMPED-CIRCULATION HEATING SYSTEM** *with radiators connected in series (two circuits) and pump installed in the return pipe*

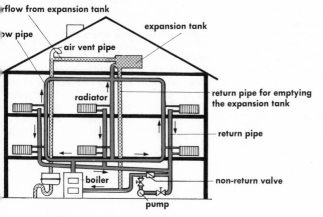

Fig. 2 **TWO-PIPE SYSTEM** *with pump installed in the return pipe*

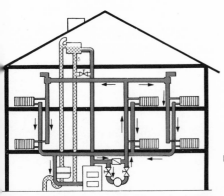

Fig. 3 **TWO-PIPE SYSTEM** *with pump installed in the flow pipe*

STEAM HEATING

In this type of central heating the heat-conveying medium is not hot water, but steam. In the radiators the steam gives off its heat and condenses. It thus flows back as water to the boiler, where it is again turned into steam (Fig. 1). In houses, low-pressure steam heating systems are used; these usually have an excess pressure of about 0.5 atm. (7 lb./in².) in relation to the external air, with which the system is in communication through valves. The hot steam used has a temperature of around 105° C.

From the boiler the steam rises to the main distribution pipe, which is installed either in the basement (Fig. 2a) or in the top storey (Fig. 2b) of the building. From this pipe the steam flows into the radiators; the condensation water flows back to the boiler through the same pipe. This return flow pipe may be situated above the level of the water in the boiler. This arrangement may be described as "dry" condensate return. To prevent steam from also flowing back into the boiler, steam traps are installed in this pipe. In the second system the return flow pipe is situated below the boiler water level and is entirely filled with water and thus prevents the return flow of steam ("wet" condensate return).

In the two-pipe system, which is more often employed, the steam and the condensate flow in separate pipes. Here again bottom (Fig. 3a) or top distribution (Fig. 3b) may be employed. In both cases, however, the steam always enters the radiators from above and subsequently emerges (as condensate) from below. When the system is started up, and the pipes and radiators become filled with steam, the air that was present in them is forced to the bottom of the system (as steam is specifically lighter than air), where it must be discharged through vent cocks.

To prevent the pressure in the boiler from becoming excessively high, the steam pipe is connected by means of a branch pipe to a relief valve, which may be of the type illustrated in Fig. 4. Increasing steam pressure in the boiler forces the water down in pipe I and up in pipes II and III. If the pressure becomes excessive, the water in pipe I is forced down so far that steam can escape through pipe II and pipe IV. The water displaced from pipe II is collected in the tank and subsequently, when the pressure goes down, flows back into pipe III.

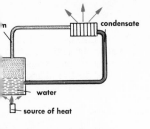

water turns to steam by heating

**1   PRINCIPLE OF CIRCULATION
IN A STEAM HEATING SYSTEM**

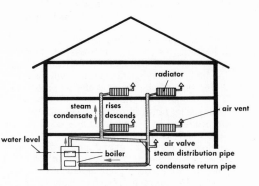

**Fig. 2a   SINGLE-PIPE LOW-PRESSURE SYSTEM WITH
BOTTOM DISTRIBUTION AND "WET"
CONDENSATE RETURN**

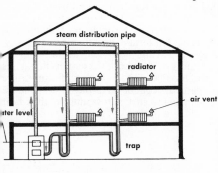

**Fig. 2b   SINGLE-PIPE LOW-PRESSURE SYSTEM WITH TOP
DISTRIBUTION AND "DRY" CONDENSATE RETURN**

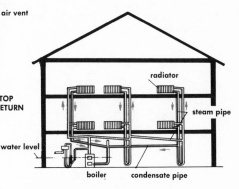

**Fig. 3a   TWO-PIPE LOW-PRESSURE SYSTEM WITH BOTTOM
DISTRIBUTION AND "DRY" CONDENSATE RETURN**

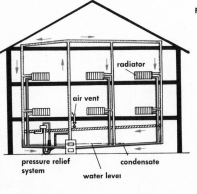

**3b   TWO-PIPE LOW-PRESSURE SYSTEM WITH TOP
DISTRIBUTION AND "WET" CONDENSATE RETURN**

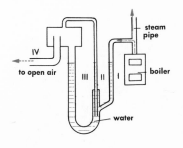

Fig. 4   PRESSURE RELIEF SYSTEM

GAS HEATING

Gas heating systems are usually fired with normal town gas. Like any other form of heating, gas heating functions on three physical principles: thermal radiation, convection, and conduction. Which of these three heat transmission effects predominates in any particular case will depend on the type of heating appliance.

One type of gas heater is the so-called infra-red radiator, whose heating action is based mainly on the emission of infra-red rays (these are heat rays and occur in the invisible range beyond the red end of the spectrum of visible light). These rays are produced by burning gas in special burners (Fig. 1a) whose heat is directed at panels of fireclay, steel fabric or some other suitable material, which are thus heated to glowing temperature and emit radiant heat. For heating halls and large rooms these radiant panels may be fitted to the ceiling (Fig. 1b). The radiation becomes more intense according as the panels are hotter.

So-called convection heaters represent a different heating principle. In this case the hot gases of combustion mainly give off its heat indirectly to the surrounding air. The most well known type of heating appliance functioning on this principle is the gas radiator, in which the burners are usually arranged in a row at the base. The hot combustion gases from the flames flow upwards through the radiator ribs which in turn give off the heat to the air. The latest form of construction of the gas-fired convection heater is the chimneyless type (Fig. 3), which can be mounted against any external wall. After giving off most of their heat, the combustion gases are discharged through a vent pipe straight into the open air. The significant feature of these convection heaters is that the hot gases are conducted through the appliance by the longest possible path, so as to enable them to part with as much of their heat as possible.

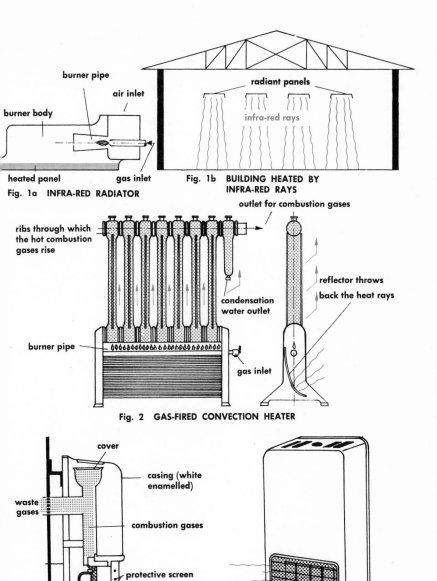

burner pipe

air inlet

burner body

heated panel   gas inlet

Fig. 1a   INFRA-RED RADIATOR

radiant panels

infra-red rays

Fig. 1b   BUILDING HEATED BY INFRA-RED RAYS

outlet for combustion gases

ribs through which the hot combustion gases rise

reflector throws back the heat rays

condensation water outlet

burner pipe

gas inlet

Fig. 2   GAS-FIRED CONVECTION HEATER

cover

casing (white enamelled)

waste gases

combustion gases

protective screen

gas supply connection

radiant burner

Fig. 3   CHIMNEYLESS GAS HEATER

HEAT PUMP

The principle of the heat pump is similar to that of the compression refrigerator (see page 276). It has the same components: compressor, condenser, throttle valve and evaporator. But whereas the refrigerator extracts heat from a chamber by the evaporation of the refrigerant and thereby lowers the temperature, the heat pump supplies heat to a room by condensation of a heat-transfer medium. The phenomenon utilised for this purpose is that fluids which are under high pressure evaporate at a higher temperature than fluids under a lower pressure. In Fig. 1 two chambers are interconnected by a passage in which a vessel which completely seals it off can move from right to left and back. Atmospheric pressure exists in the left-hand chamber, while the right-hand chamber is under a much lower pressure (i.e., a partial vacuum). If energy is supplied to a quantity of water in the right-hand chamber, this water will evaporate ("boil") already at a temperature below 100° C. When a vessel containing water vapour formed by this process is shifted from the right-hand to to the left-hand chamber, the steam will at once condense at the higher pressure which prevails in the latter chamber. On condensing, it gives off heat. In this way a substantial proportion of the heat input in the right-hand chamber is recovered in the left-hand chamber (there can never be complete recovery, since some energy must be expended in pushing the vessel to the left, against the higher pressure).

In the heat pump (Fig. 2) the fluid heat-transfer medium—e.g., ammonia—is evaporated at low pressure in the evaporator. The heat needed for this may be obtained from various sources. For a small installation, the evaporator may, for example, merely be buried in the ground. The soil at all times contains sufficient heat to evaporate the heat-transfer medium. Other heat-transfer media that can be employed under suitable conditions are water and air. The work of transporting the medium from low to high pressure is done by the compressor. It draws in the vapour and compresses it to the desired higher pressure. Then, in a condenser, the steam is condensed at that higher pressure and gives off heat in doing so. This condensation is effected by passing the vapour through pipes with water flowing around them. The heat from the vapour of the condensing heat-transfer medium is thus transferred to this water, which is thereby heated to about 60°–70° C. and can be used as a second heat transfer medium to feed the radiators of a heating system. It cools in the radiators and flows back to the condenser, where it is heated up again. In so far as this circulating water is concerned, the condenser of the heat pump therefore performs the function of an ordinary central heating boiler. The vapour which condenses in the system is expanded to a lower pressure through a valve and is again evaporated in the evaporator.

By means of this cycle the heat-transfer medium within the heat pump is "pumped up" from a low temperature (e.g., the temperature of river water, about 10° C, say) to a higher temperature (high enough for a central heating system), the necessary work being done by the compressor. Heating systems based on this principle can be advantageous where electricity to drive the compressor is cheap. They are also sometimes installed in buildings where both cooling and heating are necessary, e.g., in dairies. The cellars can be cooled by the extraction of heat by the evaporator, while the heat evolved in the condenser heats the upper storeys.

Figs. 3a and 3b show a heat pump, which can be used for heating or cooling the room, depending on the setting of the four-way valve.

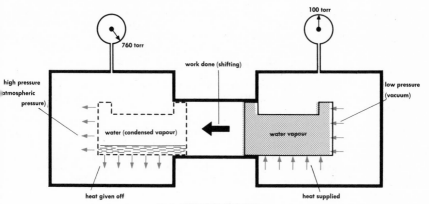

Fig. 1 PRINCIPLE OF HEAT PUMP

high pressure (atmospheric pressure)

760 torr

work done (shifting)

water (condensed vapour)

heat given off

100 torr

low pressure (vacuum)

water vapour

heat supplied

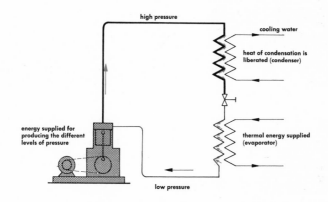

Fig. 2 DIAGRAM SHOWING OPERATION OF HEAT PUMP

high pressure

cooling water

heat of condensation is liberated (condenser)

energy supplied for producing the different levels of pressure

thermal energy supplied (evaporator)

low pressure

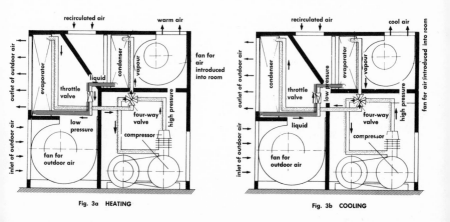

Fig. 3a HEATING

recirculated air

warm air

outlet of outdoor air

evaporator

throttle valve

liquid

condenser

vapour

fan for air introduced into room

low pressure

four-way valve

high pressure

inlet of outdoor air

fan for outdoor air

compressor

Fig. 3b COOLING

recirculated air

cool air

outlet of outdoor air

condenser

throttle valve

low pressure

evaporator

vapour

fan for air introduced into room

liquid

four-way valve

high pressure

inlet of outdoor air

fan for outdoor air

compressor

249

VALVES, COCKS AND TAPS

Devices known as valves, cocks, taps and faucets are used for controlling the flow of liquids and gases. "Valve" is the general term. The familiar water tap (or faucet) is technically therefore a valve. A plug cock (Fig. 1) is a simpler device in which the fluid passage is a hole in a rotatable plug which has a slightly tapered shape and is fitted in the body of the cock. Opening and closing the cock is done by rotating the plug through an angle of 90°. Some degree of flow control is possible by setting the plug of the cock in an intermediate position. Much more accurate control of the rate of flow of the fluid is provided by a valve, of which there are a number of different types. A feature common to most manually operated flow control valves is the stem (a screw spindle) surmounted by a handwheel. The fluid (gas or liquid) flows through an opening whose edge forms the valve seat. The ordinary domestic water tap illustrates the principle (Fig. 2). The stem is provided with a disc which is usually provided with a replaceable sealing washer to make the actual contact with the seat and thus stop the flow of water. To open the tap, the disc is raised by rotating the handwheel (or simple cross-bar handle) in the anti-clockwise direction, so that the stem is screwed out of the valve body. Clockwise rotation brings the valve disc into contact with the seat and thus closes the tap. In some valves the stem, instead of being provided with a disc, ends in a conical point which is inserted into the hole of the seat and closes it when the stem is screwed right home. This type is known as the needle valve. Another variant is the angle valve (Fig. 3). Larger valves used for controlling the flow of liquids in pipelines, water mains, etc. are often of the kind illustrated in Fig. 5. It is known as a gate valve or sluice valve. In this valve a wedge-shaped gate, actuated by a stem (with screw thread) and a handwheel, moves up and down. The gate bears against two seat faces to shut off the flow. The fluid flows through the gate valve in a straight line, so that the flow resistance is minimised. The valve stem must be suitably sealed at its point of entry into the valve body, in order to prevent leakage of the fluid. The seal is usually formed by a so-called stuffing box (Fig. 4), which is a cylindrical recess filled with packing which is compressed by a sleeve (known as a gland) to make a tight joint. The material inserted in the stuffing box is called packing. It may be a compressible material such as hemp or asbestos. The pressure exerted by the gland (screwed or bolted on) keeps the packing tightly pressed against the valve stem.

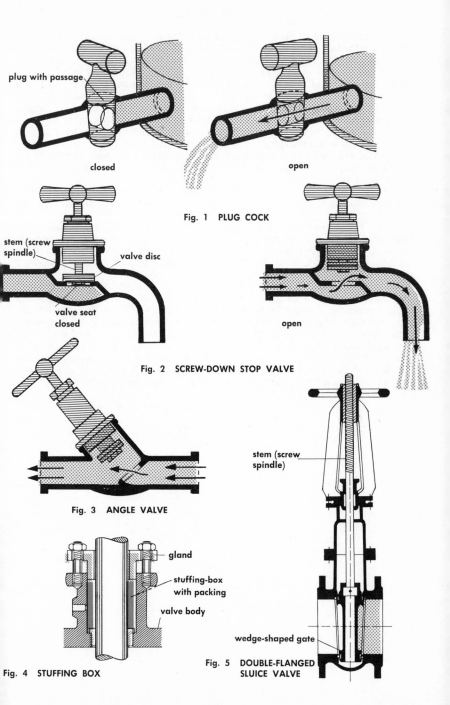

plug with passage

closed

open

Fig. 1   PLUG COCK

stem (screw spindle)

valve disc

valve seat
closed

open

Fig. 2   SCREW-DOWN STOP VALVE

Fig. 3   ANGLE VALVE

stem (screw spindle)

gland

stuffing-box with packing

valve body

wedge-shaped gate

Fig. 4   STUFFING BOX

Fig. 5   DOUBLE-FLANGED SLUICE VALVE

DOOR LOCKS

The simplest kind of door lock is the so-called rim lock, whose metal case is screwed to the face of the door (Fig. 7). The lock is provided with a bolt which can be slid out or withdrawn by the action of the key. When the key is turned, it first presses the tumbler—which is kept engaged with the bolt by the pressure of a spring—upward and thus releases the bolt. The key bit (the lateral projection at or near the end of the key) then engages with the first notch on the underside of the bolt. Further rotation of the key causes the bolt to slide until the catch of the tumbler engages with the next notch on the top of the bolt. In simple locks, as on cupboard doors, this completes the locking action; but doors of rooms usually have double-action locks, in which the same operation is repeated and the bolt is moved along a further distance. Safeguard against unauthorised entry is provided merely by the individual shape of the bit (Fig. 2) and the corresponding hole into which it is inserted.

Greater safety is provided by a lock having not one, but several tumblers (Fig. 3). In such a lock the bolt is provided with a "stop" (a projecting pin). The tumblers are not notched at the top edge as in Fig. 1, but have their notches formed on the inside of a slot. The stop on the bolt engages with these notches. The undersides of the tumblers are variously shaped, and the key bit is provided with corresponding cuts and projections (Fig. 4). When the key is turned in the lock, the projections of the bit raise all the variously shaped tumblers an exact specified amount, whereby a clear passage for the stop through the slot is provided.

A further safeguard is obtained by the use of one or more wards. A ward may take the form of a ring (as in Fig. 5a) or a number of studs which are arranged in a circle around the centre of rotation of the key. The key bit is then additionally provided with grooves (Fig. 5b) which engage with the wards. If the key is not provided with such grooves in the correct position, it cannot be turned in the lock. The wards are fixed to the back plate of the lock or to a separate mounting plate (Fig. 6a); in that case the key has a divided bit (which fits over the plate), the grooves for the wards being arranged as shown in Fig. 6b. The lock illustrated in Fig. 7 has multiple lever tumblers similar to those in Fig. 3. For cylinder locks see page 254.

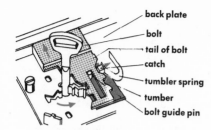

back plate
bolt
tail of bolt
catch
tumbler spring
tumbler
bolt guide pin

Fig. 1   LOCK WITH ONE TUMBLER

Fig. 2   KEY BITS

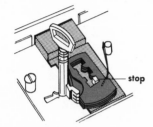

stop

Fig. 3   LOCK WITH
SEVERAL TUMBLERS

Fig. 4   KEYS FOR LOCKS WITH
SEVERAL TUMBLERS

annular ward fixed to
back plate of lock

Fig. 5a   WARD

Fig. 5b   KEY FOR LOCK
PROVIDED WITH A WARD

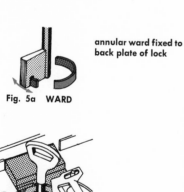

ward
mounting plate

Fig. 6a   WARDS FIXED TO SEPARATE
MOUNTING PLATE

Fig. 6b   KEY FOR LOCK IN FIG. 6A

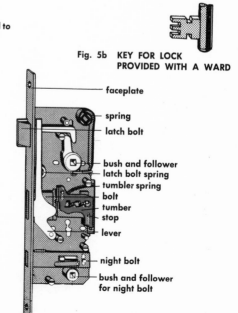

faceplate
spring
latch bolt
bush and follower
latch bolt spring
tumbler spring
bolt
tumbler
stop
lever
night bolt
bush and follower
for night bolt

Fig. 7   RIM LOCK

253

CYLINDER LOCK

The central feature of the cylinder lock is a rotatably mounted plug or cylinder. In the locked position (Fig. 1) a number of pin tumblers of different lengths and comprising an upper and lower segment are pressed down by springs to engage with holes in the cylinder, thereby preventing the latter from rotating. When the key is inserted into the lock (Fig. 2), the lower segments of the pin tumblers are raised by exactly the correct amount to bring their tops flush with the outer surface of the cylinder. As the two segments of each tumbler are separate, i.e., not interconnected, the cylinder is then free to rotate when the key is turned. The cylinder actuates the bolt, so that door can be opened. If the wrong key is inserted, it will not raise all or any of the lower tumbler segments to the correct height, and the cylinder cannot be rotated (Fig. 3).

Another and generally cheaper type of cylinder lock is the disc tumbler lock, in which the locking action is provided, not by segmented pins, but by movable discs which lock the cylinder.

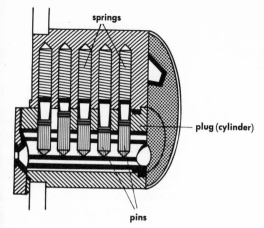

springs

Fig. 1 LOCKED: PINS PREVENT
PLUG FROM ROTATING

plug (cylinder)

pins

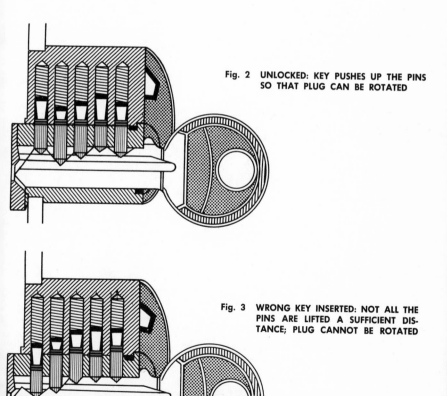

Fig. 2 UNLOCKED: KEY PUSHES UP THE PINS
SO THAT PLUG CAN BE ROTATED

Fig. 3 WRONG KEY INSERTED: NOT ALL THE
PINS ARE LIFTED A SUFFICIENT DIS-
TANCE; PLUG CANNOT BE ROTATED

255

ELECTRIC BELL

In an electric bell the to-and-fro movement of the hammer is produced by electro-magnetic action. A two-pole electromagnet (comprising two cores interconnected by an iron yoke) is energised and attracts the armature to which the hammer is attached. At that instant the circuit is broken by the contact which is likewise attached to the armature; the electromagnet immediately releases the armature, which springs back, whereupon the contact re-establishes the circuit and thus causes the electromagnet to be energised again; and so on. This continues for as long as the push-button is pressed. A bell of this kind (or a buzzer, which is, in fact, nothing but an electric bell which has no hammer and no gong) can work on direct current or on low-frequency alternating current. For alternating current an alternative type of bell can be used, which requires no make-and-break contact (Fig. 2). The armature is polarised, i.e., it is permanent magnet. The electromagnet varies its polarity in the rhythm of the frequency of the current, so that the armature is periodically attracted and repelled. The hammer thus moves to and fro in time to the alternation of the current. Bells of these kinds are chiefly used in telephones.

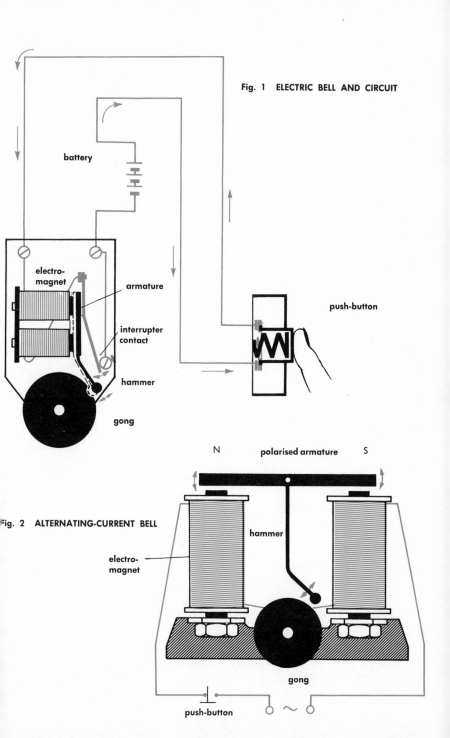

Fig. 1 ELECTRIC BELL AND CIRCUIT

battery

electro-
magnet

armature

interrupter
contact

hammer

gong

push-button

N   polarised armature   S

Fig. 2 ALTERNATING-CURRENT BELL

hammer

electro-
magnet

gong

push-button   ~

257

DOOR-CLOSER

The door-closer is the familiar device that automatically closes an opened door. The simplest type (Fig. 1) works merely with a coil spring. It has the disadvantage that the door is shut rather violently. For this reason a more sophisticated device is used, which develops a slow closing movement. Door-closers of this kind operate on the principle of the shock absorber (see page 508): a piston moving in a cylinder forces oil through small openings. When the door is opened, the piston is withdrawn; and the oil in the cylinder opens a ball valve in a passage provided in the piston and flows into the space to the right of the piston (Fig. 2). When the door is released, it is closed by the action of the spring; the piston travels back to the right and forces the oil through the return passages (Fig. 3) into the space to the left of the piston. At first, the movement proceeds quite rapidly because the oil can flow back through two passages; but it becomes slower and slower, because the oil escape is progressively cut off by the advance of the piston.

The regulating screw provides the means of compensating for differences in the viscosity of the oil at different temperatures. In cold weather the oil is relatively thick. By unscrewing the regulating screw the flow passage through which the oil escapes is enlarged, so that the door can be closed just as briskly as in warmer weather, when the oil is thinner and therefore flows more easily. However, this adjustment is unnecessary if special silicone oils, which have an almost unvarying viscosity, are used in the door-closer.

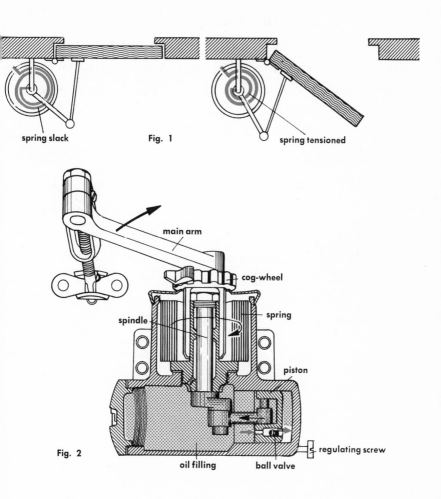

spring slack Fig. 1 spring tensioned

main arm

cog-wheel

spindle spring

piston

Fig. 2

oil filling ball valve regulating screw

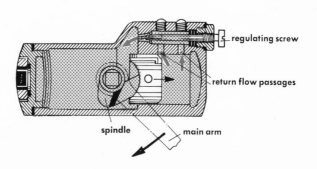

regulating screw

return flow passages

spindle main arm

Fig. 3

WATER CLOSET (TOILET)

When the chain attached to the lever of the flushing cistern is pulled (Fig. 2), the hollow iron bell-shaped unit rises and opens the passage to the flush pipe. As soon as water flows down this pipe, a vacuum is formed in the cavity of the bell and causes more water to flow from the cistern through the bell and down the pipe. The cavity inside the bell thus acts as a siphon (Fig. 1). When a vacuum is formed at C (by initially applied suction), water is drawn through the siphon tube. Once the flow has been started, it will continue. For the siphon to function, its outlet must always be below the level of the water in the tank. When the chain of the water closet has been briefly pulled and released, the bell falls back into position over the inlet of the flush pipe, but the flow of water down the pipe continues—thanks to the siphon effect—until the cistern has been drained. As the water level in the cistern goes down, the float descends and opens the water supply valve, so that the cistern fills up again. When the float has risen to a certain level, the inflowing water is cut off by the valve. The capacity of the flushing cistern is usually 2 gallons.

Fig. 3 illustrates another type of cistern. When the rod is briefly pulled up and then released, the water here, too, continues to flow until the cistern is drained. The rod is provided with a freely movable float which is prevented from floating to the surface of the water by two stops on the pull rod. When the rod is raised and the inlet of the flush pipe is opened, the closing pressure which is developed by the water column in the full tank is reduced. The buoyancy of the float predominates and keeps the pipe inlet open. Then the rod descends and the rubber valve disc is thrust against its seat by the inflowing water.

In some systems the flush pipe is connected to the water supply through a lever-operated (Fig. 4) or a push-button-operated valve (Fig. 5). In the former the flushing operation is initiated and terminated by hydraulic pressure equalisation which is effected by the composite valve system. In the push-button type, actuation of the button initiates the flow, which is subsequently likewise cut off by pressure equalisation and spring action.

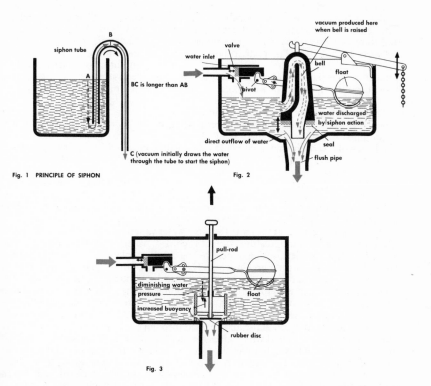

siphon tube

B

A

BC is longer than AB

C (vacuum initially draws the water
through the tube to start the siphon)

Fig. 1 PRINCIPLE OF SIPHON

valve

water inlet

pivot

vacuum produced here
when bell is raised

bell

float

water discharged
by siphon action

direct outflow of water

seal

flush pipe

Fig. 2

pull-rod

diminishing water
pressure

increased buoyancy

float

rubber disc

Fig. 3

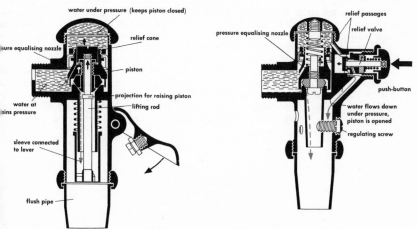

water under pressure (keeps piston closed)

relief cone

...sure equalising nozzle

piston

projection for raising piston

water at
...ains pressure

lifting rod

sleeve connected
to lever

flush pipe

Fig. 4 LEVER-OPERATED FLUSHING SYSTEM

relief passages

pressure equalising nozzle

relief valve

push-button

water flows down
under pressure,
piston is opened

regulating screw

Fig. 5 PUSH-BUTTON-OPERATED FLUSHING SYSTEM

AIR CONDITIONING

The function of an air-conditioning system is to keep the temperature and humidity of the air in rooms at values which provide a sense of comfort for human beings. The upper temperature limits of comfort are about 20° C and 25° C in winter and and summer respectively. At the same time, the relative humidity of the air must be between 35 and 70%. The relative humidity denotes the amount of water vapour actually present in the air as a percentage of the maximum amount that could be present at that particular temperature, i.e., if the air were saturated with moisture. It is therefore the ratio of the pressure of water vapour present to the saturated vapour pressure at the same temperature.

The central feature of an air-conditioning system is the air-conditioning plant (Fig. 1). Fresh air, together with a proportion of the air returned from the air-conditioned rooms (recirculated air) is drawn into a mixing chamber, the relative quantities of fresh air and recirculated air being controlled by valves. This air is cleaned by means of filters. These usually have glass-wool filter elements in which dust is retained.

After filtering, the air is preheated. This is done by means of heating pipes through which steam or hot water is passed and which are provided with fins which serve to increase their heat-exchange surface area. The air to be preheated flows along these fins and absorbs heat from them. Excess moisture is removed from a portion of the air by cooling. The warmer the air is, the more water vapour it can absorb. Conversely when air with a certain moisture content is cooled, water condenses in the form of myriads of tiny droplets, which appear as fog. In the cooler of the air-conditioning plant the moisture is thus precipitated. The moisture content and temperature of the air emerging from the cooler are determined by the temperature of the cooler. This air is then mixed with the air coming straight from the preheater, so as to obtain an air mixture of the desired temperature. If the moisture content of the mixture is too low, finely atomised water is added by spray nozzles. This causes some cooling of the air, and for this reason the air is passed through a reheater which is essentially similar to the preheater and which gives the air its desired final temperature. Behind the reheater is the fan which forces the conditioned air through ducts to the various parts of the building. The constant supply of air to the rooms produces a slight excess pressure in them, which causes the exhaust air to flow back through return ducts. Some of this exhaust air is discharged to the open air, while a certain portion (the recirculated air) is returned to the conditioning plant. In smaller air-conditioning units the air sometimes is divided into two streams, one of which is heated and the other cooled (Fig. 2). In each room these two air streams are mixed in the proportions to produce the temperature desired by the occupants of that particular room.

The system described in the foregoing is what is known as a centralised air-conditioning system, i.e., all the air is treated in a central conditioning plant and conveyed through ducts to the rooms. There are many variants of the centralised system. Decentralised systems operate either in conjunction with a central conditioning plant which treats only the proportion of outside air that is introduced into the system, or they may be fully decentralised, using only self-contained cabinet or box-type air-conditioning units in the various rooms.

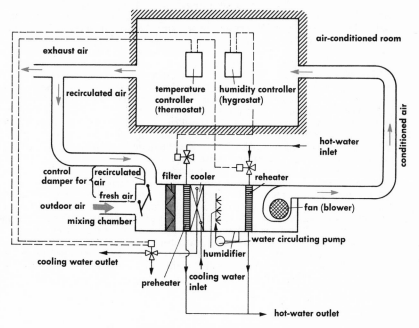

Fig. 1 CENTRALISED AIR CONDITIONING SYSTEM

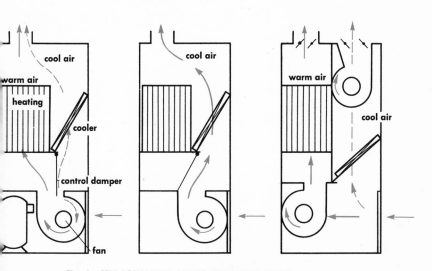

Fig. 2 SELF-CONTAINED AIR-CONDITIONING UNITS

FANS, BLOWERS AND CENTRIFUGAL COMPRESSORS

Mechanical devices for moving air or other gases and operating on the centrifugal principle—as also applied in centrifugal pumps (cf. page 24)—are sometimes classified as fans (high rates of delivery at low pressure), blowers (high rates of delivery at medium pressure), and compressors (high-pressure delivery). In semi-technical language, however, the term "fan" is more often applied to any propeller-type device which imparts motion and acceleration to air (Fig. 2).

The operating principle is the same for all three classes of centrifugal machine. The air is drawn in at the centre of the casing (Fig. 1a) by the rotating impeller which is driven by an electric motor and contains a number of passages arranged in a spiral pattern (Fig. 3). On flowing through these passages the air is given an acceleration and emerges under pressure from the spiral casing (volute) of the fan (Fig. 1b). To obtain higher delivery pressures, a number of such impellers, mounted on the same shaft, can be installed one behind the other (in series), whereby the desired high pressure is achieved in several successive stages (Fig. 4).

Air can also be compressed by rotary methods based on positive displacement. Fig. 5 illustrated the functioning of a rotary compressor of this kind. A cylindrical rotor is disposed eccentrically in a cylindrical casing. The rotor is provided with approximately radial plates which are movably inserted in slots. As a result of the high speed of rotation, these plates are flung outwards by the centrifugal force and are thus passed against the inside of the casing. Because of the eccentricity of the rotor, the compartments between these plates become alternately larger and smaller, so that the air drawn into the compartments from the inlet pipe is compressed and discharged under pressure from the outlet pipe. In the Roots blower (Fig. 6) two mating lobed impellers, driven by two gear wheels which are in mesh with each other, revolve in opposite directions within a casing.

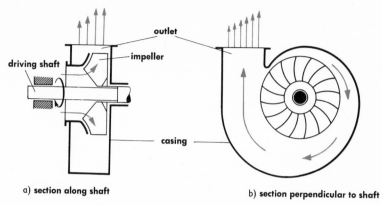

a) section along shaft

b) section perpendicular to shaft

Fig. 1 CENTRIFUGAL COMPRESSOR

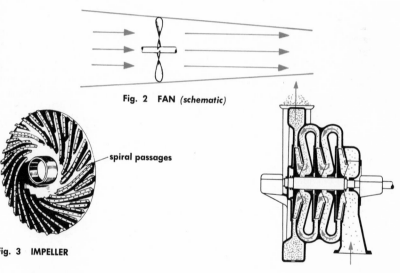

Fig. 2 FAN (schematic)

Fig. 3 IMPELLER

Fig. 4 MULTI-STAGE COMPRESSOR

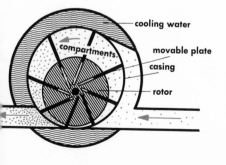

Fig. 5 ROTARY COMPRESSOR

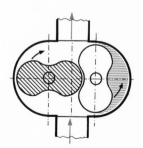

Fig. 6 ROOTS BLOWER

265

ROOM-HEATING STOVE

The most familiar type is the coal-burning slow-combustion stove (Fig. 1). It has a combustion chamber, lined with fireclay, which is charged with coal. The air for combustion enters the combustion chamber from below (by the action of natural draught). In another type of stove the air is drawn through the fuel in the downward direction (Fig. 2). Combustion takes place more particularly at the bottom of the combustion chamber; the narrower portion above it serves as a feed hopper from which fresh coal is supplied as the coal on the grate burns away (base-burner stove).

For better heat utilisation the combustion gases must not be directly discharged up the chimney, but should be compelled to make a detour so as to give off more of its heat. For this purpose the gases are made to pass through a system of ducts called flues. An efficiently designed stove embodying this principle can achieve as much as 80 per cent heat utilisation. Even so, the temperature of the gases discharged up the chimney is still about 200° C; the surface of the stove has approximately the same temperature when it is operating at full capacity.

A further development is represented by the so-called tile stove (Figs. 3a and 3b), which consist of an iron stove surrounded by a kind of jacket or casing constructed of tiles or some other ceramic material. The flue gases additionally give off heat to this casing, which stores up the heat and gradually gives it off to the air in the room.

Oil-fired stoves (Figs. 4 and 5) operate as follows: The oil from the supply tank flows into a small control tank which contains a float-operated valve that cuts off the inflow when the oil in the control tank has reached a certain level. In this way an approximately constant oil feed pressure to the burner is ensured. From the control tank the oil flows through a control valve which can be set to deliver the oil to the burner at a certain rate. By varying the valve setting, the heat output of the stove can be regulated. The burner is usually of the pot type, in which the oil first vaporises as a result of coming into contact with the hot walls of the combustion chamber. Combustion air flows into the chamber through holes, and the oil vapour burns continuously. The hot gases of combustion flow upwards and heat the combustion chamber walls. These in turn give off their heat to the air in the room. Some stoves are equipped with small fans to assist the flow of combustion air, thus making this largely independent of chimney draught. The fuel used is a relatively light fuel oil. The hot gases discharged up the chimney have a temperature of 300°–400° C.

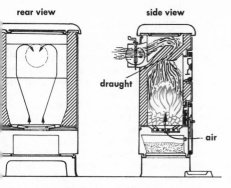

rear view   side view

draught

air

Fig. 1   COAL-BURNING SLOW-COMBUSTION STOVE

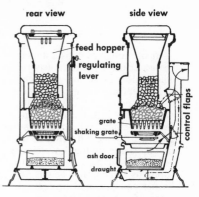

rear view   side view

feed hopper

regulating lever

grate

shaking grate

control flaps

ash door

draught

Fig. 2   BASE-BURNER STOVE

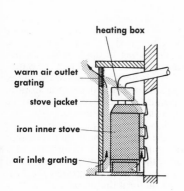

heating box

warm air outlet grating

stove jacket

iron inner stove

air inlet grating

Fig. 3a   TILE STOVE

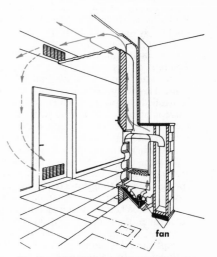

fan

Fig. 3b   TILE STOVE WITH FAN-ASSISTED AIR CIRCULATION

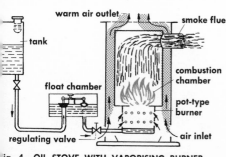

warm air outlet

smoke flue

tank

combustion chamber

float chamber

pot-type burner

regulating valve

air inlet

Fig. 4   OIL STOVE WITH VAPORISING BURNER

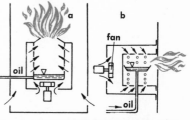

a) fan mounted under the burner

b) fan mounted on one side of the burner

oil

fan

oil

Fig. 5   VAPORISING BURNER WITH FAN

267

GAS-FIRED WATER HEATER (GEYSER)

In the so-called "instantaneous" gas-fired water heater (flow heater or geyser) the water flows continuously through the appliance, i.e., there is no storage vessel. The mode of functioning of such a heater is illustrated by the accompanying diagram.

The central feature is the heat exchanger through which the water flows and which is surrounded by the hot combustion gases produced by the burners. In the heat exchanger, which has a large heat transfer surface area, a large proportion of the heat contained in these gases is transferred to the water. The heat transfer is chiefly governed by the difference in temperature between the water to be heated and the hot gases and by the flow velocity of the water through the heat exchanger.

The pilot flame is kept alight and instantly lights the burner when the main gas supply is turned on. The gas flow controller keeps the rate of supply of gas to the burner constant and protects the appliance from overloading. The gas valve in the gas flow controller is itself controlled by the water flow acting through the agency of a diaphragm and a venturi tube (see page 226). The water flow controller keeps the water flowing at the desired pre-set rate by throttling down the mains pressure. With this device the flow of water through the heat exchanger can be regulated, and the final temperature of the hot water can thus be varied.

To get hot water, it is necessary first to move the gas control lever to the igniting position and light the pilot flame (assuming that this has not been done already). The heat of this flame causes the end of a bimetallic spring (see page 20) to move downwards, causing the ignition safety valve of the burner to open. When the gas control lever is moved farther, to the "on" position, gas is admitted under the water-controlled gas valve (which is still closed, however). Now when the hot-water outlet valve is opened, the flowing water causes an excess pressure to develop in front of the venturi tube and a suction at the throat of this tube. The excess pressure and the suction act on the underside and on the top of the diaphragm respectively. As soon as a certain minimum quantity of water is flowing through the venturi, the diaphragm is—by the combined action of pressure and suction—lifted to such an extent that the water-controlled gas valve is fully opened (against the restraining force of a spring). The gas thus flows to the burner and is lit by the pilot flame. The combustion gases rising from the burner flames heat the water as it flows through the heat exchanger. When the water is subsequently turned off (or if the supply accidentally fails), the pressure on the two sides of the diaphragm becomes equal, the diaphragm descends, and the spring-loaded water-controlled gas valve closes, so that the burner (except the pilot flame) goes out. If the gas is turned off (or if the pilot flame is extinguished by whatever cause), the bimetallic spring cools, and the ignition safety valve is closed by the spring, so that no unburned gas can escape even with the water turned full on.

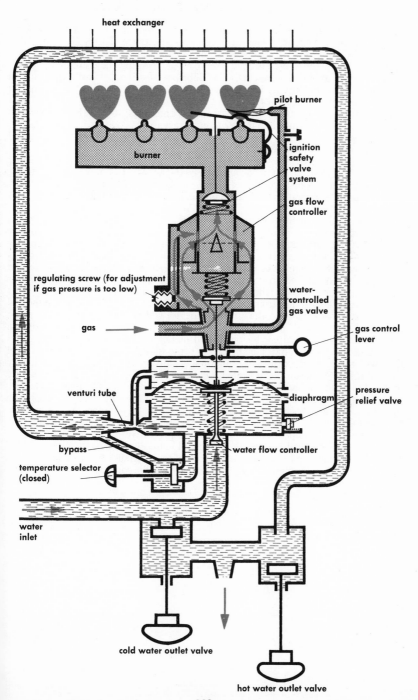

heat exchanger

pilot burner

ignition
safety
valve
system

burner

gas flow
controller

regulating screw (for adjustment
if gas pressure is too low)

water-
controlled
gas valve

gas

gas control
lever

venturi tube

diaphragm

pressure
relief valve

bypass

water flow controller

temperature selector
(closed)

water
inlet

cold water outlet valve

hot water outlet valve

THERMAL ELECTRIC DOMESTIC APPLIANCES

Thermal electric domestic appliances utilise the property of electric current of being able to develop heat when it encounters resistance. The electric current is conveyed by electrons. These transfer some of their kinetic energy to the atoms of which the conductor (the resistance wire) consists, causing these atoms to vibrate more violently about their respective equilibrium positions. It is this agitation of the atoms that manifests itself as a rise in temperature, i.e., heat. For a constant voltage, the heat produced by the current is proportional to the square of the current strength times the resistance of the wire, i.e., proportional to I^2R (Joule's law). To obtain a good heat output it is therefore necessary to use conductors having a high electric resistance. Various forms of tubular heating elements containing coiled resistance wire are illustrated in Fig. 1.

The simplest electric heating devices are *immersion heaters*, which may be either of the tubular type (Fig. 2a) or the annular type (Fig. 2b). The heat produced in the heating element is transferred to the surrounding liquid. The heat losses are small, and immersion heaters therefore have a high efficiency, nearly all the heat being given off to the liquid.

The principal component of an electric cooker is the *hot plate* (or boiling plate) (Fig. 3). Temperature control is usually effected by means of a bimetallic strip device (cf. page 20). A bimetallic strip consists of two strips of metal, with different coefficients of thermal expansion, bonded together. On being heated the two metals undergo different amounts of expansion, so that the strip curves and its free end (assuming the other end to be fixed) therefore deflects. This deflection, which is greater in proportion as the temperature is higher, can be used for actuating a contact or a switch. If the distance from the switch to the home ("cold") position of the end of the strip is made variable, the bimetallic device will be able to switch the current on and off over a whole range of operating conditions. Another device for utilising the difference in thermal expansion of two metals for performing a temperature-controlling function in domestic appliances is the Invar rod. Invar is an iron–nickel alloy with a very small coefficient of thermal expansion, so that it undergoes hardly any change in length on being heated. One end of such a rod is fixed in a slightly shorter brass tube. When the tube becomes hotter, it expands and increases its length, so that the end of the Invar rod disappears into the tube. When the tube cools, the end of the rod emerges again. The relative movement of the tube and the rod can be used for operating a switch (e.g., through suitable levers). A *water-boiling pan* (Fig. 4) may be equipped with a temperature-protective device (thermal release) which must automatically switch off the current in the event of overheating and then be capable of resetting to normal functioning of the appliance by pushing a button. a thermal release of this kind often comprises a bimetallic contact.

(Continued)

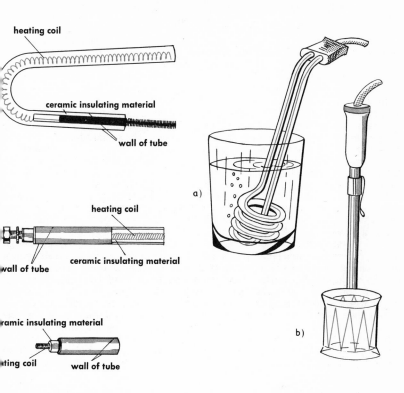

heating coil

ceramic insulating material

wall of tube

heating coil

ceramic insulating material

wall of tube

ceramic insulating material

heating coil

wall of tube

a)

b)

TUBULAR HEATING ELEMENTS USED IN
SMALL DOMESTIC HEATING APPLIANCES

Fig. 2   IMMERSION HEATER: (a) *tubular type*
(b) *annular type*

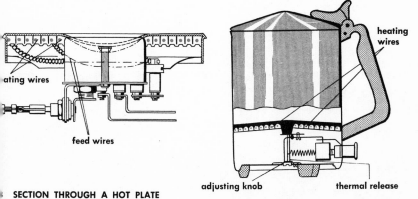

heating wires

feed wires

SECTION THROUGH A HOT PLATE

heating
wires

adjusting knob   thermal release

Fig. 4   SECTION THROUGH A WATER-BOILING PAN

With the immersion heater, water boiling pan and hot plate the transfer of heat is effected mainly by conduction and convection. In the *electric toaster* (Fig. 5), however, the heat is transferred by radiation. The slices of bread are inserted into two slots which have heating elements on both sides. When the toast is ready, a bimetallic device releases a spring, causing the slices of toast to "pop up".

In some warming pads the temperature can be pre-set to one of three maximum values, e.g., 80°, 70° or 60° C. When the pre-selected temperature is reached, the current is automatically switched off by means of a bimetallic device. When the temperature drops, the current is switched on again. The settings for these various temperatures are obtained by varying the degree of preheating of the bimetallic strip (Fig. 6). With the lowest preheat setting the highest temperature stage is obtained. In addition, a bimetallic safety device is provided, which breaks the circuit in the event of an excessively high temperature being reached (about 85° C).

Electric water heating appliances may be subdivided into storage heaters, boilers, and flow heaters (geysers). A *storage heater* comprises a water tank which is provided with efficient thermal insulation and whose contents are heated by a kind of immersion heater. Fig. 7a illustrates a small heater of this kind. The temperature control is "infinitely-variable" by means of a bimetallic controller of special design (Fig. 7b). When the bimetallic strip is heated, it curves upwards and thrusts against an actuating lever which is, at first, kept pressed down by a spring. When the force exerted by the bimetallic strip overcomes the counteraction of the spring, the actuating lever springs up and opens the contacts. With the heating element thus switched off, or when hot water is tapped from the tank (which is then replenished with cold water), the bimetallic strip cools and the operation is reversed, causing the contacts to be closed. By rotating the control knob for pre-selecting the temperature, the setting of the lever mechanism in relation to the bimetallic strip is varied, so that the device can be made to control the temperature over a fairly wide range (e.g., from 35° to 85° C).

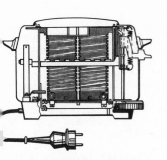

Fig. 5   ELECTRIC TOASTER

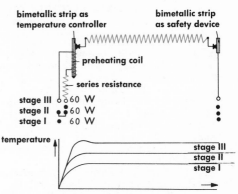

bimetallic strip as
temperature controller

bimetallic strip
as safety device

preheating coil

series resistance

stage III ○○60 W

stage II ●60 W

stage I ● 60 W

temperature

stage III

stage II

stage I

time

Fig. 6   CIRCUIT DIAGRAM OF ELECTRIC BLANKET
WITH PRE-SELECTED TEMPERATURE CONTROL

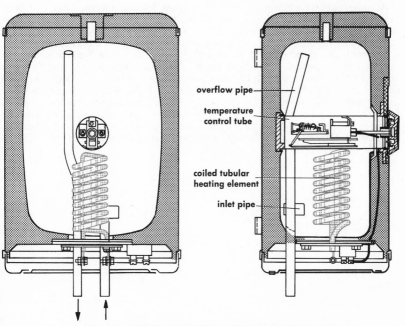

overflow pipe

temperature
control tube

coiled tubular
heating element

inlet pipe

Fig. 7a   SECTION THROUGH A SMALL STORAGE HEATER

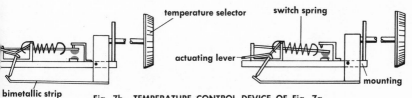

temperature selector

switch spring

actuating lever

mounting

bimetallic strip

Fig. 7b   TEMPERATURE CONTROL DEVICE OF Fig. 7a

273

A different temperature control device for hot-water storage heaters is illustrated in Fig. 8. It is installed in a protective tube beside the heating element and in close thermal communication with the hot water. Its principal component is an Invar rod (cf. page 270) which is fixed to an expansion tube. When it is heated, this tube expands, so that its end moves in relation to the end of the rod. This movement is transmitted through a lever mechanism to a mercury tube switch which tilts at a pre-set temperature and thus switches off the heating element.

In a *flow heater* (geyser) the water is not heated until just before it is actually needed. An appliance of this kind must heat the water very rapidly and must therefore have a very considerable heating capacity (about 12 kW, as compared with 2 kW for a small storage heater). See Fig. 9.

Electric *boilers* differ from storage heaters more particularly in having no thermal insulation. In this type of appliance, too, the water is heated only a short time before it is actually required. Once heated, it must be used quickly, for otherwise uneconomically large heat losses will occur. These appliances are relatively cheap and are moreparticularly suitable in cases where hot water is needed only at particular times.

A wide range of electric appliances for *room heating* purposes has also been developed. Wall-mounted (Fig. 11) and portable electric radiant heaters emit powerful heat rays which exercise their effect within a relatively small distance. The radiating unit comprises a parabolically curved reflector in whose line of focus a heating element is mounted. This reflector, more particularly if it is of the adjustable type, directs the heat rays in the desired direction. A heater of this kind does not efficiently heat up any significant volume of air. It has an effective "range" of only a few feet, and is used chiefly for auxiliary heating purposes (in bathrooms, bedrooms, etc.). More efficiently "space heating" is provided by the *fan heater* (Fig. 10). In this appliance the air drawn in by the fan is passed over a system of heating coils and then discharged into the room. A bimetallic cut-out is usually provided as a safeguard against overheating, more particularly if the fan fails to perform its proper function or if the free discharge of air is obstructed.

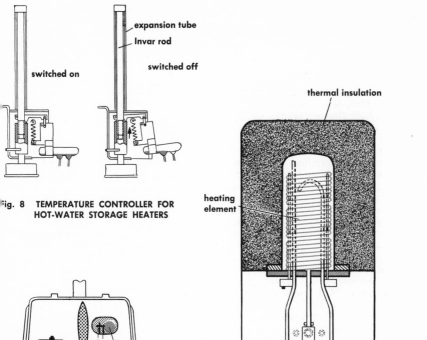

expansion tube
Invar rod
switched off

switched on

Fig. 8 TEMPERATURE CONTROLLER FOR
HOT-WATER STORAGE HEATERS

thermal insulation

heating
element

draining valve

hot water ◄-------   -------◄ cold water

Fig. 9 FLOW HEATER

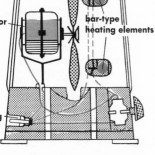

motor
bar-type
heating elements

plug

Fig. 10 FAN HEATER

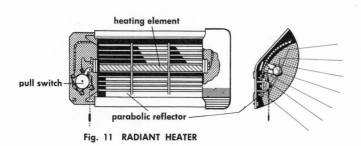

heating element

pull switch

parabolic reflector

Fig. 11 RADIANT HEATER

275

REFRIGERATORS

Refrigerators lower the temperature inside them by extracting heat from the interior. Two laws of physics are utilised in achieving this: 1. The boiling point of a liquid, i.e., the temperature at which it is turned into vapour, depends on the ambient pressure. Thus at a pressure of 1 atmosphere (normal atmospheric pressure), water boils at 100° C, but at a pressure of 0.1 atmosphere it will boil at only 46° C. This means that, conversely, water vapour of, say 50° C and 0.1 atmosphere pressure can be condensed, i.e., converted back into liquid water, simply by increasing the pressure to, for example, 1 atmosphere. 2. On passing from the liquid to the vaporous state, every liquid absorbs heat and subsequently gives off this heat again on condensing. If we choose a liquid whose boiling point at normal atmospheric pressure is below the low temperature that we wish to obtain, such a liquid will already evaporate ("boil") at that low temperature and will absorb heat while it does so. This heat is extracted from the surroundings. Now if the vapour formed in this way is compressed, it will condense even at ordinary room temperature because the higher pressure produced by compression is associated with a higher boiling point. On condensing, it gives off heat. If the pressure is then reduced back to normal, the cycle can be repeated. In order to obtain the desired effect, so-called refrigerants are employed (these are liquids with low boiling points or liquefied gases, e.g., ammonia, ethyl chloride or Freon). Fig. 1 shows the cycle of operations: the heat needed for evaporation of the refrigerant is extracted from the refrigerating compartment, so that the temperature inside the latter goes down. Next, the refrigerant is condensed, giving off heat in the process, and then made to evaporate again.—There are two kinds of refrigerator:

Compression refrigerator (Figs. 2 and 3): The refrigerant, which is under low pressure, is evaporated in the evaporator. The latter is a coiled pipe installed in the freezer compartment. The evaporation lowers the temperature in the refrigerating compartment. A small compressor draws away the vapour, compresses it, and passes it to a condenser, where it parts with its heat. As a result of the combination of increased pressure and loss of heat, the refrigerant condenses. Finally, the now liquid refrigerant is expanded to the lower pressure and is returned to the evaporator. The temperature inside the refrigerator is regulated by a thermostat (see page 20) which switches the compressor motor on and off through a relay (see page 94).

Absorption refrigerator (Fig. 4): The absorption refrigerator operates without a compressor. The pressure is built up in a so-called boiler or generator, which is usually heated by electricity and is filled with water containing a high concentration of dissolved ammonia. When this solution is heated, the ammonia is driven off as vapour and the water remains behind. As this ammonia evaporation continues, the pressure rises until it is high enough to cause the ammonia vapour to condense in the condenser. Just as in the compression refrigerator, the liquid is then expanded by means of a special valve and thereupon evaporates again, absorbing heat (from the interior of the refrigerator) in doing so. The water which remains behind in the boiler after most of its ammonia has been driven out, and which is still very hot, is passed through a heat exchanger in which it gives off some of its heat. It then goes to the absorber, where it re-absorbs, and becomes saturated with, the pure ammonia vapour coming from the evaporator. The ammonia solution formed in this way is pumped back through the heat exchanger, where it absorbs heat from the hot water flowing from the boiler, to the boiler by a small circulation pump. The cycle of events then starts all over again.

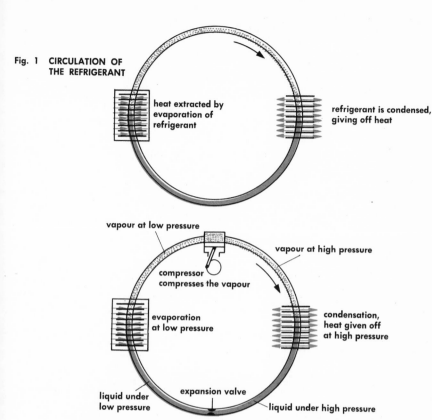

Fig. 1 CIRCULATION OF THE REFRIGERANT

heat extracted by evaporation of refrigerant

refrigerant is condensed, giving off heat

vapour at low pressure

vapour at high pressure

compressor compresses the vapour

evaporation at low pressure

condensation, heat given off at high pressure

liquid under low pressure

expansion valve

liquid under high pressure

Fig. 2 OPERATING PRINCIPLE OF COMPRESSION REFRIGERATOR

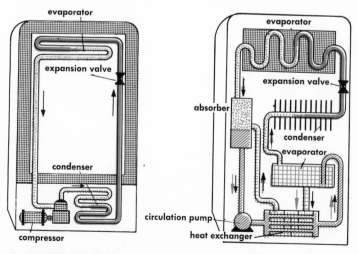

evaporator

expansion valve

condenser

compressor

Fig. 3 COMPRESSION REFRIGERATOR

evaporator

expansion valve

absorber

condenser

evaporator

circulation pump

heat exchanger

Fig. 4 ABSORPTION REFRIGERATOR

277

VACUUM CLEANER

A modern vacuum cleaner develops its suction by means of a fan which discharges a powerful stream of air from the rear end of the casing. This sets up a powerful inflowing current of air which carries along any dust particles from the carpet or floor to which the suction nozzle is applied. The fan is usually driven by a small high-speed universal motor (i.e., a motor which can be worked either on alternating current or direct current). The fan has a large number of blades set at an angle. Their rotation sets up a flow of air in the axial direction (Fig. 1). The air stream is passed through a filter in which the dust is precipitated and collected without appreciably obstructing the flow.

Many vacuum cleaners have bag-type filters (Fig. 3) through which the air passes from the inside to the outside, the dust being collected in the bag, which has to be emptied from time to time. The disadvantage is that the suction power gradually diminishes because of the increasing air flow resistance as the bag fills up with dust. In the arrangement illustrated in Fig. 2 this disadvantage is obviated. Here the dust is precipitated in the dust collecting chamber in front of the filter. This system is used more particularly in good-quality hand vacuum cleaners; these have small dust collecting chambers, and it is therefore essential that they retain their suction efficiency unimpaired for as long as possible. In general, the power input stated on the rating plate of a vacuum cleaner does not necessarily provide a reliable indication of the suction performance. A sufficiently powerful airflow to carry along dust and grit particles must be set up. Such an air flow can only be induced by the suction developed by the fan. There are thus two factors involved: air flow rate (m3/min.) and suction (mm water column). These can be plotted against each other in a graph (Fig. 4), whereby a flow rate/pressure characteristic is obtained, which—depending on the type of fan—may be very steep or relatively flat. The suction performance is the product of these two factors. From the graph it appears that the suction is zero when the flow rate is maximum, and vice versa. At both these extreme points the suction performance is therefore zero. For a vacuum cleaner with a straight-line characteristic the best performance is obtained in the middle, i.e., at half the maximum suction and half the maximum air flow rate. In a well designed vacuum cleaner the various nozzle attachments must therefore be so dimensioned and shaped that the resulting performance is within the suitable working range.

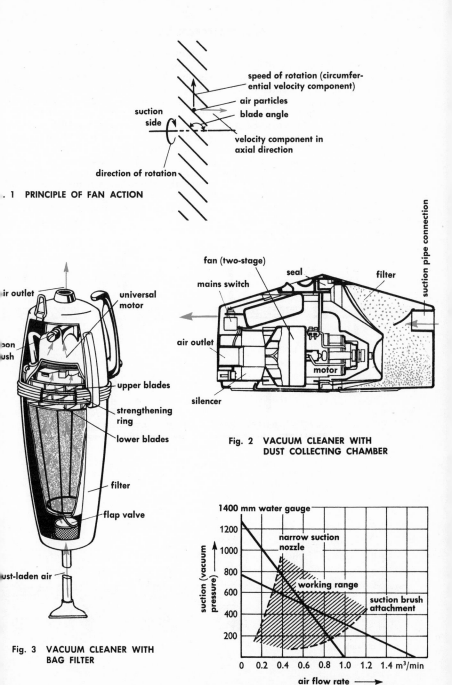

speed of rotation (circumferential velocity component)

air particles

blade angle

suction
side

velocity component in
axial direction

direction of rotation

Fig. 1 PRINCIPLE OF FAN ACTION

suction pipe connection

air outlet

universal
motor

carbon
brush

upper blades

strengthening
ring

lower blades

filter

flap valve

dust-laden air

Fig. 3 VACUUM CLEANER WITH
BAG FILTER

fan (two-stage)

mains switch

seal

filter

air outlet

motor

silencer

Fig. 2 VACUUM CLEANER WITH
DUST COLLECTING CHAMBER

1400 mm water gauge

narrow suction
nozzle

working range

suction brush
attachment

suction (vacuum pressure)

1200
1000
800
600
400
200

air flow rate

0 0.2 0.4 0.6 0.8 1.0 1.2 1.4 m³/min

Fig. 4 AIR FLOW/SUCTION CHARACTERISTICS OF
DIFFERENT VACUUM CLEANERS

SEWING MACHINE

The stitches made by a sewing machine are formed by two threads which are interlocked. In the vibrating shuttle machine the upper thread is carried by the needle, while the under thread is unreeled from the bobbin. The descending needle penetrates the fabric and carries the thread along (a). When the needle rises again, the thread forms a loop on the underside of the fabric. The shuttle, which contains the bobbin of under thread, goes through this loop and pulls the under thread along behind it (b). The shuttle thread is thus enclosed in the loop of the needle thread. The fabric is then moved forward; while this is happening, the needle remains stationary and the shuttle returns to its initial position. This causes the slack loop to be pulled tight and close up, so that the two threads interlock in the middle of the fabric (c). When the forward movement of the fabric has ceased, the operation is repeated (d). This method produces the lock stitch, which forms a strong but rather rigid seam with no "give" in it.

A chain-stitch sewing machine produces seams having greater resilience. This machine works with only one thread, which is linked at the underside of the fabric by means of a gripper hook (e and f). A variant of this stitch is the overcasting stitch which enwraps the edge of the material.

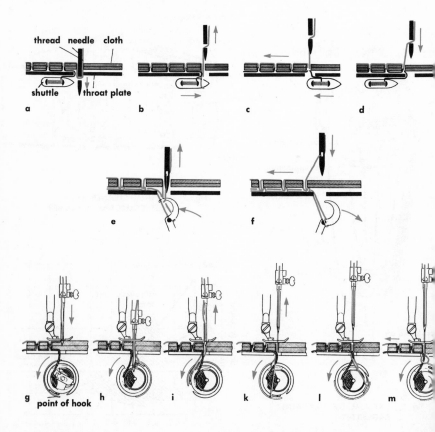

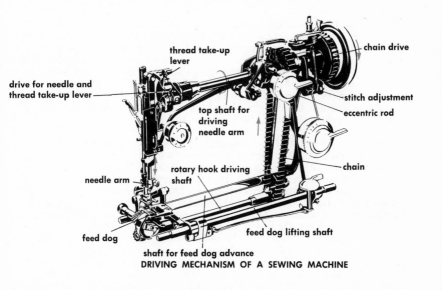

drive for needle and
thread take-up lever

thread take-up
lever

chain drive

stitch adjustment

eccentric rod

top shaft for
driving
needle arm

rotary hook driving
shaft

needle arm

chain

feed dog

feed dog lifting shaft

shaft for feed dog advance
DRIVING MECHANISM OF A SEWING MACHINE

In modern domestic sewing machines the so-called rotary hook is frequently employed. This type of machine functions as follows. The needle descends through the fabric, and the point of the hook advances to meet the needle (g). The return movement forms the loop, and the point of the hook enters it (h). The hook enlarges the loop, the front of which is held in a recess in the bobbin case (i), while the hook pulls away the other side of the upper thread loop over the bobbin case (k). The loop slips off the point of the hook, while the thread take-up lever (see illustration below) pulls the excess thread up again (l). During the unwinding of the thread, the side of the loop that was held in the recess is released and the loop is pulled tight (m).

The present-day domestic sewing machine is usually driven by an electric motor through a chain drive. The rotary motion is transmitted through the top shaft to the crank drive for the thread take-up lever. In addition, the bottom shaft (rotary hook drive shaft) is driven by a chain from the top shaft. An eccentric cam mounted on the top shaft actuates eccentric rods and thus drives the feed mechanism under the base plate whereby the fabric is moved forward. The length of the stitch can be adjusted by means of the stitch regulator. The stitch is made longer or shorter by varying the eccentric stroke and thus varying the amount of rotation that the feed motion shaft undergoes at each stroke.

INCANDESCENT LAMP

An incandescent lamp comprises an electrical conductor through which a current is passed which causes it to glow at white heat. The conductor is usually a wire, or filament, which is carried on a glass mount and whose ends are welded to thicker support wires (leads) through which the current is supplied to the filament. In order to prevent oxidation (burning away), of the filament by exposure to air, it is enclosed in a glass bulb, which is sealed together with the mount. The lead-in wires are sealed into the glass. The bulb is either evacuated, i.e., a vacuum is formed inside it, or it is filled with a neutral gas or gas mixture (e.g., nitrogen and argon). The filaments used in the early incandescent lamps were made of carbon. As it was not possible to raise the temperature of such filaments to white heat without seriously shortening the service life of the lamps, the light they gave was rather dim. For this reason carbon filaments were abandoned in favour of metal filaments. A suitable metal for the purpose was tungsten, which has a high melting point and can be heated to $3000°$ C. Tungsten is obtained, from its ore, in the form of a black powder, which is then processed, by sintering at about $1000°$ C in a neutral gas atmosphere, into pencil-size rods. The material is homogenised by hammering and stretched to rods about 18 in. long and $\frac{1}{8}$ in. in diameter. Further treatment is effected by drawing (see page 342). The drawing dies consist of pierced diamonds, by means of which it is possible to produce tungsten wire down to about $\frac{1}{100}$ mm (0.0004 in.) diameter. Some idea of the extreme thinness of such wire is conveyed by the fact that nearly 200 miles of $\frac{1}{100}$ mm wire can be produced from 1 lb. of tungsten. These extremely thin wires are then formed into doubly coiled (coiled-coil) filaments which are secured to the mount in the manner described above. The total length of the filament wire in a 15-watt lamp is about 0.75 m (30 in.); the first coil has about 3000 turns; this coiled wire is then coiled in 100 larger turns, so that the overall length of the filament is reduced to about 3 cm ($1\frac{1}{4}$ in.). The sealed bulb of the lamp is cemented into a metal base, which may be of various types, the commonest being the bayonet type and the screw type. The bayonet base is cylindrical in shape, with two small pins projecting from the sleeve to engage lock slots in the lamp socket; the two lead-in wires terminate at two metal contacts at the foot of the base. In the screw-type lamp (see illustration) one wire is connected to an insulated central metal contact plate at the foot, while the other is connected to the screw-threaded metal side of the base.

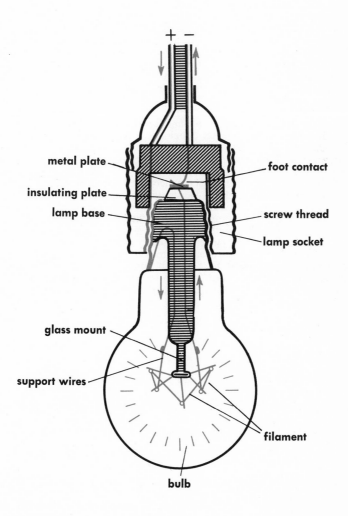

+ −

metal plate

insulating plate

lamp base

glass mount

support wires

foot contact

screw thread

lamp socket

filament

bulb

FLAT-IRON

The modern electric iron comprises a sole plate, an intermediate plate, a cover with handle, an electric heating element, a selector disc, and a glow lamp. By means of the selector device the temperature can be set to values suitable for different fabrics (nylon, rayon, silk, wool, cotton, linen). This adjustment is achieved by means of a thermostat. The three-wire A.C. connection comprises an earthed safety wire. The heating element is shown in red in the accompanying diagram. The current goes through the element, the outer contact spring and contact pin, the inner contact spring and contact pin, the connecting rod, and the flexible metal strip.

When the selector dial is, for example, set to "linen", the glow lamp lights up, and the current heats the heating element to the required temperature. The lamp then goes out. The iron is thereafter kept at constant temperature by the thermostat. For example, when the iron cools a little, the temperature of the freely movable intermediate plate, to which the thermostat is attached, also goes down. As a result of this, the intermediate plate contracts and causes the thermostat strip, which is made of Invar (a nickel-iron alloy with a very small coefficient of thermal expansion, so that it hardly expands or contracts due to temperature changes), to buckle outwards and push the connecting rod against the inner contact spring thrusts the latter against the outer contact spring, so that the circuit is restored and the heating element switched on again. The glow lamp also lights up. When the pre-set ironing temperature has been reached again, the thermostat causes the contacts to separate and thus break the circuit. The glow lamp is thereby also switched off. The switching on and off of the lamp indicates that the thermostat is functioning and automatically keeping the temperature constant. Depending on the setting of the selector dial, the heating element is switched on and off at a higher or lower temperature. Rotation of the disc moves the rod of ceramic material in the axial direction. The outer contact spring is so installed that it tends always against the inner contact spring. When the iron heats up, and the Invar strip consequently elongates, the outer spring follows the inner spring until its end encounters the ceramic rod. This causes the contacts to separate. The farther forward this rod protrudes, the sooner this occurs, i.e., the lower the temperature at which the heating element is switched on and off. A thermostat of this kind controls the temperature to within about 10° C accuracy.

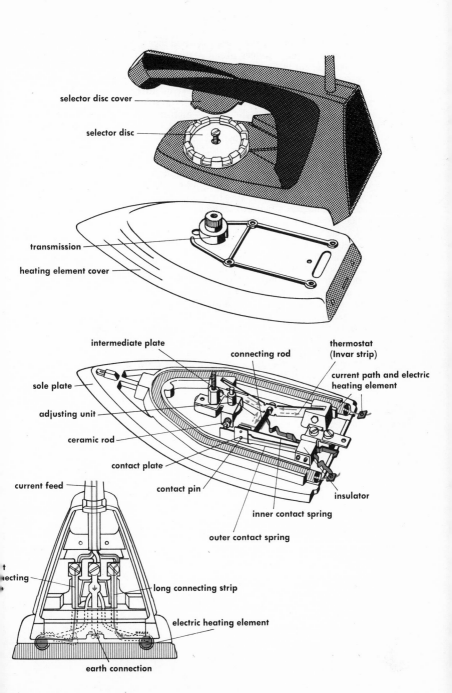

selector disc cover

selector disc

transmission

heating element cover

intermediate plate

connecting rod

thermostat (Invar strip)

sole plate

current path and electric heating element

adjusting unit

ceramic rod

contact plate

contact pin

insulator

current feed

inner contact spring

outer contact spring

ecting

long connecting strip

electric heating element

earth connection

MATCH

In the manufacture of safety matches, softwood logs (e.g., poplar) are peeled into a thin continuous shaving, or veneer, about $\frac{1}{10}$ inch thick (veneer process). The ribbon of wood is then cut up into splints at a rate of about two million per hour. These splints are soaked in a bath of sodium silicate, amonium phosphate or sodium phosphate and then dried. This impregnation prevents afterglow. Next, the splints are fed into a continuous match machine in which the splints, standing on end in wide belts, are passed through a paraffin bath, which treatment aids ignition. Next the machine dips the ends of the matches in a liquid composition which becomes the striking head when dry. This composition consists of the oxygen carrier (potassium chlorate, lead oxide, potassium chromate, manganese dioxide, etc.), the inflammable ingredient (sulphur, etc.), frictional additives (powdered glass), colouring matter, and binding agents (dextrin, gums). The striking surface on the matchbox consists of powdered glass, red phosphorus, colouring matter, and binding agents.

Safety matches are so called because they can be ignited only by friction against the striking surface of the box. On the other hand, there are universal matches which have heads of such composition that they can be lit by striking them on any friction surface. The heads of such matches have a somewhat different chemical composition from ordinary safety matches. The round wooden matches manufactured in America have two-colour heads and are produced by a double dipping process. The large bulb of the match consists of mainly inert substances, while the "eye" contains the readily ignitible ingredients. The bulb having the larger diameter prevents the sensitive "eyes" from rubbing together after packing. Another American invention, now in worldwide use, is the paper book match. These matches are packed in printed cardboard folders with a striking surface on the outside.

When the head of a safety match is rubbed against the striking surface, frictional heat is generated at a small area of the head. The heat liberates oxygen from the oxygen carrier ingredient, and this oxygen combines with the sulphur (sulphur dioxide is formed in this reaction), whereby additional heat is evolved, causing more oxygen to be liberated and react with sulphur. The chemical process thus initiated by friction proceeds very rapidly, so that the entire match is soon alight. The paraffin-impregnated splint also catches fire. The impregnation of the splint prevents it from continuing to glow after the flame is extinguished.

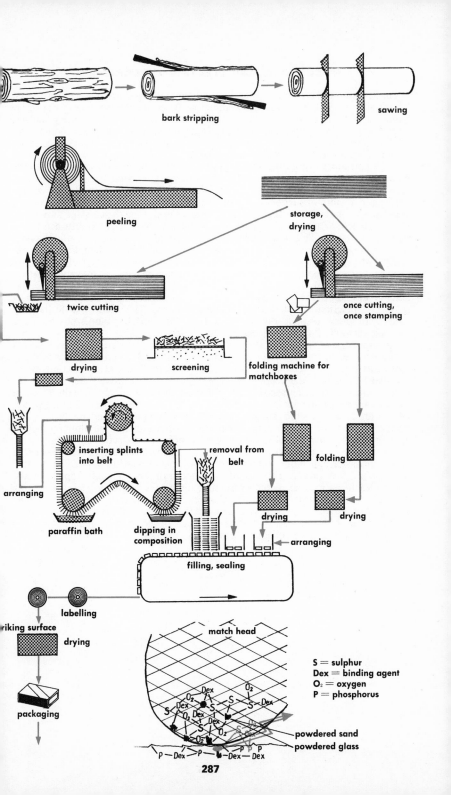

bark stripping

sawing

peeling

storage, drying

twice cutting

once cutting, once stamping

drying

screening

folding machine for matchboxes

arranging

inserting splints into belt

removal from belt

folding

paraffin bath

dipping in composition

drying

drying

arranging

filling, sealing

labelling

riking surface

drying

packaging

match head

S = sulphur
Dex = binding agent
O₂ = oxygen
P = phosphorus

powdered sand
powdered glass

287

MECHANICAL AND ELECTRIC TYPEWRITERS

The first practical typewriter by present-day standards was commercially produced in America in 1874. This was the Remington, based on the machine invented by Sholes. The mechanical typewriter generally functions on the following principle: when any particular key of the keyboard is pressed, a system of levers and linkages (Fig. 1) causes the corresponding type bar to strike the paper through an inked ribbon. The imprint of the raised type on the type bar is thereby formed on the paper which is partially wrapped round the cylinder (or platen). The type bars all strike the paper at a common centre. Each time a key is released after being pressed, the carriage on which the cylinder is mounted moves a certain fixed distance to the left corresponding to a width of a letter. This motion is arrested by an escapement mechanism (pawl and ratchet wheel) which is briefly released each time the carriage moves one step to the left. When the end of the line is reached, the carriage is returned to the right by the typist. This is normally done by pusing a lever which works the line-spacing mechanism, i.e., it rotates the cylinder a certain fixed amount. Each type bar carries two types, e.g., a capital and a small letter. The capitals are typed by pressing a special key which operates the cylinder-shift mechanism whereby the capital instead of the small letter strikes the paper when the key corresponding to any particular letter is pressed. A typewriter embodying this now universal principle is known as a shift-key typewriter. The first shift-key typewriter was produced in 1878. Its early rivals were so-called single-key machines; they had twice the number of keys—one for every character, whether capital or small letter.

An important advance was the development of the electric typewriter, which is basically a mechanical typewriter in which the typing stroke is powered by an electric motor drive (Fig. 2). The key stroke, the carriage motion and other controls are initiated by touching the proper key. The motor rotates a drive roller at constant speed. When the typist presses the key a short distance, a cam (usually made of nylon) is brought into contact with this roller. The latter moves the cam along with it by friction. This causes the cam lever to move back and thereby actuate the type bar. All the functions of the electric typewriter are performed on this or a similar principle, whereby a 95% saving in physical energy expenditure is effected, so that operator fatigue is greatly reduced. Another advantage of the electric typewriter is that it makes for faster and more uniform typing. All the strokes are applied with equal power, since they are independent of the amount of force actually applied by the typist. Despite various refinements and improvements of detail, the basic functioning principle of the typewriter remained unchanged for many years until the advent of the typing-head system (see page 290). The so-called "noiseless" typewriter is a mechanical typewriter utilising a special type bar to reduce the noise of the impact of the type bar on the paper. It is not, of course, absolutely noiseless.

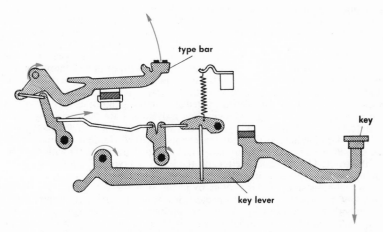

Fig. 1   MECHANISM OF A MECHANICAL TYPEWRITER

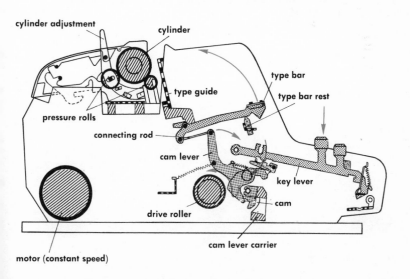

Fig. 2   SECTION THROUGH AN ELECTRIC TYPEWRITER

Instead of having 44 type bars, a machine of this kind has a spherical typing head of about $1\frac{3}{8}$ in. diameter, provided with 88 characters and moves along the line as it types. The head is made of nickel-plated moulded plastic. Owing to its light weight, combined with toughness and resilience, it can perform lightning-quick movements. It can speedily be replaced by another head whenever a different type of lettering is required for a particular purpose. The 88 characters are arranged in four rows round the head. In Fig. 1 the type marked by a cross is positioned ready to strike the paper on the cylinder. The actual striking is performed by a simple mechanism. To type a character situated at another of the 88 positions on the typing head, the latter must be appropriately swivelled and tilted so as to bring this other type into the striking position. These tilting and swivelling movements are performed by means of two steel band systems which begin and end at the slide which carries the typing head and inked ribbon holder. The tilting mechanism provides for four different positions; the swivelling mechanism has to move the head to 22 positions (11 with small letters on the front; 11 with capital letters on the back). To type any particular character, the machine must therefore select the appropriate position from four tilting and 22 swivelling positions. This is done by means of a selector system (Fig. 3). Under each key is a selector lever with projections on its underside. For each key these projections are arranged in a different combination. On being depressed by the key, the selector lever is moved forward by a rotating shaft of special shape. The projections on the underside thrust against various selector rods which operate through a system of selector catches and thereby bring about the requisite movements of the swivel arms of the steel band systems. As soon as the selected character is in the striking position facing the cylinder, the typing head is momentarily locked so as to r̩ vent tilting and swivelling. The stroke is then delivered.

In this ̩ay a typing speed of $15\frac{1}{2}$ strokes per second, i.e., 930 per minute, can be attained. A notable feature is that the proper functioning of the machine cannot be upset by an excessively rapid succession of typing strokes by the typist. If a stroke is followed too quickly by another stroke, the latter is "stored" until the previous stroke has been duly completed.

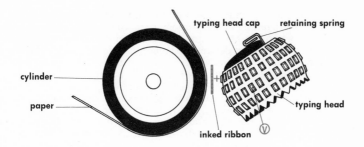

Fig. 1 TYPING HEAD AND CYLINDER (*side view*)

Labels: typing head cap, retaining spring, cylinder, paper, inked ribbon, typing head

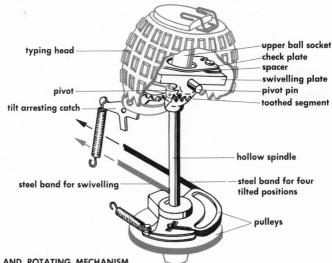

Fig. 2 TILTING AND ROTATING MECHANISM

Labels: typing head, upper ball socket, check plate, spacer, swivelling plate, pivot, pivot pin, tilt arresting catch, toothed segment, hollow spindle, steel band for swivelling, steel band for four tilted positions, pulleys

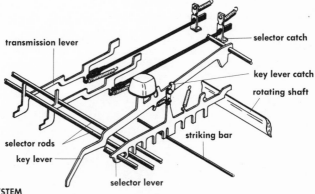

Fig. 3 SELECTOR SYSTEM

Labels: transmission lever, selector catch, key lever catch, rotating shaft, selector rods, key lever, selector lever, striking bar

CASH REGISTER

The primary function of a cash register is to record cash transactions on a strip of paper and add up the figures. For this purpose the machine is provided with a setting mechanism from which the figures are transferred to an adding mechanism, an indicator device, and a printing device. The latter prints a check strip, which remains in the machine, and a receipt slip, which is handed to the customer. A subsidiary function of a cash register is to serve as a till in which the money is kept. For this purpose it is provided with one or more cash drawers.

There are, in the main, two types of cash register which differ from each other in the setting mechanism and, consequently, in the entire adding and recording mechanism: (1) cash registers with lever action, in which the amounts are fed into the machine by setting various levers; (2) cash registers with key action, in which this is done by pushing various keys.

Lever-type cash register (Fig. 1):

When the lever for setting the amount is shifted to the desired position, the amount appears in a window on the back of the machine. At the same time, a cog-wheel rotated by the setting lever sets the printing mechanism to the selected amount. In addition, the setting lever, acting through a tension spring, shifts the adding segment lever and the adding segment guide to the working position. By pressing a button, an electric motor is started, which drives a camshaft in the clockwise direction. Cam 1 causes the adding segment to engage with the intermediate cog-wheel of the adding mechanism; cam 2 and the roller transfer the amount to the adding wheel. The camshaft is a frequently used device for producing reciprocating motions of various kinds. depending on the shape of the cams. The principle of the cam action is illustrated in Fig. 1a. It is also used for working the valves in internal combustion engines (cf. page 466). With regard to the adding mechanism see also page 294.

Key-type cash register (Fig. 2):

When a key is depressed, the electric motor is started which drives the camshaft anti-clockwise. This causes the block, which is rotatably mounted on the shaft, to thrust against the sickle-shaped lever, so that this lever rotates clockwise about its pivot. This causes the swivel arm to swivel until it is stopped by the key bar; as a result of this, the bottom pivot of the sickle-shaped lever becomes a fixed point. The sickle-shaped lever is thus compelled to rotate in the clockwise direction. In doing this, it carries the counting arm along with it until this arm, too, is arrested by the key bar. Acting through the link rod 1, the counting arm moves the adding segment into position. The pin and segment 1 rotate the type transfer wheel and thereby set the printing wheels in position. The link rod 2, attached to the segment 1, works the indicator roll through the agency of the segment 2. The adding segment engages with the intermediate cog-wheel of the adding mechanism. Then the sickle-lever differential opens, and the counting arm and the swivel arm return to their initial positions. The amount is transferred both to the top adding wheel and to the bottom sectorised adding wheel. On release of the adding segment, the camshaft rotates and performs the transfer of the tens (cf. page 294).

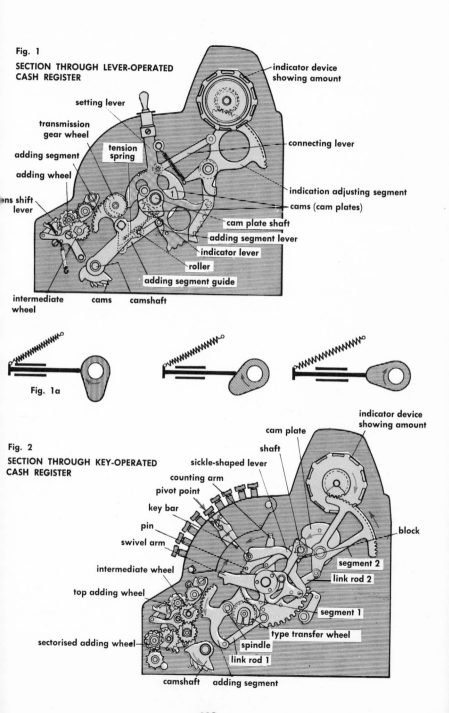

Fig. 1
SECTION THROUGH LEVER-OPERATED
CASH REGISTER

indicator device
showing amount

setting lever

transmission
gear wheel

tension
spring

adding segment

adding wheel

ens shift
lever

connecting lever

indication adjusting segment

cams (cam plates)

cam plate shaft

adding segment lever

indicator lever

roller

adding segment guide

intermediate
wheel

cams

camshaft

Fig. 1a

indicator device
showing amount

cam plate

shaft

sickle-shaped lever

Fig. 2
SECTION THROUGH KEY-OPERATED
CASH REGISTER

counting arm

pivot point

key bar

pin

swivel arm

block

segment 2

link rod 2

intermediate wheel

top adding wheel

segment 1

type transfer wheel

sectorised adding wheel

spindle

link rod 1

camshaft   adding segment

293

CALCULATING MACHINE

A desk calculating machine for performing addition and subtraction operations comprises the cog-wheel mechanism and the product register which records the result of the calculation. The product register is a counter mechanism with "tens" transfer function. Multiplication is carried out by continued addition, subtraction by reversal of the direction of rotation, and division by continued subtraction. A number is fed into the mechanism by pressing keys on a keyboard and is added to, or subtracted from, the number already in the product register. The mechanism is illustrated in Fig. 1. Under the keyboard are ten racks (toothed rods), each of which has on its underside a pin which engages with a groove in a cross-bar, the "proportional lever". When the machine is set to "addition", the rearmost rack (as shown in Fig. 1) is immovably locked. When the handle is turned through one revolution, the proportional lever is swivelled around the pin of this rack to the right and back again. In the course of this operation the front rack moves nine places, the next rack immediately behind it moves eight places, etc. Over the racks are mounted as many square shafts with slidable cog-wheels as there are places in the product register. Associated with each two keys of the keyboard is a slidable cog-wheel on the square shaft. This cog-wheel is moved by a sliding mechanism. In the neutral position only the locked rack is meshed with a cog-wheel. If, for example, the key bearing the figure 3 is pressed, this cog-wheel is disengaged, and another cog-wheel meshes with the rack which, on actuation of the handle by the machine operator, moves a distance corresponding to three teeth (Fig. 2). At the start of the forward motion, the coupling between the product register and the square shafts is moved into position. As a result of this, in each decimal place the counting wheel is rotated a number of teeth which corresponds to the figure on the keyboard. If the number exceeds 9 the counting wheel moves a marker slide for the tens transfer operation (see below). The coupling is disconnected before the racks reverse their direction of rotation.

When subtraction is carried out, the front rack is immovably locked. Now each rack moves to and fro a distance corresponding to (9-n) teeth instead of n teeth as in the case of addition. Instead of actually subtracting a from b, i.e., $a - b$, the machine performs the operation $a + (999 \ldots 999 - b)$. At the end of the subtraction the result is increased by one unit. The result $a + (1000 \ldots 000 - b)$ is equivalent to $a - b$ on the machine as the addition of $1000 \ldots 000$ affects only the next higher place, not present on the machine.

In the second half of the revolution performed by the operating handle the "tens" transfer is effected. Eccentric cams mounted in a staggered arrangement on a shaft successively raise the "tens" levers in the product register, starting with the units place. When the marker slide has been shifted, the "tens" lever can no longer slide between the cog-wheels; instead, it deflects to the left and thereby moves the cog-wheel of the next higher position a distance of one tooth. The displacements necessary for effecting a "tens" transfer are indicated by dotted red arrows in Fig. 4.

As already stated, multiplication and division are carried out as continued addition and subtraction respectively. In a multiplication the multiplier is registered in a special register called the revolution register. The multiplicand is set on the keyboard. The revolution and product registers can be moved sideways on a carriage to facilitate calculation with multi-digit multipliers. When the product register moves n places, one revolution of the operating handle adds 10^n times the number set on the keyboard. In that case the corresponding place of the revolution register must be reduced by 1. Fully-automatic machines perform the necessary displacements and terminate the calculation when the revolution register is at zero. Division is performed on similar lines.

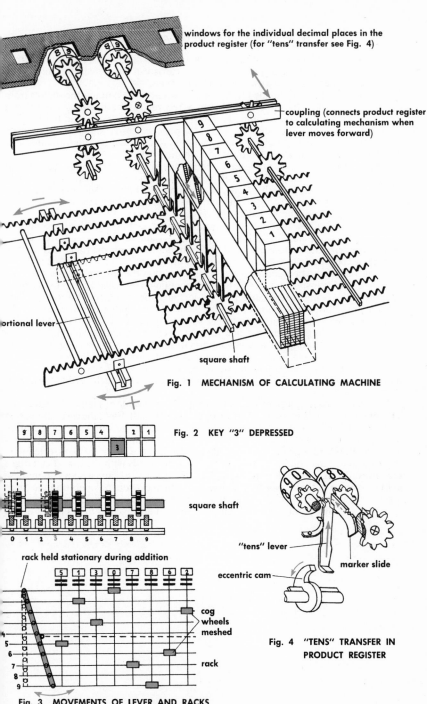

windows for the individual decimal places in the product register (for "tens" transfer see Fig. 4)

coupling (connects product register to calculating mechanism when lever moves forward)

proportional lever

square shaft

Fig. 1   MECHANISM OF CALCULATING MACHINE

Fig. 2   KEY "3" DEPRESSED

square shaft

rack held stationary during addition

cog wheels meshed

rack

Fig. 4   "TENS" TRANSFER IN PRODUCT REGISTER

"tens" lever

marker slide

eccentric cam

Fig. 3   MOVEMENTS OF LEVER AND RACKS
(cog wheels not in mesh are not shown)

HOLLERITH PUNCHED-CARD SYSTEM

Punched cards (like punched tape) can be used for effecting the input and output of data in mechanised data processing. Such cards can be sorted at rates of over 100,000 cards per hour and arranged in various ways.

A punched card is subdivided into columns whose rows contain the figures from 0 to 9. For example, if the number 403 has to be recorded in the first three columns of a card, the row 4 in the first column, the row 0 in the second column, and the row 3 in the third column must be punched. The usual punched cards comprise 80 columns. In addition, appropriate holes for conveying non-numerical code information can be punched in rows in which the places are not numbered.

When the punched cards are passed through any of various machines, the punched holes cause transmission of impulses. Basic machines are the punching machine which punches data into the cards, the sorting machine which sorts out cards according to various classifications, and the tabulating machine which prepares printed reports from the sorted cards.

Figs. 1 and 2 show the operating principle of a sorting machine. The stack of cards for sorting is placed in the feed hopper on the right, in which to-and-fro-moving feed blades seize the bottom card and push it under the transport roller (Fig. 2). The card passes between a contact roller and a scanning spring. The latter scans the rows 9 to 0 in the selected columns. In the neutral position the sorting springs are close above the card transport track. Cards which contain no punched hole in the scanned column will pass unhindered under all the sorting springs and fall into the receiving box for unperforated cards. On the other hand, if the column contains a hole, the card concerned will slide along under the sorting springs only until the hole reaches the scanning spring. When that happens, an electrical circuit is completed which energises an electromagnet, whereby an armature, on which the sorting springs are resting, is pulled down. Those sorting springs whose front edges have then not yet been reached by the card will thereby drop below the level of the card, with the result that the card slides in between two of these springs and is thus delivered to the appropriate receiving box.

A stack of cards may also be sorted with regard to the value of a multi-digit number. This involves several successive sorting operations (Fig. 3). First, the cards are sorted according to the figure in the units column. Before the second sorting operation takes place, the cards must be stacked in the feed box in the sequence of their end digits (first the end digit 0, then 1, etc. up to 9). When the cards are now sorted with regard to the "tens" digit, it is thus assured that the cards with the lowest end digits are lowest down in the relevant "tens" box; the other cards are stacked upon these in the sequence of their respective end digits. In the next sorting operation the cards are sorted with regard to the "hundreds", then the "thousands", etc. Thus, with only four sorting operations 10,000 cards have been arranged in their correct order.

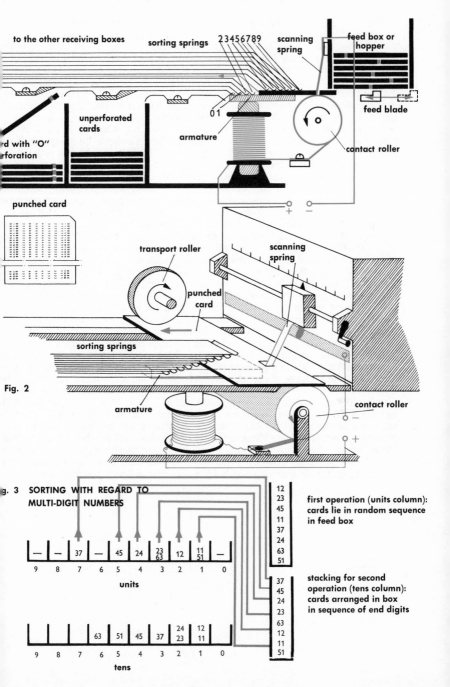

Fig. 1

to the other receiving boxes   sorting springs   23456789   scanning spring   feed box or hopper

unperforated cards

01

armature

feed blade

contact roller

...rd with "O" ...rforation

punched card

transport roller   scanning spring

punched card

sorting springs

Fig. 2

armature   contact roller

Fig. 3 SORTING WITH REGARD TO MULTI-DIGIT NUMBERS

| 12 |
| 23 |
| 45 |
| 11 |
| 37 |
| 24 |
| 63 |
| 51 |

first operation (units column): cards lie in random sequence in feed box

9	8	7	6	5	4	3	2	1	0
—	—	37	—	45	24	23 63	12	11 51	—

units

| 37 |
| 45 |
| 24 |
| 23 |
| 63 |
| 12 |
| 11 |
| 51 |

stacking for second operation (tens column): cards arranged in box in sequence of end digits

9	8	7	6	5	4	3	2	1	0
		63	51	45	37	24 23	12 11		

tens

297

DATA PROCESSING: PRINCIPLES

The term "data" in the mathematical and technical sense denotes any facts o information, particularly as taken in, operated on, or put out by a computer or othe machine for handling information. Inferences can be drawn from data. Thus th information "A is of age" and "A is a German citizen" leads to the inference "A i entitled to vote", this being so by virtue of the German election law. This selectio of significant information from a set of given data is known as "data processing". I a more general sense this refers to all the operations performed on data according t prescribed plans. These operations range from the collection of raw data to the repor ing of the results of calculations involving the data. If a large number of data have t be processed according to the same rules, this can be done by machines. For a limite range of subjects, any description can be replaced by a number of questions which ar answered by "yes" or "no" (binary number system). With the aid of a code of thi kind it is possible to represent and store data. To this end, it is necessary to hav components with two readily distinguishable conditions. Depending on the spee with which the "yes" and "no" conditions are recorded and subsequently retrievec various devices are used for the purpose: punched cards, paper tape, magnetic tape magnetic cores, magnetic drums, tubes, transistors, in conjunction with electri impulses. A binary digit, i.e., a digit in the binary scale of notation, is commonl abbreviated as "bit". As a basic unit of information the bit is the information con tained in a decision between "yes" and "no". In a data processing machine a numbe of bits, are combined into what is known as a "machine word". Each machine wor is stored in a so-called "store location" or a "register"; the latter term refers mor particularly to a device for storing one word at a time while it is actually being used Data processing means making up a new machine word — in accordance with certai rules — from the contents of one or more registers. All conceivable rules for dat processing can be built up from a limited number of simple connections such as, fo example, "and", "or" and "negation". In the above example, the right to vote ca be ascertained from a punched card index of the population by means of a simpl "and" circuit. At the output this yields a "yes" only if there is a "yes" at both inputs A circuit which adds the contents of a particular "storage location" as a binar number to the contents of a register is much more complex, but can nevertheless b built up from simple connective circuits. This principle is not a rational one for purely mechanical data processing machine. It is used only for machines whicl operate with relays, electronic tubes or transistors. Circuits for the most frequentl occurring arithmetical operations are pre-installed in the machine. Complex dat processing operations (e.g., long numerical computations) can be composed fron these "basic instructions". A programme-controlled machine carries out instruc tions in the sequence in which these occur in consecutive storage locations of storage (a device for receiving and holding information) or a punched tape.

(Continued

splitting-up of various items of information into elementary statements

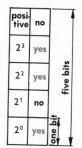

posi-tive	no
2^3	yes
2^2	yes
2^1	no
2^0	yes

five bits · one bit

the number 13 represented in the binary system

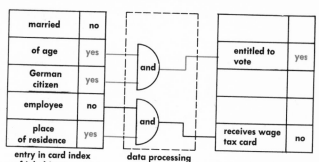

married	no
of age	yes
German citizen	yes
employee	no
place of residence	yes

entry in card index of inhabitants

and

and

data processing

entitled to vote	yes
receives wage tax card	no

the number −618 represented by a pulse train

2^{10} 2^9 2^8 2^7 2^6 2^5 2^4 2^3 2^2 2^1 2^0 +

representation of the number −618
by four parallel pulse trains
the "+" sign is coded as "12",
the "−" sign is coded as "11"

2^3 —————————————————————
2^2 —————————————————————
2^1 —————————————————————
2^0 —————————————————————

− 0 0 0 0 6 1 8

elementary logical connections and the usual symbols employed for them

A	B	C
no	no	no
yes	no	no
no	yes	no
yes	yes	yes

A	B	C
no	no	no
yes	no	yes
no	yes	yes
yes	yes	yes

A	C
no	yes
yes	no

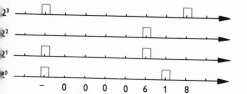

and

A ——
B —— C

or

A ——
B —— C

negation

A —○— C

Circuits for the elementary logical connections are the elements for the building up of computer circuits. The accompanying diagram shows circuits for the case where "yes" is represented by a positive voltage pulse, "no" by a negative pulse on the absence of a pulse.

In the "and" circuit no current flows in the rest position (black); the output C therefore has a voltage of $+20$ V, like A and B. If at least one of the inputs A and B is given a voltage 0 V, a current will flow through the diode, and a voltage drop will occur in the resistance R. Since the diode offers practically zero resistance to this direction of flow, C acquires the voltage 0 V. In the "or" circuit both diodes block the flow of current if A and B are both at 0 V. If A or B or both these inputs are at $+20$ V, then C is likewise connected to $+20$ V, without the interposition of a resistance. In the circuit for "negation" the grid of the tube is negative in relation to the cathode. The tube then blocks the flow of current, and the time pulses proceed undisturbed via the two conductors at the anode. When a positive pulse occurs at A, the tube allows current to pass; the time pulses are suppressed or greatly diminished. The input pulses of the connective circuits are often not of a form suitable for further processing. For example, the "or" circuit gives -20 V instead of 0 V for "no"; the negation circuit does not entirely suppress the negated pulses. So-called "triggers" produce rectangular pulses of uniform height from positive pulses of arbitrary shape. In the trigger circuit illustrated, tube 2 conducts current in the rest position (black); tube 1 blocks the current, since its grid is negative in relation to the cathode; its high anode voltage gives a positive voltage (through a voltage divider) to the grid of tube 2. When a positive pulse is fed in at the input, tube 1 will begin to conduct electricity when a certain grid voltage is exceeded. Its anode voltage decreases in consequence of this, and through the voltage divider the grid voltage of tube 2 also becomes so low that this tube now blocks the flow of current. At the same time the voltage at the output rises. The transition between the two states of the circuit is therefore effected suddenly, so that positive input pulses of sufficient height will, irrespective of their shape, produce sharp rectangular pulses at the output. If the circuit is so arranged as to function symmetrically, it is called a "flip-flop" circuit. In general, a flip-flop is an electronic device or circuit with two stable states. The circuit remains in either state until the application of a signal causes it to change. It consists of two symmetrical halves, each with its own input and output terminals. The activation of one of the two halves automatically brings about the deactivation of the other half, thereby reversing the state of the flip-flop. Thus, in a vacuum-tube flip-flop, as envisaged here, when one tube is conducting, the other is cut off, and vice versa. If the digits 0 and 1 of the binary number system are associated with the two respective states, counters (totalising devices) can be constructed. The output pulse occurring at the transition from 1 to 0 is fed to the flip-flop circuit for the next higher binary place.

A commonly used device for memory storage is the magnetic core, which is a tiny ring made of ferrite, an easily magnetisable material. These cores are strung on insulated wires. The cores can be magnetised in either of two directions, depending on the direction of current flow in a wire. If the direction of the current is reversed the magnetic state is changed. This bi-stable nature of the cores makes them suitable for binary representation: a core may be magnetised in one direction to store a binary 1, or in the other direction to store a binary 0. Each core stores one bit of information at a time. The cores are disposed at the intersections of a network of vertical and horizontal wires. If one-half of the current necessary to magnetise a core is sent through each of the two intersecting wires associated with any particular core, only that one core is affected. In this way the cores can be magnetised individually. The information stored in the cores is read by means of the sense wire, which passes through all the cores. When a core is switched, a pulse of current is created in the sense wire. Thus, coded information is stored by sending pulses through the appropriate cores. Reading is accomplished by detecting the effect of negative pulses on the cores.

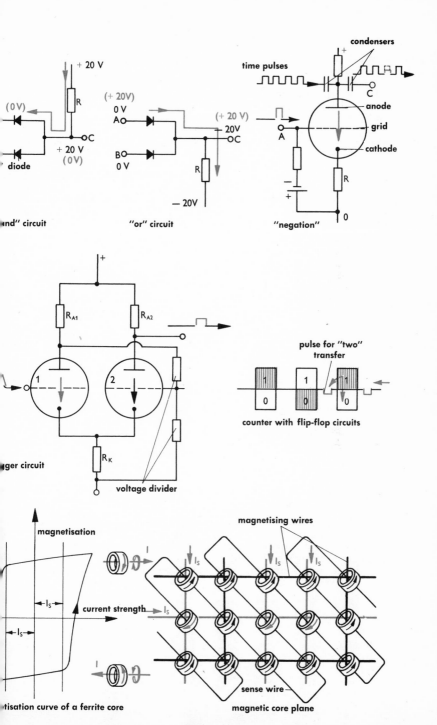

"and" circuit

"or" circuit

"negation"

condensers

time pulses

anode
grid
cathode

R

R

trigger circuit

R_{A1} R_{A2}

1   2

R_K

voltage divider

pulse for "two"
transfer

1	1	1
0	0	0

counter with flip-flop circuits

magnetisation

current strength

I_s

magnetisation curve of a ferrite core

magnetising wires

I_s

sense wire

magnetic core plane

PROGRAMME-CONTROLLED ELECTRONIC COMPUTER

An electric computer is a universal data processing machine. Large numerica calculations are merely one of the many things it can do.

The accompanying diagram shows the principal parts of a computer, in which th individual "bits" (see page 298) of a machine word are consecutively processed a voltage pulses (serial computer). The registers consist of chains of delay elements i which a pulse is delayed for a length of time equal to the time interval between tw pulses. From the end of the chain the pulse train returns to the input. When th last pulse of a word has been received, each bit can be read from the correspondin element of the chain. In the working register (WR) an addition circuit is include through which the pulse trains coming from the contents of the working register an from the magnetic drum pass synchronously and are added together, bit by bi starting with the lowest binary digit. The accumulator (A) accepts only eight binar digits; its contents are increased by 1 at each revolution. The computer functions i two cycles: In the first cycle the accumulator determines which word from th magnetic drum is passed to the control register (CR). Some binary digits of th instruction word, the operation part, actuate electronic switches in the pulse circui and thus determine the operations to be performed in the next circuit. In this secon cycle the eight lowest digits of the control register, the so-called address part of th instruction, determine the choice of the storage locations. In the accompanyin illustration the number in the accumulator is 148. In the previous cycle the conten of location 148 was fed into the control register. This instruction contains a pulse a the position for A and closes the switch A. The address part is 75. At the instant whe the location 75 reaches the read–write head of the magnetic drum, the "secto selection" switch closes for the duration of a word, and the stored pulse train, t gether with the hitherto existing contents of the working storage, passes through th addition circuit. Meanwhile the position of the accumulator has risen to 149; in th next cycle the instruction "P201" in location 149 is fed into the control register. Th following instructions are additionally embodied in the accompanying schemat diagram:

N: Resetting of the working register. The cycle in the working register is interrupte for the duration of a word.
Tn: The pulse train cycling in the working register is written in location n.
Sn: Jump of the computer operation to location n.
Pn: Jump to location n, if the contents of the working register are positive.
D: Printing out a teleprinter character corresponding to the five lowest digits ◦ the working register.
L: The combination of holes in the punched tape scanner yields the five lowe digits of the working register.

To be a practical machine, a computer requires additional instructions for shiftir the contents of a register to the right or left, for reversing the algebraic sign, e Separate instructions for multiplication and division can, if necessary, be replaced t programmes embodying additions only. More convenient are machines in which th decimal digits 6 to 9 are represented and processed on four parallel pulse circui (series-parallel machines).

LAYOUT OF A PROGRAMME-CONTROLLED COMPUTER

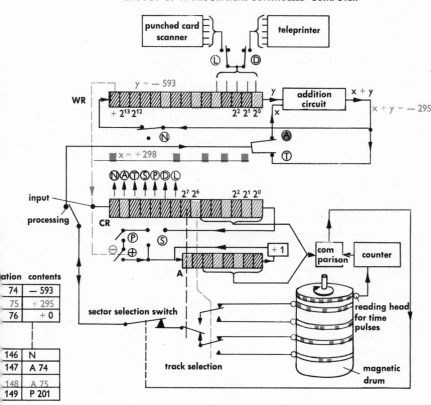

ation	contents
74	− 593
75	+ 295
76	+ 0
146	N
147	A 74
148	A 75
149	P 201

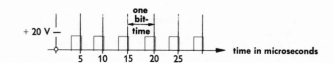

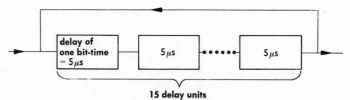

15 delay units
register for the storage of a pulse train with a length of 15 bits

PROGRAMME FOR A PROGRAMME-CONTROLLED COMPUTER

The exponential function $y = e^x$ can be expanded into an infinite series:

$$e^x = 1 + x + \frac{x^2}{1.2} + \frac{x^3}{1.2.3} \ldots + \frac{x^k}{1.2 \ldots k} \ldots$$

As the terms of the series steadily diminish in value, the summation can be terminated when the last term calculated is smaller than the number E which prescribes the accuracy required. We shall consider a programme for an electronic computer with decimal notation on four parallel pulse circuits. A machine word will contain 12 decimal digits and the sign digit (designation of algebraic sign, i.e., plus or minus). Decimal fractions such as, for example, 0.00347 will be written 0.347×10^{-2}, and for the first ten places behind the decimal point we shall use ten digits of the machine word. The exponent of the factor 10 (in this example: -2), increased by 50, is called the characteristic and occupies the last two places. The machine must be able to carry out the following instructions (cf. page 302):

Bn: transfer contents of storage location n to working register
Tn: transfer contents of working register to location n
$+$n: add contents of location n to contents of working register
$\times$n: multiply contents of working register by contents of location n
:n: divide contents of working register by contents of location n
V: make sign of contents of working register positive
Pn: transfer address n to accumulator if contents of working register are positive
Rn: transfer address in location n to accumulator
Z: stop programme

The flow diagram yields the following programme for calculating e^x:

Location	Contents	Location	Contents	Location	Contents
00100	empty	00110	$+121$	00120	Z (R 100)
1	T 123	1	T 125	1	1.0
2	T 122	2	B 122	2	a
3	B 121	3	$\times$123	3	X
4	T 124	4	: 125	4	Y
5	T 125	5	T 122	5	K
6	B 124	6	V	6	$0.00001 = e$
7	$+122$	7	-126	7	empty
8	T 124	8	P 1106		
9	B 125	9	B 124		

It is here assumed that, to begin with, the independent variable x is in the working register. At the stop the result is in the working register. This programme must be written on a punched tape in the number code that the machine can utilise (see accompanying illustration). In the "reading-in" of the punched tape the first five digits determine the switches for selecting a storage location, in which the 13 further characters are then stored. The calculation of e^x for an individual value of x can be done as follows: input of x into the working register, setting the accumulator to 00101, starting the computer operation. The programme only acquires practical value as a so-called subroutine, i.e., a selection of a programme which is stored once and can be used over and over again during the course of the programme to accomplish a certain operation. A fresh instruction Un, if it is in the location x, must transfer the address $x + 1$ to location n and set the accumulator at n + 1. As a result of the instruction Rn the jump back to $x + 1$ is then effected. Thus, at any position of a large programme the calculation of e^x can be initiated by U100 as a separate instruction.

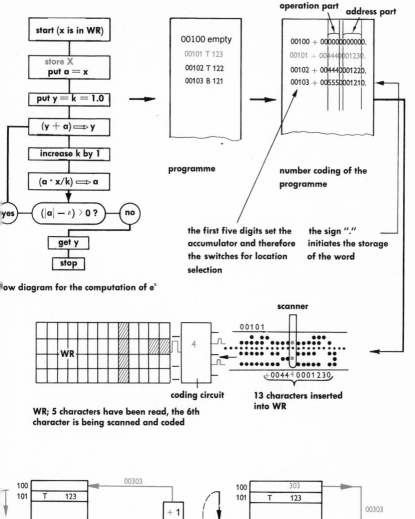

start (x is in WR)

store X
put a = x

put y = k = 1.0

(y + a) ⟹ y

increase k by 1

(a · x/k) ⟹ a

(|a| − ε) > 0 ?   yes   no

get y

stop

flow diagram for the computation of eˣ

00100 empty
00101 T 123
00102 T 122
00103 B 121

programme

operation part   address part

00100 + 000000000000.
00101 + 004440001230.
00102 + 004440001220.
00103 + 005550001210.

number coding of the
programme

the first five digits set the
accumulator and therefore
the switches for location
selection

the sign "."
initiates the storage
of the word

WR

4   coding circuit

scanner

00101

+00444 0001230

13 characters inserted
into WR

WR; 5 characters have been read, the 6th
character is being scanned and coded

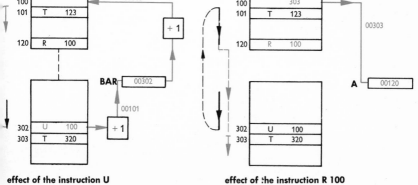

100
101 T   123
120 R   100

00303

+ 1

BAR   00302

00101

302 U   100
303 T   320

+ 1

effect of the instruction U

100   303
101 T   123
120 R   100

00303

A   00120

302 U   100
303 T   320

effect of the instruction R 100

subroutine jump

TRANSLATION PROGRAMME FOR A
PROGRAMME-CONTROLLED COMPUTER

For translation into another language, a text must first of all be coded as a sequence of machine words. For example, one of the numbers 01 to 32 can be assigned to each of the 32 characters of a teleprinter. A word of n letters will then occupy $2n$ decimal places in the storage and may, in certain circumstances, occupy several consecutive storage locations.

In this way it is possible to store ("memorise") a "dictionary" with entries relating to the grammatical properties of each word. The rough translation of a sentence involves comparing the words read from a punched tape with the entries in the "dictionary". If the latter contains each word in every one of the forms in which it can occur, then the process of translation will consist merely in seeking out that number in the storage which corresponds to the number read into the machine. For reasons of available storage space in the "memory" it is more advantageous only to store a list of the root words and another list containing the endings and first syllables. The root word is then sought as that number which agrees in as many digits as possible with the read-in number.

The rough translation printed out by the machine is similar to what would be obtained if each word of the text had been looked up in a dictionary, except that this laborious task has been performed by the machine. The translation then still has to be "licked into shape". However, the machine can go further than this. The "dictionary" entries stored in its "memory" can, by means of distinctive characteristics for nouns, verbs, etc., also take account of the syntax of a sentence. For example, a German sentence comprising a series of qualifying adjectives or adjectival clauses can be divided by means of parentheses, rather in the manner of a mathematical formula. In the German language the sequence of noun and reflexive pronouns corresponds to opening a parenthesis, while the verb in its active forms corresponds to closing a parenthesis. In the English translation these parentheses must be removed. This can be done by starting a new section for the storage of the translation whenever the characteristics for noun and reflexive pronoun occur in succession. When the verb occurs, the programme is again changed over to storage in the previously used storage section.

Translation programmes require a very considerable amount of storage space for "dictionaries". For this reason magnetic tapes are used as external storage media for the various "dictionaries". To obtain the information directly from the tapes would be too slow, as the tapes cannot be moved fast enough to give a sufficiently short "access time" (the time interval between the instant when information is called for from the storage and the instant when delivery is completed). For this reason those "dictionaries" which are needed at any particular stage of the translation procedure are temporarily transferred to the working storage (which may be a magnetic drum or a magnetic core storage), in which the information can be very quickly located (short access time).

306

text to be translated:

DER EINTRAG, DER MIT DEM GELESENEN WORT ÜBEREINSTIMMT, WIRD GESUCHT.

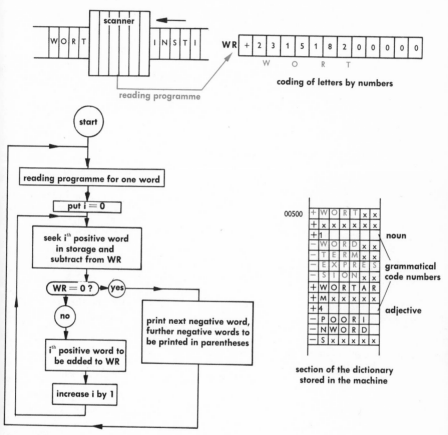

coding of letters by numbers

section of the dictionary stored in the machine

flow diagram for the production of a rough translation by computer

rough translation of text into English:

THE REGISTRATION, THAT WITH THE READ WORD (TERM, EXPRESSION) AGREES, IS SEEKED (SEARCHED).

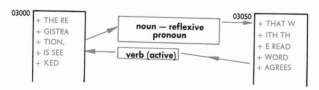

sentence construction taken into account by interchanging the storage sections when certain grammatical code numbers occur

AUTOMATIC LETTER SORTING

Sorting and classifying letters at main post offices is a laborious operation requiring a considerable number of staff to carry it out. This can be greatly reduced by automation. The essential requirement for an automated sorting system is that the machine shall be able to "read" the place of destination in the address on a letter. One way to achieve this is to provide the name of each town with a distinctive number written before the name. Ideally, the automatic sorting machine would have to be able to "read" the number direct from the envelope, but this is a problem that has not yet been reliably solved. Instead, the distinctive number has to be translated into characters that the machine can suitably distinguish (coding). The code elements employed for the purpose are markings applied with a special fluorescent or magnetisable paint. These are "read" in the machine, i.e., they are converted into electric pulses which are used to control mechanical selector devices in the distributing system.

The smallest unit of a letter sorting installation comprises a feed device for coded and for non-coded letters respectively, six coding stations with pre-distributors and a distributing machine (Fig. 1). Letters which have already been coded are automatically scanned and directly delivered into the channels of the distributor belt.

At the coding station (Fig. 2) the appropriate code—according to the address— is printed on the envelope. The receptacles of the intermediate stacker are swung round to the selector unit, from where they are called for by the coder. The empty receptacles swing back to the refilling position. After the code has been imprinted, the following automatic operations are performed: the letter (I) in the code printer is pushed by a carrier pin into a receptacle of the pre-distributor. The letter in the reading position (II) is brought within reach of the carrier pin by the rotation of a star rotor, which pin conveys it to the printing unit. The receptacle on the vertical conveyor opens, and another letter (III) drops into the reading position. The letter IV is passed from the selector unit to the receptacle; the selector unit then picks up another letter by suction.

The receptacles of the pre-distributor have destination stores which control the opening action of the receptacles. The latter are swung down and allow their contents to drop into one of the ten ducts (depending on the destination of the letter concerned) whence they are delivered to the appropriate receiving boxes.

From these boxes the letters are delivered to the intermediate stackers of the distributing machine (Fig. 3), in which a ring of receptacles and a ring of boxes rotate in opposite directions. The distributed letters are collected in these rotating boxes. To each receptacle is assigned an adjustable destination marker, and to each box is assigned a fixed "key" formed by magnetically controlled protective-gas contacts. The letters from the intermediate stackers or the feed device are fed individually to the synchronising device; they then pass through the code scanner and are delivered into the receptacles of the distributing machine. A code imprint in magnetic paint is scanned by means of magnetic heads; alternatively, an imprint in fluorescent paint is scanned by a device termed a photomultiplier (see page 118). The result is fed into an electronic translator which controls the magnetisation of the receptacles. When the "keys" and the boxes correspond to one another in the course of the rotation of the rings in the distribution machine, the protective-gas contacts close, the bottom of the receptacle opens, and the letter drops into the appropriate box.

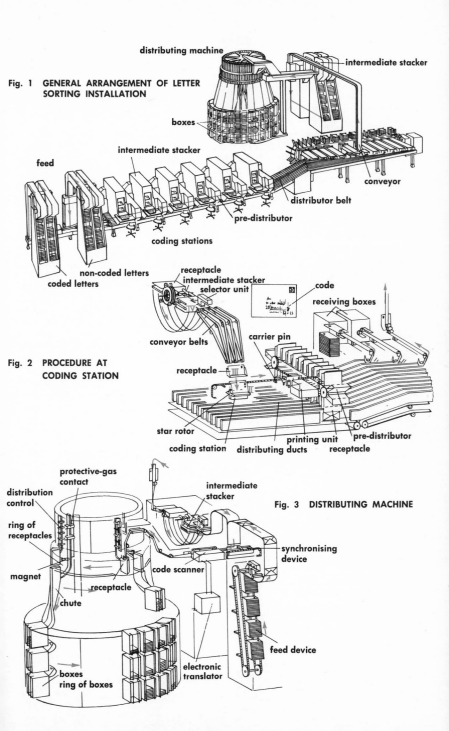

distributing machine

intermediate stacker

Fig. 1   GENERAL ARRANGEMENT OF LETTER SORTING INSTALLATION

boxes

intermediate stacker

feed

conveyor

distributor belt

pre-distributor

coding stations

non-coded letters

coded letters

receptacle

intermediate stacker

selector unit

code

receiving boxes

conveyor belts

carrier pin

Fig. 2   PROCEDURE AT CODING STATION

receptacle

star rotor

printing unit

pre-distributor

coding station

distributing ducts

receptacle

protective-gas contact

intermediate stacker

distribution control

Fig. 3   DISTRIBUTING MACHINE

ring of receptacles

synchronising device

magnet

code scanner

receptacle

chute

feed device

boxes

ring of boxes

electronic translator

309

FOUNTAIN PEN

In the *piston type fountain pen* a screw spindle is connected to the filling cap and engages with a screw thread with which the hollow piston rod is internally provided. Attached to the front end of this rod is the piston which forms an air-tight and liquid-tight seal to the rear of the ink reservoir. When the filling cap is rotated, the screw spindle, rotating inside the piston rod, causes the latter to move longitudinally (Fig. 1a). When the filling cap is turned anti-clockwise (Fig. 1b), the piston travels forward. A small passage allows air to get behind the piston and thus prevents suction that would hinder the forward movement of the piston. When the piston is subsequently retracted, the air escapes by the same path. The return movement of the piston is produced by turning the filling cap clockwise (Fig. 1c). The suction that is thereby developed in the bore of the reservoir draws ink into the pen and causes the reservoir and the ink channels to be filled (up to the air hole of the nib). The pen must, during filling, be dipped in ink to above the level of the air hole.

When the pen is in use, the ink flows from the reservoir through capillary grooves in the feed; it thus reaches the underside of the nib and eventually finds its way along the slit to the tip of the nib. The pressure exerted by the writer causes the two points of the nib to be splayed farther apart, so that the slit widens and allows more ink to reach the tip and thus be transferred to the paper. In proportion as ink flows out of the reservoir, air must enter it. For this purpose the feed is provided with an air passage through which tiny bubbles of air make their way into the reservoir (Fig. 1d).

The ink cartridge of the *cartridge type fountain pen* (Fig. 2) is made of flexible plastic and sealed by a glass ball. It contains about 1 cm^3 of ink. When the cartridge is inserted into the pen, the ball is thrust back into the cartridge by a pin and thus releases the flow path of the ink. The function of the feed is to conduct the ink from the cartridge to the nib (Fig. 2b). At the end of the feed is a tongue which extracts the ink from the cartridge. Besides, the feed is so designed as to allow air to enter the cartridge. An internal sealing cap prevents ink escaping sideways from the mouth of the cartridge and seeping into the barrel of the pen. The "thermic regulator" consists of two tubes, one within the other, in the feed. The space between these tubes is so dimensioned that the ink clings to the walls by capillary action. The object of this system is to accommodate the excess ink which may flow out of the cartridge as a result of a rise in temperature (caused by body temperature in holding the pen) and which, in the absence of any compensation system, would cause a blot on the paper. The compensation "chambers" (i.e., the spaces between the tubes) absorb and hold the ink by their capillary action and thus provide a safeguard against blots.

Fig. 1 PISTON-TYPE FOUNTAIN PEN

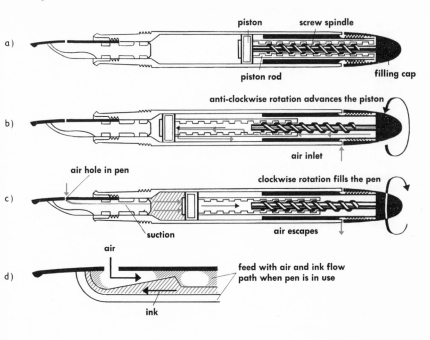

a)

piston   screw spindle

piston rod   filling cap

b)

anti-clockwise rotation advances the piston

air inlet

c)

air hole in pen

clockwise rotation fills the pen

suction   air escapes

d)

air

ink

feed with air and ink flow
path when pen is in use

Fig. 2 CARTRIDGE-TYPE FOUNTAIN PEN

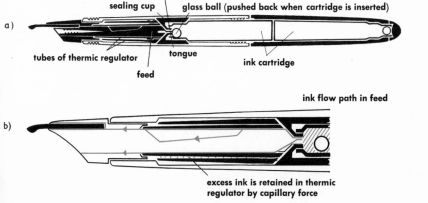

a)

pin

sealing cup   glass ball (pushed back when cartridge is inserted)

tubes of thermic regulator

tongue

feed

ink cartridge

b)

ink flow path in feed

excess ink is retained in thermic
regulator by capillary force

BALLPOINT PEN

The ballpoint is a writing instrument in which a small rolling ball, housed in a socket at the tip, transfers a viscous ink on to the writing surface. The ball is lubricated by the ink, which moves downwards in the reservoir chiefly by the action of gravity. When the pen is not in use and the ball is therefore not moving, it seals the end of the reservoir and thus prevents the ink from drying out. The ink is a viscous liquid containing either an oil-soluble dye or a spirit-soluble dye. The ball is usually made of steel, but in some pens synthetic sapphire balls have been used. Most manufacturers use a ball 1 mm (0.04 in.) in diameter.

In some ballpoint pens the reservoir and the tip comprising the ball can be retracted into the body of the pen when the pen is not in use. There are various mechanical contrivances for retracting and extending the tip of the pen. In one type of mechanism (Fig. 1), when the push-button is pressed, it pushes forward the thrust tube together with the ink reservoir. When the push-button is pressed, the catches of the thrust tube are fully inserted into the fixed slots with which the top part of the body of the pen is provided (Fig. 2a). When the button is released, the action of the large spring retracts the reservoir. The catches of the thrust tube (connected to the reservoir) engage with the small teeth on the rotating sleeve. The reservoir is then in the writing position (Fig. 2b). When the push-button is pressed again, the catches of the thrust tube plunge into the fixed slots (Fig. 2c). The rotating sleeve, which is spring-loaded by a small spring bears on the sharp edges of the fixed slots, while at the same time the sleeve rotates an amount corresponding to one tooth.

When the thrust tube moves back, the rotating sleeve is first lifted and, at the same time, turned. The catches of the thrust tube can then plunge into the large tooth gaps of the sleeve, so that the reservoir is fully retracted (Fig. 2d). The action is again controlled by the sleeve, which performs a small rotational movement whenever the push-button is actuated.

A much simpler form of retraction mechanism is illustrated in Fig. 3. It embodies a ball catch. When the push-button is pressed, the steel ball rotates in the clockwise direction in a heart-shaped cam recess the side of a cylindrical sleeve attached to the push-button (Fig. 4b). The position of the ball within the cam recess determines the position of the ink reservoir (Fig. 4c). When the push-button has been pressed, the ball is at the top holding point of the recess. It is held there by the pressure of the spring. The reservoir is then in the writing position. When the button is pressed again, the ball goes to the bottom holding point of the recess, and the reservoir slides back into the body of the pen.

Fig. 1 BALLPOINT PEN WITH ROTATING-SLEEVE PUSH-BUTTON ACTION

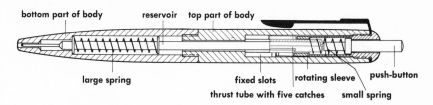

bottom part of body   reservoir   top part of body

large spring   fixed slots   rotating sleeve   push-button

thrust tube with five catches   small spring

Fig. 2 OPERATING PRINCIPLE

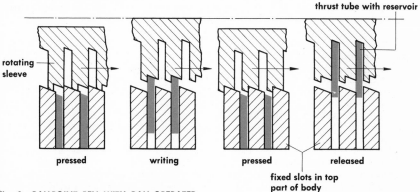

thrust tube with reservoir

rotating sleeve

pressed   writing   pressed   released

fixed slots in top part of body

Fig. 3 BALLPOINT PEN WITH BALL-OPERATED PUSH-BUTTON ACTION

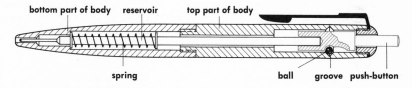

bottom part of body   reservoir   top part of body

spring   ball   groove   push-button

Fig. 4 OPERATING PRINCIPLE

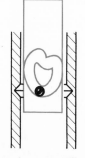
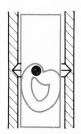
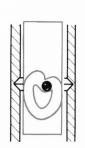

initial position: ball in bottom holding point

button pressed: ball in recess

position of ball determines position of reservoir

313

RECORD PLAYER

The record player (gramophone or phonograph) reproduces the sound waves from the grooves in the gramophone record (see page 318). The vibrations set up in the stylus of the pickup are converted into electric signals. To make these sufficiently strong to work a loudspeaker, they have to be amplified and, if necessary, corrected by means of equalisers and tone controls. The record player (pickup and turntable), amplifier and loudspeaker constitute a reproduction system (Fig. 1). They are frequently combined into one unit, but for purposes of high-fidelity reproduction they are usually kept separate from one another, as they are otherwise liable to have an adverse effect on the quality of one another's performance (heat, vibrations, reaction).

A record player comprises a turntable with drive mechanism and a pickup mounted on a tone arm.

The drive mechanism (Fig. 2) must rotate the record (or disc) as noiselessly and free from vibration as possible at the correct speed. Vibrations in the running of the mechanism, causing irregular running, manifest themselves as objectionable "rumble" in the reproduction of the sound. To obviate this, the drive motor is resiliently mounted, and its motion is transmitted to the turntable through vibrator-damping drive components, such as a rubber friction gear. The latter usually also serves as a change-speed device, the change being effected by shifting the rubber friction disc longitudinally in relation to the motor shaft which is "stepped" so as to vary its diameter.

"Studio quality" drive mechanisms are usually provided with a heavy, accurately balanced turntable whose mass helps to equalise and compensate for any irregularities in the drive. Fluctuations in the speed of rotation manifest themselves as "wow" or "flutter" when they exceed about 3 per mille of the speed. The turntable should be made of a non-magnetic material (e.g., pressure die-cast zinc) in order to avoid adversely affecting the performance of the magnetic pickup (the type most frequently employed).

The function of the tone arm (Fig. 3) is to support the pickup and counterbalance its weight, so that the only forces acting upon the stylus are the deflecting forces exerted by the grooves. Any other force results in deterioration of the quality of reproduction. The "angular error" (Fig. 5a) cannot be entirely eliminated. When the grooves are being cut, the recording cutter moves radially, whereas the tone arm of a record player swivels about a pivot, so that its end, carrying the pickup, describes a circular arc. This difference between the direction of movement of the cutter and of the stylus causes distortion of the sound. However, by suitably shaping the tone arm (as in Fig. 5b), the angular error can be kept within acceptably low values throughout the path of the stylus on the record. Ideally, the tone arm should have frictionless motion. In high-quality arms the friction is virtually eliminated by means of precision ball bearings or jewelled bearings.

(Continued)

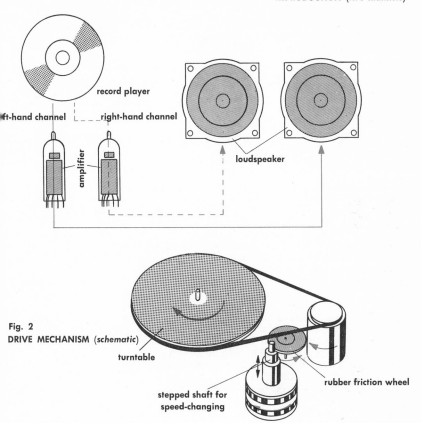

Fig. 1 PRINCIPLE OF STEREOPHONIC REPRODUCTION (*two channels*)

record player

left-hand channel   right-hand channel

amplifier

loudspeaker

Fig. 2
DRIVE MECHANISM (*schematic*)

turntable

stepped shaft for
speed-changing

rubber friction wheel

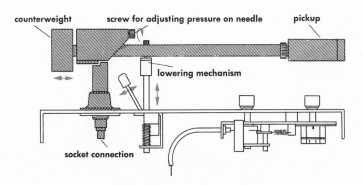

counterweight   screw for adjusting pressure on needle   pickup

lowering mechanism

socket connection

Fig. 3 SECTION THROUGH TONE ARM

315

The effect of the inertia forces due to up-and-down movements of the tone arm can never be entirely eliminated. There is a limit to the reduction of the mass of the arm, as the latter must retain a degree of rigidity in relation to the modulations of the groove, so as to enable them effectively to move the stylus in relation to the pickup. A well-designed tone arm is carefully balanced. With regard to the vertical direction of movement this is achieved by means of an adjustable counterweight. Horizontal equilibrium is usually pre-adjusted by the design (mass distribution) of the arm and cannot subsequently be varied. The necessary vertical force to keep the needle in proper contact with the groove is produced either by a spring or by a weight.

Modern high-performance tone arms sometimes have a further refinement, namely, compensation for "skating", which is caused by the fact that the stylus presses harder against the inner than against the outer side wall of the groove. This is because of the transverse force component (Fig. 4). The compensating system must exert a counteracting (i.e., outward) force of the same magnitude upon the arm.

A tone arm must not resonate with the vibrations of the stylus, but should display rigid behaviour over the entire range of reproduction. Some tone arms are made of wood, which, because of its cellular structure, has particularly high vibrational rigidity. Steel tone arms of torsionally rigid tubular cross-section are widely used.

The pickup converts the movements of the stylus—imparted to it by the groove—into corresponding electric signals in the form of an alternating voltage. In a crystal pickup (Fig. 6) the deflections of the stylus cause a thin plate of Seignette salt (sodium potassium tartrate) to undergo flexural movements, which give rise to an electric potential difference in consequence of the piezoelectric effect (see page 86). In a magnetic pickup (Fig. 7) the electric output is due to the relative motion of a magnetic field and a coil (or two coils in the case of a stereophonic pickup) located in the field. Magnetic systems are generally more complex and more expensive than crystal systems, but produce less distortion and are therefore almost exclusively used for high-fidelity reproduction. The stylus must have a rounded tip suited to the cross-sectional dimensions of the groove, so as to ensure that the tip is maintained in contact with the sloping side walls of the groove and clears the bottom (Fig. 8). The movable system in the pickup must be so mounted that the stylus can follow every rapid change of direction of the groove virtually without resistance; and for the same reason the mass of all the moving parts must be as small as possible. Pickups with very resilient stylus mountings can be operated with a relatively small vertical force on the stylus. Modern pickups combining high resilience with small moving mass so greatly reduce distortion and groove wear that deterioration of records due to repeated use has been virtually eliminated.

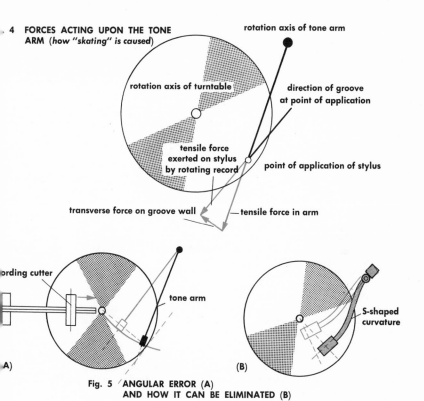

4 FORCES ACTING UPON THE TONE ARM (*how "skating" is caused*)

rotation axis of tone arm

rotation axis of turntable

direction of groove at point of application

tensile force exerted on stylus by rotating record

point of application of stylus

transverse force on groove wall

tensile force in arm

recording cutter

tone arm

(A)

S-shaped curvature

(B)

Fig. 5 ANGULAR ERROR (A) AND HOW IT CAN BE ELIMINATED (B)

rear rubber bearing

front rubber bearing

crystal

needle

Fig. 6 CRYSTAL PICKUP (*schematic*)

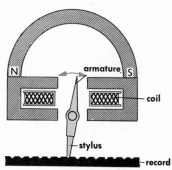

armature

N   S

coil

stylus

record

Fig. 7 MAGNETIC PICKUP (*schematic*)

standard, micro, stereo

Fig. 8 COMPARISON OF THE THREE GROOVE SIZES

GRAMOPHONE RECORD

A gramophone record (or disc) is a circular plastic disc on which the sound is recorded in a spiral groove. The sound vibrations of the air can be transmitted to a sharp recording cutter which scratches a wavy groove into a plastic-coated metal disc, the cutter being guided in a spiral path from the edge to the centre of the disc. The wavy pattern of the groove determines the frequency and the amplitude of the sound vibrations; these correspond respectively to the pitch and the loudness of the sound. On playing back this disc in a gramophone (at the same speed as the recording speed), the wave pattern of the groove will produce corresponding vibrations in the reproducing stylus, and these mechanical vibrations can be either directly (by means of a diaphragm, as in the early phonographs and gramophones) or indirectly (through a process of electrical amplification) be reproduced as audible vibrations of the air. In present-day recording techniques the master record is, of course, not itself used for playing back. The plastic surface of the disc is given a lacquer coating which is subsequently stripped off again after being metallised (plated with metal) by an electrochemical process known as electroforming. In this way an electroformed metal master disc is obtained. This disc is a "negative" in that the grooves in the master record are here represented by ridges. The negative can be used in a plastic moulding press to produce records. For commercial production of records in very large numbers, however, more durable negatives made of high-grade steel may be produced. These are then used as pressing masters. Modern fine-groove records rotate at $33\frac{1}{3}$ r.p.m. (long-playing records) or at 45 r.p.m. (extended-play records). The older standard records rotated at 78 r.p.m. Records for rotation at $16\frac{2}{3}$ r.p.m. are also produced for special purposes. The material of which the records are made plays an important part in determining reproduction quality. The cheaper records are made of synthetic thermoplastic resins containing fillers. With the introduction of fine-grooved records it became necessary to use high-quality compounds without fillers, as the filler particles produce a certain amount of background noise. A fairly wide range of synthetic materials are used for gramophone records; the vinyl plastics are most commonly used for the purpose, e.g., polyvinyl chloride. These are so-called "unbreakable" records. The moulding of records is done under pressure, with the aid of heat.

Stereophonic records are recorded with the aid of two separate microphones. Reproduction is accomplished by means of a single stylus with its axes of movement inclined at 45° to the record surface, the pickup being designed to produce two independent signals in accordance with the motion components along the two (90° displaced) axes. The two signals are amplified and fed to two separate loudspeakers.

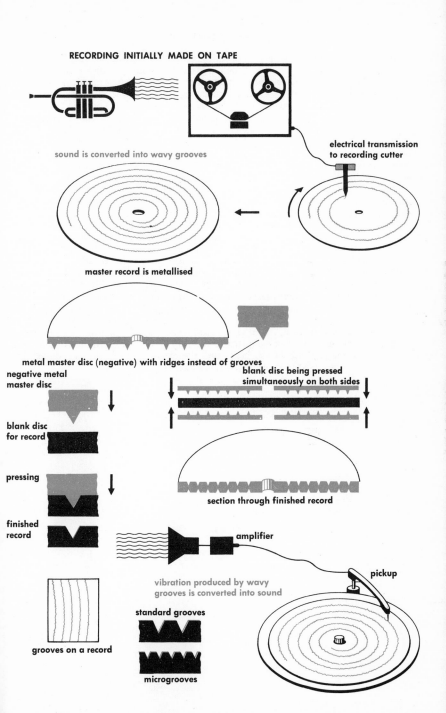

RECORDING INITIALLY MADE ON TAPE

electrical transmission
to recording cutter

sound is converted into wavy grooves

master record is metallised

metal master disc (negative) with ridges instead of grooves

negative metal
master disc

blank disc being pressed
simultaneously on both sides

blank disc
for record

pressing

section through finished record

finished
record

amplifier

pickup

vibration produced by wavy
grooves is converted into sound

standard grooves

grooves on a record

microgrooves

319

TAPE RECORDER

Many radio broadcasts, all repeat broadcasts, and nearly all automatically repeated telephonic information (e.g., the "speaking clock" time service) are recorded on magnetic tape. To produce a tape recording, the sound (speech or music) is converted into corresponding electric signals by means of a microphone in conjunction with amplifier equipment. These electric signals (voltage oscillations) produce variations in the strength of a magnetic field. The signals are thereby recorded on a magnetic tape which is magnetised along its length in accordance with the signals impressed on it. In early tape recorders steel wire or tape was used, but nowadays a plastic tape provided with a coating of powdered red iron oxide (gamma-Fe_2O_3) is most often used as a magnetic recording medium. Red iron oxide particles, needle-shaped and about 1 micron in length, are widely used. The black oxide of iron (Fe_3O_4) is sometimes used for the same purpose. The oxide particles, which are applied to the tape in a coating mixed with a binder substance are strongly magnetisable and retain their magnetic properties almost indefinitely.

Sound is transmitted as pressure waves in the air. The lowest musical notes have a frequency of about 30 cycles per second; the highest notes of musical significance are about 4000 cycles per second (the highest audible frequencies are in the 12,000–16,000 cycles/sec. range). The "tone colour" (timbre), however, consists of a complex mixture of frequencies, due to harmonics which may have as much as six times as high a frequency as that of the fundamental tone of the sound. All these vibrations are picked up by the microphone, amplified and converted into variations in the magnetic field of an electromagnet in the recording head (Fig. 1), whereby these variations are recorded on the magnetic tape. To reproduce the sounds, the tape is passed over a similar head, called the reproducing head, at the same speed as that used in recording. The magnetism stored up in the tape induces voltage oscillations in the electromagnet coil of the head, and the electric signals thus produced are amplified and then used to energise a loudspeaker (Fig. 2).

(Continued)

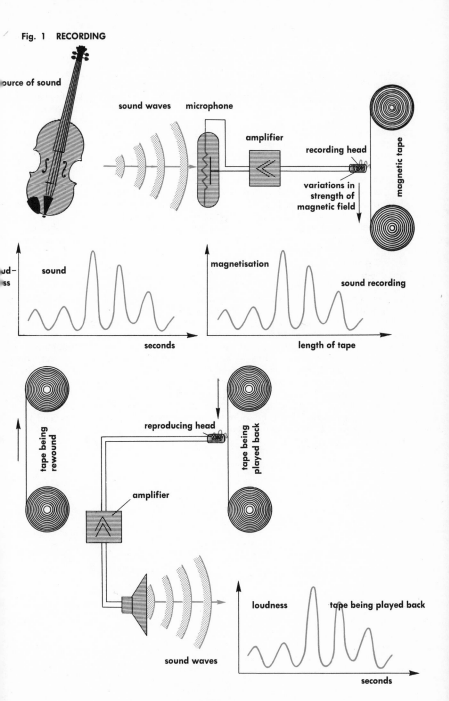

Fig. 1 RECORDING

source of sound

sound waves   microphone

amplifier

recording head

magnetic tape

variations in
strength of
magnetic field

loud-
ness

sound

seconds

magnetisation

sound recording

length of tape

tape being
rewound

reproducing head

tape being
played back

amplifier

loudness   tape being played back

sound waves

seconds

Fig. 2   REPRODUCTION

TAPE RECORDER
(continued)

The recording head consists of a coil wound around a core of magnetic iron which has a gap at the point where the tape moves across its surface. The current in the coil magnetises the particles in the tape (Fig. 3). During playback, the whole process is reversed; indeed the recording head can also be used as the reproducing head (Fig. 4). The faster the tape travels past the recording head and, subsequently, past the reproducing head, the more faithful will be reproduction of the sound. This is because a higher tape speed provides more space for accommodating the highest frequencies on the tape. In order to record an overtone of, for example, 5000 cycles/sec. it is necessary to record 5000 oscillations in the strength of the magnetic field on the tape during each second of its passage past the recording head. In radio broadcasting studios a tape speed of 15 in./sec. is usually employed, i.e., each of the 5000 oscillations has a space of 15/5000 in. = 0.003 in. Tape recorders for amateur use are usually operated at tape recording and playing speeds of $7\frac{1}{2}$ in., $3\frac{3}{4}$ in. or $1\frac{7}{8}$ in. per second, many machines being provided with facilities for using any of these three speeds, as desired. The widths of tape available for the recording of each oscillation of the overtone of 5000 cycles/sec. are thus 0.0015 in., 0.00075 in. and 0.000375 in. respectively. There is a progressive decline in recording and reproduction quality as the speed is lower, since the width of the gap in the recording and/or reproduction head cannot be reduced indefinitely; each oscillation requires a certain minimum amount of space, which is greater according as the head (and more particularly the gap) is of coarser construction. The greater the fineness and precision of the head is, the more expensive is the tape recording equipment concerned. To achieve high-fidelity recording and reproduction, it is necessary to take a large number of technical factors into account. Sound recorders for professional purposes usually have three motors: one on the supply reel, one on the take-up reel, and a third the drive the tape. Extreme care is taken to provide smooth and uniform drive. Tape recorders for amateur use record usually on one-half of the $\frac{1}{4}$ in. wide tape. Some machines are designed to record four tracks on a $\frac{1}{4}$ in. tape. A great advantage of magnetic recording is that recordings can be erased and tapes re-used over and over again. Erasure is done by an erasing head, which produces a powerful high-alternating field that demagnetises and thus erases the tape just before the latter passes the recording head.

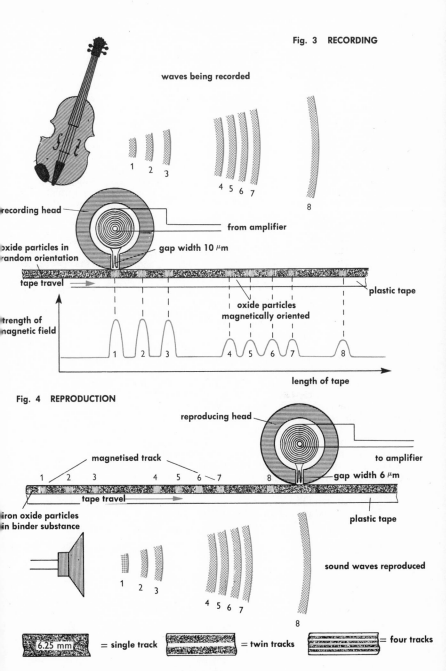

Fig. 3 RECORDING

waves being recorded

1 2 3

4 5 6 7

8

recording head

from amplifier

oxide particles in random orientation

gap width 10 μm

tape travel

plastic tape

oxide particles magnetically oriented

strength of magnetic field

1 2 3 4 5 6 7 8

length of tape

Fig. 4 REPRODUCTION

reproducing head

to amplifier

magnetised track

1 2 3 4 5 6 7 8

gap width 6 μm

tape travel

plastic tape

iron oxide particles in binder substance

1 2 3

4 5 6 7

8

sound waves reproduced

6.25 mm = single track   = twin tracks   = four tracks

track widths

323

COIN TESTERS

A feature common to all "slot machines" (automatic vending machines, etc.) is the coin testing unit which rejects counterfeit or defective coins before they can release the locking mechanism. Every coin tester checks at least the diameter and thickness of the coin inserted into the slot; further tests relate to the weight, alloy composition, and magnetic properties. The coin inserted into the slot—which is just wide enough to admit the right coin—rolls through a chute and lands in the weighing device, which also serves to check the diameter of the coin: the two hook-shaped bent-round ends of the two balance arms are so spaced that a coin of the correct diameter will press down on the right-hand arm. A coin deficient in diameter will drop down between the hooks and into the receptacle for returned coins (vertical black arrows). Oversize coins are retained by the hooks, but as their centre of gravity coincides with the pivot of the balance, the latter will then not rotate. When the coin return button is pressed, the side flap of the coin tester is swung aside, so that the oversize coin is tipped over sideways and likewise falls into the returned coins receptacle. The counterweight on the left-hand arm of the balance ensures that only a coin having at least the same weight as this counterweight can pass. The "correct" coin now presses down the right-hand balance arm and rolls down a short incline, during which journey it passes through the field of a strong permanent magnet. Depending on the alloy of which it consists, the coin will be allowed to pass or will be retarded by this magnetic field. If the iron content is high, the coin may be stopped altogether. In that case it can be retrieved by pressing the coin return button, whereby a wiper dislodges the coin from the magnet, while the side flap is swung aside to allow the coin to drop into the return receptacle (black arrows on right). When the coin has passed the magnet, it drops on to a rebound stop. If the coin is "correct", it will have the right mass (depending on the alloy) and the right speed (depending on the degree of slowing-down by the magnetic field) and thus have the right amount kinetic energy to jump over the rejector pin and run down into the outlet giving access to the release mechanism of the machine (red arrows). Coins which fall short of this requirement will strike the pin and drop into the return receptacle. A somewhat different testing mechanism is used for coins made of plated steel (Fig. 2), as are used in some countries. The coin rolls along an inclined path whose slope is such that only a coin with a sufficient amount of kinetic energy will continue to move, whereas a coin that is too light will come to a standstill. Next, the coin is weighed in a device which functions like a trap-door: if the coin is too heavy, it will fall through the flap (right-hand black arrow). In the following stages the diameter and thickness of the coin are tested. The whole coin testing device is inclined sideways, so that, at a certain point, coins deficient in diameter automatically fall out sideways through an aperature between lateral guide plates. The thickness test is performed by letting the coil roll along a narrow ridge beside a gap. If the coin is too thin, it will drop into the gap (left-hand black arrow). Coins that are too thick are rejected by the slot in the first place and cannot enter the machine at all.

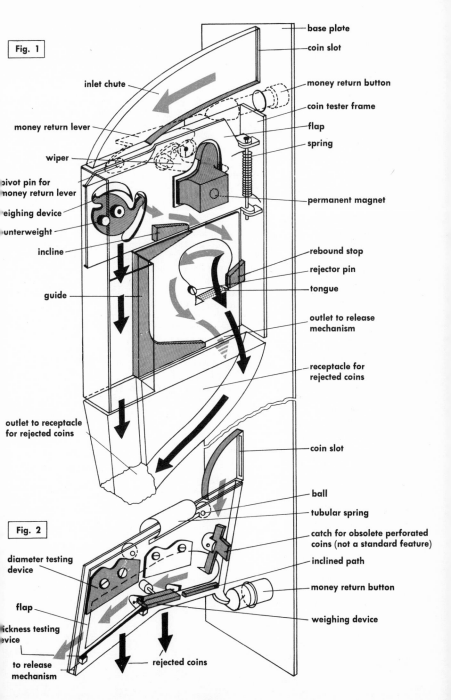

Fig. 1

base plate
coin slot
inlet chute
money return button
coin tester frame
money return lever
flap
spring
wiper
pivot pin for money return lever
weighing device
counterweight
permanent magnet
incline
rebound stop
rejector pin
guide
tongue
outlet to release mechanism
receptacle for rejected coins
outlet to receptacle for rejected coins
coin slot
ball
tubular spring
Fig. 2
catch for obsolete perforated coins (not a standard feature)
diameter testing device
inclined path
money return button
flap
weighing device
thickness testing device
to release mechanism
rejected coins

325

AUTOMATIC VENDING MACHINES

These machines are usually equipped with a number of compartments which contain the goods for sale and which can be opened after the appropriate coins have been inserted into the slot of the machine. The operating principle of a typical machine of this kind is illustrated in the accompanying diagram. Each compartment is closed by a cover, or flap, provided with a glass window through which the goods can be viewed. Connected to each flap is a lateral control cam (curved path) which is in contact with a roller. After insertion of the appropriate coin or coins (in the machine illustrated it is assumed that three coins of equal value are required to work the machine) the purchaser pulls one of the flaps. This causes the cam to lift the roller and the vertical push-rod to which the latter is attached. Through levers this upward movement is transmitted to a toggle (elbow lever) which has a slot engaging with a pin on the coin slide, whereby the latter is given in a horizontal movement (to the left in the illustration). The top coin in the slide lifts the catch lever of a tongue projecting into the coin path. The coin slide can thus travel its full distance, allowing the flap of the compartment to be opened to its full extent and at the same time causing the coins to drop into the collecting chute. If on the other hand, no (or not enough) coins have been inserted, the coin slide travels only a very short distance, when a stop pin on the slide encounters the front of the catch lever. This locks the entire mechanism and prevents the flap from being opened. Any coin or coins inserted can, in that case, be retrieved by pressing the coin return button, which causes the bottom plate under the coin slide to swing down and allow the coins to drop in the return chute. In addition to this operating mechanism, a vending machine has to be equipped with various devices to prevent misuse, more particularly in the form of attempts to open more than one flap at a time after insertion of the money. This is prevented by a ridge at the edge of each control cam. When one flap is opened, the ridge on its cam slides under a projection on the push-rod under it, thus locking the push-rod and preventing the other flaps from being opened. After a flap has been opened, an additional locking rod frustrates any further attempts to open other flaps. This locking rod is connected to the top horizontal lever and extends down to the bottom flap. At the level of each locking pin (approximately at the centre of each control cam) the locking rod is provided with a projection which, when the rod is lifted, locks all the other—as yet closed—flaps. Cigarette vending machines operate on the same principle, except that, instead of compartments, there are slides or drawers which have to be pulled out and which are automatically refilled from a stack of packets.

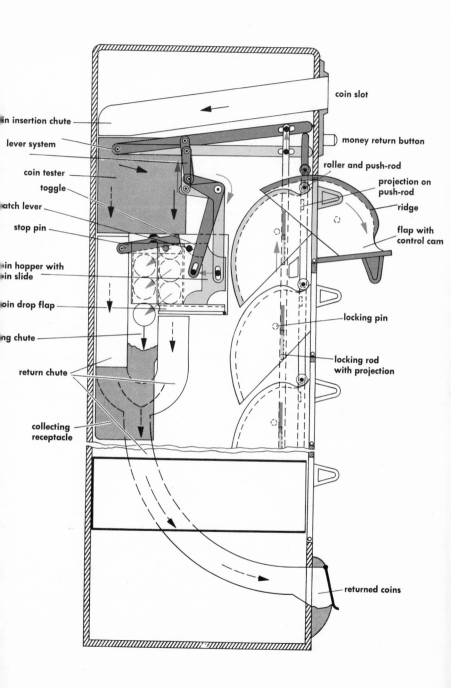

coin slot

coin insertion chute

lever system

coin tester

toggle

catch lever

stop pin

coin hopper with
coin slide

coin drop flap

ng chute

return chute

collecting
receptacle

money return button

roller and push-rod

projection on
push-rod

ridge

flap with
control cam

locking pin

locking rod
with projection

returned coins

JUKE BOX

Present-day juke boxes almost invariably use 7-inch records played at 45 r.p.m. Magnetic tape recordings and other recording media have not proved popular for the purpose. Most juke boxes hold between 30 and 100 records, which can be played on both sides.

The following components are common to all machines of this type (Fig. 1): record magazine or hopper, playing unit, programme panel, selecting device (usually provided with keys or buttons), coin tester and coin storage unit, amplifier, and loud-speakers. These components are built into a case with a transparent cover. Some juke boxes are additionally provided with a counting mechanism for the various records played (so-called popularity meter) and a remote-action selector (wall box) for remote control of the machine.

There are many design variants. The operation of a juke box will here be described with reference to a typical machine as illustrated in Fig. 1. After passing through the coin tester (see page 324), which may be equipped for testing two or three different values of coins, the coins drop into the corresponding coin hopper and actuate a micro-switch, which transmits an electric pulse to energise a magnet in the coin storage unit. This magnet in turn actuates a device which rotates the so-called adding cog-wheel, which has the same number of cogs as there are records in the juke box, e.g., 60. For example, the juke box may be so designed that it will play one record

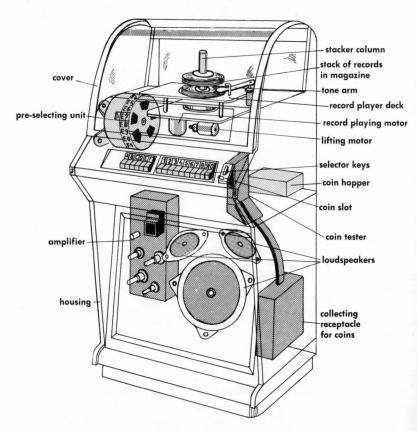

Fig. 1

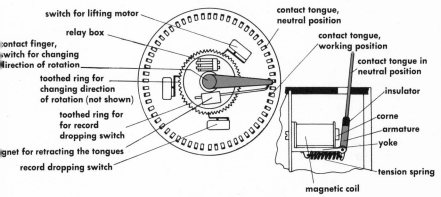

Fig. 2   PRE-SELECTING UNIT (*schematic*)

for sixpence, two for a shilling and five for a florin. (In the United States, one for a dime, three for a quarter.) On insertion of these coins the adding wheel will be rotated a distance corresponding to one cog, two cogs and five cogs respectively.

As a result a contact—situated between the adding cog-wheel and a second cog-wheel (called the subtracting cog-wheel)—is closed, so that current flows to the two unlocking magnets which then release the locking device that normally (i.e., so long as no coins have been inserted) prevents the selector keys from being operated. When the appropriate coins have been inserted, the desired record can be selected by pressing a letter key and a numeral key respectively (e.g., ten numeral keys numbered from 1 to 9 and 0, and six letter keys A to F, so that 60 combinations are possible). This causes micro-switches to energise a magnet, which causes the subtracting cog-wheel to rotate a distance corresponding to one cog. In this way the successive cog movements of the adding disc are cancelled one by one until the inserted money has been used up and the subtracting cog-wheel has caught up with the adding cog-wheel. When this happens the energising current of the unlocking magnets is cut-off and the keys become locked again. Simultaneously with the above-mentioned operations in the coin storage unit, an electric pulse travels from the actuated selector keys to the so-called pre-selecting unit, where it is stored.

The pre-selecting unit (Fig. 2) is the "brain" of the machine. It ensures that the pulse emitted by any particular selector key is transmitted to the desired record. This is accomplished as follows. An electromagnet associated with the selected key combination (there are, in this case, 60 such magnets) actuates a contact "tongue" (there are likewise 60 of these) which connects two contacts and thus completes an electric circuit to the selector motor (in the pre-selecting unit) and to a brake connected in parallel with this motor.

The selector motor drives a so-called relay box which has a contact finger that scans the contact tongues at the perimeter of the pre-selecting unit. When it encounters a tongue which has been pulled out by an electromagnet, the selector motor circuit is interrupted, and the motor is immediately stopped with the aid of the brake.

Until then a micro-switch which is connected to a toothed ring around the relay box produces a number of electric pulses corresponding to the number of teeth on the toothed ring (which is the same as the number of non-protruding contact tongues). These pulses are then fed to a dropping magnet inside the stacker column (Fig. 3). This magnet retracts three catches and, at the same time, causes three retaining tongues to protrude. Each pulse arriving at the magnet causes a gramophone record to be dropped down from the stack until the selected contact tongue has been reached. The stacked records actually rest on a carrier disc (Fig. 4), which descends a certain distance, according to the number of records dropped. See also Fig. 5.

Since each contact tongue corresponds to a particular piece of music, the "right" record has now been reached. Whether this record, too, is dropped down will depend on whether the protruding contact tongue corresponds to the "front" (top) or "back" (underside) of the record. In the selector key system (in this particular type of machine) an odd number corresponds to "back" and an even number to "front". For example, if the piece of music chosen is characterised by the combination B1, then, starting from the record A1/2 (which is at the bottom of the stack) the records A1/2, A3/4, A5/6, A7/8 and A9/0 will have to be dropped. Since B1 is the back (underside) of the sixth record, it is not dropped (the contact tongue B1 is protruding no dropping pulse is transmitted): the swivelling tone arm, which has a pick-up provided with two stylus systems, plays the underside of this record from underneath. If B2 is chosen instead, i.e., the piece of music on the front (top) of this record, then the contact finger moves past the contact tongue B1; the corresponding tooth on the toothed ring of the relay box causes the micro-switch to emit a pulse; the dropping magnet is energised; the record B1/2 is dropped. Now the pick-up plays the front (top) of this record from above.

The swivelling motion of the tone arm is produced by the record playing motor (Fig. 5), which drives the turntable and (through rubber rollers) the stacker column and furthermore drives the mechanism for swivelling and lifting the tone arm. These various movements are performed by appropriate reversals in the direction of rotation of the motor. For example, when the turntable rotates clockwise, the tone arm is swung inwards and the pickup stylus applied to the record. When the record has been played, the direction of the motor is reversed, so that the turntable then rotates anti-clockwise and tensions a spring which lifts the stylus off the record and swings the tone arm outwards. At the same time, a lifting mechanism (comprising a motor, chain and lifting attachment) carries the stack of records upwards and thus returns it to its initial position. The protruding contact tongues are retracted by the action of an electromagnet (incorporated in the relay box) which is energised through a micro-switch.

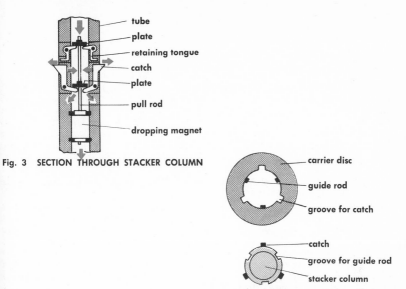

Fig. 3   SECTION THROUGH STACKER COLUMN

- tube
- plate
- retaining tongue
- catch
- plate
- pull rod
- dropping magnet

- carrier disc
- guide rod
- groove for catch

- catch
- groove for guide rod
- stacker column

Fig. 4   CO-OPERATION OF STACKER COLUMN
           AND CARRIER DISC

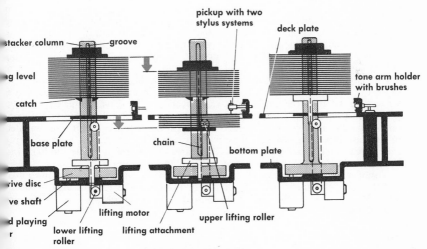

- stacker column
- groove
- pickup with two stylus systems
- deck plate
- ...g level
- tone arm holder with brushes
- catch
- base plate
- chain
- bottom plate
- ...rive disc
- ...ve shaft
- ...d playing
- ...r
- lifting motor
- lower lifting roller
- lifting attachment
- upper lifting roller

Fig. 5   RECORD PLAYING UNIT

331

BLAST-FURNACE

The blast-furnace is a shaft furnace, 100 ft. or more in height, consisting of a cylindrical bottom portion (hearth with hearth bottom), from which rises an upward-widening conically tapered portion (bosh) surmounted by a taller tapered structure (shaft) which narrows towards the top where it is closed by means of a system of double conical gates (bells) (Fig. 2). This form of furnace is eminently suited to the process of ore reduction and smelting that takes place inside it. The furnace walls are lined internally with fireclay refractory bricks. The hottest part (hearth and bottom plate) has a carbon brick lining. The steel shell of the furnace is cooled. From the top, or throat, the blast-furnace is charged with metallurgical coke, iron ore and fluxes, these various materials being placed in alternate layers. Air at a pressure of around 10–20 lb./in.^{2} is blown through blast pipes into the lower part of the furnace. This air, which has first been heated to 500°–900° C in hot blast stoves (Cowper stoves), causes part of the coke to burn and form carbon monoxide. The heat of combustion raises the temperature of the coke to incandescence, drives the carbon dioxide out of the fluxes (mostly limestone) and dries the ore in the upper zones of the furnace (Fig. 1). Just above the level of the blast inlet the temperature in the furnace charge is about 1600° C. In the bosh the temperature is 1200°–1400° C; here the blast-furnace gas is composed of approximately 40% CO, 2% H_2 and 57% N_2. The rising carbon monoxide reduces some of the ore to iron and some of it to iron monoxide and escapes from the top of the furnace as "top gas" with a composition of 28–36% CO, 12% CO_2 and 52–60% N_2. The reduction process commences with the indirect reduction in the shaft at 400°–700° C, converting part of the ore to iron and part of it to iron monoxide. In the bosh, direct reduction with the glowing hot carbon in the coke at 750°–1400° C converts all the ore into metallic iron which absorbs 3–4% of carbon (in the form of elementary carbon and as iron carbide) as it trickles down into the hearth. The pig iron which collects on the hearth bottom is discharged through the tap hole at intervals of 3–6 hours and issues from the furnace at a temperature of 1250°–1450° C. It flows through the iron runner into the pig bed (sand moulds for ingots) or into the mobile ladle. Molten slag, which floats on the pig iron at the bottom of the furnace, is discharged through the slag notch and passed into moulds in which it solidifies in the form of blocks (which are used as building or paving stones) or is processed into slag wool, road stone, fertilisers, or so-called granulated slag (which is used in the manufacture of certain kinds of cement). The slag consists of lime-alumina silicates with heavy metal oxides and is formed by the silicates present in the ore and by the coke ash. Some of the top gas from the furnace is used as fuel for heating the air in the hot blast stoves or is utilised for driving large gas engines. Besides carbon, the pig iron contains manganese, phosphorus, sulphur and silicon. Grey pig iron—in which part of the carbon is precipitated as graphite—is remelted in cupola furnaces to grey cast iron, which is not particularly brittle. In white pig iron the carbon is dissolved mainly as iron carbide; this iron is brittle and hard and is processed into malleable cast iron and chilled cast iron.

A modern blast-furnace produces 500–1200 tons of pig iron per day, for a coal consumption of around 0.6 ton per ton of pig iron. The furnace also produces 200–500 tons of slag and 2000–5000 tons of top gas per day, while it consumes about 2000–5000 tons of air.

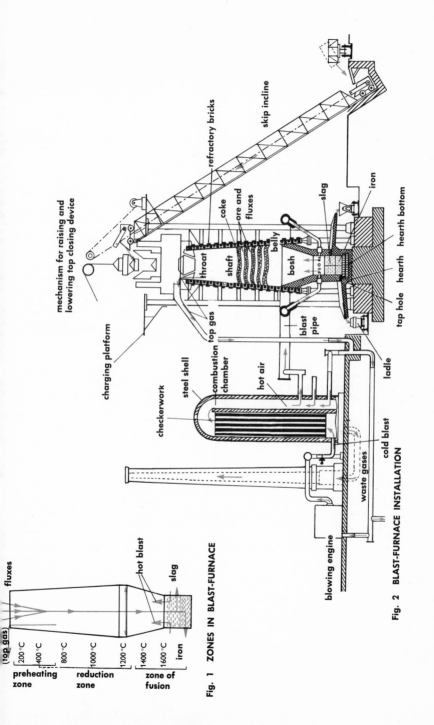

Fig. 1 ZONES IN BLAST-FURNACE

Fig. 2 BLAST-FURNACE INSTALLATION

333

STEEL

Steel differs from pig iron in that it has a lower content of carbon. Steel-makii
is therefore really nothing but the removal, by combustion, of the carbon contain
in the iron. As a result, the structure of the metal becomes more resilient, mo
flexible and—what is very important—cuttable. Steel is therefore stronger ai
better workable than iron.

In addition to carbon, steel contains other admixtures, e.g., sulphur and pho
phorus. All these substances are removed from the pig iron by oxidation. This
achieved by bringing the molten metal into contact with air, with the result that t
impurities are burned, i.e., they are transformed into their oxides by the oxygen
the air. These oxides are lighter than the molten steel and float on it as liquid sla
they must therefore be drained off before the steel itself is tapped.

Open-hearth steel-making

The central feature of a steelworks using this process is the open-hearth furna
(Fig. 1a). The pig iron, together with a certain amount of scrap iron, is deposited
the furnace hearth by a special crane. Then a gas-and-air mixture is burned over t
iron, which melts at a temperature of about 1800° C. The gas burned in the furna
is preheated by a regenerative firing system. The gas, together with the air need
for combustion, enters the furnace on one side of the furnace and is preheated
the heating chamber. This mixture of gas and air is burned over the hearth; the h
waste gases flow through flues on the other side of the furnace and are discharg
up the chimney. Before being discharged, however, the gases give off a considerat
proportion of their heat to—initially cold—brick-lined heating chambers. T
lining of these chambers consist of refractory bricks, which are heated to red-h
temperature. Then the gas flow is reversed (regenerative heating), i.e., the gas ai
air are admitted through the—now hot—heating chambers and absorb heat fro
them. This preheating of the gas and air enables the combustion temperature
the flame to be considerably raised (Fig. 1b). The air needed for the oxidation
the undesirable admixtures is provided by the combustion air. In the case of t
open-hearth furnace this oxidation process is sometimes referred to as "hear
refining".

The slag produced in this steel-making process is composed of the oxides of t
impurities and admixtures. It floats as a liquid on the molten steel. When it is tapp
off, cooled and ground, it yields a valuable fertiliser because of its high phosphor
content. The properties of the refractory brick lining of the furnace hearth are al
important, as these bricks must be able to absorb some of the sulphur and phosphor
contained in the iron.

Basic Bessemer steel-making

In this process the carbon content of the pig iron is reduced in a so-called co
verter—a basic Bessemer steel converter—which is an approximately pear-shap
refractory-lined steel vessel capable of holding 20–60 tons of pig iron (Fig. 2). A
is blown through the molten iron from nozzles (tuyeres) in the bottom and oxidis
the carbon and other admixtures.

(Continue

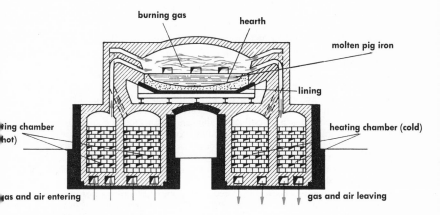

burning gas **hearth**

molten pig iron

lining

ing chamber (hot)

heating chamber (cold)

gas and air entering

gas and air leaving

Fig. 1a   OPEN-HEARTH FURNACE

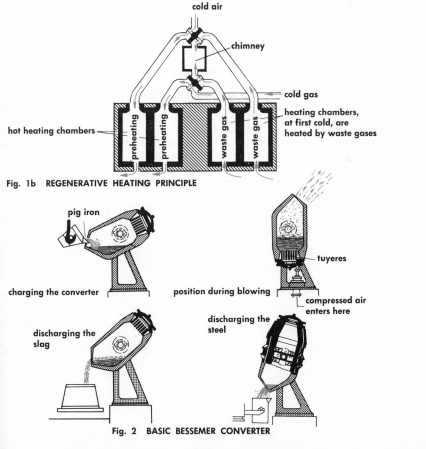

cold air

chimney

cold gas

hot heating chambers

preheating **preheating** **waste gas** **waste gas**

heating chambers, at first cold, are heated by waste gases

Fig. 1b   REGENERATIVE HEATING PRINCIPLE

pig iron

tuyeres

charging the converter

position during blowing

compressed air enters here

discharging the slag

discharging the steel

Fig. 2   BASIC BESSEMER CONVERTER

The converter is provided with trunnions and is rotatably mounted. The empty converter is tilted and filled with molten pig iron from a ladle (Fig. 2a). On completion of filling, the converter is swung to the upright position, and compressed air is blown through the pig iron from the tuyeres in the bottom (Fig. 2b).

This operation is known as blowing, and the converter steel-making process is referred to as "air refining"—as distinct from "hearth refining" in the open-hearth furnace. The oxygen in the blast air burns the carbon and the other admixtures. The lime which has been added to the converter charge promotes the separation of the oxides formed, which collect as slag on the surface of the molten metal. The latter would gradually cool and eventually solidify as a result of air-blowing, but for the fact that the combustion of the phosphorus in the pig iron produces additional heat, which not only maintains but even further raises the temperature of the molten bath. For this reason the converter method of steel-making is used chiefly for pig iron with a high content of phosphorus.

When oxidation has been completed (this is judged from the colour of the flames emerging from the top of the converter), the converter is tilted, the molten slag is first poured off, and then the molten steel—mild steel—is discharged into ingot moulds (Figs. 2c and 2d).

The conventional Bessemer—as distinct from the "basic" Bessemer—steel-making process operates on the same principle, except that the converters employed are usually smaller and the refractory lining is of a different composition, the pig iron treated in this process having a low content of phosphorus and sulphur.

Manufacture of electric furnace steel

Another steel-making process, which yields mild steel of exceptionally high purity, is the electric process. The requisite heat is in this case not produced by the burning of gas or coal, but by an electric current. The raw material for the process is usually molten open-hearthed steel, which is thus further purified and refined in quality. However, the electric furnace can alternatively be charged with cold scrap iron with a certain quantity of added pig iron. In most electric furnaces the requisite heat is produced by an electric arc whicn is formed between a number of carbon electrodes and the surface of the molten bath (see page 100). No combustion air for oxidising the undesirable admixtures is supplied to the electric arc furnace (Fig. 3); instead, iron oxides are added, which give off their oxygen.

Oxygen steel-making

The application of pure oxygen in the refining process has, in recent years, led to the emergence of new steel-making methods. The steels made by these methods are as good as open-hearth steels. A feature common to all of them is that almost pure oxygen—produced in large quantities by so-called "tonnage oxygen" plants—is blown onto or into the molten pig iron. In the LD process (Fig. 4a) a jet of oxygen is blown at high pressure through a tube (called a lance) onto the surface of molten iron in a converter-type vessel. An offshoot, differing chiefly in the technique employed, is the LD–AC process, which can deal with iron having a higher phosphorus content, the converter being additionally charged with lime. In the OLP process powdered lime is injected with the stream of oxygen. The rotor process (Fig. 4b) uses a long cylindrical kiln which is slowly rotated (about $\frac{1}{2}$ r.p.m.). A primary oxygen jet blows oxygen into the molten bath itself, and a secondary oxygen nozzle above the bath ensures heat economy by burning the Co generated to CO_2. In the Kaldo process (Fig. 4c) a converter rotating on an inclined axis at speeds up to 30 r.p.m. is used; an oxygen jet is blown against the surface of the bath.

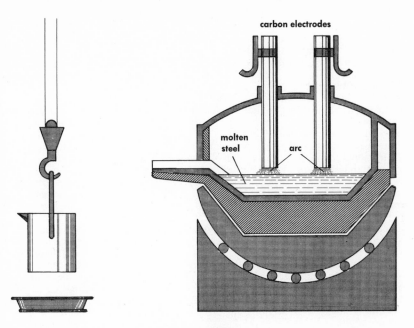

carbon electrodes

molten
steel

arc

Fig. 3   ELECTRIC ARC FURNACE

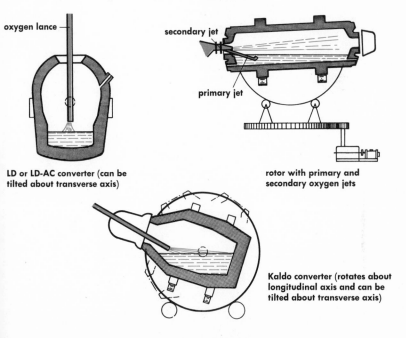

oxygen lance

secondary jet

primary jet

LD or LD-AC converter (can be
tilted about transverse axis)

rotor with primary and
secondary oxygen jets

Kaldo converter (rotates about
longitudinal axis and can be
tilted about transverse axis)

Fig. 4   VARIOUS OXYGEN STEELMAKING PROCESSES

In a rolling mill, ingots (pieces of steel of square cross-section) and slabs (of rectangular cross-section) are rolled, i.e., they are passed between rolls whereby they undergo an increase in length and a reduction in height (or depth). The white-hot ingot of steel is inserted between two rotating rolls made of cast iron or cast steel. The gap between these rolls is smaller than the thickness of the ingot. The top and bottom rolls are separately driven. Quite often they are both driven by one and the same electric motor, but in that case the drive is divided in a reduction gear unit interposed between the motor and the rolls. The thickness of the rolled ingot is varied by adjustment of the top roll (Fig. 1). The ingot or slab which is fed to the rolls is gripped by them and pulled through the gap between the top and the bottom roll by frictional action. The cross-section of the ingot is thereby reduced, and at the same time it undergoes an increase in length. The rolls used in rolling mills present a wide variety of shapes, depending on the type of rolled section to be produced. The rolls of sheet mills are smooth. The slabs (in smaller sizes they are known as "sheet bars") are rolled so as to increase their width. Of course, it is not possible to reduce a large slab of steel to a $\frac{1}{16}$ in. sheet in a single rolling operation. The reduction in thickness has to be effected in several successive operations, the slab either being passed again and again between the same pair of rolls, whose distance from each other is progressively reduced, or between a series of pairs (with gaps of diminishing width) installed one behind the other. An installation of this kind is called a rolling train. For producing rolled steel structural sections and the like, the ingots are first rough-rolled and then passed between a series of grooved rolls (Figs. 2a–2c). The shape of the grooves successively approximates to the final shape of the rolled section. I-sections, angles, bulb sections, etc. are produced in this way (Fig. 3).

(Continued)

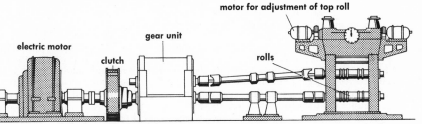

Fig. 1 ROLLING MILL WITH DRIVE MACHINERY

electric motor

clutch

gear unit

motor for adjustment of top roll

rolls

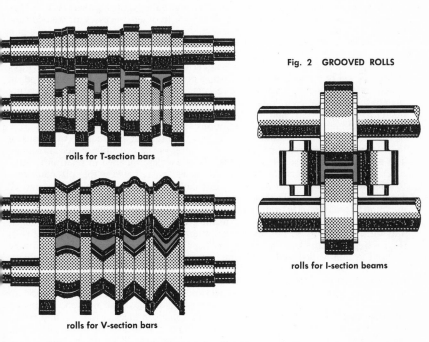

Fig. 2 GROOVED ROLLS

rolls for T-section bars

rolls for V-section bars

rolls for I-section beams

rolled steel bars

rolled steel shapes

bulb sections

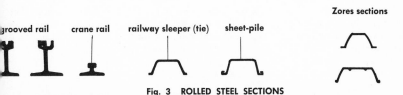

grooved rail   crane rail   railway sleeper (tie)   sheet-pile

Zores sections

Fig. 3 ROLLED STEEL SECTIONS

339

Broadly speaking, steel tubular products (pipes) may be subdivided into: welded pipes and seamless pipes. Welded pipes are produced from steel strip which is bent to a tubular shape and whose edges are then joined by welding. Seamless pipes are produced from cast or rolled round billets at rolling temperature. Depending on the pipe diameter and wall thickness required, a number of different methods of manufacture are used for both types of pipe.

The oldest continuous pipe-welding process is the Fretz-Moon process, based on the principle of "forge welding". An endless strip of steel (called the skelp) is passed through a furnace in which it is heated to about 1400° C and is then fed through shaping rolls which bend the skelp to a tubular shape (Fig. 1). It next passes through welding rolls which press the edges of the longitudinal slot together, so that they become welded to each other by their own heat. In other processes for welded tube manufacture the skelp is shaped in the cold condition, only the edges of the slot being heated to enable the weld to be formed. Various methods of electric arc welding are used, one of the most common being the submerged-arc method (in which the welding is shielded by a blanket of granular fusible material, or flux). Induction welding and resistance welding processes are also widely employed, in which electric induction and electric resistance are respectively utilised for heating the edges. In resistance welding the electrodes are copper discs, on each side of the opening to be welded. A special kind of pipe is the spiral-wound pipe made of steel strip wound and welded with a continuous spiral seam.

The oldest method of manufacturing seamless tubular products is by means of the Mannesmann piercing process, which employs the principle of helical rolling. The machine comprises two steel rolls whose axes are inclined in relation to each other. They both rotate in the same direction. The space between the rolls converges to a minimum width called the gorge. Just beyond the gorge is a piercing mandrel. A solid round bar of steel is heated to about 1300° C and, revolving in the opposite direction to the rolls, is introduced between the rolls (on the left in Fig. 2a). When the leading end of the bar has advanced to the gorge, it encounters the mandrel, which thus forms the cavity in the bar as the latter continues to move through the rolls (Figs. 2b, c). The thick-walled tube produced by this process can subsequently be reduced to thin-walled tube by passing it through special rolls in a so-called Pilger mill. These rolls vary in cross-sectional shape round their circumference. The tube, fixed to a mandrel, is gripped by the narrow part of the rolls (Fig. 3a) and its wall thickness is thereby reduced (Figs. 3a–c) until the rolls have rotated to such an extent that the wider part of their cross-section is reached and the tube is thus no longer gripped. The tube is then pulled back some distance, so that again a thick-walled portion is gripped by the rolls. The mandrel is rotated at the same time in order to ensure uniform application of the roll pressure all round the tube.

In the Stiefel piercing process for seamless tube manufacture a round bar is first pierced on a rotary piercing mill and the heavy-walled shell obtained in this way is then reduced in a second piercing operation, on a two-high rolling stand, to a tube with a thinner wall (Fig. 4).

In the rotary forge process a square ingot, heated to rolling temperature, is shaped to a shell closed at one end. This shell is then reduced and stretched on a rotary piercing mill and finally passed through sets of four rolls whereby the diameter is progressively reduced (Fig. 5).

The latest method of seamless tube manufacture is by hot extrusion: a hot billet is forced through a die provided with a mandrel for piercing the hole. In this way the tube of the correct final diameter and wall thickness is produced in a single operation.

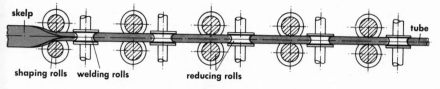

skelp

tube

shaping rolls   welding rolls   reducing rolls

Fig. 1   FRETZ-MOON PROCESS FOR WELDED TUBE
MANUFACTURE

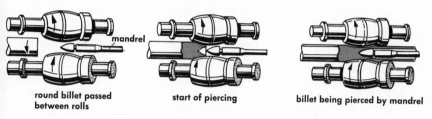

mandrel

round billet passed
between rolls

start of piercing

billet being pierced by mandrel

Fig. 2   ROTARY PIERCING MILL FOR SEAMLESS TUBE
MANUFACTURE (MANNESMANN PROCESS)

thick-walled shell being
advanced between the rolls

rolls grip a portion
of the shell

shell is reduced and stretched on
the mandrel and is then advanced again

Fig. 3   PILGER STEP-BY-STEP ROLLING PROCESS

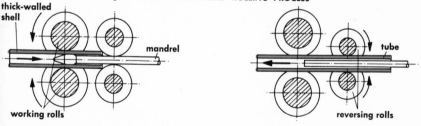

thick-walled
shell

mandrel

tube

working rolls

reversing rolls

thick-walled shell being reduced on mandrel

withdrawing the finished tube

Fig. 4   STIEFEL PIERCING PROCESS

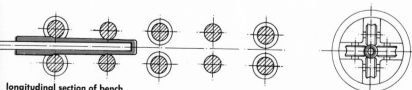

longitudinal section of bench
with sets of rolls

arrangement of rolls
in each set

Fig. 5   ROTARY FORGE PROCESS

WIRE MANUFACTURE

The preliminary treatment of the material to be manufactured into wire is done in the rolling mill (see page 338). Billets (square section ingots) about 7 cm ($2\frac{3}{4}$ in.) thick are rolled to round wire rod of about 5 mm (0.4 in.) diameter. The action of atmospheric oxygen causes a coating of mill scale to form on the hot surface of the rod and must be removed. This descaling can be done by various mechanical methods (e.g., shot-blasting) or by pickling, i.e., immersion of the wire rod in a bath of dilute sulphuric or hydrochloric acid. After pickling, the wire rod may additionally undergo a jolting treatment on the device illustrated in Fig. 1, which operates on the drop-hammer principle and dislodges the scale loosened by the acid. The remaining acid is removed by immersion of the wire rod in lime water.

The actual process of forming the wire is called drawing and is carried out on the metal in the cold state—not hot, as in rolling. The wire is pulled through a draw plate (Fig. 3a), which is a steel plate provided with a number of holes (dies) of various diameters. These dies have holes which taper from the diameter of the wire that enters the die to the smaller diameter of the wire that emerges from the die. Each passage through a die reduces the diameter of the wire by a certain amount. By successively passing the wire through dies of smaller and smaller diameter, thinner and thinner wire is obtained (Fig. 3b). To pass a wire through a die, the end of the wire is sharpened to a point and threaded through the die. It is seized by a gripping device and rapidly pulled through the die. This is assisted by lubrication of the wire. The actual minimum diameter (d_2) of the die is smaller than the final diameter (d_3) of the wire, as the elasticity of the metal causes it to expand to d_3 (Fig. 3). Copper and brass wire is manufactured from strips of sheet metal whose sharp edges are rounded by means of rollers. These strips are then drawn through dies (Fig. 2). The thick wire rod is coiled on a vertical spool called a swift and is pulled through the die by a rotating drum mounted on a vertical shaft which is driven by bevel gearing. The drum can be disconnected from the drive by means of a clutch.

The dies used in the modern wire industry are precision-made tools, manufactured in tungsten carbide for larger sizes or diamond for smaller sizes. Tungsten carbide dies are more accurate and much longer lasting than steel draw plates or steel dies.

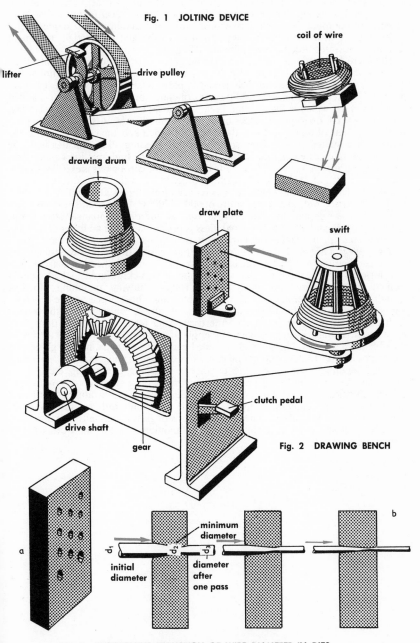

Fig. 1 JOLTING DEVICE

lifter

drive pulley

coil of wire

drawing drum

draw plate

swift

drive shaft

gear

clutch pedal

Fig. 2 DRAWING BENCH

a

minimum diameter

d_1

initial diameter

d_2

d_3

diameter after one pass

b

Fig. 3 PROGRESSIVE REDUCTION OF WIRE DIAMETER IN DIES

343

GLASS

The raw materials for glass manufacture are now still—as they were in ancient times—sand, soda and limestone or chalk. From the chemical point of view glass consists of compounds of silicates with alkaline and alkaline-earth oxides. After melting, glass with the correct composition and subjected to the right treatment (cooling), must not become crystalline on solidifying.

There are hundreds of recipes for making glass. One of these is the following: 59 parts of quartz sand, 17 parts of soda, 15 parts of dolomite, $4\frac{1}{2}$ parts of limestone, 3 parts of sodium sulphate and carbon, and $1\frac{1}{2}$ parts of felspar. These ingredients are intimately mixed together. 20 to 30 per cent of cullet (broken waste glass) is added to this mixture, which is then melted in tank furnaces with capacities of up to 1500 tons of material, or in pot furnaces containing a number of pots, each holding up to about 2 tons of material. First, the fluxes, e.g., soda and the cullet added to the mixture, are melted. The melting soda forms low-melting alkali silicates with the sand; these silicates enter into further reaction with the high-melting constituents and form the final glass melt. The carbon dioxide of the carbonates is expelled during melting and also at the end of the melting process, when the temperature is raised somewhat. Thereafter the temperature is reduced from the 1400°–1500° C, at which melting is carried out, to a temperature of 900°–1200° C. Undesirable discoloration of the glass is removed in various ways, e.g., by addition of manganese dioxide, antimony oxide and arsenic. Coloured glass is produced by the addition of metallic oxides (iron, copper, manganese, chromium, etc.). Glass melting furnaces are heated with gas or oil. The gas and the combustion air are passed through a heat exchanger; this raises their temperature before combustion takes place in the furnace (regenerative furnaces). Depending on the composition, the thickly liquid melted glass is formed to the required shapes by casting, rolling, drawing, moulding, blowing, spinning or pressing, either with or without blowing. These processes are generally applied by machines. Hand forming processes, usually in conjunction with blowing with blowpipes, are now relatively little used. After forming has been done, it is most essential that cooling be correctly applied, so as to keep the glass as free as possible from stresses. The sheet glass, rolled glass, pressed glass, hollow glassware, etc. can be further worked and manufactured by cutting, drilling, milling, cementing, welding, bending, etching, grinding, engraving, polishing, enamelling, etc.

Special glasses for technical and scientific purposes (e.g., filter glasses, refractory glasses, chemical-resisting glasses, malleable glasses, etc.) are produced by the use of additives to the standard recipe or are made from quite different raw materials from those mentioned above. These special kinds of glass are usually manufactured in fairly small pots (which are constructed of aluminium oxide or some other highly refractory material).

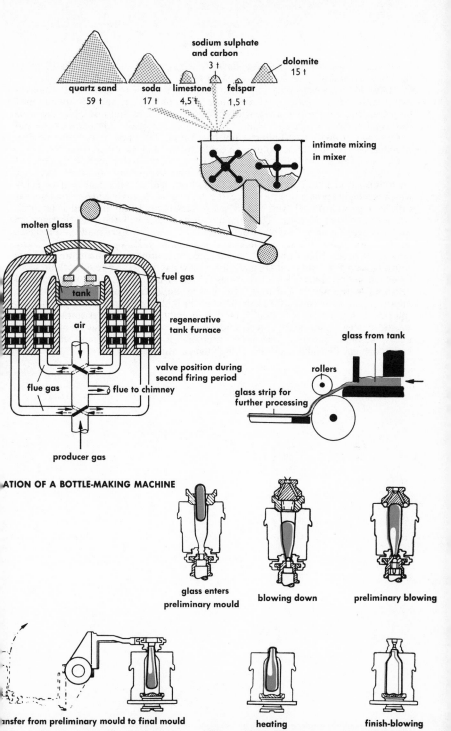

sodium sulphate
and carbon
3 t

dolomite
15 t

quartz sand
59 t

soda
17 t

limestone
4,5 t

felspar
1,5 t

intimate mixing
in mixer

molten glass

fuel gas

tank

regenerative
tank furnace

air

glass from tank

rollers

valve position during
second firing period

flue to chimney

glass strip for
further processing

flue gas

producer gas

ATION OF A BOTTLE-MAKING MACHINE

glass enters
preliminary mould

blowing down

preliminary blowing

ansfer from preliminary mould to final mould

heating

finish-blowing

345

PLEXIGLAS

Plexiglas is a synthetic "organic glass" which is produced in large quantities by the chemical industry and which has two major advantages over inorganic glass (see page 344): it weighs only half as much and it is very easy to work. Plexiglas is manufactured from acetone, hydrocyanic acid, sulphuric acid and alcohol and may be polymerised in various ways, whereby it becomes hard and insoluble. Plexiglas has even better transparency than ordinary window glass; ultraviolet rays and X-rays pass through it unhindered, but heat rays are stopped by it. It can be produced in any desired shape (solution, powder, plates, blocks, tubes, etc).

Plexiglas can be drilled, turned, filed, cast, sawn, ground, punched, welded, cut and polished. A further important property is its completely non-toxic character (as a finished product), although it is made from hydrocyanic acid (prussic acid), which is a highly poisonous substance. It is finding increasingly widespread application in surgery: artificial eyes, ears, noses, fingers, entire hands and limbs, dentures, etc. are made from Plexiglas. The human tissues coalesce with the synthetic parts, so that it is even possible to replace defective heart valves by ones made of Plexiglas. Because of its good stability to light and transparency, Plexiglas is used for many optical purposes. Many physical instruments, measuring instruments and models which have to be transparent are made from Plexiglas (protective goggles, fluorescent tubes, etc.). This material is also extensively used in the manufacture of musical instruments, ornaments and toys. Also, it is an important material in aircraft and motor engineering and is furthermore used in building construction. Plexiglas is resistant to temperatures of 100° C (and even higher); it is also resistant to water, caustic alkalies, dilute acids, petrol,[1] and mineral oils. However, it swells in alcohols, esters, ketones, benzene (and other aromatic hydrocarbons), and chlorinated hydrocarbons. Plexiglas can burn at high temperatures.

1. Gasoline in U.S.A.

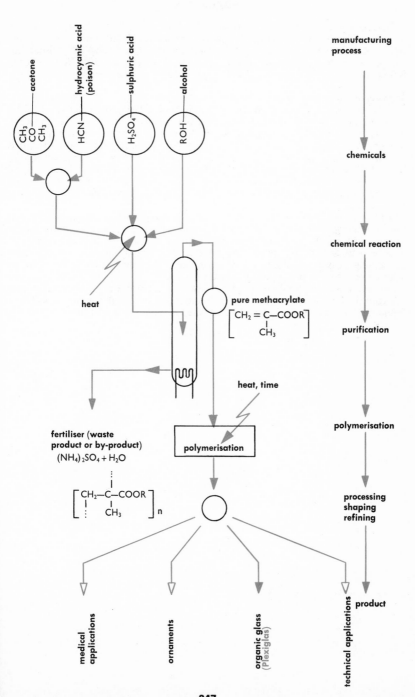

manufacturing
process

↓

chemicals

↓

chemical reaction

↓

purification

↓

polymerisation

↓

processing
shaping
refining

↓

product

acetone — CH₃ CO CH₃

hydrocyanic acid (poison) — HCN

sulphuric acid — H₂SO₄

alcohol — ROH

heat

pure methacrylate
$$\left[CH_2 = C - COOR \atop CH_3 \right]$$

heat, time

fertiliser (waste product or by-product)
$(NH_4)_2SO_4 + H_2O$

$$\left[CH_2 - C - COOR \atop CH_3 \right]_n$$

polymerisation

medical applications

ornaments

organic glass (Plexiglas)

technical applications

347

PORCELAIN

Porcelain is a translucent non-porous ceramic material. It is made by firing a mixture of kaolin (porcelain earth), quartz and felspar. Hard porcelain is usually made from a mixture comprising 50% kaolinite, 25% quartz and 25% felspar; for soft porcelain the corresponding proportions are 25%, 45% and 30%. Soft porcelain is fired at lower temperatures and is therefore cheaper to manufacture.

Manufacturing procedure:

Kaolinite is a clay mineral which is present in kaolin. The latter material is washed, screened and thoroughly mixed with finely ground quartz and felspar, in conjunction with the addition of water. Soda and other additives are added. The plastic porcelain mixture is kneaded and moulded or cast in plaster moulds. After it has dried, it is fired in a kiln at about 900° C. The porcelain has then become hard and watertight, but dull. This treatment is followed by glazing. The objects are dipped into a liquid containing the same ingredients as the material, but in which quartz and felspar predominate. They are then fired at a temperature of about 1400° C. The glazing thereby becomes a continuous, firmly adherent coating. In this heating treatment, which lasts from 20 to 30 hours, the fine raw material particles of the porcelain mixture are sintered (partially fused) together. Coloured decorative patterns can be produced by painting the glazed porcelain with dyes. In order to make these melt together with the glazing and become durable, the painted objects are heated in an enamelling furnace to about 800° C. In modern ceramic technique the paint is, alternatively, sometimes applied before the glazing.

Porcelain is used for household purposes, in laboratories, in industry (more particularly as an insulating material in electrical engineering). It is impermeable to liquids and gases and is very largely unaffected by temperature variations.

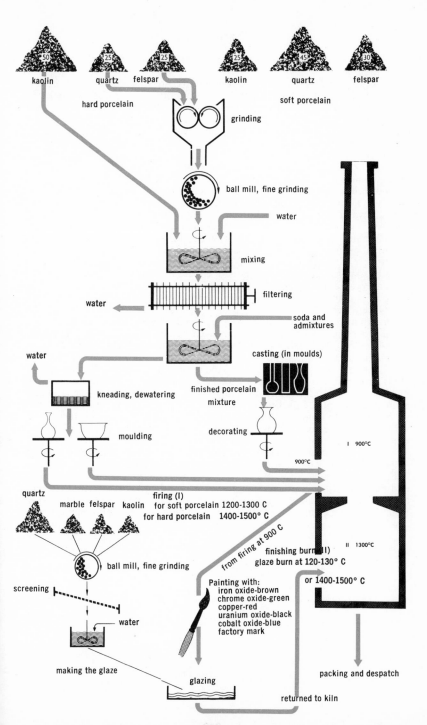

kaolin

quartz   felspar

50

25   25

hard porcelain

kaolin

quartz   felspar

25

45   30

soft porcelain

grinding

ball mill, fine grinding

water

mixing

filtering

water

soda and
admixtures

water

kneading, dewatering

casting (in moulds)

finished porcelain
mixture

moulding

decorating

900°C

I 900°C

quartz

marble felspar kaolin

firing (I)
for soft porcelain 1200-1300 C
for hard porcelain 1400-1500° C

from firing at 900 C

II 1300°C

ball mill, fine grinding

finishing burn (II)
glaze burn at 120-130° C

screening

or 1400-1500° C

Painting with:
iron oxide-brown
chrome oxide-green
copper-red
uranium oxide-black
cobalt oxide-blue
factory mark

water

making the glaze

glazing

returned to kiln

packing and despatch

ENAMEL

Enamel is a vitreous glaze, of inorganic composition (chiefly oxides), fused on a metallic surface.

Glass (see page 344) is particularly resistant to corrosion by atmospheric influences and chemicals and has a smooth and very strong surface. But glass is fragile. When the good properties of glass are combined with the strength of steel or cast iron, the objects made from these materials (kitchen utensils, baths, pipes, basins, etc.) have excellent service properties. The name "vitreous enamelling" or "porcelain enamelling" is applied to such materials. In particular cases the two materials supplement each other so well that entirely new material properties are obtained: jet engines, the internal surfaces of certain parts of marine propulsion engines, etc. are enamelled in order to make the surfaces resistant to high temperatures.

Enamel has been known since ancient times, when it was used (as it still is) for ornamental purposes on precious and non-ferrous metals. In the last few hundred years, however, it has been used chiefly for improving the surface properties of steel and cast iron objects and protecting them against corrosion. An enamel consists of glass-forming oxides and oxides that produce adhesion or give the enamel its colour. A normal enamel may consist, for example, of 34 (23) parts of borax, 28 (52) parts of felspar, 5 (5) parts of fluorspar, 20 (5) parts of quartz, 6 (5) parts of soda, 5 (2.5) parts of sodium nitrate, 0.5–1.5 parts of cobalt, manganese and nickel oxide, (6.5) parts of cryolite. The figures not in parentheses relate to a ground-coat enamel, while those in parentheses relate to a cover enamel, to which 6–10% of an opacifier (a substance which makes the enamel coating opaque, e.g., tin oxide, titanium silicate, antimony trioxide) and a colour oxide is added. This mixture is ground to a very fine powder and melted; the hot melt is quenched by pouring it into water, and the glass-like "frit" that is thus produced is ground fine again. During grinding, water (35–40%), clay, and quartz powder are added; opacifiers and pigments may also be added. The enamel "slip" (thick slurry) obtained in this way must be left to stand for a few days before use. The metal objects to be enamelled are heated thoroughly, pickled in acid, neutralised in an alkaline bath, and rinsed. Next, the ground-coat enamel slip is applied to them by dipping or spraying and is fired at 850°–900° C, so that it fuses to form a glass coating. The ground-coated objects are then provided with one or more coats of cover enamel, each coat being fired at 800°–850° C in a muffle furnace.

As an enamel coat is always more brittle than the underlying metal, the enamel will crack or spall if the object is deformed or roughly knocked.

From the chemical point of view enamel is a melted mixture of silicates, borates and fluorides of the metals sodium, potassium, lead and aluminium. Colour effects are produced, for example, by the admixture of various oxides to the melt (oxides of iron, chromium, cadmium, cobalt, nickel, gold, uranium and antimony).

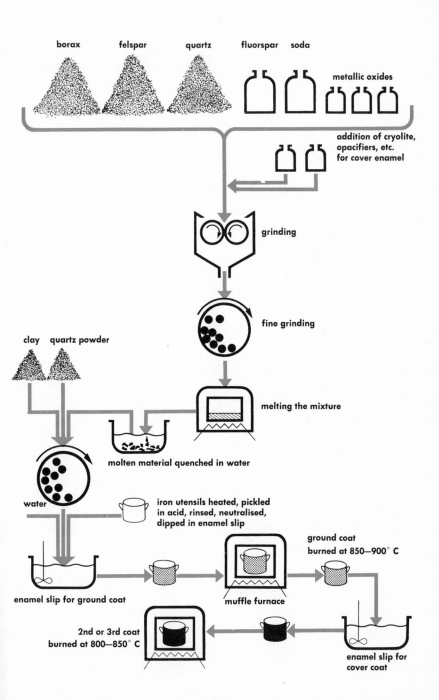

borax   felspar   quartz   fluorspar soda

metallic oxides

addition of cryolite,
opacifiers, etc.
for cover enamel

grinding

fine grinding

clay   quartz powder

melting the mixture

molten material quenched in water

water

iron utensils heated, pickled
in acid, rinsed, neutralised,
dipped in enamel slip

ground coat
burned at 850—900° C

enamel slip for ground coat

muffle furnace

2nd or 3rd coat
burned at 800—850° C

enamel slip for
cover coat

RUBBER

Rubber or indiarubber is the name applied to the vulcanised (see page 356) final product of a natural vegetable gum (caoutchouc). Natural rubber is present in the form of tiny droplets in the juice (latex) of the rubber tree (Hevea brasiliensis) which attains a height of 60–80 ft. and is grown in plantations in tropical countries. Tapping the trees for latex consists in removing a shaving of bark with a sharp knife. The cut passes through the latex tubes and there is a flow of latex in consequence. Most trees yield about 5 lb. of rubber per annum on an average. To transform the milky latex into a serviceable product, it is necessary to remove the water by spraying and drying, or by acidification, coagulation, washing and rolling, or the latex may be coagulated by treating it with smoke. The two most important forms of plantation rubber are sheet and crepe. Sheet is generally dried in smoke and is dark brown in colour. Crepe, which is air-dried, has a much lighter colour and is passed through heavy rollers prior to drying.

The raw rubber is cleaned, chemicals and fillers are added to it, and it is finally vulcanised with sulphur. As a result, a highly elastic product is obtained. This property is due to the structure and form of the rubber molecule. Pure rubber (caoutchouc) is a compound containing carbon and hydrogen only. It consists of long chains of interconnected isoprene molecules. A rubber molecule contains upwards of two thousand of such elementary units joined together in a linear arrangement. The vulcanised polyisoprene molecule has an angular pattern and polar groups. When a filament of rubber is stretched, the positions and angles of the entangled individual rubber molecules are temporarily changed. When the rubber is released, the molecules spring back to their original shape. These changes in shape involve no permanent mechanical changes and can be repeated indefinitely or, at any rate, until the rubber fractures for other reasons (e.g., aging due to the action of oxygen and exposure to strong light). Rubber does not acquire its high degree of elasticity until it has been vulcanised, whereby the rubber molecules become slightly interlinked by "sulphur bridges". Untreated raw rubber is very sensitive to heat and would, in that condition, be unsuitable for the manufacture of, for example, motor tyres.[1]

Because of its extraordinary elastic properties, rubber is a raw material for a vast range of products (something like fifty thousand different applications). It is only since about the middle of the last century that rubber has been manufactured on a technically important scale. There have been great technological improvements, and the quality of the product has been greatly enhanced, as is exemplified by modern motor tyres which have a far longer service life than their early forerunners. Rubber originally came from South America and was used by the native population for making balls which had exceptional bouncing properties. It was in this form that Columbus got to know rubber. Three centuries elapsed before the material was brought into commercial use in Europe, and at first it was used not for its elastic properties but to rub out lead pencil marks.

The world's annual output of natural rubber (plantation rubber) is now about 2 million tons. In addition, various kinds of synthetic rubber is being used on an ever increasing scale. See page 354.

1. Tires in U.S.A.

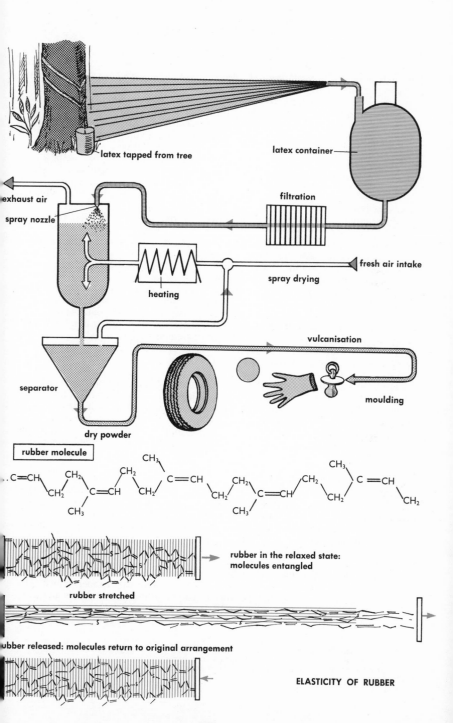

latex tapped from tree

latex container

exhaust air

spray nozzle

filtration

fresh air intake

spray drying

heating

vulcanisation

separator

moulding

dry powder

rubber molecule

rubber in the relaxed state:
molecules entangled

rubber stretched

rubber released: molecules return to original arrangement

ELASTICITY OF RUBBER

353

SYNTHETIC RUBBER (BUNA)

The name "Buna" is applied to a group of synthetic rubbers first developed in Germany and is produced by a process of polymerisation from *bu*tadiene with sodium (*na*trium) as a catalyst.[1] The process used to be carried out at a temperature of about $+50°$ C and yielded "lettered" Buna rubbers such as, for example, Buna S (butadiene styrene rubber). Nowadays copolymerisation of butadiene and styrene is mostly done in aqueous phase. With the newer activators it is possible to carry out this process at about $+5°$ C, whereby the present form known as "cold rubber" is obtained. By appropriate variation of the monomers, their proportions (chiefly about 75% butadiene and 25% styrene) and the polymerisation conditions, a number of different types of Buna rubber are obtained, and this range of types can be further extended by various methods of processing and by using various admixtures. Latterly, with aid of so-called Ziegler catalysts, a product bearing a closer resemblance to natural rubber can also be produced from butadiene or isoprene, e.g., Buna CB (poly-cis-butadiene).

In the emulsion copolymerisation process carried out at $+5°$ C (as referred to above), the hydrocarbons to be polymerised (e.g., butadiene and styrene) are in emulsion and contain a constituent of the activator system dissolved in them. The second part of the activator system is present in the aqueous phase (the watery medium of the emulsion). The combined activator system initiates the process of polymerisation. The molecule size of the polymer obtained can be regulated by certain added substances. The macromolecules (giant molecules of very great length) formed in this way have a filamentary structure with branches, so-called side chains. The polymerisation of the monomers is stopped after about 60% of these substances have reacted. The resultant product at this stage is a latex rather like the latex of natural rubber (see page 352). The unreacted monomers are removed from this latex, and stabilisers are added to it, whereafter the latex is coagulated by the addition of acids and salts. The solid matter obtained in this way is washed and dried in several stages.

For processing Buna into rubber goods, it is treated in masticating machines or on mixing rollers, various substances being added whereby the workability of the rubber and/or the properties of the vulcanisates are controlled. Such admixtures are, for example: oils, paraffin, fatty acids, tars, bitumen, carbon black, zinc oxide, chalk, silica, kaolin, finely divided organic and inorganic substances. For vulcanisation, which is usually carried out under pressure at approximately $150°$ C, the mixture moreover has sulphur and vulcanisation accelerator (e.g., mercapto benzothiazole) added to it.

In the process of vulcanisation the filamentary molecules become interlinked into a three-dimensional network, the "links" between the molecules being formed by sulphur. The process is known as cross-linking. As a result, the rubber largely loses its plastic properties and, instead, acquires a high degree of elasticity and other properties associated with manufactured rubber (e.g., wear resistance). Buna is used for making motor tyres,[2] rubber conveyor belts, and many other technical products.

There are many other synthetic rubbers besides the Buna rubbers. For example, Perbunan, Hycar, Chemigum and Butaprene are nitrile-butadiene rubbers of the oil-resistant type. During the Second World War a synthetic rubber named GR-S (Government Rubber, styrene type) was developed in the United States and extensively used. Other rubbers are butyl (GR-I) and neoprene (GR-M).

1. Polymerisation: a reaction involving a successive addition of a large number of relatively small molecules (monomers) to form the final compound or polymer.
  Polymer: giant molecule (macromolecule) formed when thousands of the original molecules have been linked together end to end.
  Copolymer: a mixed polymer; a giant molecule formed when two or more unlike monomers are polymerised together.
2. Tires in U.S.A.

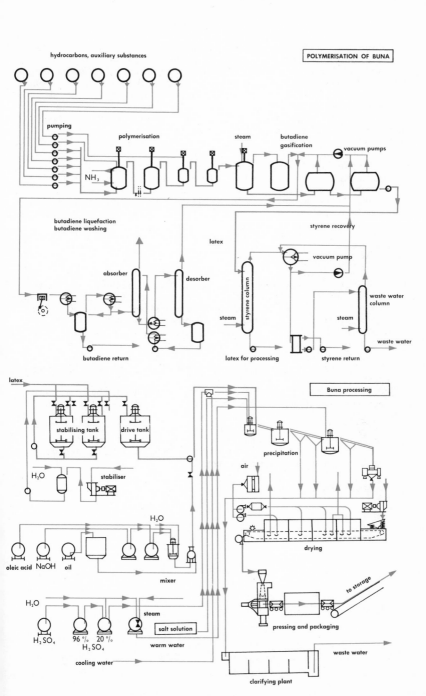

hydrocarbons, auxiliary substances

pumping

polymerisation

steam

butadiene gasification

vacuum pumps

NH_3

butadiene liquefaction
butadiene washing

styrene recovery

latex

absorber

desorber

vacuum pump

styrene column

waste water column

steam

steam

waste water

butadiene return

latex for processing

styrene return

latex

Buna processing

stabilising tank

drive tank

precipitation

H_2O

stabiliser

air

H_2O

oleic acid NaOH oil

drying

mixer

H_2O

steam

salt solution

to storage

H_2SO_4

96 %
20 %
H_2SO_4

warm water

pressing and packaging

cooling water

waste water

clarifying plant

355

VULCANISATION

Vulcanisation or curing is a chemical reaction whereby the filamentary molecules of rubber are interlinked into a three-dimensional network, this being usually achieved with the aid of sulphur. Sometimes peroxides are used for the purpose, however. It was Goodyear who, in 1839, first masticated crude rubber with sulphur and heated the mixture to 130° C. After undergoing this treatment, the rubber was no longer plastically deformable but, instead, acquired a high degree of resilience which was retained over a wise range of temperatures. The solubility of crude rubber in petrol[1] is greater than that of vulcanised rubber.

Because of the wide range of products for which rubber is used (e.g., motor tyres,[2] tubing, seals, footwear, gloves, etc.), it is necessary to incorporate other admixtures besides sulphur into the crude rubber. Various substances are mixed into the rubber in masticating machines or on roll mills, e.g., carbon black (for high abrasion resistance), silica, chalk, asbestos (more particularly for brake linings), oils (for better workability of the mixture), paraffin (for better resistance to light), antioxidants (usually: aromatic amines or phenol derivatives), activators (usually zinc oxide), and various organic and inorganic colouring substances. In order to speed up the vulcanisation process and to improve the properties of the vulcanisates, various accelerators are added, e.g., dithio carbamic acid derivatives, mercapto benzothiazole derivatives, diphenylguanidine, etc.

Vulcanisation is carried out under pressure in moulds at temperatures around 150° C and takes from a few minutes to several hours, depending on the vulcanisation temperature and the size of the rubber article concerned. Vulcanising an ordinary motor tyre takes about half an hour. By using special combinations of accelerators it is also possible to perform the vulcanisation process at ordinary room temperature. Some rubber mixtures are manufactured into various special sections (tubes, sealing gaskets for car windows, etc.) by extrusion. Such extruded articles are vulcanised under pressure in vulcanising vessels. Other mixtures are processed by calendering, i.e., the rubber is pressed between rolls to form sheets of predetermined size and thickness.

Sponge rubber is usually produced from latex, which is foamed by various methods and then vulcanised. Certain rubber mixtures can be bonded to metals so as to establish a permanent connection. Soft rubber contains about 1.5–5.5 and hard rubber contains about 15–30% sulphur. In cases where rubber goods have to fulfil special requirements—e.g., high resistance to swelling in organic solvents, to the action of light, or to high temperatures—it may be necessary to use certain synthetic rubbers, such as Perbunan or butyl rubber (see page 354).

1. Gasoline in U.S.A.
2. Tires.

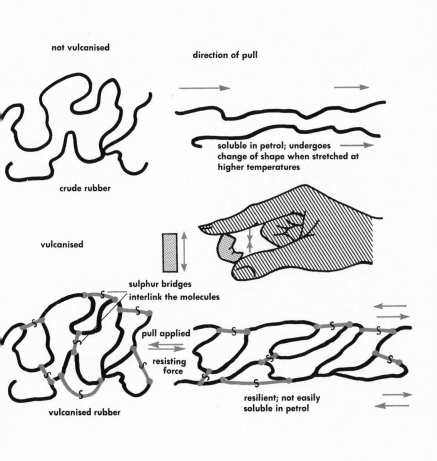

not vulcanised

direction of pull

crude rubber

soluble in petrol; undergoes change of shape when stretched at higher temperatures

vulcanised

sulphur bridges interlink the molecules

pull applied

resisting force

vulcanised rubber

resilient; not easily soluble in petrol

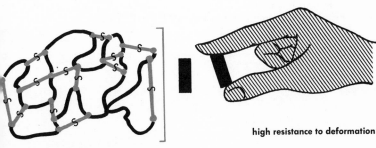

hard rubber (very large number of sulphur bridges)

high resistance to deformation

TIMBER

Along with stone, timber is one of mankind's oldest building materials. It is still a very important commercial commodity. At the present time, however, timber is being felled at a far greater rate than it can grow, so that it is bound to become increasingly scarce. Wood cannot be produced synthetically in the laboratory. With the aid of the sun's light and heat, plants convert carbon dioxide from the atmosphere and moisture from the soil into glucose, some of which they store up in the form of starch, while another portion is converted into cellulose, from which elongated cells are formed. In this way. complex bundles of tubes (called fibres) are formed through which water and other substances essential to plant life are conveyed and which also serve to give mechanical strength to the plant stems. The individual glucose molecules which are synthesised in the leaves undergo a process of polymerisation whereby they form chain molecules containing something like six to eight thousand glucose monomers. About a hundred of such chain molecules form a crystallite filament (about 6–8 millionths of a millimetre thick); between ten and a hundred of these filaments in turn form a microfibril (about 20–80 millionths of a millimetre thick). A bundle comprising 10–100 microfibrils form a fibril—the smallest unit which is just visible under an ordinary microscope when a wood fibre is finely ground up. The fibrils are arranged side by side, in so-called day rings, and are helically twisted. The individual fibrils are bonded together by a substance called lignin (a compound similar to cellulose). The day rings are shaped like hollow cylinders, a large number of which are disposed one around the other; at the centre of a composite tube of this kind is an air-filled cavity (lumen), which is 2-3 ten thousandths of a millimetre thick. Finally a number of such tubes firmly bonded together form a wood fibre, which is usually about $\frac{1}{30}$ mm (0.0013 inch) thick and is interpenetrated by tiny passages ranging in diameter from $\frac{1}{10}$ to $\frac{1}{100,000}$ mm.

Green timber contains 40–60%, seasoned timber contains 10–20% moisture. Completely dehydrated wood consists of 40–50% cellulose and 20–25% lignin, the remaining constituents being minerals, tanning agents, fats, oils, resins, carbohydrates, and hemicelluloses. Wood is a particularly useful material on account of low thermal conductivity, its high absorptive capacity for radiation (heat rays, etc.), and its strength.

A main distinction is made between softwoods (mainly from coniferous trees: pine, deal, fir, etc.; also poplar, willow, etc.) and hardwoods (oak, beech, etc.). The seasoning of timber is of paramount importance for the majority of purposes for which it is used. In green timber there is a large amount of free water present within the cells. It is the drying-out of the free water and a certain amount of moisture from the cell walls that constitutes seasoning. There are two main methods of seasoning: air seasoning (boards are stacked up in such a way as to obtain a good air flow throughout the stack and thereby evaporate the moisture) and kiln seasoning (this is done in a kiln, which is a brick-built chamber equipped with heating pipes, fans to keep the air circulating, and a number of jets for the introduction of steam).

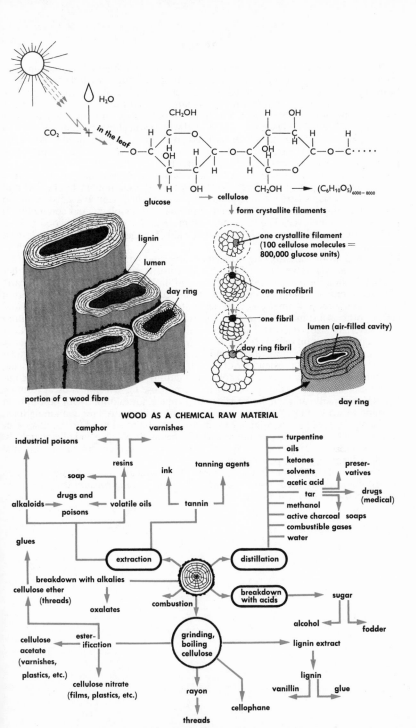

glucose → cellulose

form crystallite filaments

$(C_6H_{10}O_5)_{6000 \sim 8000}$

one crystallite filament
(100 cellulose molecules =
800,000 glucose units)

one microfibril

one fibril

lumen (air-filled cavity)

day ring fibril

lignin

lumen

day ring

portion of a wood fibre

day ring

WOOD AS A CHEMICAL RAW MATERIAL

camphor   varnishes

industrial poisons

resins

soap

ink   tanning agents

alkaloids   drugs and   volatile oils   tannin
                 poisons

glues

breakdown with alkalies

cellulose ether
(threads)

oxalates

extraction

combustion

turpentine
oils
ketones
solvents
acetic acid   preser-
                   vatives
tar   drugs
           (medical)
methanol
active charcoal   soaps
combustible gases
water

distillation

**breakdown
with acids**   sugar

alcohol   fodder

cellulose
acetate
(varnishes,
plastics, etc.)

ester-
ification

**grinding,
boiling
cellulose**

lignin extract

lignin

cellulose nitrate
(films, plastics, etc.)

rayon

cellophane

vanillin   glue

threads

359

PAPER

Paper is the general name for the substance used for writing or printing upon or for packaging and wrapping, as well as for many special purposes. It derives its name from the papyrus plant from which the ancient Egyptians produced a paper-like material for writing on. Modern paper is manufactured from a mixture of various fibres, chiefly of vegetable origin, which are mixed with a large quantity of water and shredded very fine. The mixture is treated with size (a glue-type admixture which makes it water resistant), and a filler, such as clay or chalk, may be added to give some special property to the paper. The result of this preparation is called "stuff". It is poured out on wire screens on which the water is extracted.

The fibrous ray material that is used in present-day paper making is wood from coniferous trees (pine, fir, spruce), deciduous trees (beech, poplar, birch, chestnut, eucalyptus), grasses (straw from rye, wheat, oats, barley, rice), alfa grass, bamboo and cotton. Biochemical or chemical and mechanical dissolving and comminution processes are employed. The principal raw material for newsprint—wood pulp— is obtained by grinding up whole logs with the aid of special grindstones and adding a considerable quantity of water. Small quantities of other fibrous materials such as hemp, linen, wool, asbestos, slag wool, glass fibres and synthetic fibres are sometimes added to the vegetable fibres. The fibre mixture is chemically bleached, further broken down in beaters, mixed with fillers and more water (about 100 to 200 parts of water to one part of fibre) and constantly stirred, in conjunction with the addition of colophony soap, animal glues, starch paste, casein or synthetic resin glues and certain other substances. These admixtures ensure that, despite the great dilution with water, the size is deposited almost entirely on the fibrous constituents. The paper pulp is poured out on screens (in paper machines these may be endless wire screens), dewatered, pressed, watermarked, and (in some cases) it undergoes subsequent sizing treatment, drying, calendering (whereby a smooth finish is obtained by passing the paper through highly polished rolls), and cutting to the required size. The composition of the paper varies according to the purpose for which it is used. Roofing felt, which is really an asphalted cardboard, is made, for example, with peat fibre in addition to wood pulp; document papers consist of fibre mixtures containing linen and hemp; special papers contain certain textile and animal wool fibres; newsprint comprises 80% wood pulp (ground wood), 15% cellulose, 5% glue and filler materials. The method of processing also plays an important part (surface treatment, very fine grinding for transparent paper, etc.).

Paper manufacturing machines are among the longest and most delicately adjusted pieces of machinery used in any industry. They are so long because the paper web has to be dried, smoothed and cooled.

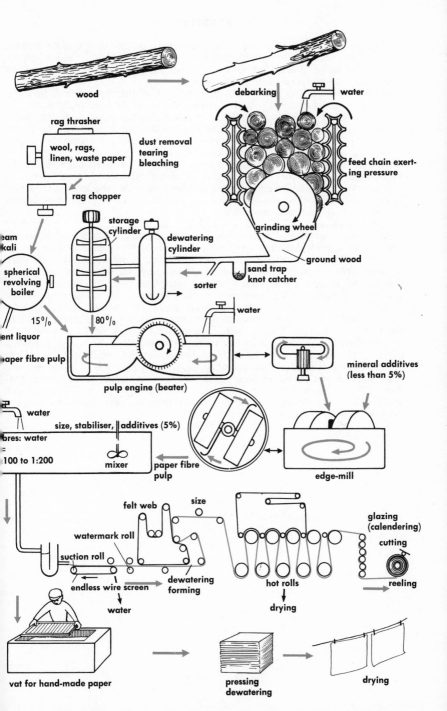

wood

debarking

water

rag thrasher

wool, rags, linen, waste paper

dust removal
tearing
bleaching

feed chain exert-
ing pressure

rag chopper

grinding wheel

ground wood

steam
alkali

storage
cylinder

dewatering
cylinder

spherical
revolving
boiler

sand trap
knot catcher

sorter

15%

80%

water

spent liquor

paper fibre pulp

pulp engine (beater)

mineral additives
(less than 5%)

water

size, stabiliser, additives (5%)

fibres: water
= 1:100 to 1:200

mixer

paper fibre
pulp

edge-mill

felt web

size

glazing
(calendering)

watermark roll

cutting

suction roll

endless wire screen

dewatering
forming

hot rolls

reeling

water

drying

vat for hand-made paper

pressing
dewatering

drying

361

PLASTICS

Plastics are materials consisting of macromolecular organic compounds which are produced from animal or vegetable matter or from raw materials derived therefrom. The general name "plastics" is based on the fact that these materials are of plastic consistency at some stage of their manufacture.

Man-made fibres and other synthetic substances of this type are not, however, included in the definition of "plastics" in the more restricted sense of the word.

Plastics are produced from a variety of raw materials: wood, coal, petroleum, plants, vegetable juices, proteins. In some respects they are superior to comparable natural products because they are produced under scientifically controlled conditions and can be given specific properties not found in nature.

All plastics consist of very large organic molecules, so-called macromolecules, which usually contain from 500 to 10,000 equal "structural units" chemically bounded together. Hard, inelastic (rigid) plastics consist mainly of spherical, highly cross-linked macromolecules; plastics possessing rubber-like elastic properties consist chiefly of thread-like macromolecules.

Some plastics such as celluloid, nitrocellulose and chlorinated rubber are derived from naturally pre-formed macromolecules; such plastics, are, in effect, chemically modified or improved natural substances. The fully synthetic plastics such as synthetic butadiene rubber (Buna rubber), polystyrene, acrylo-nitrile, polyvinyl chloride, etc. must, however, be built up from small molecules by processes called polymerisation and polycondensation. Some of the good properties of plastics are: low specific gravity, easy deformability, resistance to many corrosive chemicals, non-toxicity, excellent electrical properties, etc. Plastics are used in electrical engineering (insulation for cables, wires, equipment), in the clothing industry, in the manufacture of sheeting, films, threads, brushes, adhesives, artificial leather, linoleum, paints, etc. These materials have become indispensable for industrial and domestic purposes, as they are increasingly replacing metals and other materials which are not available in sufficient quantity or at a low enough price, and they are opening up entirely new possibilities in mechanical engineering, in vehicle construction, in the furniture industry, and in the packaging of perishable goods. The first "plastic" was produced about a hundred years ago—at the present time these synthetic materials are still in full process of development.

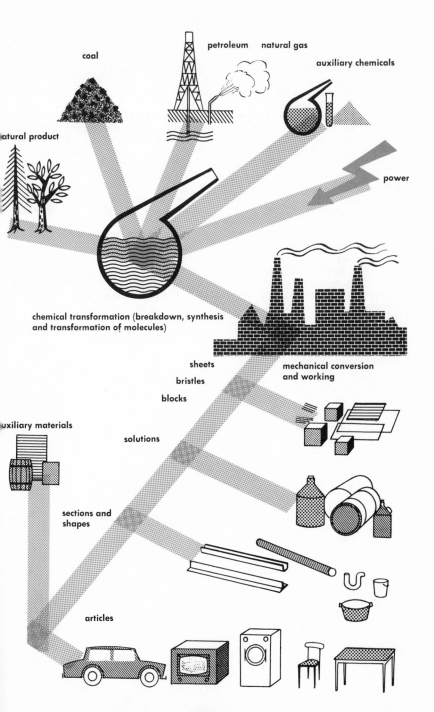

coal

petroleum   natural gas

auxiliary chemicals

natural product

power

chemical transformation (breakdown, synthesis
and transformation of molecules)

sheets

bristles

mechanical conversion
and working

blocks

solutions

auxiliary materials

sections and
shapes

articles

363

CELLULOID

Celluloid is one of the oldest plastics. It was first produced in 1869. It consists of slightly nitrated cellulose (nitrocellulose with 10–11.5% nitrogen; chemical name: dinitrocellulose) and camphor as a softener.

Nitrocellulose is made from cotton by nitration with nitric acid and sulphuric acid. The dried nitrocellulose is thoroughly kneaded with a solution of camphor in alcohol: 30–40 parts of camphor to 100 parts of nitrocellulose. The kneaded mixture is now rolled into plates or is shredded, dried, and then hot-moulded. Celluloid is hard and resilient, colourless, and used to be very extensively employed in the manufacture of photographic films. It dissolves very well in acetone and softens at temperatures above 80° C. The one great disadvantage of this versatile plastic is its inflammability, and for this reason its use for films was soon abandoned.

As celluloid can be easily worked, it is still extensively used for manufacture of a wide variety of objects, e.g., toys, dolls, ping-pong balls, brushes, combs, knobs, and many others. As such it serves as a substitute for such natural materials as ivory, horn and tortoiseshell. The addition of substances called stabilisers to the mixture of nitrocellulose and camphor gives the final product better fastness to light and helps it retain its resilience for a longer time. Celluloid achieved its greatest popularity in the early days of the film industry. At the present time it is being superseded more and more by materials which are non-inflammable or harder or with better elastic properties. Such materials are usually not so universally applicable as celluloid, but they are better suited to specific purposes. Nevertheless the celluloid manufacturing industry still consumes over two-thirds of the present-day output of synthetic camphor.

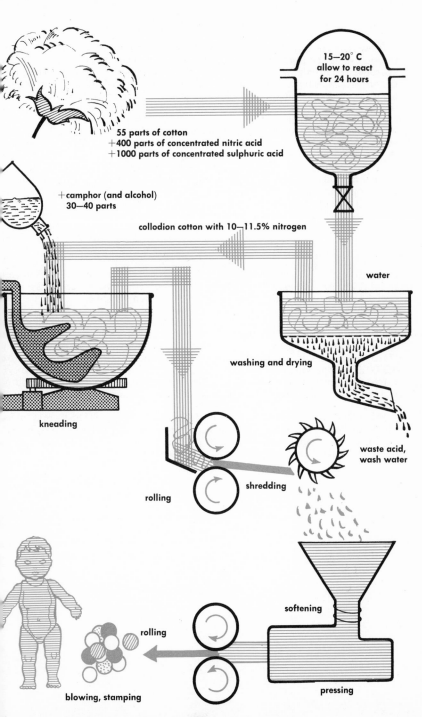

55 parts of cotton
+400 parts of concentrated nitric acid
+1000 parts of concentrated sulphuric acid

15—20° C
allow to react
for 24 hours

+camphor (and alcohol)
30—40 parts

collodion cotton with 10—11.5% nitrogen

water

kneading

washing and drying

waste acid,
wash water

rolling

shredding

softening

rolling

blowing, stamping

pressing

BRIQUETTING

Brown coal (or lignite) may contain as much as 60% moisture and often has a low calorific value. To obtain a higher-grade product, brown coals can be briquetted i.e., squeezed into compact lumps by a suitable pressure-moulding process. To do this the brown coal is pulverised, dried to a water content of 16-18%, and then pressed to briquettes. As a result, the calorific value is more than doubled in comparison with that of raw brown coal. The brown coal, which is usually mined by open-cast methods, is dug out of the ground by an excavator and conveyed to a receiving hopper From here it is passed through crushing and pulverising machinery (e.g., hammer mills). The pulverised brown coal is screened, the oversize material being returned to the pulverising mills or sold as "screened rough coal". The coal that passes the screens still contains a high percentage of moisture. It is passed to dryers whereby its moisture content is reduced to 17-20%. A modern rotary dryer is an inclined rotating drum heated by steam, into which the wet material is fed at the higher end and from which the dried material is discharged at the lower end.

The coal, which is heated to 80°-90° C in the drying process, is then cooled to 40°-50° C in a special cooler provided with baffle plates. It now contains about 15-18% water and is fed to the briquetting presses. These may operate on the extrusion principle: a certain quantity of the dried pulverised brown coal is thrust forward and compressed by each stroke of a reciprocating ram which forces it through a tapered opening. The ram has a stroke of about 200 mm (8 in.) and develops a pressure of 700-1000 kg/cm^2 (10,000-14,000 lb./in.^{2}). The process generates a great deal of heat, and the freshly formed briquettes are given time to cool before they are loaded into vehicles for transport to the consumers. A large press may have an output of 250 tons of briquettes per day. The briquettes are formed by pressure alone, no binder being employed. Another type of briquetting press is the ring roll press which attains similar outputs. If the dried screened coal has a low water content (7-10% moisture), it is necessary to use a pressure of about 2000 atm. (approx 30,000 lb./in.^{2}) in order to obtain firm briquettes. The dust produced in the process is extracted by suction equipment, and, where possible, used in pulverised-coal firing systems for boilers. Ovoid (egg-shaped) briquettes are produced in special roll presses.

Briquetting is not confined to brown coal. Ordinary coal dust and fines are moulded into briquettes with the aid of pitch and coal tar as binders. Coal briquettes are used for domestic and industrial purposes. Brown coal briquettes are chiefly employed as household fuel in the neighbourhood of their manufacture.

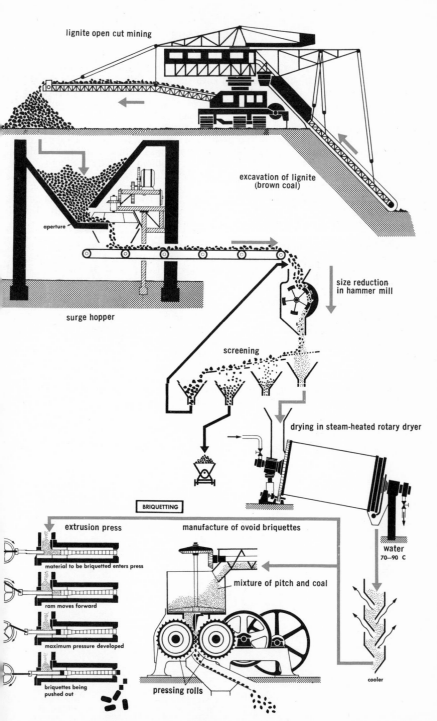

lignite open cut mining

excavation of lignite
(brown coal)

aperture

surge hopper

size reduction
in hammer mill

screening

drying in steam-heated rotary dryer

BRIQUETTING

extrusion press

manufacture of ovoid briquettes

material to be briquetted enters press

ram moves forward

mixture of pitch and coal

maximum pressure developed

water
70—90 C

briquettes being
pushed out

pressing rolls

cooler

367

CELLULOSE

Cellulose (wood pulp) is prepared from wood by a process of dissolving and chemical softening. It serves as a raw material for the manufacture of paper, nitro-cellulose, explosives, varnishes, wood sugar (xylose), collodion, celluloid, and cell wool. Depending on the solvent solution used, the following pulping processes are distinguished: sulphite process; soda process; sulphate process. The pulp is pro-duced from pine, fir, spruce and beech wood and also from other cellulose-containing vegetable matter, such as sugar-cane waste, straw, reeds, maize and sunflower stalks. These materials are subjected to a preliminary cleaning treatment, chopped up by mechanical processes, and then boiled in large tanks with hot solutions (calcium bisulphite solution or a mixture of caustic soda, sodium sulphide, sodium sulphate, sodium carbonate). The lignin which causes the cellulose fibres to adhere together is dissolved by this treatment and is, in part, chemically decomposed, leaving a soft pulp which consists of cellulose (see timber, page, 358). The raw pulp thus obtained is reduced by mechanical processes, washed, bleached and again carefully cleaned. Finally, the pulp is dewatered and formed into strips or boards. To make 1000 lb. of cellulose requires about 3 yd.^{3} of wood, 500 lb. of coal, nearly 100 lb. of sulphur (if the sulphite process), and 90 kWh of electric energy. About 10 million tons of cellulose are produced each year. As already stated, this material is used for the manufacture of paper (see page 360), nitrocellulose, explosives (see page 450), varnishes, wood sugar, celluloid (see page 364), cellite, cellon collodion, cellulose ether, cellulose ester, cellophane, and other products. Man-made fibres (see page 370) and cell wool are also manufactured from cellulose. For the manufacture of cell wool, cellulose is chemically dissolved and spun into threads in precipitating baths. The skein of threads is washed, cleaned, and cut up into 1–6 in. long pieces. These staple fibres are curled, prepared, dried, opened up, and worked into a spun yarn. The lustre, curliness, fineness, and length of cut are made similar to those of natural wool or cotton. The properties of cell wool have been steadily improved in recent years, with the result that it has attained and even surpassed the quality of cotton. Cell wool is used by itself and also in a mixture with natural wool. Most of the cellulose produced is consumed by the textile industry and the paper industry.

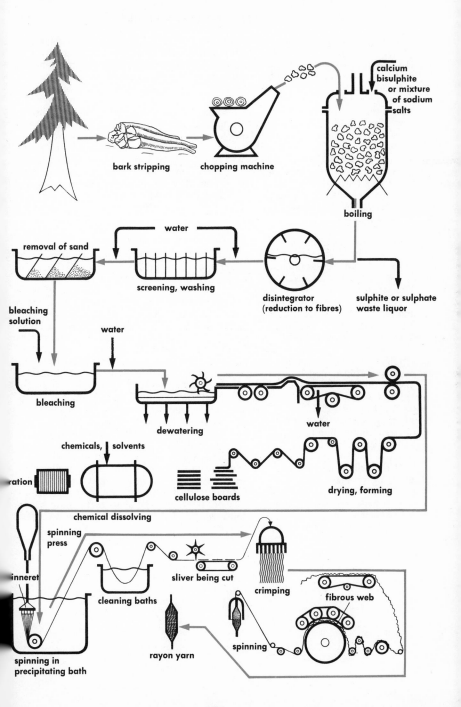

bark stripping

chopping machine

calcium
bisulphite
or mixture
of sodium
salts

boiling

water

removal of sand

screening, washing

disintegrator
(reduction to fibres)

sulphite or sulphate
waste liquor

bleaching
solution

water

bleaching

dewatering

water

drying, forming

chemicals, solvents

cellulose boards

...ration

chemical dissolving

spinning
press

sliver being cut

crimping

...inneret

cleaning baths

fibrous web

spinning in
precipitating bath

rayon yarn

spinning

As long ago as 1664 the English scientist Robert Hooke occupied himself with the question how silk filament might be produced without the intervention of silkworms. His experiments yielded no useful results, however. To produce a fibre from any particular raw material, three problems have to be solved. In the first place it is necessary to have a raw material which can be melted or dissolved; secondly, it must be possible to extrude the melted material or the solution from very fine holes or to form it into coagulable threads in some other way; thirdly, the threads must be very flexible and yet very strong, they must not dissolve in water, they must have some degree of heat resistance, and they must possess the necessary textile properties.

The vast field of man-made fibres (synthetic fibres) is subdivided into two main groups: fibres made from cellulose, and true synthetic fibres (see page 374). In both groups filaments and spinning fibres are produced. The former are thousands of yards long (virtually "endless"), whereas the latter are only a few inches in length; they are cut or torn to the length of the natural fibres with which they are often used in combination. Cellulose-based fibres are at present still a commercially far more important commodity than true synthetic fibres.

Cellulosic man-made fibres

At present these fibres are manufactured by three different processes: the viscose process, the cuprammonium process, and the acetate process.

Viscose process

The initial material is cellulose, produced by chemical processing of wood, straw and various other vegetable substances (see page 368). If cellulose is treated with caustic soda, the low-molecular components are dissolved in it, while the high-molecular components (which are the useful ones for the production of man-made fibres) form a salt which can react with hydrogen sulphide at 20°–25° C to produce cellulose xanthate. This thick yellow substance dissolves in 7% caustic soda (sodium hydroxide solution) at 15°–17° C to form a viscous solution (viscose), which is then filtered and freed from gas (by vacuum treatment) because even the tiniest gas bubbles would cause the filament to snap during spinning. The spinning solution must mature at 12°–15° C for 2–4 days before spinning. It is then pumped through spinning nozzles into spinning baths. Each nozzle is provided with a large number (up to 150) very fine holes called spinnerets ($\frac{1}{20} - \frac{1}{10}$ mm = 0.002–0.004 in. diameter) and are made of a chemically resistant metal such as tantalum. The spinning bath contains a solution of sulphuric acid and salts in water. In an acid solution of this kind the cellulose xanthate is decomposed into cellulose in the form of filaments emerging from the nozzle. These are then passed through various cleaning, bleaching, hardening, and refining baths. After drying, 10–20 filaments are spun together to form the rayon yarn. Depending on the pre-treatment and after-treatment to which it has been subject, the rayon is colourless or already spun-dyed (a very wash-fast dyeing process), lustrous or dull, fine or coarse.

(Continued)

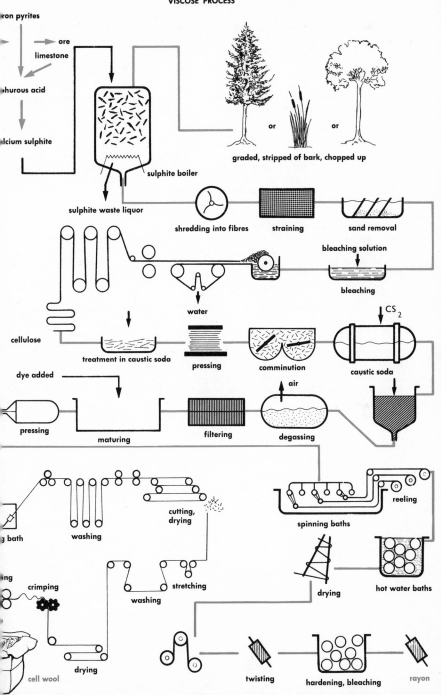

VISCOSE PROCESS

iron pyrites

→ ore

limestone

sulphurous acid

calcium sulphite

sulphite boiler

graded, stripped of bark, chopped up

sulphite waste liquor

shredding into fibres   straining   sand removal

bleaching solution

bleaching

water

cellulose

treatment in caustic soda   pressing   comminution   caustic soda

CS_2

dye added

pressing   maturing   filtering   degassing

air

cutting, drying

bath   washing   reeling

spinning baths

crimping   stretching   drying   hot water baths

washing

cell wool   drying   twisting   hardening, bleaching   rayon

When the bundles of filament extruded from a number of nozzles are grouped together into a "cable", cut up into lengths of only a few inches, and curled, the material known as cell wool (rayon staple) is obtained.

One of the products made from cell wool is motor tyre[1] cord, which is superior to cord made from cotton.

Rayon and cell wool produced by the process described above are still chemically the same substance that forms the main constituent of wood, namely the polysaccharide cellulose with the formula $(C_6H_{10}O_5)_n$.

Cuprammonium process

For the cuprammonium process and the acetate process it is necessary to use linters (short cotton fibres) or particularly pure wood cellulose (refined pulp). If pure cellulose, after undergoing a preliminary treatment with caustic soda and bleaching solutions, is treated with copper sulphate and ammonia, the macromolecular cellulose will, under the right conditions of concentration, dissolve as cellulose cuprammonium complex in aqueous alkaline solution. This viscous solution is filtered and extruded through spinnerets into a so-called spinning funnel. The filaments that are formed are drawn out in a powerful stream of water (wet spinning process), the cellulose is precipitated in the form of coherent filaments from the complex compound and is at the same time drawn out to very fine filaments—even finer than those produced by the silkworm. The washed product is dried and reeled up. After some further processing the final product is available as filament or cut staple.

Acetate process

Cellulose can be converted into numerous derivatives by chemical processing. These include cellulose acetate, which can suitably yield a serviceable synthetic fibre. Pure cellulose is acetylated with acetic acid and acetate anhydride in conjunction with sulphuric acid until the washed dry acetate becomes soluble in acetone. The solution is filtered and is extruded through spinnerets into warm air to form filaments. The acetone is thereby expelled from the filaments, carried away by the warm air, and recovered for re-use (dry spinning process). The dry filaments are reeled up, processed in various ways, and made available in the form of filament or cut staple.

1. Tire in U.S.A.

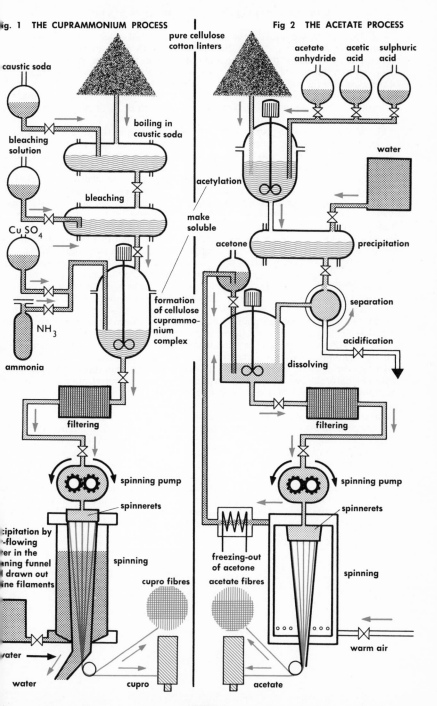

Fig. 1 THE CUPRAMMONIUM PROCESS

Fig 2 THE ACETATE PROCESS

pure cellulose
cotton linters

acetate
anhydride

acetic
acid

sulphuric
acid

caustic soda

boiling in
caustic soda

water

bleaching
solution

bleaching

acetylation

make
soluble

Cu SO₄

precipitation

acetone

separation

NH₃

formation
of cellulose
cuprammo-
nium
complex

acidification

ammonia

dissolving

filtering

filtering

spinning pump

spinnerets

spinning pump

spinnerets

cipitation by
-flowing
ter in the
nning funnel
drawn out
ine filaments

spinning

freezing-out
of acetone
acetate fibres

cupro fibres

spinning

water

water

cupro

acetate

warm air

373

SYNTHETIC FIBRES (SYNTHETIC POLYMERS)

Cellulosic fibres are manufactured from raw materials such as wood and other woody vegetable matter, i.e., naturally formed materials whose molecules are merely rearranged by means of the viscose, cuprammonium or acetate process (see page 370 *et seq*). In the case of true synthetic fibres ("man-made" fibres in the true sense of the word), on the other hand, the molecules first have to be synthetically built up from the elements carbon, hydrogen, nitrogen and oxygen and formed into macromolecules. Four main groups of synthetic fibres are to be distinguished: polyvinyl, polyamide, polyacrylic, and polyester fibres.

The diagram shows diagrammatically, by way of example, the production process for the synthetic polymer called perlon, a German synthetic fibre resembling nylon. Both these products belong to the group of polyamide fibres which derive their name from the so-called amido group (CONH) in the molecule. Nylon and perlon are extensively manufactured from coal or petroleum, air, and hydrogen. Phenol is obtained from coal, and cyclohexanol from petroleum; these two raw materials are equally suitable for the purpose. Ammonia is produced from air and water, and oxygen is used in the manufacturing process. The substance eventually obtained, namely, caprolactam (for perlon) or the salt of adipic acid and hexamethylene diamine (e.g., for nylon 66), is polycondensed, with the result that the separate molecules become linked together to very long giant molecules. A substance which melts above 260° C is formed, which is filtered and is then extruded through spinnerets whereby the perlon (or nylon) filaments are formed. The filaments are drawn out, washed, dyed, and chemically processed to produce the finished synthetic fibres.

Perlon differs from nylon in that it contains up to 10% of monomeric constituents. For this reason the perlon melt remains stable, whereas the nylon melt is readily decomposable. From a given quantity of phenol as the raw material a larger quantity of perlon than nylon can be produced. Generally speaking, perlon and nylon have similar properties, but perlon has a greater affinity to dyes. Nylon, on the other hand, is better resistant to solvents. Fabrics made from these synthetic fibres are abrasion-resistant, tear-resistant and have better folding resistance than those produced from cotton or natural wool. They can withstand the action of putrefactive bacteria (for example, cotton fabrics buried in earth in which these bacteria abound will rot away completely in six months, whereas perlon or nylon will survive such conditions) and are also more resistant to attack by many chemicals than natural fibres are. Dirt does not penetrate into nylon and perlon fibres, and fabrics made from them therefore remain clean longer and are easier to clean than fabrics from natural fibres.

Both nylon and perlon are used for the manufacture of stockings, socks, sewing thread, upholstery fabrics, lingerie, carpets, artificial furs, bandages, surgical suturing material, nets and ropes for the fishing industry, motor-tyre[1] cord, straps, cable sheaths, filter cloths, clothing of all kinds, felt, brushes, sheeting, etc. In addition, they are used for a number of technical purposes, e.g., the manufacture of gear wheels and other components. Nylon was first obtained by the American chemist W. H. Carothers in 1932. Perlon was discovered by P. Schlack, a German, in 1938.

1. Tire in U.S.A.

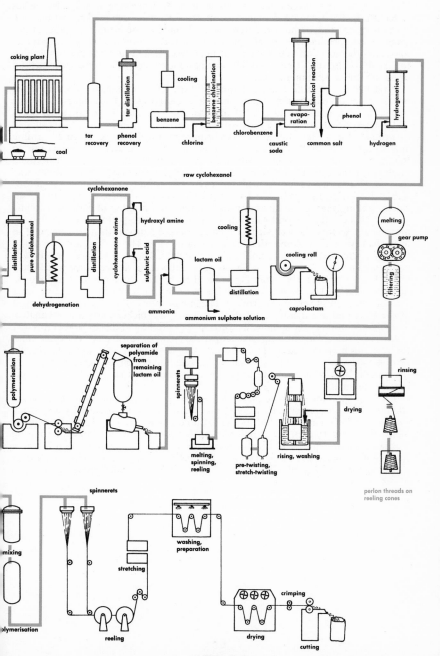

coking plant

coal

tar recovery

tar distillation

phenol recovery

cooling

benzene

chlorine

benzene chlorination

chlorobenzene

caustic soda

evapo- ration

chemical reaction

phenol

common salt

hydrogenation

hydrogen

raw cyclohexanol

cyclohexanone

distillation

pure cyclohexanol

dehydrogenation

distillation

cyclohexanone oxime

hydroxyl amine

sulphuric acid

ammonia

ammonium sulphate solution

lactam oil

distillation

cooling

cooling roll

caprolactam

melting

gear pump

filtering

polymerisation

separation of polyamide from remaining lactam oil

spinnerets

melting, spinning, reeling

pre-twisting, stretch-twisting

rising, washing

drying

rinsing

perlon threads on reeling cones

mixing

polymerisation

spinnerets

reeling

stretching

washing, preparation

drying

crimping

cutting

SPINNING

Spinning is the process of making yarns or threads by the twisting of vegetable fibres, animal hairs, or man-made fibres, i.e., filament-like elements only a few inches in length. In the spinning mill the raw material is first disentangled and cleaned. Various grades and, perhaps, different kinds of fibre may be blended together at this stage so as to produce the correct quality of yarn. The fibres are spread out parallel to one another in a thin web, from which, in the next stage, a yarn-like material (called the "rove" or "roving") is formed. This can be done either by the web divider method or by the stretch-spinning process.

In the *web divider method* the raw material (fibres) is first untangled and straightened on a machine called a carding willow or breaker card (Fig. 1). Then comes the roving (preparatory spinning). The tufts of material are separated into individual fibres and the web is formed. The web is divided into narrow strips which are then rounded to produce the roving, this operation being performed by two or three carding engines (or cards) in a row. The material is fed at an accurately controlled rate to the first carding engine (Fig. 2) which further unravels the fibres and draws them accurately parallel by the action of the cylinder, worker rolls and clearers. In this way the so-called carded yarn is formed. On leaving the third carding engine the fibrous web is divided into strips by the divider (Fig. 3). These strips are then fed to the so-called rubbing gear, or condenser, which comprises a number of endless "rubbing leathers" which, in addition to a rotational movement, also perform axial to-and-fro movements, so that the web strips which are passed between them are rounded to form the roving. Next comes the fine spinning process. The rovings are drawn and thereby attenuated and more uniformly distributed. They are twisted into threads and are then wound on to reels. This is done either on a device called a self-actor mule (Fig. 4), or on a ring spinning frame (Fig. 5). The mule operates as follows: first the carriage travels out, the spindles revolve slowly, while the feed cylinder supplies the requisite amount of roving. The thin portions of the roving take up most of the twist and are thereby strengthened, while the thicker parts are attenuated. At each revolution of the spindle, the yarn springs off the end thereof and in this way acquires its twist. Then the carriage stops; the spindles revolve at high speed until the yarn has been twisted to the desired number of turns. Next, the spindles briefly revolve in reverse to uncoil the windings between the bobbin of yarn and the tip of the spindle. Finally, the carriage travels in again and winds up the spun yarn (intermittent spinning).

The ring spinning machine performs its task in a single operation (continuous spinning). The roving coming from the feed cylinder is pre-twisted by a drawing mechanism and is passed by the traveller to the bobbin which is fixed on to the spindle. When the latter rotates, the length of yarn between the spindle and the drawing mechanism is drawn taut, so that the traveller is pulled in the direction of rotation of the spindle. Because of its weight and the friction on the ring, the traveller rotates at a slower speed than the spindle. Each revolution of the traveller produces one turn of yarn on the bobbin.

(Continued)

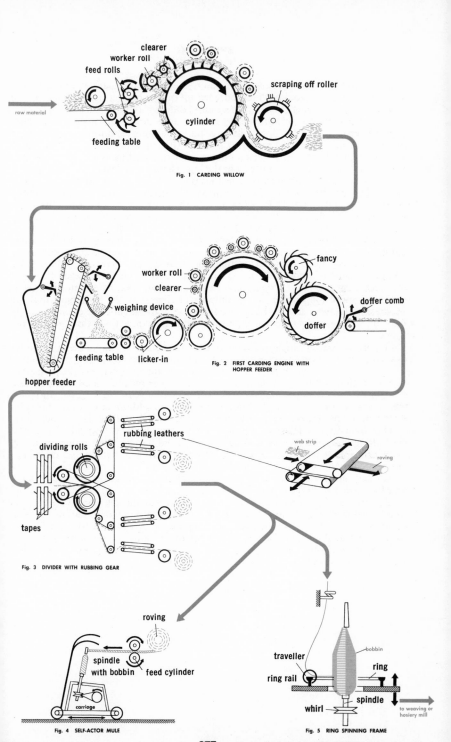

Fig. 1 CARDING WILLOW

Fig. 2 FIRST CARDING ENGINE WITH HOPPER FEEDER

Fig. 3 DIVIDER WITH RUBBING GEAR

Fig. 4 SELF-ACTOR MULE

Fig. 5 RING SPINNING FRAME

377

In the *stretch-spinning process* (here described more particularly with reference to cotton) the bales of wool are first loosened up on the hopper bale-breaker (Fig. 6) and then on the opener (Fig. 7). If necessary, different types of fibre are blended at this stage. The picker (or scutcher) forms the loose cotton into a sheet (the "lap") (Fig. 8). Separation of the fibre tufts into individual fibres and forming the web are done on a machine called a revolving flat card (Fig. 9), which is a particular type of carding engine. The taker-in roller (or licker-in) of this machine is set with teeth which tear away small bunches of fibre from the lap. These are stripped from the licker-in by a large cylinder with steel wire teeth. Over the cylinder are narrow bars (flats) carried by an endless belt and likewise provided with teeth which exercise a combing action and remove impurities. After leaving the card, the web is pulled through a funnel-shaped hole and is thus formed into a so-called "card sliver". To produce a yarn, the sliver has to be attenuated and twisted. Four, six or eight slivers are fed to the draw frame (Fig. 10); these are blended into one, and this operation is accompanied by attenuation, or drafting, so that the combined sliver becomes four, six or eight times as long but no thicker than the original card slivers. The draw frame comprises pairs of smooth rollers which are so driven that their speed of rotation increases from one pair to the next, until the front pair rotating at four, six or eight times the speed (depending on the number of slivers) as the back pair. It is this progressive increase in speed that produces the above-mentioned attenuation. To improve the regularity of the sliver, it is passed two or three times through the draw frame.

For producing very high-quality yarns, the card sliver is (before being fed to the draw frame) subjected to a process called combing in which up to 20% of the shorter fibres may be removed, thereby improving the spinning properties of the remainder. The yarn thus produced is called worsted yarn. The machine used is the comber (Fig. 11). The slivers are advanced so as to present a fringe to a set of revolving combs which remove the loose short fibres. The slivers are additionally drawn through a fixed comb. The combed fringe is then combined with the tail of the previous fringe.

The attenuation of the sliver after leaving the draw frame is completed on a series of drafting machines (known collectively as "speed frames") which operate on the same principle as the draw frame. In this way the roving is produced. At each stage, the drafted product must be twisted in order to increase its strength. This twisting is performed on flyer spindles (Fig. 12). The bobbin fits loosely on a vertical spindle to whose top is fixed the hollow inverted U-shaped flyer. The roving passes through the flyer to the bobbin, which it drags round. Because of the high speed of the spindle and flyer, the roving acquires a twist as it passes from the flyer to the bobbin. Fine spinning, i.e., the final operation in producing the finished yarn, is now usually done on a ring spinning frame or on a self-actor mule (however, the latter method is obsolescent for cotton spinning). These machines are similar in principle to those described with reference to the web divider method.

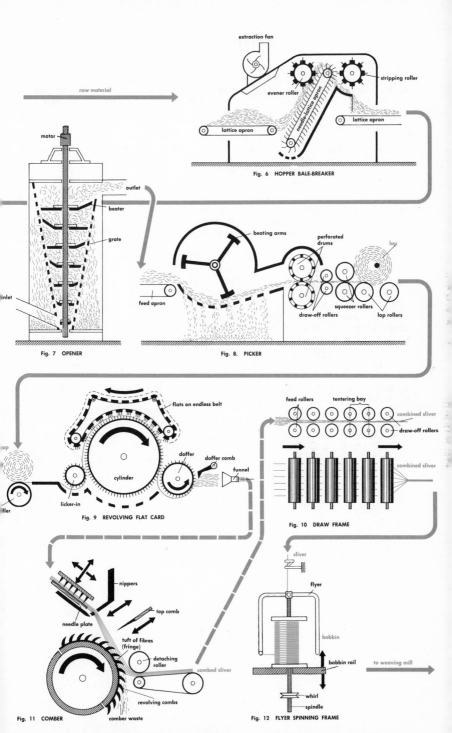

raw material

extraction fan

evener roller

needle-lattice apron

stripping roller

lattice apron

lattice apron

Fig. 6 HOPPER BALE-BREAKER

motor

outlet

beater

grate

inlet

Fig. 7 OPENER

beating arms

perforated drums

lap

feed apron

draw-off rollers

squeezer rollers

lap rollers

Fig. 8. PICKER

flats on endless belt

doffer

doffer comb

funnel

ap

cylinder

ller

licker-in

Fig. 9 REVOLVING FLAT CARD

feed rollers

tentering bay

combined sliver

draw-off rollers

combined sliver

Fig. 10 DRAW FRAME

nippers

top comb

needle plate

tuft of fibres (fringe)

detaching roller

combed sliver

revolving combs

comber waste

Fig. 11 COMBER

sliver

flyer

bobbin

bobbin rail

to weaving mill

whirl

spindle

Fig. 12 FLYER SPINNING FRAME

379

FABRIC STRUCTURE

For making textile fabrics (cloth) two systems of threads crossing each other at right angles are required. The longitudinal threads in a loom are called the warp, and the transverse threads are called the weft. The principle of weaving can best be explained with reference to the hand loom (Fig. 1). The warp threads, which are wound on the warp beam, pass over the back rest, through the eyes of the healds (or heddles), through the interstices in the reed behind which the shuttle plies to and fro, and then over the breast beam and on to the cloth beam (or cloth take-up roller). The shedding harness—comprising the heald shafts[1] with the steel wire healds and the treadles—forms the "sheds" for the shuttle to be passed through. The weaver works the treadles with his feet. When treadle 2 is depressed, shaft 2 (with the warp threads passing through the heald eyes) is lowered; at the same time shaft 1 (with the warp threads 1, 3, 5, 7, etc.) is raised. The shed is now open, and the shuttle containing the bobbin of weft thread is shot in. Next, the shed is closed, the swinging batten is moved forward, and the inserted weft thread is beaten into position in the cloth. Now treadle 1 is depressed, the shed is opened again; shaft 2 (with the warp threads 2, 4, 6, 8, etc.) is raised. The shuttle can again be inserted, and so on.

The warp and weft can intersect in many different ways. These can, however, be classified in three fundamental systems: (a) linen or plain weave; (b) twill weaves; (c) satin weaves. From these a large number of so-called "derived weaves" can be formed. The technical design of a weave is called its pattern. This is drawn on squared paper, on which the vertical lines of squares represent warp threads, whilst the horizontal lines represent weft threads. A filled-in square indicates that the warp thread it represents is above the weft, whereas a blank means weft above warp. Every weave has a certain number of "ups" and "downs" of the warp in relation to the weft. This can be represented by a symbolic notation. For instance, plain cloth is represented by 1/1 (i.e., one lifted, one depressed). Every pattern repeats itself. The area comprising the minimum number of warp and weft intersections constituting the pattern is called a "round of weave". In this area the warp threads are shown black; in the rest of the design they are in red.

The *linen weave* (L) has the smallest "repeat" of the pattern, L 1/1. It has a checker-board pattern and presents the same appearance on both sides (see Fig. 2). The bottom diagram in Fig. 2 shows a section through the warp threads (small red circles) with the weft threads (in black) passing in and out between them. On the right, a similar section through the weft threads is shown. The linen weave is very widely applied (cambric, chiffon, cretonne, georgette, muslin, poplin, calico, etc.).

(Continued)

1. Heddles in U.S.A.

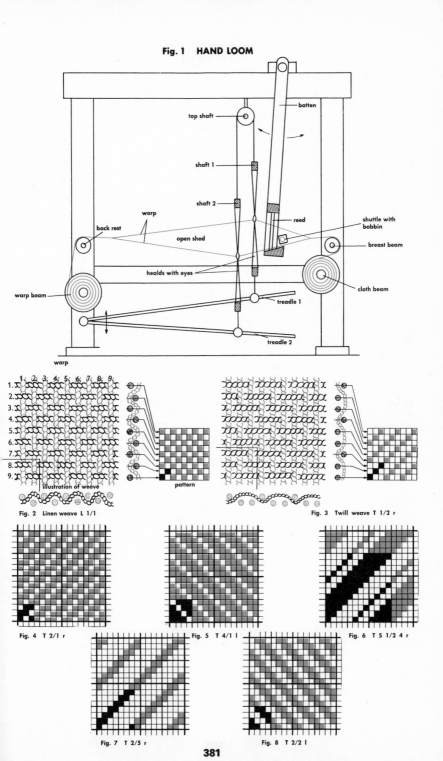

Fig. 1 HAND LOOM

batten
top shaft
shaft 1
shaft 2
reed
shuttle with bobbin
back rest
warp
open shed
breast beam
healds with eyes
cloth beam
warp beam
treadle 1
treadle 2
warp

illustration of weave
pattern

Fig. 2 Linen weave L 1/1

Fig. 3 Twill weave T 1/2 r

Fig. 4 T 2/1 r

Fig. 5 T 4/1 l

Fig. 6 T 5 1/2 4 r

Fig. 7 T 2/5 r

Fig. 8 T 2/2 l

Twill weaves (T) are characterised by diagonal ribs (twill lines). If these ribs run from bottom left to top right, the fabric is called right-hand twill (designated by r); if they run from top left to bottom right, it is called left-hand twill (designated by l). For equal density of warp and weft the ribs run at an angle of 45°. If the warp density is greater than the weft density, the ribs run at a steeper angle (steep twill), and vice versa (reclining twill). The simplest twills have the symbols T 1/2 r (Fig. 3) and T 2/1 r (Fig. 4). In the former there is more weft material on the face of the fabric (weft twill). Other twill weaves are shown in Figs. 5, 6 and 7. In the case of a double-faced twill (Fig. 8) the fabric presents the same appearance on both sides. A distinction is made between "simple" and "fancy" twills. In the former the same number of warp threads are placed successively above or below each weft thread, and the ribs are of uniform width (Fig. 8). In the latter more warp threads may be above one weft thread than another, the ribs may vary in width, and small ornaments may be introduced between the ribs (Fig. 6).

Satin weaves (S) differ from twills in having each warp thread lifted, or depressed, separately. Again a distinction can be made between warp satins and weft satins (or sateens). The simplest weft satin is S 1/4 (2) (Fig. 9), and the corresponding warp satin is S 4/1 (2) (Fig. 10). The distance from one point of intersection to the other is called the "progressive number" and is indicated by the figure in parentheses behind the symbol of the weave, e.g., (2), (3), (5). From five to upwards of thirty threads of warp and weft are required to complete the various schemes of intersecting. In satins and twills (as distinct from plain cloth) the finest or best threads can be made to predominate on the face ("right side") of the fabric. Some well known satin fabrics are charmelaine, duchesse, moleskin, velveteen, etc.

"Derived weaves" are obtained by modifying the fundamental weaves in various ways. Common variants of the linen weave are the *rib weaves* (repps) in which two or more warp or weft threads form ribs of various widths. In "weft repp" the ribs extend in the warp direction (Fig. 11) and the weft material is most in evidence on the face of the fabric; in "warp repp" the ribs extend in the weft direction (Fig. 12) and the warp material predominates on the face. Figured repps are formed by varying the width of the ribs (Fig. 13). Other popular variants of the linen weave are the *panama weaves*, in which two, three or four warp threads are lifted over, or depressed below, the same number of weft threads (Fig. 14). A figured panama weave is illustrated in Fig. 15.

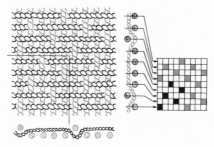

Fig. 9   Satin weave S 1/4 (2)

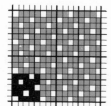

Fig. 10   S 4/1 (2)

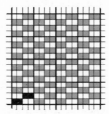

Fig. 11   Weft repp 1/1 2 f

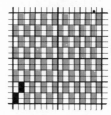

Fig. 12   Warp repp 2/2

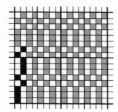

Fig. 13   Figured repp 3 1 1/1 3 1

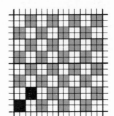

Fig. 14   P 2/2

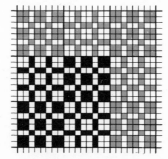

Fig. 15

383

PREPARING WARP AND WEFT FOR WEAVING

Before weaving can commence, a variety of preparatory operations, involving a number of complex machines, have to be carried out. The most important of these operations are summarised in Fig. 1.

In the process known as *doubling*, two or more yarns are wound on to a bobbin without undergoing any twisting, as distinct from spinning, in which the fibres are twisted together to obtain the requisite strength (see page 376). In *twisting doubling*, however, two or more yarns (threads) are twisted round one another, the yarns being fed by means of delivery rollers, whereas in spinning the draft passes through a drawing frame (see page 378). Another preparatory treatment is *singeing* (see page 392).

Bleaching and *dyeing* (see page 394) the yarns now tend to be done as the latest possible stage in the process because all the waste fibre material thus remains white and provides greater scope for utilisation.

Preparing the warp is called *warping*, i.e., providing a sufficient number of parallel threads. There are three methods: beam warping, mill warping, and sectional warping. A beam warper has a bobbin frame carrying some hundreds of bobbins. The threads are drawn separately through the interstices of an adjustable reed, then under and over a series of rollers, through the teeth of an adjustable comb, and on to a warp beam. The threads are thus drawn from the bobbins and wrapped in even coils upon the beam. In mill warping the warp threads are wrapped spirally round a very large reel rotating on a vertical axis. The distinctive feature of sectional warping (Fig. 2) consists in contracting the threads to form a 3–12 in. wide ribbon, which is coiled on to a warp cylinder. A number of these ribbons, or sections, are coiled side by side on this cylinder, which thus provides a means of intermediate storage. The threads are then transferred to a warp beam (loombeam), each section contributing its own width to that of the warp. Sectional warping is employed chiefly for coloured threads.

Sizing is a treatment for making the warp threads smooth so as to reduce the friction of the threads in the shedding harness (see page 380) of a loom. This is accomplished either by coating the threads or by saturating them with an adhesive paste (size). In one method the yarn for the warp is passed in the form of a sheet between a pair of rollers, the lower roller being partly immersed in liquid size.

Drawing-in, or entering, is the operation of passing warp threads through the eyes of a shedding harness in a sequence depending on the pattern to be produced. *Twisting* is the operation of joining the ends of a new warp with those of the previous one already in the loom. This is done by twisting the ends together, either by hand or with the aid of a special device.

Fig. 1 PREPARING WARP AND WEFT FOR WEAVING

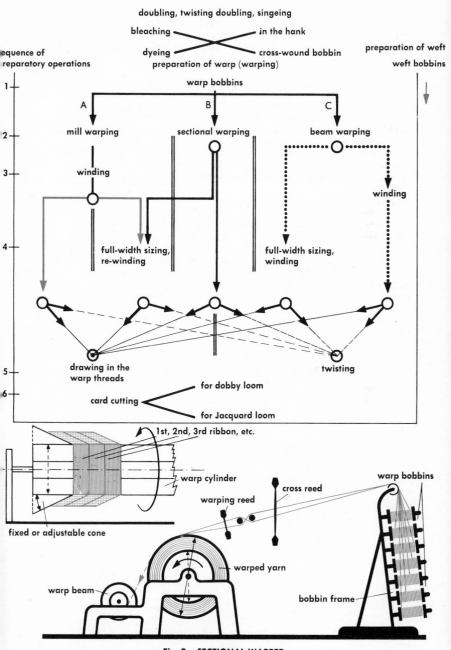

doubling, twisting doubling, singeing

bleaching ——————— in the hank

dyeing ——————— cross-wound bobbin

preparation of warp (warping)

sequence of preparatory operations

preparation of weft

weft bobbins

1 —

warp bobbins

A   B   C

2 —

mill warping   sectional warping   beam warping

3 —

winding   winding

4 —

full-width sizing, re-winding   full-width sizing, winding

drawing in the warp threads   twisting

5 —

6 —

card cutting   for dobby loom

for Jacquard loom

1st, 2nd, 3rd ribbon, etc.

warp cylinder

fixed or adjustable cone

cross reed

warping reed

warp bobbins

warped yarn

warp beam

bobbin frame

Fig. 2 SECTIONAL WARPER

WEAVING

The power loom was developed in the late 18th and early 19th century. Its operating principle was, and still is, basically similar to that of the hand loom (see page 380). Hand looms have not been entirely superseded, however, and are still used for special purposes. The most important improvement applied to the hand loom was the development of the Jacquard machine in the 18th century. In a machine of this kind the warp threads are raised by rows of upright wires called hooks. The machine also comprises a series of horizontal needles which move to and fro. This system is used to operate the shedding and control the figuring of the fabric. Machines vary in size from 100 needles and hooks up to 1600.

Over the years a number of different loom types have been evolved for different kinds of work. As a rule, looms for the weaving of fabrics with small patterns are provided with healds for shedding (i.e., raising and lowering the warp threads in a predetermined sequence, so that they form a "shed" or passage for the shuttle; after a weft thread has been inserted, the shed is changed; cf. page 380); those for large patterns are provided with Jacquard equipment.

All these systems have certain main operations in common (a) shedding (see above); (b) inserting weft threads between the divided warp (this is done by the shuttle and is called "picking"); (c) beating-up, i.e., striking each weft thread into position in the fabric (this is done by the reed). In addition, the loom must have devices for holding the warp taut and delivering it as weaving proceeds, and for drawing away the cloth manufactured. In a power loom the above equipment acts automatically, and a number of additional features are provided to ensure trouble-free functioning. In Fig. 1 the main functional elements of a modern power loom are schematically indicated: (1) warp beam; (2) fabric take-off; (3) picking (by the shuttle carrying the weft bobbin); (4) beating-up of the weft; (5) shuttle-changing (with drop box or revolving box, so that yarns of different colours and/or qualities can be used); (6) forming the selvages on both sides of the cloth; (7) shedding: this can be done by means of tappets (7a), or by means of the so-called dobby mechanism (7b), or by means of the Jacquard machine (7c).

A post-war development is the jet loom (Fig. 2). This type of machine has no shuttle, the weft thread being carried along in a jet of air or water.

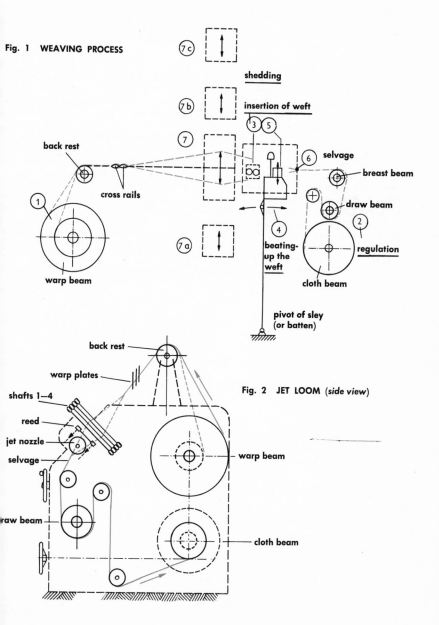

Fig. 1 WEAVING PROCESS

(7c)

shedding

(7b)

insertion of weft

(7)

(3) (5)

back rest

(6) selvage

cross rails

breast beam

(1)

draw beam

(2)

regulation

warp beam

(4)

beating-
up the
weft

cloth beam

pivot of sley
(or batten)

back rest

warp plates

Fig. 2 JET LOOM (side view)

shafts 1—4

reed

jet nozzle

warp beam

selvage

raw beam

cloth beam

In British usage the term "hosiery" includes all types of knitted fabrics, whereas in the United States its meaning is restricted to stockings and socks. Knitting is used for the production of underwear and outer garments, curtain fabrics, lace fabrics, etc. The materials used are yarn and threads of cotton, wool and man-made fibres, also blended yarns and paper yarns. The products are either in the form of flat fabrics (subsequently made up into garments) or are ready-fashioned garments (pullovers, vests, stockings, etc.).

Hosiery is formed of looped fabric. There are two main types: weft fabric (Fig. 2) and warp fabric (Fig. 3). In weft fabric the threads extend crosswise across the fabric, whereas in warp fabric the threads extend lengthwise. The loops more particularly in a weft fabric form so-called "courses" (extending crosswise) and "wales" (extending lengthwise), as indicated in Fig. 2. For stockings and socks weft fabric is usually employed, as its elasticity or stretch is mainly crosswise and so provides a better fit for the leg. Warp fabric has less elasticity and is not much used for this purpose. The back of weft fabric is characterised by ridges running crosswise, the spaces between them being the courses. The face of the fabric displays the wales as a series of vertical lines. The back of the fabric is not so smooth as the face. On the other hand, warp fabrics are almost identical on the face and back. Some knitted fabrics derived from weft fabric are indicated in Figs. 4–6, and some derived from warp fabric in Figs. 7-9. An almost unlimited variety of design is possible, for example, by using combination warp and weft fabrics in which loops of the warp type are superimposed over weft fabric loops.

In the manufacture of full-fashioned women's hosiery the stocking blank is knitted in two pieces; the seam is a characteristic feature. Seamless stockings are produced on circular hosiery knitting machines. Other types of machine are also used for the purpose.

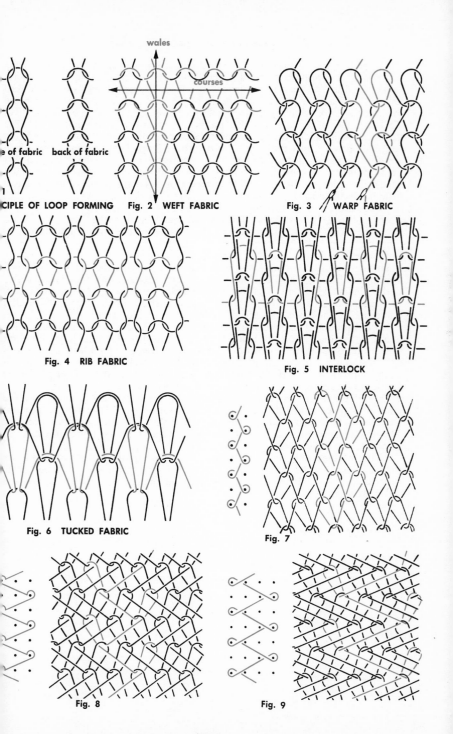

CIPLE OF LOOP FORMING   Fig. 2   WEFT FABRIC   Fig. 3   WARP FABRIC

e of fabric   back of fabric

wales

courses

Fig. 4   RIB FABRIC

Fig. 5   INTERLOCK

Fig. 6   TUCKED FABRIC

Fig. 7

Fig. 8

Fig. 9

HOSIERY AND KNITTING MACHINERY

The needles used for producing knitted fabrics on knitting machines are of two main types: the spring beard needle (Fig. 1) and the latch needle (Fig. 2). The operation of the beard needle is illustrated in Figs. 3a–d: The new thread, which is kinked around the shank below the open beard of the needle, slides past the open beard towards the hook, while the previously formed loop, resting a little below the tip of the beard, also slides upwards after the beard is closed over the new thread. The previously knitted loop thus passes over the beard and is moved towards the hook, so that the new thread in the hook is drawn through the previously formed loop, which is cast off as the new loop is formed. The latter then slides down the shank and past the open beard. The next loop can now be formed. Fig. 4 illustrates how the latch needle forms loops: The previously formed loop is on the shank of the needle, a little below the open latch. As the needle moves downwards with the new thread in its hook, the previously formed loop touches the open latch and swings it to the closed position. The previously formed loop can then be cast off over the closed hook, the new thread being formed into a loop by the hook. This new loop thereupon slides down, opens the latch, and finally slides off the lower end of the open latch on to the needle shank.

The best hosiery (women's stockings) is produced on the flat full-fashioned knitting machine (Cotton's machine, so named after the inventor). A modern machine of this kind may be as much as 60 ft. long and may comprise up to 32 sections, each of which produces a piece of flat hosiery fabric. Each section has about 400 needles set vertically. These needles perform a rather complex movement.

Hosiery produced on circular knitting machines, usually fitted with latch needles, is of the seamless type. The quality is coarser than that of stockings produced on full-fashioned flat machines. This is because latch needles cannot be constructed to such fine dimensions as spring beard needles. The stockings are shaped to fit the leg by varying the size of the loops, but the resulting fit of the tubular product is inferior to that obtained with full-fashioned hosiery.

Other types of knitting machine used for the manufacture of stockings are the circular rib machine and the Lamb type flat machine (Fig. 6). The latter can produce flat fashioned fabrics or it can produce seamless fashioned hosiery or other garments. The needles (usually of the latch type) are arranged in grooved beds placed at an acute angle to each other.

All the machines described can also be used for the manufacture of garments other than stockings. There are various other types of knitting machines used for particular purposes, e.g., the Milanese warp machine, the circular body machine, and the sinker wheel machine.

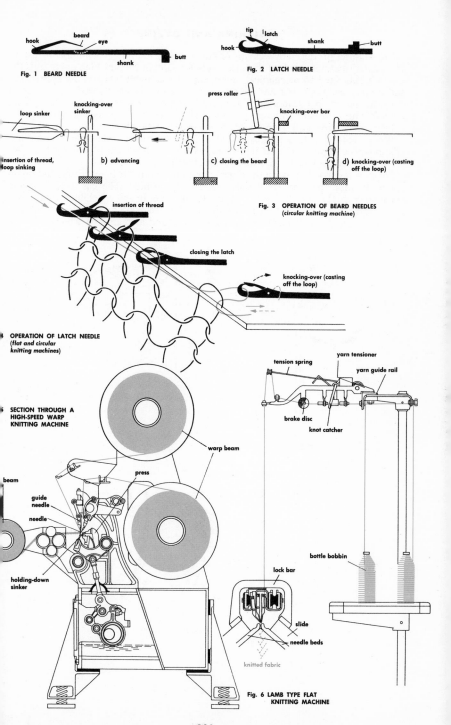

Fig. 1 BEARD NEEDLE

hook · beard · eye · shank · butt

Fig. 2 LATCH NEEDLE

tip · latch · hook · shank · butt

loop sinker · knocking-over sinker · press roller · knocking-over bar

insertion of thread, loop sinking

b) advancing

c) closing the beard

d) knocking-over (casting off the loop)

Fig. 3 OPERATION OF BEARD NEEDLES (*circular knitting machine*)

insertion of thread

closing the latch

knocking-over (casting off the loop)

OPERATION OF LATCH NEEDLE (*flat and circular knitting machines*)

tension spring · yarn tensioner · yarn guide rail

brake disc · knot catcher

SECTION THROUGH A HIGH-SPEED WARP KNITTING MACHINE

warp beam

beam

press

guide needle

needle

holding-down sinker

bottle bobbin

lock bar

slide

needle beds

knitted fabric

Fig. 6 LAMB TYPE FLAT KNITTING MACHINE

FINISHING AND DYEING

Most fabrics produced by weaving or knitting have to undergo a number of further processing treatments before they are ready for sale. In the finishing operations the fabric is subjected to mechanical and chemical treatment whereby its appearance and quality are improved and its commercial value thus enhanced. Each type of fabric has its own particular finishing operations. For example, textile produced from vegetable fibres require different treatment—raising, singeing, dyeing, printing, etc. —from those produced from animal fibres or synthetic fibres.

Woven cotton cloth is usually boiled with dilute caustic soda to remove natural oils and other impurities. Next, it is rinsed, scoured in an acid bath, processed in other ways, and then bleached, e.g., with sodium chlorite.

Singeing is carried out with the object of removing any fibres on cotton and rayon materials, more particularly if these have to be printed. The gas flame singeing machine (Fig. 1) is usually employed for the purpose. In this machine a continuous web of fabric is moved past burners acting on the face or on both sides of the fabric. It then passes through a pair of squeezer rollers and a steam box which acts as a

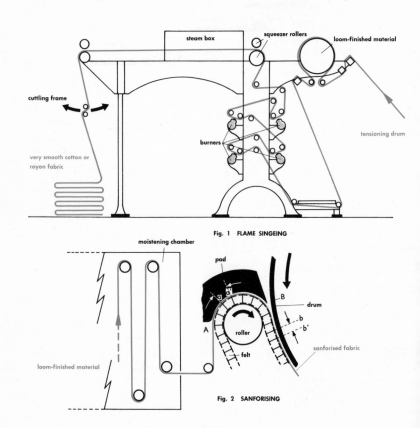

Fig. 1 FLAME SINGEING

Fig. 2 SANFORISING

spark extinguisher. "*Sanforising*" is the proprietary name of a treatment which is applied more particularly to garments which are required to retain their shape well. In the course of spinning, weaving and finishing, the fabric is subjected to a good deal of pull and stretch, so that internal stresses are produced in it. When the material gets wet (rain or washing), these locked-up stresses are released and the fibres revert to their original length: the cloth shrinks. Sanforising produces a mechanical shortening of the fibres, so that it will not subsequently shrink in the wash. In this treatment (Fig. 2) the material first goes through the moistening chamber to soften the fabric. It then passes over a felt belt on to which it is firmly pressed by a heated pad. So long as the felt and the material are running over the roller together, they undergo a greater amount of stretch on the outside (between A and B) than on the inside. When the felt and material are then curved in the opposite direction (from the point B onwards), the stretched outer surface of the material is shortened (for instance a certain portion is first stretched to a length a–a' and is then shortened to b–b').

Raising (or napping) is a treatment in which small steel hooks (Fig. 3) tear some of the fibres, or the ends of fibres, out of the weft yarn, so that fabrics acquire a woolly surface called "nap". This improves their heat-retention and absorptive properties (as in flannel fabrics), besides making them softer to the touch. Certain types of raising treatment can improve the water-repellent properties of fabrics. Raising is used chiefly for cotton, rayon and woollen fabrics. It can be applied to one or to both sides. The raising machine, or napper, comprises a large drum provided with a number of peripherally mounted rollers which are covered with closely spaced steel hooks. All these rollers rotate in the same direction, but the hooks are curved in opposite directions on alternate rollers. The material passes continuously through the machine; the revolving brushes clean the napping rollers; the roller brush smoothes the material.

(Continued)

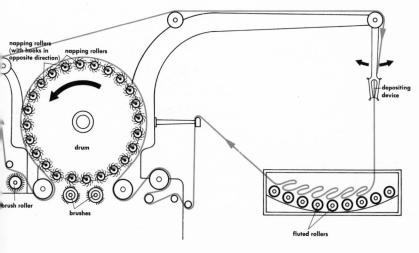

napping rollers (with hooks in opposite direction) napping rollers

depositing device

drum

brush roller

brushes

fluted rollers

Fig. 3 RAISING MACHINE (24 *rollers*)

FINISHING AND DYEING
(continued)

Textile printing: The dyes are dissolved in water. Thickening agents (e.g., starch) are added to the solutions in order to increase their viscosity. The oldest method is *block printing*, usually from wooden blocks in which the design is carved. *Stencil printing* is done with the aid of paper or thin metal stencils. Of greater practical importance is *silk screen printing*. The design is formed on a silk screen, usually by photographic methods, whereby a lacquer image is finally formed on the screen, which can then serve as a stencil. Most cloth is printed by *roller printing*, which is faster than other methods. The printing area is engraved on a copper roller so as to form a recessed pattern (intaglio), which is coated with the colour paste. Excess paste is scraped off by a steel blade. The roller then transfers the paste to the cloth. In multicolour printing, a number of rollers, each printing a single colour, are arranged around the lower part of the central cylinder. Each impression must fall accurately upon the appropriate area within the complete pattern. Fig. 4 shows an eight-colour roller printing machine. The printing rollers may be hand-engraved, or etched, or the designs may be produced by photogravure methods.

The *dyeing* of textiles is a complex field of technology. There are two main types of dyeing machines. In one type the dye solution is circulated through the fabric, which is at rest; in the other, the fabric is passed through a stationary bath of the dye solution. Fig. 5 shows a machine of the latter type; the two squeeze rollers press the dye thoroughly into the fabric.

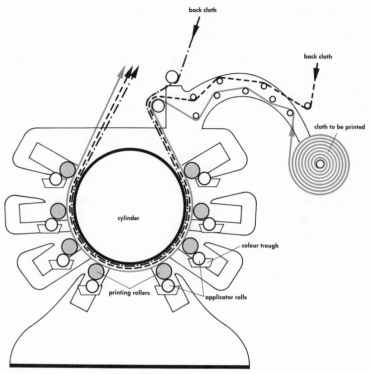

Fig. 4   ROLLER PRINTING MACHINE

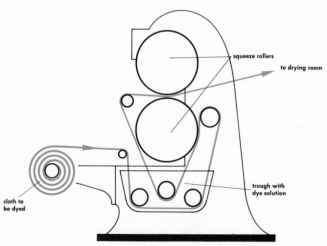

Fig. 5   DYEING MACHINE (*Foulard*)

395

ZIP FASTENER (ZIPPER)

The main parts of a zip fastener are the two chains of teeth, which are attached to strips of textile material, and the slide, which opens and closes the fastener.

Each chain consists of a large number of teeth, usually of metal, which are provided with small protrusions on the top surface and with corresponding recesses on the underside (Fig. 1). The protrusion on each tooth engages accurately with the recess in the tooth above. The two chains of teeth are slightly staggered in relation to each other. To close the fastener, the two chains must be so brought into engagement that the teeth on the two chains can interlock in pairs. This is achieved by the slide. At its upper end the slide comprises two divergent ducts, which join each other and merge into one duct as the lower end. The slide is so designed that the two chains of teeth are brought together at exactly the correct angle to make the protrusions interlock or one tooth engage with the recess on the opposite tooth (Fig. 2). At each end of the zip fastener are end pieces which prevent the slide from coming off. In some zips the two halves can be separated, in which case the bottom end piece is so designed that one chain of teeth can be withdrawn from the slide, while the latter is retained by the other chain.

Zip fasteners sometimes have plastic teeth (e.g., perlon), which are of a shape rather different from that of metal fastener teeth. The chains do not consist of individual teeth, but of loops formed by a spiral coil (Fig. 3). Fasteners of this kind have the advantage that, because of the resilient properties of plastic, they are not destroyed by tearing open. In addition to the types of zip fastener described above, there are many others, all of which operate on the same principle, however, and differ only in the particular form of the teeth employed.

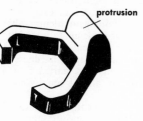

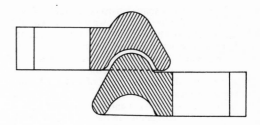

Fig. 1a

Fig. 1b

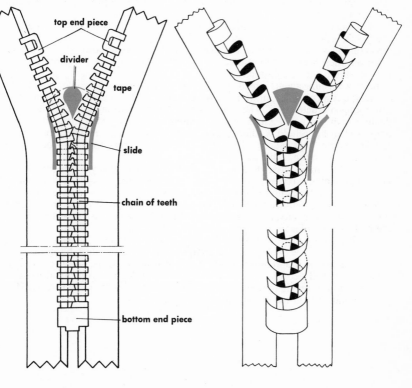

Fig. 2
ZIP FASTENER WITH METAL TEETH

Fig. 3
ZIP FASTENER WITH PLASTIC TEETH

DETERGENTS

Conventional soap consists essentially of the sodium or potassium salts of higher fatty acids and has been known for hundreds of years. The drawback is that such soap washes effectively only in "soft" water (rainwater, water containing no calcium salts). In many districts the available water supply contains dissolved calcium salts ("hard" water), which form greyish deposits with soap, which cling firmly to the textile fabric.

It was particularly on account of the sensitivity of ordinary soap to hardness of water that the manufacture of so-called synthetic detergents was started over a hundred years ago. These are substances which develop an almost equally good washing action in hard and in soft water.

Synthetic detergents are the main ingredients of all washing agents and determine the washing power by their "surface-activity". This group comprises soap and other substances with soap-like behaviour which are for the most part synthetically manufactured from petroleum products or chemically decomposed fats.

Polyphosphates or complex phosphates are major constituents of any good washing agent. By forming complex compounds they neutralise the hardness of the water and combine with the heavy-metal salts, thereby increasing the washing power of the surface-active detergent. All washing preparations also contain bleaching agents, so-called "per-salts", which give off oxygen at temperatures above about 60° C. In the presence of suitable stabilising agents this oxygen bleaches any dirt or stain that is not removed by the detergent. This bleaching action is based on oxidation.

Whiteners are substances which convert ultraviolet rays into visible light and give the wash a brilliant whiteness—provided that it is really clean. Washing preparations also contain substances which increase the dirt-absorbing power of the lather. In addition, they contain fibre-protecting and dispersing agents, perfumes, colouring matter, skin-protective cosmetics, etc.

Besides washing agents intended more particularly for woollen or for boiling, there are various "special" preparations on the market, e.g., anion-active, cation-active and non-ionogenic detergents. These are intended for particular kinds of fibre or for dealing with particular kinds of dirt. Anion-active detergents are predominantly employed in household washing preparations. Non-ionogenic detergents are used to a less extent. Cation-active detergents have hitherto been used only for industrial purposes, e.g., in the textile industry.

Important anion-active detergents are alkyl sulphates, alkyl sulphonates, alkyl-aryl sulphonates. Alkyl phenol polyglycol ether and the polyglycol esters of fatty acids are examples of non-ionogenic detergents.

Wetting power, emulsifying capacity, dispersive and protective colloidal action, dirt absorbing capacity, and foaming power are the significant properties by which the performance of a washing preparation is judged.

Another requirement that washing agents will have to fulfil in the near future is that they should be biologically decomposable, i.e., they must be destroyed by bacterial action in watercourses and sewage purification plants, otherwise rivers and other waters will become increasingly polluted with foam, especially at weirs.

The various stages in the manufacture of a modern washing preparation are shown diagrammatically in the accompanying illustration.

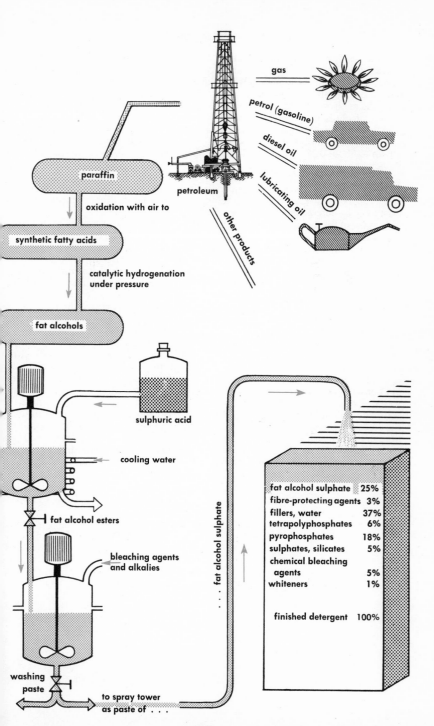

gas

petrol (gasoline)

diesel oil

lubricating oil

paraffin

petroleum

other products

oxidation with air to

synthetic fatty acids

catalytic hydrogenation
under pressure

fat alcohols

sulphuric acid

cooling water

fat alcohol esters

bleaching agents
and alkalies

... fat alcohol sulphate

fat alcohol sulphate

fat alcohol sulphate	25%
fibre-protecting agents	3%
fillers, water	37%
tetrapolyphosphates	6%
pyrophosphates	18%
sulphates, silicates	5%
chemical bleaching agents	5%
whiteners	1%
finished detergent	100%

washing
paste

to spray tower
as paste of . . .

WASHING

100 lb. of domestic washing is soiled with about 1.8 to 4 lb. of dirt as the result of normal use. This dirt consists mainly of fatty substances, proteins, dust and soot particles. Such dirt is very largely insoluble in water or is, indeed, water-repellent. Chemical analysis of this dirt shows that the following substances can (on an average) be extracted from 100 lb. of domestic washing: 0.9 lb. of protein-free organic matter (waxes, alcohols, hydrocarbons, etc.), 0.3 lb. of proteins (particles of skin, hairs, etc.), 0.15 lb. of fatty acids from sweat and greasy excretions, etc., as well as sand, dust and other inorganic constituents. A used shirt is soiled with greasy substances constituting up to about 0.25% of its weight; the collar may even contain as much as 1.2% of its weight of greasy dirt.

The dirt may be held by the fibres in various ways: mechanically (pigments are "jammed" between the fibres), chemically (fruit, oil or ink stains, etc., which in some cases can be removed only by bleaching), by absorption (feebler chemical bond, dissoluble by detergents), and by electrical forces.

As most of the dirt is relatively firmly held by the fibre, pure water by itself is not a very effective washing agent; it is necessary to add detergents (cf. page 398).

Very heavily soiled garments must first be left to soak in a detergent solution. However, this preliminary treatment is not usually necessary for normal domestic washing when modern washing agents are used. The actual washing process is determined by temperature, the mechanical treatment applied (rubbing, scrubbing, action of the washing machine, etc.), and chemical actions. The effect of these factors can be varied within certain limits; but on no account must any of these factors be overdone or neglected.

By adding a detergent to water, the surface tension of the latter is lowered: the water becomes more "fluid". The hydrophobic (water-repellent) end of the detergent molecule strives to escape from the water, while the hydrophilic (water-attracting) end wants to remain in the water. As a result, all the boundary surfaces of the water (e.g., between the water and the air or the wall of the wash-tub or the clothing itself) are densely packed with molecules of detergent. In their effort to escape from the water, detergent molecules penetrate in between the dirt and the fibre, where the water alone could not go. Aided by the mechanical actions applied (scrubbing, etc.), the detergent molecules manage to push farther and farther between the dirt and the fibre until in the end the dirt is completely dislodged. By the same process, particles of dirt which are stuck together, as well as oil and grease, are finely divided and are absorbed by the lather, which must retain the dirt in suspension and not re-deposit it on the clothing before the latter is finally rinsed with clean water.

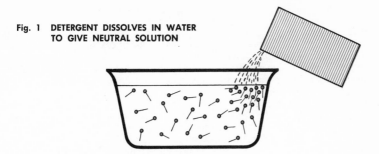

Fig. 1 DETERGENT DISSOLVES IN WATER TO GIVE NEUTRAL SOLUTION

Fig. 2 DIAGRAM OF DETERGENT MOLECULE

hydrophilic part (attracts water)   hydrophobic part of molecule (repels water)

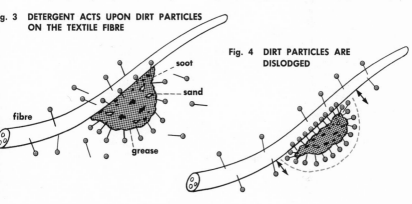

Fig. 3 DETERGENT ACTS UPON DIRT PARTICLES ON THE TEXTILE FIBRE

soot

sand

fibre

grease

Fig. 4 DIRT PARTICLES ARE DISLODGED

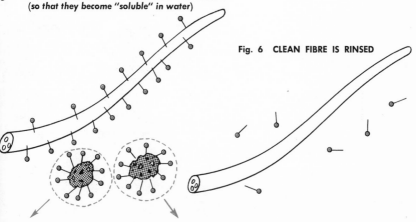

Fig. 5 DIRT PARTICLES ARE COMPLETELY ENVELOPED (so that they become "soluble" in water)

Fig. 6 CLEAN FIBRE IS RINSED

401

WASHING MACHINES

There are two main types of washing machines: (a) Tub type machines (e.g., agitator machines, nozzle machines, paddle-wheel machines). (b) Drum type machines (fully automatic, semi-automatic).

In all tub type washing machines the load to be washed is moved about suspended in water. In an agitator machine the movement is produced by fins or blades slowly revolving on a central shaft (Fig. 1). In a nozzle machine it is produced by water jets streaming from nozzles at the bottom of the tub, and in a paddle-wheel machine it is produced by a flat paddle wheel rotating at high speed. Tub type machines are provided with a draining pump, are often independently heatable by electricity, and usually embody semi-automatic features, i.e., the temperature and the washing time can be pre-set to required values. When the desired temperature is reached, the agitator mechanism or paddle wheel is started automatically and continues to run for the predetermined time. Water is extracted in a separate power-driven spinner or wringer.

In the drum (or cylinder) type machines (Figs. 2a and 2b) a perforated steel drum is rotated inside a tank. In some machines the drum turns in one direction only,

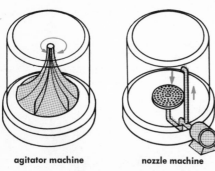

agitator machine   nozzle machine

Fig. 1   TUB TYPE WASHING MACHINES

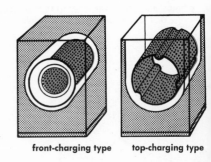

front-charging type   top-charging type

Fig. 2   DRUM TYPE WASHING MACHINES

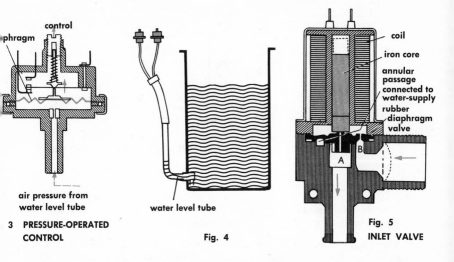

control
phragm
coil
iron core
annular
passage
connected to
water-supply
rubber
diaphragm
valve
A   B

air pressure from
water level tube

water level tube

**3 PRESSURE-OPERATED
CONTROL**

Fig. 4

**Fig. 5
INLET VALVE**

whereas in others it reverses at intervals. Projections (baffles) inside the drum cause the clothes to drop back into the water as the drum revolves. A fully automatic machine of this kind pre-soaks, washes, rinses and extracts water with no attention from the operator after the load is placed in the machine, the power switched on and the timing device set. A semi-automatic machine has to be filled by hand (through a hose connected to the water supply), and at the end of the washing operation the water must be drained from the tank by switching on a pump.

The following is a description of the principal components and the mode of functioning of a fully-automatic washing machine.

The inflow of water and the water level in the tank is controlled by a pressure-operated control device (Fig. 3). It comprises a diaphragm which is forced upwards as the pressure under it increases and which actuates a contact when the predetermined pressure (and therefore depth of water) has been reached. The contact completes an electric circuit which causes the water inlet valve to close. Different quantities of water are required for rinsing and for washing, and for this reason there are usually two control devices. These are connected to a side tube communicating with the tank. As the water rises in the tank, it also rises in this tube and compresses the air in the upper part thereof. It is this air pressure that actuates the diaphragms in the control devices (Fig. 4).

The inlet valve (Fig. 5) is controlled by the control device. When no current is flowing, the iron core rests on the rubber diaphragm and keeps the opening A closed. As the active area upon which the water pressure acts above the valve is larger than below it, the diaphragm is pressed firmly on the valve seat, so that the water, by its own pressure, keeps the valve closed. When the coil is energised, the magnetic core is pulled into the coil, so that A opens. Equalisation of pressure now occurs through the openings A and B. The pressure acting on the rubber diaphragm from below increases and lifts the diaphragm off its seat.

The programme control unit emits the electric impulses which control the various operations that the machine performs (Fig. 6). It comprises the drive, reversing mechanism, washing time selector, step-by-step switching device, and programmed switching device. The control unit as a whole is driven by a synchronous electric motor which drives various cams, each of which has a particular shape that controls

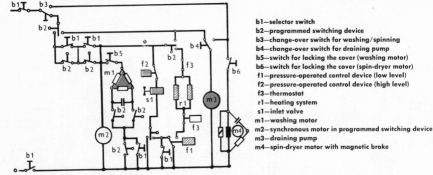

b1—selector switch
b2—programmed switching device
b3—change-over switch for washing/spinning
b4—change-over switch for draining pump
b5—switch for locking the cover (washing motor)
b6—switch for locking the cover (spin-dryer motor)
f1—pressure-operated control device (low level)
f2—pressure-operated control device (high level)
f3—thermostat
r1—heating system
s1—inlet valve
m1—washing motor
m2—synchronous motor in programmed switching device
m3—draining pump
m4—spin-dryer motor with magnetic brake

Fig. 6 ELECTRICAL CIRCUIT OF AN AUTOMATIC WASHING MACHINE

a certain sequence of operations. The edges of the cams are "scanned" by spring contacts and thus, for example, cause the drive motor of the washing drum to reverse its direction of rotation at intervals (Fig. 8) or determine the length of the washing and/or rinsing time, which can be varied as desired by means of the washing time selector.

The purpose of the step-by-step switching device is to transform the rotation of the synchronous motor into a stepwise motion for the programming and control of the washing and rinsing operations. A control diagram of the programme control unit is shown in Fig. 9: the heating system and the inlet valve (low level) are not switched on during the whole of the time span indicated. The heater is switched on and off by a thermostat (see page 20), while the inlet valve is actuated by the pressure-operated control device. The washing temperature can be pre-set to any value between 30° and 100° C, and the thermostat keeps the actual temperature to within a degree or two of this selected value. The waste washing water and the water extracted from the clothes by spin-drying is removed by means of a draining pump. For water extraction by centrifugal action (spin-drying) the drum is rotated at high speed (about 2800 r.p.m.).

Modern washing machines are equipped with a number of safety devices. The rotation of the drum is automatically switched off when the cover is opened, and a magnetic brake quickly stops the motion, so that there is no danger of the operator's hand being caught in the revolving drum. Another protective device prevents the tank being heated unless it contains water up to the correct level. In the event of an interruption of the water supply to the machine during operation, a safety device stops the programme and switches off the heating.

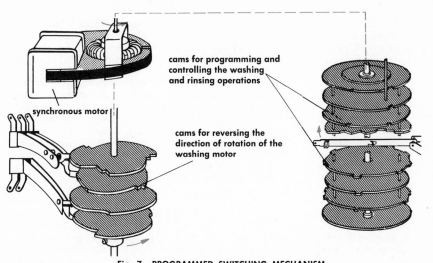

cams for programming and controlling the washing and rinsing operations

synchronous motor

cams for reversing the direction of rotation of the washing motor

Fig. 7   PROGRAMMED SWITCHING MECHANISM

preliminary and main washing operation

anti-clockwise clockwise

6 9 6 9 9 6 9 6 6 9 6 9 9 6 9 6 9 6 6 9 6 9

time

cycle repeated 41 times
(complete operation: 105 minutes)

fine washing

anti-clockwise clockwise

9 6 9 6 9 6 9 6 9 6 9 6 9 6 9 6 9 6 9 6 9 6

time

cycle repeated 15 times
(complete operation: 40 minutes)

Fig. 8   REVERSAL OF WASHING MOTOR

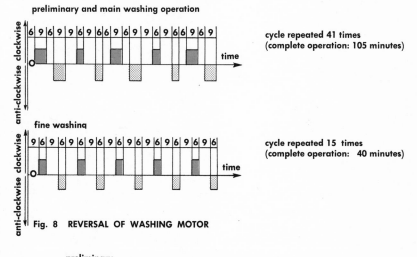

operation	preliminary washing	main washing	rinsing
running time (min.)	19.5	61.5	24
heating			
draining pump			
inlet valve (low level)			
inlet valve (high level)			

Fig. 9   CONTROL DIAGRAM OF PROGRAMME CONTROL UNIT

DRY CLEANING

In most cases dirt remains adhering to the fibres of textile fabrics by two kinds of forces: first, by sticking to a coating of grease or a dried coating of substances which swell up in water or other solvents (e.g., starch, proteins and other glue-like substances); second, by direct adhesion because of the physico-chemical character of the fibres and the dirt (cf. page 400).

"Dry" cleaning (more properly called "chemical cleaning") uses liquids other than water for the cleaning of fabrics. In this treatment, adhering dirt of the first kind is removed by dissolving the grease or other sticky matter to which the dirt particles are clinging. A wide range of solvents are employed: carbon tetrachloride, trichloro-ethylene, tetrachloro-ethylene, naptha (petroleum ether), benzene, etc. (Carbon tetrachloride is a toxic substance and its use has largely been discontinued). A modern dry cleaning plant comprises a number of specialised machines and appliances. The soiled garments are treated with the solvents in rotating drums. The contaminated solvent is drained off and purified for re-use. The cleaned garments are dried, impregnated (if desired), and re-shaped.

In some cases, however, it is necessary to use water as an additional solvent or swelling agent. The second type of dirt is dislodged from the fabric by means of detergents added to the water. After this "wet" treatment the fabric is usually treated in very weak acid solutions (to revive the colours), rinsed, centrifuged and dried. Impregnation treatment may be applied at an intermediate stage to stiffen the fabric and make it water- and dirt-repellent. Garments are finally pressed on special machines operated with steam and air.

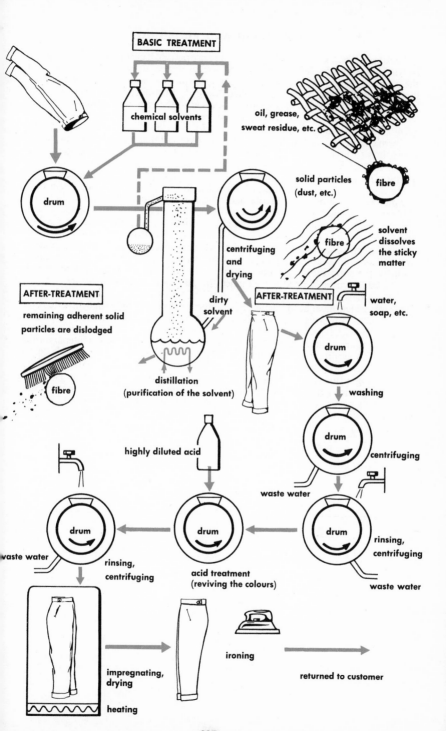

BASIC TREATMENT

chemical solvents

oil, grease, sweat residue, etc.

fibre

drum

solid particles (dust, etc.)

centrifuging and drying

fibre

solvent dissolves the sticky matter

AFTER-TREATMENT

remaining adherent solid particles are dislodged

fibre

dirty solvent

distillation (purification of the solvent)

AFTER-TREATMENT

water, soap, etc.

drum

washing

drum

centrifuging

waste water

highly diluted acid

drum

acid treatment (reviving the colours)

drum

rinsing, centrifuging

waste water

drum

rinsing, centrifuging

waste water

impregnating, drying

heating

ironing

returned to customer

407

STARCHING AND FINISHING

The appearance, glaze and shape-retaining properties of garments may be impaired by washing. Starching helps to restore them. This treatment consists in impregnating the garment, before ironing, with a solution of starch in water. A similar but much more comprehensive process is applied to newly manufactured fabrics. The term "finishing" or "dressing" is collectively applied to the various treatments involved. These comprise mechanical treatment and processing by chemicals to improve the glaze, shape-retaining properties, crease resistance, "feel", smoothness and drape of the material. In addition, depending on the kind of material and the purpose for which it is to be used, it can be made shrinkproof, water-repellent, supple, soft or heavy. Mechanical finishing treatments may consist in mangling, pressing, rolling, milling, shearing, calendering, raising and/or singeing (cf. page 392). Before undergoing these treatments, the material is passed through liquid baths or steam baths in which various substances (textile auxiliaries) are applied to the fibres. Solutions or suspensions in water of starch or starch derivatives, vegetable gums, glues, gelatins and mucilages improve the shape-retaining properties after the material has been dried and smoothed. In recent years, these vegetable substances have in part been superseded by more water-resistant synthetic substances, such as suitable solutions or emulsions of various synthetic resins. Oils, alcohols (e.g., glycerine), fats or tallow improve the suppleness; gypsum, kaolin, wax and binders such as albumen, glues and suitable synthetic products enhance the glaze and weight of fabrics.

Various designations, such as "non iron" or "rapid iron", are applied to textile materials which have been treated by chemical impregnation with synthetic resins and/or cellulose derivatives, usually followed by mechanical treatment applied in conjunction with heat. In particular, the tendency to crease and the swelling capacity of the fabric are reduced. White fabrics may be treated with special whiteners which enhance the impression of whiteness. Many of the organic or vegetable textile auxiliaries are liable to be affected by bacterial or fungoid decay in warm and damp surroundings; this is prevented by the addition of antiseptic substances (salicyclic acid, boric acid, zinc salts, formaldehyde compounds, etc.). Such substances may additionally perform a dirt-repellent or deodorising function. The various substances incorporated into the fabric may constitute as much as 10–20 per cent of the weight of the fabric.

rough fabric

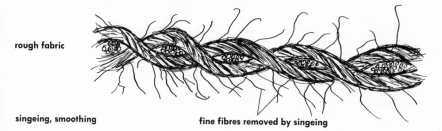

singeing, smoothing

fine fibres removed by singeing

straightened

improving the glaze

water drop

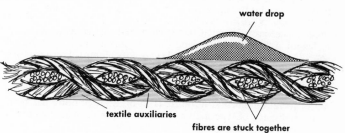

textile auxiliaries

fibres are stuck together

making water-repellent

water drop

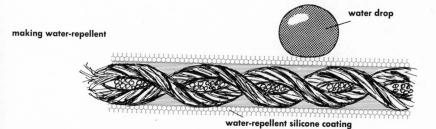

water-repellent silicone coating

 silicone molecule

TYPESETTING: HAND COMPOSITION

The letters (types) used in modern printing are made of metal consisting of approximately 70% lead, 25% antimony and 5% tin. On the front of each letter is a groove, called the "nick" (Fig. 1b), which provides a means of distinguishing the various kinds of type from one another and also enables the compositor to check the type he has set.

Printing type is available in a wide variety of designs and styles (often named after the designer who first conceived them) and in a number of different sizes (e.g., nonpareil, cicero, etc.; in English terminology, however, the type size is usually indicated as a certain number of points, ranging from 6-point, which is the smallest size used in commercial printing, to 48-point) and thicknesses (light, medium, bold, extra bold, etc.). Those parts of type matter which remain blank are filled up with what are called furniture and spacing materials, e.g., spaces between words, "reglets" (for increasing the spacing between the lines of type), and "pieces of furniture" for forming relatively large blank spaces.

The compositor works at a composing frame (Fig. 2) which has a sloping top carrying the case. The case comprises about 130 compartments of various sizes in which the letters (types) are accommodated. In the upper part of the case are the capitals, while the small letters are disposed in the lower part. For this reason capitals and small letters are referred to as "upper case" and "lower case" respectively. The latter are so arranged that the most frequently used letters come most conveniently to hand. In addition, the case contains a range of other types, such as figures, punctuation marks, and spaces for insertion between words.

In his left hand the compositor holds his composing stick (or setting stick), adjusted to the required length of the line of type. With his right hand he builds up the line, letter by letter, the letters being held in position by the thumb of the left hand. By feeling the nicks the compositor can tell that the letters are set the right way up. Spaces are inserted between the words. When the complete line has been set, these spaces are somewhat increased or reduced so as to make all the lines equal in length. When the composing stick is full, the lines of type are transferred to a so-called galley. In this way a whole page (or column) of type is assembled and is then tied up with a strong cord (Fig. 4). A proof, called a "galley proof", is then printed on a hand press and is corrected to remove any misprints. For the actual printing operation the type matter is gripped in a rectangular frame, called a chase, with the aid of metal quoins and furniture (Fig. 5). After printing has been completed, the forme (the page of type matter) is broken up and the letters are returned to their compartments in the compositor's case (Fig. 6).

In modern printing practice, hand composition is little used except for so-called jobbing work (letterheads, leaflets, etc.) and for difficult scientific typesetting (formulae, tables, etc.). For other kinds of work (books, newspapers, magazines) mechanical composition is almost exclusively employed (see page 412).

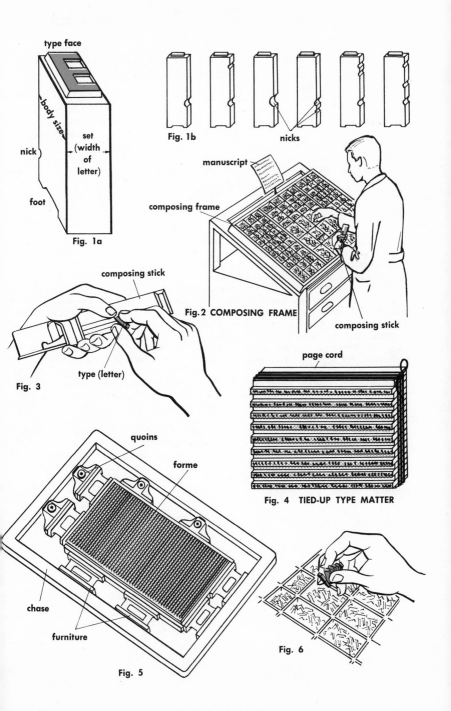

type face

body size

nick

set (width of letter)

foot

Fig. 1a

Fig. 1b   nicks

manuscript

composing frame

Fig. 2 COMPOSING FRAME

composing stick

composing stick

type (letter)

Fig. 3

page cord

Fig. 4   TIED-UP TYPE MATTER

quoins

forme

chase

furniture

Fig. 5

Fig. 6

411

TYPESETTING:
MECHANICAL COMPOSITION, COMPOSING MACHINES

The advantages of mechanical composition over hand composition are the much greater speed of setting and the use of newly cast clear type which does not have to be broken up after printing but is simply melted for recasting.

In *line casting machines* (e.g., Linotype) the typesetting—i.e., the setting up of the matrices side by side—and the casting of the lines of type are performed in the same machine. The operator sits at the machine and works a keyboard resembling that of a typewriter. Each time a key is pressed, a matrix is released from the magazine (Fig. 3) and slides on to a moving belt which conveys it to the assembler (Fig. 1). Special matrices, which are kept available in boxes on the right of the keyboard, can be inserted by hand, as required. When a complete line of matrices has been assembled, the operator presses a lever and the entire line is raised and transferred to the casting mechanism. Here the spacebands (sliding wedges) between the words are pushed home so that the line fills out to its full length. Then molten metal is pumped from the melting pot (Fig. 2) into the matrices, so that the line of type is cast (Fig. 4). The "slug" (line of cast type) is ejected and trimmed by knives. The line of matrices is transferred to grooves and they are automatically returned to their appropriate channels in the magazine. The matrices are provided with teeth cut in particular combinations; in the distributing mechanism these teeth engage with corresponding grooves, so that each matrix drops into its proper channel. The matrices are thus in constant circulation while the machine is in operation.

The Lino–Quick system operates on the same principle as the Linotype, but the operator's keyboard punches holes in a paper tape which is fed into a casting machine and controls the type-casting. Another device of this kind is the Teletypesetter. The holes are punched in the tape by a perforating machine by electrical impulses received over telephone wires, the operator being many miles away.

In the *Monotype* system the typesetting and the type-casting operations are performed by separate machines. A keyboard machine (Fig. 5) punches holes (according to a certain code) in a paper tape (Fig. 6). The tape is then fed into an automatic composition caster (Fig. 7). The letters are cast as single types (Fig. 8); this makes for greater convenience of correction, as the letters can be replaced individually, whereas with Linotype a whole line has to be recast if there is an error in it.

There are various kinds of *filmsetting machine*. One of these is the Monophoto (Fig. 9). This machine is controlled by a paper tape perforated on a Monotype keyboard. The tape controls the movements of a matrix case comprising a number of transparent plastic matrices through which a beam of light photographs each required letter in turn. When the line is completed, the strip of film is advanced on a revolving drum.

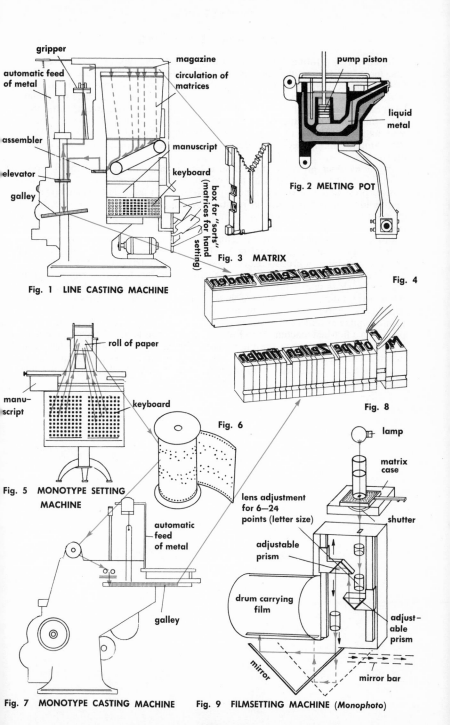

gripper

automatic feed of metal

magazine

circulation of matrices

assembler

manuscript

elevator

keyboard

galley

box for "sorts" (matrices for hand setting)

Fig. 1 LINE CASTING MACHINE

pump piston

liquid metal

Fig. 2 MELTING POT

Fig. 3 MATRIX

Fig. 4

roll of paper

manuscript

keyboard

Fig. 6

Fig. 8

Fig. 5 MONOTYPE SETTING MACHINE

automatic feed of metal

lamp

matrix case

shutter

lens adjustment for 6—24 points (letter size)

adjustable prism

drum carrying film

adjustable prism

galley

mirror

mirror bar

Fig. 7 MONOTYPE CASTING MACHINE

Fig. 9 FILMSETTING MACHINE (Monophoto)

LETTERPRESS PRINTING

In letterpress printing the image is printed direct from type or other relief surfaces (the term "relief printing" is sometimes used to denote this more particularly). Early printing was done on hand-operated presses, as illustrated in Fig. 1. A press of this kind comprised a screw spindle operated by a long bar, causing the platen to be pressed down on to the paper. This simple method is still used by artists for obtaining prints from woodcuts, etc. The same principle is applied in the modern sheet-fed automatic platen press (Fig. 2). Inking the printing plate in a modern machine calls for a complex inking mechanism comprising a number of rollers for evenly distributing the ink.

In the cylinder press an impression cylinder takes the place of the flat platen. The printing plate is mounted on a flat bed which is thrust to and fro under the cylinder. A letterpress machine of this kind is illustrated in Fig. 3. The sheets enwrap the impression cylinder, are held in position by grippers, and are pulled between the cylinder and the plate. With this printing system it is possible to operate at high speeds and use larger plates.

For still higher speeds, more particularly for newspaper and magazine production, web-fed rotary presses are used (Fig. 5). The curved printing plates for these machines are cast in metal by a process called stereotyping. A matrix (Fig. 4) is a mould which is formed by making an imprint of the printing forme (type and engravings) in a material such as papier-mache. A mixture consisting of 75–82 parts of lead, 15–20 parts of antimony, and 3–5 parts of tin is poured into the matrix. Up to about twenty castings (stereotypes) can be obtained from one and the same matrix. The metal printing plate produced in this way is placed round a cylinder (instead of being placed on a flat-bed machine as in Fig. 2). The continuous web of paper coming from large rolls passes between the impression cylinder and the plate cylinder, both of which rotate. Web-fed rotary letterpress newspaper machines can attain very high production rates. Sheet-fed rotary letterpress machines are used mainly for producing catalogues, magazines, etc.

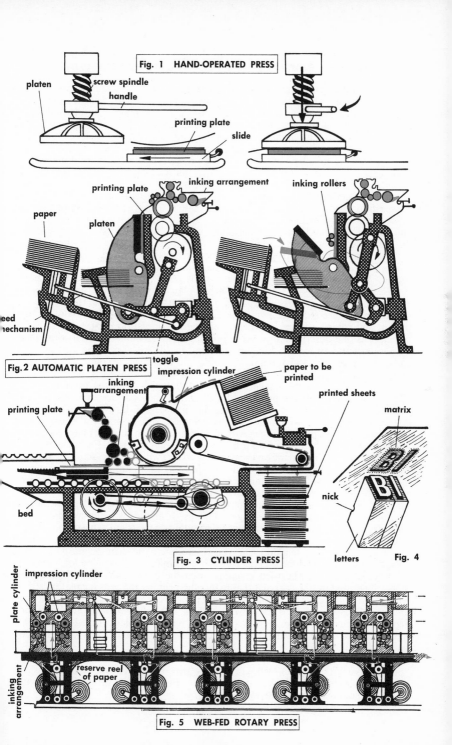

Fig. 1 HAND-OPERATED PRESS

platen — screw spindle — handle — printing plate — slide

Fig. 2 AUTOMATIC PLATEN PRESS

printing plate — inking arrangement — inking rollers — paper — platen — feed mechanism — toggle

Fig. 3 CYLINDER PRESS

inking arrangement — impression cylinder — paper to be printed — printed sheets — printing plate — bed

Fig. 4

matrix — nick — letters

Fig. 5 WEB-FED ROTARY PRESS

impression cylinder — plate cylinder — reserve reel of paper — inking arrangement

415

INTAGLIO PRINTING (PHOTOGRAVURE, ROTOGRAVURE)

In relief printing (letterpress printing: see page 414) the lines or points to be printed are raised above the general level of the printing plate. On the other hand, in intaglio printing they are below the surface of the plate. The oldest intaglio printing process is line engraving, in which the design is produced by lines cut in the surface of a copper plate. To obtain prints, ink is applied to the face of the plate and fills the lines, any excess ink being wiped off; prints are made by laying sheets of paper on the inked plate and applying pressure by means of a roller (Fig. 2). Etching is a development of this technique; a polished copper plate is covered with so-called etching ground (a thin coating of a varnish-like substance) in which the design is scratched with a sharp needle, so that the coating is removed and the bare copper thus exposed along these lines. The plate is then treated with sulphuric acid or iron chloride, which eats away some of the exposed copper by chemical action and thus etches the design into the plate (Fig. 1b). In the allied techniques called dry point no etching chemicals are used, the design being scratched direct in the plate with a steel needle (Fig. 1a). It is therefore really a variety of engraving, but differs from it in technical details. In all these processes, therefore, the lines forming the design are below the general surface of the plate. A thick and absorbent paper is used for printing from engraved or etched plates, so that the paper will to some extent allow itself to be pressed into the lines in the surface of the plate. These centuries-old techniques are still used by artists. Commercial printing makes use of cylinder presses and rotary presses, but the actual printing operation is based on the same principle as that described above. The printing forme is almost invariably produced by photographic processes. Intaglio printing can, like relief printing, be used for a wide variety of purposes ranging from fine line drawings to colour photographs. Half-tone illustrations, such as photographs, have to be converted into a printable form by breaking up the image into small dots which form the printing surface after etching. The dots are produced by making a photographic exposure through a glass screen divided into small squares by intersecting dark lines. In this way a dot image on the photographic plate is obtained. For printing on cheap coarse paper (such as newsprint) a screen with 60 lines to the inch is used; plates made with finer screens must be printed on a better-quality coated paper. From the negative thus obtained a print is made on copper plate coated with a photo-sensitive solution. The plate is then etched, whereby the non-printing areas are removed, leaving the dots standing in relief. The technique of producing pictures by this method is known as the half-tone process. It comes under the more general heading of photo-engraving. For intaglio printing the dots are not raised above, but are "wells" depressed below the non-printing areas; the latter have no ink on them, the ink being concentrated in the wells, which are deeper or shallower, depending on the tonal value of the original. These plates are produced by a method similar in principle to that for making relief printing plates, but using a different type of screen and different technical processes.

Intaglio printing is done on presses generally similar to those used for letterpress printing, such as the sheet-fed machine (used more particularly for high-quality work) illustrated in Fig. 4, except that in intaglio printing the printing plate is always wrapped round a cylinder (instead of a flat plate, as in the cylinder press described on page 414). The plate is inked with a thick soft ink which fills the "intaglio" depressions, and any excess ink is scraped off by a steel blade (called a "doctor"). There are many different inking systems; Fig. 5 shows one of these. A web-fed rotary press is illustrated in Fig. 6.

The intaglio printing process described here is known as "gravure printing" or "photogravure". The term "rotogravure" is used more particularly for high-speed printing on web-fed machines, such as that in Fig. 6, which produces catalogues, newsprint supplements, packaging materials, etc.

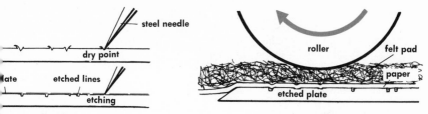

Fig. 1 ETCHING

Fig. 2 PRINTING

steel needle

dry point

late   etched lines

etching

roller   felt pad

paper

etched plate

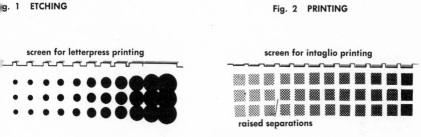

screen for letterpress printing

screen for intaglio printing

raised separations

Fig. 3 SCREEN

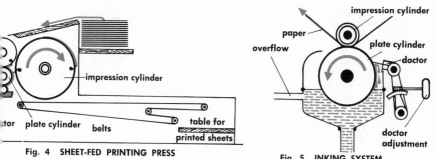

impression cylinder

paper

overflow

impression cylinder

plate cylinder
doctor

tor   plate cylinder   belts

table for
printed sheets

Fig. 4 SHEET-FED PRINTING PRESS

doctor
adjustment

Fig. 5 INKING SYSTEM

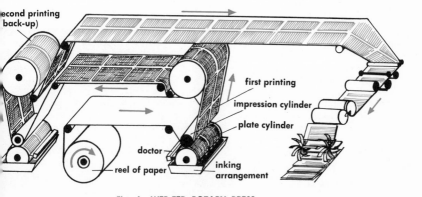

econd printing
back-up)

first printing

impression cylinder

plate cylinder

doctor

reel of paper

inking
arrangement

Fig. 6 WEB-FED ROTARY PRESS

417

PLANOGRAPHIC PRINTING PROCESSES:
LITHOGRAPHY AND OFFSET PRINTING

In planographic processes the matter to be printed is not raised above the surface of the plate (as in letterpress or "relief" printing) nor sunk below the surface (as in intaglio printing), but remains on the surface. Lithography is based on the principle that grease and water are mutually repellent. Ink is applied to grease-treated printing areas, while the non-printing parts, which absorb and hold water, reject the greasy ink. The process was invented by Senefelder, a German, in 1798. The drawing is made with a greasy medium on a special kind of stone, which is then lightly etched. Next, the stone is treated with gum arabic and the drawing is washed off with turpentine. Finally, the stone is coated with water and inked (Fig. 1a). Printing is done by applying sliding pressure exerted by a wooden scraper. The stone is covered with dampened paper and a backing board. Then the stone (on the bed of the press) is moved horizontally (Fig. 1b).

A similar technique can be applied to metal plates instead of stone. These have the advantage that they can be wrapped around the cylinder of a printing press and can thus be used for printing by rotary methods. As a rule, the image is not printed direct from the plate on to the paper, but is first transferred to an intermediate rubber cylinder (blanket cylinder) which then transfers (offsets) the image to the paper. This procedure has the great advantage that, because of the flexibility of the rubber cylinder, the image can be transferred not only to paper, but also to various other materials, rough or smooth. The offset printing press thus comprises three rotating cylinders (Fig. 2): the plate cylinder (carrying the printing plate), the blanket cylinder (covered by a sheet of rubber), and the impression cylinder (which presses the paper against the blanket cylinder). Moistening rollers apply a film of water to the plate, which then comes into contact with inking rollers (Fig. 3). The ink is rejected by the water-holding areas but is accepted by the greasy image. The process is used for the printing of copy (text) as well as pictures and is widely used for the production of books and magazines. Fig. 5 is an illustration of a four-colour offset printing press comprising two plate cylinders, each with four sets of inking rollers (one set for each colour) and each printing on one side of the web of paper. The printing plates for offset lithography are produced by photographic processes, the metal plate (zinc or aluminium) being given a sensitised coating. The exposed plate then undergoes various treatments (developing, washing, etching, etc.) before it is ready for use as a printing plate. The offset lithography process is also known as photo-lithography.

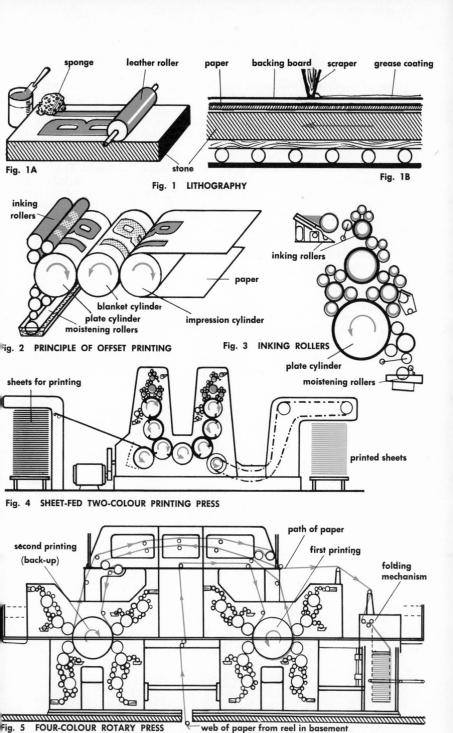

Fig. 1A

sponge · leather roller

Fig. 1B

paper · backing board · scraper · grease coating

stone

Fig. 1   LITHOGRAPHY

inking rollers

paper

blanket cylinder
plate cylinder
moistening rollers
impression cylinder

Fig. 2   PRINCIPLE OF OFFSET PRINTING

inking rollers

plate cylinder

moistening rollers

Fig. 3   INKING ROLLERS

sheets for printing

printed sheets

Fig. 4   SHEET-FED TWO-COLOUR PRINTING PRESS

path of paper

second printing (back-up)

first printing

folding mechanism

Fig. 5   FOUR-COLOUR ROTARY PRESS — web of paper from reel in basement

PLANOGRAPHIC PRINTING PROCESSES: COLLOTYPE

The collotype, or photogelatin, printing process differs from letterpress, offset and photogravure in that the image is not broken up into dots by means of a half-tone screen. This enables it to make more closely accurate reproductions than any of the other processes. It resembles photolithography (see page 418) in that it is based on the fact that water and grease repel each other. The non-printing areas of the plate hold the moisture and reject the greasy printing ink, while the relatively dry printing areas accept the ink. A glass or aluminium plate is coated with a light-sensitive solution containing gelatin and potassium bichromate. The image of a photographic negative is then projected on to this plate. Where the light passes through the transparent areas of the negative, the gelatin is hardened; darker areas prevent hardening to a greater or less degree. Next, the plate is soaked in glycerin, which is absorbed chiefly by the soft (non-printing) gelatin areas. The plate is exposed to a moist atmosphere, and the soft areas absorb moisture. When the plate is inked, these areas repel the greasy ink, whereas the hardened areas, which do not absorb moisture, do accept the ink. Printing is done on flat-bed presses or on cylinder presses.

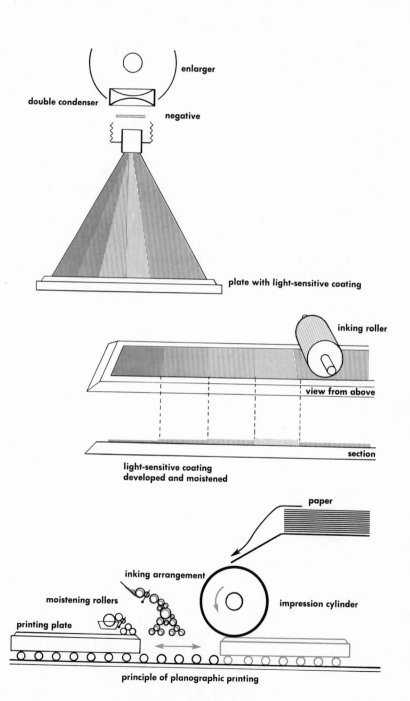

enlarger

double condenser

negative

plate with light-sensitive coating

inking roller

view from above

section

light-sensitive coating
developed and moistened

paper

inking arrangement

moistening rollers

printing plate

impression cylinder

principle of planographic printing

SILK SCREEN PRINTING

This is essentially a stencil printing method, the stencil being formed by bolting silk stretched over a wooden or metal frame. For fine detail a fine-meshed silk will be used. Steel wire gauze or plastic screens are sometimes used for special purposes. The design can be applied directly to the screen by painting it with a greasy medium (paint, ink, etc.). A water-soluble gum is then applied to the screen and closes the pores of the silk. However, the greasy areas reject the gum. The greasy paint is then washed away with a solvent (e.g., turpentine), so that the corresponding areas of the silk become pervious to ink. The screen is placed on the surface to be decorated and ink is applied to the screen by means of a rubber squeegee. Some of the ink soaks through the pervious areas of the silk and is printed on to the surface (paper, metal, wood, glass, rubber, textile fabric, etc.). The screen-printing of textiles is carried out on long tables, the screen being moved along step by step to successive positions (as shown in the bottom illustration). To obtain fine detail in the pattern, it is necessary to produce the stencil by a photographic process. This is done by applying a light-sensitive coating to the screen. The image is developed by washing: this removes the coating from those areas where it has not been hardened by the action of light. The silk screen process is very versatile with regard to the wide range of materials to which it can be applied, but it is not suitable for reproducing fine detail and gradations of tone. Simple designs can be made by sticking paper, celluloid or metal patterns to the screen. The screen can be wrapped round a cylinder for rotary printing (see illustration).

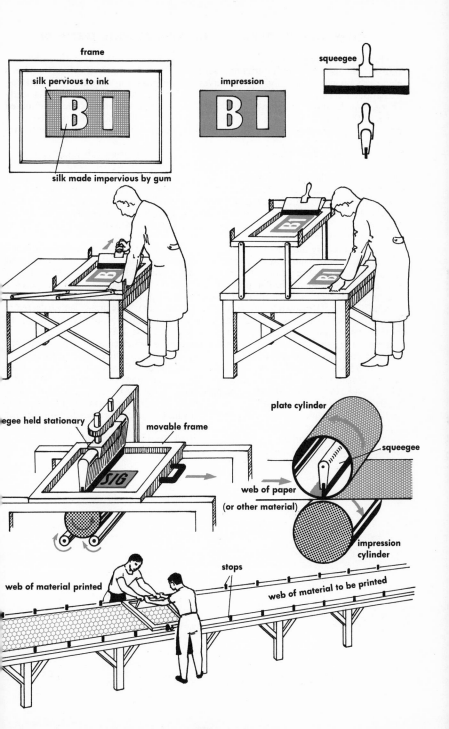

frame

silk pervious to ink

B I

silk made impervious by gum

impression

B I

squeegee

egee held stationary

movable frame

SIG

plate cylinder

squeegee

web of paper

(or other material)

impression cylinder

web of material printed

stops

web of material to be printed

423

COPYING AND DUPLICATING (XEROGRAPHIC METHOD)

The xerographic process was evolved by Carlson in America in the nineteen-thirties. He used a photoconductive semi-conductor, a material which conducts electricity on exposure to light but behaves as an insulator in the dark. This material was applied in layers to a conducting plate. The semi-conductor was electrostatically charged in the dark, and a pattern was then projected on to it. In the illuminated areas of the design the electric charge was dissipated, but the unilluminated areas retained as residual charge which was made "visible" by dusting the plate with a suitable powder (e.g., rosin powder).

In the present-day application of this principle a colouring substance is applied to an electric charge pattern formed in a semi-conductor, which nowadays consists of coatings of selenium, selenium/arsenic or selenium/tellurium. What is known as the cascade method of development has come into widespread use in modern xerographic reproduction technique: A very fine synthetic powder (called the toner) with special frictional electric properties are mixed with small steel and quartz balls provided with a coating of special plastic. As soon as this mixture is set in motion, the balls and the synthetic powder induce electric charges in each other, the charge acquired by the powder being of opposite sign to that of the semi-conductor. If a mixture of this kind is moved about on the coated plate, particles at first adhering to the carrier balls are detached from these and remain adhering to the more highly charged areas of the plate. The powder thus makes the pattern of electric charges in the plate "visible". As a result of the development process, which takes only a few seconds, a complete powder image emerges on the plate. This image is transferred to paper likewise by means of electrostatic forces. The paper is simply laid upon the powder image and is electrically charged from the back. This causes the powder to adhere to the paper. To fix the powder, heat is applied, which causes the thermoplastic powder particles to melt and thus remain permanently adhering to the paper. In other methods the powder is sprayed with a solvent or is fixed by a varnishing treatment. Alternatively, some methods print the powder image on to paper coated with plastic and zinc oxide, the image being directly fixed by the semi-conductive zinc oxide coating. Xerographic processes are used not only for copying and multiplying but also, for example, for obtaining rapid printing-out of results from data-processing equipment (cf. page 298 *et seq.*). The electric image is produced by electrodes in printing heads controlled by impulses emitted by the equipment, the image then being made visible and fixed in the manner described.

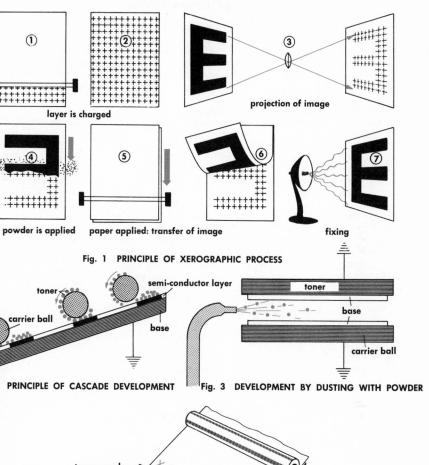

layer is charged

projection of image

powder is applied

paper applied: transfer of image

fixing

Fig. 1 PRINCIPLE OF XEROGRAPHIC PROCESS

toner

semi-conductor layer

carrier ball

base

toner

base

carrier ball

PRINCIPLE OF CASCADE DEVELOPMENT

Fig. 3 DEVELOPMENT BY DUSTING WITH POWDER

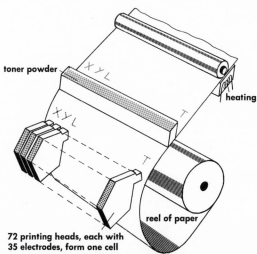

toner powder

heating

72 printing heads, each with
35 electrodes, form one cell

reel of paper

Fig. 4 HIGH-SPEED PRINTING EQUIPMENT (BORROUGHS)

MACHINE BOOKBINDING

The sheets arriving from the press are folded into 8-, 16-, 32- or 64-page sections (known as signatures). First, however, the sheets arriving in the bookbinding works are accurately placed in stacks and are then cut to the correct size by means of a *cutting machine* (or guillotine). The sheets are then passed to the *folding machine* in which the sheets are folded halfway down their length a number of times until the correct page size for the book and the correct sequence of page numbering is obtained.

The folded signatures are placed in the receiving hoppers of the *collating machine* (or gatherer). As many hoppers are needed as there are signatures in the book and the signatures are arranged consecutively in the hoppers. From each hopper one signature at a time is deposited on a travelling belt, which then moves it along to the next hopper, where the next signature is deposited on the first, and so on. Each cycle of the machine delivers one complete gathered book.

The gathered signatures, or sections, are then ready for sewing. This operation is done on a *book sewing machine*, nowadays usually a semi-automatic or fully automatic machine. The operator places the sections over a saddle from which they are moved automatically to the sewing position or, in the fully automatic machine, merely feeds them into a hopper. For better joining the pages together, book back glueing is applied, i.e., the backs of the sewn sections are passed over rollers which put glue on them. When the glue has dried, the treatments known as "smashing" or "nipping" are applied. Nipping is pressure applied to the back only and is usually sufficient for novels, whereas larger books are subjected to smashing (all-over compression applied to the book block). Trimming the book blocks is done on a *three-knife cutting machine* that trims all three sides.

For cheaper books ("paper-backs") threadless or unsewn binding[1] is now widely used. In this system the backs of the sections are cut off, so that the book block consists of single leaves. A strip of gauze linen and glue are then applied.

After trimming, the books undergo rounding (putting the round into the back), which is done on a special machine, and backing (glueing the backbone, applying the head and tail bands[2] and the paper backbone lining).

Casing-in machines fix each book into its case (or cover) and are semi-automatic or fully automatic. The book is split by an ascending blade which moves it upwards between paste rollers. These apply adhesive to the end papers. The case, which has been treated on a forming iron to achieve correct shaping of the backbone, is then placed in position over the ascending book. From the casing-in machine the books are fed to a forming and pressing machine in which the cases are firmly bonded on by the application of pressure and heat.

The cases (covers) are made entirely by mechanised processes on casemaking machines. Some of these machines, which again are semi-automatic or fully automatic, make cases from sheets of cloth already cut to size; others have the cloth fed to them in a continuous web from a roll.

1. Called perfect binding in U.S.A.
2. Foot bands in U.S.A.

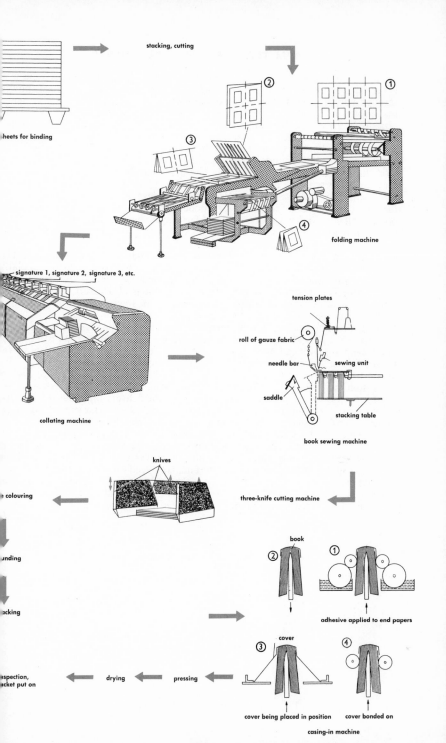

stacking, cutting

② ①

sheets for binding

③

④

folding machine

signature 1, signature 2, signature 3, etc.

tension plates

roll of gauze fabric

needle bar   sewing unit

saddle

stacking table

collating machine

book sewing machine

knives

colouring

three-knife cutting machine

book

② ①

unding

adhesive applied to end papers

acking

cover

③

④

inspection,
acket put on   drying   pressing

cover being placed in position   cover bonded on

casing-in machine

427

FARM TRACTOR AND ATTACHMENTS

The tractor is an important aid in modern farming. In most essential respects it is very similar to an automobile. A diesel engine (see page 470) transmits its power through a propeller shaft to the eight- or ten-speed gearbox (cf. page 490) and is thence transmitted to the drive wheels through the differential gear (cf. page 500). The propulsive force and therefore the tractive force (pull) developed by the tractor depends not only on the force that the engine transmits to the big rear drive wheels but also on the load on these wheels. If the axle load is too small, the wheels will slip and fail to grip the ground. To increase the load and thus press the drive wheels more firmly against the ground, ballast weights may be provided at the rear, or sometimes the tyres are filled with water instead of air. Often the attached implements drawn by the tractor are so designed as to develop an additional downward force on the rear axle of the tractor. A modern tractor is also extensively used as a power unit for driving various kinds of farm machinery and is, for this purpose, usually provided with three power take-off shafts. Two of them are mounted under the trailer coupling and rotate at 1000 r.p.m. and 540 r.p.m. respectively, power being transmitted to the attached machinery through an articulated shaft. The third power take-off shaft protrudes forward and is intended more particularly for driving an attached grass or grain cutting machine (see page 430). The speed is 1000 r.p.m. The hydraulic equipment of the tractor is also a very useful adjunct which serves not only for adjusting the positions of the towing control rods but also for hydraulic control of attached machinery.

The hydraulic system is shown schematically in Fig. 2. The pressure is generated by a hydraulic pump (e.g., a geared pump, as shown, or alternatively a piston pump or a vane pump), which forces the oil through the delivery pipe to the control valve. In the "lifting" position the slide opens the passage to the working cylinder. The piston travels slowly out of the cylinder. Through an appropriate linkage system this piston movement raises the two bottom towing control rods. If the load to be lifted is too heavy, the pressure that builds up in the delivery pipe causes the safety valve to open and thus bypass the oil to the oil supply tank. This prevents damage to the hydraulic system. In the "neutral" position on the slide closes the passage to the working cylinder, so that the piston is locked. However, since the pump continues to deliver oil, the slide simultaneously opens a passage leading the oil, via the oil filter, back to the supply tank. The oil filter is provided with a relief valve which allows the oil to flow to the tank even if the filter is clogged with dirt. In the "lowering" position the slide again opens the passage to the working cylinder. The pressure of the attached load causes the oil to flow out of this cylinder and be discharged, along with the oil delivered by the pump, via the filter to the supply tank.

(Continued)

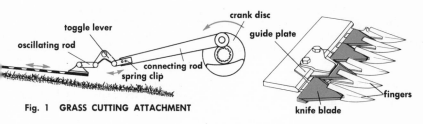

Fig. 1 GRASS CUTTING ATTACHMENT

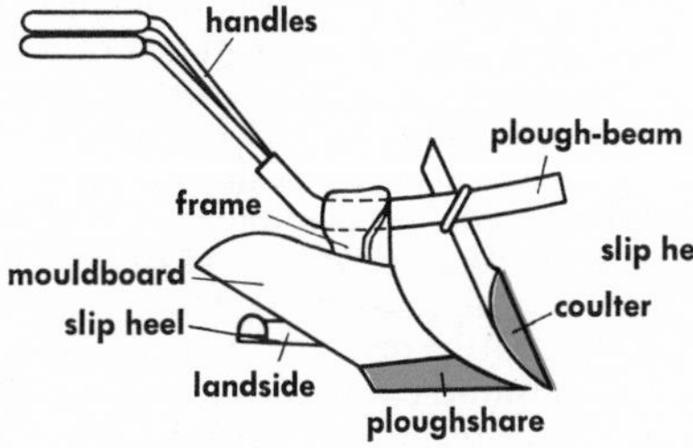

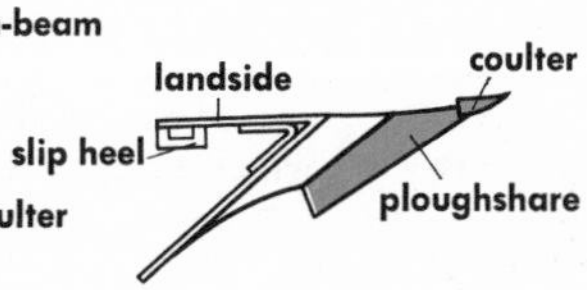

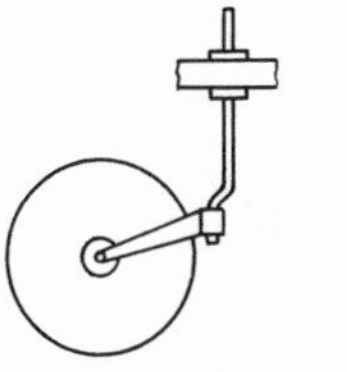

oscillating rod
toggle lever
connecting rod
spring clip
crank disc
guide plate
fingers
knife blade

handles
plough-beam
frame
mouldboard
slip heel
landside
ploughshare
coulter

landside
slip heel
coulter
ploughshare

coulter

Fig. 2c DISC COULTER

Fig. 2a PLOUGH

Fig. 2b PLOUGH (top view)

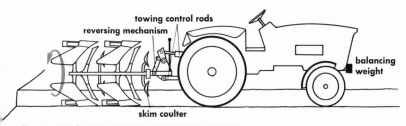

a   b

Fig. 3 OPERATION OF SKIM COULTER: (a) ploughing
without, and (b) ploughing with skim coulter

towing control rods
reversing mechanism
balancing weight
skim coulter

Fig. 4a TWO-WAY PLOUGH WITH SKIM COULTER

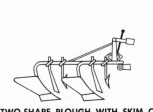

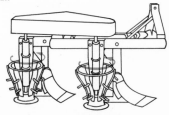

Fig. 4b TWO-SHARE PLOUGH WITH SKIM COULTER

Fig. 4c ROTARY PLOUGH

COMBINE HARVESTER AND THRESHER

The combine harvester is a combination of a grain harvesting machine and a threshing machine. The grain is cut, threshed and cleaned in one operation. The machine may be self-propelled or be towed by a tractor.

The wheatstalks are cut by an oscillating knife while the revolving reel pushes them back towards the knife and auger (feed screw). Grain flattened by wind or rain is raised by the spring prongs on the reel. The cut wheat is conveyed into the machine by the auger and reaches the threshing cylinder which rubs the grain out of the heads against a "concave". The grains of wheat, together with the chaff and short fragments of straw fall through the interstices between the bars of the concave and into the cleaning "shoe". Some of the grain is carried along with the straw, is stopped by check flaps, and is shaken out of it on shaking screens on the straw rack of the machine. The straw drops out of the back of the machine and is left in a windrow for later baling, or is baled directly by a baling attachment or press, or is scattered over the ground by a fan-like straw spreader. The grain shaken out of the straw is also delivered to the cleaning shoe. In the shoe the grain is separated from the chaff and cleaned by sieves and a blast of air. The chaff and fragments of straw are thrown out from the back of the machine. The grains of wheat fall through the sieves and into the clean-grain auger (screw conveyor) which conveys them to an elevator and on into the storage tank or into bags. Any heads of wheat which fail to go through the sieves and are thrown backwards by the air blast fall short in comparison with the lighter chaff and drop into a return auger which, via an elevator, returns them to the threshing cylinder. Correct adjustment of the air blast—by throttling the intake of the fan and by altering the setting of baffles—is important in determining the degree of cleaning of the grain and the magnitude of the grain losses that occur.

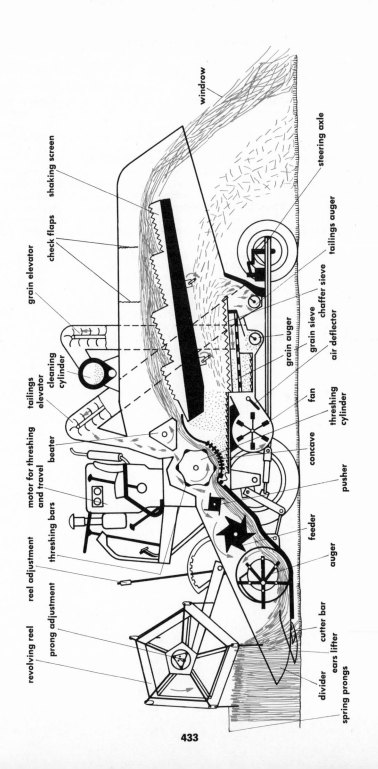

revolving reel

prong adjustment

reel adjustment

threshing bars

motor for threshing
and travel

beater

tailings
elevator

cleaning
cylinder

check flaps

grain elevator

shaking screen

divider

ears lifter

spring prongs

cutter bar

auger

feeder

pusher

concave

threshing
cylinder

fan

air deflector

chaffer sieve

grain sieve

grain auger

tailings auger

steering axle

windrow

433

BEET-HARVESTING MACHINE

The beet harvesting machine (Fig. 1) cuts off the top of the beet (this operation is called "topping"), lifts the beet out of the ground, cleans the earth off it, and delivers it to a hopper or to a wagon travelling along with the machine. Topping is performed by a topping device which may either comprise a knife (Fig. 3) or a revolving inclined disc (Fig. 4). In the former arrangement a spiked roller moves along the ground. When it travels over a beet, the topping knife is automatically set to the correct height. The cut-off beet head with the leaves is fed by the action of the spiked roller to an elevator and is discharged into a hopper (not shown) or is deposited in a windrow beside the machine (as in Fig. 2). The lifting mechanism operates on the adjacent row of beet, already dealt with by the topping device. The guide skids keep the lifting fork at the correct pre-set working depth. The fork seizes the beet below its point of greatest girth, loosens it from the ground, and passes it to the cleaning wheel which flings the beet against a surrounding cage and there removes adhering earth. The beet is then delivered to an elevator which conveys it to the beet hopper. From time to time the contents of this hopper are emptied into a wagon. This is done by means of the discharging conveyor which forms one side of the beet hopper and which can be swung down to deliver the beet into the wagon. In addition, the hopper can (by hydraulic power) be tilted about the axis $A-A$ in Fig. 1. The lifting mechanism can be swivelled by the operator, if necessary, in order to seize any beet that may be somewhat out of the row. The power for driving the beet harvesting machine is supplied through a drive shaft from the tractor that tows it. The machine may be provided with two sets of rubber beater arms to follow up the topping device. The beet can then be cut off at a somewhat higher level above ground (see Fig. 5); the short leaves that are then still left standing on the beet top are removed by the beater arms, which revolve in opposite directions.

Fig. 1

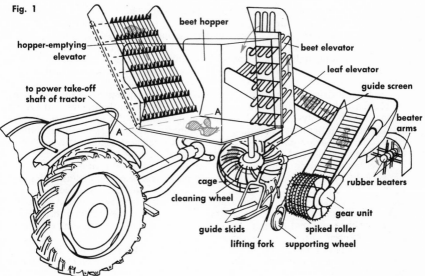

hopper-emptying elevator

beet hopper

to power take-off shaft of tractor

beet elevator

leaf elevator

guide screen

beater arms

rubber beaters

A

A

cage

cleaning wheel

gear unit

guide skids

spiked roller

lifting fork

supporting wheel

Fig. 2

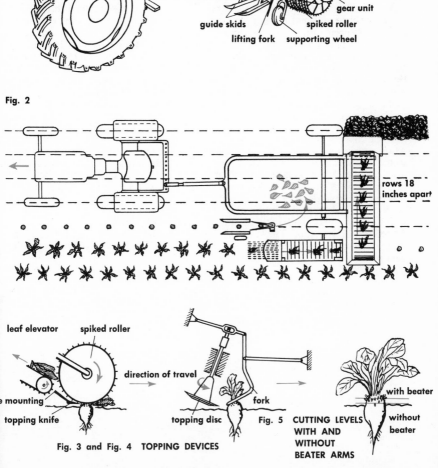

rows 18 inches apart

leaf elevator

spiked roller

direction of travel

e mounting

topping knife

topping disc

fork

Fig. 5

with beater

without beater

CUTTING LEVELS WITH AND WITHOUT BEATER ARMS

Fig. 3 and Fig. 4   TOPPING DEVICES

The pick-up baler is used to bale hay (or straw) directly from the windrow in the field. The hay is picked up by prongs and passed to the auger (feed screw) which pushes it to the feed prongs. These deliver the hay to the bale chamber on each stroke of the compressing plunger. The latter compresses the hay into compact layers; protruding stalks which are liable to cause jamming are cut off by knives. A number of layers are tied to form bales (whose length and density can be adjusted) (Fig. 1).

The baler is driven by an internal combustion engine mounted on the baler itself or, alternatively, it is driven by a power-take-off shaft from the tractor that tows it (cf. page 428). The flywheel equalises the power thrusts of the compressing plunger and carries the latter past its "dead-centre" point (i.e., when it is rammed fully home). It thus helps to achieve smoother running. As a safeguard against damage due to the possible presence of stones or pieces of wood or iron in the hay, the flywheel is driven by a shearing pin mounted on the shaft. In the event of overloading, the pin shears through, allowing the flywheel to rotate freely, without transmitting any of its stored-up energy to the plunger. When the obstruction has been removed and the shearing pin replaced by a new one, the machine is ready for operation again. Additional protective devices against overloading are provided in the form of friction clutches which develop slip and thereby shed part of the load before fracture of working parts of the machine can occur.

The bales of hay are automatically tied with wire or twine. The main functioning parts of the twine tying mechanism are illustrated in Figs. 2a–c. The successive stages of the tying operation are shown in Fig. 3. To start with, the twine is threaded through the needle (not shown) and is inserted into the mechanism as indicated in Fig. 3a. While the bale is being compressed and thrust forward by the plunger, the twine is looped round it. When the bale has reached the requisite length, the tying mechanism comes into operation (Fig. 3b). As the plunger is withdrawn, the needle raises the twine, so that the latter encircles the bale, and inserts both ends of the loop into the discs of the twine-holder, which rotate and thus securely hold the twine. At the same time, the knotter begins to turn (Fig. 3c) and, in so doing, opens its jaws so that both ends of the twine are gripped between them (Fig. 3d). The twine-holder discs meanwhile continue their rotation so that the twine attached to the needle is held in the second notch (Fig. 3e). The knotter has now completed its turning motion and its jaws have closed again. The knife swivels round and cuts the twine between the knotter and the twine-holder discs. A continuation of this swivelling movement slips the twine off the ends of the knotter jaws (Fig. 3f), the two cut-off free ends being passed through the loop. The knot has thus been formed, and the knife lever returns to its initial position. Meanwhile the needle descends, thus clearing the way for the next plunger stroke.

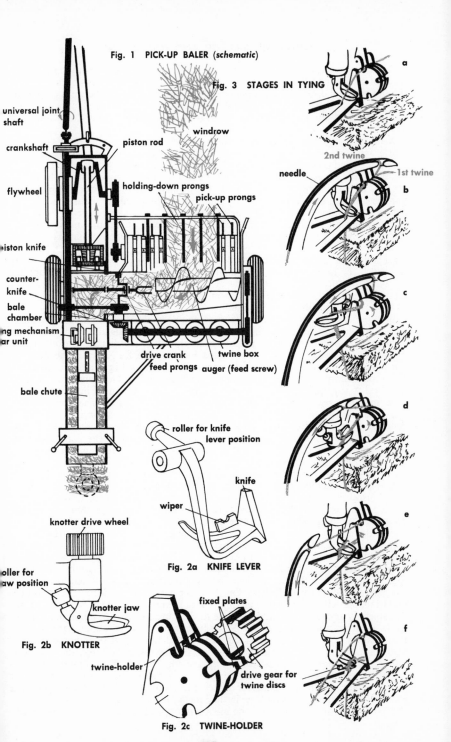

Fig. 1 PICK-UP BALER (schematic)

universal joint shaft

crankshaft

piston rod

flywheel

windrow

holding-down prongs

pick-up prongs

piston knife

counter-knife

bale chamber

ng mechanism
ar unit

drive crank
feed prongs

twine box

auger (feed screw)

bale chute

roller for knife
lever position

knife

wiper

Fig. 2a KNIFE LEVER

knotter drive wheel

oller for
aw position

knotter jaw

Fig. 2b KNOTTER

fixed plates

twine-holder

drive gear for
twine discs

Fig. 2c TWINE-HOLDER

Fig. 3 STAGES IN TYING

a

2nd twine

needle

1st twine

b

c

d

e

f

437

Radiology is the branch of medicine that deals with the use of X-rays in the diagnosis of disease and the use of X-rays, gamma rays and other forms of radiation in the treatment of disease. Thus a major distinction is to be made between diagnostic radiology and therapeutic radiology. Depending on the purposes for which they are intended, a number of different types of X-ray apparatus and X-ray tubes are available.

X-rays are short-wave electromagnetic vibrations which can penetrate solid matter (cf. page 106). They are produced when, in a vacuum, electrons are released, accelerated and then abruptly retarded. This takes place in the X-ray tube. To release electrons, the tungsten filament in the tube is heated to incandescence (white heat) by passing an electric current through it. The electrons are accelerated by a high voltage (ranging from about ten thousand to some hundreds of thousands of volts) between the anode (positive) and the cathode (negative) and impinge on the anode, whereby they are abruptly slowed down. In modern X-ray tubes the anode—usually referred to as the "target"—is often of the rotating disc type, so that the electron beam is constantly striking a different point of the anode perimeter. The X-ray tube itself is made of glass, but is enclosed in a protective casing, which is filled with oil to absorb the heat produced. The high voltage for operating the tube is supplied by a transformer (cf. page 92). The alternating current is rectified by means of rectifier tubes (or "valves") (Fig. 4) or, in the most up-to-date equipment, by means of barrier-layer rectifiers (see page 80).

Bones and internal organs into which a suitable contrast medium has been introduced appear most distinctly in X-ray photographs. Various arrangements of the X-ray apparatus and other equipment are employed for the diagnostic examination or therapeutic treatment of various organs. For example, for X-raying the stomach, intestines, heart and lungs an installation as illustrated in Fig. 1 may be used. For X-ray photographs of small appendages, such as teeth, fingers and toes, a small spherical X-ray apparatus, in which the transformer is mounted integral with the tube, may be used. In modern radiology the exposures can be timed by means of multiplier phototubes (see page 118) (phototiming). X-ray films consist of an acetate cellulose base coated on both sides with an emulsion of silver halide and gelatin. In addition, so-called intensifying screens are used, whereby the contrast of the image can be enhanced. The clinical usefulness of the X-ray examination of certain internal organs (e.g., stomach and intestines) depends on the use of a contrast medium—usually barium sulphate—which is introduced into the organs by various means and makes them show up distinctly in the photograph. Examination by direct visual inspection of the "live" X-ray image on a fluorescent screen, as distinct from photography, is called fluoroscopy. It is not so widely used as photography, as the photographic image shows a greater amount of detail.

For therapeutic purposes—e.g., the treatment of tumours, etc.—the X-rays employed are in some cases generated at much higher voltages (over 4 million volts). Also the rays emitted by radium and artificial radioisotopes, as well as electrons, neutrons and other high-speed particles (for instance, produced by a betatron, Fig. 1), are used in radiotherapy. The tissues of the body are unaffected by radiation that merely passes through them. On the other hand, if a particular tissue absorbs radiation, the cells of that tissue are injured. In the treatment of cancer, for example, the object is to cause maximum damage to the cancer cells with minimum damage to the adjacent normal tissue. The X-ray tube may be moved about, so that, while its radiation remains focused on the deep-seated tumour, it does not constantly pass through the same intermediate tissues. In diagnostic radiology the technique known as tomography, consisting in taking "layerwise" X-ray photographs, is sometimes employed. This is based on the use of rays varying in penetrating power and thus photographing the interior of the body at different depths, thus enabling the exact location of an infection (e.g., in the lungs) to be ascertained. For this purpose the X-ray tube and the film may be moved in opposite directions in curved paths (Fig. 2).

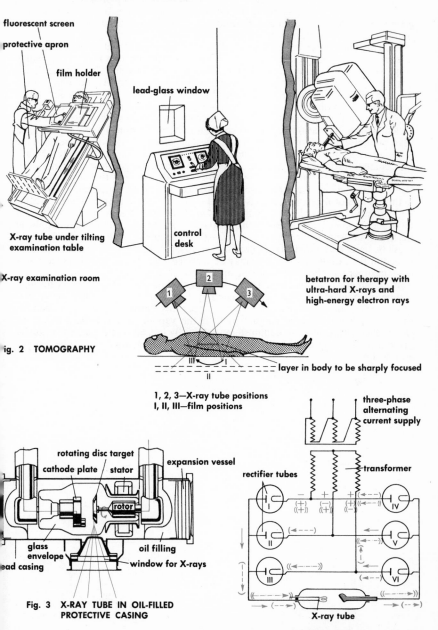

Fig. 1   EQUIPMENT FOR DIAGNOSTIC AND
THERAPEUTIC RADIOLOGY

fluorescent screen

protective apron

film holder

lead-glass window

X-ray tube under tilting
examination table

control
desk

X-ray examination room

betatron for therapy with
ultra-hard X-rays and
high-energy electron rays

Fig. 2   TOMOGRAPHY

layer in body to be sharply focused

1, 2, 3—X-ray tube positions
I, II, III—film positions

rotating disc target

cathode plate   stator

expansion vessel

rotor

glass
envelope

oil filling

lead casing

window for X-rays

Fig. 3   X-RAY TUBE IN OIL-FILLED
PROTECTIVE CASING

three-phase
alternating
current supply

rectifier tubes

transformer

X-ray tube

Fig. 4   CIRCUIT DIAGRAM OF A
SIX-TUBE INSTALLATION

439

Anaesthesia means loss of feeling or sensation, so that no pain is felt. In surgery this result is obtained by using an anaesthetic. A distinction is to be made between general anaesthesia (total unconsciousness) and local anaesthesia (only one area of the body is deprived of sensation).

General anaesthesia can be produced in various ways, including intravenous injection with thiopental sodium or other agents. The older and still most widely employed method, however, is by inhalation of a gaseous or volatile anaesthetic. Early anaesthetics were ether, nitrous oxide, and chloroform. At the present time a range of other agents are available. In modern surgery, especially for major operations, a combination of two or more anaesthetic agents may be employed, the gaseous or volatile anaesthetic being administered by means of a special apparatus, which enables the various agents to be accurately proportioned and controlled, so as to minimise the risk of overdosing. A typical anaesthetic apparatus is shown in the accompanying illustration. The underlying principle is that the patient's breath is circulated through the apparatus, in a closed circuit, the gas flow rate being controlled by means of valves and flow meters. The advantage of the closed circuit is that loss of body heat and moisture is prevented. Besides, a considerable economy in the amount of anaesthetic used is effected. Also included in the circuit are a breathing bag (which shows the breathing movements and their frequency and which can be squeezed in order to intensify the inhalation), an inlet attachment for supplying fresh air, an evaporator for volatile anaesthetic agents (e.g., diethyl ether) should these be used, and a cartridge containing an absorbent for the carbon dioxide contained in the exhaled air. This air may be recycled through the breathing circuit or may, in other varieties of anaesthetic apparatus, be discharged from the apparatus. The anaesthetic is administered to the patient either through a face mask or through a tube introduced into the trachea (windpipe), the latter method now being considered safer and more effective. In the apparatus illustrated, the anaesthetic is nitrous oxide gas used in conjuction with the vapour of a volatile anaesthetic. Before having this mixture administered to him by inhalation the patient is usually given a preliminary anaesthetic by intravenous administration, i.e., in the form of an injection.

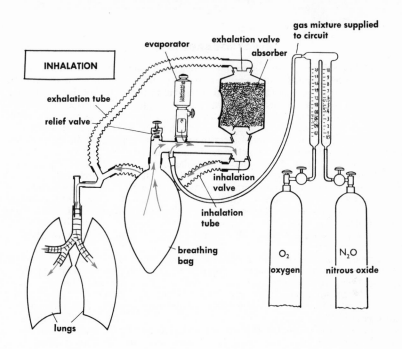

INHALATION

gas mixture supplied
to circuit

exhalation valve

evaporator

absorber

exhalation tube

relief valve

inhalation
valve

inhalation
tube

breathing
bag

O₂
oxygen

N₂O
nitrous oxide

lungs

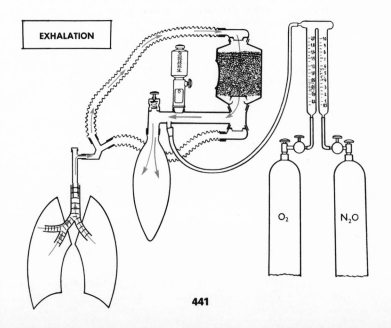

EXHALATION

O₂

N₂O

441

ELECTROCARDIOGRAPH

Every muscle can perform only one movement, namely, the shortening of its fibres by contraction. This also applies to the heart muscle. Each action of a muscle is associated with electric currents which change in the course of the contraction and which, after passing through the various tissues, reach the surface of the body. There they can be picked up by electrodes and be recorded with the aid of a suitable apparatus, the electrocardiograph. The record thus obtained on a chart is called an electrocardiogram. In its original form the instrument was based on the principle of the string galvanometer, which was invented in 1903 by Einthoven, a Dutch physiologist (Fig. 1). A silver-plated quartz filament is brought into a magnet field. The electric currents produced by the contraction of the heart muscle and picked up by the electrodes applied to the patient's body are passed through this filament, which undergoes a deflection whose direction and magnitude will depend on the direction and strength of the current. This movement of the filament is projected, by means of an optical system, as a spot of light on to a moving paper strip chart which is coated with a light-sensitive compound. When no current is flowing through the filament, a straight line is traced on the chart. Currents associated with the muscular action of the heart cause the spot of light to oscillate and thus trace a typical curve on the light-sensitive chart. Any irregularities in the functioning of the heart appear as corresponding irregularities in the curve which enable the heart specialist to diagnose the disease or other cause of these deviations from the normal pattern.

The string galvanometer instrument has now been superseded by the electronic cardiograph which operated with amplifier tubes (Fig. 2). The currents from the body electrodes enter the amplifier at E_1 and E_2. The greatly amplified currents are fed to a mirror galvanometer. The movements of the mirror cause a reflected spot of light to oscillate on the light-sensitive chart (film) and thus trace the required curve.

The electrodes are affixed to the human body at certain definite points (Fig. 3): left arm and right arm (1), left leg and right arm (2), left leg and left arm (3). These were the points originally selected by Einthoven. Nowadays other points of attachment to the limbs and also to the wall of the chest are used. Modern cardiograph records do not record these various curves separately, in successive operations, but record them simultaneously. The normal electrocardiogram presents the appearance shown in Fig. 4. The portion of the curve between P and Q corresponds to the contraction of the auricles, while the portion between Q and T corresponds to the contraction of the ventricles of the heart.

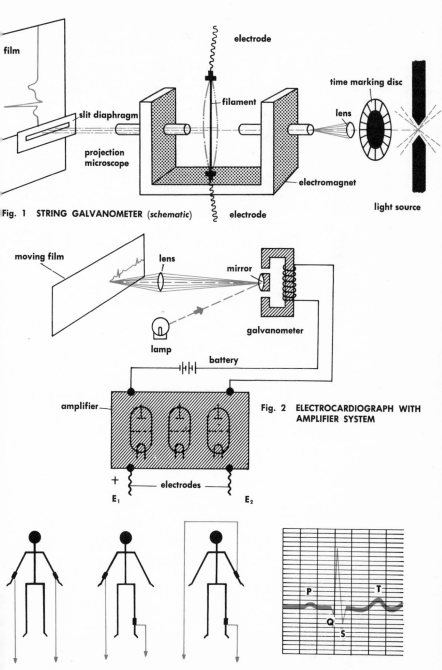

film

electrode

time marking disc

slit diaphragm

filament

lens

projection microscope

electromagnet

light source

Fig. 1   STRING GALVANOMETER (*schematic*)   **electrode**

moving film

lens

mirror

galvanometer

lamp

battery

amplifier

Fig. 2   ELECTROCARDIOGRAPH WITH AMPLIFIER SYSTEM

$+$

electrodes

E_1 E_2

P   **T**

Q
S

Fig. 3   POINTS OF ATTACHMENT FOR ELECTRODES
(*according to Einthoven*)

Fig. 4   NORMAL ELECTROCARDIOGRAM

In cases where paralysis or other causes impair normal breathing, the machine popularly known as the iron lung can help the patient to breathe and thus remain alive indefinitely or until his recovery. In the iron lung an excess pressure (in relation to the atmospheric air pressure) alternates rhythmically with a reduced pressure. When the pressure surrounding the patient's body is reduced, his chest expands, so that air streams into his lungs. Then when the pressure is increased, the air is automatically expelled from the lungs.

In the machine illustrated (Type E 52 manufactured by the German firm of Dräger) the patient lies on a foam-rubber-cushioned bed, with his head protruding out of the end of the machine and reclining on an adjustable head-rest. At the other end is a likewise adjustable foot-rest. In the chamber under the bed is a movable intermediate diaphragm which is moved up and down by the drive mechanism (powered by electricity) and thus performs a bellows function. As the chamber is airtight, this alternate increase and decrease of its volume produces the reduced pressure and excess that enables the patient to breathe in and out. In the event of a power cut, a warning signal is sounded. The iron lung can then be operated by hand. The rate of rise and fall of this intermediate diaphragm determines the breathing frequency. For washing or examining the patient the cover of the machine can be swung open. The patient's head is then temporarily enclosed in a plastic dome in which the air pressure is alternately raised and lowered, so that he can continue to breathe.

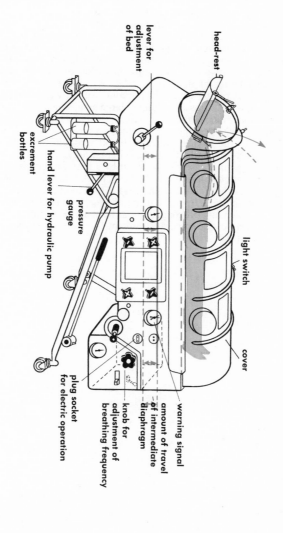

head-rest

lever for
adjustment
of bed

excrement
bottles

hand lever for hydraulic pump

pressure
gauge

light switch

cover

warning signal

amount of travel
of intermediate
diaphragm

knob for
adjustment of
breathing frequency

plug socket
for electric operation

Surgery of the heart usually involves opening the heart muscle. For operations of short duration it is possible to apply hypothermy (deep cooling) and thus temporarily stopping the blood circulation altogether. However, for major operations it is necessary to maintain the circulation, and this is achieved by means of the heart-lung machine. This has the twofold function of keeping the replacement blood in circulation by means of a pumping system and of enriching with fresh oxygen the blood of low oxygen content coming from the patient's body. The system described here is the one used at Heidelberg University Hospital and elsewhere.

The venous blood, before it enters the right auricle of the heart, is diverted out of the vena cava and passed into plastic tubes (a). This blood, which has already circulated through the body and consequently has a low oxygen content, is circulated through an artificial lung (b). In a horizontal glass cylinder partly filled with blood a number of steel discs rotate, which thus become wetted with blood. The blood on the surface of these discs forms a thin film of large area, which is exposed to a stream of oxygen in the upper part of the glass cylinder. The red blood cells are thus able to absorb oxygen in much the same way in which they do this in the human lung. The pump 1 now passes the oxygen-saturated blood through a heat controller and a filter and then back to the patient's arterial circulation. Losses of blood occurring in the course of the operation are compensated by a blood reservoir. A second pump (pump 2) extracts venous blood from the heart itself, this being blood reaching the heart through veins other than the vena cava. This blood is defoamed and likewise passed to the artificial lung. Before starting, the machine is filled with three or four litres of blood to which an anti-coagulant has been added so that it cannot congeal. All the internal parts of the apparatus (except the steel discs) are silicone-treated to make them unwettable.

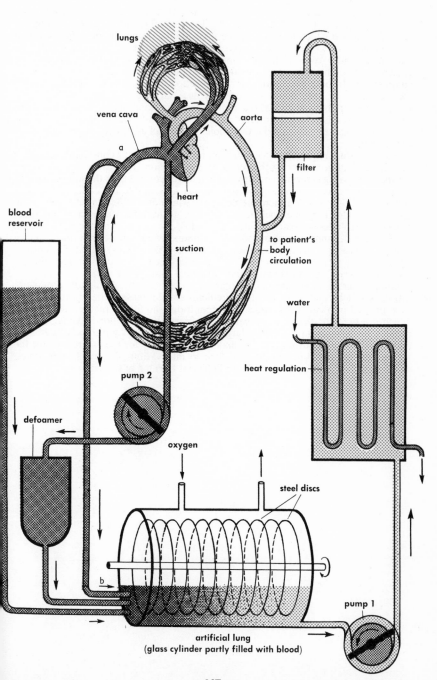

lungs

vena cava

aorta

a

heart

filter

blood
reservoir

suction

to patient's
body
circulation

water

heat regulation

pump 2

defoamer

oxygen

steel discs

b

pump 1

artificial lung
(glass cylinder partly filled with blood)

GUNPOWDER

Gunpowder is an explosive which has a relatively low detonation velocity. Its action is propellant rather than shattering. The general term "propellant" is applied to any explosive which can suitably be used for the propelling of projectiles fired from guns or of rockets. These explosives consist either of intimate mixtures of substances which react with one another and release a considerable amount of energy while doing this, or of chemical compounds which release energy on decomposition. In both cases, however, the reaction does not take place at ordinary temperatures: ignition of the explosive is necessary, i.e., the reaction has to be initiated by supplying energy at one point. Once the reaction has thus been started, the energy that is released initiates the reaction at adjacent points. This "chain reaction" can spread throughout the whole quantity of explosive in a small fraction of a second.

The significant requirement for a suitable propellant is that a considerable increase in volume shall occur during the course of the reaction. The reaction products are for the most part gases which occupy a much larger volume than the solid explosive. If the reaction takes place in a confined space (as, for example, in a cartridge fired in a rifle), a very high pressure therefore develops, which drives the projectile out of the barrel. The oldest known propellant is, of course, ordinary black powder (gunpowder). When this explodes, the reaction forms about 45% gases (nitrogen, carbon monoxide, carbon dioxide) and 55% vaporised salts. A pound of gunpowder will thus produce about 5 cubic feet of gas and about 300 kilocalories (1200 B.T.U.) of heat. The bottom left-hand diagram shows how much gas (the large circle) is evolved from the explosion of a small quantity of powder (represented by the black dot).

Gunpowder is a mixture of granular ingredients, namely, sulphur, potassium nitrate (saltpetre) and charcoal. The ingredients are ground separately or two by two, then pressed into cakes in a moistened condition, and finally reduced to granules which are used for the filling of cartridges, fireworks, fuses (for blasting, etc.). In modern fire-arms gunpowder has largely been superseded by nitrocellulose-based and other smokeless explosives. To make these suitable for use as propellants, the nitrates are dissolved in solvents and formed into various shapes (threads, tubes, small plates, etc.) which assist rapid and efficient burning of the explosive.

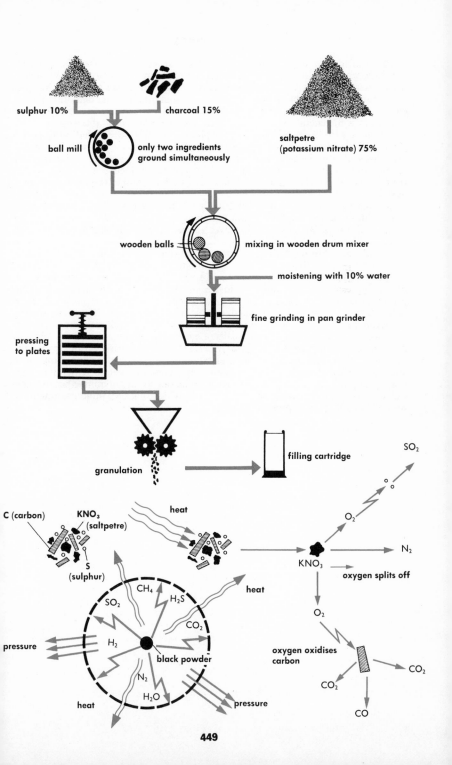

sulphur 10%

charcoal 15%

ball mill

only two ingredients ground simultaneously

saltpetre (potassium nitrate) 75%

wooden balls

mixing in wooden drum mixer

moistening with 10% water

fine grinding in pan grinder

pressing to plates

granulation

filling cartridge

SO_2

O_2

N_2

heat

C (carbon)

KNO_3 (saltpetre)

S (sulphur)

KNO_3

oxygen splits off

O_2

oxygen oxidises carbon

CO_2

CO_2

CO

heat

CH_4

SO_2

H_2S

heat

CO_2

pressure

H_2

black powder

N_2

H_2O

heat

pressure

449

EXPLOSIVES

The explosives more particularly considered here are of the "brisant" or "shattering" type which explode on heating as a result of a blow, or friction, or ignition and which then develop a very rapid and shattering action. These explosives are used more particularly for blasting in quarrying, mining, tunnelling, demolition work, etc., i.e., in cases where large masses of solid material have to be broken up quickly and cheaply. In general they are too violent and therefore unsuitable as propellants.

By varying the composition of the explosive, its "brisance" (shattering power) can be adjusted to suit the particular purpose for which it is to be used. The various explosives differ in the amount of gas that is produced per pound of explosive, in the amount of heat liberated per pound, in the detonation velocity, in the pressure that the hot gases exert upon their immediate surroundings, and in the shattering power developed.

For instance, one pound of blasting gelatine (nitroglycerine with about 8% nitrocellulose added) exploding at a temperature of over 4700° C produces about 680 kilocalories (2700 B.T.U.) of heat, over 9 cubic feet of gas is formed, and a pressure of about 13,000 atm (190,000 lb./in.^{2}) is developed as the explosion takes place in an enclosed space. Although the amounts of heat and gas liberated in the explosion are not very much than twice those produced in the explosion of one pound of gunpowder, which is a much slower explosive (see page 448), the shattering power of blasting gelatine (and similar explosives) is very much greater than that of gunpowder, this being due mainly to the greater suddenness of the explosion reaction.

Dynamite as originally invented by Nobel consisted of 75% nitroglycerine (glycerol trinitrate, a yellow liquid) compounded with 25% kieselguhr (a diatomaceous earth consisting of the tiny shells of microscopic marine creatures). The term "dynamite" is nowadays used in a wider sense to comprise various explosives consisting of nitroglycol, ammonium nitrate, saltpetre, aromatic nitro compounds, and wood meal. By adding up to about 40% common salt to dynamites, their shattering power is so reduced that they become safe for use in mining because they can then be exploded without attendant risk of igniting any mine gas (methane) or coal dust that may be present in the air.

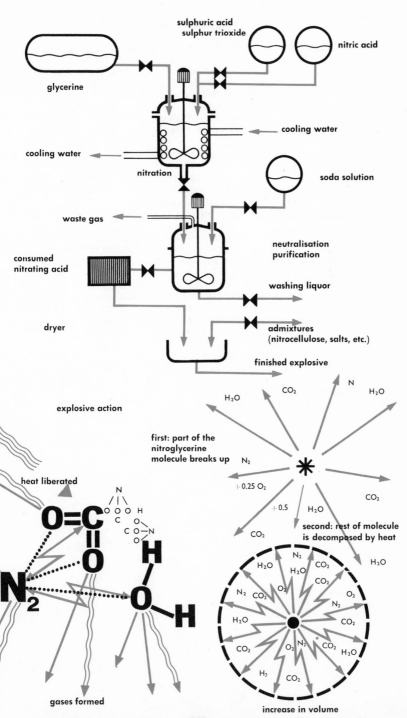

sulphuric acid
sulphur trioxide

nitric acid

glycerine

cooling water

cooling water

nitration

soda solution

waste gas

neutralisation
purification

consumed
nitrating acid

washing liquor

dryer

admixtures
(nitrocellulose, salts, etc.)

finished explosive

explosive action

CO_2 N

H_2O H_2O

first: part of the
nitroglycerine
molecule breaks up

N_2

heat liberated

$+ 0.25\ O_2$

$+ 0.5$ H_2O

CO_2

CO_2

second: rest of molecule
is decomposed by heat

O=C=O

N_2

H
O
H

N_2 CO_2 H_2O
H_2O H_2O CO_2
N_2 CO_2 CO_2
O_2 O_2
N_2 CO_2
H_2O CO_2 H_2O
CO_2 O_2 N_2 CO_2 H_2O
H_2 CO_2 N_2

gases formed

increase in volume

451

DETONATORS

To be safe and efficient in use, explosives should explode only when they are required to do so. Under ordinary conditions of handling they should be stable, insensitive to pressure, impact and heat, and even (in some cases) withstand the effect of sparks or a small flame without exploding. On the other hand, they should be highly effective on being exploded. Alfred Nobel, in 1867, found that a "safe" (insensitive) explosive can be efficiently exploded by detonating it—initiating its explosion—with a small quantity of a highly sensitive, and in itself therefore dangerous, explosive. Such explosives (called "priming explosives" or "primers") explode easily on being subjected to a blow, heating or friction.

There are various types of detonating devices depending on the purpose for which they are employed : for blasting, for military use (in cartridges, artillery ammunition, bombs, etc.). Detonation can be effected by heat (fire), by an electric spark, by impact, etc. An ordinary small-arms cartridge is usually of the centre-fire type, i.e., the metal cartridge case containing the propellant is provided at the centre of its base with primer cap containing a small quantity of priming which is exploded by a blow from the hammer or firing pin. For ordinary blasting as used in quarrying, mining, tunnelling, etc. the main explosive is detonated by means of a detonator (or blasting cap). This consists of a small metal tube containing a small quantity of priming explosive, e.g., mercury fulminate or lead azide, together with a larger quantity of a secondary explosive such as trinitrotoluene (T.N.T.). The detonator may be designed for electric detonation, for which purpose it is provided with a filament in the priming. Alternatively, a detonator may be ignited by a slow-burning fuse (generally called "safety fuse") inserted into one end of the detonator or by so-called detonating cord or fuse, which burns at a very much higher speed and is particularly useful in cases where two or more charges have to be detonated more or less simultaneously or in accurately timed rapid succession. The cord consists of a plastic sheath enclosing a core of fast-burning explosive (the burning rate is about 20,000 ft./sec., whereas the ordinary safety fuse burns at only about 2 ft./sec.) and must itself be ignited by a detonator. Modern artillery shells are sometimes fitted with relatively elaborate fuse and detonation equipment designed to ignite the charge by impact and/or after a certain predetermined length of time (time fuse).

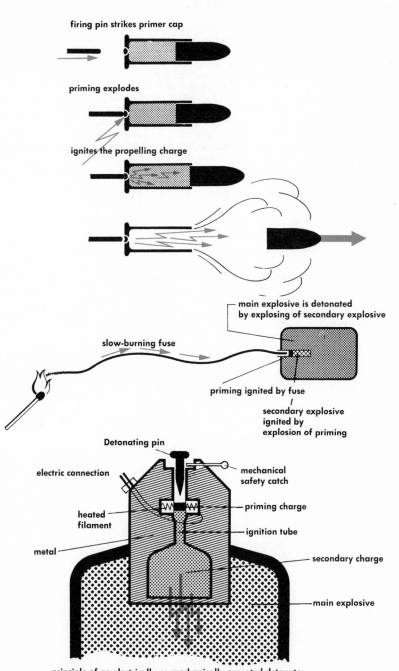

firing pin strikes primer cap

priming explodes

ignites the propelling charge

main explosive is detonated
by explosing of secondary explosive

slow-burning fuse

priming ignited by fuse

secondary explosive
ignited by
explosion of priming

Detonating pin

electric connection

mechanical
safety catch

heated
filament

priming charge

ignition tube

metal

secondary charge

main explosive

principle of an electrically or mechanically operated detonator

AUTOMATIC RIFLE

An automatic weapon can fire a number of rounds in quick succession, all the functions of firing and reloading being performed by the weapon itself: firing the cartridge, withdrawing the bolt, ejecting the spent cartridge case, cocking the hammer, forcing the bolt forward, and inserting a fresh cartridge into the chamber ready to fire. The energy for performing these functions is provided by the pressure of the gas produced by the firing of the cartridges (gas-operated weapons) or by the recoil of the weapon. Well-known gas-operated rifles are, for example, the Garand rifle, which was widely used by the United States forces in World War II, and the more recent FN rifle, of Belgian origin, which was adopted by the British army in 1954.

The rifle illustrated in Fig. 1, on the other hand, is a recoil-operated weapon—designated as the G3—and designed to fire the NATO standard 7.62 mm calibre cartridge. Its operating principle is shown in Figs. 2 and 3. To start with, the weapon is loaded, cocked and ready for firing. When the trigger is pulled, the cocked hammer is released and strikes the firing pin whereby the cartridge is fired. The gases produced by the explosion propel the bullet out of the barrel. At the same time the gases thrust the cartridge case and, with it, the breech block backwards. The gas pressure is so great that the sealing rollers are forced against the sloped shoulders of the bolt. The latter slides backwards, and the rollers are withdrawn into the breech block until the bolt is disengaged. The rear shoulders of the bolt strike the bolt carrier and thrust it backwards. In its backward movement the extractor of the breech block extracts the cartridge case (which is ejected by the ejector) and cocks the hammer. When the breech block has completed its backward motion, it is returned forward by the action of a spring. In the course of this return movement the end face of the breech block strips the top cartridge from the magazine and thrusts it into a chamber ready to fire. The extractor engages with the corresponding groove at the base of the cartridge. The sealing rollers are pushed outwards by the sloped shoulders of the bolt until they engage with the recesses in the breech wall. The firing cycle has thus been completed and the rifle is ready to fire the next round. The rifle can be operated either automatically—i.e., so long as the trigger is kept pulled, the weapon continues to fire until the magazine is empty—or as a semi-automatic (self-loading) rifle, a separate squeeze of the trigger being necessary to fire each shot.

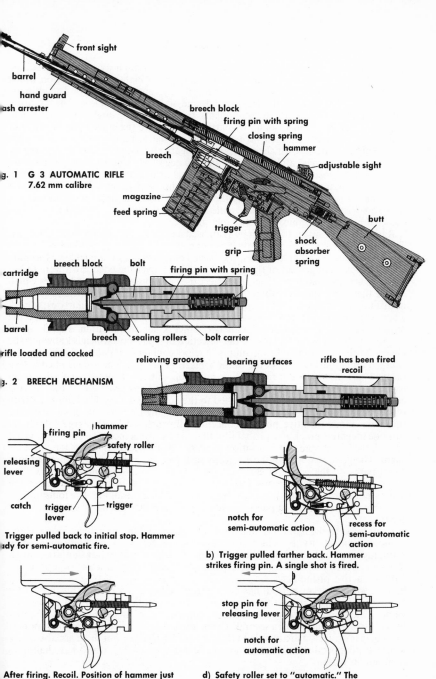

front sight

barrel

hand guard

flash arrester

breech block

firing pin with spring

closing spring

hammer

breech

adjustable sight

Fig. 1 G 3 AUTOMATIC RIFLE
7.62 mm calibre

magazine

feed spring

trigger

grip

butt

shock
absorber
spring

cartridge

breech block   bolt

firing pin with spring

barrel

breech   sealing rollers   bolt carrier

rifle loaded and cocked

Fig. 2 BREECH MECHANISM

relieving grooves   bearing surfaces   rifle has been fired
recoil

firing pin   hammer

safety roller

releasing
lever

catch   trigger
lever   trigger

Trigger pulled back to initial stop. Hammer
ready for semi-automatic fire.

notch for
semi-automatic action

recess for
semi-automatic
action

b) Trigger pulled farther back. Hammer
strikes firing pin. A single shot is fired.

After firing. Recoil. Position of hammer just
before engagement of catch. Trigger lever acts
only with semi-automatic fire.

Fig. 3 TRIGGER MECHANISM

stop pin for
releasing lever

notch for
automatic action

d) Safety roller set to "automatic." The
trigger has to be pulled back a longer
distance. Trigger lever does not act now.
Hammer is released by means of releasing
lever instead.

RADIOACTIVITY

Radioactivity is the spontaneous disintegration of certain heavy elements (radium, uranium and others) accompanied by the emission of high-energy radiation which consists of three kinds of rays: alpha-rays, beta-rays, and gamma-rays. The ultimate end product of radioactive disintegration is one of the isotopes of lead. The radiation can be split up into its three components by passing it through a magnetic field (Fig. 1). Alpha-rays consist of alpha-particles, which are the nuclei of helium atoms which are positively charged on account of having lost two electrons. Beta-rays consist of beta-particles, which are electrons (negatively charged elementary particles). The positively charged alpha-particles and the negatively charged beta-particles are deflected in opposite directions by the magnetic field. Gamma-rays are an electromagnetic radiation of very short wavelength and high penetrating power (about 10^{-12} cm); they are not deflected by the magnetic field. All three kinds of radiation cause blackening of a photographic plate and ionisation of gases, so that they can be detected by photographic or electric methods.

Radioactive disintegration can be visualised as follows (according to G. Gamow): The nucleus of the radioactive atom is conceived as a kind of pot-like receptacle (Fig. 2) containing alpha-particles, the basic components of the nucleus. Normally these particles can get out of the pot only by flying over the edge. However, alpha-particles are not merely particles of matter; they also possess wave properties which enable them (in limited numbers) to penetrate the wall of the pot. Particles escaping in this way constitute the alpha-radiation. Beta-radiation can be similarly explained, whereas gamma-radiation is associated with changes in energy states inside the atomic nucleus in conjunction with two other kinds of radiation. Fig. 3 shows diagrammatically an apparatus for the detection of alpha-rays which is known as the Geiger-Müller counting tube (or simply "Geiger counter"). It detects the electrically charged alpha-particles by virtue of the ionisation of a gas. The tube is filled with a rarefied gas in which the radioactive radiation initiates a process called impact ionisation whereby a voltage impulse of short duration is produced in the external circuit. This impulse is amplified and fed to the counting device. The high sensitivity of the Geiger counter is due to the geometrical configuration of its electrodes. The thin wire anode (positive pole) is concentrically enclosed by the large cylindrical cathode (negative pole). The probability that the electrons (negative particles) which are released in the impact ionisation process will immediately fly to the anode is slight. The great majority of the electrons rush past the anode and are directed into spiral paths by the powerful electric field of force around the anode. In travelling along these paths the electrons initiate a large number of further impact ionisation processes before they end their flight by finally reaching the anode. The ionisation in the tube gives rise to the impulse by causing a momentary discharge of electricity in the tube.

In addition to the natural radioactivity of radium and uranium there is artificially induced radioactivity, by which is understood a state of radioactivity induced in normally non-radioactive elements by means of artificial atomic transmutation. Such elements are now obtained as waste products from nuclear reactors (see page 54). All radioactive phenomena die away after a certain length of time. The so-called half-life (or half-decay period) has been introduced as a criterion of this. It denotes the period in which the activity of a radioactive substance falls to half its original value. It varies considerably for different substances and ranges from a vast number of years to a tiny fraction of a second. The half-lives of the radioactive fission products of a nuclear explosion are mainly in the range of 10–60 days, but there are also much longer-lasting products such as strontium 90 and caesium 137, which have half-lives of about 30 years.

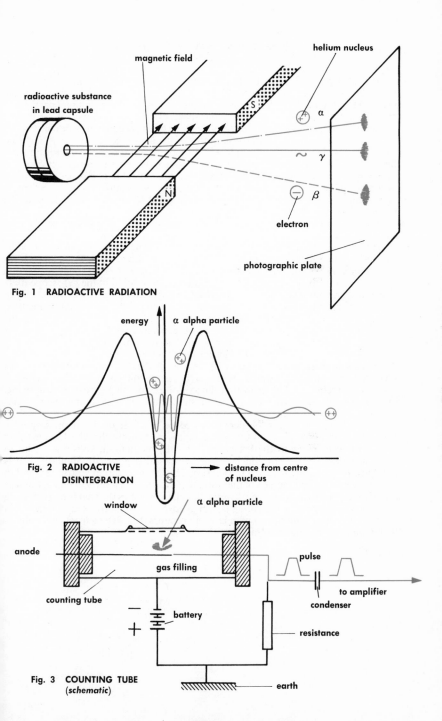

helium nucleus

magnetic field

radioactive substance
in lead capsule

S

α+ α

~ γ

− β

electron

N

photographic plate

Fig. 1 RADIOACTIVE RADIATION

energy

α alpha particle

++

Fig. 2 RADIOACTIVE
DISINTEGRATION

distance from centre
of nucleus

window

α alpha particle

anode

pulse

gas filling

to amplifier

counting tube

condenser

battery

−

+

resistance

Fig. 3 COUNTING TUBE
(schematic)

earth

GYROSCOPES AND SPINNING TOPS

In a general sense the term "gyroscope" can be applied to any solid object rotating about a fixed point. For practical purposes a gyroscope consists of an axially symmetrical rotating body. It has a certain rotational momentum ("spin") which depends on the mass of the gyroscope, the square of the distance of the individual particles of mass to the axis of rotation, and on the speed of rotation (number of r.p.m.). To increase the rotational momentum, the gyroscope can advantageously be constructed as a disc with a thickened rim, so that most of its mass is concentrated as far from the axis as possible. The significant feature of a gyroscope is that the momentum and the rotational axis preserve their direction so long as no external forces act upon the gyroscope. Because of this tendency to keep the direction of its axis constant in space, the gyroscope can suitably be used for the stabilisation of movements. A convenient form of gyroscope (spinning top), in which the point of rotation coincides with the centre of gravity, is illustrated in Fig. 1a.

In the diagrams, forces are represented by black arrows, rotational momentum (N) and turning moments (M) by red arrows. The red arrows actually represent the so-called vector of the momentum or the turning moment; it can be conceived as the axis about which the momentum or moment rotates, the rotation being seen clockwise on looking towards the tip of the arrow. In the case of the rotational momentum (spin) the vector obviously coincides with the axis of rotation of the gyroscope itself. Now the behaviour of a gyroscope conforms to the following law: when a rotational moment is applied to a spinning gyroscope, the vector of the rotational momentum (and therefore the axis of the gyroscope) will tend to move in the direction of the vector of that applied moment. This can be explained with reference to Fig. 1b, where a gyroscope is shown tilted over to the left. Its own weight thus produces an overturning moment, which is in fact an applied moment in the sense envisaged above. This moment (M) has a vector represented by the thick red arrow, which must be conceived as pointing towards the viewer, i.e., perpendicular to the plane of tilting. It is in the direction of this arrow that the axis of the spinning gyroscope will swing. The axis thus swings round and round in the manner familiar to any one who has observed a child's spinning top.

The gyroscope effect can be demonstrated on a wheel mounted on a spindle. When it is spun round (Fig. 2a) and an attempt is made to tilt the wheel to the left — i.e., a turning moment to the left is applied — the momentum vector will tend to move in the direction of the thick red arrow (pointing forward). Similarly, if it is attempted to swivel the wheel to the left (Fig. 2b), the momentum vector will tend to swing upwards (so that the axis of the wheel tends to move in a vertical plane, whereas in Fig. 2a it tends to move in a horizontal plane). In ballistics the spin imparted to the projectile from a gun by the rifling (spiral grooves) of the barrel keeps it steady in flight. Some ships are equipped with large gyroscopes (Fig. 3) which act as stabilisers by damping the rolling movements.

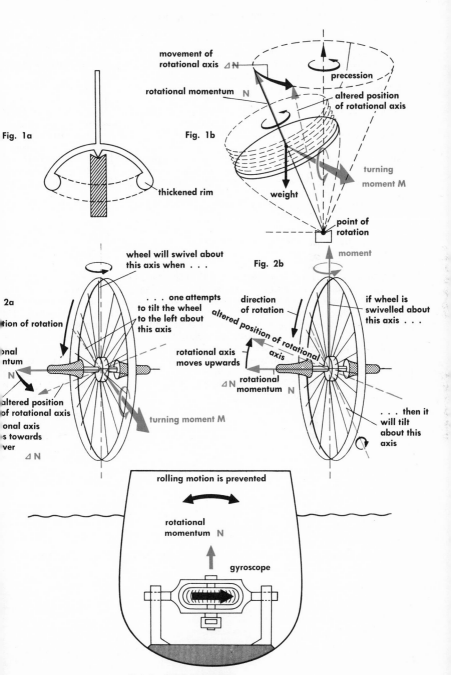

Fig. 1a

Fig. 1b

movement of rotational axis △N

rotational momentum N

thickened rim

precession

altered position of rotational axis

turning moment M

weight

point of rotation

moment

2a

tion of rotation

onal ntum

N

altered position of rotational axis

onal axis es towards ver

△N

wheel will swivel about this axis when . . .

. . . one attempts to tilt the wheel to the left about this axis

rotational axis moves upwards

△N rotational momentum N

turning moment M

Fig. 2b

direction of rotation

altered position of rotational axis

if wheel is swivelled about this axis . . .

. . . then it will tilt about this axis

rolling motion is prevented

rotational momentum N

gyroscope

Fig. 3   GYRO-STABILISER

459

The freewheeling hub performs three functions: transmission of the driving power via the chain to the rear wheel in the course of normal forward motion of the pedals; freewheeling when the pedals are at rest; braking when the pedal motion is reversed.

The first two functions are performed by bringing a series of drive rollers into contact with a rotating cylinder and by releasing them respectively (Fig. 1). These rollers are disposed inside a guide ring. The drive wheel is fixed to a special ratchet which is so designed that when the pedals move forward (Fig. 1a) the sloped faces on the ratchet bear against the rollers so that the latter are jammed between the ratchet and the hub sleeve. In this way the power is transmitted through the rollers to the sleeve, which is fixed to the rear wheel of the bicycle and thus drives it round. When freewheeling, the ratchet remains stationary while the rear wheel continues to rotate (Fig. 1b). The rollers are then in the depressions formed in the surface of the ratchet and are no longer jammed against the hub sleeve. The latter is thus able to rotate freely in relation to the ratchet.

When the cyclist "back-pedals", the brake comes into action. The braking mechanism functions as follows. Two more or less conical components are slid into a slotted cylinder (the brake sleeve), causing this to expand, so that it is forced against the inside of the hub sleeve of the wheel, thus developing the braking action (Fig. 2). The inside of the roller guide ring is provided with two claws (Fig. 3) which hold the braking cone when back-pedalling takes place. The brake cone thus remains stationary, slides into the brake sleeve and, at the same time, pushes this sleeve on to the lever cone. It is this action that causes the expansion of the brake sleeve from both ends. The lever cone is provided with a lever (externally visible) secured to the frame of the bicycle and thus develops the reaction to the braking force applied. To do this, the lever cone must be prevented from rotating, and for this purpose it is provided with two flat surfaces (Fig. 5). Between each of these surfaces and the grooved inner surface of the brake sleeve is a roller, held in position by a spring. When the pedals are moved backwards, one end of each flat surface presses the roller into a groove, with the result that the cone is immovably gripped. The thrust exerted by the claws on the roller guide ring then forces the brake-sleeve over the lever cone. Fig. 4 shows a section through the hub.

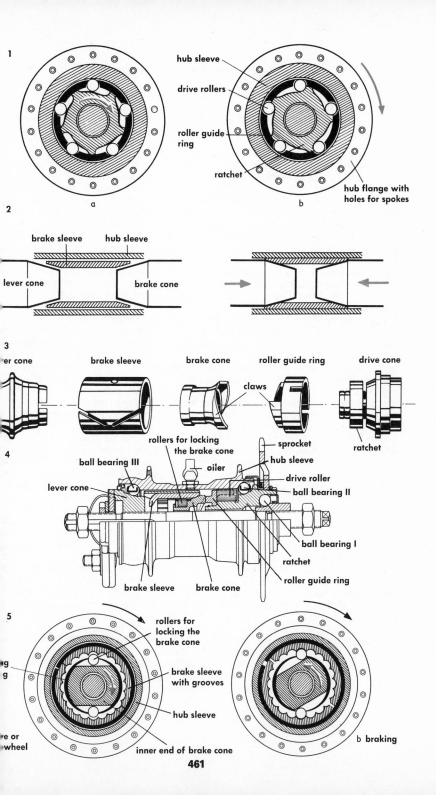

1

hub sleeve

drive rollers

roller guide ring

ratchet

hub flange with holes for spokes

a

b

2

brake sleeve   hub sleeve

lever cone

brake cone

3

er cone   brake sleeve   brake cone   roller guide ring   drive cone

claws

ratchet

4

rollers for locking the brake cone

ball bearing III

sprocket

oiler

hub sleeve

lever cone

drive roller

ball bearing II

ball bearing I

ratchet

brake sleeve   brake cone

roller guide ring

5

rollers for locking the brake cone

brake sleeve with grooves

hub sleeve

g

inner end of brake cone

e or wheel

b braking

461

There are two different systems of changing the gear ratios on a bicycle: the variable gear hub and the derailleur system.

The *variable gear hub* embodies a planetary (or epicyclic) gear set (Fig. 3) comprising a central cog-wheel, called the sun wheel, surrounded by three other cog-wheels called planet wheels. The latter engage with the sun wheel and also with internal gear teeth on a gear ring (annulus). The principle is illustrated in Figs. 1a and 1b, with reference to a system comprising only one planet wheel (the additional planet wheels in no way alter the principle). If the sun wheel is held stationary and the line connecting the centre of this wheel to the centre of the planet wheel is swung through a quarter circle, the planet wheel will rotate along the circumference of the sun wheel (with whose teeth it meshes) and will, in so doing, drive the annulus through a distance of more than a quarter circle (so that point A of the annulus thus arrives at A' in Fig. 1b). The annulus thus rotates faster than the connecting line. Conversely, if the annulus is rotated, the connecting line will rotate at a lower number of revolutions than the annulus. The actual transmission ratio will, of course, depend on the relative dimensions and the numbers of teeth on all the gears involved. If the planet wheel is locked so that it is prevented from rotating about its own axis and the sun wheel is allowed to rotate about its axis, then the connecting line and the annulus will revolve at the same speed.

Fig. 2 shows a section through a three-speed variable gear hub. This hub has a planetary gear set for low gear (hill climbing gear) and another for high gear; both these gear sets engage with the same annulus. Gear-changing is effected by means of a gear control chain worked by the control wire from a lever mounted on the handlebars. The chain shifts the sun wheels of the two planetary gear sets along the hub spindle. When the sun wheel (which is additionally provided with internal teeth, Fig. 3) is slid over corresponding teeth on the stationary hub spindle and thus immovably locked in relation to the planet wheels, the transmission ratios envisaged above (i.e., the step-up ratio and the step-down ratio respectively) can operate. For "normal" gear, the internal teeth of the sun wheel are disengaged so that this wheel is now free to rotate on the hub spindle; at the same time the outer teeth of the sun wheel (which remain engaged with those of the planet wheels) are engaged with internal teeth of the cage which carries the three planet wheels (transmission ratio 1:1). The sprocket, driven by the chain from the pedals, is fixed to the planet wheel cage (the outer drive element) of one of the planetary gear sets. When the gear set shown on the right in Fig. 2 is engaged, the power is transmitted from the driven cage through the faster-rotating annulus to the left-hand gear set — which is now locked — and thus to the planet wheel cage (the inner drive element) of this left-hand gear set. The inner drive element is provided with a worm thread on which the drive cone runs. When this cone is moved over to the right, it carries along with it the surrounding cone of the drive sleeve. The latter is fixed to the hub and thus to the rear wheel of the bicycle. In its left-hand position the drive cone performs a braking function (see page 460). This is the situation for high gear. In low gear (for hill climbing), the gear set on the left is operative, while the right-hand set is locked instead. In "normal" gear both planetary gear sets are locked, and the drive is thus directly transmitted from the sprocket to the rear wheel of the bicycle.

A *derailleur gear* system comprises a freewheel with two or more sprockets, a mechanism that alters the line of the chain and causes it to jump from one sprocket to another, and a spring-operated jockey pulley or tension pinion to take up or let out the slack in the chain. In this way various gear ratios can be selected. Although the principle is the same in all derailleur gears, the mechanisms produced by the various manufacturers differ in detail. A typical derailleur is illustrated in Fig. 4.

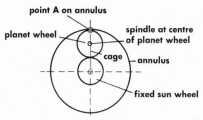

point A on annulus

planet wheel

spindle at centre of planet wheel

cage — annulus

fixed sun wheel

Fig. 1a PLANETARY GEAR SET
WITH FIXED SUN WHEEL

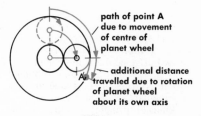

path of point A
due to movement
of centre of
planet wheel

additional distance
travelled due to rotation
of planet wheel
about its own axis

Fig. 1b POSITION AFTER A QUARTER TURN

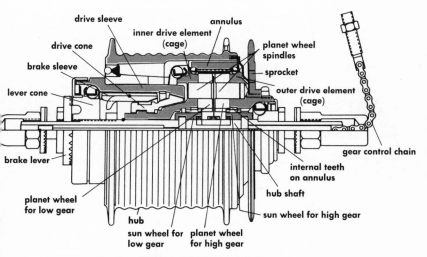

drive sleeve

inner drive element
(cage)

annulus

drive cone

planet wheel
spindles

brake sleeve

sprocket

outer drive element
(cage)

lever cone

brake lever

gear control chain

planet wheel
for low gear

internal teeth
on annulus

hub shaft

sun wheel for high gear

hub

sun wheel for   planet wheel
low gear   for high gear

Fig. 2 SECTION THROUGH A THREE-SPEED
VARIABLE-GEAR HUB
Setting: "normal" gear

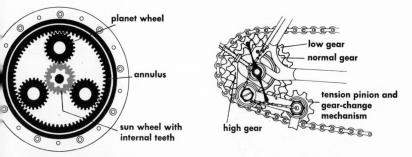

planet wheel

annulus

sun wheel with
internal teeth

3 PLANETARY GEAR SYSTEM
OF THREE-SPEED
VARIABLE-GEAR HUB

low gear

normal gear

tension pinion and
gear-change
mechanism

high gear

Fig. 4 DERAILLEUR GEAR

MOTOR CYCLE

Two-wheeled vehicles powered by internal combustion engines comprise motor cycles, motor scooters and mopeds.[1] These are all similar in principle.

The motor cycle comprises four main sections: the frame, the engine with gearbox and drive components (chain or drive shaft), the road wheels, and the petrol[2] tank (Fig. 1). The frame is of tubular pressed steel construction. The most important components of the frame are the springs for absorbing the jolts caused by the irregularities of the road surface or other obstacles encountered. There are various kinds of springing for motor cycles: (1) parallelogram suspension (Fig. 2), which is a somewhat clumsy system because the whole mass of the front wheel and fork participates in the oscillation; (2) telescopic front forks in combination with short swinging arm (Fig. 3), in which arrangement the oscillating mass is reduced; (3) telescopic front forks in combination with long swinging arm (Fig. 4): more resilient than the foregoing, but involving great oscillating mass (the same principle is applied to the rear wheel suspension in Fig. 3). The telescopic suspension system used in types (2) and (3) has the advantage that it can undergo considerable compression in conjunction with only small oscillating masses. By these or similar means it is possible to achieve very efficient suspension conditions, so that the saddle springing can be dispensed with on modern motor cycles. A foam-rubber seating cushion is usually sufficient, especially on racing machines. Sectional views of typical front and rear suspension systems are shown in Figs. 4 and 5. Spring elements in combination with oil-filled cylinders provide the necessary shock-absorbing function (see page 508).

Two-stroke and four-stroke engines are used as power units for motor cycles. The power is transmitted to the rear wheel through the gearbox (Fig. 6) and thence through sprockets and chains or through a drive shaft. Transmission through a shaft is shown in Fig. 5, the shaft being neatly accommodated in the swinging arm of the rear suspension. Motor cycles and mopeds have wire-spoke wheels, whereas scooters generally have solid wheels like those of a car.

1. "Moped" is an abbreviation of "motor-assisted pedal cycle".
2. Gasoline in U.S.A.

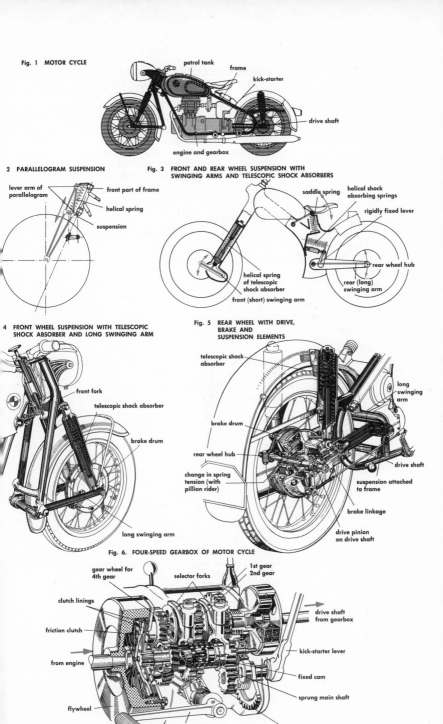

Fig. 1 MOTOR CYCLE

petrol tank
frame
kick-starter
drive shaft
engine and gearbox

2 PARALLELOGRAM SUSPENSION

lever arm of parallelogram
front part of frame
helical spring
suspension

Fig. 3 FRONT AND REAR WHEEL SUSPENSION WITH SWINGING ARMS AND TELESCOPIC SHOCK ABSORBERS

saddle spring
helical shock absorbing springs
rigidly fixed lever
rear wheel hub
rear (long) swinging arm
helical spring of telescopic shock absorber
front (short) swinging arm

4 FRONT WHEEL SUSPENSION WITH TELESCOPIC SHOCK ABSORBER AND LONG SWINGING ARM

front fork
telescopic shock absorber
brake drum
long swinging arm

Fig. 5 REAR WHEEL WITH DRIVE, BRAKE AND SUSPENSION ELEMENTS

telescopic shock absorber
long swinging arm
brake drum
rear wheel hub
drive shaft
change in spring tension (with pillion rider)
suspension attached to frame
brake linkage
drive pinion on drive shaft

Fig. 6. FOUR-SPEED GEARBOX OF MOTOR CYCLE

gear wheel for 4th gear
selector forks
1st gear
2nd gear
clutch linings
drive shaft from gearbox
friction clutch
kick-starter lever
from engine
fixed cam
sprung main shaft
flywheel
gear-change pedal
drive pinion of kick-starter

465

INTERNAL COMBUSTION ENGINE:
FOUR-STROKE PETROL (GASOLINE) ENGINE

The petrol engine, like the diesel engine (page 470), is an internal combustion engine. The thermal energy which is released when the fuel is burned is converted into mechanical energy. The petrol engine differs from the diesel in that the liquid fuel (i.e., the petrol) is mixed with air—usually in a device called a carburettor (see page 478)—to form a combustible mixture, which is compressed in the cylinder and finally ignited by an electric spark produced between the electrodes of a sparking plug (see page 484). The gases which are formed in the cylinder by the combustion of the petrol-and-air mixture expand and thrust the piston downwards. Acting through the connecting rod, the piston imparts a rotary motion to the crankshaft. The spent burned gases must then be removed from the cylinder and be replaced by fresh petrol-and-air mixture, so that a fresh cycle can begin. The energy needed for effecting this change in the contents of the cylinder is provided by the flywheel, which stores up some of the mechanical energy released by the combustion that takes place in the cylinder. The additional energy developed by the engine can be taken off at the end of the crankshaft.

With internal combustion engines—diesel as well as petrol engines—a distinction must be made between four-stroke and two-stroke operation. To perform a full cycle of operations (changing the contents of the cylinder and effecting the combustion) the four-stroke engine requires four, and the two-stroke engine requires two strokes of the piston.

Four-stroke engine:

1st stroke: induction stroke: while the inlet valve is open, the descending piston draws fresh petrol-and-air mixture into the cylinder.

2nd stroke: compression stroke: While the valves are closed, the rising piston compresses the mixture to a pressure of about 7–8 atm.; the mixture is then ignited by the sparking plug.

3rd stroke: power stroke: While the valves are closed, the pressure of the gases of combustion forces the piston downwards.

4th stroke: exhaust stroke: the exhaust valve is open and the rising piston discharges the spent gases from the cylinder.

Since power is developed during one stroke only, the single-cylinder four-stroke engine has a low degree of uniformity, i.e., the rotation of the crankshaft is subject to considerable accelerations and decelerations during a cycle. More uniform—that is to say, smoother—running is obtained with multi-cylinder engines because the "cranks" of the crankshaft are staggered in relation to one another (Fig. 3), so that the various cylinders do not develop their power strokes simultaneously, but successively (and sometimes in an overlapping sequence). Depending on the cylinder arrangement, various types of engine are to be distinguished: in-line engine (Fig. 3), horizontally opposed engine (Fig. 4), vee engine (Fig. 5), and radial engine (Fig. 6).

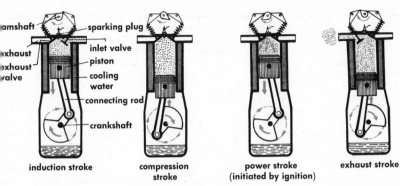

camshaft — sparking plug
exhaust — inlet valve
exhaust valve — piston
— cooling water
— connecting rod
— crankshaft

induction stroke | compression stroke | power stroke (initiated by ignition) | exhaust stroke

Fig. 1   OPERATING PRINCIPLE OF A FOUR-STROKE ENGINE

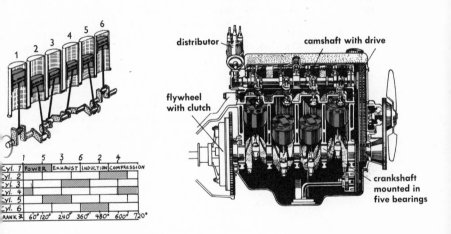

Cyl. 1	POWER	EXHAUST	INDUCTION	COMPRESSION
Cyl. 2				
Cyl. 3				
Cyl. 4				
Cyl. 5				
Cyl. 6				
CRANK	60° 120°	240°	360° 480°	600° 720°

distributor · camshaft with drive
flywheel with clutch
crankshaft mounted in five bearings

Fig. 2   WORKING SEQUENCE OF A SIX-CYLINDER IN-LINE ENGINE

Fig. 3   SECTION THROUGH A FOUR-CYLINDER IN-LINE ENGINE

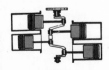

Fig. 4   HORIZONTALLY OPPOSED ENGINE

Fig. 5   VEE ENGINE

Fig. 6   RADIAL ENGINE

In this type of engine the piston periodically covers and uncovers openings—known as ports—in the cylinder wall (the two-stroke engine is seldom equipped with valves).

The operation of the two-stroke engine will be explained with reference to Fig. 7, which represents such an engine of the type provided with a scavenging fan. At the start of the first stroke, the piston is in its highest position. When the compressed petrol-and-air over the piston is ignited, the latter is thrust downwards and, in so doing, releases the exhaust port. The burned gases in the cylinder, which are still under high pressure, can thus escape through this port. When the piston descends further, its upper edge releases the inlet port, which admits fresh petrol-and-air mixture (delivered by the fan) into the cylinder, so that the remaining burned gases are flushed out. When the piston rises again (2nd stroke), all the ports are closed for a time, and during this period the petrol-and-air mixture is compressed, so that a fresh cycle can commence.

The crankcase-scavenged two-stroke engine (Fig. 8) has no scavenging fan. Instead, the crankcase is hermetically sealed, so that it can function as a pump in conjunction with the piston. When the piston ascends, a partial vacuum is produced in the crankcase, until the lower edge of the piston releases the inlet port and thus opens the way to the fresh petrol-and-air mixture into the crankcase. When the piston descends, the mixture in the crankcase is compressed a little so that, as soon as the top of the piston releases the transfer port and overflow duct (connecting the crankcase to the cylinder), it can enter the cylinder. Meanwhile, what happens above the piston is the same as in the fan-scavenged engine.

In the latter type of two-stroke engine the fan adds to the cost. However, as the overflow duct between the cylinder and crankcase is eliminated, the crankshaft can be provided with forced-oil lubrication without involving a risk that the oil in the crankcase can find its way into the cylinder. In the cheaper crankcase-scavenged engine the lubricating oil is mixed with the petrol ("petroil" lubrication) or is, alternatively, supplied to the points of lubrication dropwise by small lubricating oil pumps. The oil which enters the crankcase is liable to be carried through the overflow duct and transfer port into the cylinder, whence it passes through the exhaust port and into the exhaust system, where it may manifest itself as blue smoke in the exhaust.

Fig. 7 FAN-SCAVENGED TWO-STROKE ENGINE

A = admission port (*inlet port*)   E = exhaust port

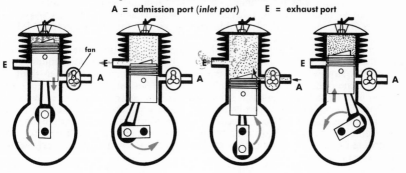

after ignition,
power is developed
as the piston descends

when the exhaust
port E is open,
the burned gas
escapes

when the admission port A
is open, the fan forces
fresh petrol-and-air
mixture into the cylinder

when the piston rises and
E and A are closed,
compression takes place

Fig. 8 CRANKCASE-SCAVENGED TWO-STROKE ENGINE

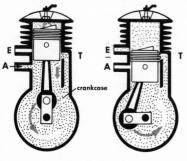 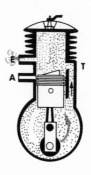 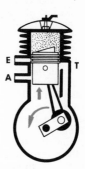

above the piston

after ignition,
power is developed
as the piston descends

when the
exhaust port E is
open, the burned
gas escapes

when the piston rises and
E and T are closed,
compression takes place

below the piston

when the admission port A
is open, fresh petrol-
and-air mixture flows into
the crankcase

when E and T (transfer
port) are closed, petrol-
and-air mixture in the
crankcase is compressed

when the transfer port T
is open, petrol-and-air
mixture flows from the
crankcase (where it has
been compressed) into
the cylinder

after A and T are closed,
further rising of the piston
produces suction in the
crankcase

The combustion processes in the petrol[1] engine and the diesel engine differ in the following significant features: in the petrol engine (see page 466) the petrol-and-air mixture is drawn into the cylinder, compressed (compression ratio ranging from 4:1 to 10:1), and ignited by a spark. In the diesel engine, on the other hand, air alone is drawn into the cylinder and is compressed to a much higher ratio (14:1 to 25:1) than in the petrol engine. As a result of this high compression the air is heated to a temperature of 700°–900° C. Only then is a certain quantity of diesel fuel injected into the cylinder. Beeause of the prevailing high temperature, the fuel ignites spontaneously. However, combustion does not take place immediately when the fuel particles enter the combustion chamber, but after an interval of about $\frac{1}{1000}$ sec. This is because the fuel droplets first have to mix intimately with the air in the combustion chamber and must then be heated up and vaporised before they can burn. The time that elapses between injection and ignition is called the ignition lag. On injection of the fuel, it is broken up by the nozzle into smaller and larger droplets, according to a certain pattern. The smaller droplets occur more particularly in the edge zone of the injected fuel spray (Fig. 1) and are the first to ignite. Next, the larger droplets in the interior of the spray are ignited. Fuel injection continues after the first flame has formed (main combustion). If some of the diesel fuel is incompletely burned in this combustion process, or if it accumulates and then burns suddenly and violently at the next main combustion, the engine is said to be "knocking". In the petrol engine, on the other hand, the petrol-and-air mixture first ignites in the vicinity of the sparking[2] plug (Fig. 2). The heat given off by the burning fuel particles causes the adjacent particles to ignite, so that a flame front, starting from the sparking plug, spreads through the combustion chamber. As a result of thermal radiation and rise in pressure, but also in consequence of the presence of "hot pockets" in the combustion chamber, a fresh ignition and flame front formation may occur in the still unburned mixture not yet reached by the initial flame front. Thus, in certain circumstances, the entire unburned mixture may undergo sudden and violent combustion, causing "knocking" of the petrol engine.

Diesel engines are designed to operate on the four-stroke or the two-stroke principle, just like petrol engines. In respect of their design features diesel engines differ more particularly in the manner in which the fuel and air are brought together and ignited. In a diesel engine with direct injection (or solid injection) the fuel is injected directly into the cylinder (or sometimes into a spherical combustion chamber formed in the piston) (Fig. 3). The injection nozzle must be so designed that its spray pervades all the air in the combustion chamber, so that complete combustion of the fuel can take place. In a diesel engine provided with a swirl chamber (Fig. 4) the air is forced into this chamber by the piston and thereby acquires a rapid swirling motion, so that mixing with the fuel is promoted. What mainly occurs in the precombustion chamber of a diesel engine as shown in Figs. 5 and 6 is mixing of the fuel and air and preliminary combustion of the mixture. As a result of the rise in pressure during this precombustion, the incompletely burned fuel-and-gas mixture flows at high velocity from the precombustion chamber into the cylinder, where it can undergo complete combustion with the air there.

1. Gasoline in U.S.A.
2. Spark plug in U.S.A.

Fig. 1 COMBUSTION PROCESS
IN A DIESEL ENGINE

Fig. 2 COMBUSTION PROCESS
IN A PETROL ENGINE

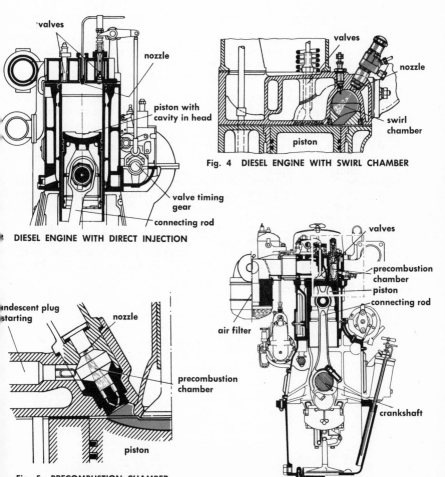

DIESEL ENGINE WITH DIRECT INJECTION

Fig. 4 DIESEL ENGINE WITH SWIRL CHAMBER

Fig. 5 PRECOMBUSTION CHAMBER
OF A DIESEL ENGINE

Fig. 6 DIESEL ENGINE WITH PRECOMBUSTION CHAMBER

ROTARY PISTON ENGINE (WANKEL ENGINE)

The rotary piston engine is an internal combustion engine which operates on the same general principle as the conventional petrol[1] engine (see page 466). In the latter, however, a rotary motion is produced by an oscillating piston and connecting rod (Fig. 1), whereas the rotary piston engine produces this motion by means of a rotating "piston". This means that there are no oscillating masses which have to be alternately accelerated and retarded, as occurs when an ordinary piston moves to and fro. Consequently, the forces of inertia associated with the oscillatory motion are obviated in the rotary piston engine. As a result, higher speeds of rotation are possible. The edges of the rotating piston open and close ports in the cylinder wall, so that the piston itself controls the "breathing" of the engine, without the aid of valves. The triangular piston with convex sides rotates in a housing whose internal cross-section presents an oval shape slightly constricted in the middle (epitrochoid). When the piston rotates, the seals mounted at its three corners continuously sweep along the wall of the housing. The three enclosed spaces formed between the piston and the wall successively increase and decrease in size with each revolution. These variations in the spaces are utilised for drawing in the fuel-and-air mixture, for compressing this mixture, for combustion, and for discharging the burned gases, so that the full four-stroke working cycle is performed (Fig. 2). The four strokes for the chamber between the corners A and C are as follows:

1st stroke: the rotary piston uncovers the inlet port: the mixture of fuel and air flows in;

2nd stroke: the mixture is compressed;

3rd stroke: the compressed mixture is ignited by the sparking plug, burns and drives the piston (power stroke);

4th stroke: the exhaust gas is discharged through the outlet port.

In the other two combustion chambers the same processes occur, but with a displacement of 120° in each case. In the course of one piston rotation there are therefore three ignitions. As appears from Fig. 2, the rotary piston engine has only two moving parts: the piston and the driving shaft. The piston is provided with concentric internal gearing which engages with a gear wheel which is concentric with the engine shaft but is firmly connected to the housing. The ratio of the number of teeth of the internal gearing and gear wheel is 3:2.

One of the major problems in the construction of the rotary piston engine is the sealing of the three chambers in relation to one another. Intercommunication between these chambers would be detrimental to the proper functioning of the engine. This problem has been solved by means of a system of sealing strips (Fig. 4).

1. Gasoline in U.S.A.

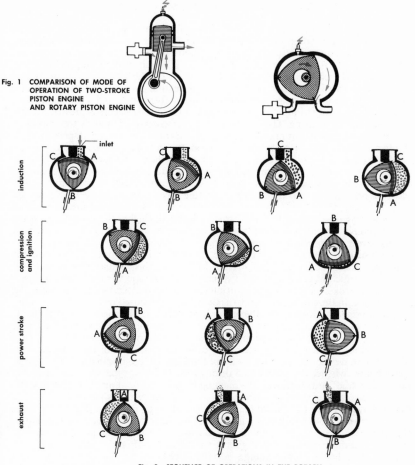

Fig. 1 COMPARISON OF MODE OF
OPERATION OF TWO-STROKE
PISTON ENGINE
AND ROTARY PISTON ENGINE

induction

inlet

compression
and ignition

power stroke

exhaust

Fig. 2 SEQUENCE OF OPERATIONS IN THE ROTARY
PISTON ENGINE
(shown for one combustion chamber)

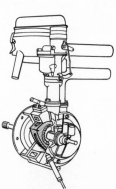

Fig. 3 SECTION THROUGH A
ROTARY PISTON ENGINE

Fig. 4 ROTARY PISTON

Fig. 5 PISTON EDGE SEAL

In a diesel engine (see page 470) the fuel-and-air mixture is formed within the cylinder itself, after compression by the piston. The fuel is injected into the highly compressed hot air and burns. The fuel injection pump has to provide the requisite high pressure (80–300 atm. = 1175–4400 lb./in.^{2}), which must be higher than the pressure developed in the cylinder at the instant of injection, and ensure that a certain quantity of fuel is injected into the combustion chamber at the correct time and with the desired velocity. The injection nozzle distributes and atomises the fuel (Fig. 1). It is mounted in the nozzle holder, and the nozzle needle is pressed against the valve seat by a spring. The needle has a larger cross-section at its top part than at the bottom. The pump pressure acts upon the transition surface (taper) between the two cross-sections (Fig. 1b), so that, when the spring pressure is overcome, the needle is raised some distance and the fuel is injected into the combustion chamber through the aperture thus formed. The nozzle holder is provided with a screw by means of which the spring pressure and therefore the injection pressure (i.e., the pressure needed to overcome the counteracting force exerted by the spring) can be varied. The nozzle holder is connected to the injection pump by a delivery pipe. The length of this pipe, and indeed its diameter and wall thickness, affect the pressure distribution in the pipe and thus also affect the injection and the combustion process.

Like every reciprocating pump (see page 24) the injection pump comprises a piston, a suction valve and a delivery valve. In addition, it is provided with a device for regulating the quantity of fuel delivered. In general, this regulation is effected by keeping the suction valve open for a certain length of time while the piston is performing its stroke. As a result, a proportion of the delivered quantity is returned to the suction pipe. In Bosch pumps (Fig. 3) the delivery rate is varied by rotating the piston. The compression chamber over the piston is connected to the space below the chamber of the piston by a longitudinal groove or hole. So long as the surface shown in red in Fig. 4 covers the opening on the right, the pump delivers fuel; when the opening is uncovered, however, delivery ceases because then the rest of the fuel, which is displaced above the piston, can flow away through the longitudinal groove into the space below, whence it is discharged through the overflow pipe. On rotation of the piston, the "red" area will cover the opening for a longer or shorter time, so that the delivery rate is varied. This adjustment by rotating the piston is performed by hand (through the agency of a toothed rack) or by a centrifugal governor (Fig. 5).

In order to achieve a rapid drop in pressure in the delivery pipe from the pump to the nozzle, and thus to ensure immediate closure of the latter, the pressure valves of Bosch injection pumps are fitted with a special device (Fig. 6). On completion of delivery, the relief piston first plunges into the valve hole and closes the delivery pipe. Then the taper of the valve body is lowered on to a seat. As a result, the volume available to the fuel in the delivery pipe undergoes an increase equal to the volume of the relief piston, and the delivery pipe is quickly relieved of pressure. Dribbling and the resultant carbonisation (coking) of the nozzle are thereby obviated.

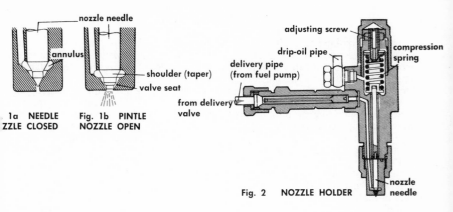

Fig. 1a NEEDLE NOZZLE CLOSED

Fig. 1b PINTLE NOZZLE OPEN

Fig. 2 NOZZLE HOLDER

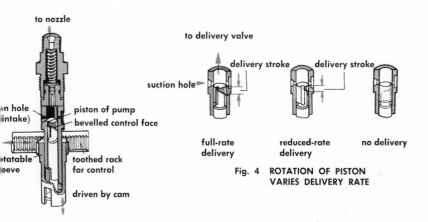

FUEL INJECTION PUMP ELEMENT

full-rate delivery

reduced-rate delivery

no delivery

Fig. 4 ROTATION OF PISTON VARIES DELIVERY RATE

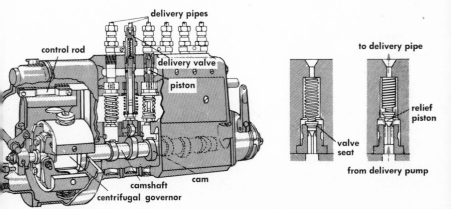

Fig. 5 INJECTION PUMP (cut-away view)

Fig. 6 PRESSURE VALVE WITH RELIEF PISTON

475

STARTERS

Internal combustion engines are generally started by rotating the flywheel until the engine fires and continues to run on its own power. The flywheel is usually rotated by a starter motor fed with current from the battery. Petrol[1] engines have to be started at a speed of 50–60 r.p.m.; diesel engines require about 100 r.p.m. The shaft of the starter is provided with a pinion (a small gear wheel) which, on commencement of the starting operation, is shifted forward until it engages with the toothed rim on the flywheel. The driving motor of the starter then rotates the flywheel. When the engine has started up, the starter pinion is disengaged from the flywheel and retracted. The various types of starter which are in present-day use differ mainly in the manner in which engagement and disengagement is effected.

Pinion shift starter (Figs. 1 and 2): When the starter button (inside the car) is actuated, the connection between the battery and the solenoid switch is established. A powerful magnetic field is set up in the magnetic coil of this switch, so that the armature of the switch is pulled forward such a distance that the tilting bridge closes the contact I, with the result that the auxiliary coil and the holding coil are energised. This causes the armature to be drawn, slowly rotating, into the magnetic field of the auxiliary coil and to engage with the toothed rim of the flywheel.

As a result of this movement the release lever is freed and closes the contact II on the tilting bridge (Fig. 1b). The main coil is now energised, the armature rotates, and the engine is turned. When the starter button is released, the current ceases to flow through the armature, and the latter is pulled back, and thus disengaged from the flywheel, by the return spring.

Inertia gear drive starter (Bendix type starter) (Figs. 3 and 4): In this type of starter the pinion can be shifted along the armature shaft on a quick screw thread. When the starter button is actuated, the armature of the solenoid switch is attracted and the pinion is pushed forward, while it rotates, by the engaging lever. In the second stage the solenoid switch closes, the current ceases to flow through the draw-in coil, the armature of the starter begins to rotate and screws the pinion completely forward until it engages with the gear rim on the flywheel. The solenoid switch is held in position by the holding coil. The starter motor can now turn the engine. When the latter fires, the engagement lever is pulled back to the home position by the return spring; when the engine begins to rotate faster than the starter, the pinion is disconnected from the armature shaft by a roller-operated freewheel device.

With all types of starter it is possible to perform the first stage of operation by means of a pedal, as exemplified by a gear-shift starter (Fig. 5). The design is simpler than in the case of the Bendix type starter because here the pinion is not rotated while it engages with the gear rim.

1. Gasoline in U.S.A.

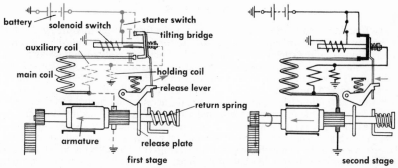

battery — solenoid switch — starter switch — tilting bridge
auxiliary coil — holding coil
main coil — release lever — return spring
armature — release plate

first stage

second stage

Fig. 1 OPERATING STAGES OF PINION-SHIFT STARTER

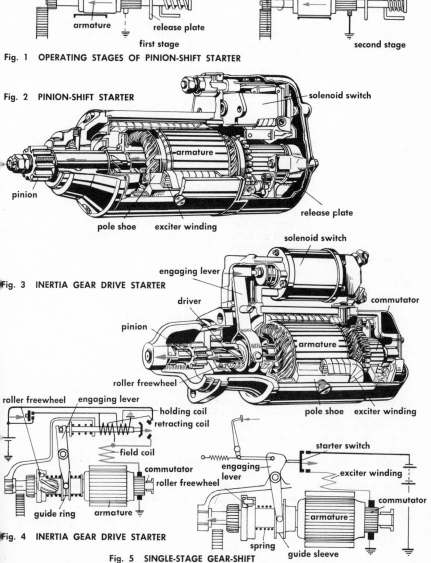

Fig. 2 PINION-SHIFT STARTER

solenoid switch
armature
pinion
release plate
pole shoe   exciter winding

solenoid switch

Fig. 3 INERTIA GEAR DRIVE STARTER

engaging lever
driver   commutator
pinion
armature
roller freewheel
pole shoe   exciter winding

roller freewheel   engaging lever
holding coil
retracting coil
field coil
commutator
engaging lever   starter switch
exciter winding
roller freewheel
guide ring   armature   commutator

Fig. 4 INERTIA GEAR DRIVE STARTER

armature
spring   guide sleeve

Fig. 5 SINGLE-STAGE GEAR-SHIFT STARTER

CARBURETTOR[1]

The function of the carburettor is to produce the fuel-and-air mixture needed for the operation of a petrol[2] engine. In the carburettor the fuel is distributed in the form of tiny droplets in the stream of air. As a result of heat absorption on the way to the cylinder these droplets are vaporised, so that the mixture thus becomes an inflammable gas. The vapour-and-air mixture thus formed enters the combustion chamber of the cylinder. A modern carburettor comprises four different systems: the main carburettor, the idling (slow-running) system, the acceleration pump, and the choke.

Combustion of the mixture in the cylinder requires oxygen; this is present in the air drawn into the cylinder when the piston descends. The air is passed through a filter (air cleaner) and a pipe called the induction pipe or intake manifold, in which the petrol is carried along with the stream of air (Fig. 1b). This effect is based on a law of physics known as Bernoulli's equation, which states that for a gas (or other fluid) flowing through a pipe the sum of the static pressure and the dynamic pressure is constant. This means that when the velocity, and therefore the dynamic pressure is increased, the static pressure decreases. If the induction pipe is narrowed to a reduced diameter at one particular section, the velocity of the air at that section will be increased, while the (static) pressure will diminish to a negative value in relation to the surroundings. In other words, a suction is developed there, which causes the petrol to be sucked out of the choke tube and be atomised (Fig. 1b). The tiny droplets are carried along into the cylinder by the air stream. The air intake pipe is preferably laid close along the exhaust pipe. The heat given off by the latter serves to preheat the intake air and helps to vaporize the petrol droplets. The main jet, which is essentially a constriction in the fuel supply pipe from the float chamber to the choke tube, limits and controls the quantity of fuel introduced into the air stream per unit of time: the jet has a small orifice which allows the fuel to flow from the float chamber only at a certain limited rate. The rate of supply of fuel to the carburettor itself is controlled by the equipment. This comprises the float chamber, the float and the needle valve. When the float chamber fills up with petrol, the hollow metal float rises until the needle is in contact with the valve seat and thus closes the petrol inlet opening. By this means the level of the petrol in the chamber can be constantly maintained at 2–3 mm (about $\frac{1}{8}$ inch) below the opening of the outlet pipe. When the float rises, the air which it displaces is forced back into the induction pipe. The throttle valve, which is operated by the accelerator pedal, is closed when the engine is idling. In this condition the main system is out of action and the pilot system comes into operation instead. The latter system provides the requisite combustion mixture for idling, i.e., when the engine is running under zero load (Figs. 3a and 3b), and operates independently of the main system. With the throttle closed, only a small amount of air can flow through the induction pipe and is unable to carry along any petrol from the choke tube. However, at a narrow gap between the throttle valve and the carburettor wall the air velocity is increased to such an extent that a powerful suction is developed behind the valve, causing petrol to be sucked from the pilot outlet. The necessary air is drawn through a passage branching off from the main air inlet at the top. Additional air is drawn through another branch passage, which is provided with an air regulating screw. By turning this screw in or out the composition of the pilot mixture (i.e., the fuel-and-air mixture for running the engine when idling) can be made leaner or richer (Fig. 3a). In another type of pilot system (Fig. 3b) it is not the quantity of additional intake air that is regulated; instead, the quantity of pilot mixture that is admitted through the pilot outlet into the induction pipe is varied by means of the mixture regulating screw. In this case, the upper outlet comes into operation when the throttle valve is slightly opened. The "idling" position of the throttle valve is determined by a stop.

(Continued)

1. Carburetor in U.S.A.
2. Gasoline in U.S.A.

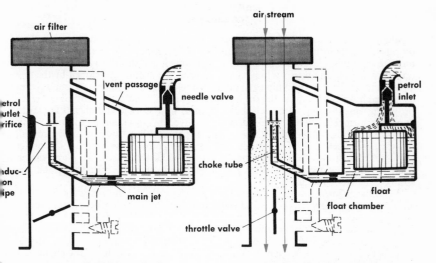

Fig. 1a MAIN CARBURETTOR SYSTEM
NOT FUNCTIONING

Fig. 1b MAIN CARBURETTOR SYSTEM
FUNCTIONING

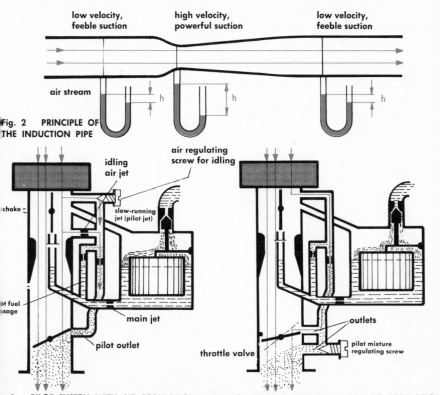

Fig. 2 PRINCIPLE OF
THE INDUCTION PIPE

Fig. 3a PILOT SYSTEM WITH AIR REGULATION

Fig. 3b PILOT SYSTEM WITH MIXTURE REGULATION

Sudden acceleration of the engine speed calls for an immediate increase in power output, and this in turn requires a momentarily richer combustion mixture, i.e., a mixture containing a higher proportion of petrol. If the throttle valve is suddenly opened when the engine is running at a low speed, the suction developed by the low air velocity in the induction pipe will not be sufficient by itself to draw enough petrol from the choke tube to raise the engine speed. This problem can be solved either by providing an extra supply of petrol in readiness in a storage chamber (Fig. 4a) to boost the normal flow when required, or alternatively by providing an injection pump (Fig. 4b) which is connected to the accelerator pedal. When this pedal is depressed, the spring is slackened by the pump linkage, and petrol flows through the outlet valve and the jet into the choke tube. When the pedal is released, the pump piston rises, the outlet valve closes, more petrol enters through the inlet valve, and the spring is tensioned again.

When the engine is started from cold, a high proportion of the fuel in the fuel-and-air mixture is precipitated on the cold wall surfaces of the induction pipe and cylinder. In order nevertheless to obtain a combustible mixture in the combustion chamber, the carburettor must temporarily supply a very rich mixture. To this end, the main air inlet in the carburettor is closed by a valve called the choke (Fig. 5). The throttle valve is then only slightly opened. When the piston in the cylinder of the engine descends, a powerful pumping action is developed in the carburettor, and the suction draws an ample flow of petrol both from the choke tube and from the pilot system. When the engine fires, a poppet valve (Fig. 6) enables a somewhat larger quantity of air to be drawn in, since an excessively rich mixture is not suitable for the engine as it warms up. The suction developed by the engine causes the plate to be lifted against the restraining force of the spring, so that the supply of air to the engine is increased. At the end of the warming-up period, the choke is opened either by hand or automatically. The automatic action is, as a rule, thermally controlled. A coil spring keeps the choke closed. This spring is a bimetallic one, i.e., it consists of two metals which undergo different amounts of expansion on heating, causing the spring tension to change. As the engine warms up, this coil spring is also warmed and opens the choke an appropriate amount.

Fig. 6 shows the construction of a down-draught carburettor. Names like down-draught, up-draught or cross-draught carburettor indicate the direction of flow of the intake air.

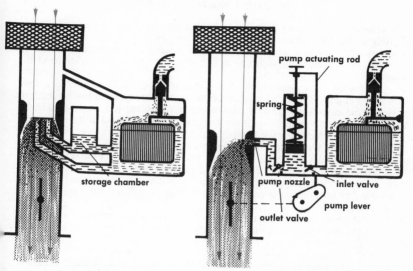

Fig. 4a ACCELERATION SYSTEM
WITH STORAGE CHAMBER

Fig. 4b ACCELERATION SYSTEM
WITH INJECTION PUMP

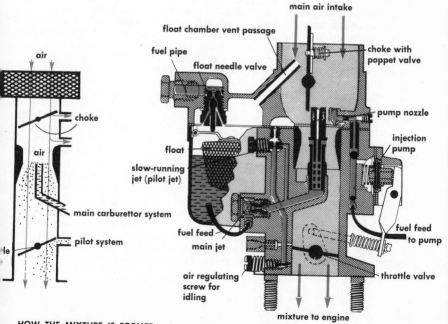

HOW THE MIXTURE IS FORMED
WHEN STARTING FROM COLD

Fig. 6 SOLEX DOWN-DRAUGHT CARBURETTOR

481

The distributor is a device for conveying electrical current to the sparking plugs according to the firing order. It comprises the contact-breaker with condenser, the ignition cam, the actual distributor, and an automatic timing control device which determines the optimum ignition timing suited to the operating conditions of the engine.

The distributor has a longitudinal shaft whose lower end is connected to a drive pinion in the engine block. This shaft is rotated at the same speed as the camshaft of the engine and carries the ignition cam, which actuates the contact lever (Fig. 1). This lever is rotatably mounted on a plate. Fitted to the upper end of the shaft is the distributor rotor, which is made of plastic and through which an electrode passes. The distributor disc is also the cover of the housing. At the centre it is provided with a carbon brush through which the current is passed to the distributor rotor. At the edge of the disc are a number of tungsten electrodes, one for each cylinder of the engine. These are so arranged that the rotor is always at a contact just when the contact-breaker interrupts the circuit of the primary winding of the ignition coil. At that instant a high voltage is induced in the secondary winding of the ignition coil, and this voltage is allowed to pass through the rotor to the appropriate sparking plug. The condenser prevents the occurrence of sparking at the make-and-break contact. The ignition spark is produced as follows: so long as the make-and-break contact has not been opened by the cam, current can flow in the primary circuit (battery, primary winding, make-and-break contact, earth; Fig. 2), so that a magnetic field is formed in the ignition coil. At the instant when the contact interrupts the primary circuit, this magnetic field breaks down. This sudden change of the magnetic field induces a high voltage in the secondary winding, which voltage is thereupon applied to one of the sparking plugs, causing it to produce a spark.

The distributor housing also accommodates the timing control. This device automatically adjusts the optimum ignition timing, which very largely depends upon the type of petrol and upon the load and speed of the engine at any particular time (e.g., idling or running under full load). To adjust the ignition timing, the distributor shaft comprises two parts. The upper end is rotatable in relation to the lower end, so that the cam can be rotated relatively to the drive which is effected from below. A device operating with centrifugal weights rotates the upper end of the distributor shaft — therefore the cam — in relation to the drive by a certain amount corresponding to the speed of rotation of the engine. As a result of this automatic adjustment, ignition takes place earlier at high than at low engine speeds. When they are at rest, the centrifugal weights are pulled inwards by springs. When the speed increases, the weights are flung outwards by the centrifugal force until the latter is balanced by the spring force. A pin engaging with a slot in the centrifugal weights forms the connection with the top part of the distributor shaft. When the weights move outwards, the pin causes the upper end of the shaft to rotate in relation to the lower end; consequently, the cam is rotated relatively to the drive, and the instant at which the make-and-break contact opens is thereby altered. Additional adjustment can be controlled by the negative pressure in the induction pipe of the engine. This negative pressure, which develops behind the throttle valve in the induction pipe (page 478), cause a diaphragm to curve, and this movement is transmitted to the contact-breaker plate. As a result, the contact lever is shifted in relation to the cam, and the ignition timing is thereby altered. This adjustment operates more particularly when the throttle valve is not fully open (i.e., in the partial load range), whereas the ignition timing adjustment by the centrifugal weights is dependent upon the engine speed.

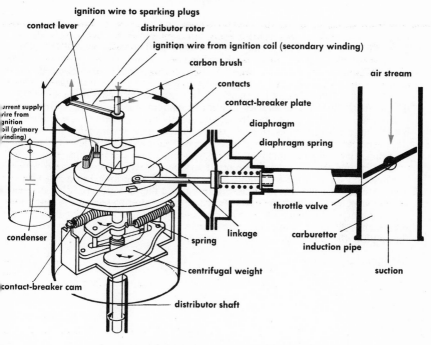

contact lever

ignition wire to sparking plugs

distributor rotor

ignition wire from ignition coil (secondary winding)

carbon brush

contacts

contact-breaker plate

diaphragm

diaphragm spring

air stream

urrent supply
wire from
ignition
oil (primary
winding)

condenser

contact-breaker cam

throttle valve

spring

linkage

carburettor
induction pipe

centrifugal weight

suction

distributor shaft

Fig. 1   DISTRIBUTOR WITH VACUUM-CONTROLLED
SPARK ADJUSTMENT

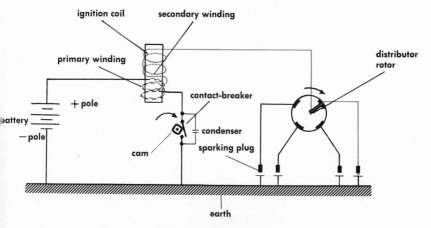

ignition coil

secondary winding

primary winding

distributor
rotor

+ pole

contact-breaker

condenser

battery

−pole

cam

sparking plug

earth

Fig. 2   DIAGRAM SHOWING OPERATION OF
CONTACT-BREAKER AND DISTRIBUTOR

The sparking plug ignites the compressed fuel-and-air mixture in the cylinder of a petrol engine by means of a spark which leaps from the central electrode to the so-called earth electrode. The sparking plug consists essentially of the two electrodes, the insulator and the body with its screw thread and connecting nut. The ignition current coming from the distributor (page 482) flows through the central electrode and produces the spark between this electrode and the earth electrode. The ignition voltage is about 25,000 volts, the spark gap between the electrodes being about 0.6–0.7 mm (0.025–0.03 in.). In engines with a low compression ratio, i.e., in which the combustion mixture is not so greatly compressed, the distance between the electrodes is made larger: this produces a longer spark, which can more readily ignite the mixture than a shorter one can. Since a highly compressed gas presents a higher resistance to the spark, a smaller spark gap is employed with high compression ratios.

The deciding factor in the choice of a sparking plug is its thermal value, which characterises the thermal behaviour of the plug. It is determined in a test engine under accurately defined conditions. For instance, a thermal value of 95 means that incandescent surface ignition occurs in the test engine after 95 seconds. A plug with a high thermal value, i.e., a plug which can be subjected to a high thermal load and yet remain cold, has a smaller insulator—so as to provide better heat dissipation— than a plug with a low thermal value.

1. Spark plug in U.S.A.

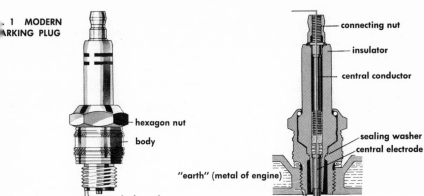

Fig. 1 MODERN SPARKING PLUG

hexagon nut
body
earth electrode

connecting nut
insulator
central conductor
sealing washer
central electrode
"earth" (metal of engine)

Fig. 2 SECTION THROUGH SPARKING PLUG (*functioning correctly*)

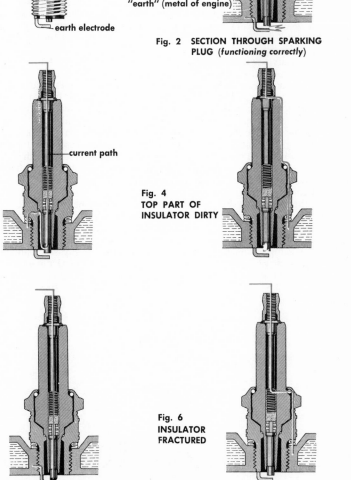

current path

Fig. 3 INSULATOR DIRTY

Fig. 4 TOP PART OF INSULATOR DIRTY

Fig. 5 SPARK GAP BRIDGED

Fig. 6 INSULATOR FRACTURED

faulty plug operation (Figs. 3 to 6)

CLUTCH

Internal combustion engines must have a certain minimum speed (approx. 300–600 r.p.m.) before they can run on their own power and develop a sufficiently high torque to drive the vehicle. While the vehicle is stationary, with its engine running, it is necessary to disconnect the engine from the gearbox; this is done by means of the clutch (Fig. 1). When the vehicle is about to move off, the clutch must first gradually raise the speed of rotation of the gearbox input shaft to the speed of the engine shaft. In so doing, the clutch has to transmit a torque while the slip due to the difference in speed between the engine shaft and the gearbox input shaft steadily decreases. Short periods of disconnection of the engine from the gearbox by means of the clutch are also necessary for gear-changing—i.e., for changing the transmission ratio of the gearbox—so as to effect the temporary disengagement of intermeshing components in the gearbox.

In the commonest form of clutch the connection of the engine shaft to gearbox shaft is effected by friction between two or more discs. The slip which occurs during the period of equalisation of the speeds of the driving shaft and the driven shaft generates heat. In the normal clutch operations the amount of heat involved is negligible, but if the clutch is allowed to slip for a considerable time, the clutch lining will quickly be destroyed.

Nowadays dry single-plate clutches are mostly used. In this form of construction a drive plate, made of steel and faced on both sides with riveted-on segmental clutch linings, is so mounted on the clutch shaft that it cannot rotate but can be shifted axially in relation to the latter (Fig. 2). The clutch shaft also forms the output shaft of the clutch to the gearbox. The drive plate is pressed between the flywheel and the clutch ring by thrust springs. This clutch ring is axially movable, but is so connected to the housing by drive elements (dogs) that it must always participate in the rotation of the housing. The clutch ring engages with the clutch release lever, the other end of which is moved by the movable clutch release sleeve. When the clutch is disengaged, the clutch release sleeve moves towards the engine, with the result that the clutch release lever shifts the clutch ring against the pressure of the thrust springs: the connection between the engine and gearbox is severed.

The multiplate clutch (Fig. 3) has been evolved from the single-plate clutch. Here again the clutch is integral with the flywheel of the engine. The housing contains the driving plates, which are non-rotatably connected to the housing, but can be shifted axially, and which are faced with clutch linings. The driven plates are secured to the pressure plate, upon which the pressure spring acts. The pressure plate is mounted directly on the drive shaft, on which it is axially movable, in order to enable the clutch to be disengaged (Fig. 3b).

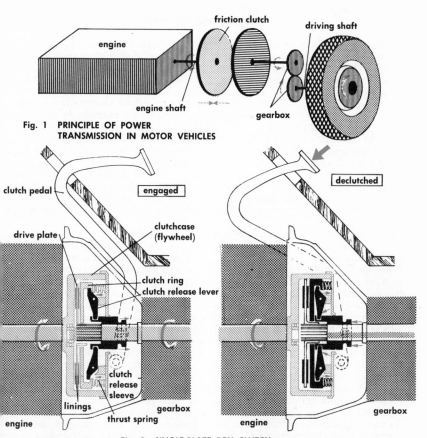

Fig. 1 PRINCIPLE OF POWER
TRANSMISSION IN MOTOR VEHICLES

Fig. 2 SINGLE-PLATE DRY CLUTCH

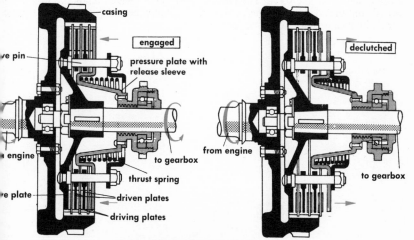

Fig. 3 MULTIPLATE DRY CLUTCH

AUTOMATIC CLUTCH

An automatic clutch installed in a motor vehicle makes for much more comfortable driving in comparison with an ordinary pedal-operated clutch (see page 486). The clutch pedal inside the vehicle is obviated, since the clutch automatically disengages when the engine is idling and also when the motorist takes hold of the gear-shift lever. In principle, an automatic clutch comprises—besides the gear selecting clutch, which may be mechanically, pneumatically, hydraulically or electrically actuated—an additional starting clutch which may be engaged, for example, by centrifugal action or may be in the form of a fluid flywheel clutch or a magnetic powder clutch.

In the Saxomat automatic clutch the *starting clutch*, which in this case is of the centrifugal type, is a plate clutch which transmits power as soon as the centrifugal weights are flung outwards when the speed of the engine exceeds the idling speed. These weights press the pressure plate against the drive plate and thrust the latter against the flywheel (Fig. 1). At low speeds of rotation this clutch disengages automatically. In order nevertheless to take advantage of the braking action of the engine when travelling downhill, a freewheel is installed (Fig. 2), which establishes the mechanical connection between the crankshaft and the gearbox drive shaft as soon as the latter tends to rotate faster than the crankshaft.

The *gear selecting clutch* is likewise a plate clutch, which is always engaged during starting and which is actuated by means of a vacuum-controlled servo mechanism. When the motorist takes hold of the change-speed lever (Fig. 3), a contact is closed, with the result that an electromagnet is energised. It moves the valve to the right, so that the intake pipe of the engine is connected to the servo mechanism. Its diaphragm is now subjected on one side to a vacuum, and on the other side it is subjected to atmospheric pressure, with the result that it pulls the clutch actuating lever to the "disengaged" position. When the change-speed lever is released, the flow of current to the electromagnet is interrupted, the valve returns to its initial position and disconnects the servo system from the induction pipe. Atmospheric air now slowly flows into the vacuum chamber of the servo through a nozzle with a very fine orifice (which is so narrow that it does not disturb the sequence of events described above). As the pressure on both sides of the diaphragm has now been equalised, the latter returns the clutch actuating lever to the "engaged" position. Engaging the clutch is expedited by depressing the accelerator pedal, as the vacuum which is developed in the choke tube of the carburettor is applied, through a special pipe, to an auxiliary diaphragm, which lifts the valve "b", so that the atmospheric air can flow much more quickly into the servo. The tension of the spring which holds the valve "b" closed, and thus determines the vacuum pressure at which this valve opens, can be varied by means of an adjusting screw.

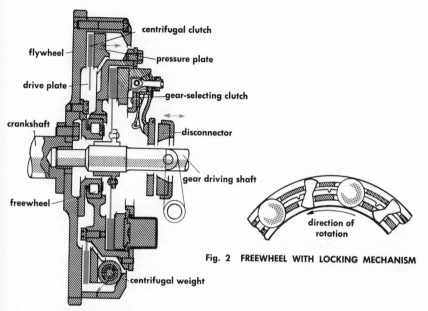

centrifugal clutch

flywheel

pressure plate

drive plate

gear-selecting clutch

crankshaft

disconnector

gear driving shaft

freewheel

direction of rotation

Fig. 2   FREEWHEEL WITH LOCKING MECHANISM

centrifugal weight

Fig. 1   SAXOMAT AUTOMATIC CLUTCH

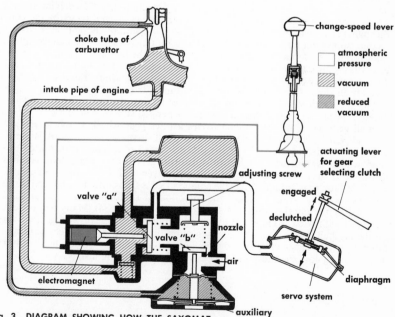

choke tube of carburettor

change-speed lever

atmospheric pressure

vacuum

reduced vacuum

intake pipe of engine

actuating lever for gear selecting clutch

adjusting screw

engaged

valve "a"

declutched

nozzle

valve "b"

air

electromagnet

diaphragm

servo system

Fig. 3   DIAGRAM SHOWING HOW THE SAXOMAT AUTOMATIC CLUTCH WORKS

auxiliary diaphragm

GEARBOX (TRANSMISSION)

The internal combustion engines generally installed in motor vehicles develop their power output at high speeds of rotation (approx. 4000–6000 r.p.m.). It is therefore necessary to reduce the speed between the crankshaft and the shaft which drives the wheels. In addition, the torque (see below) that the engine delivers can be varied only within narrow limits. For this reason it is necessary to be able to alter the transmission ratio, so that the driving forces applied to the wheels of the vehicle can be adapted to the varying road resistance conditions.

Part of the requisite total speed reduction is effected in the final drive (see differential gear, page 500). The rest of the reduction can be obtained by means of the change-speed gearbox, which is interposed between the clutch (see page 486) and the final drive. In addition, the gearbox contains the mechanism for reversing. The gearbox alters the torque that is transmitted and therefore functions as a so-called torque converter. The transmission ratio (or gear ratio) is dependent upon the ratio of the numbers of teeth of the meshing gear wheels: a gear wheel mounted on a shaft rotating at a certain speed will drive another shaft whose gear wheel has half the number of teeth at twice the speed of rotation of the first shaft. Since the forces acting upon the two gear wheels are equal, the torque—i.e., the product of the force acting tangentially upon the gear wheel and the distance from the point of application of this force to the centre of rotation of the shaft—will, for the larger gear wheel, be double that for the small one. On the other hand, the smaller wheel will revolve at twice the speed of the larger. In other words, the smaller gear wheel has the higher speed, but the lower torque; the larger wheel rotates more slowly, but transmits the higher torque. The transmission ratio is the ratio of the input speed to the output speed; the pitch circle diameters of the gear wheels and torques of the shafts are in the inverse ratio.

A change-speed gearbox usually comprises the driving shaft end, the layshaft, and the driven shaft (Fig. 1), which are installed (parallel to the longitudinal axis of the vehicle) in the gearcase. A gear wheel is rigidly mounted on the driving shaft end which protrudes into the gearcase. This gear wheel is driven directly by the engine, through the clutch, and therefore rotates at the speed of the engine. It drives a second, somewhat larger gear wheel which is mounted on the layshaft, so that this shaft rotates at a lower speed. Rigidly mounted on the layshaft are the transmission gear wheels for the low speeds (1st, 2nd and 3rd gear in a four-speed, 1st and 2nd in a three-speed gearbox). The driven shaft—i.e., the shaft which transmits the desired speed to the final drive of the vehicle—is mounted in line with the driving shaft and carries the longitudinally movable driven gear wheels corresponding to the various speeds. The layshaft is rotating all the time. When the vehicle is in "1st gear" (Fig. 1), a small gear wheel on the layshaft drives a large gear wheel on the driven shaft; in "2nd gear" a larger gear wheel on the layshaft drives an only slightly larger gear wheel on the driven shaft (Fig. 2), so that the speed of rotation transmitted to the road wheels is somewhat higher than in "1st gear". In a four-speed gearbox a third pair of gear wheels on the layshaft and driven shaft drives the vehicle in "3rd gear". In "top gear" (direct drive) the engine speed is transmitted unreduced through the gearbox. For "reverse gear" the direction of rotation of the driven shaft is reversed by the interposition of a second gear wheel (Fig. 4). Many gearboxes are equipped with what is known as an overdrive or cruising gear: a large gear wheel on the layshaft drives a smaller gear wheel on the driven shaft, thereby causing the latter to rotate faster than the engine. This means that the engine need only run at a relatively low speed even when the vehicle is travelling fast.

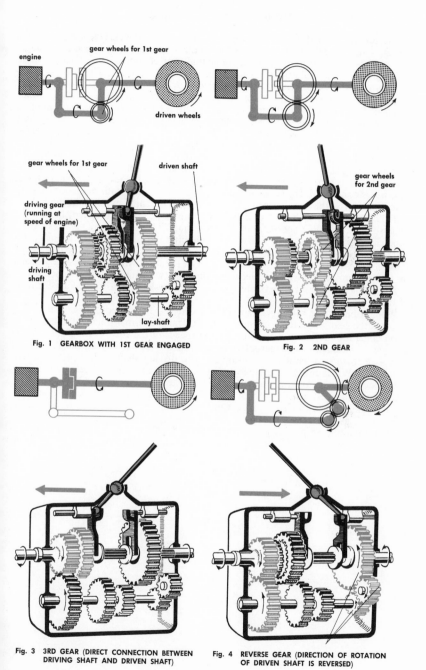

engine

gear wheels for 1st gear

driven wheels

gear wheels for 1st gear

driven shaft

gear wheels for 2nd gear

driving gear (running at speed of engine)

driving shaft

lay-shaft

Fig. 1 GEARBOX WITH 1ST GEAR ENGAGED

Fig. 2 2ND GEAR

Fig. 3 3RD GEAR (DIRECT CONNECTION BETWEEN DRIVING SHAFT AND DRIVEN SHAFT)

Fig. 4 REVERSE GEAR (DIRECTION OF ROTATION OF DRIVEN SHAFT IS REVERSED)

The fundamental difference between the conventional gearbox (see page 490) and the synchromesh (Figs. 1 and 4) is that in the former the gear wheels are brought into mesh—by sliding—only when the actual gear-change is performed, whereas in the latter all the pairs of gear wheels are constantly in mesh. The various transmission ratios are engaged by means of sleeves which are slid into position. Since the gear wheels themselves do not have to be moved in relation to one another, they can be provided with helical or spiral teeth for the sake of quiet running. In each pair of gear wheels one wheel is, for example, rigidly mounted on the layshaft, whereas the other wheel is loosely rotatable on the main shaft. To engage a particular ratio, the loose wheel of the pair of gear wheels concerned is locked to the shaft by means of dogs (locking elements). One set of dogs is mounted on the inside of a sleeve (the dog sleeve), and the other set is on the gear wheel which is to be engaged. The dog sleeve can slide axially on the main shaft but is locked to it in so far as rotation is concerned. However, before the dogs can engage with one another so as to transmit force, the dog sleeve (which is rotating at the same speed as the main shaft) and the gear wheel to be engaged (which rotates at a different speed) have to be synchronised, i.e., their speeds must become equal. This is done by means of small cone clutches or plate clutches. With cone clutches the gear wheel to be engaged is formed with a conical protrusion which slides into a conical socket in the dog sleeve. Plate clutches consist of small plates mounted on the shaft, which are pressed together by the pressure exerted by the sleeve, so that the two rotating parts, which are at first rotating at different speeds, are synchronised by slowing down and acceleration of the respective parts.

When a particular ratio (gear speed) is selected, the dog sleeve (Fig. 2) is shifted towards the gear wheel to be engaged (Fig. 3). The above-mentioned clutches thereupon come into action and synchronise the speeds of the two rotating parts. Then the dog sleeve can move farther forward and engage with the dogs on the gear wheel, just as if these two parts were stationary. The driving shaft is thus locked to the gear wheel. When engaging the selected gear, the motorist at first feels a resistance, which continues until the two rotating parts are synchronised. Only when this has been completed can the sliding sleeve be moved into its final position and the desired ratio thus definitely engaged. For the positions corresponding to the various ratios see Figs. 5–8 on page 495.

In automobile engineering a number of different kinds of synchromesh gear systems are used. They all function on the principle described here, but differ in various technical details.

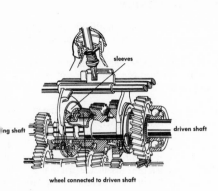

sleeves

ing shaft

driven shaft

wheel connected to driven shaft

Fig. 1 FOUR-SPEED SYNCHROMESH GEARBOX
         (3rd gear engaged)

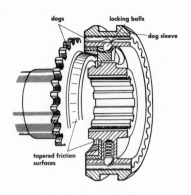

dogs   locking balls

dog sleeve

tapered friction
surfaces

Fig. 2 SYNCHRONISATION (cone clutch)

Fig. 3 HOW THE SYNCHROMESH WORKS

rive dog   sliding dog

wheel

neutral position   clutch engages   sliding dog engaged

Fig. 4 FOUR-SPEED SYNCHROMESH GEARBOX
         SHOWING WORKING PARTS

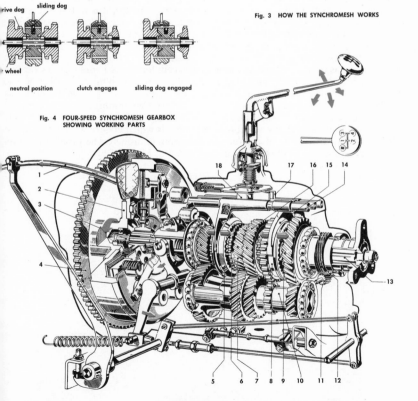

1 clutch pedal	7 spiral gear (3rd gear)
2 crankshaft	8 sliding sleeve (1st and 2nd gear)
3 driving shaft	9 spiral gear (1st gear)
4 starting gear ring	10 lay-shaft
5 sliding sleeve (3rd and 4th gear)	11 small drive wheel (speedometer drive)
6 synchronising cone	12 spiral gear

13 main shaft
14 gear-shift rods
15 selector fork (1st and 2nd gear)
16 spiral gear (2nd gear)
17 selector head
18 selector fork (3rd and 4th gear)

In European automobile engineering, manual gear-changing is being superseded by automatic gear-changing in the larger cars. American private cars already nearly all have automatic transmission systems.

The automatic transmission has no gear lever for selecting the various speeds, or ratios. Speed control is entirely effected by the position of the accelerator pedal (gas pedal). Automatic gearboxes of this kind embody a combination of hydraulic and mechanical transmission components.

The hydraulic part comprises fluid couplings and torque converters; the mechanical part comprises planetary (or epicyclic) gears. The working principle of a fluid coupling can most conveniently be explained with reference to the behaviour of two fans placed together (Fig. 1): one of the fans is driven and produces a current of air which sets the blades of the other fan, which is not driven, in motion. The transmission of the rotary motion in this case is not effected by friction (as in the friction clutch; see page 486), but through the agency of a medium. In the example of the fans the medium is air; oil is used in a fluid coupling.

A coupling of this kind comprises two rotating parts fitted with vanes, one of which is the driving member (impeller) and the other is the driven member (turbine) (Fig. 2). The impeller itself is driven by the engine. The oil with which the coupling is filled is flung outward (Fig. 3) and, since it cannot escape, it is forced in between the vanes of the turbine, where it is deflected and flung back into the impeller. The circulating oil drives the turbine round at an increasing speed until it is rotating at the same speed as the impeller. A fluid coupling thus provides a smooth "take-up", so that the vehicle moves off entirely without any jerking. This transmits the same torque as that developed by the engine, except for minor losses due to so-called "slip", which is due to the fact that the turbine is not mechanically locked to the impeller but runs with a certain amount of lag in relation to it. At low speeds this loss is relatively far greater than at high speeds. Other important components of automatic gearboxes are the planetary gears (Fig. 4). They comprise a centrally mounted sun wheel and one or more planet wheels which engage with it and which furthermore engage with an external toothed ring (annulus). The possibilities presented by a gear system of this kind are indicated in Fig. 4 (cf. also page 462).

(Continued)

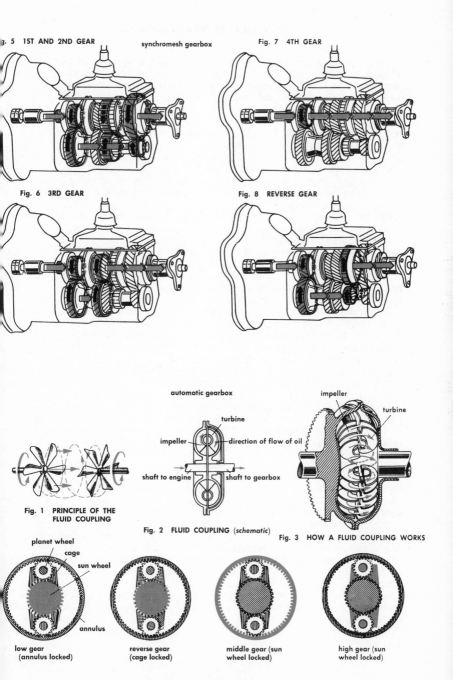

g. 5 1ST AND 2ND GEAR

synchromesh gearbox

Fig. 7 4TH GEAR

Fig. 6 3RD GEAR

Fig. 8 REVERSE GEAR

automatic gearbox

impeller

turbine

turbine

impeller — direction of flow of oil

shaft to engine — shaft to gearbox

Fig. 1 PRINCIPLE OF THE
FLUID COUPLING

Fig. 2 FLUID COUPLING (schematic)

Fig. 3 HOW A FLUID COUPLING WORKS

planet wheel
cage
sun wheel

annulus

low gear
(annulus locked)

reverse gear
(cage locked)

middle gear (sun
wheel locked)

high gear (sun
wheel locked)

Fig. 4 PLANETARY GEARS

One of the most well-known forms of construction of an automatic transmission is the Hydra-Matic (Fig. 5; Fig. 7, page 499), great numbers of which were manufactured in the U.S.A. in the post-war years. It comprises two planetary gear sets for the four forward gears and one set for reverse. Transmission of force is effected by a fluid coupling. Gear-changing is effected automatically, depending on the speed of the car (speed of rotation of the driven shaft of the transmission), engine load, and accelerator position (through a governor). The transmission of force is effected in the mechanical part of the system by means of planetary gear sets and a fluid coupling. In first and second gear the total power is transmitted through the fluid coupling, which is driven at a higher speed in second gear than in first because the planetary gear set is then locked, and the slip losses in the coupling become less. On the other hand, the greater slip that occurs in first gear ensures great smoothness in take-up of the clutch.

In third and fourth gear, however, the power is transmitted in two ways. At the point marked X the power coming from the engine via the planetary gear set 1 is transmitted partly (through the fluid coupling) to the sun wheel (S) of the planetary gear set 2 and partly (through the hollow shaft and the locked clutch K 2) to the annulus (A) of the planetary gear set 2. In the last-mentioned gear set the two flows of transmitted power converge upon the planetary gear (P). The fluid coupling is by-passed. The slip then affects only that portion of the power which is transmitted by the coupling. In third gear the drive of the fluid coupling is effected through the operative planetary gear set 1, as in first gear, with reduced speed of rotation (1.44). In fourth gear, on the other hand, the planetary gear set 1 is locked by the clutch K 1. As a result of this the fluid coupling receives a higher operating speed in relation to third gear, so that the slip is reduced. In the parking position (Pa) the clutches B2 and BR are locked. B2 locks the annulus of PL2 and therefore the sun wheel of PLR. BR locks the annulus of PLR, so that the planetary gear between the sun wheel and the annulus is likewise immobilised. The drive to the rear axle is thus locked.

The gear-changing operations are controlled by a hydraulic regulating device. Fig. 6 shows the operations associated with changing up to the next higher gear. The centrifugal governor is driven by the driving shaft of the transmission. It comprises a centrifugal piston which is eccentrically and movably mounted in a housing. Controlled by the centrifugal force, whose magnitude depends upon the road speed of the vehicle, the centrifugal piston feeds a regulated supply of hydraulic pressure oil to the control valve. This oil pressure, regulated by the centrifugal governor, is now applied to one side of a piston, while a spring thrusts against the other side. This spring pressure is augmented by the oil pressure which is developed in the load regulator by the action of the accelerator pedal. If the oil pressure controlled by the load centrifugal governor exceeds the pressure controlled by the load regulator, the piston in the control valve clears the way to the relevant planetary gear set. At the same time the brake is released and the clutch is locked, as corresponds to the gear-changing operations described above. On the other hand, if the oil pressure controlled by the load regulator is greater than the pressure controlled by the centrifugal governor, the whole operation is reversed. The transmission system is thus controlled only by the accelerator (load regulator) in relation to the road speed (centrifugal governor). When there is no pressure in the pipe from the control valve to the relevant planetary gear set, then the spring action locks the brake and keeps the clutch released. A hydraulic regulator of this kind is provided for each planetary gear set.

(Continued)

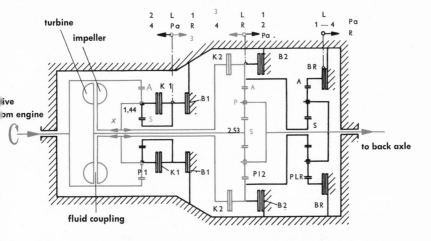

**Fig. 5   DIAGRAM SHOWING HOW THE HYDRA-MATIC
TRANSMISSION OPERATES** (*3rd gear engaged*)

The various operating positions of this transmission are as follows:
Idling: All brakes (B) and clutches (K) released.

1st gear: Both brakes (B1, B2) locked, both clutches (K1, K2) disengaged; both
   planetary gear sets (Pl 1, Pl 2) are operative. Transmission ratio = 1.44 ×
   2.53 = 3.66:1.

2nd gear: Oil pressure from governor to Pl 1, so that B 1 is disengaged, K 1
   locked. Only Pl 2 is operative; Pl 1 is locked by K 1. Transmission ratio
   2.53:1.

3rd gear: Oil pressure to Pl 2, so that B 1 is locked, K 1 is disengaged, B 2 is disengaged, K 2 is locked. Only Pl 1 is operative. Transmission ratio 1.44:1.

4th gear (direct drive): Both brakes disengaged, both clutches locked; oil pressure to Pl 1 and Pl 2; Pl 1 and Pl 2 rotate in locked condition. Transmission
   ratio 1.0:1.

Reverse: B 1 locked, K 1 disengaged; B 2 and K 2 disengaged; BR locked (in the
   four forward gears it idles [L] and is always disengaged). Consequently
   PLR becomes operative, so that the direction of rotation of the driving shaft
   is reversed.

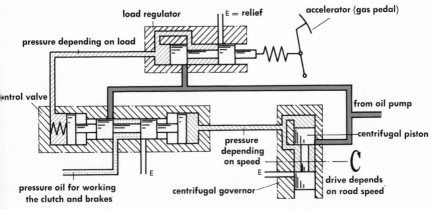

Fig. 6   HYDRAULIC GEAR-SHIFT SYSTEM OF THE HYDRA-MATIC

In other types of automatic transmission a fluid converter or hydraulic torque converter is used instead of a fluid coupling. Whereas the fluid coupling merely transmits the engine torque to the mechanical gearbox, the torque converter converts the low torque of the rapidly rotating engine into a high torque in conjunction with low speed of rotation at the output shaft of the converter. A torque converter of this kind therefore itself constitutes a transmission stage. In the fluid converter is an impeller which imparts its speed to the oil and forces it into the turbine. At low speeds of rotation the efficiency of such a device is very low, and for this reason the oil flowing out of the turbine is passed through a so-called stator (or reactor) whose fixed vanes are so curved that they redirect the oil flow into the impeller and thereby boost the action of the latter (Fig. 8). The stator vanes thus assist the conversion of the low torque of the rapidly rotating engine shaft into the high torque of the slowly rotating output shaft of the converter, so that the energy of the oil emerging from the turbine is not dissipated, but can be re-utilised. The speed of the turbine gradually becomes equal to that of the impeller, however, with the result that the efficiency diminishes again. Various arrangements are used to counteract this. In one of these the stator vanes are made adjustable, i.e., the deflection of the redirected flow is suited to the speed of rotation of the turbine at any particular time (in stationary systems). Another arrangement comprises a freewheel which thrusts against the casing during starting up. The force which restrains the freewheel is produced by the difference between the engine torque and the output torque of the transmission. When these torques finally become equal at the end of starting-up, the stator detaches itself from the housing, through the agency of a freewheel, and rotates along with the turbine. The converter has thus become a fluid coupling. The freewheel (Fig. 9) may be of the grip roller type. The transmission casing and the cage of the freewheel are rigidly interconnected. When the thrusting force of the stator acts in one direction, the grip rollers are jammed into narrowing gaps in the freewheel, so that the latter becomes locked and transmits force. When the thrusting force decreases or reverses its direction, the rollers are released, thus allowing the collar to rotate freely. The remaining gear ratios in an automatic transmission equipped with torque converters are obtained by means of planetary gear sets additionally provided (Fig. 10).

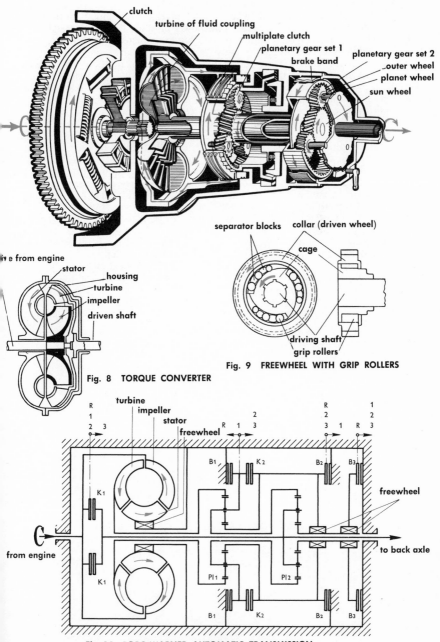

Fig. 7   SECTION THROUGH HYDRA-MATIC TRANSMISSION

clutch
turbine of fluid coupling
multiplate clutch
planetary gear set 1
brake band
planetary gear set 2
outer wheel
planet wheel
sun wheel

drive from engine
stator
housing
turbine
impeller
driven shaft

Fig. 8   TORQUE CONVERTER

separator blocks   collar (driven wheel)
cage
driving shaft
grip rollers

Fig. 9   FREEWHEEL WITH GRIP ROLLERS

R 1 2 3
turbine
impeller
stator
freewheel   R 1 2 3
R 2 3 1   1 2 R 3

B1   K2   B2   B3

K1
from engine
freewheel

K1

PI1   PI2

to back axle

B1   K2   B2   B3

Fig. 10   BORG-WARNER AUTOMATIC TRANSMISSION
WITH TORQUE CONVERTER AND FREEWHEEL

DIFFERENTIAL GEAR

When a car turns a corner, the driving wheels (the driven road wheels) rotate at different speeds, since the inside wheel has to travel a much shorter distance than the outside one (Fig. 1). For this reason the power must not be passed straight to the two wheels mounted on one continuous axle, but must, instead, act through a device called a differential gear, which drives two separate half shafts—one to each driving wheel—with the same torque, but at different speeds of rotation. The propeller drive shaft, which forms the connection from the gearbox (or transmission case) to the rear axle, is provided at its rear end with a bevel pinion (Fig. 3), which drives a larger gear wheel called the crown wheel; the latter is loosely mounted on one of the half shafts of the rear axle but is firmly connected to a box in which the four differential pinions are mounted. When this whole box rotates (as a result of the rotation of the crown wheel to which it is bolted), the differential pinions whose shafts are rotatably mounted in the box, will be carried round with it on their shafts (only two of the four differential pinions are shown in Fig. 3).

When the vehicle is travelling straight ahead (Fig. 3a), the box rotates, but the differential pinions will then not rotate on their shafts. They drive the bevel wheels which are rigidly connected to the inner ends of the driving shafts (the "half shafts" to the road wheels) and which now rotate at the same speed.

In Fig. 3b the vehicle is travelling in a bend: the right-hand half shaft is rotating at a slower speed than the left-hand half shaft. Now the differential pinions will rotate on their respective shafts, with the result that they retard the bevel wheel of the right-hand half shaft and at the same time accelerate the left-hand bevel wheel. The principle of this operation is shown in Fig. 2: the toothed racks symbolise the bevel wheels of the half shafts. If the two racks both move to the right at the same speed, the pinion will form a rigid connection between them. But if the bottom rack is retarded a little, the pinion will roll along it and, consequently, rotate in relation to both racks. The system as a whole will move in the direction represented by the arrow in Fig. 1.

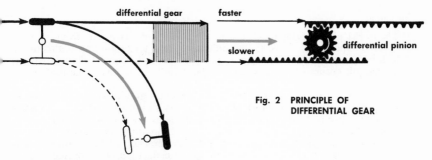

differential gear

faster

slower

differential pinion

Fig. 2 PRINCIPLE OF DIFFERENTIAL GEAR

Fig. 1 DIFFERENCE IN DISTANCE TRAVELLED BY OFFSIDE AND NEARSIDE WHEELS IN CORNERING

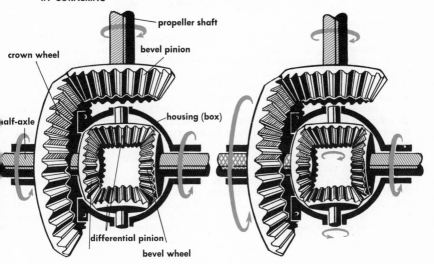

propeller shaft

crown wheel

bevel pinion

half-axle

housing (box)

differential pinion

bevel wheel

Fig. 3a DRIVING STRAIGHT AHEAD

Fig. 3b CORNERING

Fig. 4 DIFFERENTIAL GEAR

SPRINGING, AXLES, WHEEL SUSPENSION

Springing

The object of the springing is to transform the short sharp jolts from the road into soft damped oscillations, so that only quite small forces are transmitted to the vehicle body itself. Also, the spring must prevent the wheels being lifted off the road as a sudden jolt occurs and thus safeguard the "grip" or "ground adhesion" of the vehicle.

Leaf springs are the oldest—and still frequently applied—springing system. Such springs consist of a number of steel strips (spring leaves) which are stacked one upon another and are held together by spring clips. The longest leaf of the spring is formed with an eye at each end through which a mounting pin is inserted (Fig. 1).

At one end the spring is mounted in a bearing bracket, while the other end is attached to a spring shackle which takes up the elongation of the spring when it deflects. Usually leaf springs of the semi-elliptic type are used as longitudinal springs with rigid axles (Fig. 2) or as transverse springs (Fig. 3). Longitudinal springs are fixed at their ends, the sprung mass being supported at the centre of the spring, whereas transverse springs are fixed at the centre, while the sprung mass is supported by the ends.

Coil springs are increasingly used in modern automobile engineering. They are lighter than leaf springs and require less maintenance, but they do not possess oscillation-damping properties (Fig. 4). What is desired of springs is that they should be very yielding at low loads and become stiffer at higher loads. A spring is said to be stiffer than another if it requires a greater force than the other spring to shorten or lengthen it a certain amount. In the case of a coil spring the force applied is proportional to the shortening or elongation it produces, i.e., it is equally stiff for all values of the load. Fig. 5 shows a progressively acting spring which fulfils the requirement as to increasing stiffness with increasing load. In this arrangement, a load increase first brings the main spring into action; next, the auxiliary spring and finally also the resilient rubber pads come into operation.

Fig. 6 shows the functioning principle of a *torsion bar suspension* system. One end of a torsion bar is fixed in the frame of the vehicle, while the other end is connected to a lever arm (pull rod). The spring actions are transmitted to the wheel by the lever (Fig. 7). They depend upon the thickness and length of the torsion bar; thick short bars are stiffer than thin long ones. Torsion rods consisting of bundled strips of spring steel may be used instead of solid rods of circular section.

(Continued)

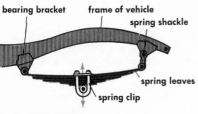

bearing bracket | frame of vehicle | spring shackle | spring leaves | spring clip

Fig. 1 LEAF SPRING

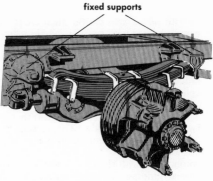

fixed supports

Fig. 2 LONGITUDINAL SPRING OF RIGID AXLE

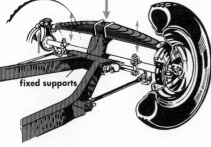

fixed supports

Fig. 3 TRANSVERSE SPRING
(*floating axle*)

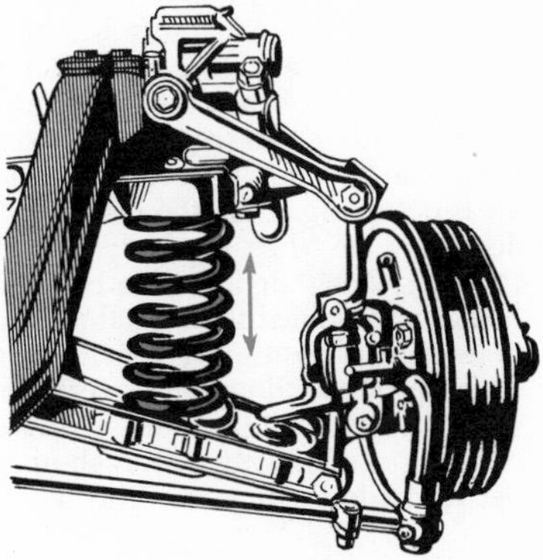

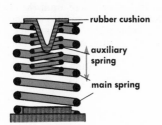

rubber cushion

auxiliary spring

main spring

Fig. 5 COIL SPRING WITH PROGRESSIVELY
ACTING AUXILIARY SPRING

Fig. 4 COIL SPRING

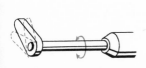

Fig. 6 PRINCIPLE OF
TORSION BAR SUSPENSION

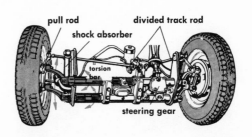

pull rod | shock absorber | divided track rod | torsion bar | steering gear

Fig. 7 FRONT AXLE WITH TORSION BAR SUSPENSION

With *air suspension* (pneumatic cushioning) the spring forces are resisted by a chamber filled with compressed air, which is formed either by a cylinder containing a piston which can move inside it or which may, alternatively, be designed as a compressible spring bellows. With this arrangement a suitably yielding suspension, well adjusted to the load, can be obtained, and the movement of the car body thereby reduced (more particularly when travelling in bends). As a result, riding comfort and safety are substantially increased. Depending on the type of suspension concerned, the air forming the cushion has a pressure of 3 to 9 atm. (45–130 lb./in.^{2}). The piston is connected directly to the sprung masses, which try to push the piston farther into the cylinder. This causes the air in the latter to become more highly compressed and thus resist this movement. The metal bellows (Fig. 8), which can absorb movements only in the direction of its longitudinal axis, is used mainly in conjunction with rigid axles. With this kind of suspension it is necessary to provide special guiding devices in order to obviate the occurrence of transverse forces (Fig. 9). Each bellows is connected to an auxiliary air vessel which ensures that there is always a sufficient quantity of air in the bellows. In the case of the roll bellows a piston-shaped movable body is directly connected to the auxiliary air vessel by the bellows (Fig. 10). It can also absorb transverse forces and can therefore be used in combination with independent wheel suspension and swinging half-axles (Fig. 11). The installation principle of air suspension systems is shown diagrammatically in Fig. 12. The road clearance is automatically always kept constant by means of the air equalising valve (height regulator). The latter is connected to the axle through a linkage system. When the load on the axle increases, the linkage rods will cause the piston of the height regulator to rise, so that air from the compressor and storage vessel can flow into the bellows, until the car body has risen so high that the inflowing air is cut off again by the piston in the height regulator. When the load on the axle decreases, or when the body lifts, the piston in the height regulator opens a hole through which air from the bellows can escape into the atmosphere, until the car body has regained its normal position and the piston in the regulator has returned to its middle position. The height regulator can be provided with a damping device, which produces a certain time lag in the response of the regulator. The regulating system will then not respond to jolts of short duration. In addition, damping prevents oscillation of the regulator about its normal position, i.e., continual alternation between admission of air into the pneumatic spring and escape of air.

(Continued)

load compresses
air in bellows

bellows

Fig. 8   AIR SUSPENSION
WITH METAL BELLOWS

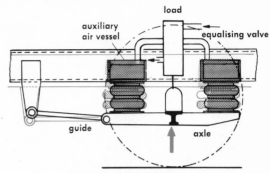

load

auxiliary
air vessel

equalising valve

guide

axle

Fig. 9   EXAMPLE OF MOUNTING OF
METAL BELLOWS SUSPENSION

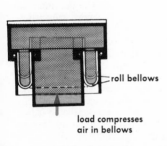

roll bellows

load compresses
air in bellows

Fig. 10   ROLL BELLOWS WITH INTERNAL
AND EXTERNAL GUIDANCE

wheel

shock absorber control rod

shock absorber

compressed air

auxiliary air vessel

front axle

equalising valve

roll
bellows

load

middle control rod
for suspension

Fig. 11   EXAMPLE OF MOUNTING OF ROLL
BELLOWS SUSPENSION

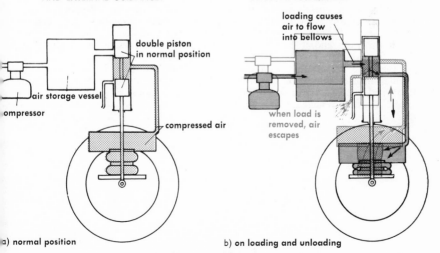

double piston
in normal position

air storage vessel

compressor

compressed air

a) normal position

loading causes
air to flow
into bellows

when load is
removed, air
escapes

b) on loading and unloading

Fig. 12   EQUALISING VALVE OF AIR SUSPENSION
SYSTEM (*height regulator*)

Axles and wheel suspension

The axles and wheel suspension determine the amount of the wheels in relation to the body of the vehicle. Various wheel movements are to be distinguished: (a) The wheel moves only in the vertical direction in its plane in relation to the body; (b) the wheel undergoes sideways displacement; (c) the angle of the wheel in relation to the body is changed; (d) sideways displacement occurs in combination with change of angle. Various forms of construction for the axles and wheel suspension are employed for eliminating these wheel movements as far as possible.

With a *rigid axle* (Fig. 14) the two wheels share the same suspension and springing. This type of axle is used chiefly for heavy vehicles, and more particularly for the rear axles. Such an axle often consists of a welded split sheet-steel casing. If one of the wheels encounters an irregularity on the road, this will cause the whole axle to tilt, with the result that the two springs are unequally stressed. The wheels undergo no parallel displacement when the axle tilts, but their angle does change. A *floating axle* (Fig. 15) is a rigid axle provided with a transverse spring above it. If the spring stop is located at the level of the centre of gravity of the vehicle, any tilting over of the body when the vehicle is negotiating a bend can be obviated. The floating axle therefore provides particularly good road-hugging ability during cornering (side-tilt stability).

The *swing axle* provides independent wheel suspension and springing, so that only the wheel that encounters a "bump" alters its position. For normal rear axle drive the independent suspension is usually provided in the form of the single-pivot swing axle (Fig. 16). The drawback of this arrangement is that the road contact surface of the wheel undergoes a certain amount of sideways displacement when the springs are compressed, for which reason it is not used for front axles (steering axles).

If it is desired to use the swing axle principle for the steering axle, the so-called wishbone suspension (Fig. 18) can be applied. This embodies a parallelogram system which ensures that the wheels are kept accurately parallel. However, here too, sideways displacement of the wheels occurs when the springs are compressed; in addition, angular displacement occurs when cornering. Another form of construction for steering axles is based on the use of double transverse springs (two leaf springs mounted one above the other: Fig. 17). The greater the deflections of these springs are, the larger will be the amounts of sideways and angular displacement of the wheels. The wheels may be mounted on arms, which are connected at one end to the frame and at the other end to the wheel axle. These arms may be single (Fig. 19) or double (Fig. 20). In this case, the springing takes the form of a torsion bar (see page 502). With suspension systems of this kind there is no sideways nor angular displacement when the springs deflect. The same is true of the arrangement illustrated in Fig. 21—in which the coil spring is enclosed in a tubular casing—except when the vehicle is cornering.

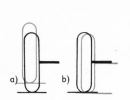

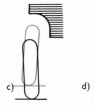

Fig. 13   WHEEL MOVEMENTS

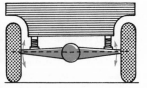

Fig. 14   RIGID AXLE

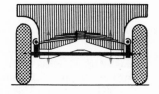

Fig. 15   FLOATING AXLE

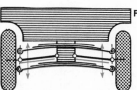

Fig. 16   SINGLE-PIVOT SWING AXLE

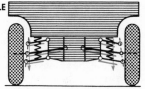

Fig. 17   DOUBLE TRANSVERSE SPRINGS

Fig. 18   WISHBONE SUSPENSION

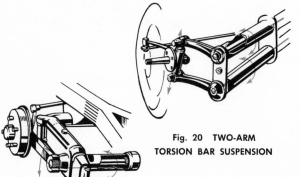

Fig. 20   TWO-ARM
TORSION BAR SUSPENSION

Fig. 19   SINGLE-ARM
TORSION BAR SUSPENSION

Fig. 21   INDEPENDENT WHEEL SUSPENSION WITH
COIL SPRING IN TUBULAR CASING

SHOCK ABSORBERS

Shock absorbers are devices which are installed between the body of a motor vehicle and the wheel suspension and which perform the function of damping the objectionable spring oscillations that may be caused by irregularities of the road surface (Fig. 1).

In modern cars the shock absorbers are almost invariably of the hydraulic type: a piston moves inside a cylinder and forces oil through narrow holes or valves. In this way a high resistance to the movement of the piston is developed, so that it is greatly retarded (Fig. 2).

In the older types of shock absorber the piston travels to and fro in an oil-filled casing (Fig. 3). The movements caused by the road irregularities are transmitted to the piston through a lever system connected to the axle of the vehicle. When the lever moves upward, the piston goes to the left and forces oil through a passage and a valve to the other side of the piston. This upward movement must be only slightly damped, in order not to impair the spring action (Fig. 3a). A valve with a large orifice is accordingly used. This allows the oil to escape quickly, so that only a small damping effect is obtained. On the other hand, the return motion of the spring-ing must be powerfully damped; for this reason a much narrower orifice is used for the other valve, which opens when the piston travels to the right and the lever moves downward (Fig. 3b). This shock absorber is therefore double-acting, but with different intensities of damping in the two directions. The type of shock absorber most frequently used nowadays is the telescopic shock absorber (Fig. 4). Its operating principle is the same as that of the lever type. It comprises two tubes, one fitting inside the other, the piston rod being connected to the outer tube; the piston moves in the oil-filled inner chamber of the inner tube. The piston contains so-called flap valves which alternately allow oil to pass in one direction only. They constitute the throttle valves that produce the damping action.

When the piston travels to the right (compression of the springs), the oil is forced through a flap valve or through holes into the left-hand chamber; when the piston moves back to the left (decompression of the springs), the oil flows through another valve back into the right-hand chamber. Since the left-hand chamber is smaller than the right-hand chamber (due to the presence of the piston rod in the former), some of the oil must, when compression of the springs occurs, flow through the bottom valve into the storage space. The bottom valve (Fig. 5) is so designed that it allows oil to pass in both directions, except that the flow resistance it presents when the springs are compressed is much higher because in that case the oil is not discharged through the orifice of the valve but is forced through the narrow gaps of the plates. On decompression of the springs, the oil which was forced into the storage space flows back into the inner chamber through the relatively large valve orifice, i.e., without encountering much resistance.

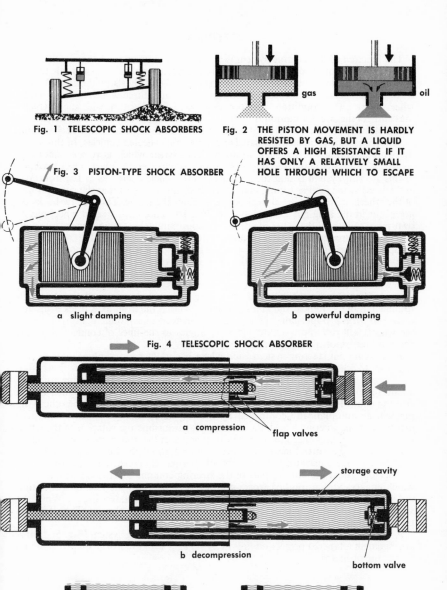

Fig. 1 TELESCOPIC SHOCK ABSORBERS

Fig. 2 THE PISTON MOVEMENT IS HARDLY RESISTED BY GAS, BUT A LIQUID OFFERS A HIGH RESISTANCE IF IT HAS ONLY A RELATIVELY SMALL HOLE THROUGH WHICH TO ESCAPE

gas

oil

Fig. 3 PISTON-TYPE SHOCK ABSORBER

a slight damping

b powerful damping

Fig. 4 TELESCOPIC SHOCK ABSORBER

a compression

flap valves

storage cavity

b decompression

bottom valve

Fig. 5 BOTTOM VALVE POSITIONS IN COMPRESSION AND DECOMPRESSION

The function of the steering system is to enable the vehicle to change its direction of travel and negotiate corners. The main requirement applicable to a good steering system is to ensure geometrically precise rolling of the wheels (without slip) when travelling in bends. In the case of motor cycles and three-wheelers with single-wheel steering this condition is automatically satisfied, because with such vehicles the centre of the circular motion is always located at the intersection of the extensions of the steered and the non-steered axle. The so-called bogie or fifth-wheel steering system (Fig. 1a) is geometrically satisfactory for four-wheeled vehicles. In this sytem the whole steering control shaft forms a rigid system which is rotated about its centre; it is usually employed on horse-drawn vehicles and trailers. The drawback of this steering system is that the stability of the vehicle decreases as the front axle and wheels swing farther round, and a further disadvantage is that the swing-round of the wheels takes up a good deal of space under the frame. These draw-backs do not occur in the king-pin steering system (Fig. 1b), since each steered wheel has its own pivot point; on the other hand, it only approximately satisfies the main condition as to slip-free geometrically accurate rolling of all the wheels on the road surface. As appears from Fig. 1b, the extension of the rear axle coincides at one point with the extensions of the two front stub axles only if the wheel on the inside of the curve has a larger angle of lock than the wheel on the outside of the curve, because only then will all the wheels be rolling on concentric circles around the centre of the circular motion. The track arms (Fig. 1b) can, however, be installed, not parallel to the longitudinal axis of the vehicle, but at an angle to it (so that the front axle, track arms and track rod form a trapezium—as in Fig. 1b—instead of a parallelogram). Then all the wheels will run approximately at right angles to the lines of connection to the common centre of the curved path.

In the king-pin steering system each wheel has its own pivot point, namely, the king pin, to which is attached the stub axle on which the wheel rotates. Each stub axle is connected to a short lever called the track arm. The two track arms are interconnected by the track rod. Thanks to this arrangement, the force applied by the steering control arm need act only at one king pin; the movements of the other king pin will be automatically controlled by the trapezium linkage system. When the driver turns the steering wheel, the steering gear transmits the rotation of the wheel to the drop arm and drag link which in turn actuates the above-mentioned steering control arm. The latter then rotates the stub axle about the king pin (Fig. 2).

Figs. 3, 4 and 5 illustrated various forms of steering gear construction. In the worm-and-sector system the bottom part of the steering column is provided with a worm which engages with a toothed worm-gear sector (Fig. 3). In the case of worm-and-nut steering a nut moves along the worm when the latter rotates (Fig. 4). When the steering column is rotated, the worm-gear sector (Fig. 3) or the nut (Fig. 4) moves up or down and transmits its movement to the drop arm.

A variant of the worm-and-nut system is the cam steering system (Fig. 5). In this arrangement a tapered projection (follower) engages with the worm-shaped cam and moves the drop arm.

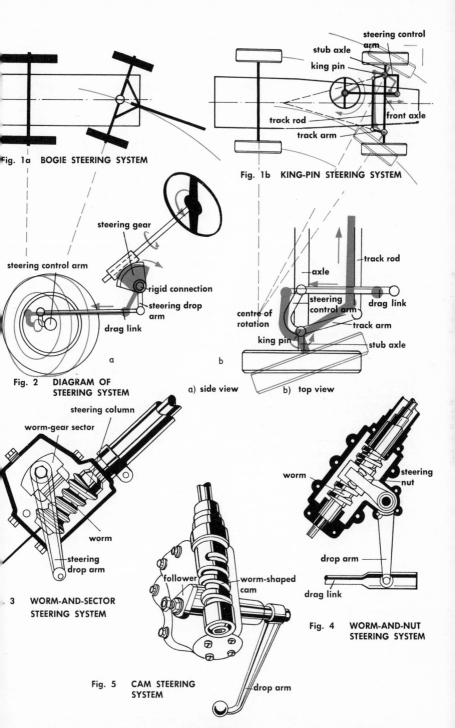

Fig. 1a BOGIE STEERING SYSTEM

Fig. 1b KING-PIN STEERING SYSTEM

steering control arm
stub axle
king pin
track rod
track arm
front axle

steering gear
steering control arm
rigid connection
steering drop arm
drag link
a

axle
track rod
centre of rotation
steering control arm
drag link
track arm
king pin
stub axle
b

Fig. 2 DIAGRAM OF STEERING SYSTEM

a) side view   b) top view

steering column
worm-gear sector
worm
steering drop arm

3 WORM-AND-SECTOR STEERING SYSTEM

follower
worm-shaped cam
drop arm

Fig. 5 CAM STEERING SYSTEM

worm
steering nut
drop arm
drag link

Fig. 4 WORM-AND-NUT STEERING SYSTEM

BRAKES

In modern motor vehicles fitted with shoe-type brakes the latter are almost invariably of the internal-expanding kind, hydraulically operated. Hydraulic actuation is based on a natural law, namely, that a pressure exerted upon a liquid is uniformly transmitted in all directions (Fig. 1): the load on the piston at the extreme left is 100 lb.; as a result of the transmission of the pressure through the liquid, which is an incompressible medium, the force developed at each of the other pistons (which are assumed to have the same area as the first) will also be 100 lb. However, the travel of the eight right-hand pistons will be only one-eighth of the travel of the left-hand piston. Fig. 2 shows the diagram of an internal-expanding brake, together with its hydraulic equipment; it comprises a main cylinder with a reserve fluid tank, the wheel cylinders, and the connecting pipelines. Application of the brakes involves the following operations: when the brake pedal is depressed, a piston in the main cylinder is moved (this piston can be regarded as corresponding to the left-hand piston in Fig. 1) and produces a pressure through the brake system. This pressure forces the two small pistons in the wheel cylinders apart. As a result, the shoes are thrust against the brake drum (Figs. 3a and 3b). The kinetic energy of the vehicle is transformed into heat energy by the friction which occurs at the brake linings. This causes heating of the brake drum. In order quickly to get rid of as much heat as possible, the brake drums must have a large external surface area and be mounted in a place where the air has proper access to them. If a brake drum becomes too hot, it will expand excessively, and then the brake shoes will not press so tightly against the inside of the drum. In addition, the braking efficiency of the brake lining diminishes at elevated temperature, as heat reduces the frictional force developed. Thus, poor heat dissipation greatly reduces the efficiency of the brake.

The central component of the brake system is the master cylinder (Fig. 4). When the brake pedal is depressed, the piston travels to the right and produces a pressure in the chamber behind it. This pressure is transmitted by the hydraulic fluid through the pipes to the wheel cylinders. To equalise any differences of pressure in the system (which differences may, for example, be caused by expansion of the brake liquid in the pipelines), a check valve is installed between the pressure chamber and the pipeline. In addition, the master cylinder ensures uniform filling: when the piston is at rest, hydraulic fluid flows from the reserve tank through the compensating port into the pressure chamber. To prevent air being drawn in when the piston returns to the home position, the space behind the back of the piston is kept filled with fluid through the auxiliary port. At one end of the master cylinder is the stop-light switch in which the hydraulic pressure moves a small piston which actuates the electrical contact that switches on the light.

There are various patterns of internal-expanding shoe-type brakes. Figs. 5a and 5b illustrate two patterns of the Simplex brake embodying mechanical arrangements whereby better braking power is obtained by so-called self-servo action.

(Continued)

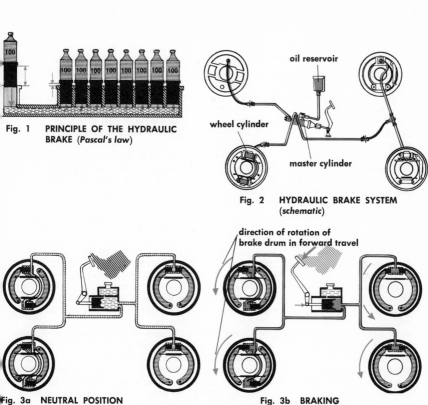

Fig. 1 **PRINCIPLE OF THE HYDRAULIC BRAKE** (*Pascal's law*)

Fig. 2 **HYDRAULIC BRAKE SYSTEM** (*schematic*)

oil reservoir

wheel cylinder

master cylinder

direction of rotation of brake drum in forward travel

Fig. 3a **NEUTRAL POSITION**

Fig. 3b **BRAKING**

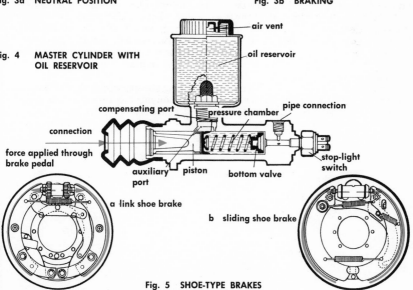

Fig. 4 **MASTER CYLINDER WITH OIL RESERVOIR**

air vent

oil reservoir

compensating port

pressure chamber

pipe connection

connection

force applied through brake pedal

auxiliary port

piston

bottom valve

stop-light switch

a link shoe brake

b sliding shoe brake

Fig. 5 **SHOE-TYPE BRAKES**

Another example of the internal-expanding brake is the Duplex brake (Fig. 6): in this arrangement each shoe has its own wheel cylinder which acts in one direction only, pressing one shoe against the drum, while the other shoe serves as a support for thrusting against. In this system the shoes are so mounted that, when the vehicle is travelling in the forward direction, the drum tends to carry each shoe around with it in the direction away from the pivot point of the shoe. This makes for efficient braking by self-servo action. On the other hand, the braking action is rather poor when the vehicle is reversing.

Besides the single-circuit brake systems described here, dual-circuit hydraulic systems comprising a tandem master cylinder which contains two pistons that are actuated by the brake pedal (Fig. 7). The front piston transmits its force to the rear one, so that hydraulic pressure is developed in two circuits. The advantage of the two-circuit braking system is that if an oil pipe in one circuit fractures, the second circuit will still continue to function.

Disc brakes

Partial disc brakes: In this arrangement the brake disc is gripped pincer-wise between two circular or kidney-shaped brake pads fitted with friction linings. The large area of the disc assures excellent dissipation of the heat generated by braking (Figs. 8a and 8b). Two-circuit hydraulic systems, when applied to disc brakes of this kind, do not separately serve the front and the rear wheels respectively; instead, each circuit serves all four wheels. For this purpose the brake disc of each of the wheels is provided with four hydraulic brake cylinders (Fig. 9).

Full disc brakes (Fig. 10): In this form of construction, fixed pads with friction linings act from inside upon both sides of a rotating casing, which has to dissipate the heat in much the same way as a shoe-type brake. In this case the self-servo or self-energising action (Fig. 10b) is obtained by means of steel balls which mount the inclined faces of sockets when the two brake discs (one fixed and one moving) rotate in relation to each other. This forces the discs apart, causing them to be pressed even more firmly against the casing. The degree of servo action developed is dependent on the inclination of the faces of the sockets. If they are flatly inclined, a considerable servo action results, but this may involve a risk of jamming and locking of the brake, as the balls may be wedged so tightly that they cannot by themselves roll back to the bottom of the sockets. Besides, the two discs must then undergo a considerable displacement in relation to each other before they are forced so far apart that they can develop a powerful braking action. Wear of the friction linings necessitates an even greater amount of displacement of the discs in relation to each other. For this reason disc brakes having a high degree of self-servo action are particularly sensitive to lining wear.

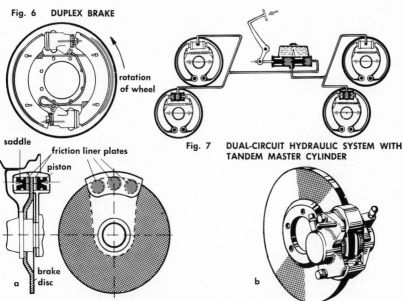

Fig. 6   DUPLEX BRAKE

rotation
of wheel

Fig. 7   DUAL-CIRCUIT HYDRAULIC SYSTEM WITH
TANDEM MASTER CYLINDER

saddle

friction liner plates

piston

brake
disc

a

b

Fig. 8   PARTIAL DISC BRAKE

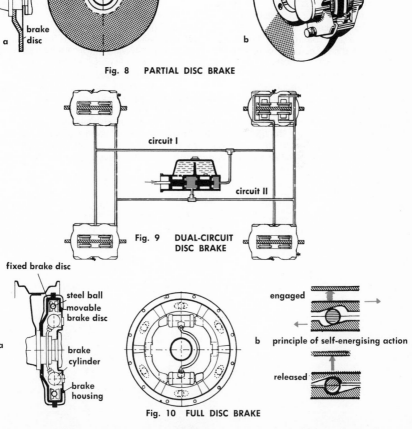

circuit I

circuit II

Fig. 9   DUAL-CIRCUIT
DISC BRAKE

fixed brake disc

steel ball
movable
brake disc

brake
cylinder

brake
housing

a

engaged

b   principle of self-energising action

released

Fig. 10   FULL DISC BRAKE

515

HEADLIGHTS

A car headlamp consists of a housing (usually recessed into the body of the vehicle), the reflector, the light-diffusing glass, and the bulbs with their sockets.

The purpose of the reflector is to concentrate the light that the bulb emits in all directions and directing it ahead of the vehicle. A reflector is a paraboloid mirror which is so shaped that all the rays of light emitted from a light source at its focus are reflected in a direction parallel to the axis of the reflector (Fig. 1; see page 138). If the light source is not located at the focus (Figs. 2 and 3), the light output of the headlamp in the desired direction will be greatly reduced by scatter of the rays. The reflectors are made of steel, the reflecting surface being "silvered", usually by a thin coating of aluminium applied as vapour in vacuum. They reflect about 89% of the light that strikes them. The headlamp glass functions as a light diffuser, i.e., it must so distribute the light that the zone on each side of the vehicle and directly in front of it must also be illuminated. This effect is achieved by providing the glass with grooves or ribs which function as prisms (Fig. 4) and deflect the light. This diffusion does, of course, reduce the brightness of the beam in the main direction.

The principal requirements that the electric bulbs have to fulfil are that the filament must be accurately located at the focus of the reflector and that the bulb should be as small as possible and yet be very bright. The first requirement is fulfilled by accurate location of the fixing tabs on the base of the bulb in relation to the filament. Thus, if the bulb is correctly fitted, the filament will be exactly at the focus of the reflector. A high light efficiency is obtained with coiled or "coiled coil" tungsten filaments enclosed in bulbs filled with an inert gas.

At the present time most headlight bulbs are of the twin-filament type, with a built-in screen (Figs. 5a and 5b). The filament for high-beam ("far beam") is located at the focus of the reflector. The filament for low beam ("dimmed light") is placed a few millimetres in front of the focus and a little higher (Fig. 5a), so that the light emitted by this filament is reflected as a downward-directed spreading beam (Fig. 6a). Rays from this filament striking the lower part of the reflector would be reflected upwards, but these rays are intercepted by the screen installed (inside the bulb) under the filament.

Most cars in the United States are equipped with sealed-beam headlights. This type of light contains the filament, reflector, and lense, all assembled into one unit. The entire sealed-beam fits into the car's headlight housing and, if replacement becomes necessary, the entire unit is removed and a new one is inserted.

reflector (paraboloid)

Fig. 1   LIGHT SOURCE AT FOCUS:
rays are reflected as a parallel beam

Fig. 2   LIGHT SOURCE ABOVE OR BELOW
FOCUS: rays are scattered

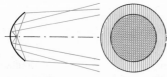 

Fig. 3   LIGHT SOURCE BEFORE OR BEHIND FOCUS:
rays are scattered

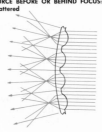

Fig. 4b   LIGHT DISTRIBUTION
BY DIFFUSING GLASS

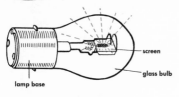

Fig. 4a   LIGHT-DIFFUSING GLASS

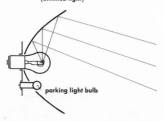 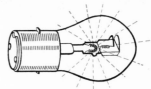

screen

glass bulb

lamp base

Fig. 5a   TWIN-FILAMENT LAMP
(dimmed light)

Fig. 5b   TWIN-FILAMENT LAMP
(far beam)

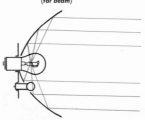

parking light bulb

Fig. 6a   DIRECTION BEAM WITH DIMMED LIGHT

Fig. 6b   DIRECTION OF FAR BEAM

517

ELECTRIC HORN

A motor horn, like any other source of sound, must set up vibrations in the air; the variations in air pressure associated with these vibrations are perceived by the ear as sound. The pitch of the sound is determined by the frequency, i.e., the number of vibrations per second. Depending on the acoustic pressure (measured in microbars, a unit of pressure corresponding to a water volume of 1/100 mm) and the frequency of the sound, the human ear perceives a certain loudness (Fig. 1). Loudness is measured in phons. For a given acoustic pressure, sounds differing in pitch are not perceived as having the same loudness. The range of audibility is bounded by the threshold of hearing at low values of the acoustic pressure, and by the threshold of pain at high values of this pressure. At frequencies of 2000–5000 cycles/secs., audibility extends down to very low acoustic pressures, i.e., the human ear is particularly sensitive in this frequency range. It so happens that the acoustic pressure of the sound emitted by motor vehicles is relatively low in this same frequency range of 2000–5000 cycles/sec. (see Fig. 2). It is therefore advantageous to ensure that the frequencies of the sounds made by a motor horn are within this range: the horn will thus better be able to make itself heard above the general noise of the traffic. Most of the horns now used as warning devices on motor vehicles are either of the impact type (Fig. 3) or klaxons (Fig. 4). Both kinds have an electromagnet whose winding is energised when the driver presses the horn button. An iron plate, called the armature, is attracted by the magnet and, in doing so, opens a contact and thus cuts off the current to the electromagnet, which now releases the armature, allowing the latter to spring back to its initial position. The whole cycle of events now repeats itself. The oscillations of the armature are transmitted to a diaphragm which in turn sets up vibrations in the air. The number of vibrations per second is called the fundamental frequency of the horn.

In the impact-type horn (Fig. 3) the entire diaphragm assembly (comprising armature plate, oscillating beam and disphragm) strikes the core of the electromagnet. Harmonic oscillations in a narrow frequency range are additionally produced. As a result of this, the sound spectrum of an impact-type horn mainly shows two narrow frequency ranges, so that it can penetrate effectively through noise. In the case of the klaxon, with its rather softer note, the diaphragm assembly does not hit the core, but can oscillate freely. The sound spectrum of the klaxon has many overtones spread out over a wide frequency range; the pitch of the fundamental tone of the horn is determined mainly by the length of the horn.

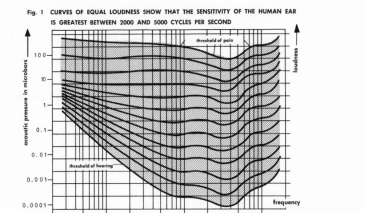

Fig. 1 CURVES OF EQUAL LOUDNESS SHOW THAT THE SENSITIVITY OF THE HUMAN EAR IS GREATEST BETWEEN 2000 AND 5000 CYCLES PER SECOND

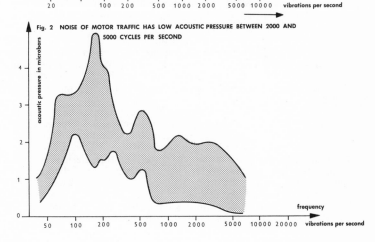

Fig. 2 NOISE OF MOTOR TRAFFIC HAS LOW ACOUSTIC PRESSURE BETWEEN 2000 AND 5000 CYCLES PER SECOND

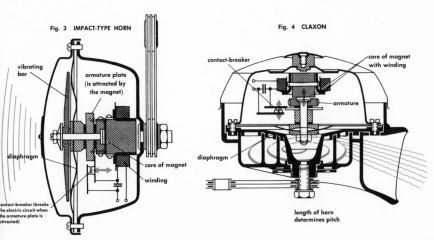

Fig. 3 IMPACT-TYPE HORN

vibrating bar

armature plate (is attracted by the magnet)

diaphragm

core of magnet

winding

contact-breaker (breaks the electric circuit when the armature plate is attracted)

Fig. 4 CLAXON

contact-breaker

core of magnet with winding

armature

diaphragm

length of horn determines pitch

FLASHING DIRECTION INDICATOR

The flashing direction indicator (or blinking trafficator) operates on the electro-thermal principal and uses bimetallic strips to open and close electrical contacts. As its name implies, a bimetallic strip consists of two strips of different metals, with different coefficients of thermal expansion, bonded together. When a bimetallic strip is heated, it will curve towards the side where the metal with the lower co-efficient of expansion is affixed. Thus, if one end of the strip is gripped, the other end will thus move a certain distance away from its home position when cold, the magnitude of this distance depending on the temperature to which the strip is exposed.

The flashing direction indicator comprises two such bimetallic strips (Fig. 2a), both of which move in the same direction on being heated. Each strip is provided with a silver contact at its end. In the neutral position these contacts touch each other. When the ignition of the motor vehicle is switched on, current from the battery flows through these contacts and through the heating coil of one of the bimetallic strips. The heat produced by this coil warms the strip, causing it to bend and thus open the contact. Now the current, instead of flowing through this contact, is passed through the heating coil of the other bimetallic strip, with the result that this strip, too, is deflected, in the same direction as the other strip (Fig. 2b). The latter now receives less current, consequently cools a little, and moves back towards its initial position; the two contacts touch each other again; and the cycle is repeated. This continues as long as the ignition is switched on, even while the direction indicator switch is not actuated by the driver of the vehicle. When he wishes to turn a corner and actuates the switch, then current will flow directly to the direction indicator when the contacts are closed (Fig. 2a). The indicator lamp then lights up. However, the process continues: the contacts separate, and the lamp goes out. The pilot light inside the vehicle always lights up just when the indicator light is out because the pilot light gets its current only when the contacts of the bimetallic strips are open (Fig. 2b). When these contacts close again, the indicator lamp lights up, while the pilot light remains dark, as it is then short-circuited by the contacts. The frequency of blinking is independent of the outside temperature. Besides, when the engine is running, the flashing indicator is already switched on and therefore comes into immediate action when the driver actuates the indicator switch.

Another widely used type of flashing indicator is based on the hot-wire principle. The thermal elongation of a thin resistance wire under the influence of a current passing through it is used for controlling the blinker contacts.

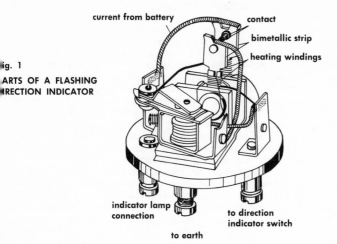

Fig. 1

PARTS OF A FLASHING
DIRECTION INDICATOR

current from battery
contact
bimetallic strip
heating windings
indicator lamp
connection
to earth
to direction
indicator switch

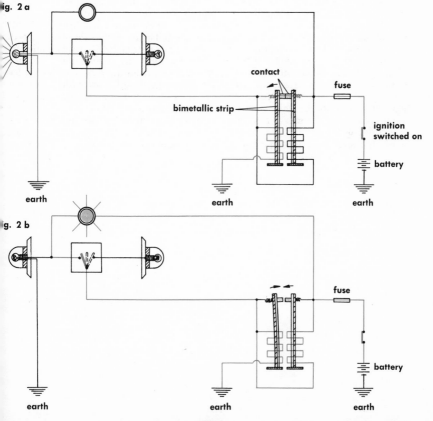

Fig. 2 a

contact
bimetallic strip
fuse
ignition
switched on
battery
earth
earth
earth

Fig. 2 b

fuse
battery
earth
earth
earth

SPEEDOMETER

A speedometer is an instrument which measures the speed at which the car is travelling and usually also embodies a mileage recording mechanism. The central feature of the device is a permanent magnet. Each magnet is surrounded by a magnetic field (Fig. 2), which can be conceived as consisting of lines of force. These can be "made visible" by strewing iron filings on a sheet of cardboard under which the magnet is held; the filings will arrange themselves along the lines of force and thus reveal the pattern of these lines. When a magnet is rotated, its field will rotate with it. The magnet in the speedometer begins to rotate as soon as the vehicle is set in motion; it is driven through a small gear unit by the speedometer shaft, which is connected to the propeller shaft or the front axle. The higher the speed of the vehicle is, the higher is the speed of rotation of the magnet. The magnet rotates concentrically in an aluminium ring, in which the rotating magnetic field induces eddy currents which in turn produce a magnetic field of their own. The interaction of this magnetic field with that of the rotating permanent magnet exercises a torque (twisting moment) on the aluminium ring. This torque tries to rotate the ring along with the magnet. The faster the magnet rotates, the higher is the torque. The ring is not free to rotate, however: it can merely swing a certain distance—depending on the magnitude of the torque—and is then restrained by the counteracting force of a spiral spring. Attached to the ring is a pointer which indicates the speed of the vehicle on a suitably graduated scale. In many types of speedometer the ring has an extension in the form of a drum to which the scale is attached. When the speed increases, this drum rotates, and the speed indication is shown in a narrow gap in a panel mounted in front of the scale. The speedometer generally also comprises a mileage recorder. This device is driven through a small worm gear, which is mounted on the speedometer shaft, by the same shaft that drives the rotating magnet. The motion of the speedometer shaft, greatly reduced by another small gear unit, is transmitted to the mileage recording mechanism. The latter therefore merely counts the number of revolutions. However, since a certain number of revolutions, of the front wheel or of the propeller shaft correspond to a certain distance travelled by the vehicle, the revolution counting mechanism can be made to give a direct reading of the mileage covered. When the disc which counts the units (i.e., miles) has performed one whole revolution, the counting disc for the tens is rotated one place (by means of a small driving catch). When the "tens" disc has performed one revolution, it similarly rotates the "hundreds" disc one place. This operation is repeated up to the "ten thousands" disc.

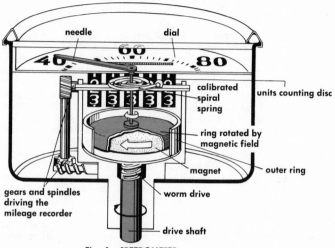

Fig. 1 SPEEDOMETER
(*schematic*)

needle

dial

calibrated
spiral
spring

units counting disc

ring rotated by
magnetic field

magnet

outer ring

gears and spindles
driving the
mileage recorder

worm drive

drive shaft

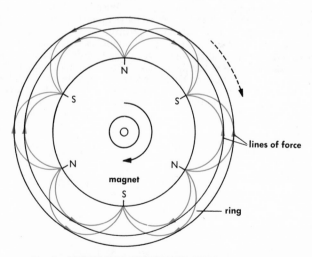

N

S

S

N

N

lines of force

magnet

ring

S

Fig. 2 PRINCIPLE OF SPEEDOMETER DRIVE

STEAM LOCOMOTIVE

A steam locomotive is powered by a reciprocating steam engine, i.e., a power unit operated by the expansion of steam which is admitted into a cylinder and moves a piston to and fro. The piston motion is transmitted to the driving wheels of the locomotive.

The drive mechanism and control gear of a steam locomotive are illustrated in Fig. 1. The steam, generated in a smoke tube boiler or flue boiler (cf. page 40 and Fig. 3), is delivered through a pipe to the slide-valve chest. From here the slide valve admits the steam to the cylinder alternately through two openings so that it enters first on one side and then on the other side of the piston and thus pushes the latter to and fro. In Fig. 1 the steam is entering the cylinder on the left-hand side of the piston, and is pushing the piston to the right. At the same time, the exhaust steam on the right-hand side is being pushed out of the cylinder by the piston and is discharged through a duct from which it excapes through the chimney into the open air. The piston rod connects the piston to the cross-head, which moves backwards and forwards in a guide. Attached by means of an articulated connection to the cross-head is the driving rod whose other end is connected to the driving pin on the driving wheel. In this way the reciprocating (to-and-fro) motion of the piston is transformed into the rotary motion of the wheel. There are usually two or more sets of driving wheels, these being coupled together by coupling rods.

The locomotive in Fig. 1 is travelling backwards; its driving wheels are revolving anti-clockwise. To reverse the motion, the slide valve would, for the piston position illustrated, have to be so altered so as to admit steam to the right instead of to the left of the piston. This adjustment of the slide valve can be done from the driver's cab by means of a handwheel which works a system of control rods and thus pulls the slide valve to the left. This adjustment system is shown diagrammatically in Fig. 2. The normal to-and-fro movement of the slide valve to admit the steam alternately on the two sides of the piston is performed by the slide valve gear. Attached to the same pin as that actuated by the driving rod is a so-called fly crank which, through a rod, moves the link to and fro. When the valve rod is above the pivot, the slide valve will move to the left when the link rod moves to the right; when the valve rod is below the pivot, the opposite occurs.

The locomotive develops its tractive force because of the "adhesion" (due to friction) between the wheels and the rails. Because of the weight of the locomotive, whereby the wheels are pressed tightly against the rails, a high frictional force and therefore a high tractive force can be developed. However, if the force applied to the wheel circumference by the steam engine exceeds the frictional force that can be developed, slip of the wheels on the rails will occur.

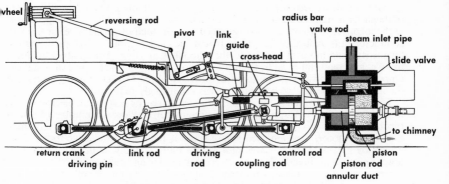

wheel

reversing rod

pivot

link

guide

cross-head

radius bar

valve rod

steam inlet pipe

slide valve

return crank

driving pin

link rod

driving rod

coupling rod

control rod

piston

piston rod

annular duct

to chimney

Fig. 1 DRIVE MECHANISM AND CONTROL GEAR OF
A STEAM LOCOMOTIVE

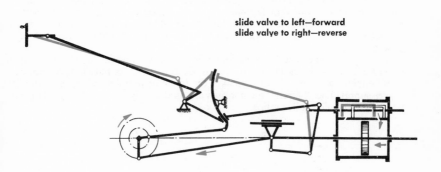

slide valve to left—forward
slide valve to right—reverse

Fig. 2 DIAGRAM SHOWING SLIDE VALVE ADJUSTMENT
(*Heusinger system*)

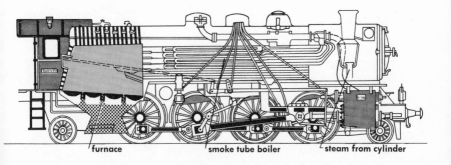

furnace

smoke tube boiler

steam from cylinder

Fig. 3 SECTION THROUGH A STEAM LOCOMOTIVE

ELECTRIC LOCOMOTIVE

As a traction unit for railway operation the steam locomotive (see page 524) has, in many countries, been superseded by the electric locomotive. One of the advantages of the latter is that the power to drive the locomotive does not have to be generated in the locomotive itself but can be supplied to it through overhead wires or through conductor rails. A further advantage is that the electric motor develops its highest torque (turning moment applied to the wheels) at starting. This enables the locomotive, and the train it pulls, to move off more swiftly after stopping at a station. Once the locomotive is in motion, the torque required to keep it going is less and the amount of electric power consumed is accordingly reduced.

The wheels or the axles can be individually driven by a separate electric motor to each axle (Fig. 1). Alternatively, one large motor may drive a number of wheels through a system of connecting rods (Fig. 2). With individual drive, relatively small high-speed motors are employed whose speed is reduced to the drive speed of the wheels by means of gears. Large motors can more suitably be designed to run at lower speeds and directly drive an intermediate driving shaft (or jackshaft). Fig. 3 represents an electric motor with individual drive. The current is collected from the overhead contact wire by means of pantograph current collectors. On many railways single-phase alternating current at 15,000 volts with a frequency of $16\frac{2}{3}$ cycles per second is used. This current is transformed down to the working voltage of the motors (usually 300–700 volts). The speed of the locomotive is controlled by connecting the motors to different tappings (output connections) of the transformer (cf. page 92). This is preferable to controlling the speed by means of variable resistances connected in series with the motors, as the latter method would entail considerable power losses.

A variant of the electric locomotive is the diesel-electric locomotive, which generates its own electric current by means of a generator (see page 64) powered by a diesel engine (see page 470). This makes the locomotive independent of an outside power supply. Diesel-electric locomotives are used chiefly on non-electrified or only partially electrified railway lines.

Fig. 1   INDIVIDUAL AXLE DRIVE

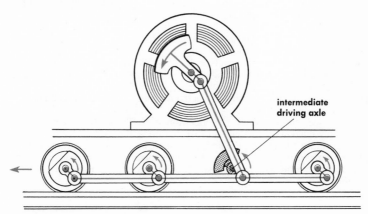

intermediate
driving axle

Fig. 2   MULTIPLE-AXLE DRIVE BY ONE MOTOR THROUGH CONNECTING ROD

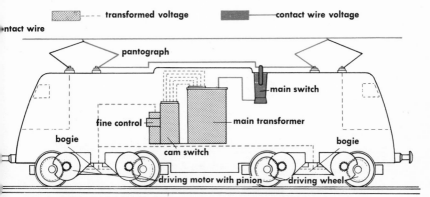

····· transformed voltage   contact wire voltage

ntact wire

pantograph

main switch

fine control

main transformer

bogie

cam switch

bogie

driving motor with pinion   driving wheel

Fig. 3   SCHEMATIC SECTION THROUGH AN ELECTRIC LOCOMOTIVE

DIESEL LOCOMOTIVE

Diesel locomotives are relatively cheap to run, can be got ready for operation and started up more quickly and conveniently than steam locomotives, and can be speedily and easily refuelled. Also, their mechanical efficiency is superior to that of steam locomotives, while they dispense with the expensive overhead contact wires and power distribution installations required by electric traction. However, they lack the robustness of steam locomotives and the operational flexibility and smooth running properties of electric locomotives.

The accompanying illustration shows a typical modern diesel locomotive, the type V 320 as used by the West-German Federal Railways. This locomotive has two independent sets of drive machinery, each associated with one bogie (or truck). The power is supplied by two 16-inch cylinder four-stroke diesel engines developing 2000 h.p. each. These are supercharged engines, i.e., the air needed for combustion of the fuel is fed to the cylinder by powerful fans (radial-flow fans) driven by small gas turbines (see page 46) which utilise the exhaust gases from the engine. Supercharging greatly increases the power of an engine in comparison with a non-supercharged engine which has to rely on mere suction for its air intake.

The engine power is transmitted through rubber-cum-metal couplings and shafts to two hydraulic gear units and thence through another shaft to a special mechanical gear unit which can be hand-controlled from low to high speed range. From this speed-control gear unit all the axles of the bogie are driven by means of a number of drive shafts. The engine itself as well as the lubricating oil and the gear oil are cooled by water which is then circulated through a fan-operated cooling unit where it gives off the heat it has collected.

The underframe and superstructure of the V 320 are of lightweight welded steel construction; the superstructure shell is welded to, and co-operates structurally with, the underframe. The locomotive is equipped with disc brakes—a pair of brakes to each wheel—and additionally an electro-magnetic rail brake which ensures short stopping distances even at high speeds.

The electrical equipment of the locomotive comprises two electric generators which supply current to the lead storage batteries, the motors for driving various items of auxiliary equipment, the lighting system, and the electric control and monitoring equipment. In addition, the V 320 diesel locomotive is provided with a boiler installation for supplying superheated steam for heating the train and for preheating the engine.

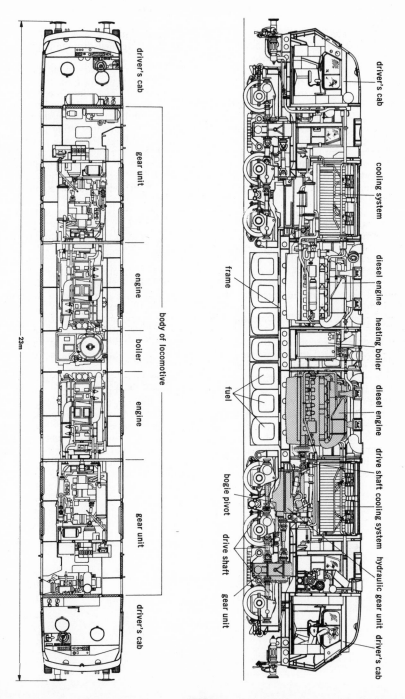

driver's cab

gear unit

engine

body of locomotive

boiler

engine

gear unit

driver's cab

23m

driver's cab

cooling system

diesel engine

heating boiler

diesel engine

drive shaft cooling system

hydraulic gear unit driver's cab

frame

fuel

bogie pivot

drive shaft

gear unit

PNEUMATIC BRAKE

The simplest method of braking a railway vehicle is by means of the hand-operated block brake (Fig. 1). The braking force in this case is applied through a system of levers worked by a handwheel mounted on a screw spindle.

For quickly stopping a train in motion, however, it is necessary to employ more powerful means, in the form of a compressed air brake (pneumatic brake) as illustrated in Figs. 2a and 2b. The system comprises a compressor which supplies compressed air to the main air reservoir and thence, via the driver's brake valve and the main brake pipe, to the auxiliary air reservoirs. The main brake pipe extends through all the carriages of the train, the connections between the carriages being formed by flexible hoses provided with quick-action couplings. When the brake is released (Fig. 2a), there is equal pressure on both sides of the valve piston. Its own weight keeps this piston pressed down on its seat and thus closes the passage through which the compressed air can reach the brake cylinder, which is in communication with the external air. Each axle is equipped with a brake cylinder whose piston actuates the brake.

When the driver wishes to apply the brakes, he moves the control lever of the brake valve to the appropriate position (Fig. 2b). As a result, the main brake pipe is put into communication with the external air, and the pressure in this pipe therefore goes down to the atmospheric pressure. Now all the auxiliary reservoirs contain air at a higher pressure than that in the main brake pipe. This causes the brake valve piston to be forced upwards, whereby compressed air, from the auxiliary reservoirs, is admitted to the brake cylinder. The compressed air entering this cylinder pushes the brake piston back against the pressure of a spring (which keeps the piston in the home position when the brake is released) and thus causes the brake blocks to be pressed hard against the wheels. On completion of the braking operation the control lever of the driver's brake valve is returned to its initial position. A slight excess pressure in the main brake pipe pushes the valve piston down again. The main brake pipe is thus reconnected to the auxiliary air reservoirs and the brake cylinders are once again in communication with the atmosphere.

In the event of a connecting hose between two carriages rupturing or bursting, the main brake pipe will lose its air pressure. As a result, the brakes will be applied all along the train, The same effect is produced by actuation of the emergency brake valve which is provided in each carriage and which can be worked from each compartment by means of a control wire. The type of pneumatic brake described here is named the Westinghouse brake, after its inventor. A further development of this system is embodied in the Kunze-Knorr brake, which has a brake cylinder comprising two chambers and two coaxial pistons. This arrangement enables the brake to be released step by step and thus makes for finer brake control.

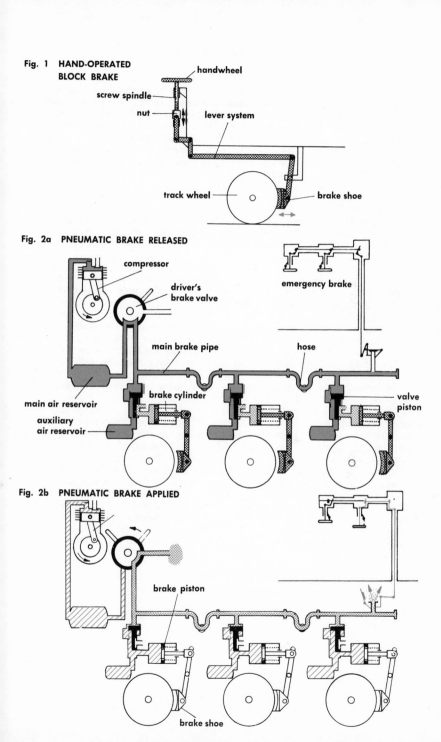

Fig. 1 HAND-OPERATED BLOCK BRAKE

handwheel
screw spindle
nut
lever system
track wheel
brake shoe

Fig. 2a PNEUMATIC BRAKE RELEASED

compressor
driver's brake valve
emergency brake
main brake pipe
hose
main air reservoir
brake cylinder
auxiliary air reservoir
valve piston

Fig. 2b PNEUMATIC BRAKE APPLIED

brake piston
brake shoe

RAILWAY SAFETY DEVICES

Automatic train stop:

Attached to the driver's control lever in a railcar or an electric locomotive is a contact which, on being depressed, breaks an electric circuit (Fig. 1). If the driver lets go of the lever, this circuit is closed, causing current to flow through the windings of an electromagnet of a monitoring valve. This valve closes the pipe leading from the main air reservoir to the main brake pipe. At the same time another valve is opened whereby the pressure is released from the main brake pipe, thus causing the brakes to be applied (see page 530), the effect being the same as if the brake valve had been actuated. When the driver's control lever is released, the driving motor is also automatically switched off.

Inductive control:

For use on busy lines various other safety devices are additionally available. One of these is the inductive system (Fig. 2) of train control. Each signal on a section of line equipped with this system has a device whereby the brakes of a passing train can be actuated. The locomotive is provided with a "transmitter" which comprises an iron-core coil and a condenser. This oscillating circuit (see page 70) is tuned to 2000 cycles/sec. and is fed with current from a high-frequency generator to which, in addition, the coil of an electromagnet for a relay (see page 94) is connected. The high-frequency generator is driven by an electric motor or a small steam turbine which also drives a 24-volt direct-current dynamo. Connected to this dynamo via the high-frequency relay is a second relay and two pilot lamps. When the system is in operation, the high-frequency generator supplies current to the oscillating circuit of the locomotive and to the high-frequency relay, so that the armature of the latter is attracted by the electromagnet and allows current to flow through the 24-volt direct-current relay. When thus energised, this last-mentioned relay interrupts a flow of current to the actuating electromagnet of a valve (corresponding in its function to the monitoring valve in Fig. 1).

The signal beside the railway track is also equipped with an oscillating circuit tuned to 2000 cycles/sec. When the signal is at "safe", its oscillating circuit is short-circuited and has no effect on the passing locomotive. However, if the signal is at "stop" and the train nevertheless fails to stop, the oscillating circuit of the signal will resonate (see page 204) in tune with that of the passing locomotive and thereby withdraw so much energy from the latter circuit that the armature of the high-frequency relay is no longer sufficiently strongly attracted by the electromagnet and is therefore released. This in turn cuts off the supply of current to the 24-volt relay, which then likewise releases its armature. This closes the electric circuit to the electromagnet that controls the monitoring valve. When this happens, the monitoring valve causes the brakes to be applied and the driving motor of the locomotive to be switched. At the same time, the pilot lamp "a" goes out and the lamp "b" lights up.

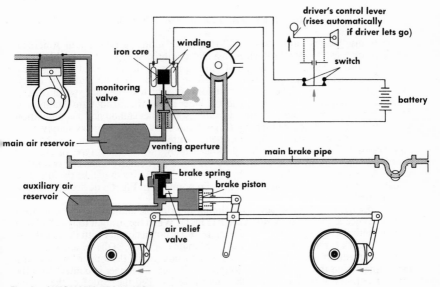

driver's control lever (rises automatically if driver lets go)

iron core

winding

monitoring valve

switch

battery

main air reservoir

venting aperture

main brake pipe

brake spring

brake piston

auxiliary air reservoir

air relief valve

Fig. 1 AUTOMATIC TRAIN STOP

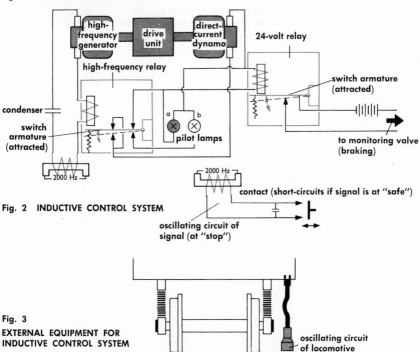

high-frequency generator

drive unit

direct-current dynamo

24-volt relay

high-frequency relay

switch armature (attracted)

condenser

switch armature (attracted)

a   b

pilot lamps

to monitoring valve (braking)

2000 Hz

2000 Hz

contact (short-circuits if signal is at "safe")

Fig. 2 INDUCTIVE CONTROL SYSTEM

oscillating circuit of signal (at "stop")

Fig. 3
EXTERNAL EQUIPMENT FOR
INDUCTIVE CONTROL SYSTEM

oscillating circuit of locomotive

oscillating circuit of signal

RAILWAY SWITCHES OR POINTS

The terms "points" and "switches" (the latter more particularly in American practice) are used to denote devices, usually comprising tapered metal blades or tongues, for setting alternative routes of running rails. In the somewhat more general sense of a curved track leading from one track to another, the term "turnout" is also used in this connection. The commonest form of switch is the split switch (Fig. 1) in which one rail of the main track and the inner rail of the turnout are continuous. There are various other types of railway switch, sometimes embodying a combination of two split switches (double turnout) (Figs. 2 and 3). Where two tracks simply cross each other without provision for trains being routed from one track to another, the term "crossing" is usually employed. Fig. 5 shows a common type of crossing (diamond crossing). In some cases, however, more particularly when the two intersecting tracks form a small angle with each other, the crossing may take the form of a so-called crossing switch (also known as "slip points"). In Fig. 4 a device of this kind is illustrated.

The operation of all these devices is similar in principle and can best be explained with reference to the ordinary split switch (Fig. 1): When the straight tongue "a" is in contact with the rail I and the curved tongue "b" is not in contact with the rail II, the switch is set for running straight ahead on the main track. When the switch is set so as to divert a train coming from the left on to the turnout track, the tongue "b" is swung into contact with the rail II and the tongue "a" is now no longer in contact with the rail I. The point of intersection of the inner rails is called the "frog" of the switch, marked by H in Fig. 1. It is usually in the form of a V-shaped unit. As a safeguard against derailment the rails opposite the frog are provided with guard rails (e), and the frog itself is assisted initially (i.e., at its point) by wing rails (f) to carry the weight of the wheels passing over it.

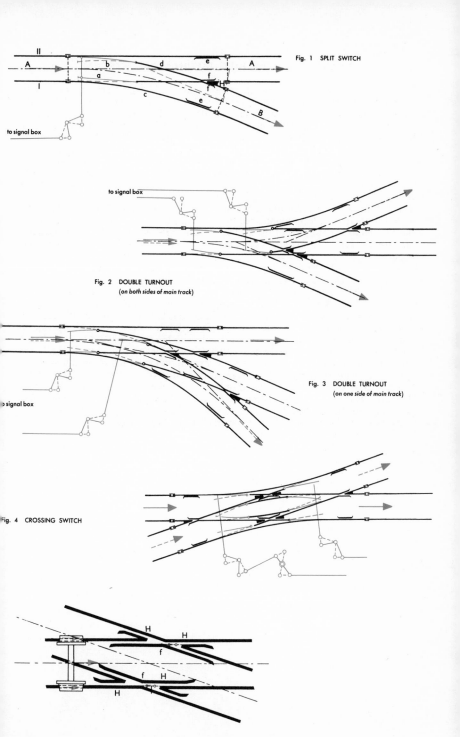

Fig. 1 SPLIT SWITCH

Fig. 2 DOUBLE TURNOUT
(on both sides of main track)

Fig. 3 DOUBLE TURNOUT
(on one side of main track)

Fig. 4 CROSSING SWITCH

5 DIAMOND CROSSING

535

RAILWAY SIGNAL BOX: MECHANICAL SYSTEM

The switches (points) and signals on a section of railway track are worked by controls accommodated in a signal box (or tower). On lines carrying scheduled train services these controls are operated in accordance with predetermined timetables.

The principle of mechanical switch and signal operation is illustrated in Fig. 1. In the signal box are pulleys, each connected to an operating lever. When the signal-man moves the lever, the pulley is rotated a certain amount, depending on the desired switch position. A catch secures the lever in position. A steel wire rope passes round the pulley. The end of this rope is attached to the switch actuating mechanism or to the operating wheel of the main signal. The tensioning device keeps the wire rope constantly taut. Now when the signalman swings the operating lever, the actuating wheel of the switch mechanism is rotated through a certain angle by the wire rope, so that the actuating lever (connected to the wheel) is likewise swung about its pivot and thus shifts the tongues of the switch to the desired position. The main signal is similarly worked, the arm of the signal being moved by a rod attached to the actuating wheel.

Fig. 2 represents the track layout of a four-track railway station. Two trains are standing on tracks 3 and 4 respectively. The train arriving on track 4 must cross the tracks 2 and 3 and continue its journey on track 1. The switches 1 and 4 and the crossing switches 3 and 2 must be appropriately set. To establish the route for the train approaching on track 4, the signalman must accordingly set the relevant switches, crossing switches and signals. When this has been done, he operates a route lever. This lever, which is associated only with the route marked in red in Fig. 2, can be operated only if all the switches and crossings for this route have first all been correctly set. This dependence of the route lever upon the switch settings is achieved by a system of interlocking controls. A separate route lever is provided for each route. None of these levers can be operated unless all the signals (1a–4a and 1e–4e) are set at "stop". When the route has been established, all the signals except 4a are locked in the "stop" position. When the route is cleared by the station inspector, the signalman shifts the signal 4a to "go". The train on track 4 can then proceed.

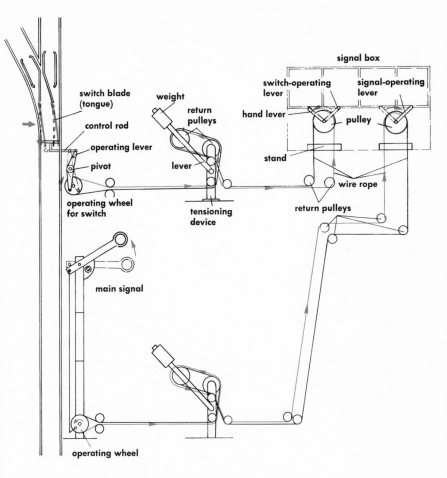

Fig. 1 SWITCH AND SIGNAL OPERATING SYSTEM

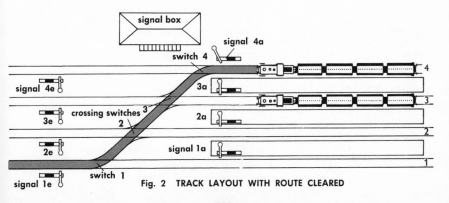

Fig. 2 TRACK LAYOUT WITH ROUTE CLEARED

537

RAILWAY SIGNAL BOX: ELECTRIC SYSTEM

Operating a mechanical signal box (see page 536) involves the exertion of considerable physical force by the signalman. For this reason in modern installations the points and signals are worked by small electric motors. On a control desk in the signal box each switch (set of points) has its own control key (electric switch). Also, there are similar keys for controlling the signals. The signal box also contains, at eye level, an illuminated diagram showing the track layout and all the switches, crossings and signals of the section of railway line concerned. The switch and signal positions are indicated on this diagram by means of small coloured lights. A glance at the panel also shows whether any particular track is free or occupied by a train. An illuminated diagram of this kind greatly facilitates the signalman's task. A further development, providing even greater convenience and sureness of operation, is the "track plan" signal box. In this arrangement the signalman's control desk itself is laid out as a track plan showing all the signals and switches. Each of these is provided with a key or push-button by means of which the corresponding signal or switch on the track can be operated. The tracks themselves are represented on the control desk by small illuminated compartments (Fig. 2). Unoccupied tracks and track sections which at any particular moment are not in use as a train route remain dark, i.e., not lighted up. The switches in the track plan are additionally marked by yellow lamps installed in slots. When these lamps light up, they indicate in which position the switch has been set (Figs. 1a and 1b). In Fig. 1c the switch is set at "straight ahead", but is occupied by a vehicle (compartment lighted red) and is "closed" to all other traffic. In Fig. 1d the switch is set at "straight ahead" and the route is now clear (indicated by a second yellow-lighted slot to the left of the switch). In Fig. 1e the main signal is set at "safe" (green light). Fig. 1f shows the signal at "stop".

A track plan corresponding to the layout in Fig. 2 controlled by the mechanical system described on page 536 is represented in Fig. 2a. Tracks 3 and 4 are each occupied by a train; the corresponding slots in the track plan of the control desk are accordingly lighted red. All the signals are set at "stop". The switches 13–16 are all set at "straight ahead". Now the station inspector gives instructions to clear a route from track 4 to track 1, for example. This instruction is brought to the signalman's attention by the yellow lighting-up of the (hitherto unlighted) slots along the required route. The signalman thereupon works the push-buttons 8 and 17. The winking of the yellow indicator lights of the switches 13–16 informs him that the switches are moving in to the desired positions. The winking light in the slots changes to a steadfast light. The switch positions shown in Fig. 2a change to those in Fig. 2b: the selected route is then indicated by steadfast yellow lights along its entire length. Now the signal 8 changes from red to green, and the train waiting on track 4 can proceed. All the switches on this route are now kept locked by an electric circuit and their positions cannot be altered. Also, the signals 5, 6 and 7 are set at "stop". The train on track 3 therefore cannot move ahead. When the train on track 4 travels along the route thus cleared for it, the yellow-lighted slots change to red, section by section, according to the train's position. Behind the train the red lights in the slots change back to yellow and then soon go out. The route is thus cancelled again and the signal 8 reverts to red. All the switches remain in the positions at which they have been set, however. The position of the train on the track plan is automatically indicated by the train itself.

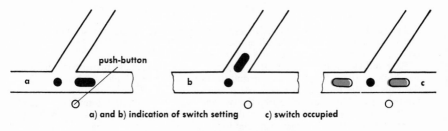

a) and b) indication of switch setting   c) switch occupied

Fig. 1 SWITCH AND SIGNAL SETTINGS

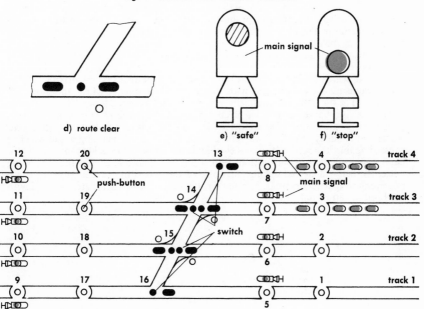

d) route clear   e) "safe"   f) "stop"

Fig. 2a TRACK PLAN WITH TWO TRACKS OCCUPIED

Fig. 2b TRACK PLAN WITH ROUTE CLEARED

An escalator is a continuously acting passenger conveying device which has about ten times the hourly handling capacity of a lift (cf. page 238). The escalator conveys passengers at a speed of 8–12 ft./sec.

Each individual step of an escalator is constructed as a carriage provided with four small wheels (Figs. 1 and 3). The top and the bottom pair of wheels each run on rails; the rails of the top pair are set farther outwards than those of the bottom pair. On the upward journey of the step the two rails are situated in the same plane, but a short distance before the top reversal point and a short distance past the bottom reversal point the rails are so displaced in relation to one another that the inner rail is below the outer rail. As a result of this arrangement the steps gradually merge into a flat horizontal surface at the top of the escalator, enabling the passengers to step off easily. Similarly, convenient stepping-on is ensured at the bottom of the upward-moving escalator. The moving steps perform the return journey on the rails which are continued on the underside of the escalator (Fig. 2). Each step is attached to two end-less chains which run on sprocket wheels at the top and bottom of the escalator; the top sprocket wheels are driven by an electric motor, whereby the steps can be made to travel upwards or downwards. A ratchet wheel is mounted on the drive shaft. If a chain fractures, a pawl engages with the teeth of the ratchet wheel and stops the escalator. The motor is automatically switched off at the same time.

The moving handrails consist of continuous belts made of rubber and canvas plies incorporated in it. They are driven by the escalator drive shaft through a gear wheel and chain system. Half-way along the escalator is a tensioning wheel which is pressed against the return strand of the handrail belt and is thus kept taut, so that it cannot slip off the top and bottom return pulleys. Before and after the tensioning wheel the belt is deflected through an angle of 180°, so as to prevent the belt surface becoming roughened by wear. The guide roller keeps the belt accurately aligned with the bottom return pulley.

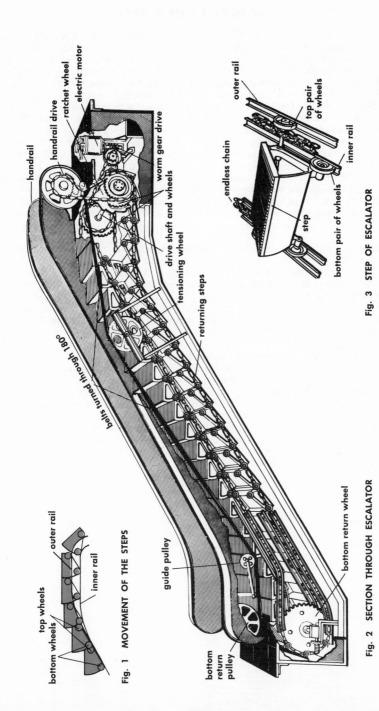

handrail

handrail drive

ratchet wheel

electric motor

worm gear drive

drive shaft and wheels

tensioning wheel

returning steps

belts turned through 180°

guide pulley

bottom return pulley

bottom return wheel

Fig. 2 SECTION THROUGH ESCALATOR

top wheels

bottom wheels

outer rail

inner rail

Fig. 1 MOVEMENT OF THE STEPS

outer rail

top pair of wheels

inner rail

endless chain

step

bottom pair of wheels

Fig. 3 STEP OF ESCALATOR

WHY DOES A SHIP FLOAT?

According to Archimedes' principle, a body which is wholly or partly immersed in a fluid undergoes a loss in weight equal to the weight of fluid which it displaces. An aluminium cube with sides 1 ft. in length weighs about 168 lb. (Fig. 1a). A cubic foot of water weighs about 62 lb. If the aluminium cube is immersed in water (Fig. 1b), its weight has apparently decreased to 106 lb. This is because the cube displaces a cubic foot of water and thereby undergoes a loss in weight equal to the weight of this displaced water. The upward force due to *buoyancy* in this case is equal to 62 lb. and acts at the centre of gravity of the displaced volume of water. If a body, on being totally immersed in a fluid, would displace a volume of fluid whose weight is greater than that of the body concerned, then that body will float on the fluid. Floating merely means that the body sinks into the fluid to such a depth that the displaced volume of fluid weighs exactly as much as the whole floating body. In that case the upward force (buoyancy), which is equal to the weight of the displaced fluid, is in equilibrium with the weight of the body. A 1 ft. wooden cube weighs about 50 lb. It will float in water; the submerged part of the cube displaces a volume of water weighing 50 lb., so that the upward force is 50 lb. and thus counter-balances the weight of the cube (Fig. 2). Hence the displacement of a floating object is equal to its weight.

This is the elementary principle of floating. However, a ship must additionally have stability, i.e., it must be able to right itself after being swung to an inclined position by an external force such as wind pressure. A ship is said to "heel" when it leans over to port or starboard (Fig. 3a); the term "trim" refers to the longitudinal position of a ship in relation to the waterline: the ship is said to be trimmed by the head (as in Fig. 3b) or by the stern, according as the head or the stern lies deeper down in the water. Stability is especially important with regard to the danger of capsising. Fig. 4a shows the ship in its normal position. Its weight can be conceived as a downward force acting at its centre of gravity S. The counterbalancing upward force acts at the centre of buoyancy W, which is the centre of gravity of the displaced volume of water. Normally the points S and W are located on the same vertical line. When the ship heels over (Figs 4b and 4c), the centre of buoyancy shifts to a different position (marked W^1), and the upward force acting here strives to rotate the ship around its centre of gravity S. The intersection M of the line of action of the upward force A with the ship's axis of symmetry is called the metacentre. If the metacentre is located above the centre of gravity S of the ship (as in Fig. 4b), the ship will return to its normal upright position; it is said to be in stable equilibrium. On the other hand, if the metacentre is below the centre of gravity S (Fig. 4c), the ship is in unstable equilibrium and will capsise when it heels over.

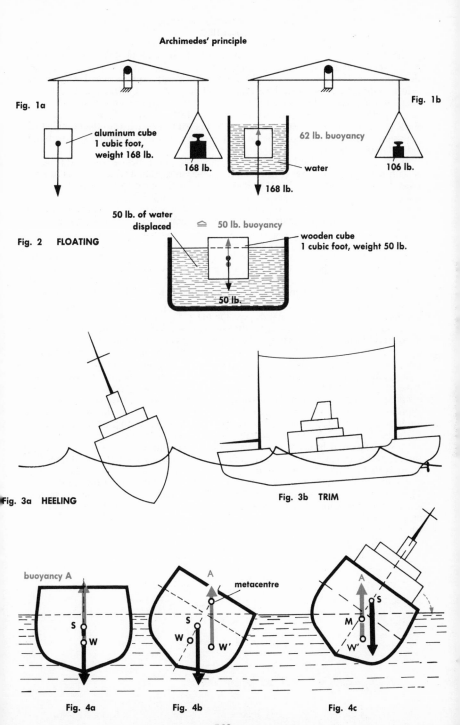

Archimedes' principle

Fig. 1a

aluminum cube
1 cubic foot,
weight 168 lb.

168 lb.

62 lb. buoyancy

water

168 lb.

106 lb.

Fig. 1b

Fig. 2   FLOATING

50 lb. of water
displaced

50 lb. buoyancy

wooden cube
1 cubic foot, weight 50 lb.

50 lb.

Fig. 3a   HEELING

Fig. 3b   TRIM

buoyancy A

metacentre

S

W

A

S

W

W'

A

S

M

W'

Fig. 4a

Fig. 4b

Fig. 4c

543

The two main types of sail are square sails and fore-and-aft sails. The former are set in a position across the longitudinal axis of the ship, whereas the latter are set along the axis. The sailing ships of olden days were mostly square-rigged. An example of fore-and-aft rig is provided by a typical sailing yacht as illustrated in Fig. 1. This boat has a mainsail, a foresail and a jib. The tall triangular mainsail has better wind-catching efficiency than a mainsail of equal area attached to a gaff fitted to the top part of the (generally lower) mast. At the base the mainsail is attached to the boom which can swing about the lower part of the mast in either direction in relation to the longitudinal axis of the boat.

In the early days of sailing, ships were only able to sail before the wind (Fig. 2a) or with wind on the quarter (Fig. 2b). If they encountered half wind (Fig. 2c) or head wind (contrary wind) (Fig. 2d), they had to wait for the wind to turn. However, as a result of gradual improvement of the design of the hull, rigging and shape of the sails, it became possible to sail a ship against the wind by a procedure known as "tacking" or "beating up against the wind", in which the ship follows a zig-zag path (Fig. 3). The precise functioning of a sail is a somewhat complex phenomenon. For one thing, it acts as a straightforward wind-catching area. Furthermore, because of its curvature under the pressure of the wind, the sail develops aerodynamic behaviour comparable to that of an aircraft wing (cf. page 554), which is associated with a forward suction effect acting on the outside (convex side) of the sail. Thirdly, there is a kind of jet propulsion effect (cf. page 562) produced by the air streaming between foresail and mainsail. It is for this latter reason that racing yachts have foresails extending backward some distance past the mast.

In Fig. 3 the arrow W represents the constant wind force. Of this force only the component S, at right angles to the sail, is effective in propelling the boat. This force S tries to push the boat in the direction of the arrow S. However, the boat encounters a high resistance from the water (pressing against hull and keel) in this direction. Hence, only the longitudinal component V of the force S acts as a forward-propelling force on the boat. On reaching the point C, the helmsman swings the boat round towards D and at the same time swings the sail so that its surface is once again approximately bisecting the angle between the direction of the wind and the longitudinal axis of the boat. The boat is now propelled in the direction C–D. At D the boat and the sail are once again swung round, and so on.

Most yachts and larger vessels have lead-ballasted fixed keels (Fig. 1), but some smaller boats have movable keels (Fig. 5). The ballast in a fixed keel is so designed in relation to the sails that, in conjunction with the lateral resistance of the water, it normally more than counteracts the overturning effect of the wind pressure (Fig. 4a). The movable keel (or centre-board) of a small boat such as a dinghy has no ballast, and to avoid capsizing, the crew must lean far out to counterbalance the wind pressure on the sail (Fig. 4b).

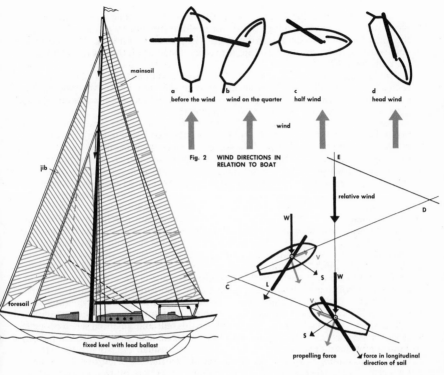

mainsail

jib

foresail

fixed keel with lead ballast

Fig. 1   YACHT WITH FORE-AND-AFT RIG

a
before the wind

b
wind on the quarter

c
half wind

d
head wind

wind

Fig. 2   WIND DIRECTIONS IN
RELATION TO BOAT

E

relative wind

D

W

V

S

W

C

L

V

S

propelling force

force in longitudinal
direction of sail

Fig. 3   TACKING

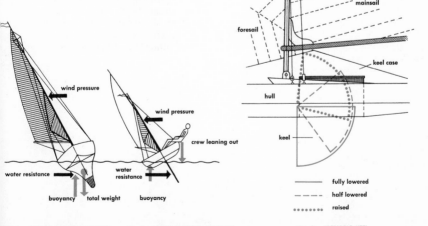

wind pressure

water resistance

buoyancy   total weight

Fig. 4a   FORCES ACTING ON BOAT
WITH FIXED KEEL

wind pressure

crew leaning out

water
resistance

buoyancy

Fig. 4b   FORCES ACTING ON BOAT
WITH MOVABLE KEEL

mainsail

foresail

keel case

hull

keel

fully lowered

half lowered

raised

Fig. 5   MOVABLE KEEL

Like all propellers, the function of the ship's propeller (technically called "marine screw propeller") is to produce the thrust to drive the ship by giving momentum to the water it displaces in an astern direction. The propeller, as it were, pushes the water backwards and this in turn develops a reaction force which thrusts the ship forward (cf. page 578) (Fig. 2).

The principle of the screw motion of a propeller is illustrated in Fig. 1. The tip of each revolving blade describes a helical curve as the propeller moves forward in the direction of movement of the ship. The pitch is the longitudinal distance corresponding to one complete revolution of the propeller (Fig. 1).

The efficiency of propulsion, i.e., the proportion of the engine power output that is utilised for propelling the ship through the water, is determined by the difference between the approach velocity of the water ahead of the propeller (which velocity is equal to the speed of the ship) and the velocity of the water displaced astern of the propeller at each revolution. When a ship starts up its engines and begins to move, small quantities of water are given a large sternward acceleration by the propeller; when the ship is under way, large quantities of water are given a relatively small acceleration.

In a solid unyielding medium, each revolution of the propeller would cause the ship to travel a distance equal to the pitch of the propeller. In reality, water is a yielding substance which gives way a little under the pressure of the propeller blades. As a result of this, the actual forward motion achieved at each revolution is only about 60–70% of the pitch. The difference in relation to 100% is known as the slip of the propeller. On the suction side of the propeller a negative pressure is produced, which is greater according as the angle of incidence of the blades is larger and their speed of rotation is higher. If the negative pressure is too great, the flow of water round the propeller blades is disrupted and bubbles filled with water vapour are formed (this phenomenon is known as cavitation); for this reason high-speed screw propellers are given very wide and flat blades with low angles of incidence (Fig. 3). On the other hand, a low-speed propeller has narrow blades with a high angle of incidence (Fig. 4). Large slow-running propellers (large masses of water, low acceleration) are preferred for ocean liners, whereas small inland navigation craft are usually provided with small fast-running propellers (small masses of water to which a high acceleration is imparted).

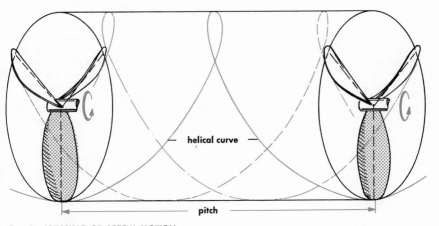

helical curve

pitch

Fig. 1 PRINCIPLE OF SCREW MOTION

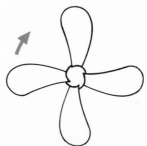

special rudder
(increases steering
efficiency)

Fig. 2 ACCELERATIVE FORCE OF WATER DISPLACED
(action) **PROVIDES THRUST** *(reaction)*

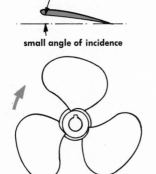

small angle of incidence

large angle of incidence

Fig. 3 HIGH-SPEED PROPELLER *(wide, flat blades)*

Fig. 4 LOW-SPEED PROPELLER *(narrow blades strongly curved in section)*

NAVIGATION

By navigation is understood the science of determining the position and course of ships and aircraft (for air navigation cf. page 568 *et seq.*). In marine navigation the ship's position is usually determined as the intersection of two or more position lines. The latter are determined by the taking of bearings on terrestrial or celestial fixed points. Terrestrial fixed points are landmarks, buoys, beacons, lighthouses, etc. Fig. 1 shows how a navigator takes his bearings on two such points. By means of his sextant (cf. page 550) he measures the angle α between the two points A and B which are a known distance apart. Also, he measures the angle β between one of the position lines and the north direction indicated by the ship's compass. As the geographical latitude and longitude of the points A and B, as well as the distance between them, are known, one side and two angles in each of the triangles ABS (or ABS') are known. The lengths of the position lines and the geographical co-ordinates of the position S (or S'). In the open sea, out of sight of land, the navigator must take bearings on a heavenly body or make use of radio direction-finding (see page 570 *et seq.*). In celestial (or astronomical) navigation the navigator, using an instrument called a sextant, sights his instrument, for example, at a star and measures its culmination altitude, i.e., the angle between the line of sight and the horizon (Fig. 2). The position of the star in the sky at that particular time can be looked up in tables (nautical almanacs). The ship's chronometer, which is a very accurate timepiece, gives the precise time at which the observation is made. From these data the position of the ship can be determined. The successive positions determined in this way are plotted on a nautical chart. Among other information, charts also show the depths of water. An important feature of navigation in coastal waters is determining the depth or taking soundings. Formerly a lead line was always used for the purpose; a more modern device for measuring depths is the echo-sounder (see page 550).

The couse plotted between two points A and B can either be an orthodrome, i.e., the shortest distance between these points measured along a great circle of the globe, or a loxodrome (Fig. 3a). The latter course is characterised by the fact that it intersects the circles of longitude always at a constant angle. On a map drawn to Mercator's projection the loxodrome therefore appears as a straight line (Fig. 3b). The loxodrome is nevertheless longer than the orthodrome.

Radio direction-finding signals and bearings on lighthouses provide the navigator with reference points. The exact geographical location and the characteristics of each lighthouse can be looked up in tables. For example, Fig. 4 shows the characteristics of a revolving light which periodically emits short and long flashes.

For keeping the ship on course, regulating its speed, and manoeuvring in harbours and in perilous situations a very important piece of equipment is the telegraph (Fig. 5). It is used for transmitting orders from the bridge to the engine-room. When the lever is moved to a particular position of the dial, a sprocket moves a chain to whose ends wires are attached which actuate a similar dial in the engine room. In the more modern form of the telegraph the signal is transmitted electrically. For example, when the lever of the bridge telegraph is moved to "half ahead", the pointer on the engine-room telegraph also moves to "half ahead", and a bell rings to attract attention. The engineer then replies by moving the lever of his telegraph to "half ahead", and by doing so operates the return pointer on the bridge telegraph, which rings a bell, thus indicating that the order has been understood.

(Continued)

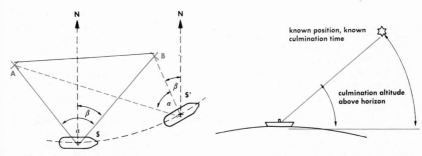

Fig. 1 TAKING BEARINGS ON TWO
FIXED POINTS

Fig. 2 TAKING BEARINGS WITH THE
AID OF A STAR

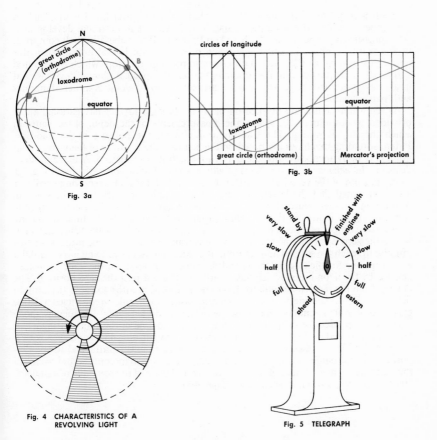

Fig. 3a

Fig. 3b

Fig. 4 CHARACTERISTICS OF A
REVOLVING LIGHT

Fig. 5 TELEGRAPH

One of the most important navigation instruments is, of course, the compass (magnetic compass or gyro compass; see page 552). The compass is used for steering and for fixing the ship's position by bearings. The chronometer and sextant have already been mentioned. The *sextant* is used in astronomical navigation for measuring the altitude of a star (or the sun) above the horizon. A simple sextant is shown in Fig. 6. Looking through the hole in the sight vane, the observer sights the instrument at the star, which he sees in the unsilvered half of the mirror. If he wishes to measure, say, the angular distance between this star and another star, the observer rotates an adjustable mirror mounted on a swivel arm until the second star (whose light is reflected from the adjustable mirror and from the half-silvered mirror, as indicated in Fig. 6) is seen to coincide with the first. The angular distance between the two stars can then be read from the graduated scale (which is usually 60°, i.e., one-sixth of a circle, hence the name "sextant"). Most modern sextants are fitted with a small telescope instead of a mere sight hole.

For plotting the course of a ship it is also important to know the speed at which it is sailing. This is measured by means of a device called a *log*. In modern navigation the so-called patent log is mostly used (Fig. 7). A small propeller, called a "rotator", is towed along behind the ship and revolves faster according as the speed is higher. The rotation is transmitted through a flexible shaft to the register fitted with a dial on which the speed (usually in nautical miles) is indicated. A more recent development is the pressure type speed recorder based on Prandtl's Pitot tube (Fig. 8). It comprises two concentric tubes, the outer one being provided with lateral holes. When this device moves through the water, a difference in pressure develops which is measured and which is proportional to the square of the vessel's speed. A similar device is used in air navigation (see page 570) and for measuring flow velocities in aerodynamics and hydrodynamics.

As the water depths are marked on nautical charts, a further navigational aid is provided by soundings, i.e., systematic measurements of the depth of the water in which the ship is sailing. The traditional device for the purpose is the lead-line. Patent sounding machines are based on the fact that the pressure of the water on an immersed body increases with the depth to which it is immersed. A more modern device is the *echo sounder*, one form of which is shown diagrammatically in Fig. 10. In the bottom of the vessel's hull a transmitting oscillator and a receiving oscillator are so mounted that the latter picks up the echo reflected back from the sea bed. A rotating contact causes a condenser to discharge through the electromagnetic transmitting oscillator, so that a sound impulse is transmitted. The time measuring equipment comprises a neon lamp rotating in front of a timing scale. When the lamp passes the zero position, the sound impulse is transmitted. The time it takes for this impulse to reach the sea bed and return to the receiving oscillator (which is essentially a microphone for picking up the sound) is marked, or read, on the scale by a flash emitted by the neon lamp, which has meanwhile rotated past the zero position. The current from the receiving oscillator has to be amplified in order to cause the lamp to light up. Echo sounders usually operate with ultrasonic frequencies (20,000 cycles/sec.), but sounders operating with an audible sound frequency (3600 cycles/sec.) are used for deep-sea soundings. The principle of the transmitting oscillator is illustrated in Fig. 9. The coil is energised by an alternating current with a frequency of 3600 cycles/sec., so that the laminated armature, attached to the diaphragm, is alternately attracted and released. The diaphragm emits sound waves of this same frequency. Other types of transmitter make use of the principle of magnetostriction or the piezo-electric effect (cf. page 208).

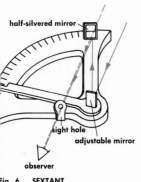

half-silvered mirror

sight hole

adjustable mirror

observer

Fig. 6   SEXTANT

register

flywheel

propeller

Fig. 7   PATENT LOG

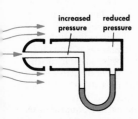

increased pressure   reduced pressure

Fig. 8   PITOT TUBE

0

10   50

20   40

30

rotating neon lamp

contact

1000 volts

amplifier

receiver   transmitter

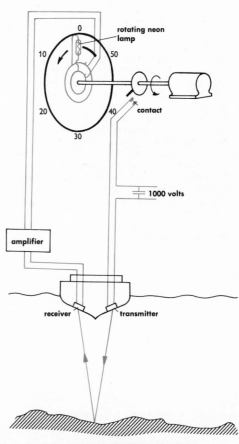

Fig. 10   ECHO SOUNDING EQUIPMENT

diaphragm

coil

iron core

coil

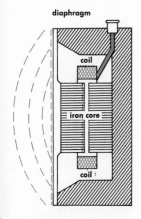

Fig. 9   ELECTROMAGNETIC TRANSMITTING OSCILLATOR

The property of natural magnetism possessed by certain iron ores can be explained with reference to a simple conception of the structure of the atom (Fig. 1). A single electron orbiting around the nucleus acts as an electric current and produces an electric field, i.e., it behaves like a tiny magnet. Iron can be conceived as consisting of a multitude of such elementary magnets which are aligned parallel to one another in groups. Externally the magnetism of these groups cancels out (Fig. 2a). However, if all the groups are aligned in the same direction as the result of external influences, this alignment will, in the main, be retained (Fig. 2b). A piece of iron in which this has happened is a natural magnet. The earth as a whole, too, is a natural magnet (Fig. 3). The magnetic axis does not coincide with the axis of rotation, so that the magnetic poles are displaced in relation to the geographical poles. In navigation the earth's magnetic field is utilised for the determining of direction. The instrument used for the purpose is the magnetic compass. It consists of a non-magnetic housing (e.g., made of brass or plastic) in which a magnetic needle, poised on a point, can rotate freely over a compass card (Fig. 4). The needle swings to such a position that one end (its magnetic north pole) points approximately—not exactly, for the reason mentioned above—to the north and, consequently, the other end points to the south. The magnetic needle's deviation from the true north direction is called the "variation". It varies from place to place and is determined by the direction of the horizontal component of the earth's magnetic field (magnetic declination). The vertical lines of force of the earth's field can be detected with the aid of a magnetic needle pivoted about a horizontal axis (Fig. 5; magnetic inclination, inclination needle). If the variation is marked on the compass card, or if the magnetic declination is known from tables, the exact northerly direction (and therefore all the other significant directions) can be determined. The gyro compass functions on a different principle: a rotor which is rotatably mounted at its centre of gravity tends to dispose its axis of rotation parallel to the earth's axis (Fig. 6). For the sake of simplicity, a gyroscope—i.e., a suitably mounted rotor—is assumed to be located at the earth's equator (Fig. 6, position I). As a result of the rotation of the earth, the gyroscope moves to position II. Since it tends to maintain the position of its axis, its centre of gravity will be raised some distance (because of the nature of the gyroscope mounting). The force of gravity then exerts a torque (twisting movement) which strives to swing the gyroscope and its mounting back to its original position (small black arrows). As a result of this the axis of rotation of the gyroscope swings in the direction of this torque, causing the gyroscope to align itself in the north-south direction. The gyro compass is the directional reference most used by modern navigators. Its advantage is that it indicates true instead of magnetic north and is subject to fewer errors. The magnetic compass is installed as a standby.

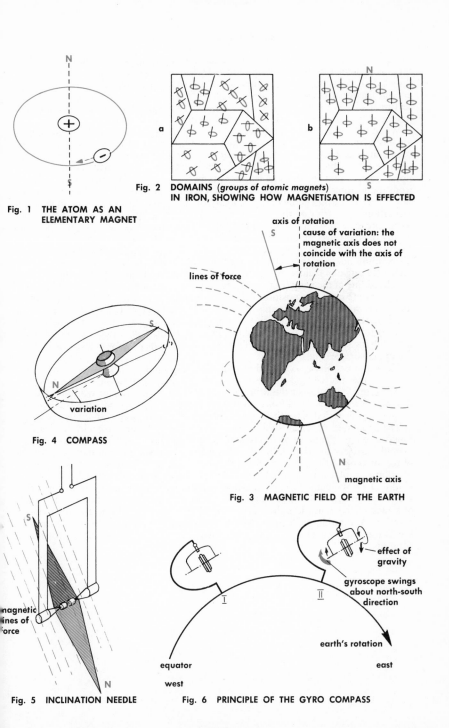

Fig. 1   THE ATOM AS AN
ELEMENTARY MAGNET

a

b

Fig. 2   DOMAINS (groups of atomic magnets)
IN IRON, SHOWING HOW MAGNETISATION IS EFFECTED

axis of rotation
cause of variation: the
magnetic axis does not
coincide with the axis of
rotation

lines of force

variation

Fig. 4   COMPASS

magnetic axis

Fig. 3   MAGNETIC FIELD OF THE EARTH

magnetic
lines of
force

effect of
gravity

gyroscope swings
about north-south
direction

earth's rotation

equator   east

west

Fig. 5   INCLINATION NEEDLE   Fig. 6   PRINCIPLE OF THE GYRO COMPASS

As an aircraft is "heavier than air", it needs an upward force to keep it aloft. This force is provided by the "lift" developed by the supporting surfaces (wings) and is directed at right angles to the direction of movement. In addition, the air offers a certain frictional resistance, called "drag" (Fig. 1). By suitable design of the cross-sectional shape of the wing (Fig. 2) the drag can be kept small in relation to the lift. A shape of this kind is known as an airfoil section.

When the wing of an aircraft (Fig. 3) moves forward through the air, the flow of air along the lower surface arrives at the trailing edge before the flow along the upper surface. The lower surface flow attempts to expand around the trailing edge. As a result of this a vortex is formed. The rotation of this vortex accelerates the upper surface flow, so that the length of time required for a particle of air to move from the leading edge to the trailing edge becomes the same for the upper and the lower surface flow. The increased velocity of the upper surface flow eliminates the formation of a vortex by the lower surface air at the trailing edge, and it produces a lower pressure at each point on the upper surface than exists at the corresponding points on the lower surface. It is this difference in pressure that produces the lift. The distribution of lift along the cross-section of a wing is illustrated by the pressure-distribution diagram (Fig. 4). The magnitude of the forces changes with the angle of attack (or angle of incidence), i.e., the angle between the direction of the air flow and the chord line of the wing (Fig. 5). The resultant aerodynamic force acts at the centre of pressure (Fig. 4); its position varies with the angle of attack. The stability of an aircraft is significantly determined by the displacement of the centre of pressure. With increasing angle of attack this point moves forward. When the angle is increased beyond the value that produces maximum lift, "stall" occurs: this results in loss of flying speed and lift and finally loss of control; the air flow detaches itself from the upper surface (Fig. 6).

The airfoil section is so shaped as to present minimum air resistance at the design speed of the aircraft and at the same time provide the necessary amount of lift. Figs. 7a and 7b represent the wing sections of a cargo-carrying aircraft and a faster aircraft respectively. The lift provided by the thick highly curved wing is about half as much again as that of the thinner and flatter wing, but its drag is about twice as high.

The principles of airfoil design are also applicable to the propeller blades. The function of the propeller is to convert the torque developed by the engine into a propulsive thrust to drive the aircraft forward. This thrust is produced by acceleration of the air around the propeller. Since the velocity at each blade section is a function of radius, the blades are twisted to maintain a favourable angle of attack all along the blade. The principal forces and velocities associated with the action of the propeller are shown in Fig. 8. The pitch angle of the propeller blade corresponds to the angle of attack of the wing; it is the angle between the blade chord line and the plane of rotation. A variable-pitch propeller is designed to maintain propeller efficiency as the forward velocity changes. The pitch setting can be changed while the propeller is rotating.

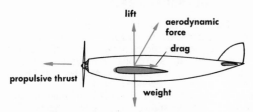

Fig. 1   FORCES ACTING ON AIRCRAFT'S WING

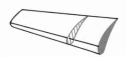

Fig. 2   AIRFOIL SECTION

longer path, higher velocity

shorter path, lower velocity

Fig. 3   AIR FLOW AT WING

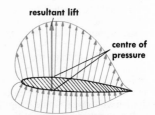

Fig. 4   PRESSURE DISTRIBUTION DIAGRAM

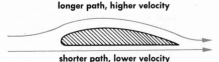

Fig. 5   VARIATION OF FORCES AND POSITION OF CENTRE OF PRESSURE WITH ANGLE OF ATTACK

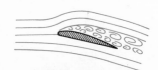

Fig. 6   CO-OPERATION OF FORCES ACTING ON PROPELLER AND WING

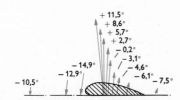

Fig. 7   DIFFERENT AIRFOILS

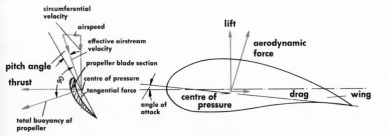

Fig. 8

SUPERSONIC SPEED

The speed, or velocity, of sound is the speed at which a disturbance is propagated through a substance (in particular: air). It depends on the elastic properties and density of the substance concerned. In air at normal atmospheric pressure, at a temperature of 15° C, sound travels at a speed of 1120 ft./sec. (340 m/sec.), i.e., about 760 m.p.h. So long as the speed of an aircraft travels at a speed below the speed of sound, the air will be displaced in all directions and behave as an entirely "soft" medium. However, when the aircraft reaches the speed of sound, the air "becomes hard" and presents a very high resistance—the "sound barrier"—which the aircraft must break through or, rather, slice through. On going through the barrier, the aircraft produces a series of elastic waves in the air. As they travel at a slower speed, these waves lag behind the aircraft. The transition from supersonic to subsonic air flow is accompanied by a shock wave.

What happens may be compared to cutting through a material with a knife. (Fig. 1). For example, when a knife cuts a sheet off a roll of paper, a "hissing" noise is heard. These sound waves are produced by the knife blade cutting through the paper. The same thing happens when a body travels through the air at supersonic speed, i.e., faster than sound. The air behaves like a solid substance towards the "knife" cutting through it. The leading part of the body, e.g., a shell fired from a gun (Fig. 2), produces a shock wave (bow wave), while other waves emanate from the rear end (tail wave). Behind the projectile a vacuum is formed, and the adjacent air rushes in to fill this, thereby producing a state of turbulence called a vortex path. To facilitate their passage through the air, projectiles, rockets and supersonic aircraft have pointed noses (Fig. 3). The wings of a supersonic aircraft are relatively much smaller than those of a subsonic aircraft in order to minimise drag. Because of the very high speed, these narrow wings are nevertheless able to develop sufficient lift to keep the aircraft in the air (cf. page 554). The bow wave produced by a supersonic aircraft spreads out in the shape of a cone (Fig. 4). The noise of the aircraft is heard in the zone formed by the intersection of this cone with the ground. The sound pressures recorded in this zone may be as high as 30 lb./ft.^{2}—high enough to shatter windows ("sonic bang").[1] However, if the aircraft flies above about 30,000 ft., such high pressures will not occur.

1. "Sonic boom" in U.S.A.

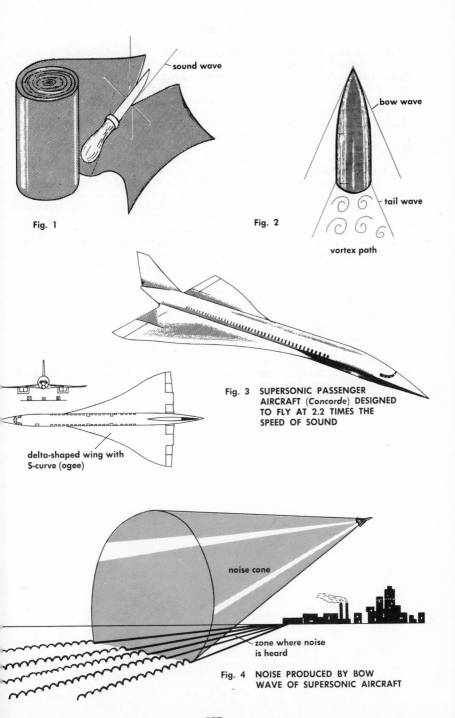

sound wave

Fig. 1

bow wave

tail wave

vortex path

Fig. 2

Fig. 3 SUPERSONIC PASSENGER
AIRCRAFT (Concorde) DESIGNED
TO FLY AT 2.2 TIMES THE
SPEED OF SOUND

delta-shaped wing with
S-curve (ogee)

noise cone

zone where noise
is heard

Fig. 4 NOISE PRODUCED BY BOW
WAVE OF SUPERSONIC AIRCRAFT

For horizontal flight the weight of an aircraft must be counteracted by the lift (cf. page 554) and the drag overcome by a propulsive thrust acting in the direction of flight. In a powered aircraft (Fig. 1) the thrust is developed by the engine. A glider has no engine. It therefore cannot perform horizontal flight (i.e., at constant height) in perfectly calm weather; under such conditions the glider is merely able to proceed along a downward-sloping path. Only then will the lift counterbalance the weight of the aircraft (or rather the component of the weight perpendicular to the flight path), while the drag is overcome by the forward component of the weight (Fig. 2). The path of the glider (Figs. 3a and 3b) is dependent upon the ratio of drag to lift (gliding angle). The greater the drag, the steeper is the slope of the flight path. The flight performance of a glider is therefore better according as the drag is smaller for a given lift.

The gliding angle determines the duration of the flight under calm weather conditions. However, the attraction of gliding as a sport consists in seeking out and utilising upward air currents which enable the skilled glider pilot to soar higher and higher and thus prolong his flight. This calls for considerable experience and knowledge of weather conditions. For example, birds soaring in the air without flapping their wings are a sure sign of a rising air current, and the experienced pilot will not fail to take advantage of this. A glider, though "heavier than air", can rise if the velocity of the rising air is greater than the velocity of descent of the glider. The rate of climb or descent is indicated by an instrument called a variometer (rate-of-climb indicator, see page 568). Rising air currents develop on hillsides (Fig. 4), over warm areas of land, and under cumulus clouds in the process of formation (thermal air currents). Suitable rising currents also occur along fronts between warm and cold air masses such as are to be found at the edges of thunderstorms.

Launching a glider is usually done by towing the aircraft into the air by an automobile at the end of a long rope (500 ft. or more in length) or by means of a high-speed winch (auto-tow and winch-tow launching technique). Alternatively, airplane tow can be employed, the glider being towed into the air behind a power-driven aircraft and released at the desired altitude.

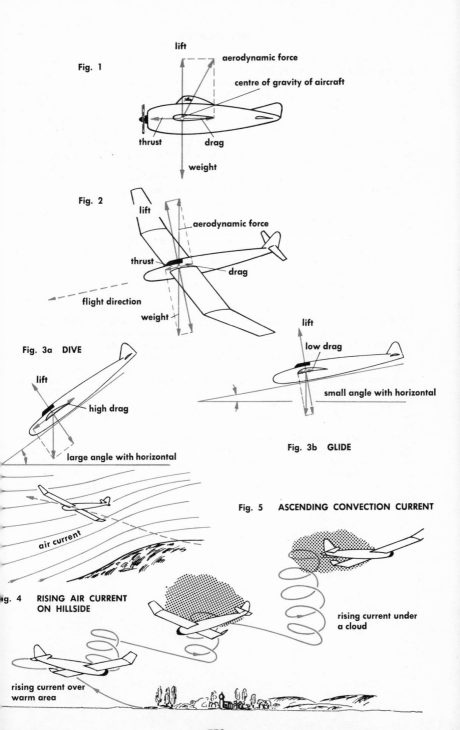

Fig. 1

lift
aerodynamic force
centre of gravity of aircraft
thrust
drag
weight

Fig. 2

lift
aerodynamic force
thrust
drag
flight direction
weight

Fig. 3a DIVE

lift
high drag
large angle with horizontal

lift
low drag
small angle with horizontal

Fig. 3b GLIDE

air current

Fig. 5 ASCENDING CONVECTION CURRENT

rising current under a cloud

Fig. 4 RISING AIR CURRENT ON HILLSIDE

rising current over warm area

559

HELICOPTER

A helicopter is equipped with one or more power-driven rotors (horizontal propellers) in lieu of fixed wings. It is able to take off and land vertically, to move in any direction, or to remain stationary in the air. The lift developed by a conventional aircraft wing depends on two factors: the angle of attack of the wing (Fig. 1) and the velocity of the air in relation to the wing. To obtain the necessary lift, the aircraft must have a forward movement (see page 554). In the case of the helicopter the (relative) air velocity is produced by the rotation of the rotor blades: when the angle of attack attains a certain value, the lift overcomes the weight of the aircraft. The aircraft then takes off vertically (Fig. 2). To achieve horizontal flight, the pilot tilts the rotor forward at a certain angle. This is done by what is known as cyclic pitch change, i.e., changing the pitch of each blade once per revolution. More particularly, the angle of attack of each blade is increased every time it sweeps over the tail of the machine, thereby temporarily developing a greater amount of thrust than the other blades. The thrust developed by the rotor can be resolved into a vertical component (the actual lift that keeps the machine in the air) and a forward component (which propels the machine horizontally) (Fig. 3). Each blade can swivel about its longitudinal axis and its pitch is changed cyclically, through a linkage system, by a so-called swash-plate, which performs a sort of wobbling rotary motion around the shaft and swivels the blades to and fro as they rotate. The tilt of the swash plate can be varied by the pilot, and the tilt of the rotor follows the tilt of the plate.

The blade root hinges (called lag hinges) shown in Fig. 4 allow "blade flapping", as represented in Fig. 6. If there were no hinges, tilting of the plane of rotation of the rotor blades relative to the helicopter causes a periodic change in the speed of the blades. This would produce severe stresses in the blades; these stresses are relieved and cancelled by the hinge. Motion about the hinge enables the blade to rotate at constant speed irrespective of how much the rotor is tilted. In forward movement of the helicopter, the velocity due to blade rotation and that due to forward speed are added together, i.e., they intensify each other, on the advancing side of the rotor; on the retreating side, however, they are subtracted from each other. If the rotor blades were rigidly fixed to the shaft, the lift would vary cyclically and cause the helicopter to roll. This is prevented by the hinge. Instead, the blade flaps cyclically as it rotates.

The rotation of the rotor tends to cause the fuselage of the aircraft to rotate in the opposite direction (on the principle that any action calls forth a reaction). To prevent this, the single-rotor helicopter is provided at its tail with a small propeller producing a counteracting sideways thrust (Figs. 2, 3 and 7). Alternatively, the helicopter may have two rotors which revolve in opposite directions and thus counterbalance each other.

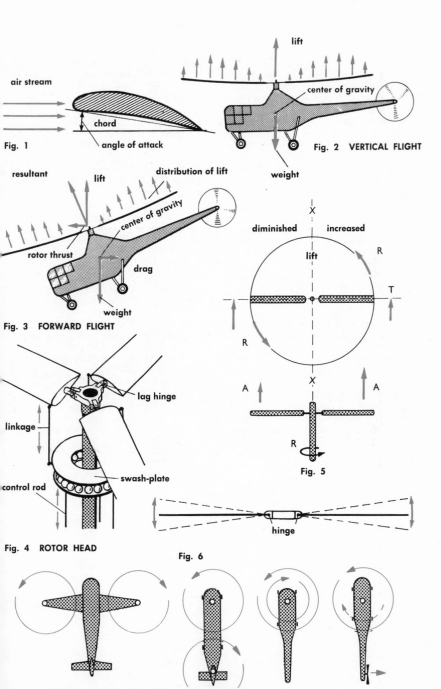

air stream

chord

angle of attack

Fig. 1

lift

center of gravity

Fig. 2   VERTICAL FLIGHT

weight

resultant

lift

distribution of lift

rotor thrust

center of gravity

drag

weight

Fig. 3   FORWARD FLIGHT

lag hinge

linkage

swash-plate

control rod

Fig. 4   ROTOR HEAD

X

diminished   increased

lift   R

T

R

X

A   A

R

Fig. 5

hinge

Fig. 6

Fig. 7   METHODS OF PREVENTING FUSELAGE ROTATION

Jet engines for aircraft propulsion are of various types: turbojet, turboprop, ramjet, turbofan. The turboprop (turbo-propeller engine) is not strictly a jet propulsion engine. Rockets have also been used for the propulsion of aircraft and are jet propulsion devices, but they will be separately considered (see pages 578 and 580).

In jet engines of all types the air is taken from the outside, compressed, heated (by combustion of fuel), and then expanded in a jet or a turbine. The air is expelled from the jet at a much higher velocity than the intake velocity, and it is this increase in velocity that produces the desired propulsive thrust. It is based on the fundamental law of mechanics which states that action is equal to reaction. The compression energy developed in the combustion chamber of the jet engine is converted into impulse (= mass × velocity). The thrust results from the impulse of the air and combustion gases streaming out of the rear of the engine—not from any "pushing" against the air behind the aircraft. The law of action and reaction is illustrated by the familiar lawn sprinkler (Fig. 1): the water emerging from the jet at the end of the arm develops the "action"; the "reaction" force, of the same magnitude but in the opposite direction, causes the arm to rotate. In the case of a propeller-driven aircraft the propeller accelerates large quantities of air to a relatively low velocity, whereas in a jet-propelled aircraft the jet engine accelerates smaller quantities of air to far higher velocities (Fig. 2). Another example illustrating the principle of action and reaction is provided by a closed vessel (Fig. 3a) in which pressure is generated by the burning of fuel. If a hole is made in one side of this vessel, the combustion gases rush out at high velocity, and the vessel itself experiences a propulsive thrust in the opposite direction. The performance of a jet engine is proportional to the density of the intake air. It therefore diminishes with increasing altitude. However, as the drag on the aircraft likewise diminishes, there is actually an increase in speed at higher altitudes.

The simplest type of jet engine is the ramjet. It has no moving parts. Air entering the front of a tube shaped as shown in Fig. 4a is slowed down in the tube (because of the larger diameter of the middle part) and undergoes an increase in pressure in consequence. If fuel is injected into the centre of the tube and burned (Fig. 4b), the hot combustion gases flow out at high velocity from the rear of the tube (the nozzle of the jet). The velocity at the nozzle exit is higher than the flight speed of the aircraft; so a thrust is produced. The ramjet produces no thrust when the aircraft is stationary, because there is then no pressure build-up in the engine because the intake air has zero velocity. This type of jet is therefore efficient only at very high speeds.

(Continued)

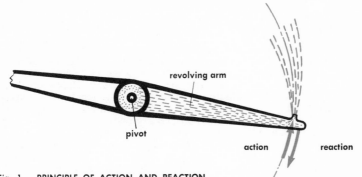

Fig. 1   PRINCIPLE OF ACTION AND REACTION

revolving arm

pivot

action   reaction

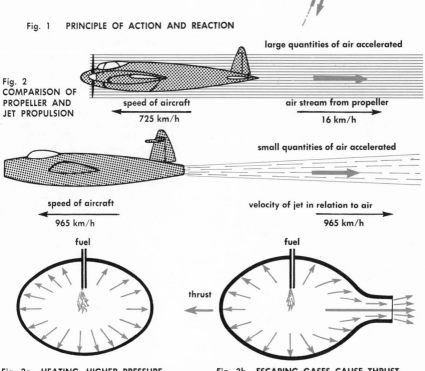

Fig. 2
COMPARISON OF
PROPELLER AND
JET PROPULSION

large quantities of air accelerated

speed of aircraft
725 km/h

air stream from propeller
16 km/h

small quantities of air accelerated

speed of aircraft
965 km/h

velocity of jet in relation to air
965 km/h

fuel

fuel

thrust

Fig. 3a HEATING: HIGHER PRESSURE

Fig. 3b ESCAPING GASES CAUSE THRUST

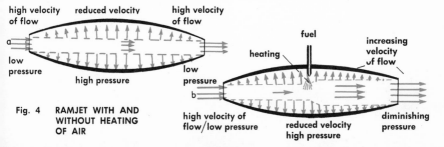

high velocity
of flow

reduced velocity

high velocity
of flow

a

low
pressure

high pressure

low
pressure

fuel

heating

increasing
velocity
of flow

b

high velocity of
flow/low pressure

reduced velocity
high pressure

diminishing
pressure

Fig. 4   RAMJET WITH AND
          WITHOUT HEATING
          OF AIR

563

A turbojet (jet turbine engine) differs from the ramjet in that it is additionally provided with a compressor driven by a turbine (Fig. 1). A multi-stage axial compressor (comprising alternate sets of rotating and stationary blades) draws in the air and compresses it. Fuel is injected into the combustion chamber. The rise in temperature produces a considerable increase in the volume of the gases, which are expelled through the exhaust nozzle at the rear. The turbine absorbs only so much energy from the gases as is necessary to drive the compressor. The greater part of the energy is utilised to develop the propulsive thrust. The performance of a turbojet can be improved by means of an afterburner, which is a second combustion chamber placed between the turbine and the propulsion nozzle. Additional fuel is injected into this chamber and combustion is effected with the oxygen unconsumed in the main combustion process.

The propeller turbine engine (turboprop) likewise comprises a compressor, combustion chamber and turbine, but in this case nearly the whole of the energy is used to drive the turbine, which not only drives the compressor but whose excess power is used to drive a propeller (through reduction gears) (Figs. 2 and 3). The turboprop is much lighter than a reciprocating engine of equal power and is easier to construct in very large sizes (over 4000 h.p.). It is nevertheless a complex piece of machinery. The gases are very largely expanded in the turbine. The exhaust gases provide a certain amount of additional thrust.

A modified form of the turboprop has two concentric shafts revolving at different speeds. A turbine unit is mouned on each shaft. One shaft drives the compressor, the other drives the propeller. This type of engine is especially suitable for speed ranges which are too high for the conventional propeller-driven aircraft and too low for the turbojet. In the low-pressure compressor stage a proportion of the compressed air is bypassed and delivered to the propulsion nozzle (Fig. 4). Because of the higher power requirement of the turbine, the exit velocity of the gases is reduced, which is equivalent to increased propulsion efficiency. The low-pressure stage of the compressor is driven by the second turbine stage (shown black), and the high-pressure stage is driven by the first turbine stage (shown dotted).

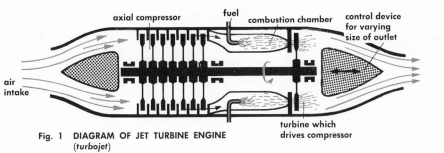

Fig. 1 DIAGRAM OF JET TURBINE ENGINE
(*turbojet*)

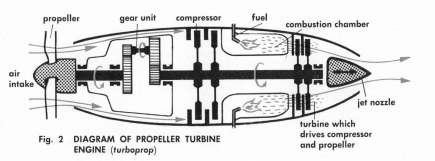

Fig. 2 DIAGRAM OF PROPELLER TURBINE
ENGINE (*turboprop*)

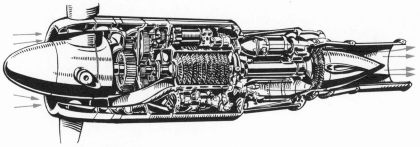

Fig. 3 TURBOPROP ENGINE

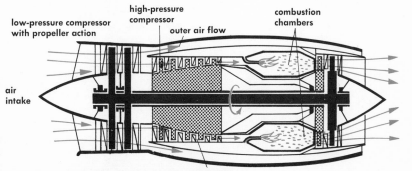

Fig. 4 DIAGRAM OF TWO-STAGE TURBOPROP

PARACHUTE

When a parachute has opened and is falling steadily, a state of equilibrium exists in which the resultant force of drag and lift acting upon the falling parachute is equal to the weight (Fig. 2). The magnitude of the drag force (W) is dependent on the square of the velocity of descent (v), the magnitude (F) of the projected area of the parachute, and the specific gravity (y) of the air:

$$W = \frac{\gamma}{2g} \cdot v^2 \cdot F.$$

If the angle of the approach velocity becomes zero, the drag force will be equal to the weight, while the rate of descent remains the same.

A parachute descent is conceived as comprising various zones (Fig. 1). In the free fall zone the parachutist falls with ever increasing velocity until a certain limiting velocity—determined by air drag and friction—is reached. The ripcord is then pulled causing the pilot parachute to open; this is a small auxiliary parachute attached to the top of the main parachute; it pulls the latter out of its pack. When the main parachute opens, the velocity of fall is reduced from about 110 m.p.h. to about 10–15 m.p.h. This sudden slowing-down produces the "opening shock". The further descent is then made at constant velocity. This velocity depends not only on the diameter and shape of the parachute, but of course also on the parachutist's weight, the air permeability of the parachute fabric, and the density of the air. For a normal rate of descent the impact on landing is about the same as that on jumping from a height of 5 ft.

The parachute may be opened by means of a ripcord pulled by the parachutist or by an automatic timing device. The ripcord withdraws the rip pin which secures the flaps on the parachute pack (Fig. 3). The ripcord system is used for pilot escape. For mass jumps by parachute troops, a static line attached to the aircraft pulls the parachute out of its pack. The principal parts of a parachute are the canopy, suspension lines, chute pack, pilot parachute, and harness (Fig. 4). Modern parachutes are made of nylon. A typical pilot-escape parachute has a diameter of 28 ft. Airborne troops generally use parachutes of somewhat larger diameter. The harness is so designed that it can instantly be released from the wearer's body.

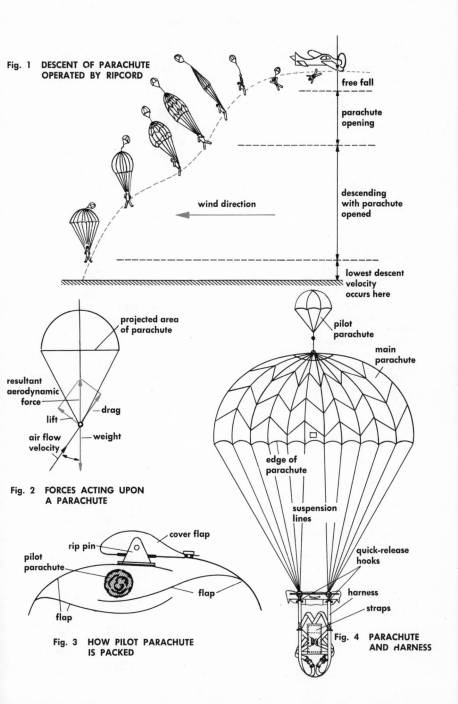

Fig. 1 DESCENT OF PARACHUTE OPERATED BY RIPCORD

free fall

parachute opening

descending with parachute opened

wind direction

lowest descent velocity occurs here

projected area of parachute

resultant aerodynamic force

drag

lift

weight

air flow velocity

Fig. 2 FORCES ACTING UPON A PARACHUTE

pilot parachute

main parachute

edge of parachute

suspension lines

quick-release hooks

harness

straps

Fig. 4 PARACHUTE AND HARNESS

cover flap

rip pin

pilot parachute

flap

flap

Fig. 3 HOW PILOT PARACHUTE IS PACKED

567

AIR NAVIGATION

The *altitude* of an aircraft above sea level is measured by means of the altimeter, which is essentially an aneroid barometer (see page 220) and provides an indication of atmospheric pressure which is calibrated—by means of a standard formula—to give readings direct in terms of altitude (Fig. 1). The instrument is affected by variations of barometric pressure, and provision is made for adjustment. The temperature also affects the altitude readings obtained. The correct use of the terms "altitude", "height" and "elevation" is indicated in Fig. 2. By setting a pointer on a subsidiary scale of air pressure values the altimeter can be made to indicate the actual elevation of the airport when the aircraft has landed on the runway. Also, by means of this adjustment the altimeter can be made to give actual readings of height above airport runway level, i.e., the "datum" (reference level) in relation to which the height is measured can be varied. This vertical adjustment of the relative height indications is represented by the full and the dotted red lines in Fig. 3. The setting of the instrument in any specific case will also depend on the atmospheric pressure existing at that particular time and place. The change-over from altitude readings to height readings is effected prior to landing. This is done on entering (from above) the statutory zone (generally at least 1000 ft. in depth) shown shaded by oblique lines in Fig. 3. When the aircraft takes off, the opposite adjustment is made on entering this zone (from below).

The height of an aircraft above ground level is additionally measured by means of a *radio altimeter*. A radio signal is transmitted to the ground, reflected back, and picked up by a receiving instrument (Fig. 4). The length of time between transmission and reception of the signal is evaluated by electronic means and provides an indication of the height. The readings obtained in this way are reliable only over flat country and over water. Surface irregularities cause inaccuracies.

The *rate-of-climb indicator* (variometer, vertical speed indicator) is a pressure gauge whose dial indicates the rate of climb or descent in thousands of feet per minute. It comprises a differential pressure element (usually a diaphragm capsule) one side of which is connected to the ambient static pressure and the other side is connected to this pressure through a constriction (a narrow orifice or the like). A change in altitude of the aircraft is associated with a change in static pressure. Because of the constriction, equalisation of pressure can only take place slowly. The differential pressure at the construction provides an indication of the vertical speed.

The direction of the flight path of an aircraft is measured in terms of the angle (the course) between the tangent to the path and a particular reference direction, e.g., compass north, true north or grid north (Fig. 6). The angle between this reference direction and the longitudinal axis of the aircraft is called the heading. If there is no wind, the two angles, i.e., the course and the heading, will be identical. To compensate for winds blowing obliquely in relation to the flight path, the heading will differ from the course (the latter being the actual desired direction). The shortest flight path between two points A and B is not the loxodrome (this being the path obtained if the course is kept constant throughout the flight: cf. page 548) but a great circle (a circle on a sphere—more particularly: the earth—whose plane passes through the centre of the sphere). In practice, the navigator determines the great circle passing through A and B and then approximates it by a "polygon" of stretches of loxodrome which can be flown with the aid of a magnetic compass or a gyrosyn compass. The gyrosyn compass system comprises a directional gyroscope (Fig. 7), a compass indicator, and a so-called flux valve (a detector of magnetic field). The directional gyroscope ensures directional stability of the compass system; the flux valve senses the earth's magnetic field and transmits signals which correct any wandering of the gyroscope.

(Continued)

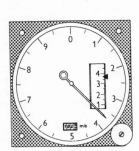

Fig. 1 ALTIMETER

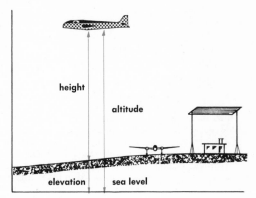

height

altitude

elevation   sea level

Fig. 2

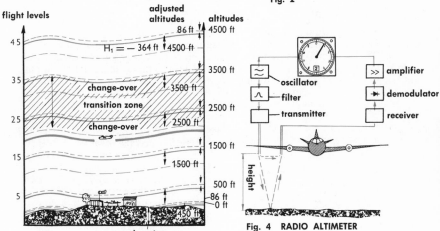

flight levels

adjusted altitudes   altitudes

45   86 ft   4500 ft

$H_1 = -364$ ft   4500 ft

35   3500 ft

change-over   3500 ft
transition zone
25   2500 ft
change-over

15   1500 ft

1500 ft

5   500 ft
                           86 ft   0 ft
                           450 ft

Fig. 3   elevation

oscillator   amplifier
filter   demodulator
transmitter   receiver

height

Fig. 4 RADIO ALTIMETER

20
10   50
                80
+
0   THOMMEN
          m/sec
−   80
10   50
20

Fig. 5 RATE-OF-CLIMB
        INDICATOR

569

Astronomical aircraft navigation is done with the aid of the astro-compass, which is a non-magnetic instrument which enables the true heading of an aircraft to be found by sighting upon a celestial body. The readings obtained with this instrument can be used for correcting the directional gyroscope from time to time.

With reference to the "speed" of an aircraft in flight a distinction is made between the airspeed (the speed relative to the air through which the aircraft moves), the groundspeed (the speed relative to the ground), and the wind velocity or speed. These speeds are represented by v_e, v_g and v_w respectively. If two of these are known, the third speed can be found as a resultant in the so-called wind triangle (Fig. 8) in which the length and direction of each vector ("arrow") corresponds to the magnitude and direction of the speed concerned.

The airspeed is generally measured by means of the *airspeed indicator*. It operates by utilising the pressure difference between static and dynamic air pressures, the instrument usually being calibrated to give readings in knots or in miles-per-hour. The dynamic pressure is produced in a so-called pitot tube (whose open end points in the direction of flight), the pressure difference being measured by means of a diaphragm capsule (Fig. 9). The instrument shows true airspeed under standard sea-level conditions (atmospheric pressure 29.92 inches of mercury, temperature 15° C). In actual practice, corrections must be applied for varying atmospheric conditions. For navigational purposes it is important to know the groundspeed, and this can be determined by means of the wind triangle if the local wind velocities are known. There are also instruments for the direct measurement of groundspeed.

In so-called contact flight the pilot establishes his position with the aid of prominent landmarks (bridges, railroads, mountains, etc.) or—at night—air beacons and other lights. However, in modern high-level flying this method has been largely superseded, the establishment of position being achieved by means of navigational instruments. For night flying over uninhabited areas, the periscope sextant (Fig. 10) is used for observing the altitudes of celestial bodies. To make an observation, the periscope tube of the instrument is extended so as to protrude out of the fuselage of the aircraft.

(Continued)

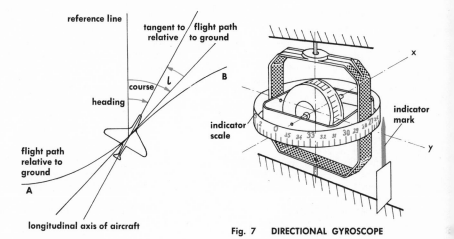

reference line

tangent to flight path
relative / to ground

course

ι

B

heading

flight path
relative to
ground

A

longitudinal axis of aircraft

Fig. 6

x

indicator
scale

indicator
mark

y

Fig. 7   DIRECTIONAL GYROSCOPE

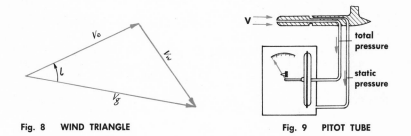

V_e

ι

V_w

V_g

Fig. 8   WIND TRIANGLE

V

total
pressure

static
pressure

Fig. 9   PITOT TUBE

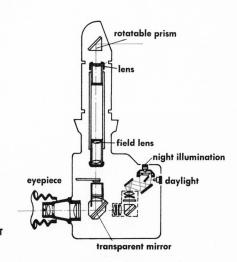

rotatable prism

lens

field lens

night illumination

daylight

eyepiece

transparent mirror

Fig. 10   PERISCOPE SEXTANT

AIR NAVIGATION
(continued)

The most widely used means of establishing an aircraft's position is by the use of *electronic aids*. Radio direction-finding (DF) equipment relies on the direction property of a loop antenna. By rotating the antenna it is possible to establish the direction from which the signals from a ground-based radio beacon are coming and thus to find the aircraft's bearing in relation to that direction, i.e., the angle between the direction of the signals and the longitudinal axis of the aircraft. Since the aircraft's heading (see above) is also known, it is possible to establish the angle between the radio signal direction and, for example, true north. The principle is illustrated in Fig. 11. By taking bearings on three different radio beacons it is possible to establish the position of the aircraft. In a modern aircraft the equipment usually takes the form of an *automatic direction finder* (radio compass) whose antenna is kept directed at a particular radio beacon by means of an electrical sensing circuit. The antenna position, and therefore the aircraft's bearing in relation to the signal direction, is indicated on a dial (Fig. 12). In the navigational system known as VOR (very high-frequency omnidirectional range), which is used chiefly in the United States, a direct indication of bearing from the transmitting station is obtained. Other well known navigation systems are Decca and loran (long range navigation), developed in Britain and in the United States respectively.

Inertial guidance systems are entirely independent of outside signals. For this reason they are valuable for missile control and submarine navigation. The operation is based on the measurement of the amount and direction of acceleration, usually in three mutually perpendicular directions. The speed at any particular instant and the distance travelled are obtained by a process of integration which is carried out with the aid of computer equipment (Fig. 13). Fixed reference axes are established by three gyroscopes. These are mounted on gimbals with mutually perpendicular axes. Deviations from the reference co-ordinates are fed to a computer.

The *instrument landing system* (ILS) is illustrated in Fig. 15. Radio signals are transmitted from two ground-based antenna systems and provide horizontal and vertical guide planes respectively. The pilot's indicating instrument (Fig. 14) comprises a pointer for horizontal and another for vertical guidance. Approximate indications of distance are obtained on passing the outer marker (OM), middle marker (MM) and boundary marker (BM) transmitters. The signals are converted to acoustic and visual indications. In another system the aircraft is tracked by ground radar and the pilot receives instructions by radio (he is "talked down"). This is known as ground controlled approach (GCA).

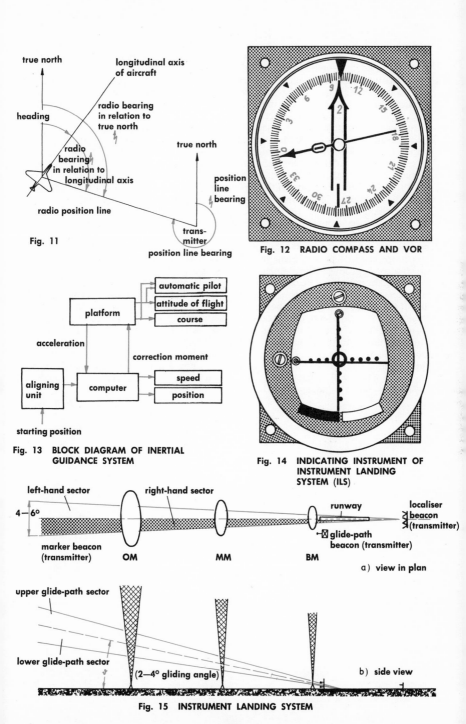

true north

longitudinal axis
of aircraft

heading

radio bearing
in relation to
true north

radio
bearing
in relation to
longitudinal axis

true north

radio position line

position
line
bearing

transmitter

position line bearing

Fig. 11

Fig. 12   RADIO COMPASS AND VOR

automatic pilot

attitude of flight

platform

course

acceleration

correction moment

speed

aligning
unit

computer

position

starting position

Fig. 13   BLOCK DIAGRAM OF INERTIAL
         GUIDANCE SYSTEM

Fig. 14   INDICATING INSTRUMENT OF
         INSTRUMENT LANDING
         SYSTEM (ILS)

left-hand sector

right-hand sector

runway

localiser
beacon
(transmitter)

4—6°

glide-path
beacon (transmitter)

marker beacon
(transmitter)

OM

MM

BM

a) view in plan

upper glide-path sector

lower glide-path sector

(2—4° gliding angle)

b) side view

Fig. 15   INSTRUMENT LANDING SYSTEM

HOVERCRAFT

Hovercraft belong to the category of what can be described as "air cushion vehicles" or "ground effect vehicles". In principle, a hovercraft comprises a body or hull in which a rotor (lift fan) is so mounted that it can produce an air cushion on which the craft is supported. There is therefore no contact between the craft and the ground and no friction to overcome. It can travel on land as well as on water. The hovercraft relies on the so-called ground effect to form the air cushion. The principle underlying this effect is illustrated in Fig. 1. The flow of air produced by a fan close to the surface of the ground acquires an annular pattern: all the flow and turbulence is concentrated at the edges, while at the centre an air cushion is formed in which the air is very nearly at rest. At the edge of this cushion an annular jet of air develops which forms a curtain that insulates the cushion from the surrounding lower-pressure atmospheric air.

A number of devices based on the hovercraft principle have been constructed and tested. Fig. 2 shows a very simple machinery comprising a lift fan and a large chamber (plenum chamber) in which the air cushion is formed. The "hovering" distance above the surface of the ground in this case is dependent on the relation between the air intake and air discharge rate. However, as the pressure in the chamber is low, it is necessary to provide a large base area in order to obtain a reasonable amount of lift.

A more efficient arrangement in this respect is the annular chamber (Fig. 3), which directly produces the annular "jet" envisaged in Fig. 1. The effect is improved by sloping the peripheral nozzles inwards. As a rule, one or more horizontal-thrusting propellers are fitted for forward propulsion of the hovercraft. Extensive tests have shown that these craft give the best performance and stability when the "hovering" height is somewhat less than one-tenth of the diameter, i.e., a craft of 20 ft. diameter should operate at a height of about 2 ft. above the surface of the ground. To reduce wind resistance, however, hovercraft are usually not constructed circular on plan— though this would be the most favourable shape from the stability point of view— but are made oval or rectangular. For example, Fig. 4 illustrates a projected large hovercraft which will be provided with an annular air jet. It will have a total weight of 400 tons and be capable of speeds of up to 100 m.p.h.

(Continued)

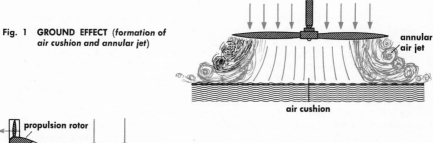

Fig. 1 GROUND EFFECT (*formation of air cushion and annular jet*)

annular air jet

air cushion

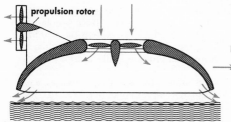

propulsion rotor

Fig. 2 HOVERCRAFT WITH PLENUM CHAMBER (*propulsion by jet impulse*)

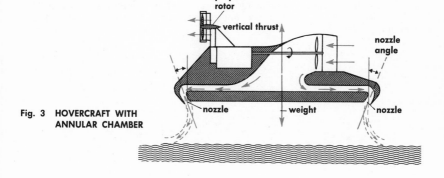

propulsion rotor

vertical thrust

nozzle angle

Fig. 3 HOVERCRAFT WITH ANNULAR CHAMBER

nozzle   weight   nozzle

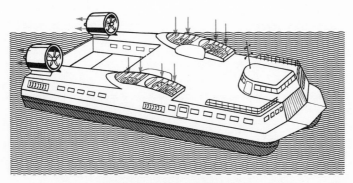

Fig. 4 PROJECTED LARGE PASSENGER HOVERCRAFT (*100 m.p.h., total weight 400 tons*)

The forces acting upon a hovercraft are indicated in Fig. 5. With increasing forward speed the aerodynamic drag plays an increasingly important part. In addition to this pure form drag, which is also associated with the forward motion of aircraft, there is an impulse drag which is caused by the acceleration of the air needed for forming the supporting cushion under the hovercraft. At low speeds this impulse drag is greater than the form drag, at high speeds the latter is greater. For forward motion the rear nozzles on the underside of the craft can be so adjusted as to develop a rearward thrust equivalent to about 20% of the total thrust necessary for propelling the craft, the other 80% being supplied by the horizontally acting propeller.

A more elaborate system of sealing the air cushion is employed in the craft illustrated in Figs. 6 and 7. Here the insulating "curtain" is formed by a circulating stream of air at the edge. Higher efficiency and reduced air losses from the cushion are claimed for this system. On the other hand, the cost of construction is higher.

Braking and steering a hovercraft are performed aerodynamically. Simple control surfaces (rudders) such as those used on aircraft may be useful at high speeds, but are ineffective at low speeds. Hence these craft are steered by thrust impulses, e.g., by means of lateral propellers. The same principle is employed for braking: the forward propulsion propellers are of the variable-pitch type; by appropriately varying the pitch angle of the blades to a negative value, these can be made to develop a backward thrust. In the design of hovercraft the problem of stability plays a major part. For example, with increasing speed of the craft its stability is impaired by the increasing dynamic pressure which tends to break down the supporting air cushion. The dynamic pressure must on no account exceed the pressure existing within the air cushion.

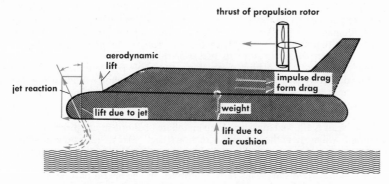

Fig. 5 FORCES ACTING ON A HOVERCRAFT IN MOTION

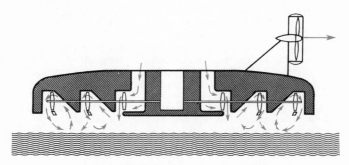

Fig. 6 HOVERCRAFT WITH AIR CURTAIN
(Weiland two-stage system)

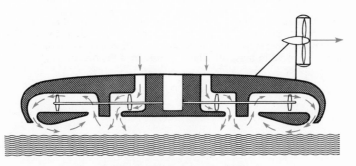

Fig. 7 HOVERCRAFT WITH AIR CURTAIN
(Miller single-stage system)

ROCKETS

A rocket is a jet-propelled missile which carries the source of its propulsive energy along with it and whose functioning is independent of the presence of an atmosphere. It is more particularly in this latter respect that a rocket differs from an aircraft jet engine (see page 562 f.). Whereas an "air-breathing" jet engine uses air to burn its fuel and can therefore operate only in the atmosphere, the propulsion of a rocket requires no external aid to burn its fuel. For this reason the altitudes and speeds attainable by rockets, as distinct from those attainable by jet aircraft, are in effect "unlimited". Every jet propulsion system is based on Newton's fundamental law of "action" and "reaction", which states that every "action" produces a "reaction" of the same magnitude but acting in the opposite direction. Some elementary examples of this principle are illustrated in Fig. 1.

When the air is allowed to escape from an inflated balloon in one direction (action), the balloon will move in the opposite direction (reaction) (Fig. 1a). Something similar happens when a gun is fired (Fig. 1b). In order to accelerate the projectile to the required muzzle velocity, the force due to gas pressure developed by the explosive must act for a certain time. This force multiplied by the length of time is called the "impulse"; it is equal to the mass of the projectile multiplied by its muzzle velocity.

Similar conditions also apply to rocket propulsion (Figs. 1c and 1d). When a hot gas under high pressure is produced by the burning of a rocket fuel (propellant) in a combustion chamber, the gas will exercise an equal pressure in all directions upon the walls of the chamber. Now if an opening is made in one side of the chamber, the gas will come streaming out at supersonic velocity; at the same time a reaction force will be exerted on the opposite side of the chamber, and it is this reaction force that thrusts the rocket forward. This propulsive force (thrust) is equal to the mass of propellant discharged per unit of time multiplied by the flow velocity. This means that the thrust becomes greater in proportion as the gas discharge rate per second and the flow velocity are higher. The thrust is therefore not produced — as is often erroneously supposed — by the outflowing gases "pushing" against the surrounding medium (atmosphere), but is developed purely as a reaction force due to the expulsion of matter at high velocity from a closed system. Rocket propulsion is therefore the only propulsive system that can function in vacuum. Fig. 2 shows some practical applications of the impulse theorem and the principle of reaction.

When the entire propellant supply carried along by the rocket has been transformed into thrust, the rocket has attained its maximum velocity. This final velocity depends upon the flow velocity of the gas and the so-called mass ratio of the rocket, i.e., the ratio of the initial mass (mass of the rocket at blast-off, including the propellant supply) to the final mass (the initial mass minus the mass of the consumed propellant). An increase in final velocity is attainable by means of the multi-stage rocket. Each stage has its own propulsion system and propellant supply; the final stage additionally carries the payload. When the propellant supply of one stage has been exhausted, this stage is mechanically detached from the subsequent stages. The thrust developed by the next stage serves to produce a further increase in the velocity of the rocket, now reduced in mass after having discarded the previous (spent) stage.

(Continued)

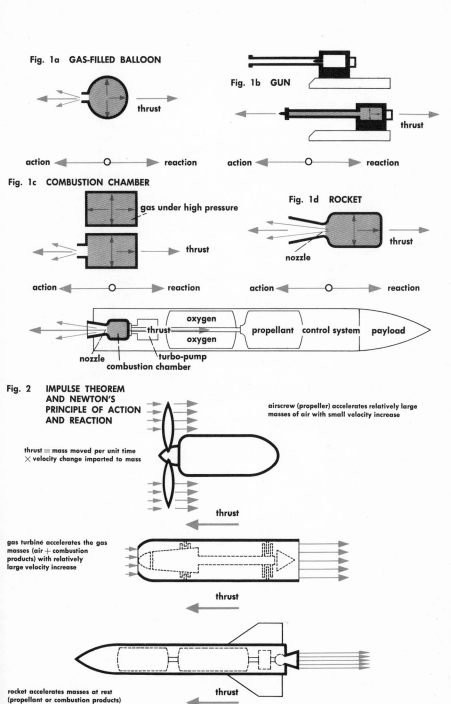

Fig. 1a GAS-FILLED BALLOON

thrust

action ⟵——O——⟶ reaction

Fig. 1b GUN

thrust

action ⟵——O——⟶ reaction

Fig. 1c COMBUSTION CHAMBER

gas under high pressure

thrust

action ⟵——O——⟶ reaction

Fig. 1d ROCKET

thrust

nozzle

action ⟵——O——⟶ reaction

oxygen
thrust
oxygen
propellant   control system   payload

nozzle
combustion chamber
turbo-pump

Fig. 2   IMPULSE THEOREM AND NEWTON'S PRINCIPLE OF ACTION AND REACTION

airscrew (propeller) accelerates relatively large masses of air with small velocity increase

thrust = mass moved per unit time × velocity change imparted to mass

thrust

gas turbine accelerates the gas masses (air + combustion products) with relatively large velocity increase

thrust

rocket accelerates masses at rest (propellant or combustion products) to very high exit velocity

thrust

579

Rocket propulsion systems:

Acceleration of the mass of a propellant to high flow velocities in a rocket motor can be achieved in various ways.

In chemical-propellant rockets, as at present employed, hot gases under high pressure are produced in a combustion chamber and acquire their velocity in a nozzle. Rockets of this class can be subdivided into solid-propellant, liquid-propellant, and hybrid rockets.

In the case of a solid-propellant rocket the propellant, which consists of the combustibles and an agent supplying the oxygen for its combustion and which may have a variety of surface configurations and arrangements, is introduced into the combustion chamber, where it burns. In so doing, it produces a hot high-pressure gas which is discharged through a nozzle and thus produces the thrust that propels the rocket. In liquid-propellant rockets the liquid combustibles are contained in tanks and fed into the combustion chamber through an injector head by a propellant supply system. Most liquid-propellant rockets use two combustibles (bipropellant system) such as liquid oxygen and kerosene. Also, a liquid oxygen supplying agent can be used in conjunction with a solid combustible (hybrid rockets), whereby better control of the thrust developed by the rocket motor is obtained.

In another method (still in the experimental stage) the hot gas is produced, not by chemical combustion, but with the aid of nuclear energy. This method involves heating a working fluid (e.g., water or hydrogen) in a nuclear reactor (cf. page 54), the gas being discharged through a nozzle in which it is accelerated and develops the thrust.

Whereas chemical-propellant rockets are characterised by high thrust for short durations and are therefore more particularly suitable for getting large payloads launched from the ground, electrical propulsion systems have been proposed which would yield a relatively low thrust over a long period of time. Such systems would be suitable for space travel, i.e., under interplanetary conditions of rocket flight.

Of the various electrical propulsion systems that have been proposed, the one most closely resembling the chemical system is the electro-thermal arc jet. This device utilises an electric arc to heat a working fluid (e.g., hydrogen, helium, etc.), which is "thermodynamically" accelerated in a nozzle.

In another system, the so-called ion rocket, electrostatic fields are used to accelerate positively-charged ions to very high specific impulse values. The system comprises an ion-producing and an ion-accelerating device, as well as a neutralising zone where electrons are added in order to restore the electrical equilibrium.

In yet another electrical propulsion system the plasma produced by an electric arc is accelerated by means of an electromagnetic field. ("Plasma" is the term applied to a gas with more than 50% of its particles ionised, i.e., electrically charged). Also, there is a somewhat different type of thrust device which operates in a pulsed fashion and utilises magnetohydrodynamics (MHD) to accelerate high-temperature gases.

To provide the necessary propulsive energy, suitable sources of electrical energy, such as nuclear power generating plants (fission, controlled fusion), have to be carried along in rockets which rely on electrical propulsion.

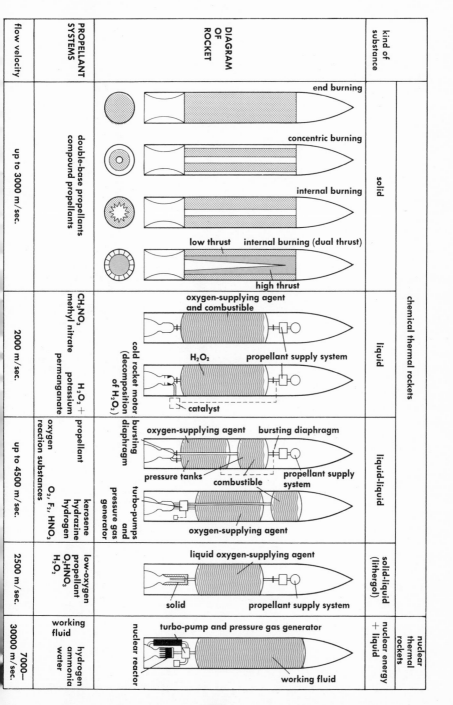

flow velocity	PROPELLANT SYSTEMS	DIAGRAM OF ROCKET	kind of substance	
up to 3000 m/sec.	double-base propellants compound propellants	end burning; concentric burning; internal burning; internal burning (dual thrust) — low thrust / high thrust	solid	chemical thermal rockets
2000 m/sec.	CH_3NO_3 methyl nitrate — H_2O_2 + potassium permanganate	oxygen-supplying agent and combustible; propellant supply system; cold rocket motor (decomposition of H_2O_2); H_2O_2; catalyst	liquid	
up to 4500 m/sec.	propellant — oxygen reaction substances O_2, F_2, HNO_3 — kerosene hydrazine hydrogen	oxygen-supplying agent; bursting diaphragm; pressure tanks; combustible; propellant supply system; turbo-pumps and pressure gas generator; oxygen-supplying agent	liquid-liquid	
2500 m/sec.	low-oxygen propellant $O_2 HNO_3$ H_2O_2	liquid oxygen-supplying agent; solid; propellant supply system	solid-liquid (lithergol)	
7000–30000 m/sec.	working fluid — hydrogen ammonia water	turbo-pump and pressure gas generator; nuclear reactor; working fluid	nuclear energy + liquid	nuclear thermal rockets

581

INDEX

584

Driving rod, 524
Driving shaft, 490
Driven shaft, 490
Drum type meter, 226
Drum-type washing machines, 402
Dry cell, 66
Dry chemical extinguisher, 14
Dry cleaning, 406
Dry gas meter, 224
Dry ice, 18
Dry point, 416
Duplex brake, 514
Duplicating, 424
Dyeing, 384, 392, 394
Dynamic loudspeaker, 86
Dynamite, 450
Dynamo, 64

E

Earthing, 90
Eccentric press, 22
Echo, 204
Echo soundings, 550
Eddy currents, 222, 522
Eidophor system, 130
Einstein's equation, 102
Electrical propulsion, 580
Electric arc, 100
Electric bell, 256
Electric blanket, 272
Electric field, 58
Electric furnace, 100
Electric furnace steel, 336
Electric horn, 518
Electric iron, 284
Electricity meters, 222
Electric lenses, 128
Electric locomotive, 526
Electric motor, 526
Electric signal box, 538
Electric toaster, 272
Electric typewriter, 288
Electrocardiogram, 442
Electrocardiograph, 442
Electrodes, 100, 118, 484
Electrodynamic loudspeaker, 86
Electrodynamics, 60, 62
Electroforming, 318
Electrolyte, 66
Electrolytic meter, 222
Electromagnet, 60, 256
Electromagnetic radiation, 68
Electromagnetic relay, 94
Electromagnetic vibrations, 76
Electromagnetic waves, 68, 70, 72
Electron beam, 122
Electron gas, 62
Electronic computor, 302, 304, 306
Electronic flash, 184
Electronic lenses, 144
Electronic navigation aids, 570
Electron microscope, 144
Electron packets, 78
Electron-ray tube, 120
Electrons, 52, 56, 62, 74, 100, 108, 118, 120, 124, 130, 144,

438, 456
Electrophotography, 198
Electrostatic lenses, 144
Electrostatic loudspeaker, 86
Electrostatics, 56, 58
Electro-thermal arc jet, 580
Elevator, 238
Emission of electrons, 74
Emulsion, 200
Enamel, 350
Energy level diagram, 82
Energy meters, 22
Engine, 466, 468, 470, 472
Engine-room telegraph, 548
Engraving, 416
Entrance pupil, 148, 162
Epicyclic gears, 462
Epidiascope, 196
Episcope, 196
Equilibrium, 230
Equipotential surface, 58
Erasing head, 322
Escalator, 540
Escapement, 214
Etching, 416
Evaporator, 10, 248, 276
Everset shutter, 158
Exhaust-steam turbine, 44
Exit pupil, 148
Expanding universe, 206
Explosives, 448, 450
Exposure control, 176
Exposure meter, 176, 180
Extended-play record, 318
Extinguishing agents, 14
Extractive distillation, 10
Extrusion, 340, 356
Eye, 140
Eyeglasses, 140
Eyepiece, 142, 146

F

Fabric structure, 380, 382
Fan, 264, 278
Fan heater, 274
Fan-scavenging, 468
Faraday cage, 90
Farenheit scale, 16
Farm tractor, 428, 430
Far-sightedness, 140
Faucet, 250
Ferrite, 300
Fibres, 358, 370, 372, 374
Fibril, 358
Field-free space, 90
Field strength, 58
Filament of lamp, 282, 516
Filaments, 370, 372
Film, 188, 190, 192, 194, 200
Filmsetting machine, 412
Finishing, 392, 408
Fire extinguisher, 14
Fire-tube boiler, 40
Firing pin, 454
Fission, 54
Fixing, 200
Flash boiler, 40
Flash bulb, 182

Flash gun, 182
Flashing direction indicator, 520
Flashlight photography, 158, 160, 184
Flash synchronisation, 158, 160
Flash-time curve, 182
Flash tube, 184
Flat chamber, 478
Flat-iron, 284
Flip-flop circuit, 300
Floating, 542
Floating axle, 506
Flow heater, 268, 274
Flue, 266
Fluid coupling, 494, 496
Fluorescent lamp, 104
Fluorescent screen, 126, 128, 438
Fluoroscopy, 438
Flutter, 314
Flyer spindle, 376
Flying, 554
Fly press, 22
Flywheel, 42
F-number, 162, 176, 180
Foam type extinguisher, 14
Focal distance, 154
Focal length, 136, 142, 146, 154, 156, 178
Focal plane shutter, 160
Focus, 136, 138, 178
Folding camera, 150
Folding machine, 426
Forced-circulation boiler, 40
Foresail, 544
Forme, 410, 416
Fountain pen, 310
Four-stroke engine, 466
Fractionating column, 30
Fraction distillation, 30
Fractioning unit, 10
Francis turbine, 50
Franklin, Benjamin, 236
Freewheel, 460, 498
Freezing point, 16
Frequency, 68, 70, 518
Frequency modulation, 72, 84, 110
Frequency ranges, 320
Frit, 350
Fretz-Moon process, 340
Fuel-and-air mixture, 478, 480
Fuel cell, 52
Fuel injection, 470
Fuel oil, 28, 36
Full-fashioned hosiery, 390
Fundamental vibration, 210
Full disc brakes, 514
Fuse, 98, 452

G

Galilean telescope, 146
Galley, 410
Galton pipe, 208
Galvanic cell, 66
Gamma rays, 456

Secondary cell, 66
Sedimentation, 12
Selector, 112
Selenium, 180, 198, 424
Self-induction, 70
Self-servo action, 512, 514
Self-timer, 158
Semaphore, 110
Semiconductor, 80, 82, 102
Semiconductor diode, 82
Semiconductor triode, 82
Servo mechanism, 488
Sewing machine, 280
Sextant, 550
Shadow-mask tube, 166
Shaft, 332
Shaft furnace, 332
Shattering explosives, 450
Shattering power, 450
Shaving mirror, 138
Shedding, 386
Sheet rubber, 352
Shift-key typewriter, 288
Ship, 542
Ship's propeller, 546
Shock absorber, 508
Shoe, brake, 514
Short circuit, 98
Short-sightedness, 140
Short waves, 84
Shrinking, 392
Shutters, 158, 160
Shutter speed, 176
Shuttle, 280
Signal box, 536, 538
Signal plate, 122, 124
Silicon, 82
Silk screen printing, 392, 422
Silver bromide, 200
Simplex brake, 512
Singeing, 384, 392
Single-lens reflex camera, 150, 156
Single-plate clutch, 486
Siphon, 260
Sizing, 384
Skating, 316
Skelp, 340
Skim coulter, 430
Slabs, 338
Slag, 332, 334, 336
Slewing, 234
Slide projector, 196
Slide valve, 42
Slip, 350
Slip-rings, 62, 64
Sliver, 378
Slot machine, 324
Slow-combustion stove, 266
Slow motion, 188
Slug, 412
Sluice valve, 250
Soap, 398
Soft water, 398
Solar battery, 102
Solid-propellant rockets, 580
Solvents, 406
Sonic bang, 556
Sorting, automatic letter, 308

Sorting machine, 296
Sound absorption, 202
Sound barrier, 556
Sound intensity, 202
Sound machine, 550
Space heating, 274
Sparking plug, 482, 484
Speaker, 86
Spectacles, 140
Spectral colours, 134
Spectroscope, 134
Spectrum, 134, 206
Speed of camera lens, 162
Speedometer, 522
Spherical aberration, 152
Spin, 458
Spin-dryer, 12, 404
Spinnerets, 370, 372, 374
Spinning, 376, 378
Spinning frame, 376
Spinning nozzles, 370
Spinning top, 458
Split-image rangefinder, 186
Split switch, 534
Sponge rubber, 356
Spring balance, 212
Spring beard needle, 390
Springing, 464, 502, 504, 506
Softwoods, 358
Squirrel-cage rotor, 68
Stability, 542
Stall, 554
Standard lens, 154, 156
Starching, 408
Star connection, 68
Starter, 476
Starting clutch, 488
Stator, 64, 498
Steam boilers, 40
Steam engine, 42, 524
Steam heating, 244
Steam locomotive, 524
Steam turbine, 44
Steel, 334, 336
Steering, 510
Stencil, 422
Stencil printing, 392
Stereophonic pickup, 316
Stereophonic record, 318
Stereophonic sound, 192
Stereotyping, 414
Stiefel process, 340
Stirling boiler, 40
Stockings, 388, 390
Storage battery, 66
Storage heater, 272
Store location, 298
Stove, 266
Straw, 436
Stretch-spinning process, 378
Stroboscopic effects, 132
Stroboscope, 132
Stuffing box, 250
Styrene, 354
Sublimation, 18
Submerged-arc welding, 340
Subtractive colour blending, 170
Subtractive process, 170
Suction, 278

Suction head, 24
Suction pad, 220
Sulphur, 356
Superheater tubes, 40
Superheterodyne receiver, 84
Supersonics, 208
Supersonic speed, 556
Suspension, 502, 504, 506
Swash-plate, 560
Swing axle, 506
Switch, 96
Switches, 534
Swivelling wedge rangefinder, 186
Synchromesh gearbox, 492
Synchronisation, 182
Synchrotron, 108
Synthetic detergents, 398
Synthetic fibres, 370, 374
Synthetic petrol, 38
Synthetic polymers, 374
Synthetic rubber, 354

T

Tabulating machine, 296
Tank furnace, 344
Tap, 250
Tape, 320
Tape recorder, 320, 322
Tap hole, 332
Target, 438
Telecommunication, 110
Telegraph, 110, 114, 548
Telephone, 112
Telephone exchange, 112
Telephoto lens, 154, 156, 162, 178
Teleprinter, 110, 114
Telescope, 146, 148
Telescopic shock absorber, 508
Teletypesetter, 412
Television, 122
Television, colour, 166–69
Television camera tubes, 124
Television picture tube, 126
Telex, 110, 114
Temperature measurement, 16
Terrestrial telescope, 146
Textile auxiliaries, 408
Textile fabrics, 380
Textile printing, 392
Thermal conductivity, 228
Thermal electric domestic appliances, 270, 272, 274
Thermal expansion, 20
Thermal insulation, 228
Thermal plasma, 100
Thermal release, 270
Thermal value, 484
Thermionic tube, 74
Thermocouple, 16
Thermo-electric potential difference, 16
Thermometer, 16
Thermopile, 16
Thermo-relay, 94
Thermostat, 20, 242, 276, 284, 404
Thickness oscillations, 86